AA

GREAT
BRITAIN
ROAD
ATLAS
1997

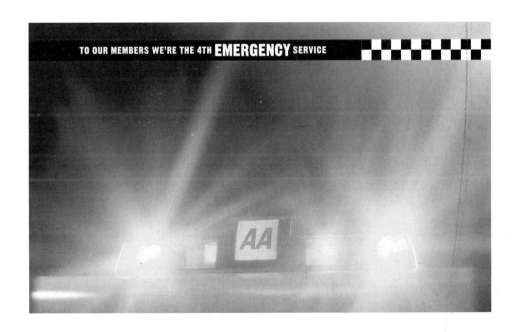

TO OUR MEMBERS WE'RE THE 4TH **EMERGENCY** SERVICE

11th edition September 1996
10th edition September 1995
Reprinted February 1996
9th edition September 1994
Reprinted June 1995
Reprinted February 1995
8th edition September 1993
7th edition September 1992
Reprinted October 1992
Reprinted November 1992
6th edition September 1991
5th edition September 1990
4th edition September 1989
3rd edition October 1988
2nd edition October 1987
Reprinted April 1988
1st edition October 1986

Published by AA Publishing (a trading name of Automobile Association Developments Limited, whose registered office is Norfolk House, Priestley Road, Basingstoke, Hampshire RG24 9NY. Registered number 1878835).

Mapping produced by the Cartographic Department of The Automobile Association. This atlas has been compiled and produced from the Automaps database utilising electronic and computer technology.

ISBN 0 7495 1375 6
ISBN 0 7495 1438 8

A CIP catalogue record for this book is available from the British Library.

Printed by: Printers Trento, S.R.L., Italy.
Bound by L.E.G.O. SpA, Vicenza, Italy.

The contents of this atlas are believed to be correct at the time of printing. Nevertheless, the publishers cannot be held responsible for any errors or omissions, or for changes in the details given. They would welcome information to help keep this atlas up to date; please write to the Cartographic Editor, Publishing Division, The Automobile Association, Norfolk House, Priestley Road, Basingstoke, Hampshire RG24 9NY.

As a result of the Local Government Review, changes to some counties and county boundaries will take place when new Unitary Authorities are introduced in England, Wales and Scotland during 1996, 1997 and 1998. New and revised County, County Borough and Council Area boundaries have been added to the atlas where appropriate, and included in the index to place names. New Unitary Authorities for towns and cities in England which are within an existing county (eg Portsmouth) are not shown on this mapping.

Information on National Parks provided by the Countryside Commission for England and the Countryside Council for Wales.
Information on National Scenic Areas in Scotland provided by the Scottish Natural Heritage.
Information on Forest Parks provided by the Forestry Commission.
The RSPB sites shown are a selection chosen by the Royal Society for the Protection of Birds.
National Trust properties shown are those open to the public as indicated in the handbooks of the National Trust and the National Trust for Scotland.

contents

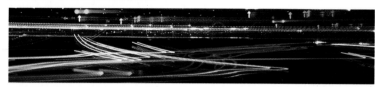

Tourism and leisure

Places of interest to note in the area you are visiting.

Red pictorial symbols and red type highlight numerous places of interest, catering for every taste. Red symbols within yellow boxes show tourist attractions in a town. Use them to plan days out or places to visit on holiday. To avoid disappointment remember to check opening times before you visit.

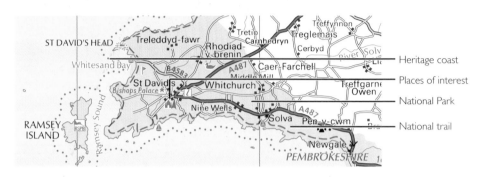

Town plans

Up-to-date, fully indexed town plans show AA recommended roads and other practical information, such as one-way streets, car parks and restricted roads, making navigation much easier.

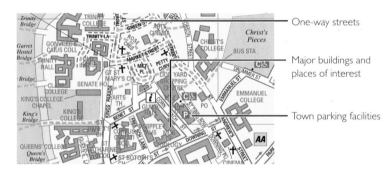

London

Easy-to-read, fully indexed street maps of inner London provide a simple guide to finding your way around the city.

Ports and airports

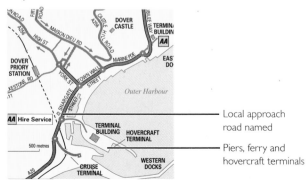

using this atlas

Road Maps

Clear, easy-to-read mapping helps you to plan more detailed journeys, and provides a wealth of information for the motorist.

All motorways, primary, A and B roads, and unclassified roads are shown. The atlas also identifies interchanges, roundabouts and those roads outside urban areas which are under construction.

Additional features include rivers, lakes and reservoirs, railway lines, interesting places to visit, picnic sites and Tourist Information Centres. To assist you in estimating journey length, distances are shown in miles between blue marker symbols.

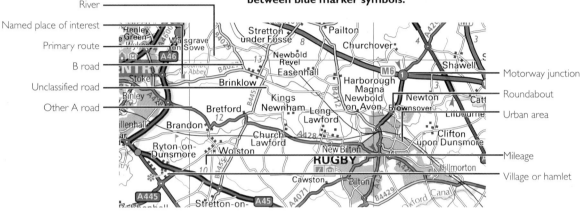

River
Named place of interest
Primary route
B road
Unclassified road
Other A road

Motorway junction
Roundabout
Urban area
Mileage
Village or hamlet

Ferry and rail routes

Useful ferry and rail information.

To assist in planning journeys overseas mapping of coastal regions provides basic off-shore information including ferry routes. Throughout the atlas, railway lines with stations and level crossings are shown to assist with general navigation or rail travel requirements.

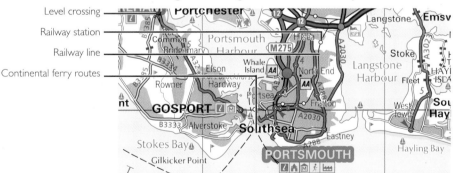

Level crossing
Railway station
Railway line
Continental ferry routes

Motorways – restricted junctions

Motorway junctions, displayed as diagrams, highlight individual restrictions.

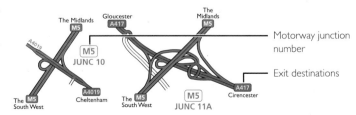

Motorway junction number
Exit destinations

Call AA Roadwatch

or listen to local radio

to avoid delays on

your journey.

Delays and hold-ups

Despite ever-increasing levels of traffic, motorways are still the quickest means of getting from A to B. Nevertheless, a hold-up on a motorway can easily delay your journey for several hours. There are a number of ways of gleaning information about the stretches of motoway to avoid: by phone, television (teletext), radio and newspaper.

AA Roadwatch

This service provides up-to-the-minute information on traffic conditions, roadworks and the weather for the whole country. See page XII for numbers to call.

Radio

Frequent radio bulletins are issued by both the BBC and independent local radio stations about road and weather conditions, and likely hold-ups. By tuning into the local radio stations you can prepare to make changes to your route and avoid delays. Local radio however, does not yet cover the entire country. A recent development is the Radio Data System Traffic Message Channel (RDS–TMC), which is becoming more widely available.

Carry out regular checks to make sure that you

and your car arrive safely.

Daily checks

Before you start every journey you should always ensure that:
- You check the dashboard warning lights before and after starting the engine
- There are no unusual noises once the engine is running
- All the lights are both clean and working
- The windscreen and all other windows are clean
- You have sufficient fuel for your journey

Weekly checks

Before you set out on a journey you should also ensure that:
- The engine oil level is correct, looking for obvious signs of leakage
- The coolant level is correct, checking the anti-freeze before the onset of winter
- The battery connections and terminals are clean and free from corrosion
- The brake (and clutch, if hydraulic) fluid is correct
- The tyres, including the spare, are properly inflated and not damaged
- The tyres are changed if the tread falls below 2mm
- The fan-belt is not worn or damaged, and that the tension is correct
- The windscreen wipers are clean and that the screen wash reservoir is full

Are you fit to drive?

Food, tiredness, drink

and medicine all affect

your driving.

Fit to drive

Many accidents are caused by one or more of the drivers involved being unfit to drive when the accident occurred. The most obvious reason for such accidents is alcohol; even the smallest quantity can affect driving. The only safe advice is: if you drive, don't drink – if you drink, don't drive. However, alcohol is just one of a number of factors that can make someone unfit to drive.

Tiredness

Some people become tired sooner than others, but the following are guidelines which you should aim to keep: for every three hours on the road, take 20 minutes rest; if possible, share the driving; limit yourself to a maximum of eight hours behind the wheel in any one day; and try to avoid driving at times when you would normally be asleep or resting. You should also avoid driving after hard exercise, a large meal and, of course, after consuming alcohol. Other factors which can contribute to tiredness are temperature inside the car and medication; a stuffy atmosphere – and some drugs – can induce drowsiness. If you are on medication, check with your doctor whether you should be driving at all. One final point: not driving during peak hours keeps delays to a minimum, reduces frustration and minimises journey time.

Driving abroad

Always ensure you know the specific legal requirements and road signs before you set out – and make sure your car conforms to such requirements. If you take an overnight ferry crossing you will probably be tired the next morning; do not set yourself too long a drive after arriving on the Continent. When you begin driving again after taking a break be especially careful to keep on the correct side of the road.

journey planning

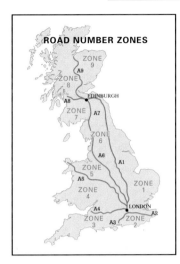

ROAD NUMBER ZONES

How to get there
Special route-planning maps on pages XII–XVII enable you to devise a basic route before referring to the main pages of the atlas for greater detail.

Road classification
London is the hub for the spokes of roads numbered A1 to A6, and Edinburgh the hub for A7, A8 and A9. Beginning with the A1, running north from London, the roads radiate clockwise from the capital: A2 runs roughly east, the A3 west, and so forth. The system has made the numbering of other roads very simple. Generally, the lower the subsequent number, the closer the road's starting point to London (or Edinburgh).

using the national grid

One of the unique

features of AA

mapping is the use of

the National Grid

System.

The National Grid
The National Grid covers Britain with an imaginary network of squares, using blue vertical lines called eastings and horizontal lines called northings. On the atlas pages these lines are numbered along the bottom and up the left-hand side.

The index
Each entry in the index is followed by a page number, two letters denoting an area on the map and a 4-figure grid reference. You will not need to use the two letters for simple navigation, but they come in useful if you want to use your map in relation to the rest of the country and other map series.

Quick reference
For quick reference, the four figures of the grid reference in the index are arranged so that the 1st and 3rd are in a bolder type than the 2nd and 4th. The 1st figure shows the number along the bottom of the grid, and the 3rd figure, the number up the left-hand side. These will indicate the square in which you will find the place name.

Pinpoint accuracy
However, to pinpoint a place more accurately you will also need to use the 2nd and 4th numbers. The second will tell you how many imaginary tenths along the bottom line to go from the first number, and the 4th will tell you how many tenths to go up from the third number. Where these two lines intersect, you will find your place name. For example: Skegness 77TF**56**63. Skegness is located on page 77 within grid square **56** in National Grid square TF. Its exact location is **5663**.

Skegness **77**TF**5663**

Skegness is located on page **77**

within grid square **56**

in National Grid square TF.

Its exact location is **5663**.

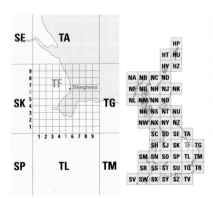

A consistent and comprehensive set of road signs

provides information and warning to the motorist.

Classes of signs

These are based on an internationally agreed system, with variations specific to Britain. Signs which give orders and prohibitions are usually circular, and if the background is blue, their instructions are compulsory. Triangular signs carry warning messages and rectangular signs give information.

There are three shapes of road signs: triangles, circles and rectangles. Red triangles warn. Red circles prohibit

Blue circles give positive instruction. Blue rectangles give general information. Green rectangles are used for direction signs on primary routes.

Warning signs lead up to a junction or

roundabout, and provide information about the

nature of the junction.

Junctions and roundabouts

Warning signs will probably be followed by a give way or stop sign. The road markings at a stop sign consist of a solid white line identifying the farthest point to which you may drive. It is obligatory to stop and look to see that it is possible to enter the major road in safety. The give way sign has different road markings – a pair of white dashed lines – and drivers are required to delay joining the main road until it is safe to do so. If the main road is clear, there is no obligation to stop completely.

| Countdown markers approaching a major junction | Crossroads | T-junction | Staggered junction | Roundabout | Mini-roundabout (roundabout circulation) | No through road | No vehicles |

| Distance to 'STOP' line ahead | Distance to 'GIVE WAY' line ahead | Stop and give way | Give way to traffic on major road |

Advance warning of the road layout ahead helps

a driver plan his/her approach.

The road ahead

The information given is generally precise about which side of the road is affected or which direction the road will take. The triangular signs give warnings, the circular signs must be obeyed.

| Bend to left | Double bend, first to left | Bend to right | Double bend, first to right | Road hump or series of road humps ahead | Worded warning sign | Dual carriageway ends | Steep hill downwards | Steep hill upwards |

| No goods vehicles over maximum gross weight shown (in tonnes) | Axle weight limit (in tonnes) | No vehicles over height shown | Sharp deviation of route | Traffic merges from left | Road narrows on left | Traffic merges from right | Road narrows on right | Road narrows on both sides |

Hazards ahead

The signs warning of hazards ahead should never be ignored, and provide valuable information about what is round the next corner or just ahead.

Pedestrian crossing

Hospital ahead with accident and emergency facilities

Slippery road

Road works

Uneven road

Wild animals

Wildhorses or ponies

Cattle

Other danger

Traffic signals

Failure of traffic light signals

Children

Children going to or from school

School crossing patrol ahead

School crossing patrol

Hump bridge

Opening or swing bridge ahead

Falling or fallen rocks

Quayside or river bank

Overhead electric cable

Traffic behaviour

Information about the way traffic should be organised is given in a series of specific signs.

These signs govern the speed and general approach at any situation. They are signs which must be obeyed.

No stopping (Clearway)

National speed limit applies

No U-turns

Give priority to vehicles from opposite direction

No overtaking

Motor vehicles prohibited except for access

No entry for vehicular traffic

Two-way traffic straight ahead

No right turn

No left turn

Turn left ahead

ONE WAY

Turn left

Vehicles may pass either side to reach same destination

Ahead only

Keep left

Level crossings

There are several different types of level crossing. Many have barriers which may cross half or all of the road.

Level crossings may be worked automatically by the approach of the train or they may be operated by an attendant. When flashing lights and bell signals are in operation you should not pass. If you are already crossing when the amber lights flash and the bells start, keep crossing.

Level crossing without barrier

Level crossing without barrier or gate ahead

Level crossing with barrier or gate ahead

Alternately flashing red lights mean YOU MUST STOP

M1 London–Leeds

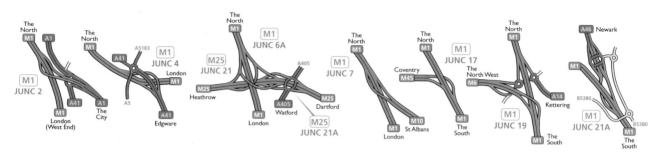

M1 London–Leeds   M2 Rochester–Faversham   M3 Sunbury–Southampton

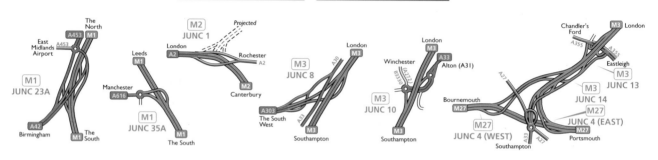

M4 London–South Wales   M5 Birmingham–Exeter

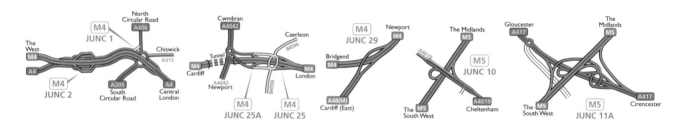

M5 Birmingham–Exeter   M6 Rugby–Carlisle

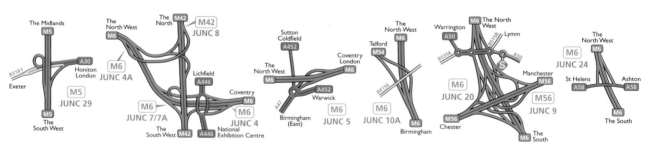

M6 Rugby–Carlisle   M8 Edinburgh–Bishopton

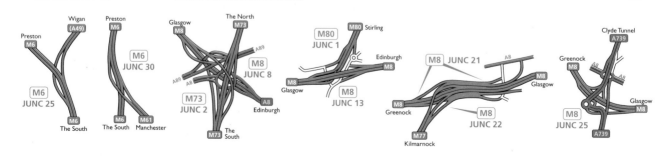

motorways – restricted junctions

Diagrams of selected motorway junctions which have entry and exit restrictions

M8 Edinburgh–Bishopton ## M9 Edinburgh–Dunblane ## M11 London–Cambridge

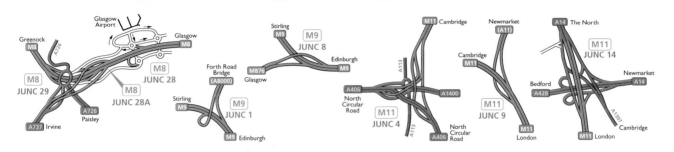

M20 Swanley–Folkestone ## M25 London Orbital ## M27 Cadnam–Portsmouth ## M40 London–Birmingham

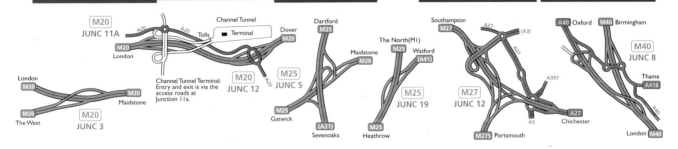

M42 Bromsgrove–Measham ## M56 North Cheshire Motorway ## M62 Liverpool–Humberside

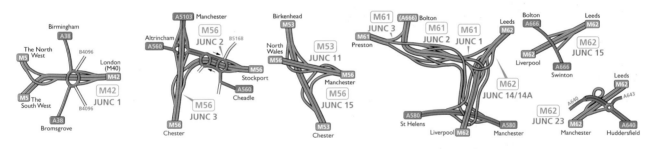

M63 Greater Manchester ## M73 East of Glasgow ## M74 Glasgow–Gretna

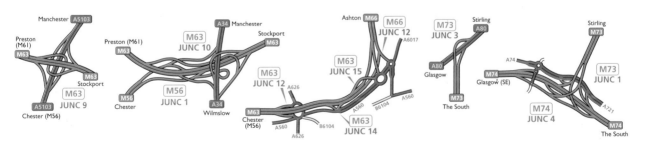

M74, A74(M) Glasgow–Gretna ## M80 Glasgow–Stirling ## M90 Forth Road Bridge–Perth ## A1(M) Scotch Corner–Tyneside

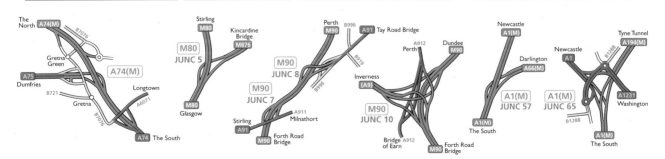

XI

route planner

Planning your route

The route-planning maps on the following pages show principal routes throughout the country and pinpoint the major towns and cities. Detailed routes can be worked out from the maps in the main atlas section of this book. You may find it useful to make a note of road numbers and route directions. You are advised to avoid driving through towns and built-up areas whenever possible, even if such routes appear to be more direct on the map. Delays caused by traffic lights, one-way systems and other road-users will almost certainly be encountered in such areas.

The length of the journey is a fundamental consideration when planning a route. The mileage chart on the inside back cover gives the distances between main towns and can be used to make a rough calculation of the total journey length. The time needed for the journey can then be estimated.

out and about

AA Roadwatch

Latest reports on traffic hold-ups and roadworks

National Traffic conditions by region Call 0336 401 plus 3 digits for the area required on the map

NATIONAL MOTORWAYS
0336 401 110

LONDON
and the **SOUTH EAST**
0336 401 122   area within M25
0336 401 123   Essex, Herts, Beds, Bucks, Oxon, Berks
0336 401 125   Hants, Surrey, Sussex, Kent
0336 401 127   M25 and link roads

AA Weatherwatch

Latest weather report followed by a 2-day forecast

National Weather Forecast Call 0336 401 plus 3 digits for the area required on the map

NATIONAL FORECAST
0336 401 130

Calls to 0336 numbers are charged at 39p per minute cheap rate, 49p at all other times, prices correct at the time of going to press.

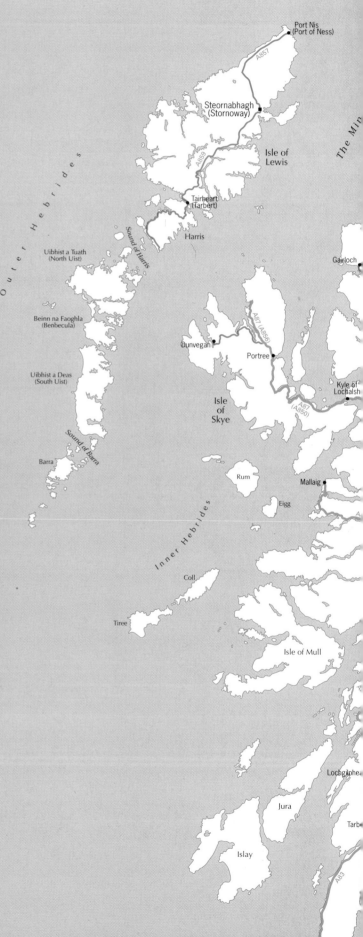

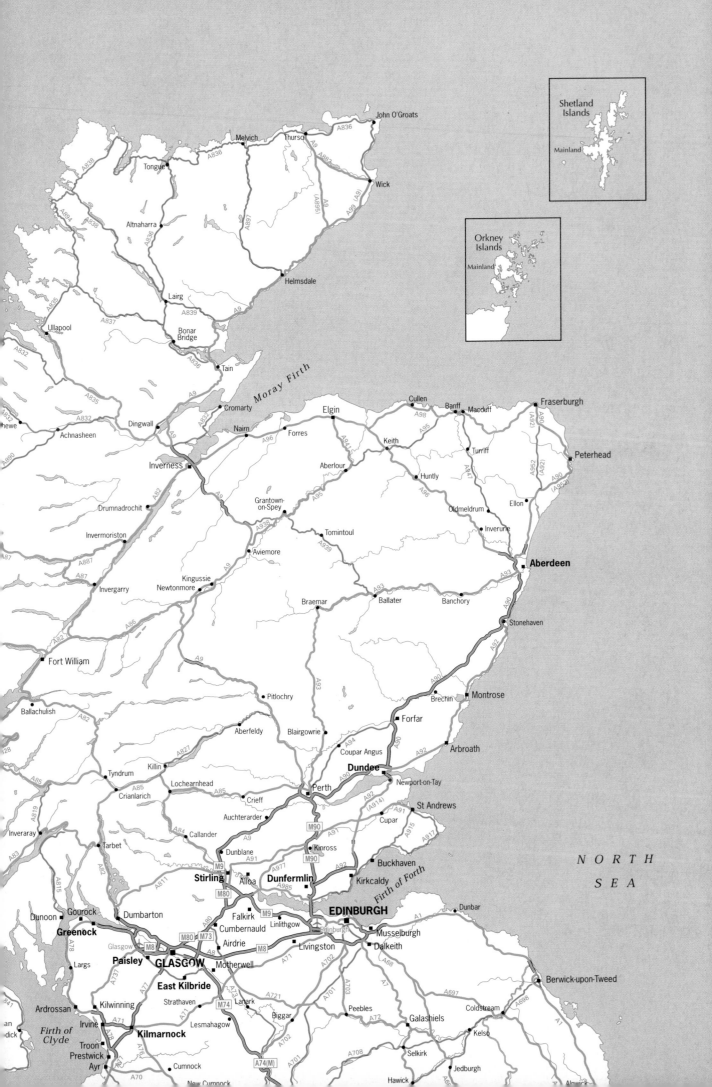

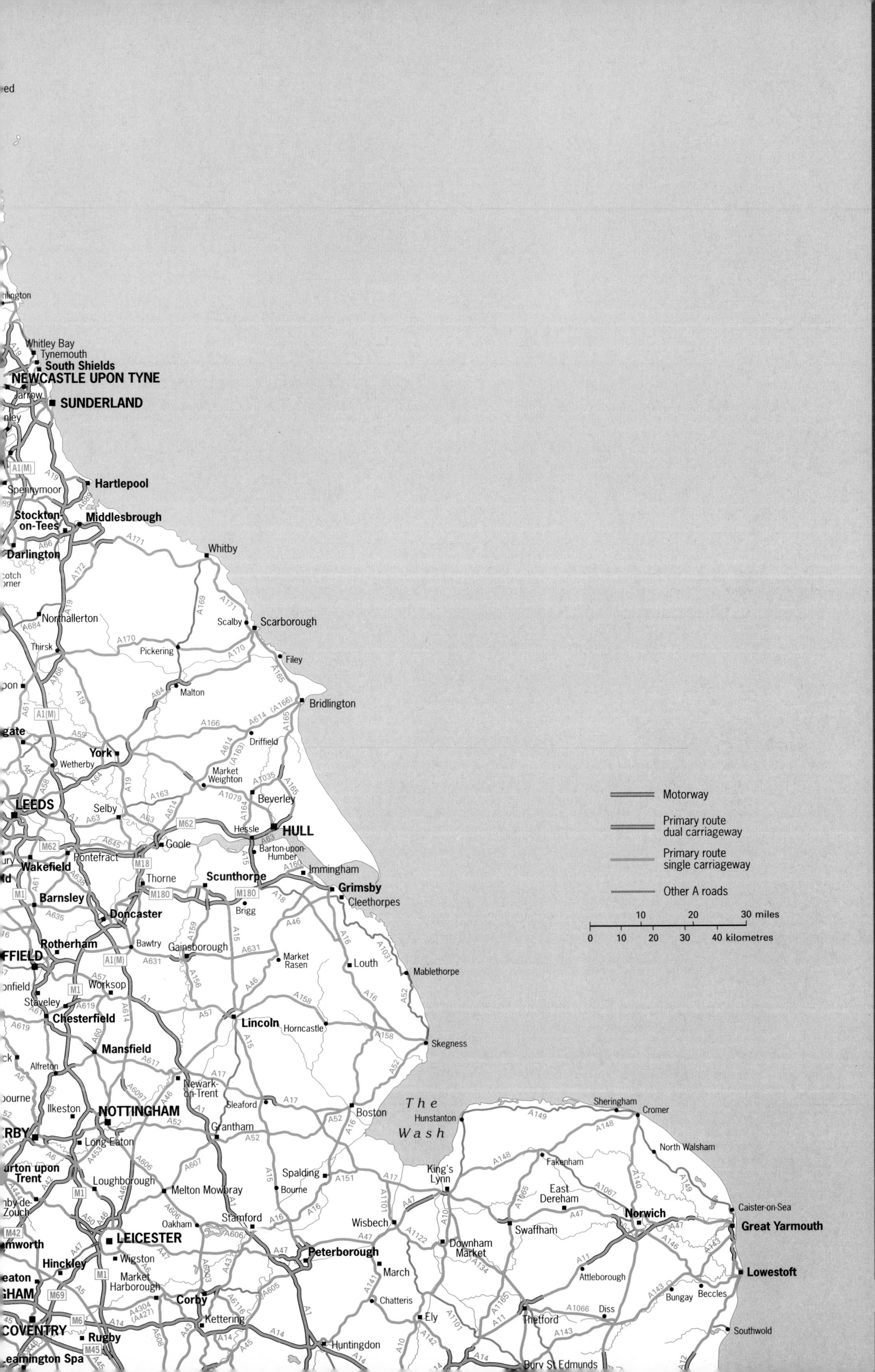

Whitley Bay
Tynemouth
South Shields
NEWCASTLE UPON TYNE
Jarrow
SUNDERLAND
A1(M)
Spennymoor
Hartlepool
Stockton-on-Tees
Middlesbrough
Darlington
Scotch Corner
Whitby
Northallerton
Thirsk
Scalby
Scarborough
Pickering
Filey
Malton
Bridlington
Driffield
York
Wetherby
Market Weighton
Beverley
LEEDS
Selby
Goole
Hessle
HULL
Barton-upon-Humber
Immingham
Pontefract
Wakefield
Thorne
Scunthorpe
Barnsley
Doncaster
Brigg
Grimsby
Cleethorpes
Rotherham
Bawtry
Gainsborough
Market Rasen
Louth
Mablethorpe
SHEFFIELD
Worksop
Staveley
Chesterfield
Lincoln
Horncastle
Skegness
Mansfield
Alfreton
Newark-on-Trent
Sleaford
NOTTINGHAM
Boston
The Wash
Hunstanton
Sheringham
Cromer
Ilkeston
Long Eaton
Grantham
North Walsham
DERBY
Burton upon Trent
Loughborough
Melton Mowbray
Spalding
Bourne
King's Lynn
Fakenham
East Dereham
Norwich
Ashby-de-la-Zouch
Oakham
Stamford
Wisbech
Swaffham
Great Yarmouth
LEICESTER
Wigston
Downham Market
Tamworth
Hinckley
Market Harborough
Peterborough
March
Attleborough
Lowestoft
NOTTINGHAM
Corby
Chatteris
Bungay
Beccles
Kettering
Ely
Thetford
Diss
COVENTRY
Rugby
Huntingdon
Southwold
Leamington Spa
Bury St Edmunds

Legend:
Motorway
Primary route dual carriageway
Primary route single carriageway
Other A roads

10 20 30 miles
0 10 20 30 40 kilometres

map pages

Orkney
Islands

155

Shetland
Islands

155

Outer
Hebrides

Steornabhagh
(Stornoway)

154

148 149 Thurso 151
150 Wick

Ullapool 146 147
144 145
Gairloch Tain

Dingwall Elgin Banff
136 137 138 139 140 141 Peterhead
Portree Inverness 142 143

Aviemore Aberdeen

Mallaig 130 131 132 133 134 135
128 129 Montrose
Fort
William Pitlochry

120 121 122 123 124 125 126 127
Oban Perth Dundee

Stirling

112 113 114 115 Edinburgh 118 119
Glasgow 116 117 Berwick-
Largs upon-Tweed

104 105 106 107 Peebles 110 111
Campbeltown Ayr 108 109 Alnwick
Moffat

98 99 100 101 102 103
Stranraer Dumfries Newcastle upon Tyne
Carlisle

92 93 94 95 96 97
Workington Penrith Middlesbrough

153 Kendal Thirsk Scarborough
Douglas 86 87 88 89 90 91
Isle of Lancaster Settle
Man York

Blackpool Burnley Leeds Hull
80 81 82 83 84 85
Liverpool Grimsby

Colwyn Manchester Sheffield 76 77
Bay 78 79 74 75 Lincoln
68 69 70 71
Caernarfon Chester Stoke Newark Boston
72 73 Nottingham King's Lynn 66 67
56 57 62 63 64 65 Norwich Great
Dolgellau Shrewsbury Stafford Leicester Peterborough Yarmouth
58 59 60 61 50 51 52 53 Bury St
Aberystwyth Newtown Birmingham Northampton Cambridge Edmunds 54 55
42 43 Ludlow Coventry Stratford-upon- Bedford Felixstowe
Cardigan 46 47 Avon 38 39 Chelmsford
44 45 Worcester 48 49 Luton 40 41
Fishguard Brecon Hereford Gloucester Oxford 37 Watford
30 31 Carmarthen Abergavenny 35 36 Reading LONDON 26 27
Pembroke 33 34 Bristol Swindon 24 25 Sevenoaks Maidstone
32 Swansea Cardiff Bath Andover Guildford 28 29 Dover
20 21 22 23 Salisbury 14 15 16 17 Folkestone
Barnstaple Yeovil Southampton Brighton Hastings
18 19 Taunton 12 13 Chichester Newhaven
Bude Lyme 10 11 Bournemouth
8 Regis Weymouth
Exeter 9
4 5 Torquay
Bodmin 6 7
2 Truro 3 Plymouth

156 Londonderry
Larne
157 Belfast
Sligo

Westport Cavan Newry

Galway Athlone DUBLIN

Limerick

158 159
Tralee
Killarney Waterford Rosslare
Cork

Isles of
Scilly 2

The Channel
Islands 152

XVIII

map symbols

motoring information

M4	Motorway with number
11	Motorway junction with and without number
3	Motorway junction with limited access
S Fleet	Motorway service area
	Motorway and junction under construction
A3	Primary route single/dual carriageway
S Oxford	Primary route service area
BATH	Primary route destination
A1123	Other A road single/dual carriageway
B2070	B road single/dual carriageway
	Unclassified road single/dual carriageway
	Roundabout
	Interchange
	Narrow primary, other A or B road with passing places (Scotland)
	Road under construction
	Road tunnel
	Steep gradient (arrows point downhill)
Toll	Road toll
5	Distance in miles between symbols

— V —	Vehicle ferry – Great Britain
BERGEN – V	Vehicle ferry – continental
— H —	Hovercraft ferry
✈	Airport
H	Heliport
F	International freight terminal
	Railway line/in tunnel
	Railway station and level crossing
	Tourist railway
AA	AA shop
☎	AA telephone
	Urban area/village
628 ▲	Spot height in metres
	River, canal, lake
	Sandy beach
	County/County Borough /Council Area boundary
	National boundary
85	Page overlap and number

tourist information

i	Tourist Information Centre
i	Tourist Information Centre (seasonal)
	Abbey, cathedral or priory
	Ruined abbey, cathedral or priory
	Castle
	Historic house
M	Museum or art gallery
	Industrial interest
❈	Garden
	Arboretum
	Country park
	Agricultural showground
	Theme park
	Zoo
	Wildlife collection – mammals
	Wildlife collection – birds
	Aquarium
	Nature reserve
RSPB	RSPB site
....	Forest drive
— — —	National trail
☀	Viewpoint
	Picnic site
	Hill-fort

	Roman antiquity
	Prehistoric monument
✕ 1066	Battle site with year
	Steam centre (railway)
	Cave
	Windmill
⚑	Golf course
	County cricket ground
	Rugby Union national ground
	International athletics ground
	Horse racing
	Show jumping/ equestrian circuit
	Motor racing circuit
	Coastal launching site
	Ski slope – natural
	Ski slope – artificial
NT	National Trust property
NTS	National Trust for Scotland property
★	Other places of interest
☐	Boxed symbols indicate attractions within urban areas
	National Park (England & Wales)
	National Scenic Area (Scotland)
	Forest Park
	Heritage Coast

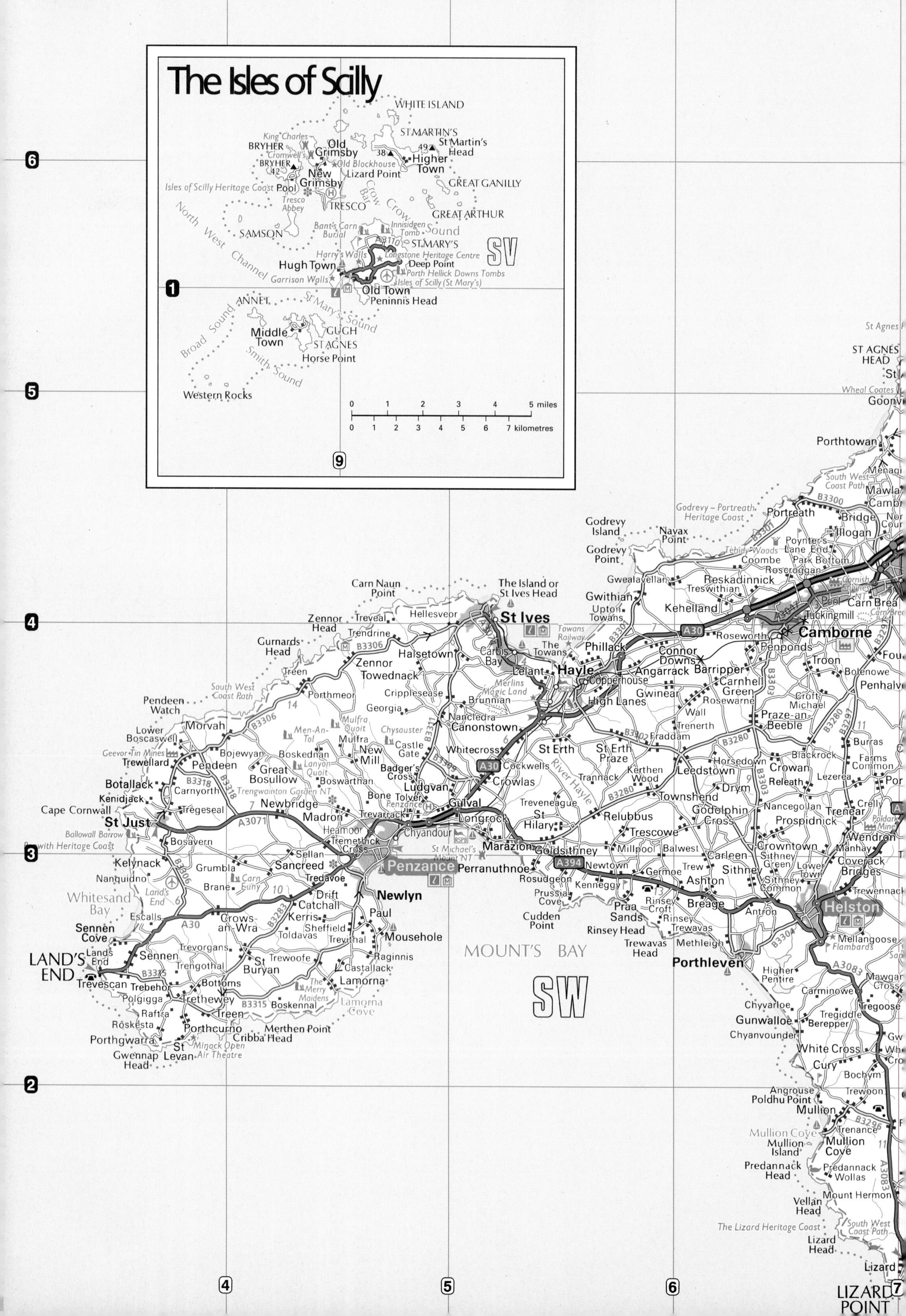

2

The Isles of Scilly

WHITE ISLAND

ST. MARTIN'S
St Martin's Head
BRYHER
Old Grimsby
King Charles
Cromwell's
BRYHER
42
New Grimsby
Old Blockhouse
Lizard Point
49
38
Higher Town
GREAT GANILLY
Isles of Scilly Heritage Coast
Pool
TRESCO
Tresco Abbey
Crow Bar
Crow Sound
GREAT ARTHUR
North West Channel
SAMSON
Bant's Carn Burial
Innisidgen Tomb
ST. MARY'S
SV
Harry's Walls
Longstone Heritage Centre
Hugh Town
Deep Point
Garrison Walls
Porth Hellick Downs Tombs
Isles of Scilly (St Mary's)
Old Town
ANNET
St Mary's Sound
Peninnis Head
Broad Sound
GUGH
Middle Town
ST AGNES
Smith Sound
Horse Point
Western Rocks

0 1 2 3 4 5 miles
0 1 2 3 4 5 6 7 kilometres

St Agnes
ST AGNES HEAD
St
Wheal Coates
Goonv
Porthtowan
Menagi
South West Coast Path
Mawla
Camb
Nor
Cour
Portreath
B3300
Godrevy – Portreath Heritage Coast
Bridge
Ilogan
Poynter's Lane End
Park Bottom
Tehidy Woods
Coombe
Roscroggan
Reskadinnick
Treswithian
Cornish Mines
Pool
Carn Brea
Godrevy Island
Navax Point
Godrevy Point
Gwealavellan
Upton Towans
Gwithian
Kehelland
A30
Roseworthy
Penponds
Tuckingmill
Carn Brea
Camborne
The Island or St Ives Head
Carn Naun Point
Treveal
Hellesveor
Trendrine
St Ives
Towans Railway
The Towans
Phillack
Connor Downs
Roseworthy
Troon
Bolenowe
Penhale
Fou
Zennor Head
Gurnards Head
Treen
Zennor
Halsetown
Carbis Bay
Lelant
Hayle
Copperhouse
Angarrack
Barripper
Carnhell Green
Croft Michael
Praze-an-Beeble
11
Burras
South West Coast Path
14
Porthmeor
Zennor Towednack
Cripplesease
Georgia
Merlins Magic Land
Brunnian
High Lanes
Gwinear
Rosewarne
Wall
Trenerth
Blackrock
Farms Common
Por
Pendeen Watch
Lower Boscaswell
Morvah
Bojewyan
Men-An-Tol
Mulfra Quoit
Nancledra
Whitecross
Canonstown
St Erth
St Erth Praze
Fraddam
Horsedown
Crowan
Releath
Lezerea
Crelly
Geevor Tin Mines
Trewellard
Pendeen
Great Bosullow
Boskednan
Lanyon Quoit
Mulfra
New Mill
Castle Gate
Badger's Cross
Cockwells
A30
Crowlas
Kerthen Wood
Leedstown
Drym
Nancegollan
Prospidnick
Trenear
Poldark Mine
Botallack
Carnyorth
Trengwainton Garden NT
Boswarthan
Ludgvan
Trannack
Townshend
Godolphin Cross
Wendron
Kenidjack
Newbridge
Madron
Bone Tolver
Gulval
St Hilary
Relubbus
Trescowe
Crowntown
Sithney
Coverack Bridges
Cape Cornwall
St Just
Tregeseal
7
Heamoor
Tremethick Cross
Chyandour
Trevarrack
Longrock
Treveague
Goldsithney
Millpool
Balwest
Carleen
Sithney
Green
Lower Town
Trewennack
Ballowall Barrow with Heritage Coast
Bosavern
Chyandour
Marazion
St Michael's Mount NT
A394
Newtown
Germoe
Ashton
Sithney Common
Helston
Kelynack
Grumbla
Sancreed
Tredavoe
Penzance
Perranuthnoe
Rosudgeon
Kenneggy
Trew
Breage
Antron
Flambards
Mellangoose
Nanquidno
Brane
Carn Euny
Newlyn
Prussia Cove
Praa Sands
Rinsey Croft
Rinsey
Trewavas
Methleigh
A3083
Sellan
Drift
Kerris
Paul
Cudden Point
Rinsey Head
Higher Pentire
Mawgan Cross
Whitesand Bay
Land's End 6
Catchall
Sheffield
Trevithal
Mousehole
MOUNT'S BAY
Trewavas Head
Porthleven
Carminowe
Tregoose
Escalls
A30
Crows-an-Wra
Toldavas
Raginnis
SW
Chyvarloe
Tregiddle
Berepper
Sennen Cove
Sennen
Trevorgans
Trewoofe
St Buryan
Castallack
Lamorna
Gunwalloe
Chyanvounder
LAND'S END
Land's End
Trengothal
Bottoms
The Merry Maidens
Boskennal
Lamorna Cove
White Cross
Cury
Gw
Cro
Trevescan
Trebehor
Trethewey
Treen
Merthen Point
Bochym
Polgigga
Raftra
Cribba Head
Angrouse
Trewoon
Röskesta
Porthcurno
Minack Open Air Theatre
Poldhu Point
Mullion
Trenance
Porthgwarra
St Levan
Gwennap Head
Mullion Cove
Mullion Island
Mullion Cove
11
Predannack Head
Predannack Wollas
Vellan Head
Mount Hermon
The Lizard Heritage Coast
South West Coast Path
Lizard Head
Lizard
LIZARD POINT

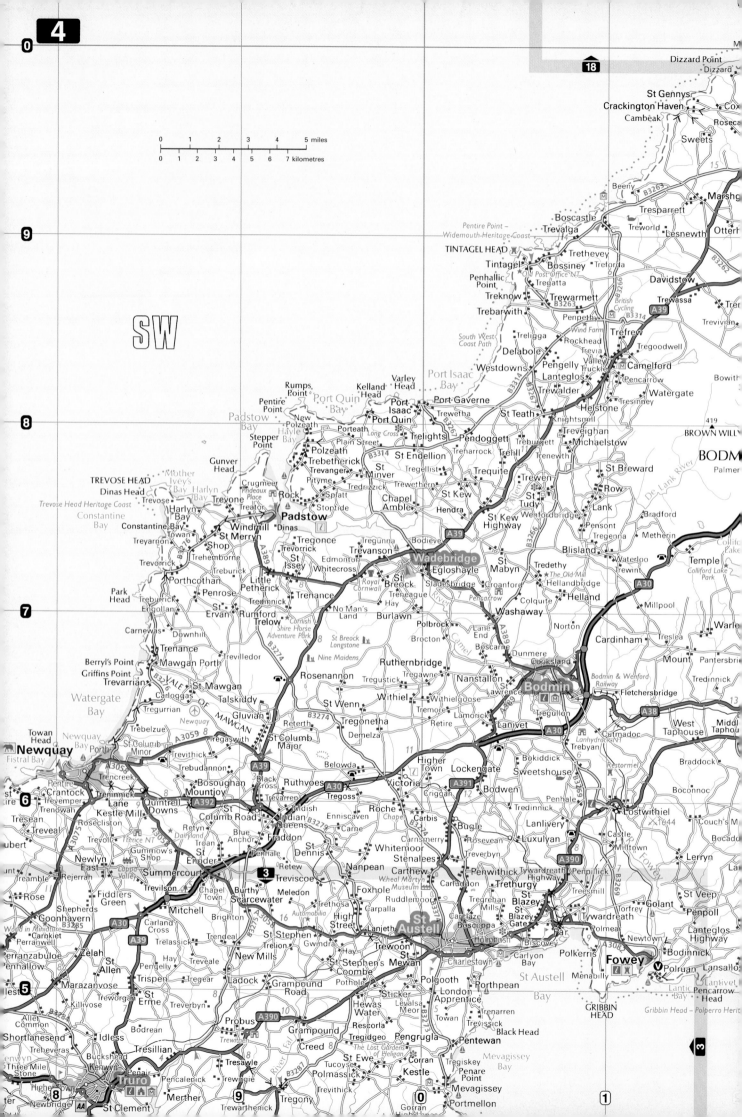

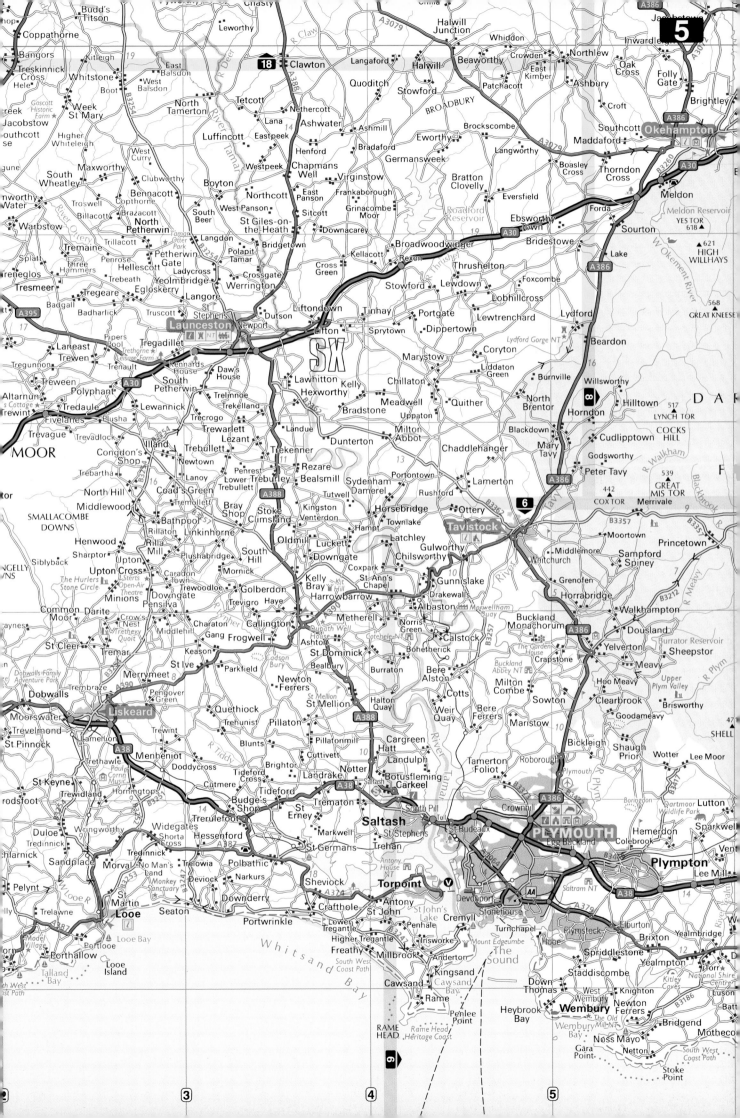

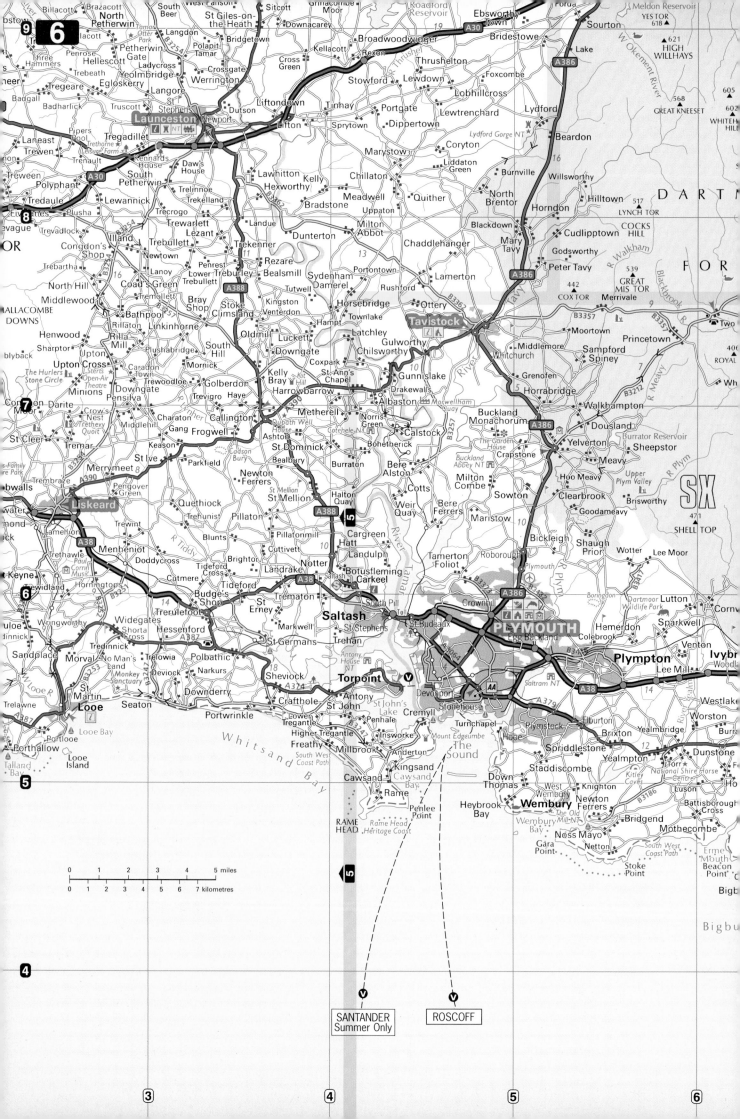

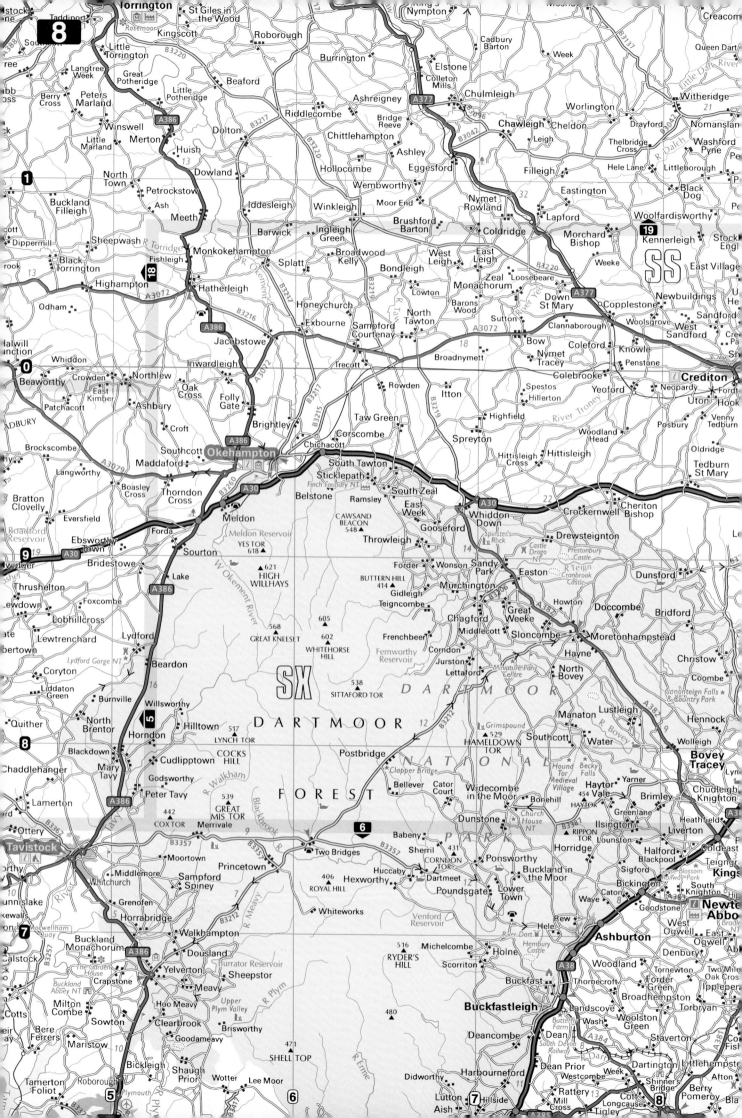

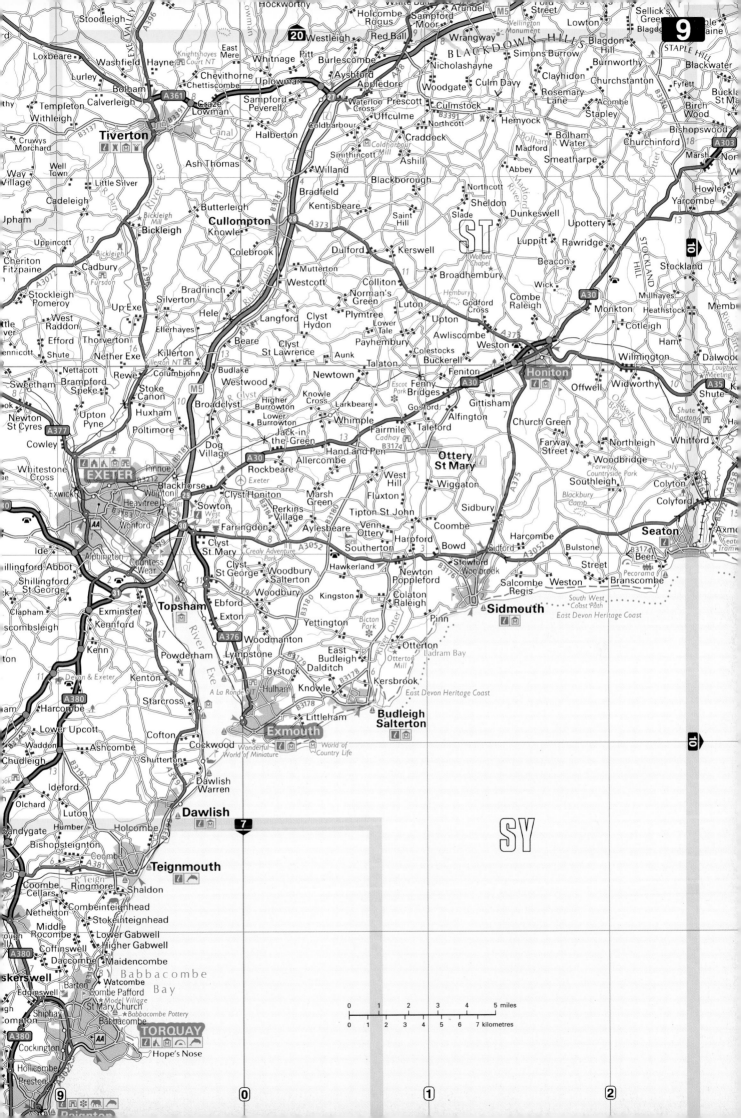

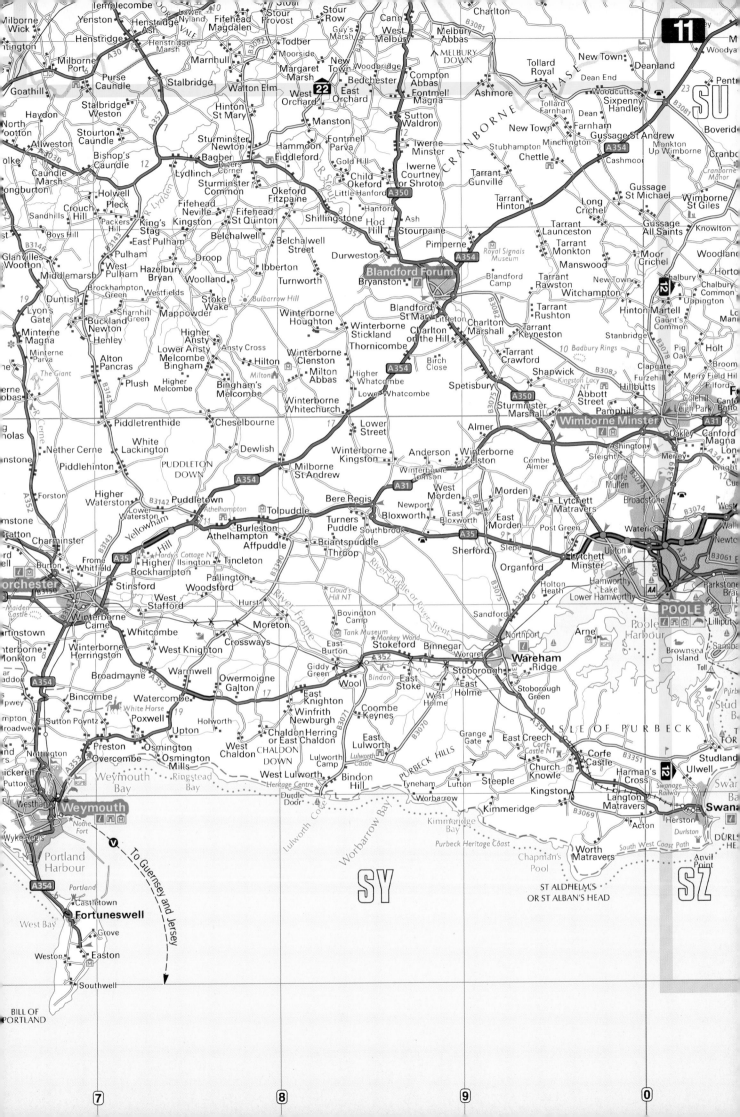

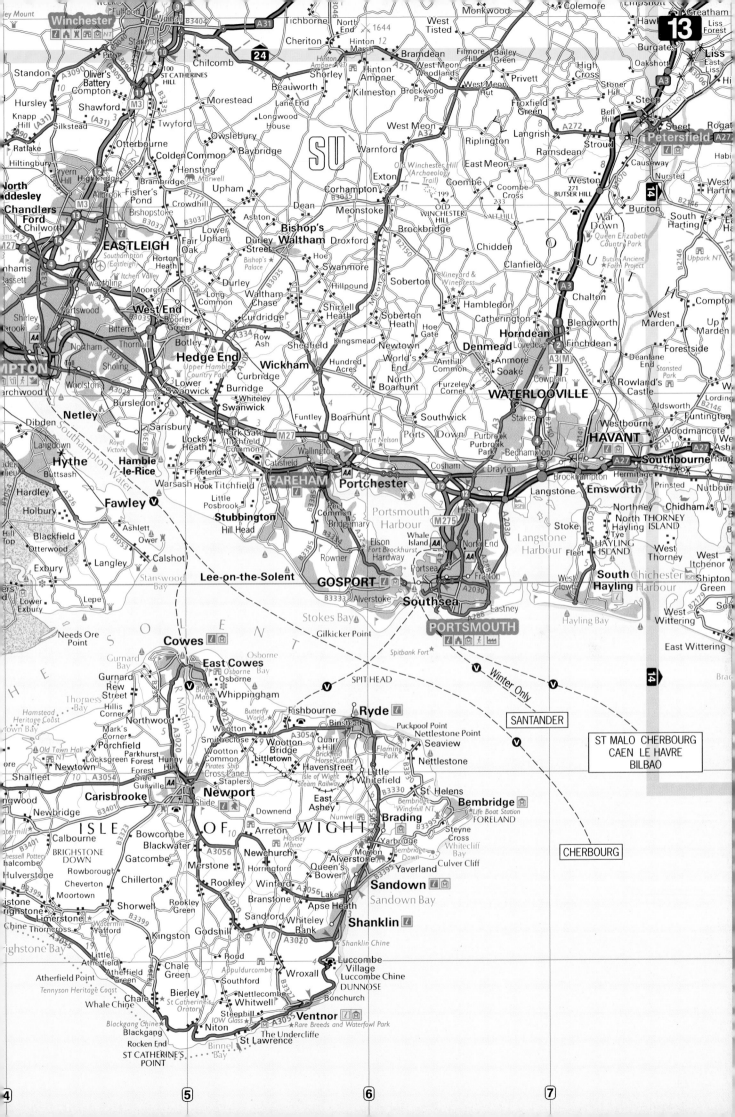

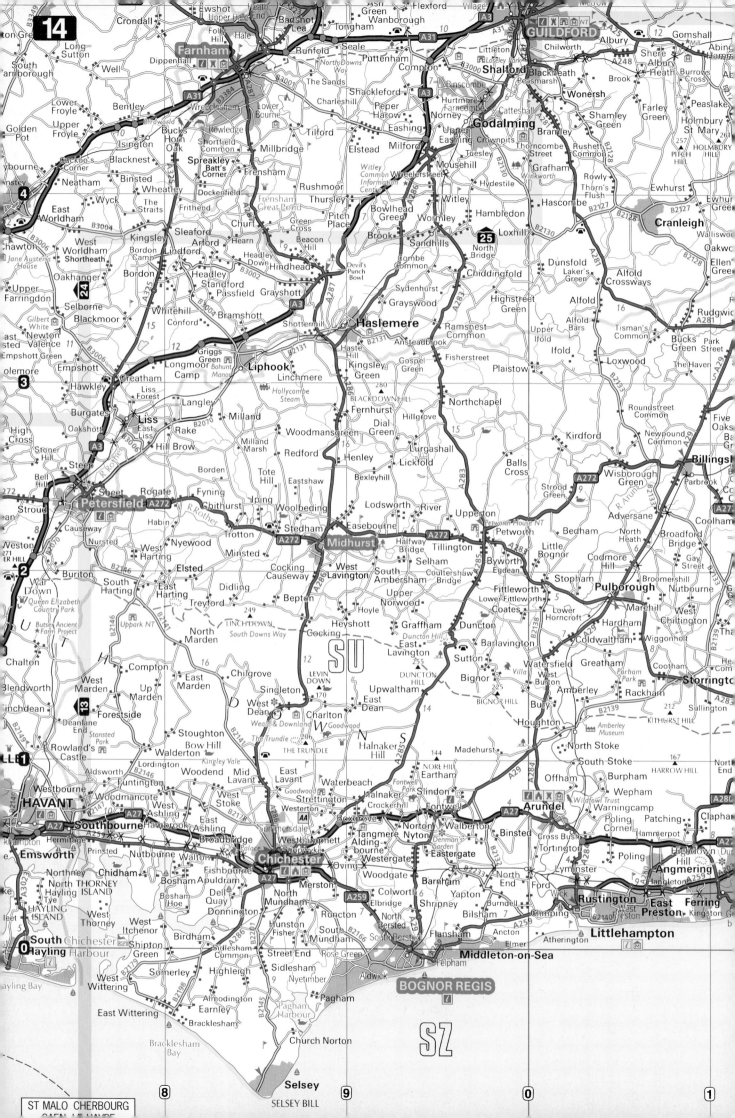

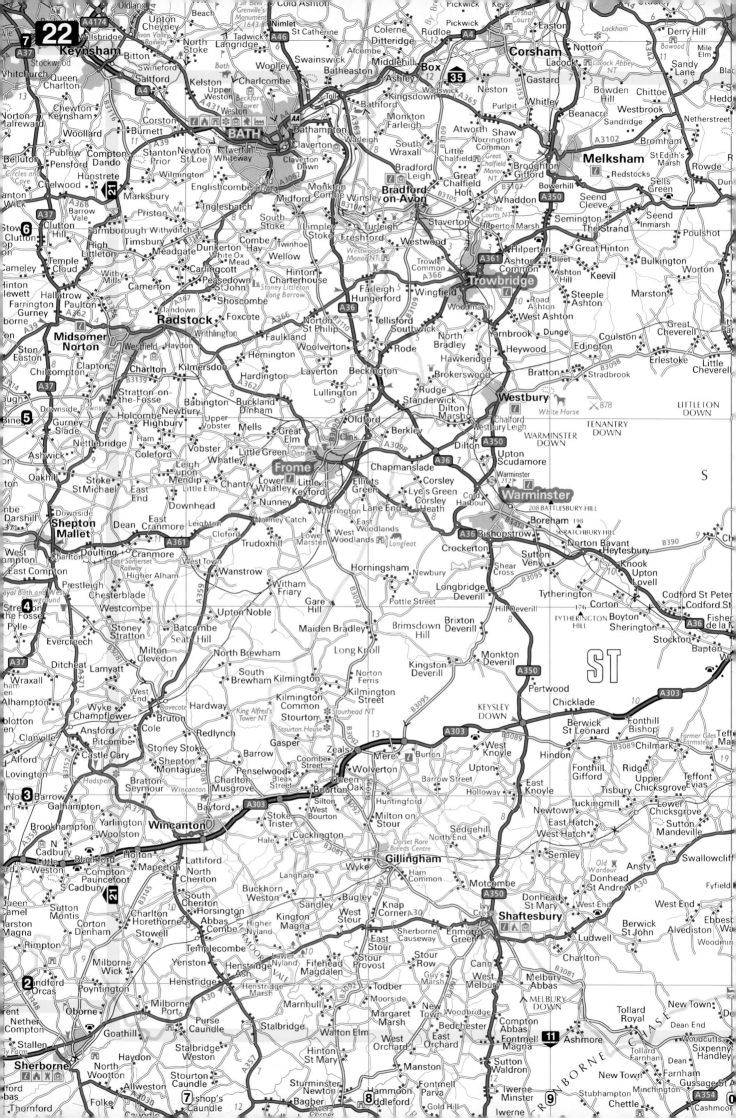

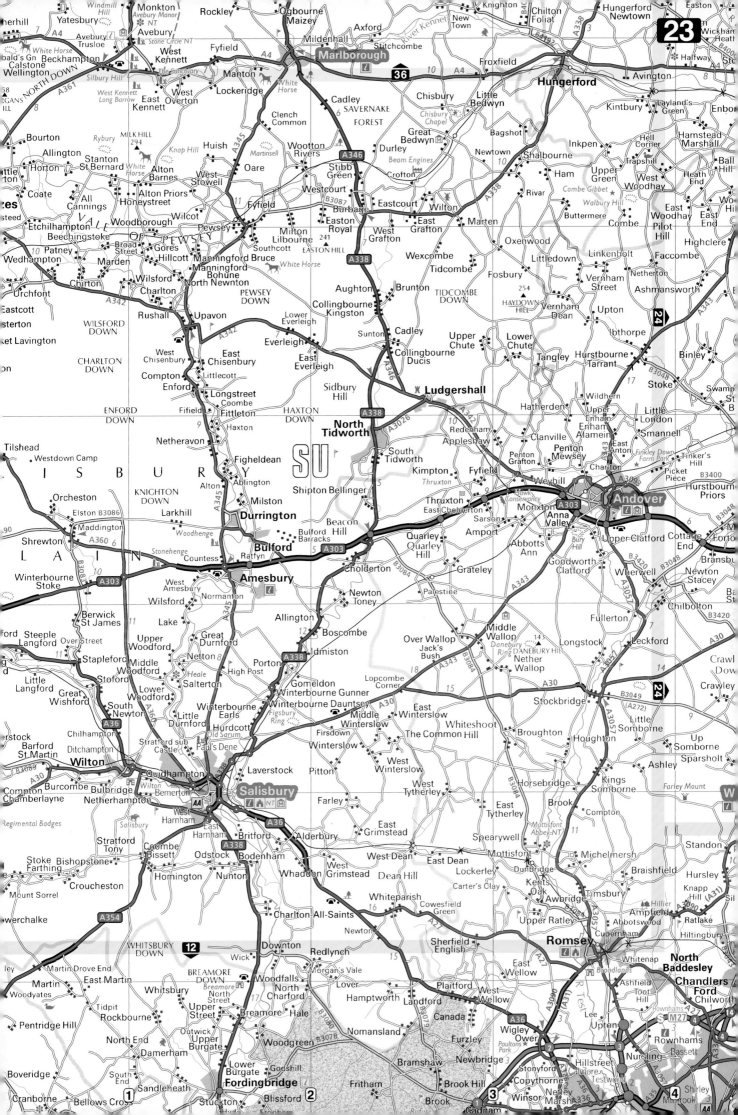

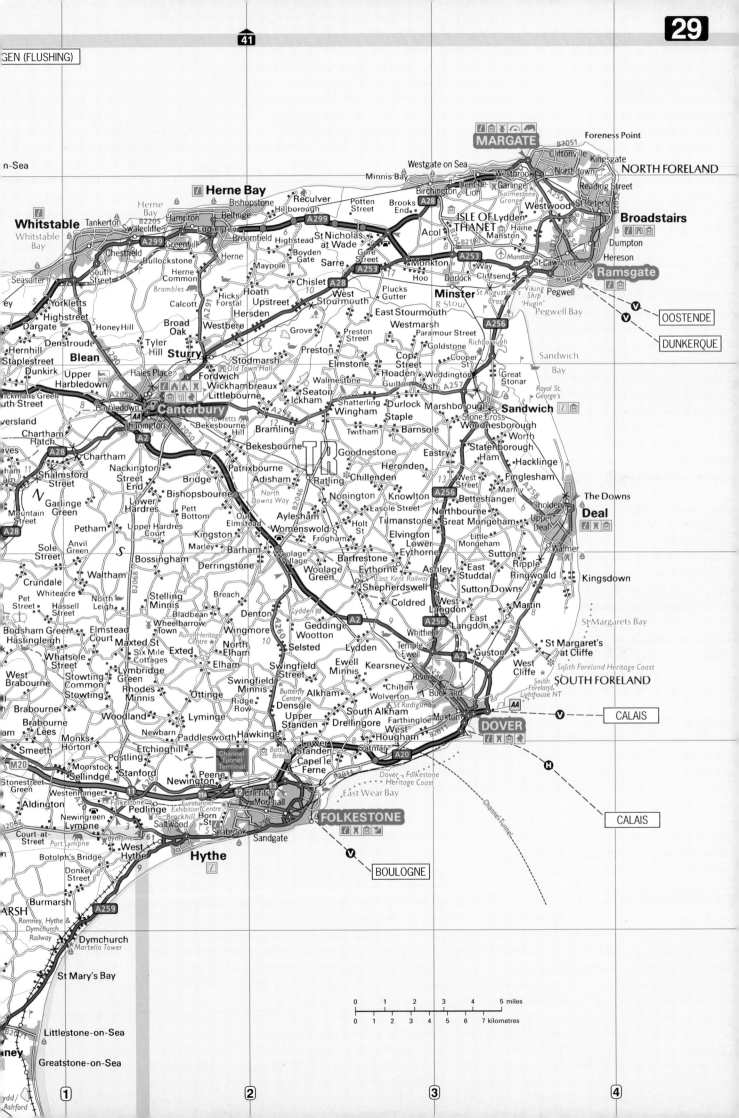

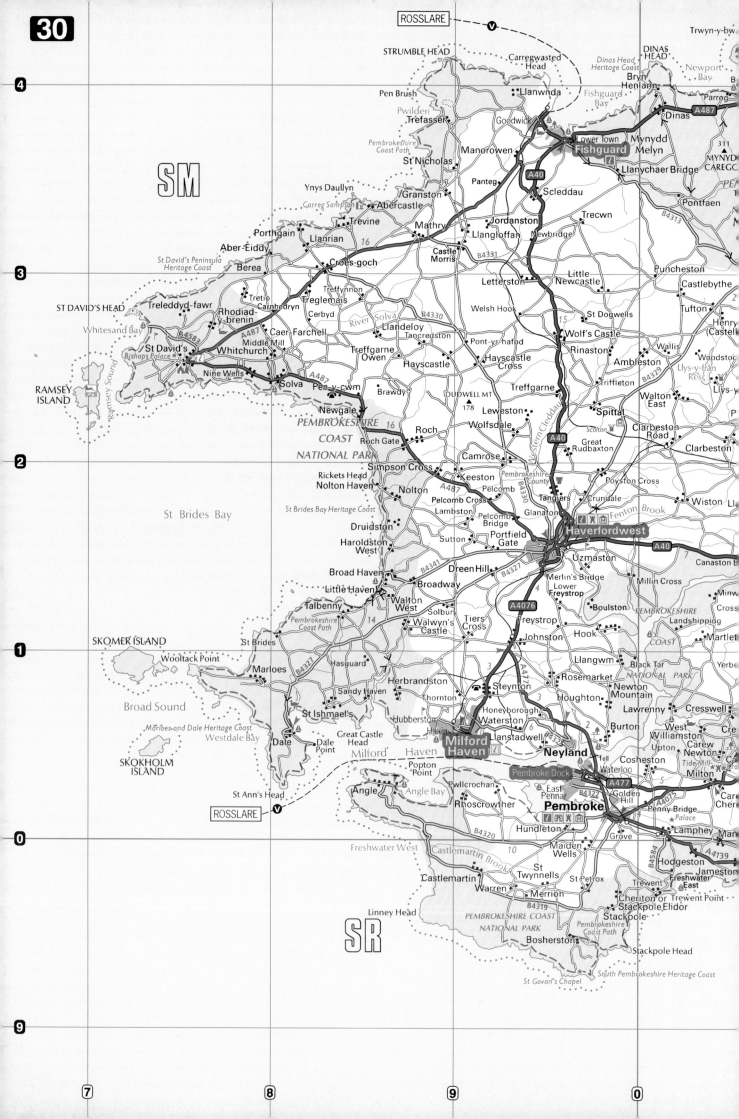

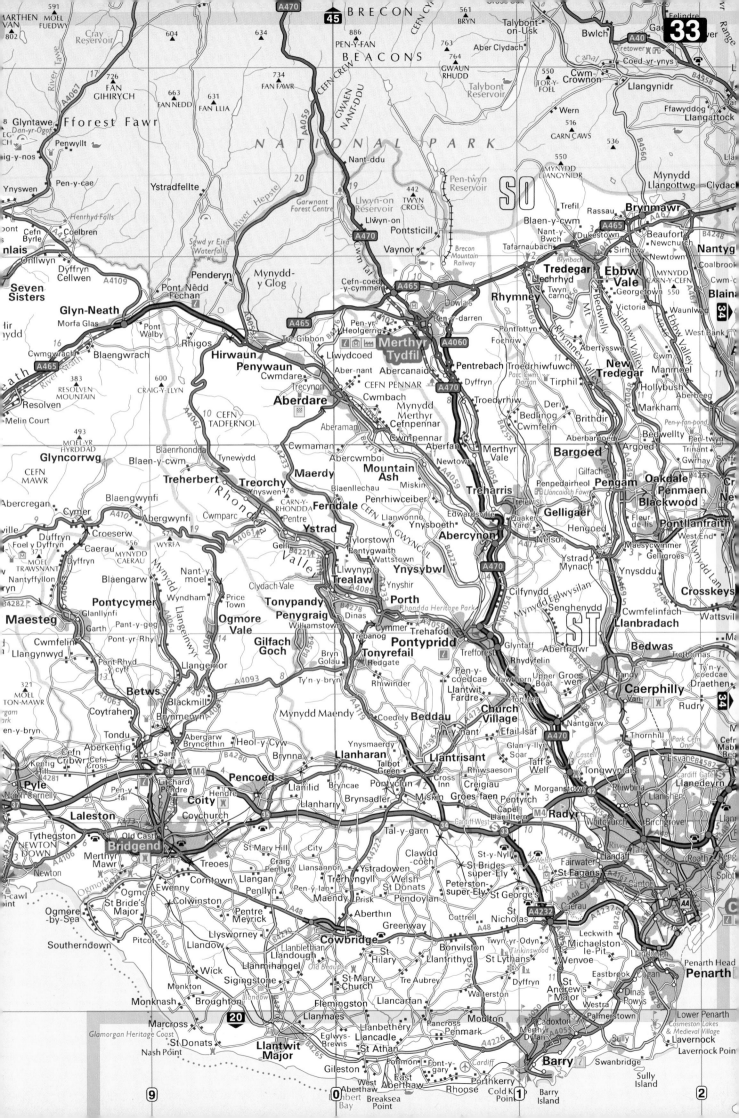

Felixstowe

Boxted
Langham
Dedham
Brantham
Gate
Horkesley Green
Boxted Cross
Castle House
Cattawade
Holbrook Bay
Parkeston Quay
Bath Side
The Redoubt
Boxted Heath
Langham Wick
Lawford
River Stour
Wrabness
AA
Parkeston
Harwich Harbour
Landguard Fort
Manningtree
New Mistley
Ramsey
A120
Upper Dovercourt
Harwich
Landguard Point
Mile End
Fox Street
Ardleigh Heath
Mistley
Mistley Heath
Bradfield
Bradfield Heath
B1352
Dovercourt
High Woods
Parson's Heath
Crockleford Heath
Ardleigh
A120
Horsleycross Street
Wix
B1414
Little Oakley
A133
COLCHESTER
Great Bromley
A120
Horsley Cross
Tendring Heath
Wix Green
Great Oakley
Pennyhole Bay
Greenstead
A133
Elmstead Market
Little Bentley
Tendring Green
Stones Green
New Quay
Beth Chatto
Frating Green
Goose Green
Beaumont
Horsey Island
The Naze
Old Heath
Wivenhoe Cross
Elmstead Heath
Tendring
Thorpe Green
ESBJERG GÖTEBORG
HAMBURG
HOEK VAN HOLLAND
Blackheath
Wivenhoe
Elmstead Row
Frating
A133
Weeley
Thorpe-le-Soken
B1034
Kirby-le-Soken
Rowhedge
Alresford
Great Bentley
B1033
Walton on the Naze
Malting Green
High Park Corner
Aingers Green
Weeley Heath
B1033
Kirby Cross
Fingringhoe
Tenpenny Heath
Great Holland
Abberton
Thorrington
Samson's Corner
Cook's Green
Little Clacton
Frinton-on-sea
Langenhoe
South Green
Hurst Green
B1442
B1032
TM
Peldon
Brightlingsea
B1027
Great Clacton
Holland-on-Sea
Great Wigborough
MERSEA ISLAND
Cudmore Grove
St Osyth
Rush Green
A133
CLACTON-ON-SEA
East Mersea
Point Clear
West Mersea
Jaywick
Colne Point

Shinglehead Point

Bradwell Waterside
Sales Point
Bradwell-on-Sea
B1021

Tillingham

Dengie

Asheldham

hminster

ham-on-ouch
Holliwell Point
Foulness Point

Courtsend

Churchend

FOULNESS ISLAND

0   1   2   3   4   5 miles
0   1   2   3   4   5   6   7 kilometres

TR

0   VLISSINGEN (FLUSHING)   2   3

CARDIGAN

BAY

56

9

0   1   2   3   4   5 miles
0 1 2 3 4 5 6   7 kilometres

8

SN

7

6

5

Llansant
Llan

A487

Aberarth
B4577

Aberaeron

Monachty

Ffos-y-ffin   Llyswen

Cilc

New Quay   Llanina   Llwyncelyn

Maen-y-groes   Gilfachrheda   Oakford

Ceredigion
Heritage Coast   Cross   B4342
Inn   Llanarth

Nanternis   A486   A487   Dihewyd   B4342

Ynys-Lochtyn   4   7   B4342

Llwyndafydd   Caerwedros   Mydroilyn

Pentre'rbryn

Llangranog   Synod Inn

Pontgarreg   Ffynnonddewi

Morfa   Plwmp

Penbryn   B4321   311

Ceredigion
Heritage Coast   Sarnau   15   Pentregat   324   B4338   Gorsgoch

Cardigan Island   Aberporth   Talgarreg   Bwlchyfadfa
Cardigan Island Coastal   Parcllyn   Traethsaith   Brynhoffnant   A486   B4459
Farm Park   B4333

Y Ferwig   Felinwynt   B4333   Capel Cynon

Gwbert on Sea   Rainforest &   Tan-y-groes   Cwrt-newydd
Butterflies   Blaenannerch   A487   Glynarthen   B4334   Penrhiw-pal   9   Pontshaen   Cwmsychbant
Centre   Rhydlewis   Efostrasol   Drefac

Penparc   Tremain   Blaenporth   Bettws Evan   Tre-groes   Rhydowen   Llanwenog
Cardigan   B4570   Hawen   12
Pembrokeshire   Beulah   Brongest   Penrhiw-pal   Croes-lan   Pren-gwyn   Li
Coast Path   St Dogmaels   Llangoedmor   A484   Ponthirwaun   Troedyraur   Coed-y-bryn   A475   Rhyddlan
Moylgrove   Bridgend   Llechryd   Llandygwydd   Maesllyn   A486
Monington   A487   Cilgerran   Llangynllo   Gorrig
Pen-y-bryn   Castle NT   31

2   3   4   5

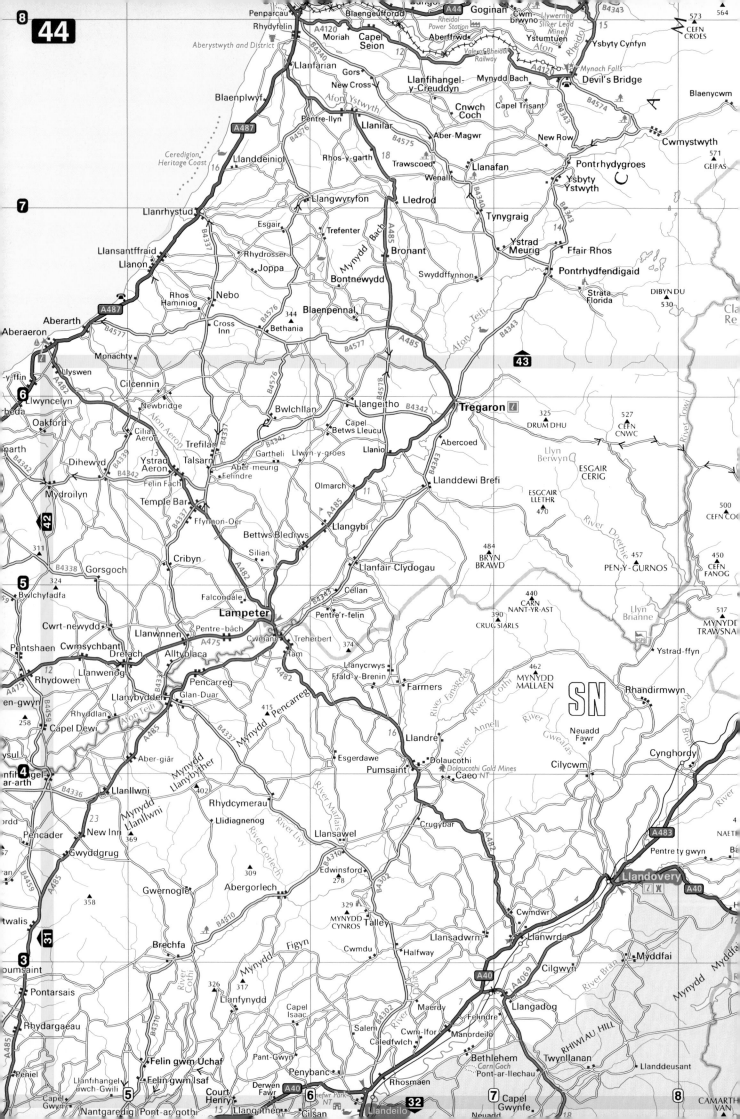

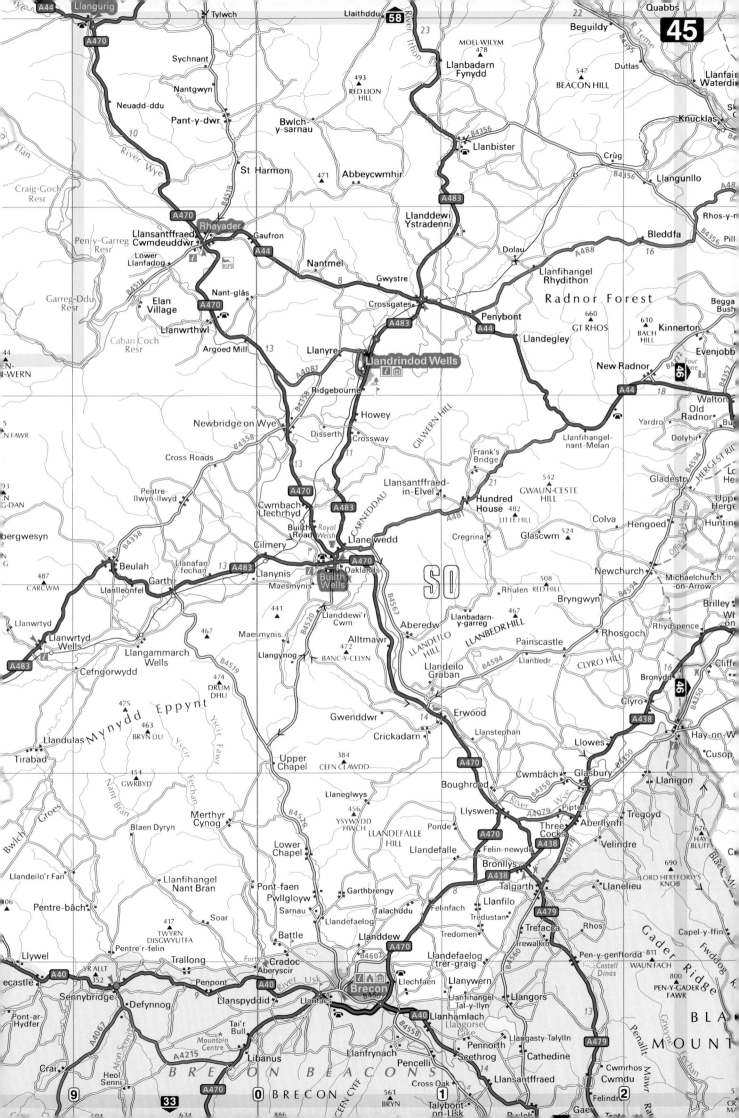

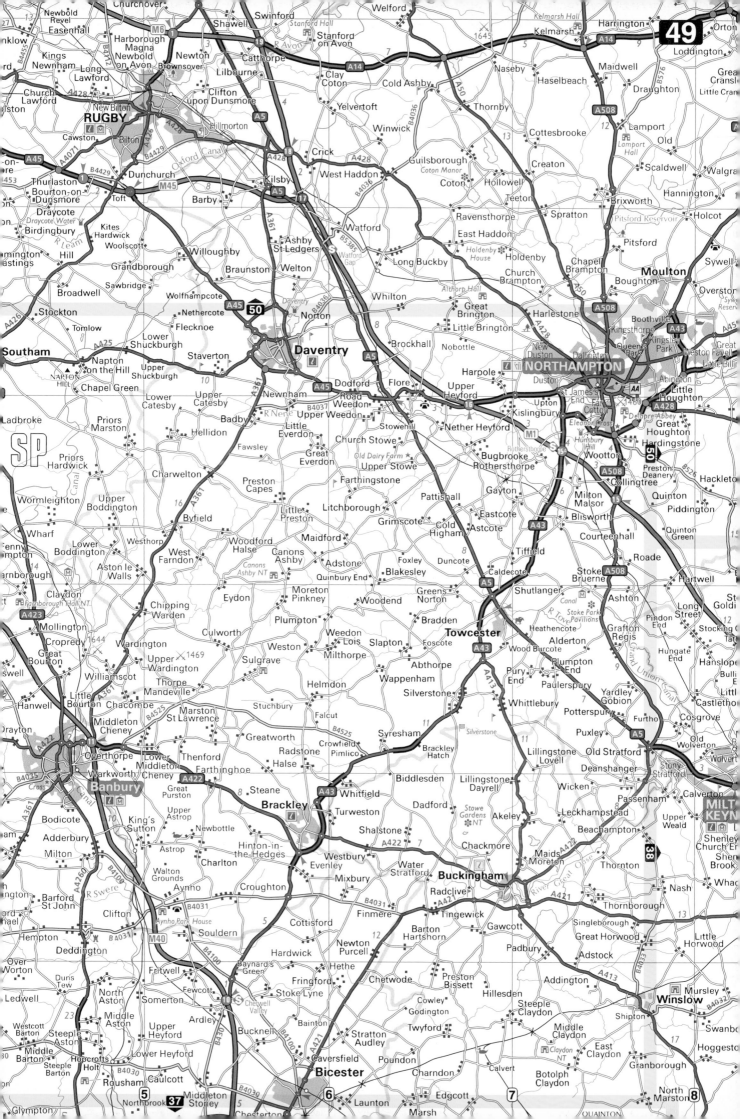

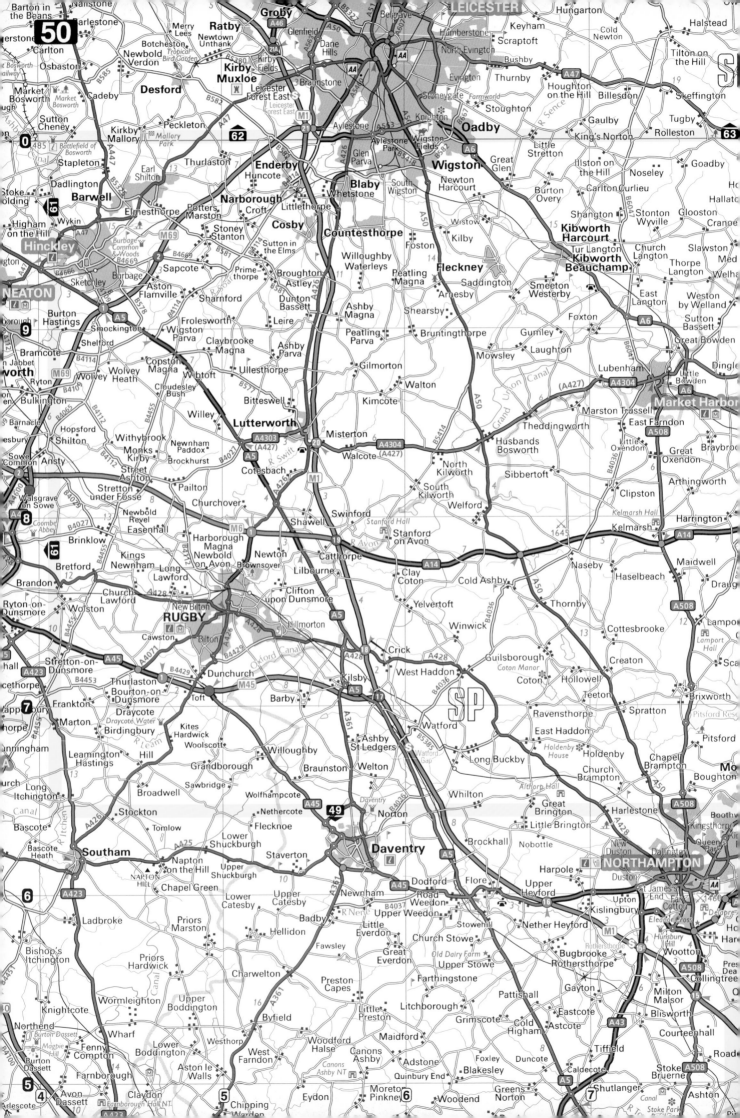

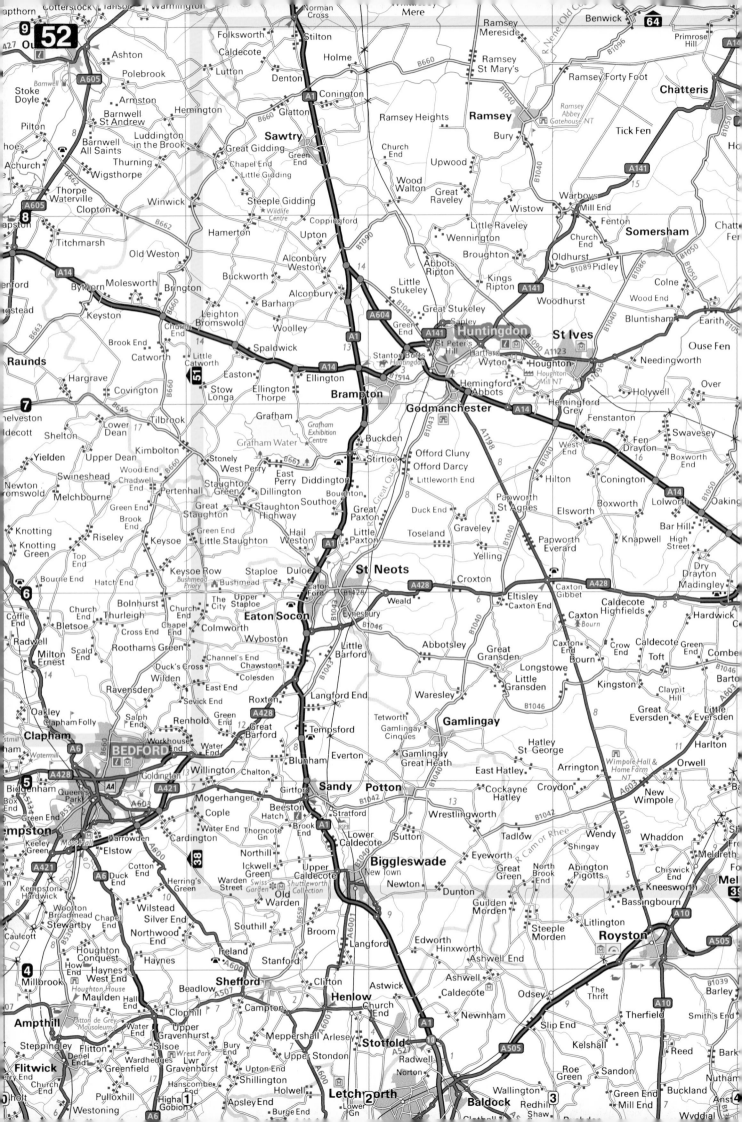

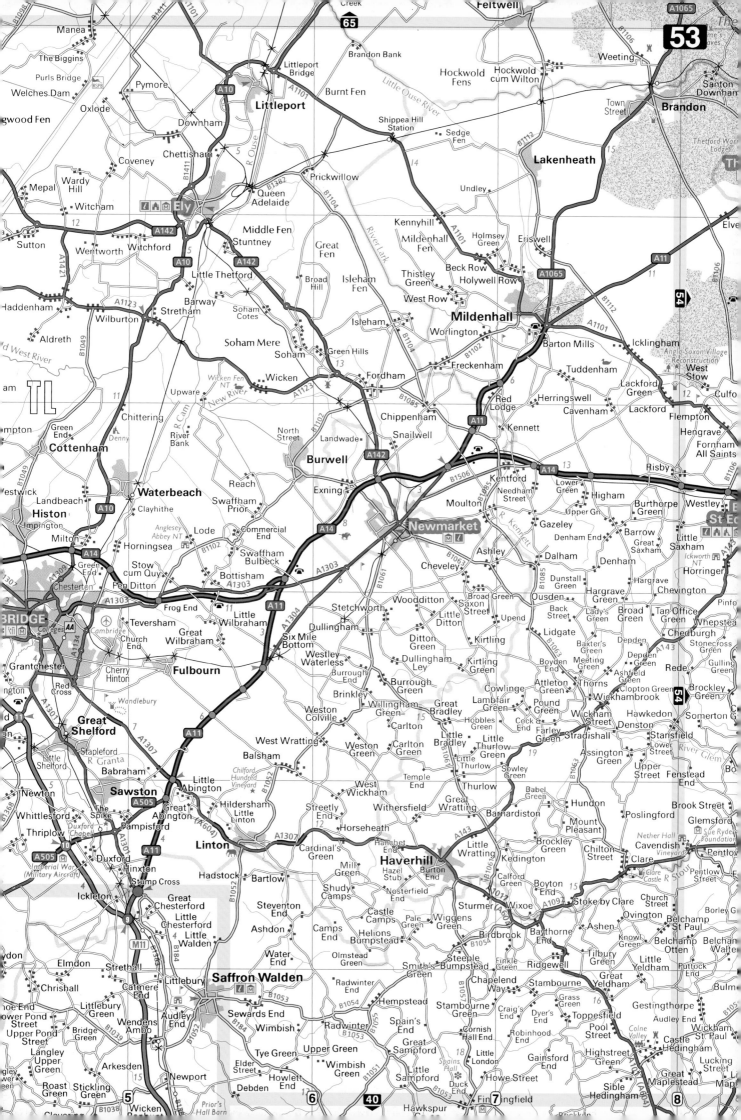

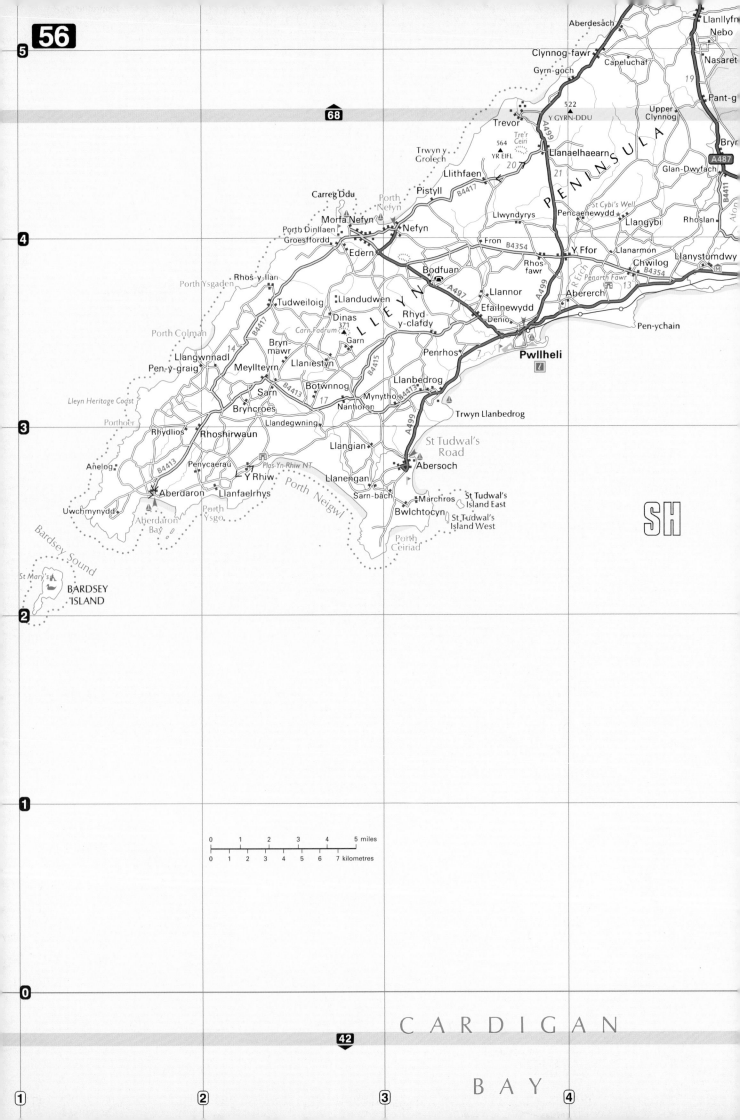

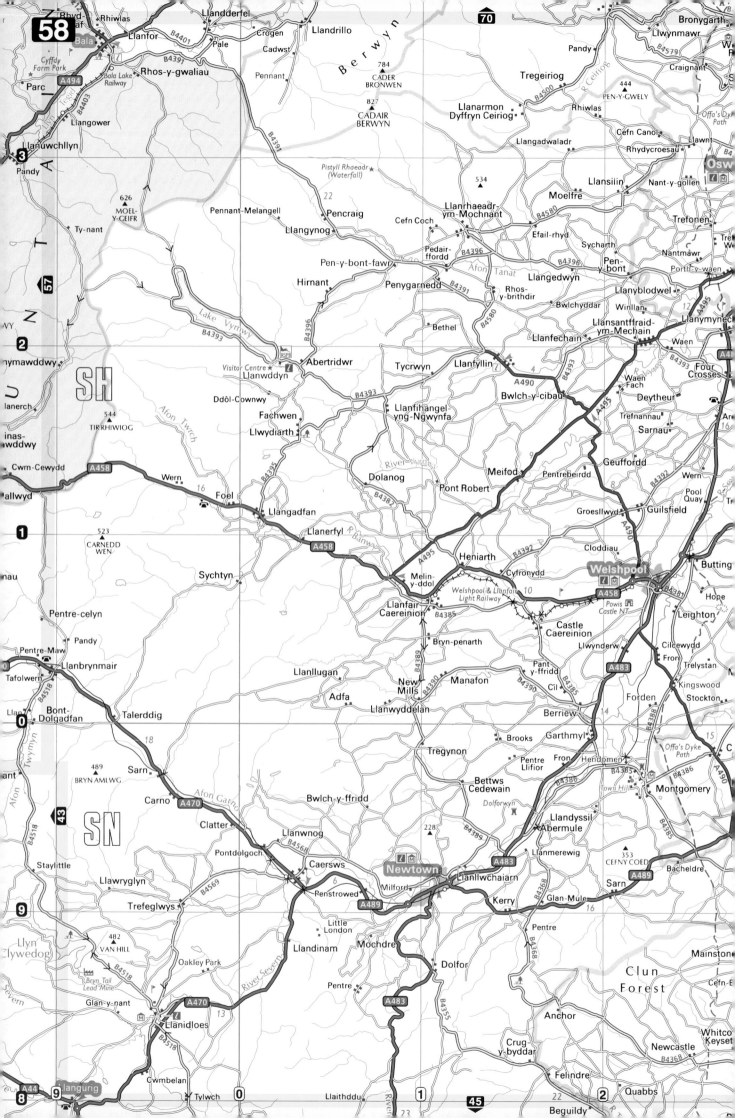

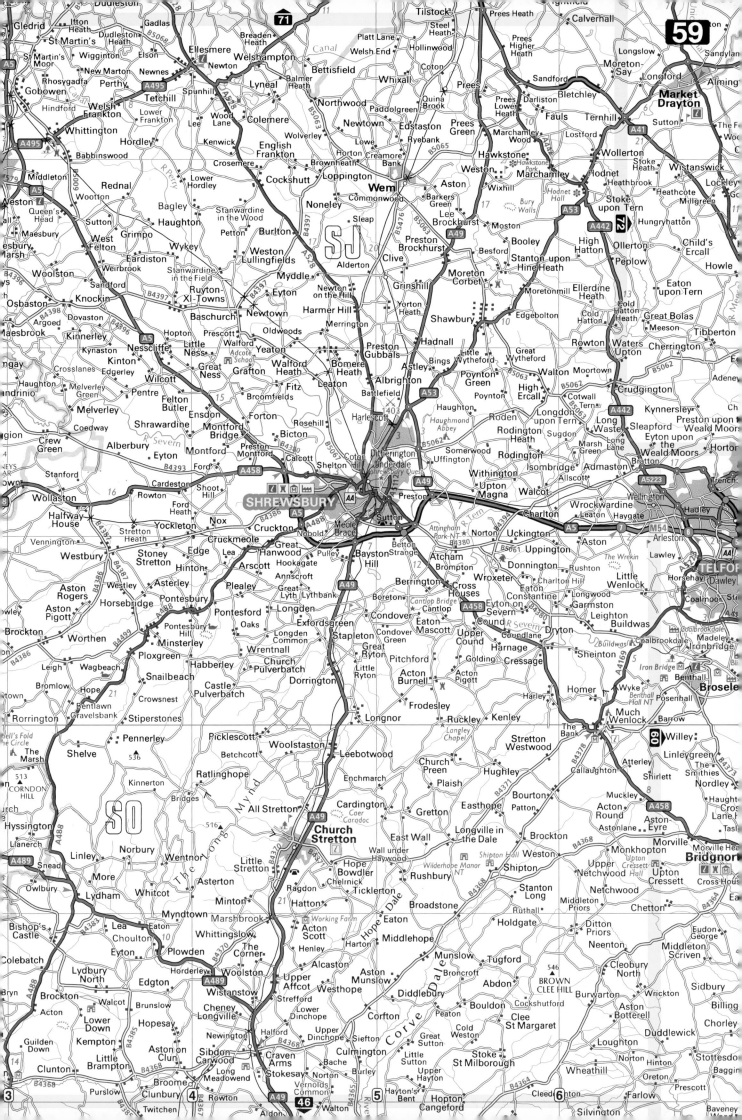

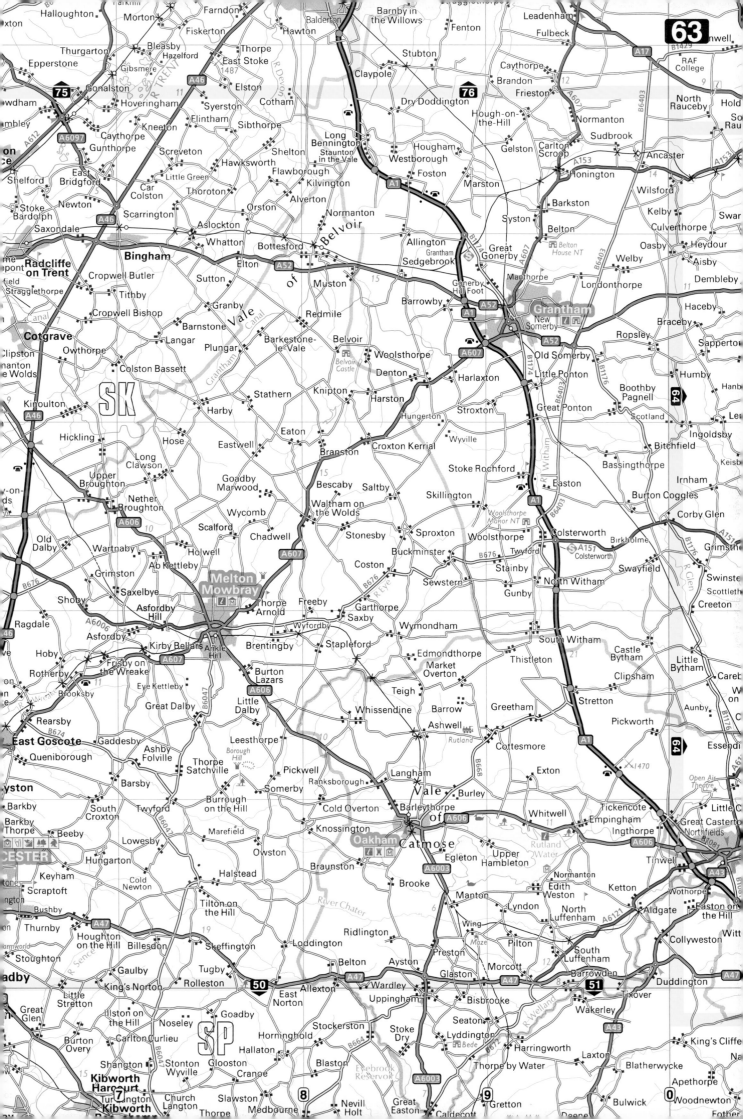

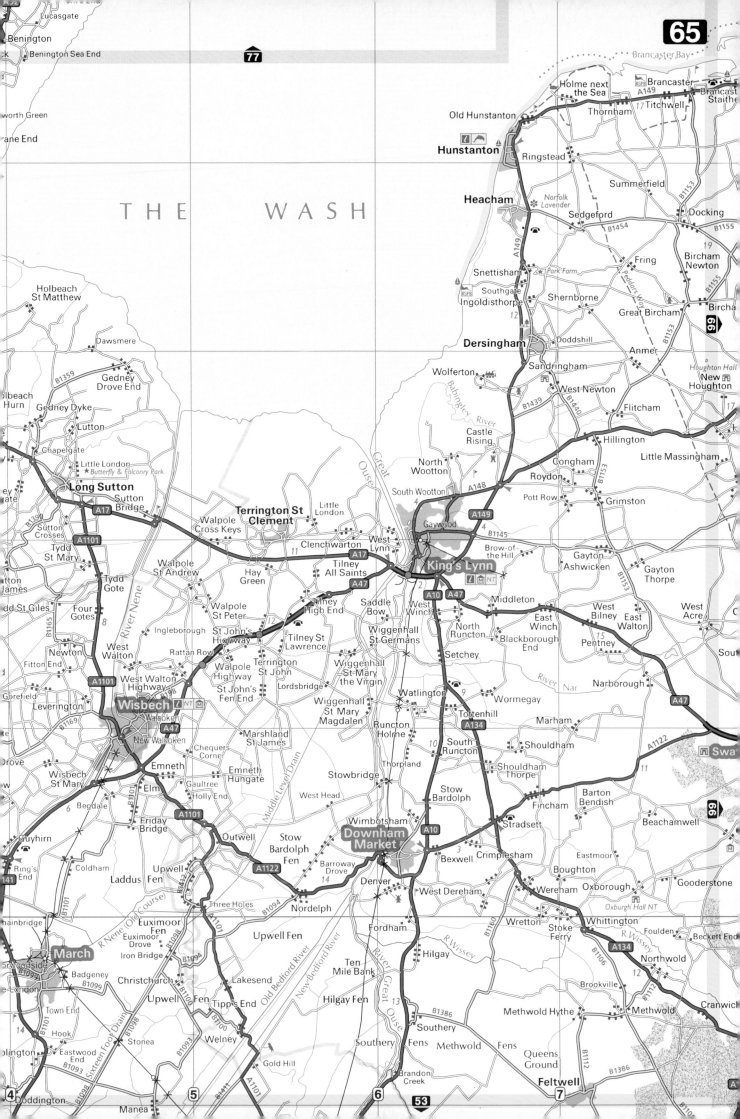

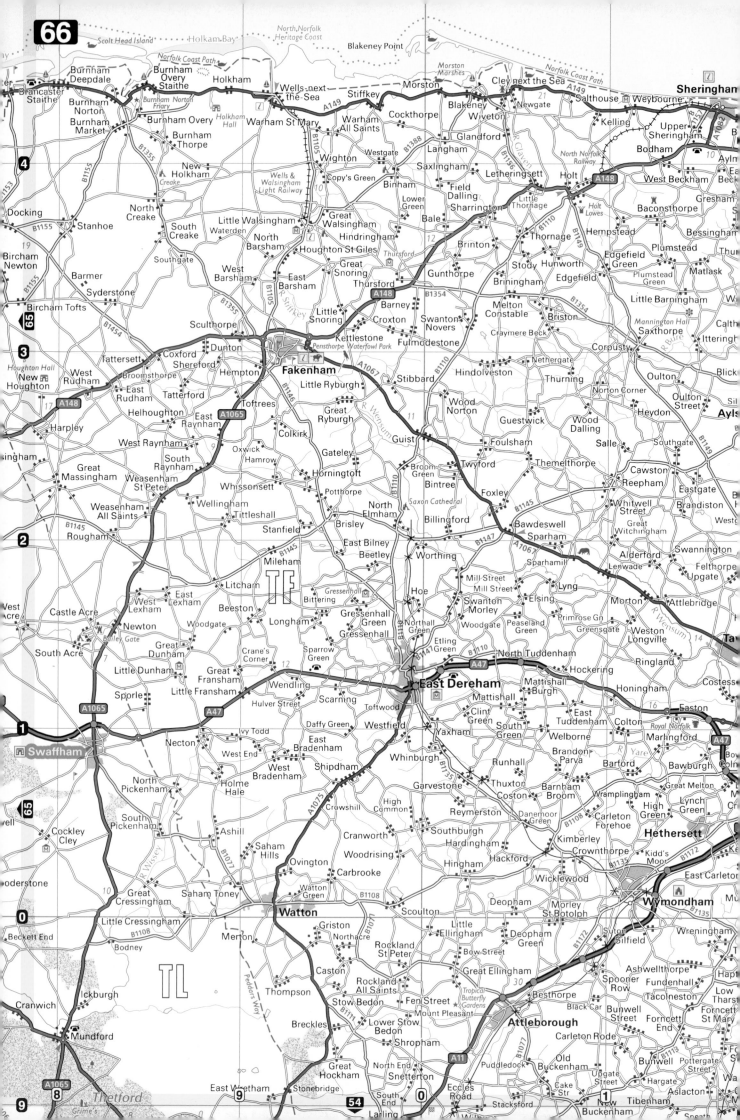

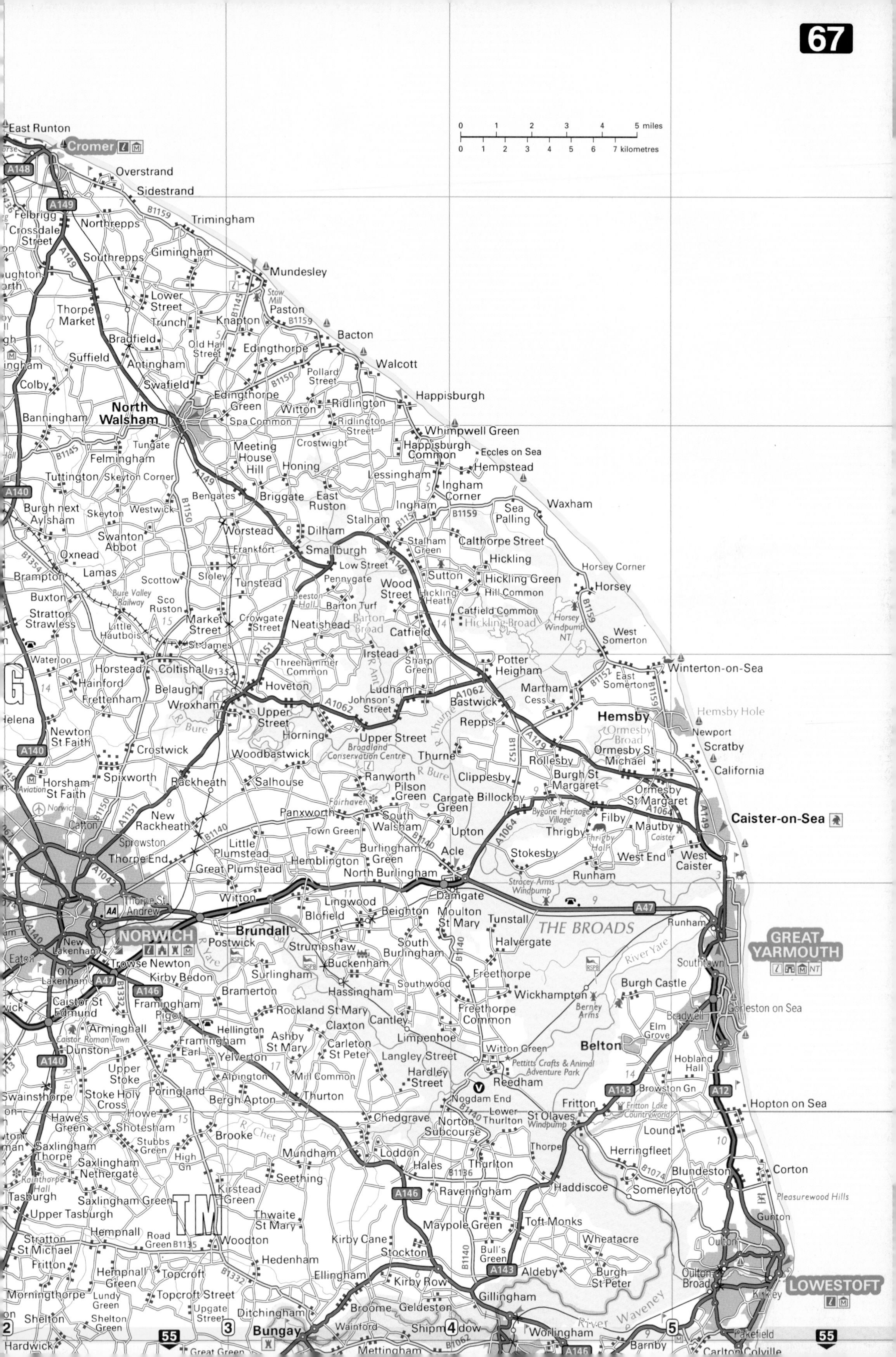

0 1 2 3 4 5 miles
0 1 2 3 4 5 6 7 kilometres
East Runton
Cromer
A148
Overstrand
Sidestrand
A149
B1159
Trimingham
Felbrigg
Crossdale Street
Northrepps
Southrepps
Gimingham
Mundesley
Stow Mill
Paston
Lower Street
Thorpe Market
Trunch
Knapton
B1145
Bacton
Bradfield
Old Hall Street
Edingthorpe
Suffield
Antingham
Walcott
Pollard Street
Colby
Swafield
Edingthorpe Green
Happisburgh
North Walsham
Banningham
Witton
Ridlington
Spa Common
Ridlington Street
Whimpwell Green
Tungate
Meeting House Hill
Crostwight
Happisburgh Common
Eccles on Sea
Felmingham
Honing
Hempstead
Tuttington
Skeyton Corner
Lessingham
A140
Bengates
Briggate
East Ruston
Ingham Corner
Burgh next Aylsham
Skeyton
Westwick
B1150
Ingham
Sea Palling
Waxham
Stalham
B1159
Worstead
Dilham
Swanton Abbot
Stalham Green
Calthorpe Street
Oxnead
Frankfort
Smallburgh
Hickling
Lamas
Low Street
Brampton
Scottow
Sloley
Tunstead
Pennygate
Wood Street
Sutton
Hickling Green
Horsey Corner
Horsey
Buxton
Bure Valley Railway
Sco Ruston
Beeston Hall
Barton Turf
Hickling Heath
Hill Common
Catfield Common
Stratton Strawless
Little Hautbois
Market Street
Crowgate Street
Neatishead
Barton Broad
Catfield
Hickling Broad
Horsey Windpump NT
West Somerton
St James
Irstead
Waterloo
Horstead
Coltishall
B1354
Threehammer Common
Sharp Green
Potter Heigham
Winterton-on-Sea
Hainford
Belaugh
Hoveton
Ludham
A1062
Martham
East Somerton
B1152
Frettenham
Wroxham
Johnson's Street
Bastwick
Cess
Helena
Upper Street
Bure
Horning
Repps
Hemsby
Hemsby Hole
Newton St Faith
Upper Street
Thurne
Ormesby Broad
Newport
Scratby
A140
Crostwick
Woodbastwick
Broadland Conservation Centre
Thurne
B1152
Rollesby
Ormesby St Michael
California
Horsham St Faith
Spixworth
Rackheath
Salhouse
Ranworth
R Bure
Clippesby
Burgh St Margaret
Norwich Aviation
Pilson Green
Cargate Green
Billockby
Ormesby St Margaret
Norwich
New Rackheath
Fairhaven
A1064
Catton
Panxworth
South Walsham
Bygone Heritage Village
Filby
Caister-on-Sea
A1151
B1140
Town Green
Upton
Thrigby
Thrigby Hall
Mautby
Caister
Sprowston
Little Plumstead
Burlingham Green
Stokesby
West End
West Caister
Thorpe End
Hemblington
Acle
A1042
Great Plumstead
North Burlingham
Runham
Stracey Arms Windpump
Thorpe St Andrew
Witton
Damgate
A47
Lingwood
Beighton
Moulton St Mary
Tunstall
THE BROADS
Runham
AA
Brundall
Blofield
GREAT YARMOUTH
NORWICH
Postwick
Strumpshaw
South Burlingham
Halvergate
River Yare
New Lakenham
R Yare
RSPB
Buckenham
Southtown
Eaton
Trowse Newton
Surlingham
Freethorpe
Old Lakenham
A47
Kirby Bedon
Hassingham
Southwood
Burgh Castle
A146
B1332
Bramerton
Wickhampton
Berney Arms
Gorleston on Sea
Caistor St Edmund
Framingham Pigot
Rockland St Mary
Cantley
Freethorpe Common
Bradwell
Arminghall
Hellington
Claxton
Elm Grove
Caistor Roman Town
Framingham Earl
Ashby St Mary
Carleton St Peter
Limpenhoe
Belton
Dunston
Yelverton
Langley Street
Witton Green
A140
Upper Stoke
Alpington
Hardley Street
Pettitts Crafts & Animal Adventure Park
Hobland Hall
Poringland
Mill Common
Reedham
Swainsthorpe
Stoke Holy Cross
Bergh Apton
Thurton
Nogdam End
A143
Browston Gn
A12
Fritton
Fritton Lake Countryworld
Hopton on Sea
Howe
Chedgrave
Norton Subcourse
Lower Thurlton
St Olaves Windpump
Hawe's Green
Shotesham
Lound
Brooke
R Chet
Thorpe
Saxlingham Thorpe
Stubbs Green
High Gn
Mundham
Loddon
Herringfleet
Saxlingham Nethergate
Hales
Thurlton
Corton
B1136
Blundeston
Rainthorpe Hall
Seething
Haddiscoe
B1074
Pleasurewood Hills
Tasburgh
Saxlingham Green
Kirstead Green
A146
Raveningham
Somerleyton
Upper Tasburgh
TM
Thwaite St Mary
Maypole Green
Toft Monks
Gunton
Hempnall
Road Green
B1135
Woodton
Kirby Cane
Wheatacre
Stratton St Michael
B1140
Bull's Green
Oulton
Fritton
Hedenham
Stockton
Hempnall Green
Topcroft
B1332
Ellingham
A143
Aldeby
Burgh St Peter
Oulton Broad
LOWESTOFT
Morningthorpe
Lundy Green
Topcroft Street
Kirby Row
Gillingham
Kirkley
River Waveney
Upgate Street
Ditchingham
Broome
Geldeston
Shelton
Shelton Green
Bungay
Wainford
Shipmeadow
Worlingham
Pakefield
Hardwick
Great Green
Mettingham
B1062
Barnby
Carlton Colville
A146
2
3
4
5
55
55

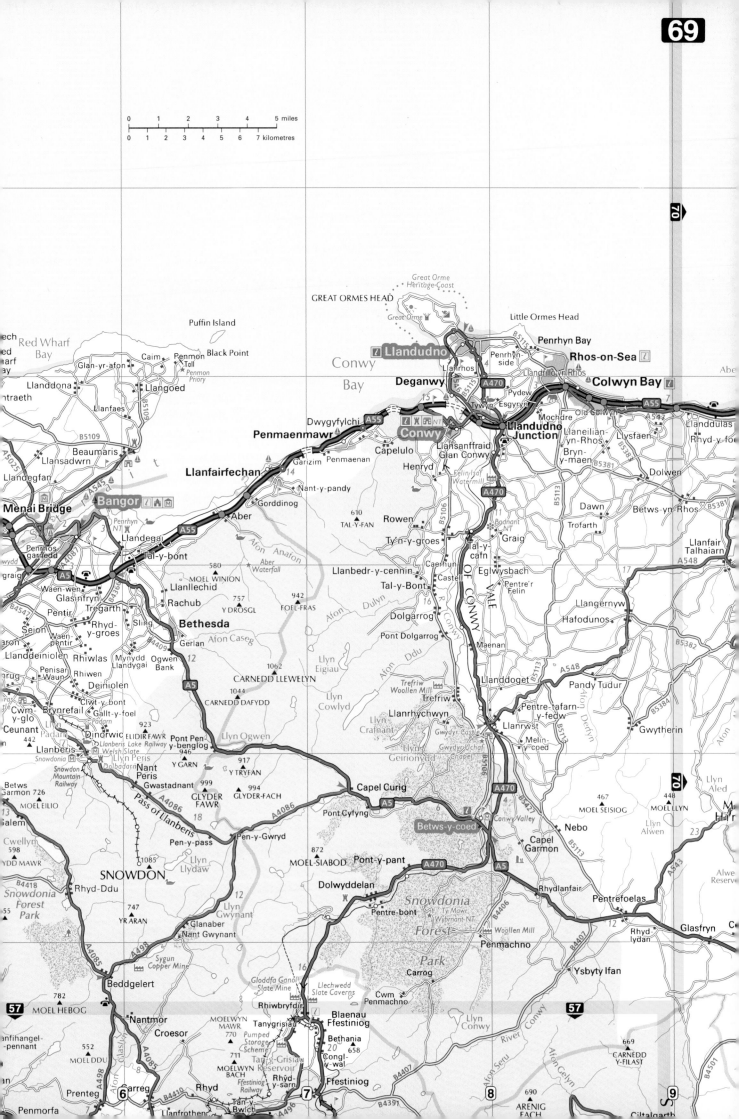

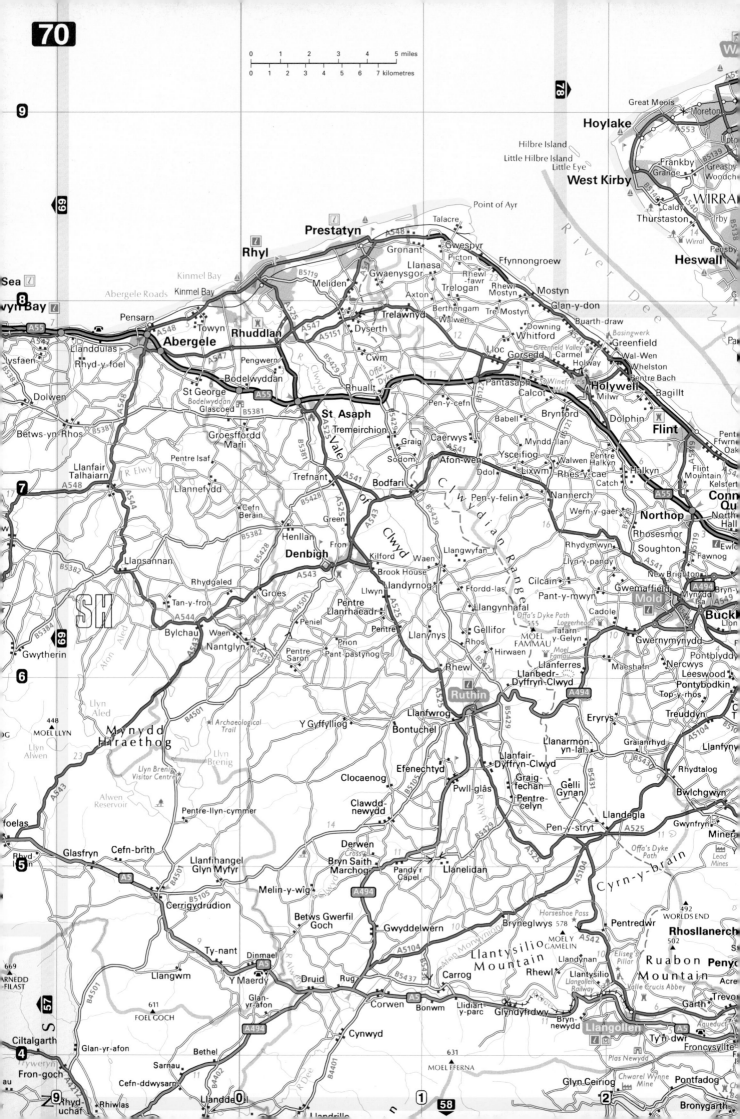

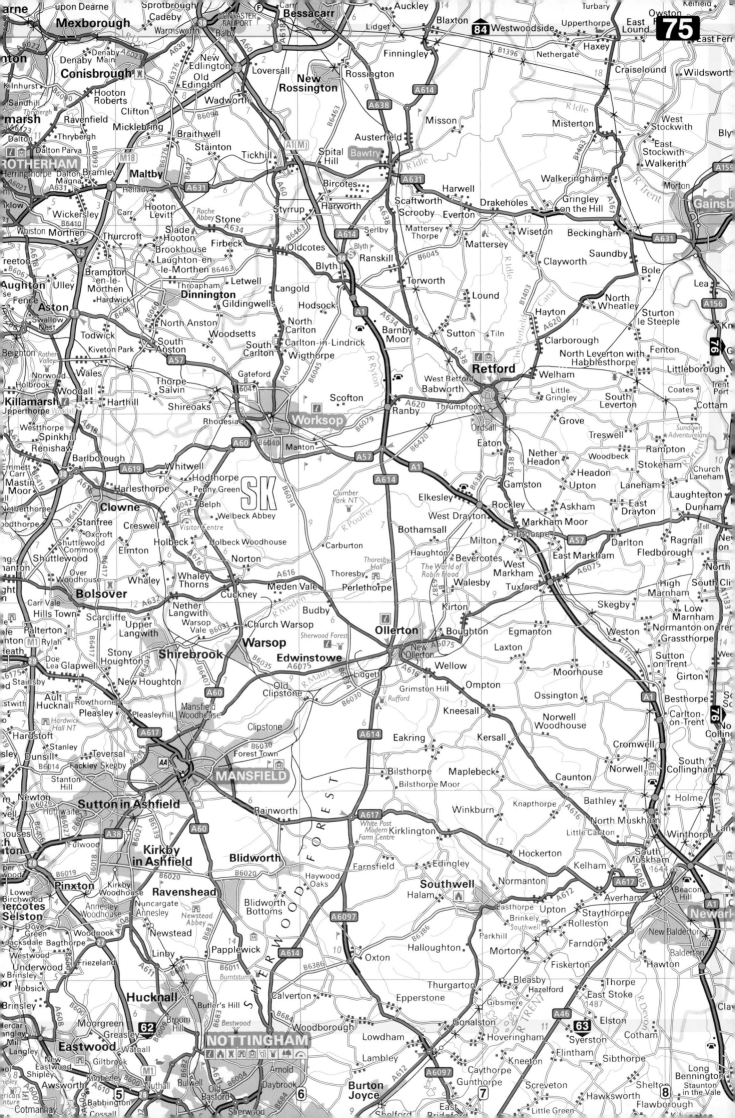

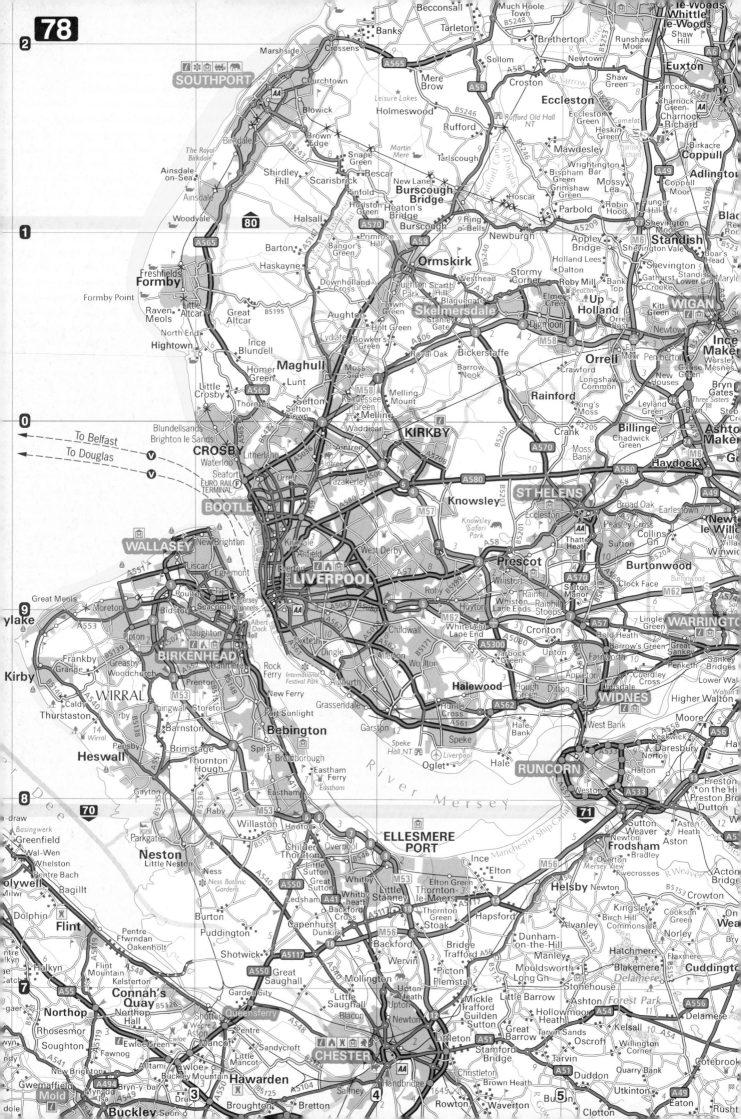

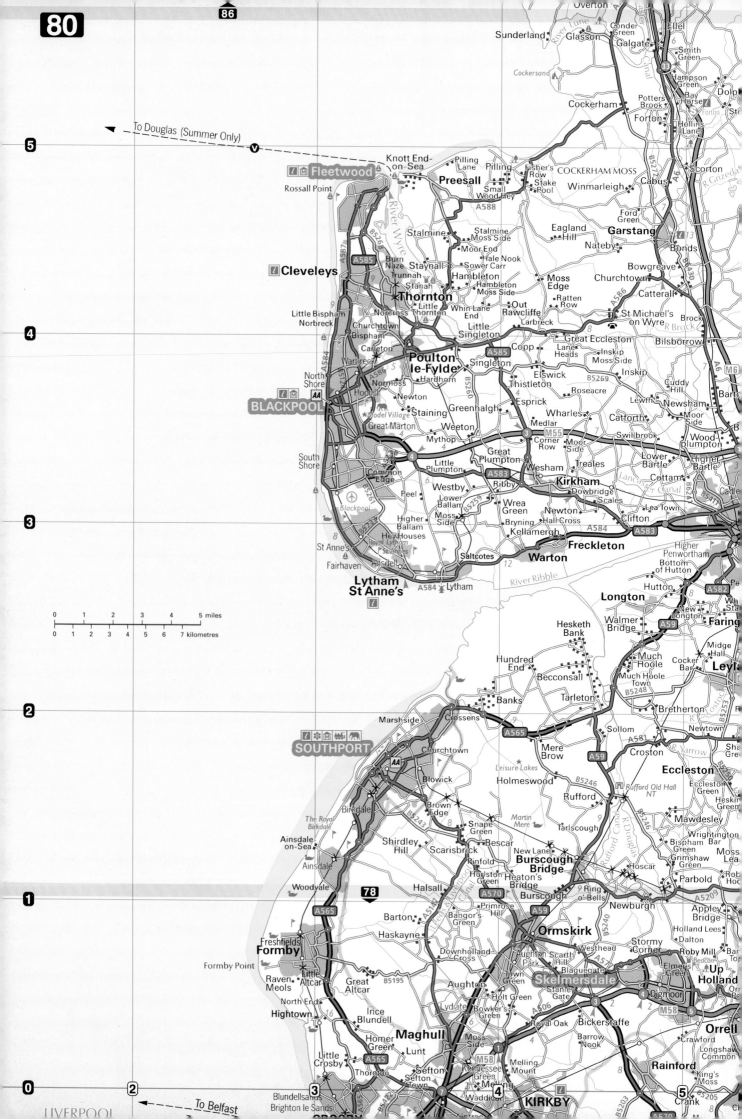

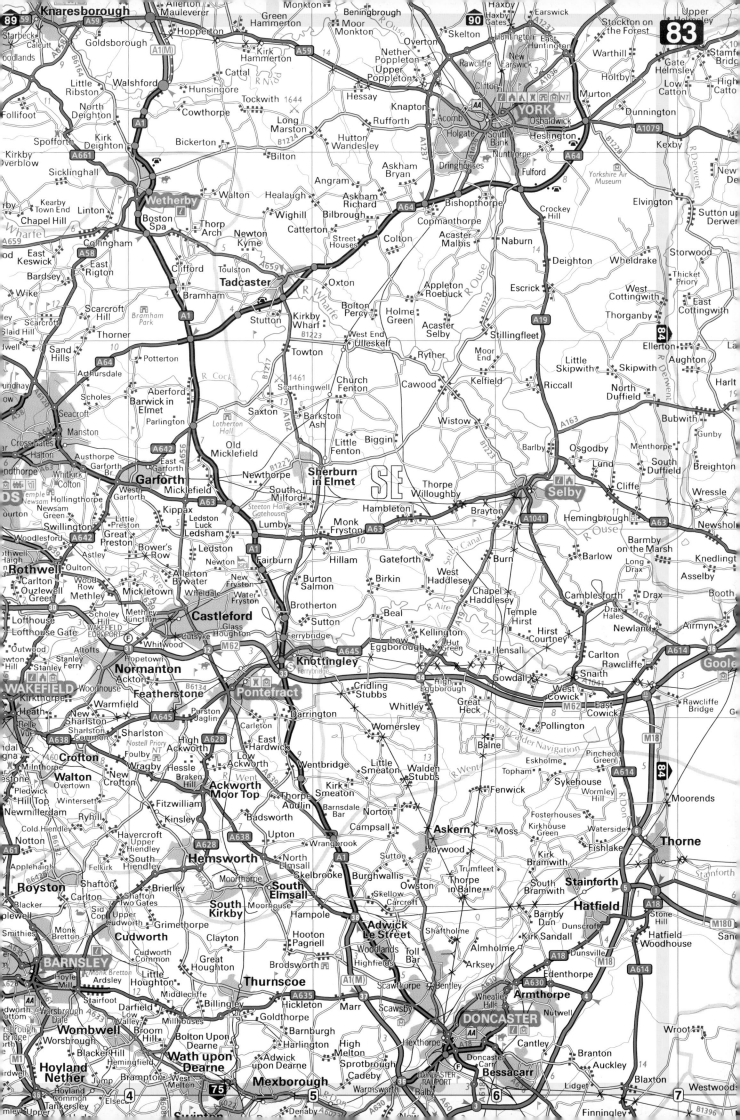

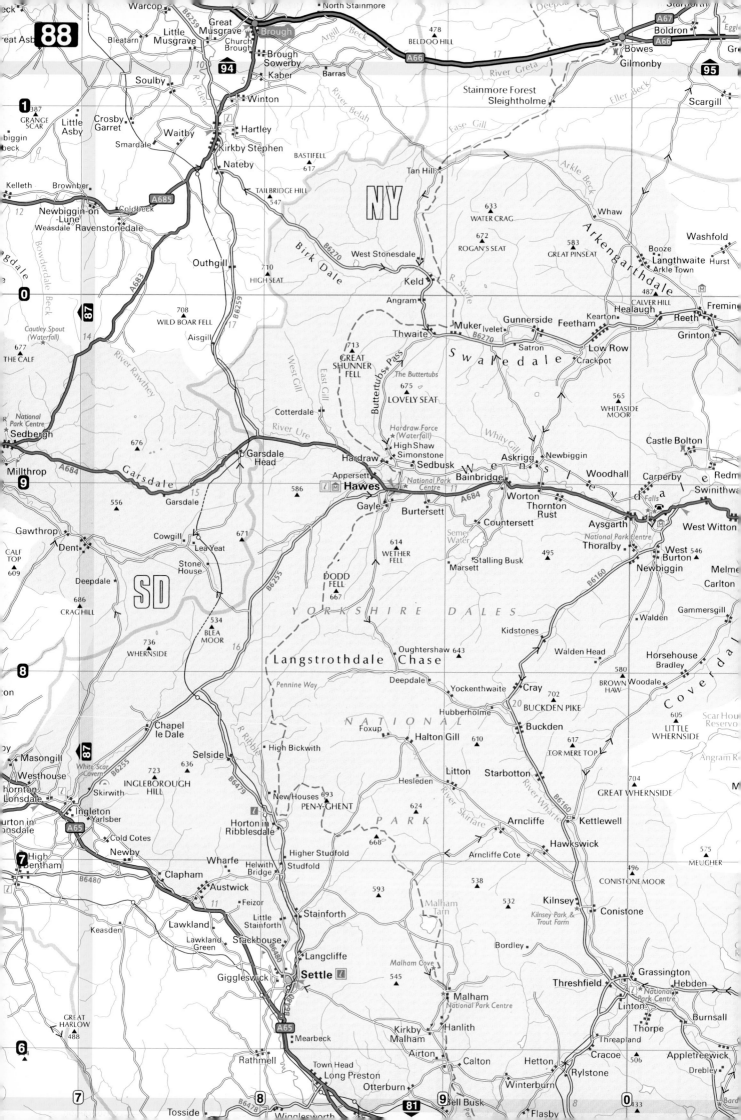

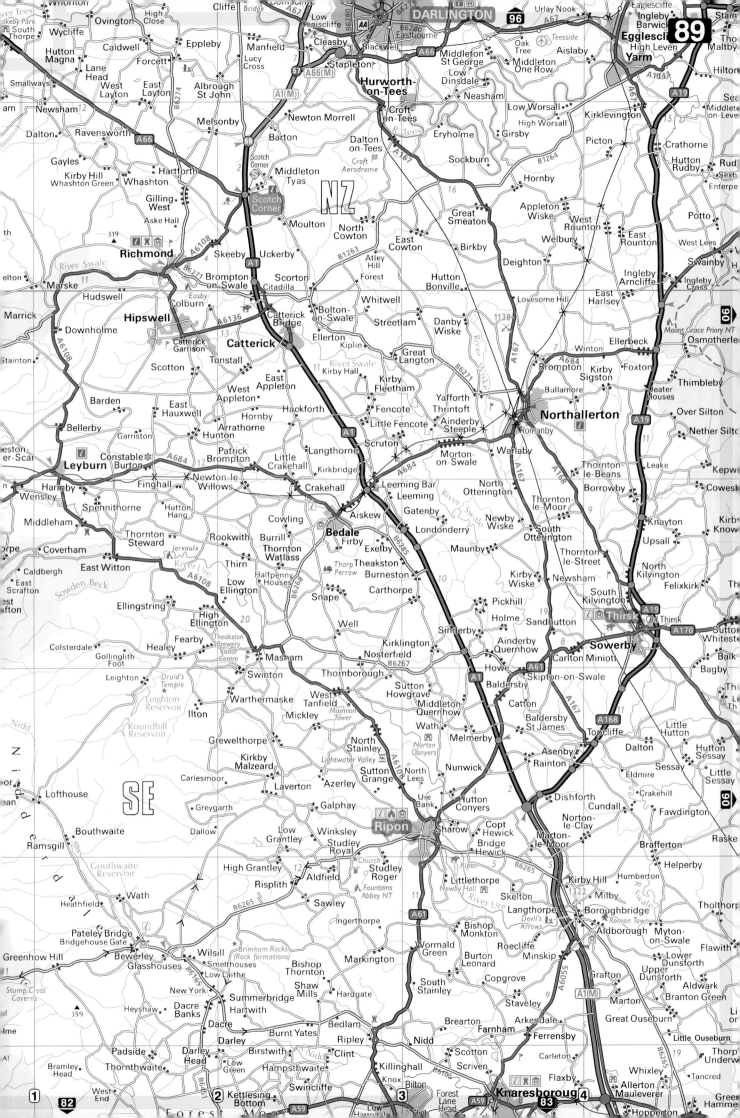

Whitby
Saltwick Bay
Stainsacre
Sneaton High Hawsker
barnby Low
Hawsker
neatonthorpe Raw Ness Point or
North Cheek
Robin Hood's Bay
Fylingthorpe
Robin Hood's
Bay
Old Peak or
South Cheek

Ravenscar

Cleveland Way

20
A171
Staintondale
Hayburn Wyke
Cloughton
Newlands
Cloughton Wyke
Bickley
Silpho
Broxa
Cloughton
Burniston
Cromer Point
Langdale
End Hackness Suffield
Scalby Newby
Wrench Green Everley

Forest Park Falsgrave

Scarborough

River Derwent
Sea Cut

A170
Oliver's Mount

West East
Ayton Ayton
A165
Sawdon Hutton Irton Osgodby Cayton Bay
Buscel Eastfield
Ebberston Ruston Seamer Crossgates High Killerby The Wyke
B1261 Cayton Lebberston Filey Brigg
Wykeham
A170 Brompton Gristhorpe A1039 Filey
Snainton 17 R Hertford Folkton Muston
Yedingham Willerby West Filey Bay
A1039 Flixton Flotmanby
Staxton 7
Sherburn Ganton A165
16 A64 Hunmanby
East Heslerton Potter Reighton
Brompton Speeton
West B1249
Heslerton Fordon B1229
RSPB Thornwick Bay
Wold Buckton
Foxholes Newton Burton Bempton
Fleming Flamborough Headland
Heritage Coast
Butterwick North Landing
Weaverthorpe Grindale Selwicks Bay
FLAMBOROUGH
Helperthorpe Marton HEAD
Thwing Boynton Flamborough
West Octon B1253 B1255
Lutton East Lutton BRIDLINGTON
Kirby B1253 Rudston Monolith Sewerby
Grindalythe Bondville BAY
Low Langtoft Model Village
owthorpe Bridlington
Sledmere Bessingby Hilderthorpe
Cottam Carnaby
Kilham Haisthorpe
owthorpe B1252 Thornholme
B1251 Ruston Parva Burton A165
12 Agnes Norman
Manor House Fraisthorpe
A166 Harpham
Garton-on- Lowthorpe Gransmoor
the-Wolds Nafferton Barmston
orpe Wetwang (A166) A614 Little Great
Elmswell Kelk Kelk Lissett Ulrome
9 Little Driffield 1 Gembling 85 2
Driffield Foston
Wansford

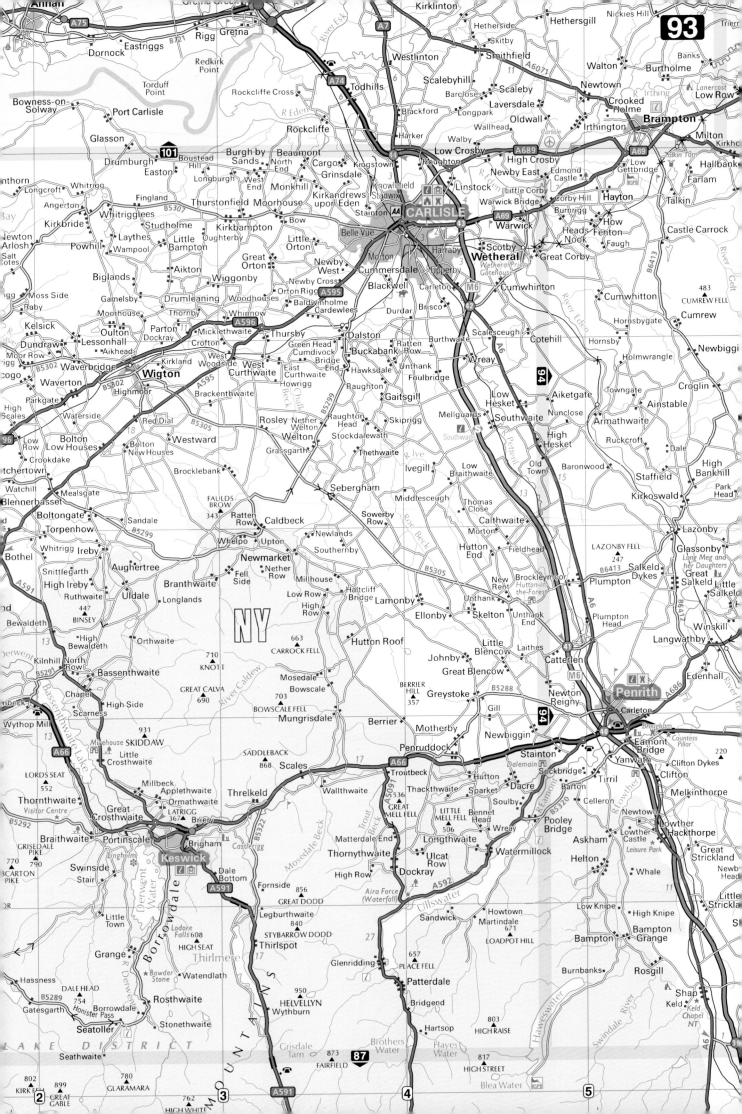

BERGEN
STAVANGER

GÖTEBORG
Summer Only

HAMBURG
Summer Only

AMSTERDAM
Summer Only

ND

NZ

agton
liery

be

erlee ⓘ
den

Blackhall Colliery
Blackhall Rocks
Blackhall

Hart
Station

on Hart

High
Throston
Elwick

Historic
Quay Middleton

HARTLEPOOL

AA

Dalton
Piercy

Hartlepool Bay

Brierton

Seaton Carew

Greatham

Tees Bay

A689

Graythorpe

Newton
Bewley

Hartlepool Power
Station Visitor
Centre

Billingham

Seal
Sands

Coatham

Cowpen
Bewley

Warrenby

Redcar

Haverton Hill

Teesport

Marske-by-the-Sea

Port
Clarence

Kirkleatham

Saltburn-by-the-Sea ⓘ

Grangetown

Saltburn
Smugglers

New
Brotton

Hummersea Scar

Toll

Lazenby

Yearby

New Marske

Brotton

North
Ormesby

South
Bank

Lackenby

Wilton

Upleatham

Skelton

Skinningrove

Boulby

Eston

Dunsdale

New
Skelton

Carlin
How

Street
Houses

MIDDLESBROUGH

Teesside Park

AA

Normanby

Tocketts

Boosbeck

North
Skelton

Kilton

Kilton
Thorpe

Loftus

Staithes

Acklam

Ormesby

Lingdale

Liverton
Mines

Easington

Dalehouse

Port Mulgrave

Marton

Ormesby Hall NT

Margrove
Park

Stanghow

Handale

Roxby

Newton
Mulgrave

Hinderwell

Runswick
Bay

Nunthorpe

Liverton

Borrowby

Runswick

Stainton

Hemlington

Pinchinthorpe

Newton

Hutton

Hutton
Hall

Guisborough

90

Moorsholm

Scaling

B1266

llerby

Goldsb

North Yor

Lythe

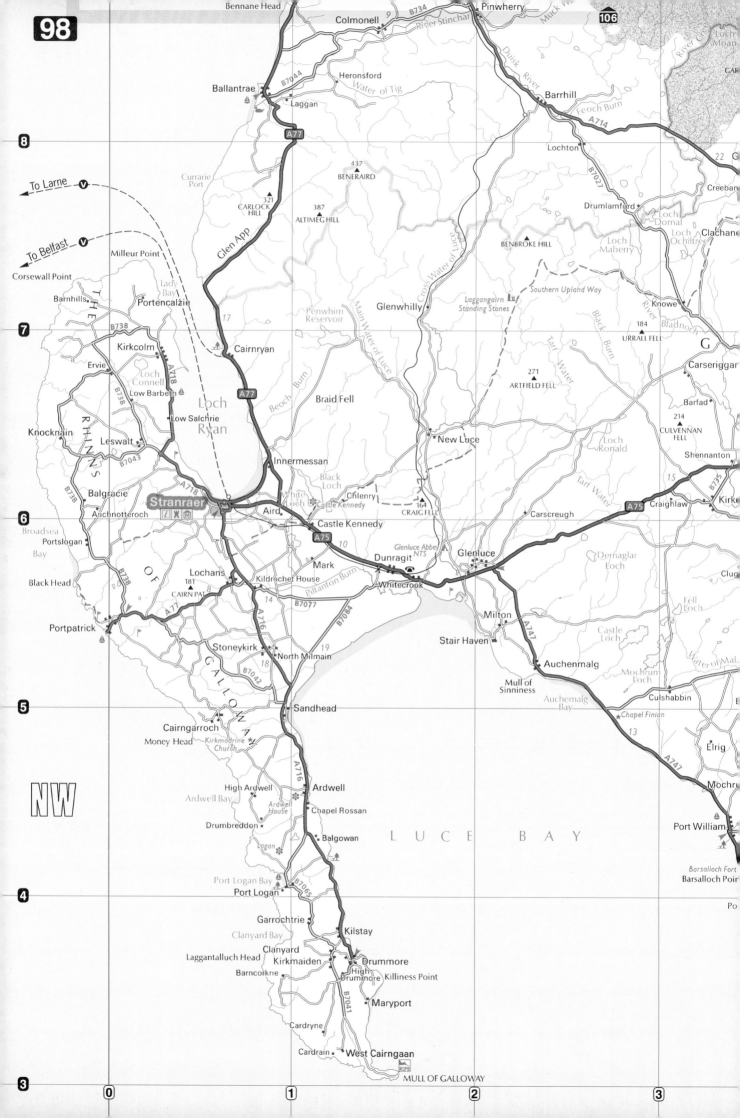

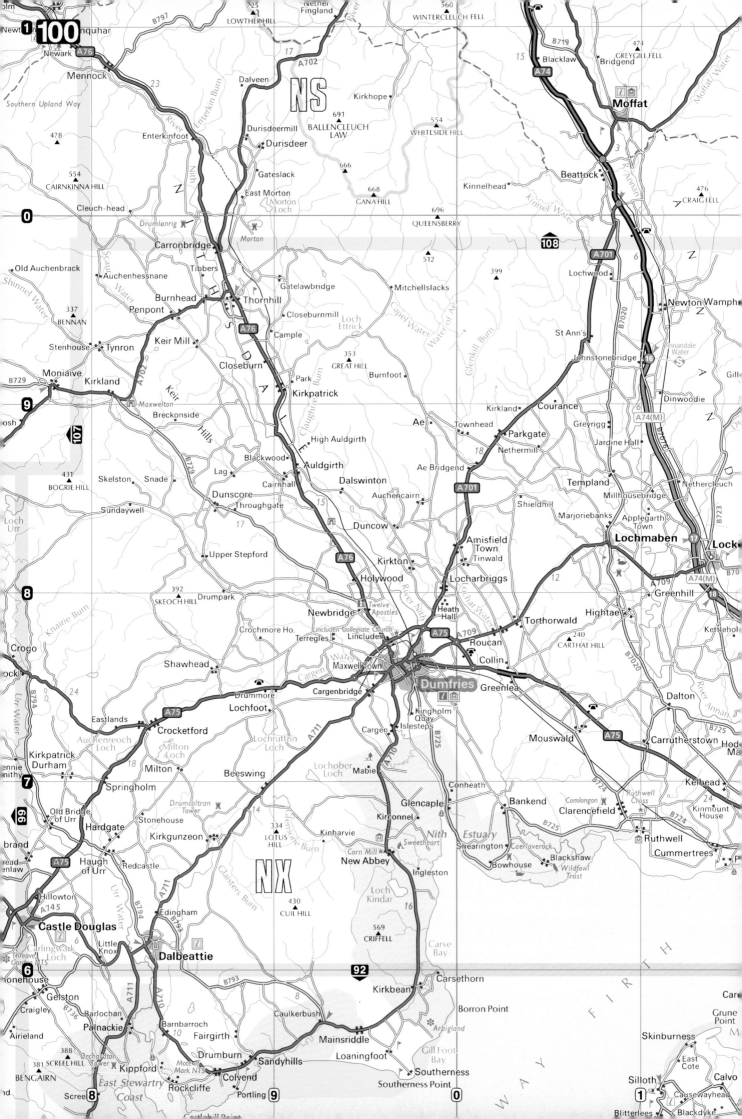

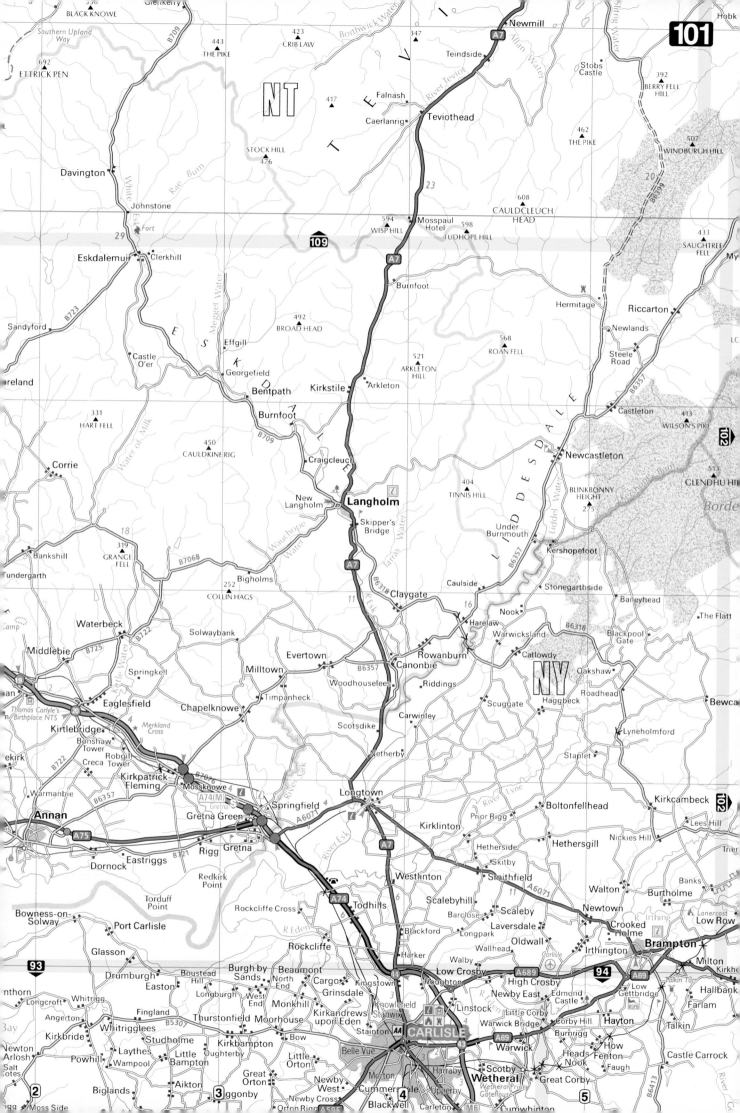

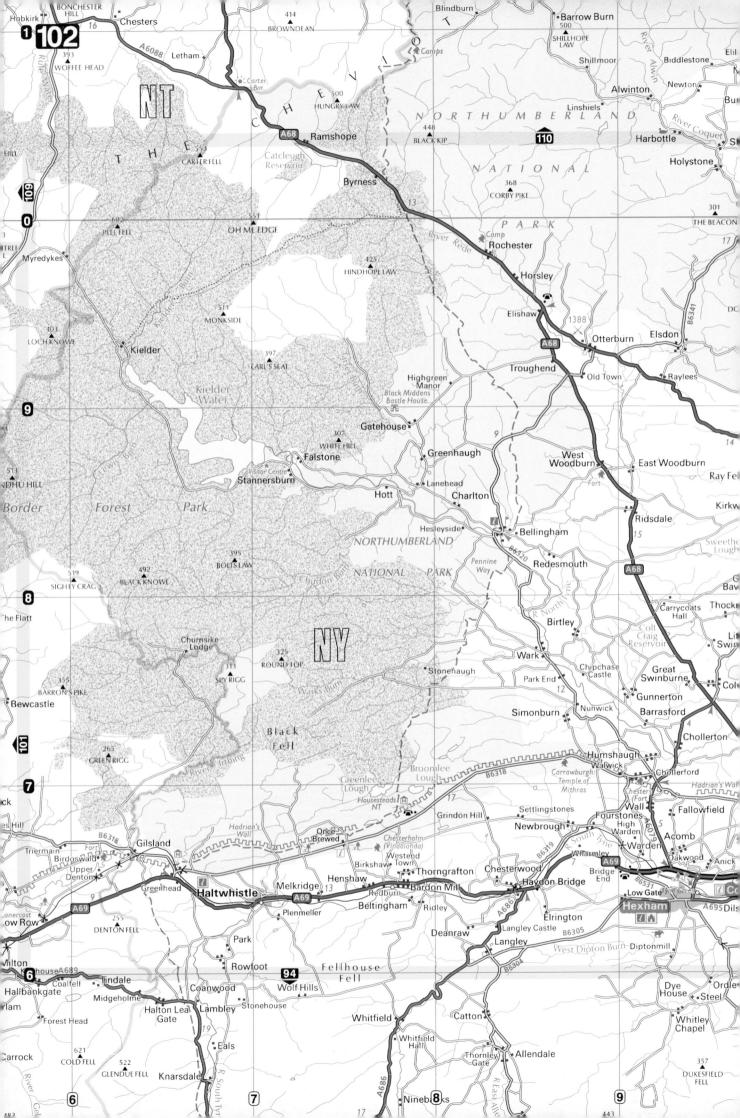

River Laggan
Duich R
490
BEINN BHEIGEIR
Rudha Liath
454
Ardtalla
BEINN URAIRAIDH
Loch Uraraidh
Claggain Bay
B8016
A846
11
Laggan
Bay
Glenegedale
Kintour
Islay
(Port Ellen)
Ardmore Point
5
112
346
Kildalton Cross
BEINN SHOLUM
Eilean
a'Chuirn
Rudha Mòr
165
MAOL BUIDHE
Lagavulin
Ardbeg
Rudha na
Gainmhich
A846
The   Oa
Port
Ellen
Laphroaig
Lower
Killeyan
Risabus
Kinnabus
Texa
4
American
Monument
Loch
Kinnabus
OF OA
Rudha nan
Leacan

Port Askaig – Kennacraig
v
Port Ellen – Kennacraig
Tarbert
Ardail
v
113
GIGHA
Ardminish
Achamore
Cara

3
Glenacardoch Po

Bellochantuy

0   1   2   3   4   5 miles

0   1   2   3   4   5   6   7 kilometres

NR

Machrihanish
Bay
Machrihanish
2
Drumler
Earadale Point
385
THE STATE
446
CNOC MOY
Dalsmeran
1
Glen Breake
Strone Glen
BEINN NA LICE
428
Carskey
MULL OF
KINTYRE
Borgadelmor
Point

0

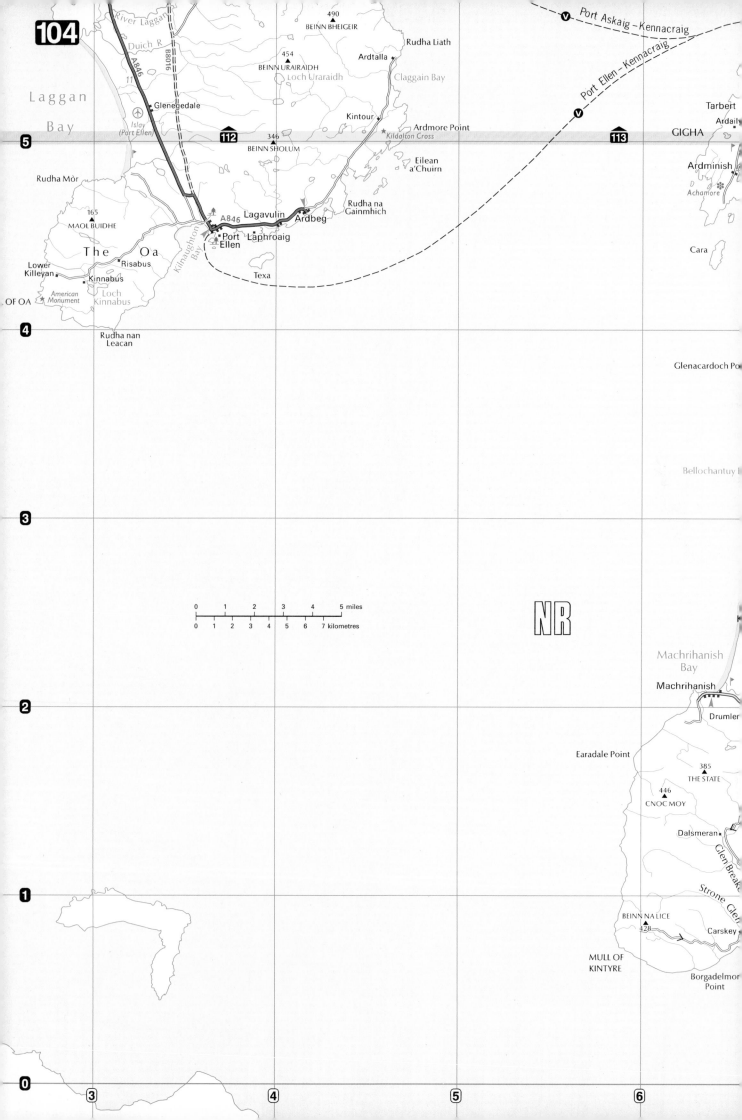

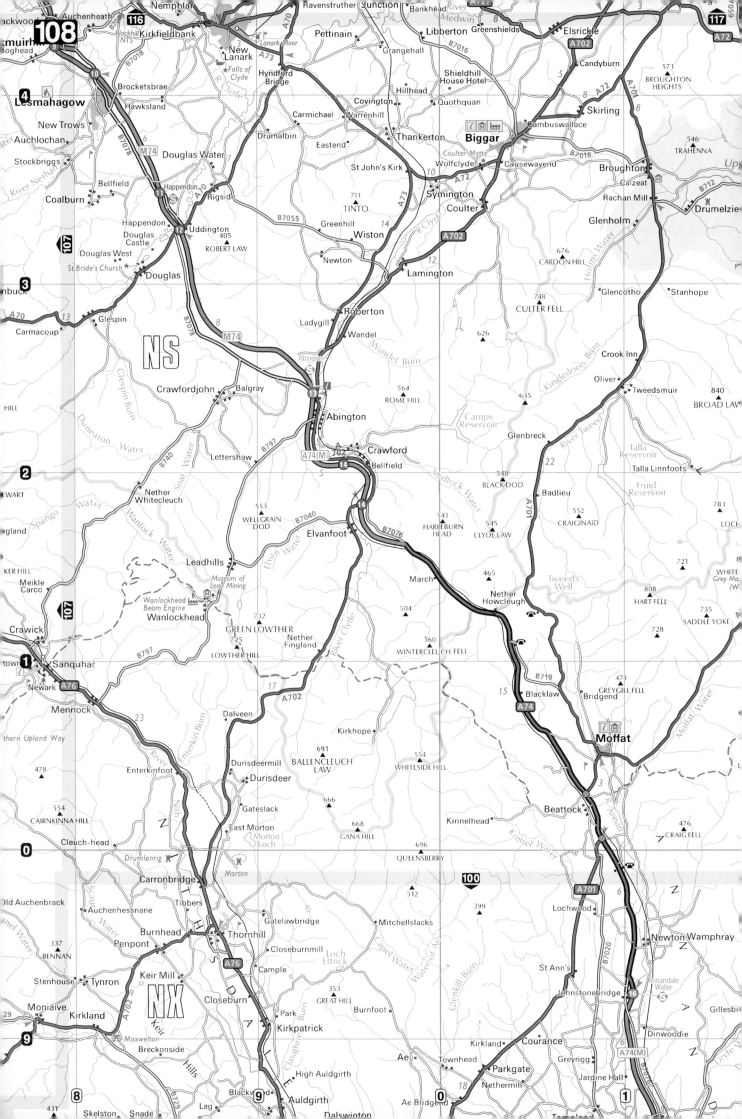

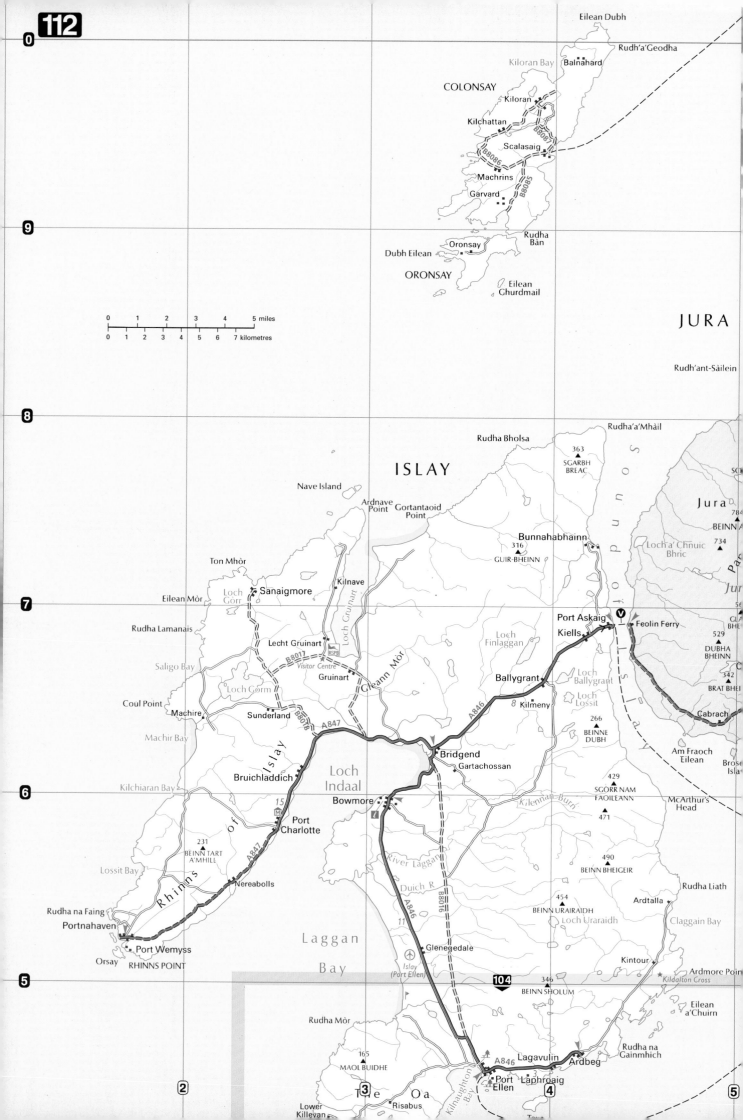

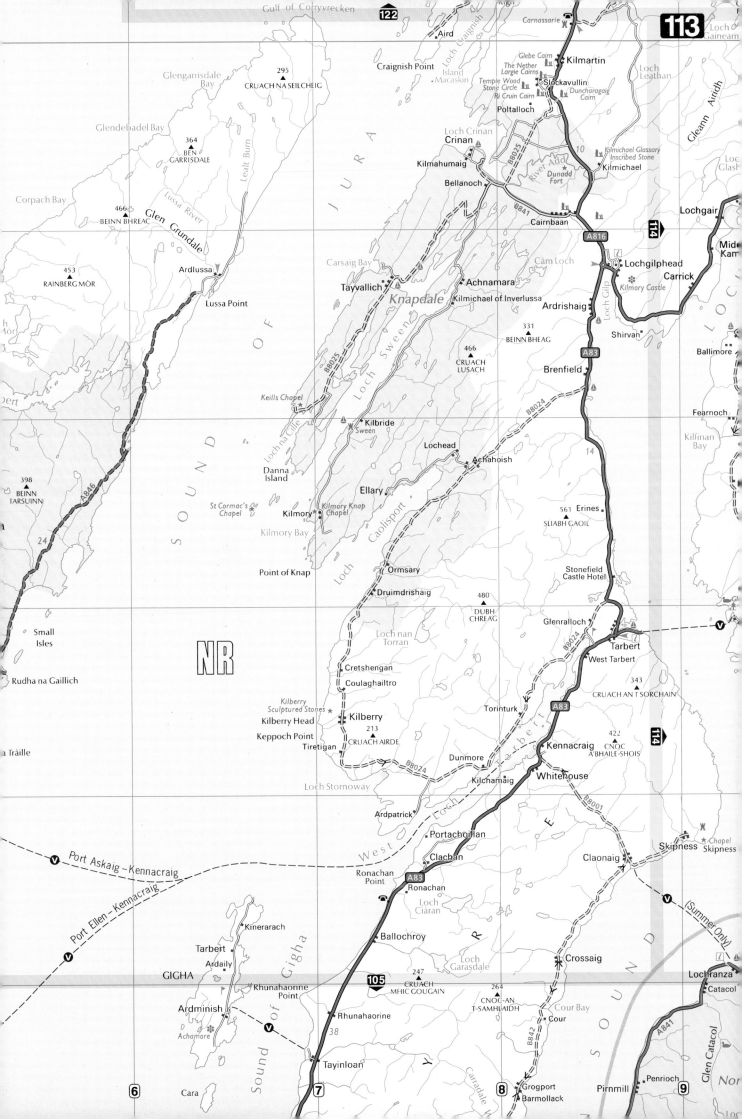

Gulf of Corryvrecken

122

Loch Gaineam

Loch Leathan

Loch Airidh

Gleann Airdh

Aird

Carnassarie

Kilmartin

Craignish Point

Island Macaskin

Glebe Cairn
The Nether Largie Cairns
Temple Wood Stone Circle
Ri Cruin Cairn

Slockavullin

Duncharagaig Cairn

Glengarrisdale Bay

295
CRUACH NA SEILCHEIG

Glendebadel Bay

Poltalloch

Kilmichael-Glassary Inscribed Stone

Kilmichael

Loch Crinan

Crinan

10

Loch Glash

Corpach Bay

364
BEN GARRISDALE

Kilmahumaig

River Add

Dunadd Fort

Lochgair

Bellanoch

B8025

B841

Cairnbaan

114

466
BEINN BHREAC

Glen Grundale

Lussa River

Loch

A816

Lochgilphead

Mid Kam

Lealt Burn

Ardlussa

Carsaig Bay

Tayvallich

Knapdale

Achnamara

Kilmichael of Inverlussa

Carrick

Kilmory Castle

Ardrishaig

453
RAINBERG MÖR

Lussa Point

Loch Sween

B8025

Câm Loch

Shirvan

Ballimore

A83

331
BEINN BHEAG

Brenfield

466
CRUACH LUSACH

B8024

Keills Chapel

Fearnoch

14

Kilbride Sween

Kilfinan Bay

398
BEINN TARSUINN

A846

Lochead

Achahoish

Danna Island

Ellary

561
Erines

SLIABH GAOIL

St Cormac's Chapel

Kilmory Knap Chapel

Kilmory

24

Kilmory Bay

Loch Caolisport

Ormsary

Stonefield Castle Hotel

NR

Loch nan Torran

Druimdrishaig

480
DUBH CHREAG

Glenralloch

B8024

Tarbert

West Tarbert

Small Isles

Point of Knap

Cretshengan

Coulaghailtro

343
CRUACH AN T SORCHAIN

Rudha na Gaillich

Kilberry Sculptured Stones

Kilberry

Torinturk

A83

114

Loch Stornoway

422
CNOC A'BHAILE-SHOIS

Kilberry Head
Keppoch Point

213
CRUACH AIRDE

Dunmore

Kennacraig

a Tràille

Tiretigan

B8024

Kilchamaig

Whitehouse

B8001

Ardpatrick

West Loch Tarbert

E

Portachoillan

Port Askaig – Kennacraig

Clachan

Skipness

Chapel Skipness

Ronachan Point

A83

Claonaig

Port Ellen – Kennacraig

Ronachan

(Summer Only)

Kinerarach

Loch Ciaran

Ballochroy

R

Tarbert

Ardaily

Loch Garasdale

Crossaig

Lochranza

GIGHA

Rhunahaorine Point

105

247
CRUACH MHIC GOUGAIN

264
CNOC AN T-SAMHLAIDH

Catacol

Ardminish

Achamore

Rhunahaorine

Cour Bay

Cour

A841

Glen Catacol

Sound of Gigha

38

B842

Tayinloan

Carradale

Grogport

Pirnrioch

Glen Nor

6

7

8

Barmollack

Pirnmill

9

Cara

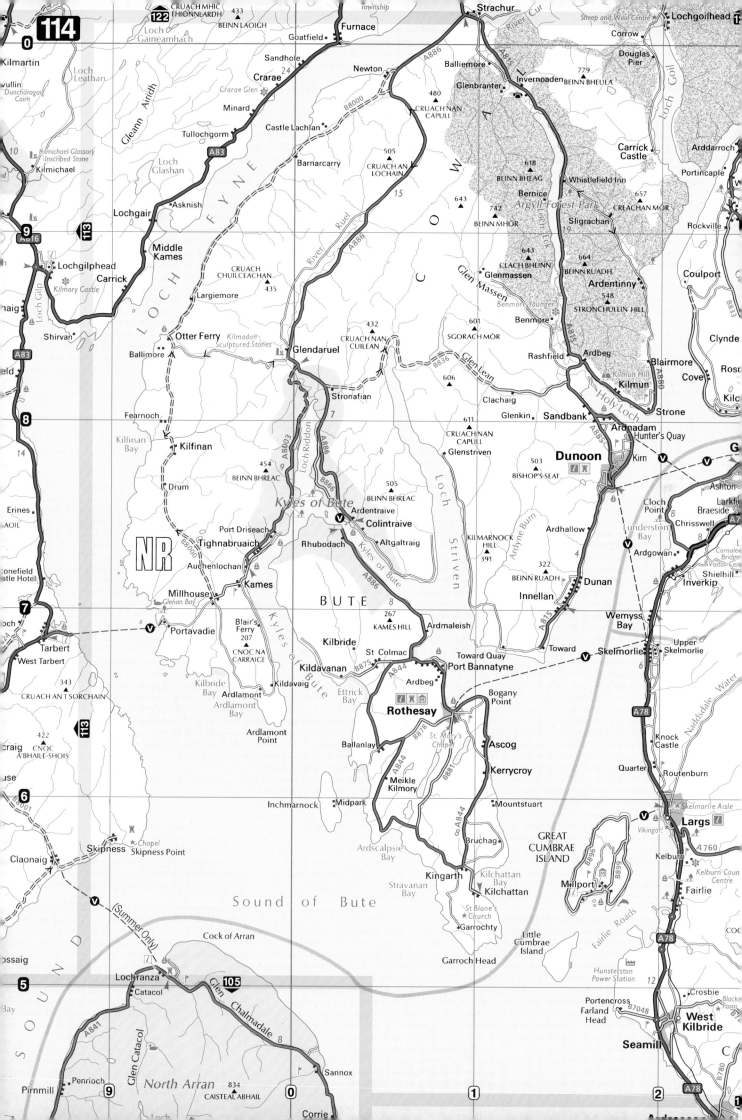

127

0 1 2 3 4 5 miles
0 1 2 3 4 5 6 7 kilometres

NU

xburn
650
Barns Ness
East Barns
12
Chapel Point
Skateraw
Torness Power Station
Thorntonloch
Innerwick
Crowhill
Reed Point
319
Dunglass
Cove
Pease
COCKLAW HILL
Collegiate
Bay
Siccar Point
Fast Castle Head
Oldhamstocks
Church
Cockburnspath

A1
A1107
196
BROWN RIG
ST ABB'S HEAD

Ecclaw
Southern
Upland Way
St Abbs
391
HEART LAW
Grantshouse
Coldingham
Coldingham Bay
Eye
Butterdean
21
Houndwood
22
Water
Quixwood
Heugh Head
Cairncross
Eyemouth
A6112
262
HORSELEY HILL
Reston
A1
Abbey St Bathans
Edin's
14
B6438
Ayton
Burnmouth
Ellemford
Hall Broch
Auchencrow
325
COCKBURN
Marygold
LAW
B6437
ERMUIR
B6355
Lintlaw
Lamberton
Primrosehill
Preston
Chirnside
B6355
Marshall Meadows Bay
B6365
Cumledge
Edrom
15
North Northumberland
Church
Chirnsidebridge
Foulden
A1
Heritage Coast
9
Duns Castle
Broadhaugh
Edington
Whiteadder
1333
A6105
T LAW
Manderston
Allanton
Hutton
Barracks
A6105
Town Ramparts
Duns
Paxton
Berwick-upon-Tweed
Gavinton
Blackadder
B6461
Tweedmouth
B6456
Sunwick
East
Spittal
Sinclair's
Paxton
Ord
Polwarth
Nisbet
Whitsome
Hilton
Loanend
Huds Head
Hill
Fishwick
13
A1
Scremerston
110
Fogo
6
B6461
A698
111
7
B6460
Horndean
Murton
Unthank
A6105
Forgorig
Ladykirk
Thornton
Greenlaw
Charterhall
11
Swinton
Norham
West Allerdean
Cheswick
Ladykirk
Shoreswood
Simprim
Ho.
B6354
Ancroft
A1
Göswick
7
8
Leitholm
10
B6437
Upsettlington
River Tweed
9
Grindon
Shellacres
Felkington
Haggerston
0

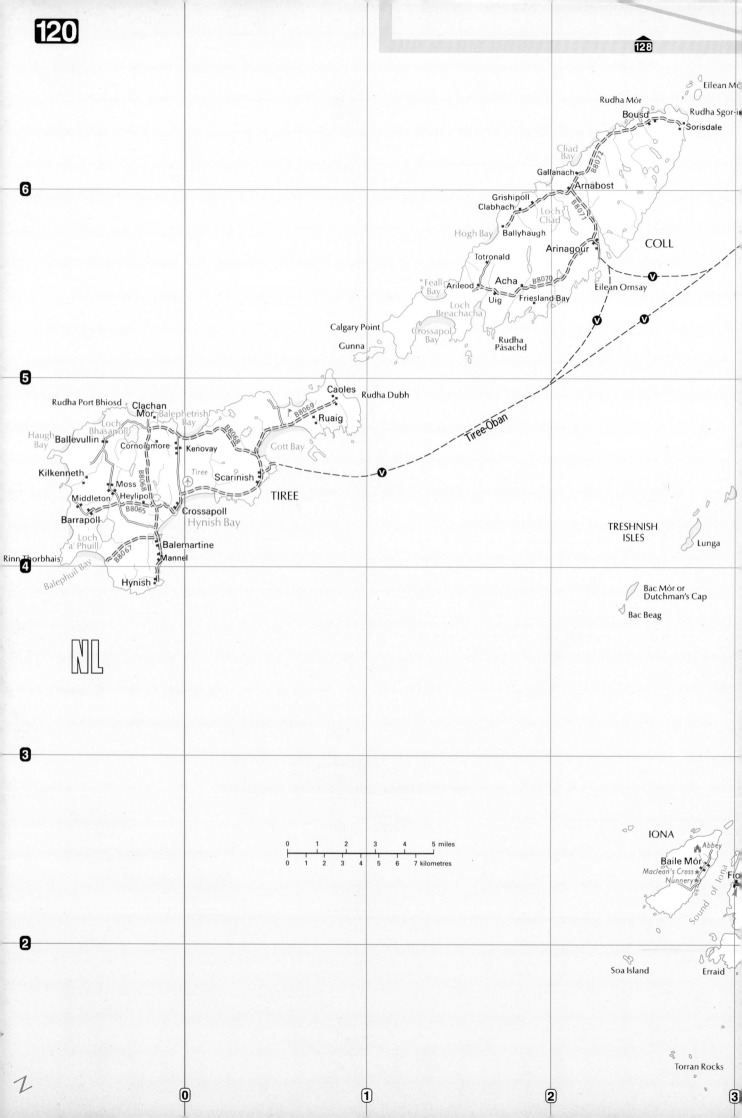

128

Eilean Mò

Rudha Mòr

Rudha Sgor-i

Bousd

Sorisdale

Cliad
Bay

Gallanach

B8072

Arnabost

Grishipoll

Clabhach

B8071

Loch
Cliad

Hogh Bay

Ballyhaugh

COLL

Totronald

Arinagour

Feall
Bay

Arileod

Acha

B8070

Uig

Friesland Bay

Eilean Ornsay

Loch
Breachacha

Calgary Point

Crossapol
Bay

Gunna

Rudha
Pàsachd

5

Caoles

Rudha Dubh

Rudha Port Bhiosd

**Clachan
Mor**

B8069

Ruaig

Balephetrish
Bay

B8068

Tiree-Oban

Loch
Bhasapoll

Haugh
Bay

Ballevullin

Cornaigmore

Kenovay

Gott Bay

Kilkenneth

B8068

Tiree

Scarinish

Moss

Heylipoll

TIREE

Middleton

B8065

Crossapoll

TRESHNISH
ISLES

Lunga

Barrapoll

Hynish Bay

Loch
a' Phuill

Balemartine

Rinn Thorbhais

B8067

Mannel

Bac Mòr or
Dutchman's Cap

Balephuil Bay

Hynish

Bac Beag

NL

3

0   1   2   3   4   5 miles

0 1 2 3 4 5 6 7 kilometres

IONA

Abbey

Baile Mór

Maclean's Cross

Nunnery

Fio

Sound of Iona

2

Soa Island

Erraid

Torran Rocks

4

6

0   **1**   **2**   **3**

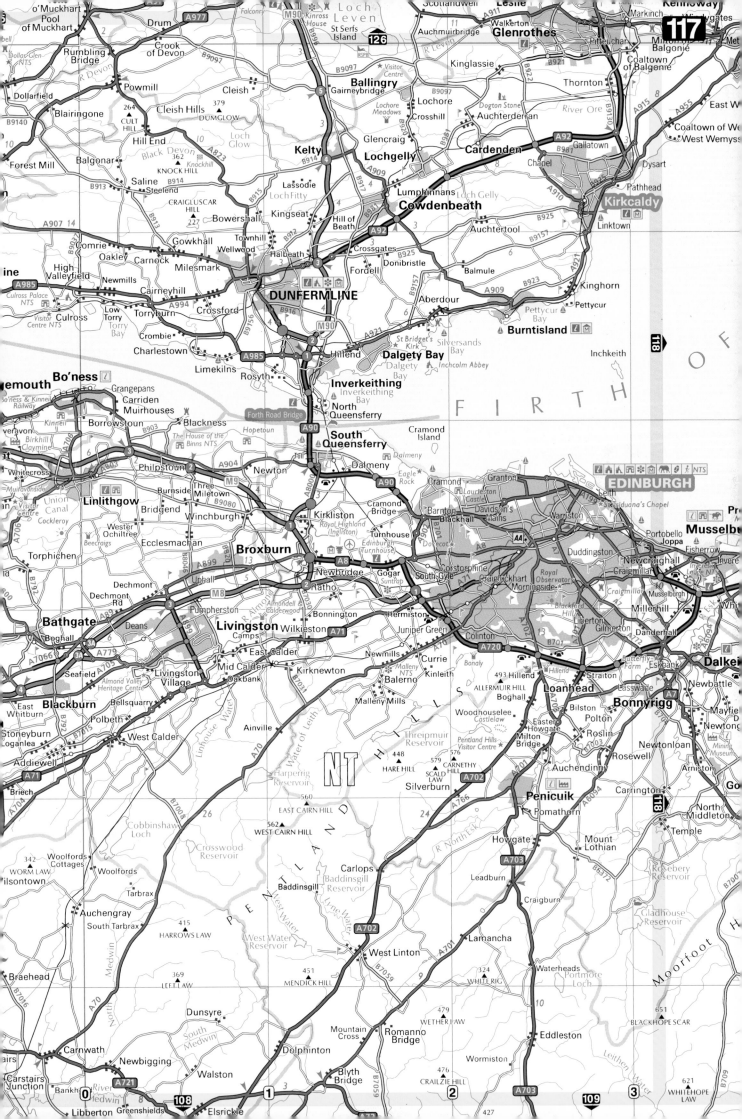

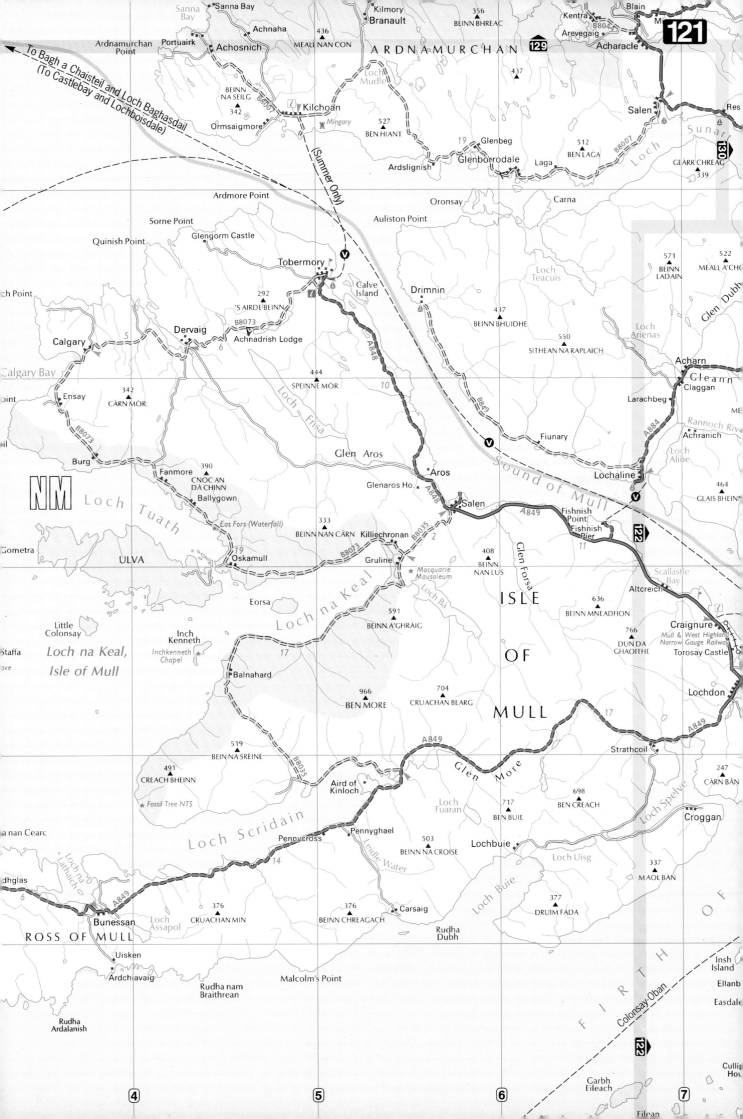

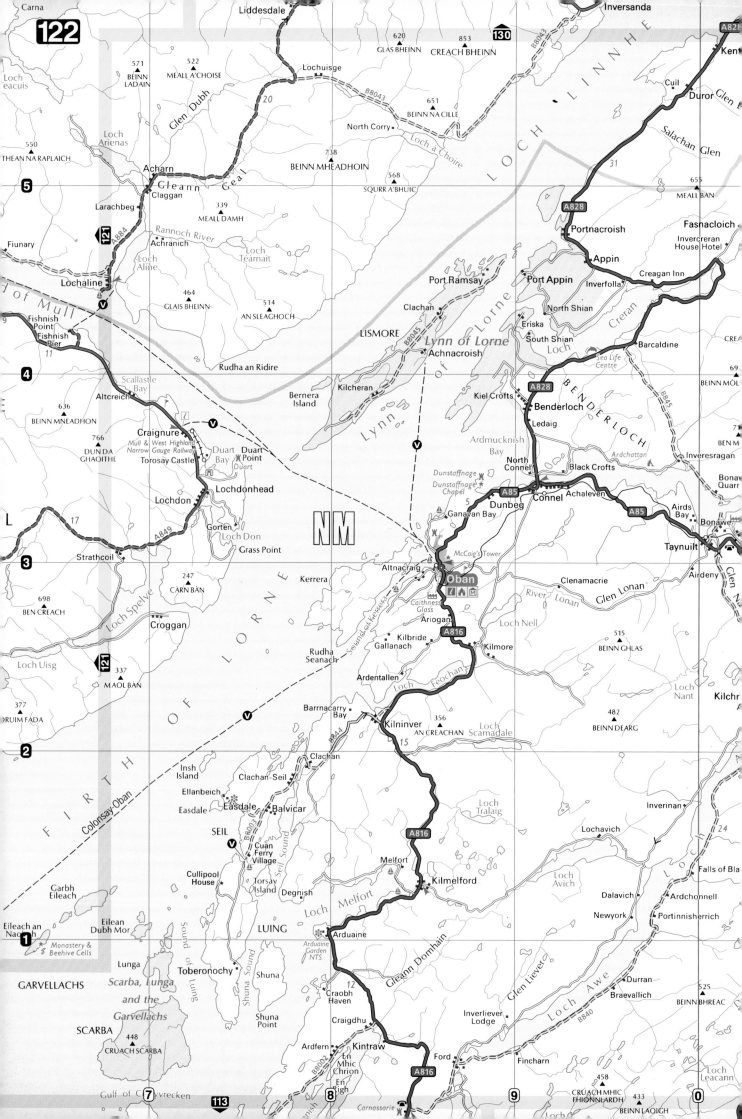

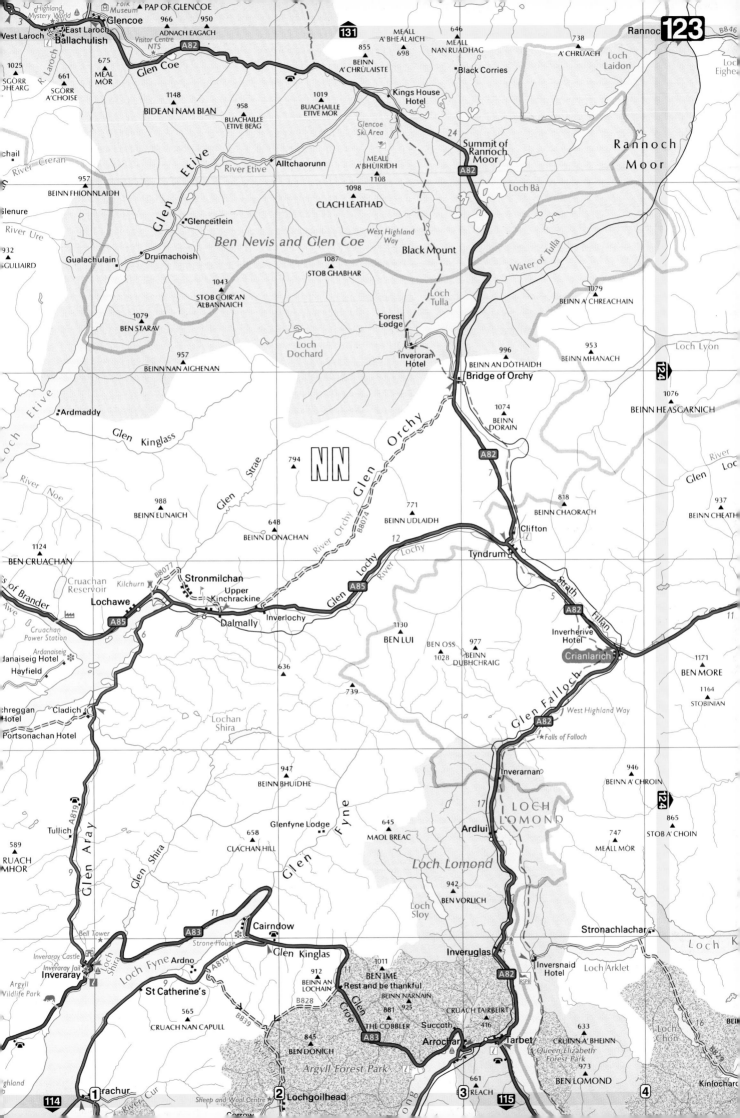

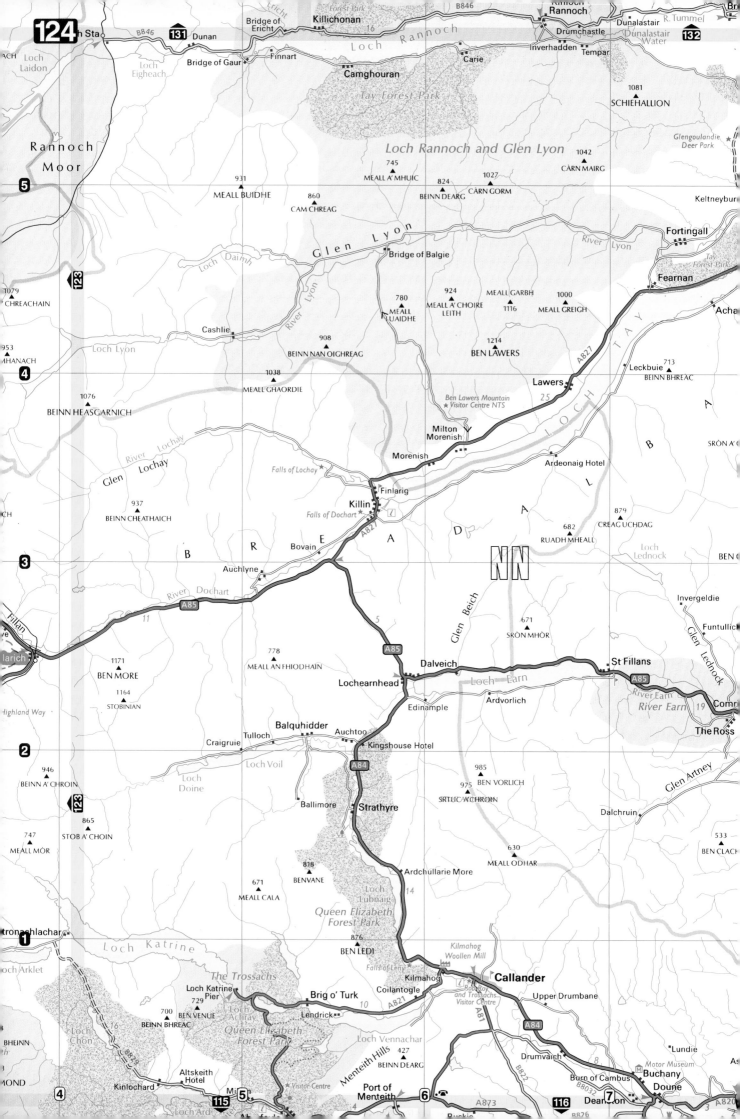

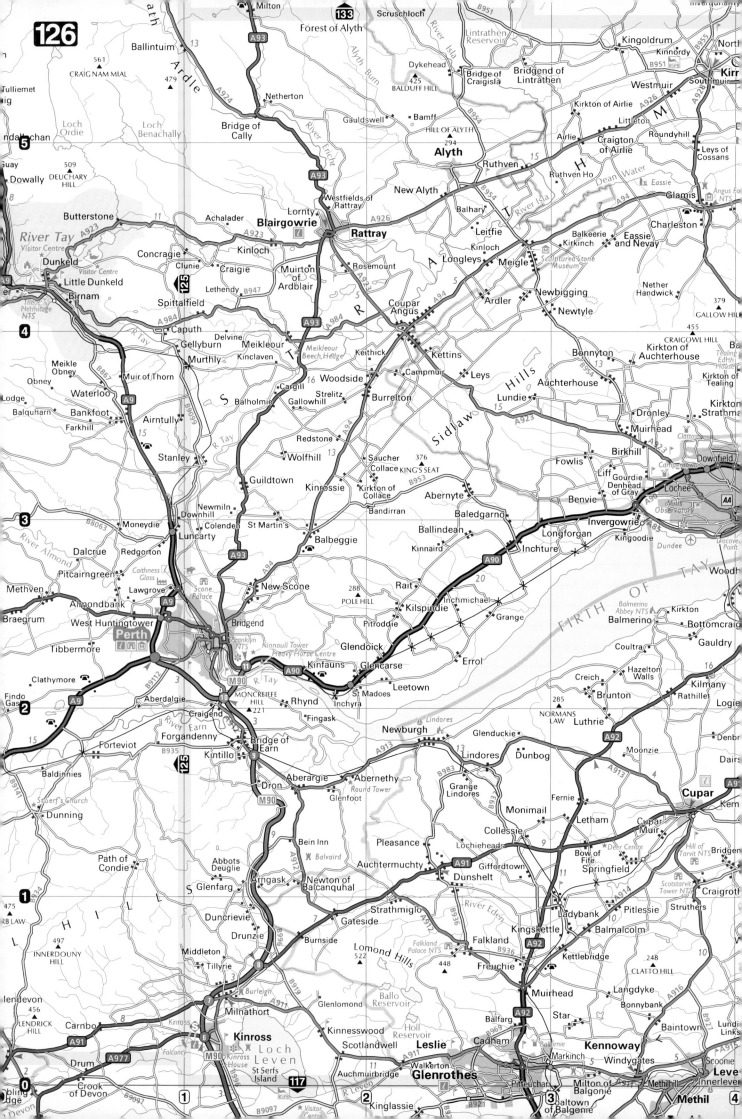

2

1

136

Loch Eynort

The Cuillin Hills

434
AN CRUACHIN ▲

974
SGÙRR A' GHEADAIDH

Cuillin Hills

927

Glenbrittle
House ▪

Bualintur ▪

1009
SGÙRR ALASDAIR ▲

Loch
Coruisk

Loch
Crèithea

BLAVE

Camas
Ki ▪

Loch Brittle

894
GARS BHEINN ▲

Loch
Scavaig

225
CEANN NA BEINNE ▲

Rudh'an Dùnain

Soay Sound

139
BEINN BHREAC ▲

BENN

Elg ▪

▪ Mol-chlach

SOAY

St

Rudh' Aonghais

CANNA

210
CÀRN A' GHAILL ▲

A'Chill ▪

CUILLIN

NG

Garrisdale Point

Canna Harbour

Rudha Shamhnan
Insir

SOUND

Sanday

Sound of Canna

302
MULLACH MÒR ▲

0

A Bhrideanach

570
ORVAL ▲

Rudha na Roinne ▪

Kinloch ▪ Loch
Scresort

Oigh-sgeir

RUM

810
ASKIVAL ▲

763
SGÙRR NAN ▲
GILLEAN

The Small Isles

Rudha nam Meirleach

9

Sound of Rum

Bay of
Laig

Cleadale ▪

EIGG

Rudha an
Fhasaidh

Laig ▪

299
AN ▲
CRUACHAN

Sandavore ▪
393
AN SGÙRR ▲

Kildonnan ▪

Galmisdale ▪

Eilean
nan Each

Sound of Eigg

Eilean
Chathastail

MUCK

8

Port Mor ▪

0	1	2	3	4	5 miles

0	1	2	3	4	5	6	7 kilometres

7

Sanna Point

Ockle

Sanna
Bay

▪ Sanna Bay

Achnaha ▪

Ki
Bra

120

Ardnamurchan
Point

Portuairk ▪

436
MEALL NAN CON ▲

2

3

◄ To Bagh a Chaisteil
(To Castleb

Eilean Mòr

Achosnich ▪

121

4

5

Loch
Mudl

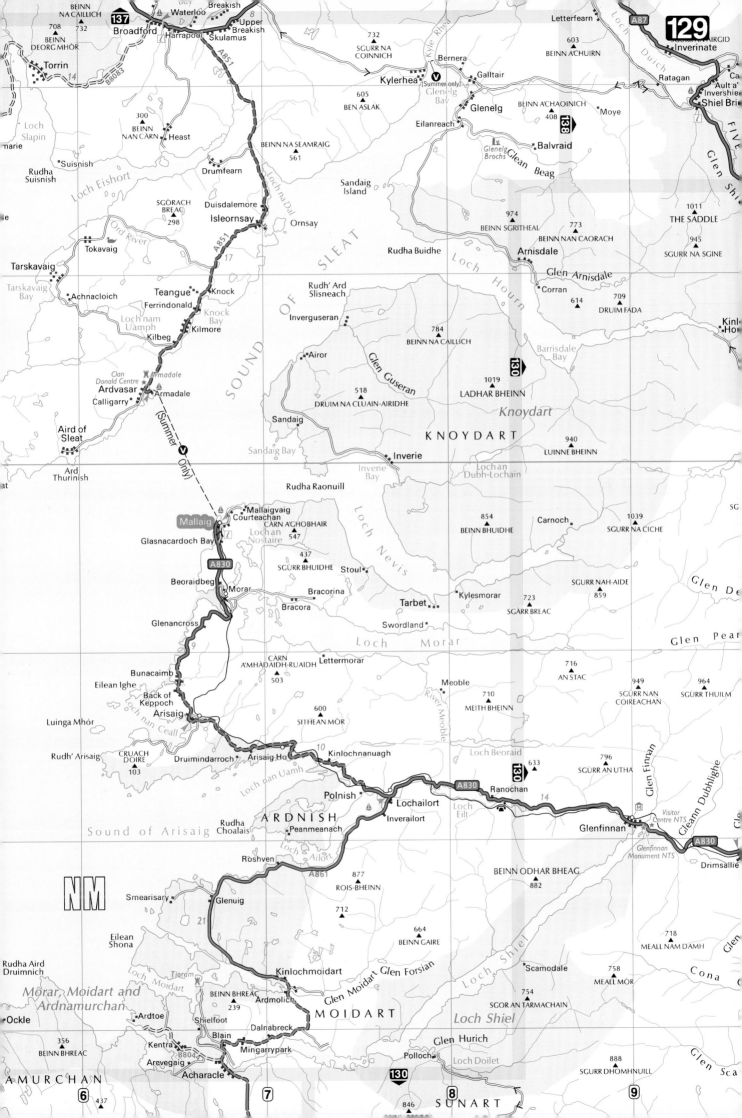

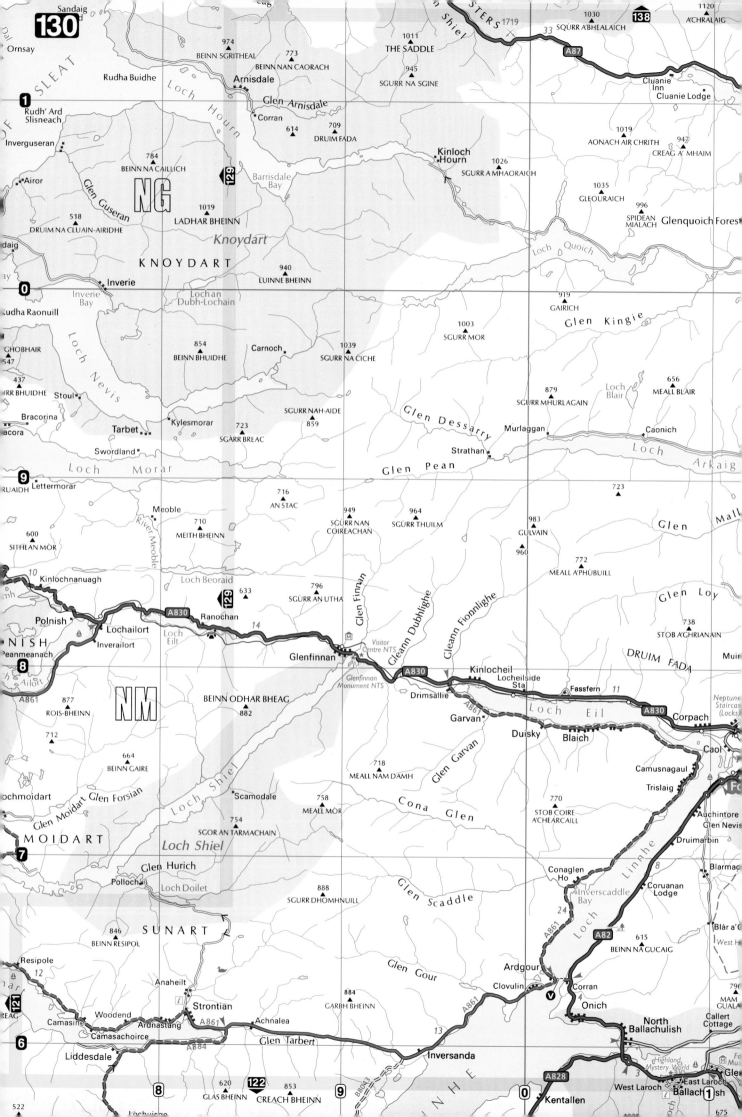

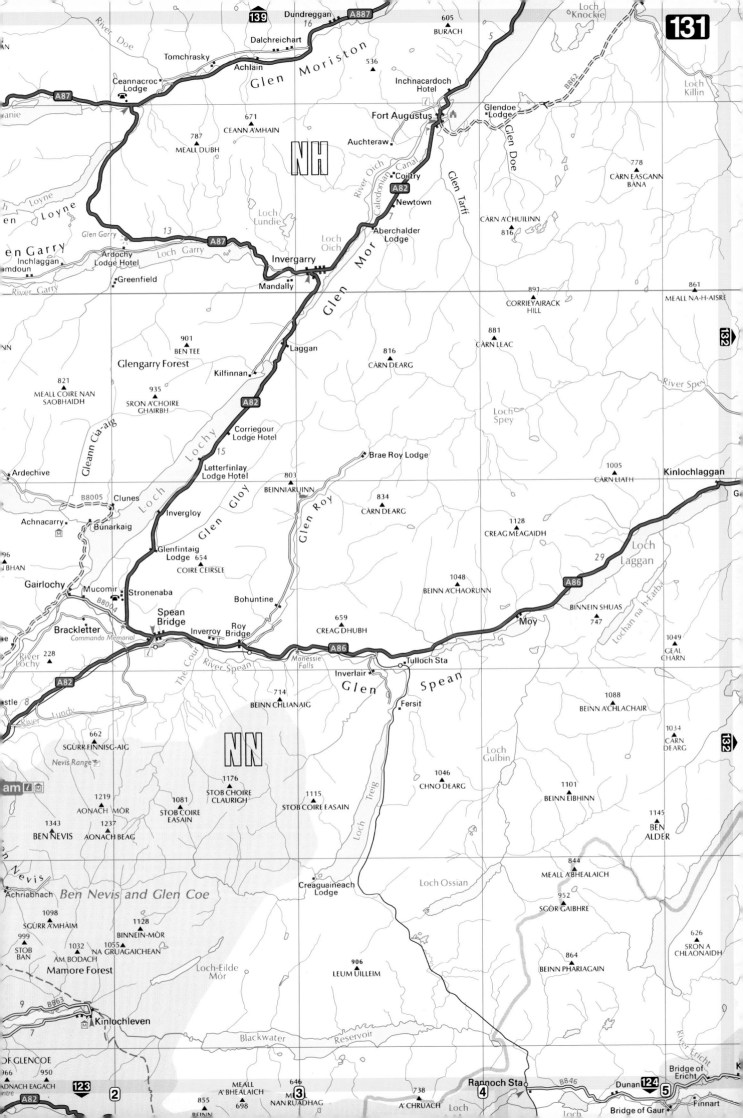

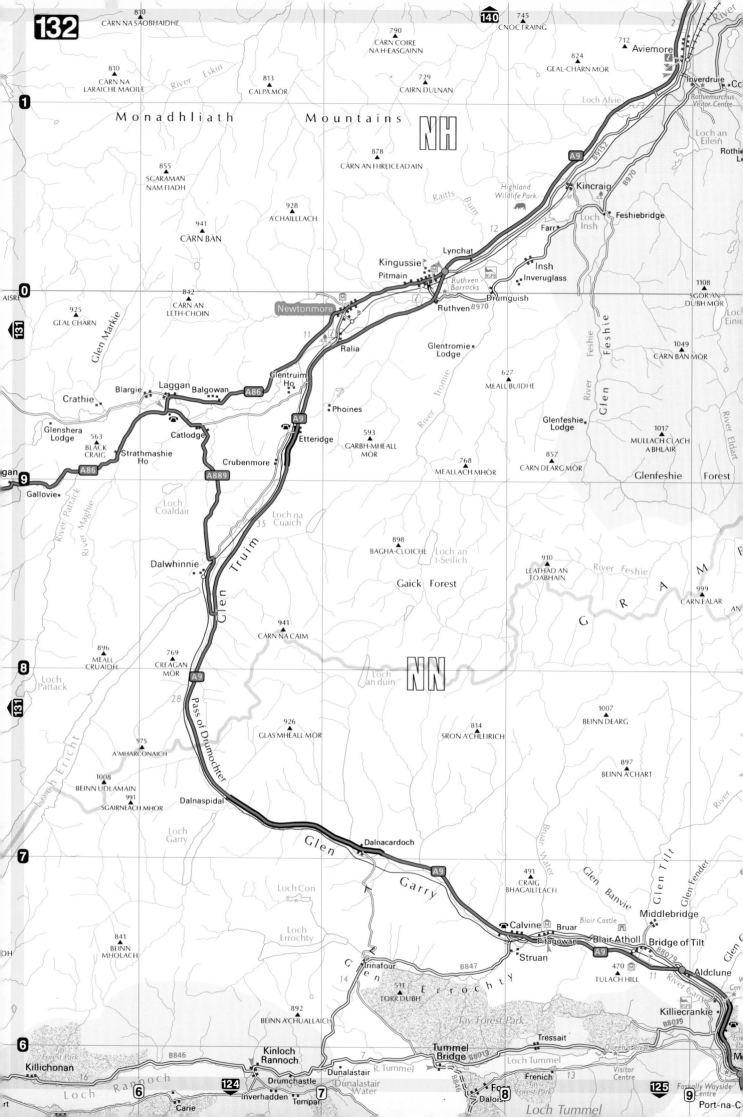

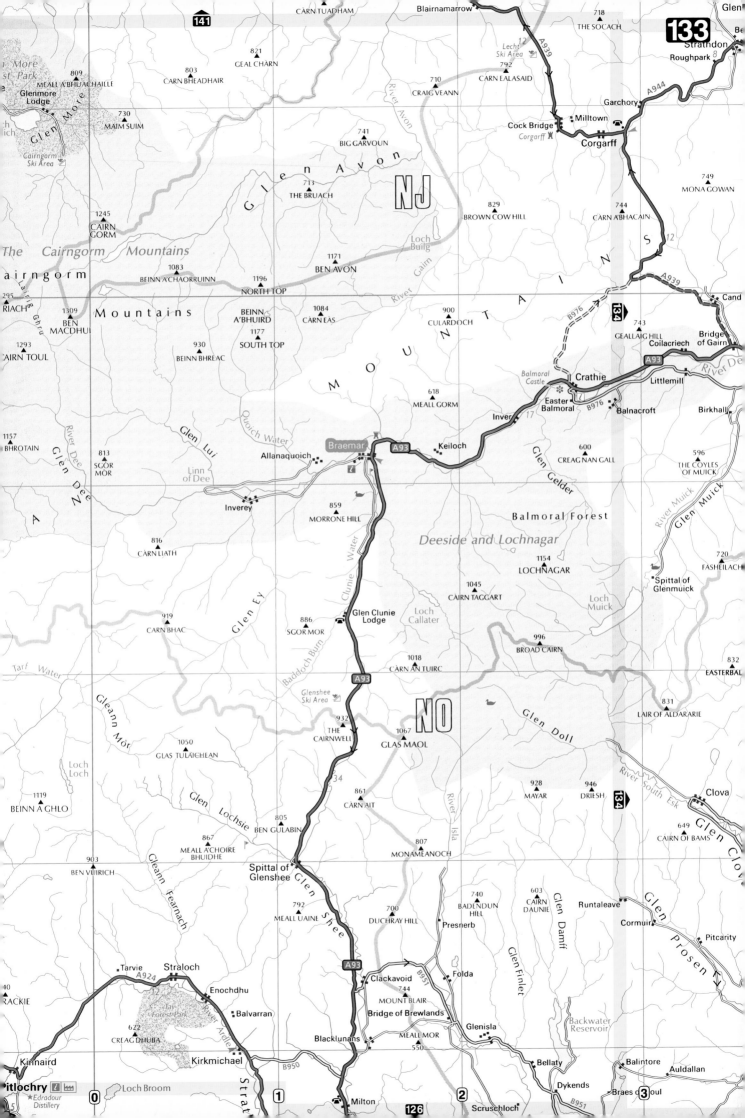

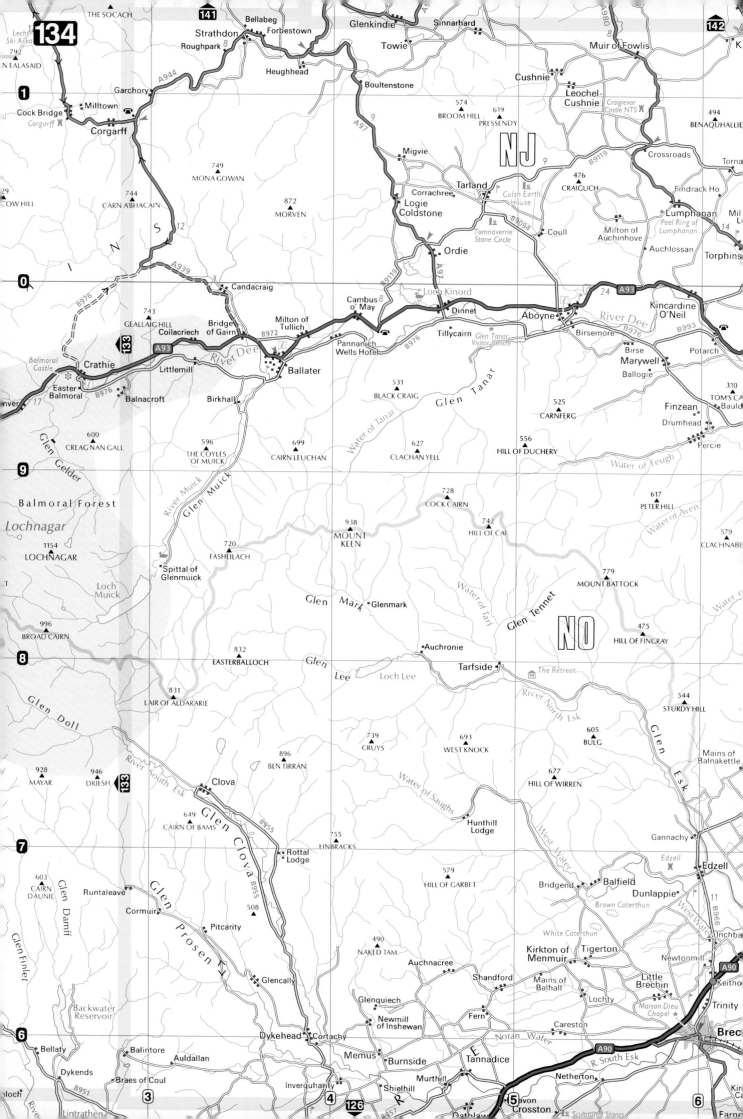

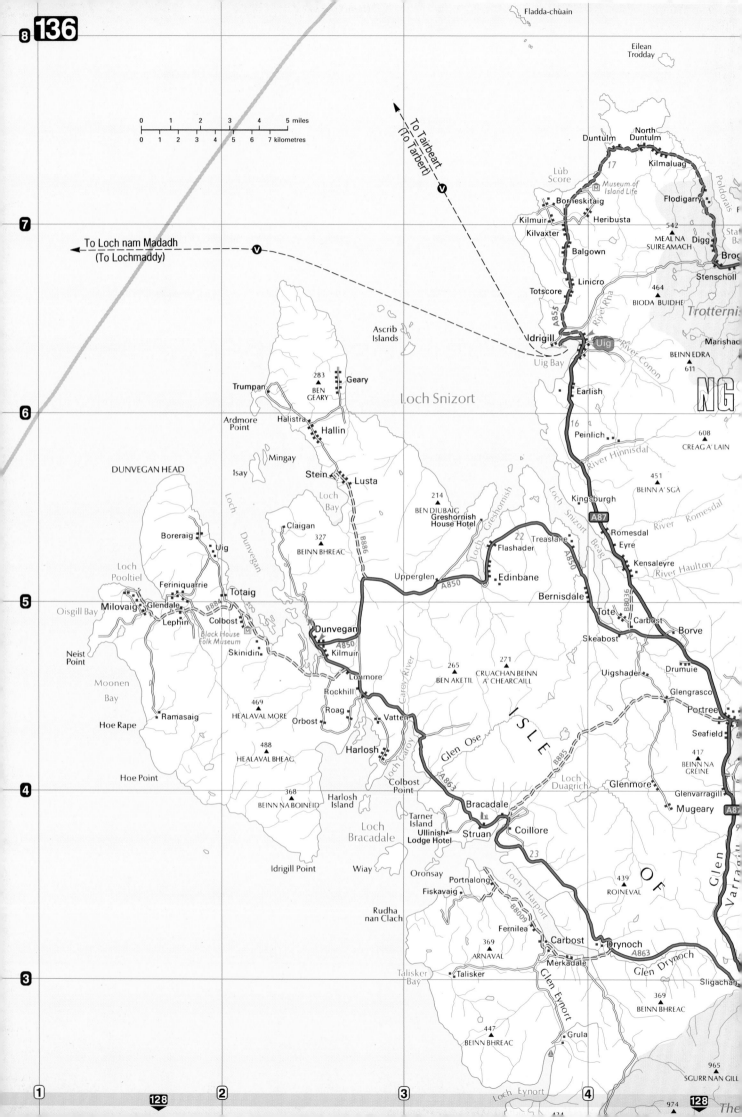

0 1 2 3 4 5 miles
0 1 2 3 4 5 6 7 kilometres

To Tairbeart
(To Tarbert) Ⓥ

To Loch nam Madadh
(To Lochmaddy) Ⓥ

Fladda-chùain

Eilean
Troddday

Duntulm
North
Duntulm
Kilmaluag

Lùb
Score
17
Museum of
Island Life
Borneskitaig
Flodigarry

Poldorais

Kilmuir
Heribusta

Kilvaxter
542
MEAL NA
SUIREAMACH
Digg
Brog

Balgown

Linicro
Stenscholl

Totscore
464
BIODA BUIDHE
Trotternis

Ascrib
Islands

Idrigill
Ⓤ Uig

Uig Bay

River Conon

Earlish

NG

Loch Snizort

Trumpan
283
BEN
GEARY
Geary

Ardmore
Point
Halistra
Hallin

16
Peinlich

River Hinnisdal

608
CREAG A' LAIN

DUNVEGAN HEAD
Mingay
Isay
Stein
Lusta

Loch
Bay

214
BEN DIUBAIG
Greshornish
House Hotel

451
BEINN A' SGÀ

Kingsburgh

A87

Romesdal

Boreraig
Uig

Claigan
327
BEINN BHREAC

B886

22
Treaslane
Flashader

Romesdal
Eyre

River

Loch
Pooltiel
Feriniquarrie
Totaig

Upperglen
A850
Edinbane

A850
Kensaleyre
River Haulton

Oisgill Bay
Milovaig
Glendale
Colbost

B884

Bernisdale

B8036

Tote
Carbost
Borve

Neist
Point
Lephin
Black House
Folk Museum
Skinidin

Dunvegan
Kilmuir

A850

Lonmore

Skeabost

Uigshader
Drumuie

Moonen
Bay
469
HEALAVAL MORE
Rockhill
Roag
Orbost
Vatten

265
BEN AKETIL
271
CRUACHAN BEINN
A' CHEARCAILL

Glengrasco
Portree

Hoe Rape
Ramasaig

488
HEALAVAL BHEAG
Harlosh

Glen Ose
ISLE
B885
Loch
Duagrich
Glenmore

Seafield

417
BEINN NA
GREINE

Hoe Point
368
BEINN NA BOINEID
Harlosh
Island
Colbost
Point
A863

Glenvarragill
Mugeary
A87

Idrigill Point
Wiay
Loch
Bracadale
Tarner
Island
Ullinish
Lodge Hotel
Bracadale
Struan
Coillore

Glen
Varragill

Oronsay
Portnalong
Fiskavaig

23
Loch Harport
439
ROINEVAL

OF

Rudha
nan Clach
B8009
Fernilea
Carbost
Drynoch
A863
Glen Drynoch
Sligachan

369
ARNAVAL
Merkadale

Glen Eynort
Talisker
Bay
Talisker
369
BEINN BHREAC

447
BEINN BHREAC
Grula

965
SGURR NAN GILL

974

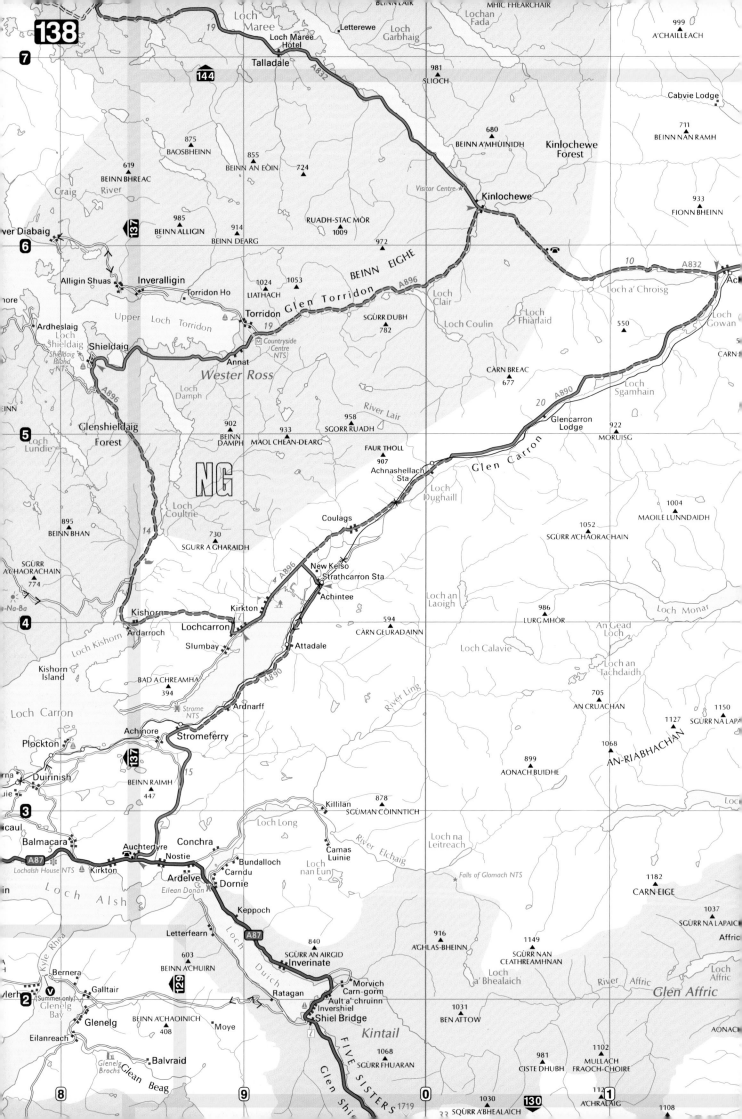

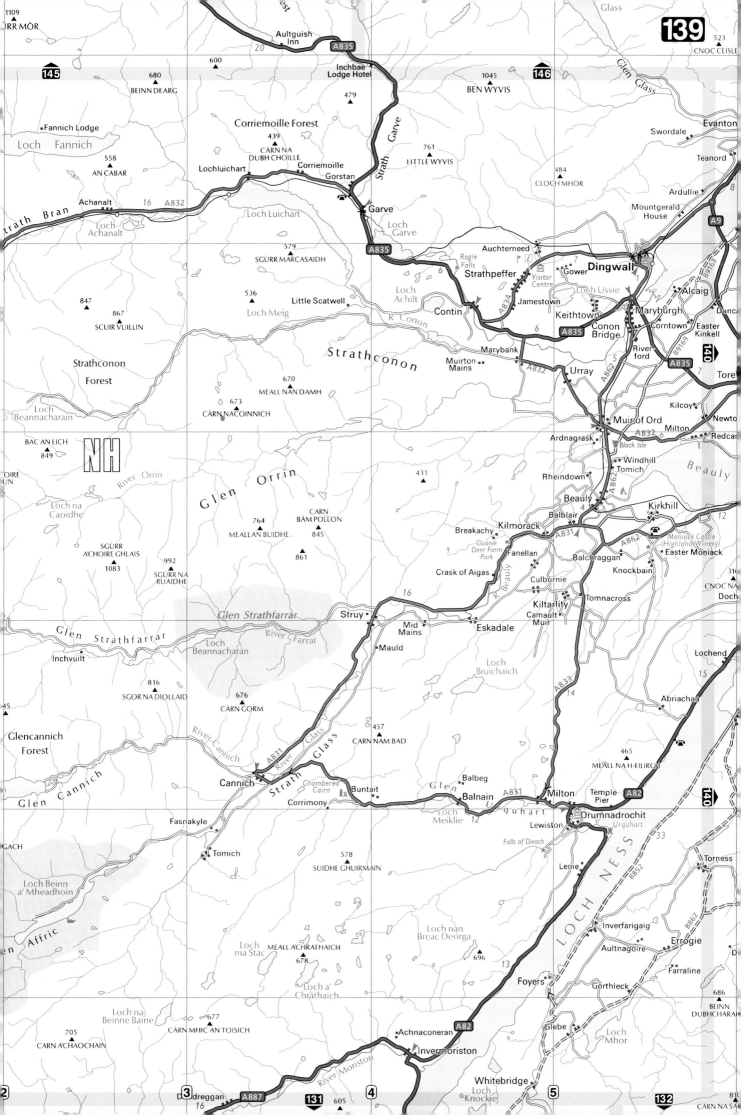

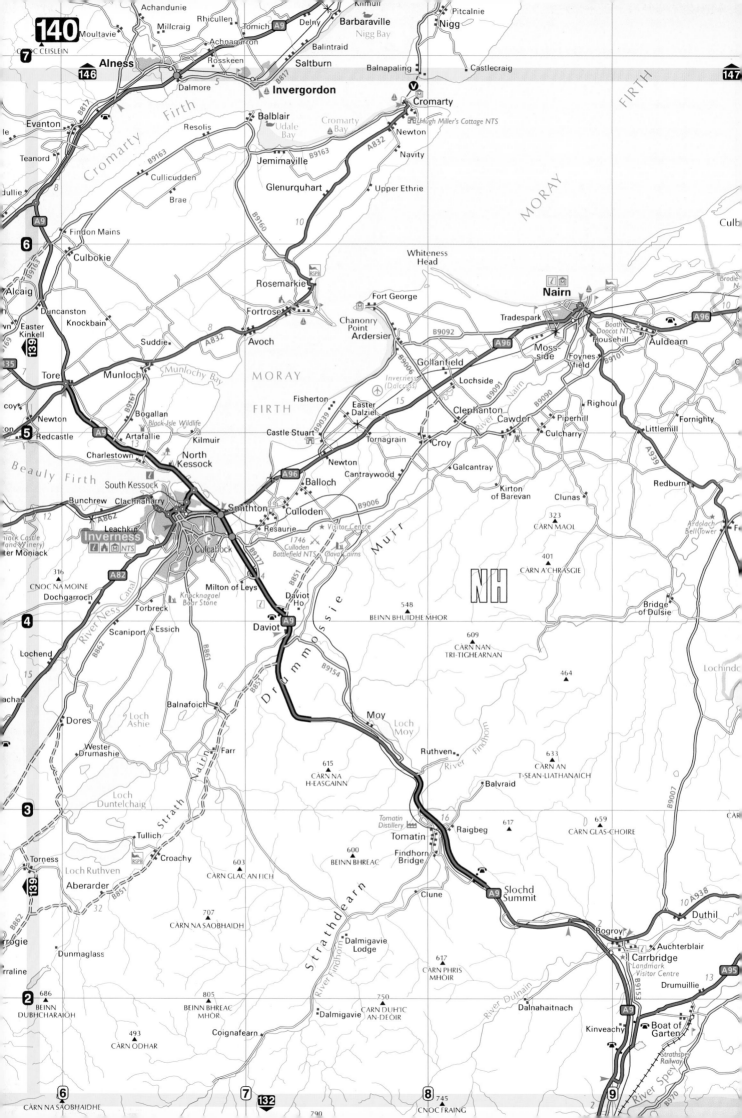

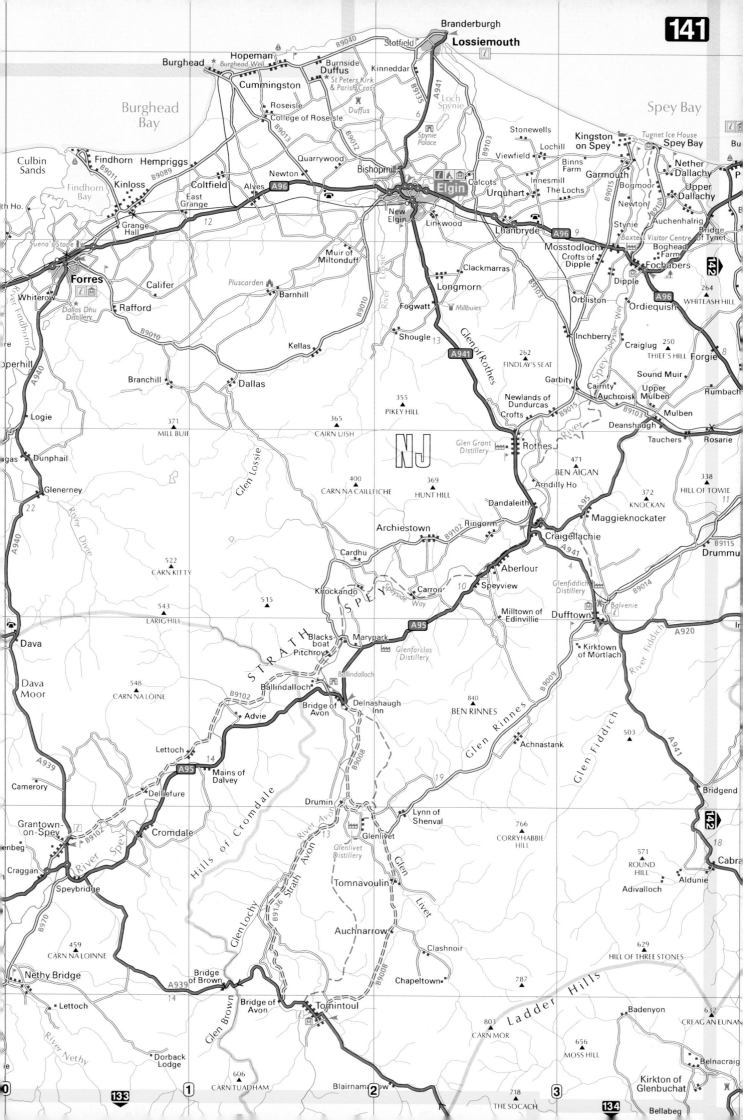

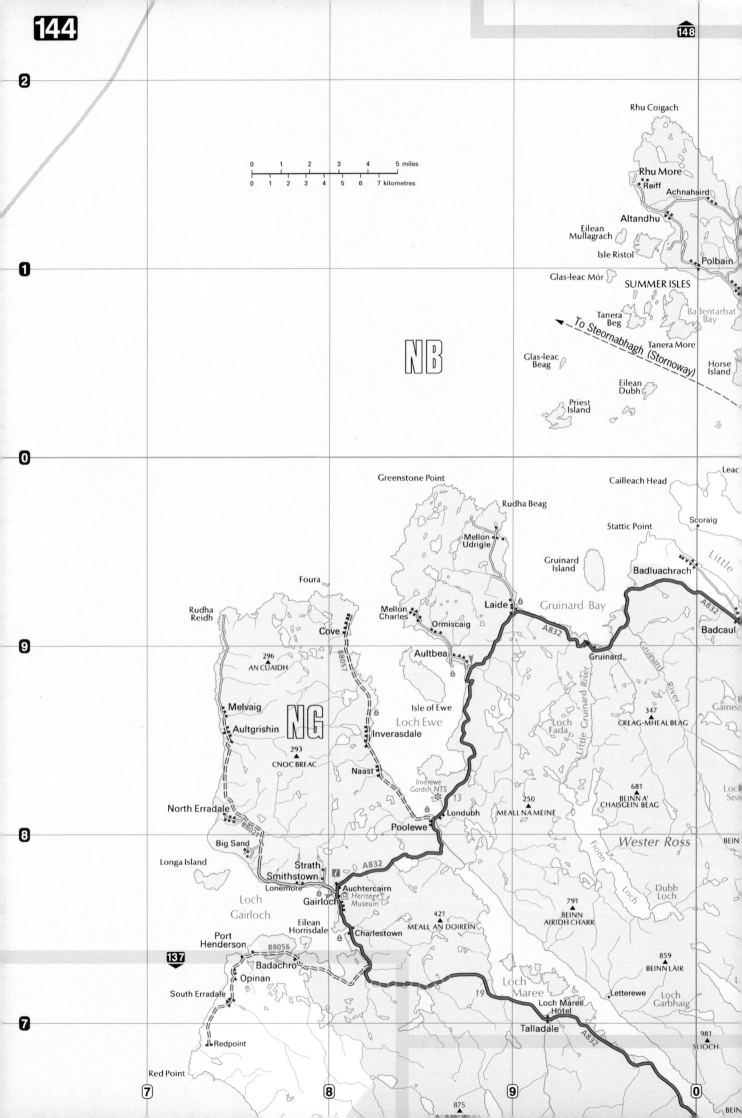

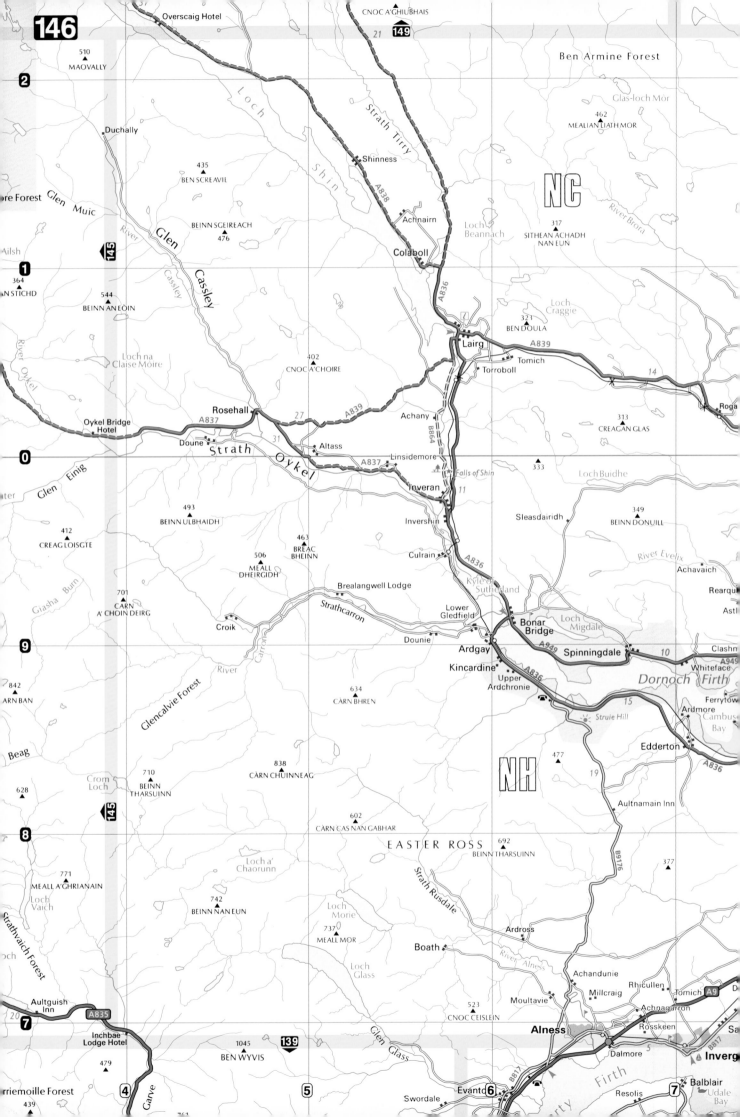

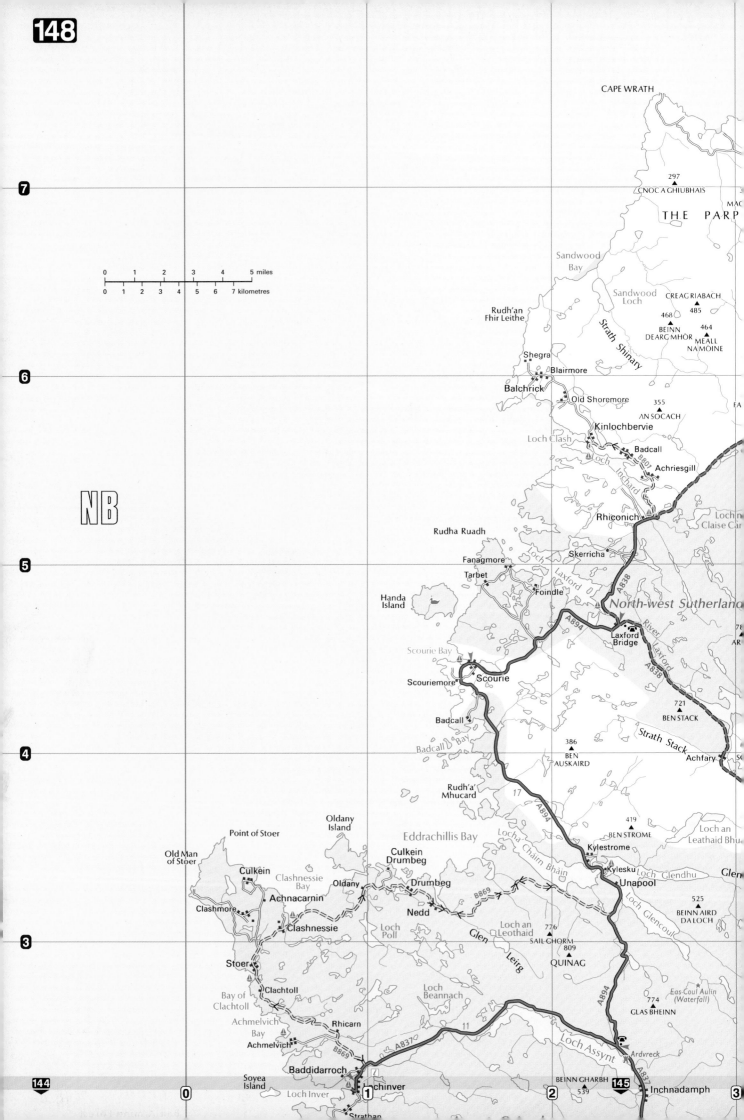

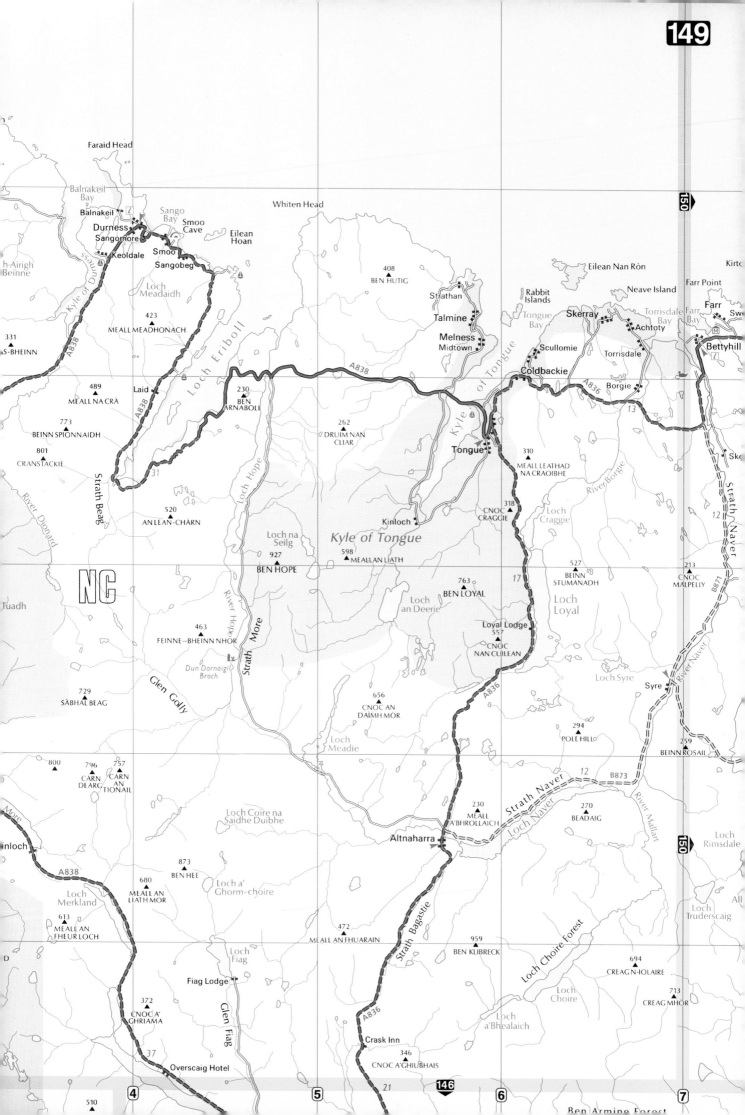

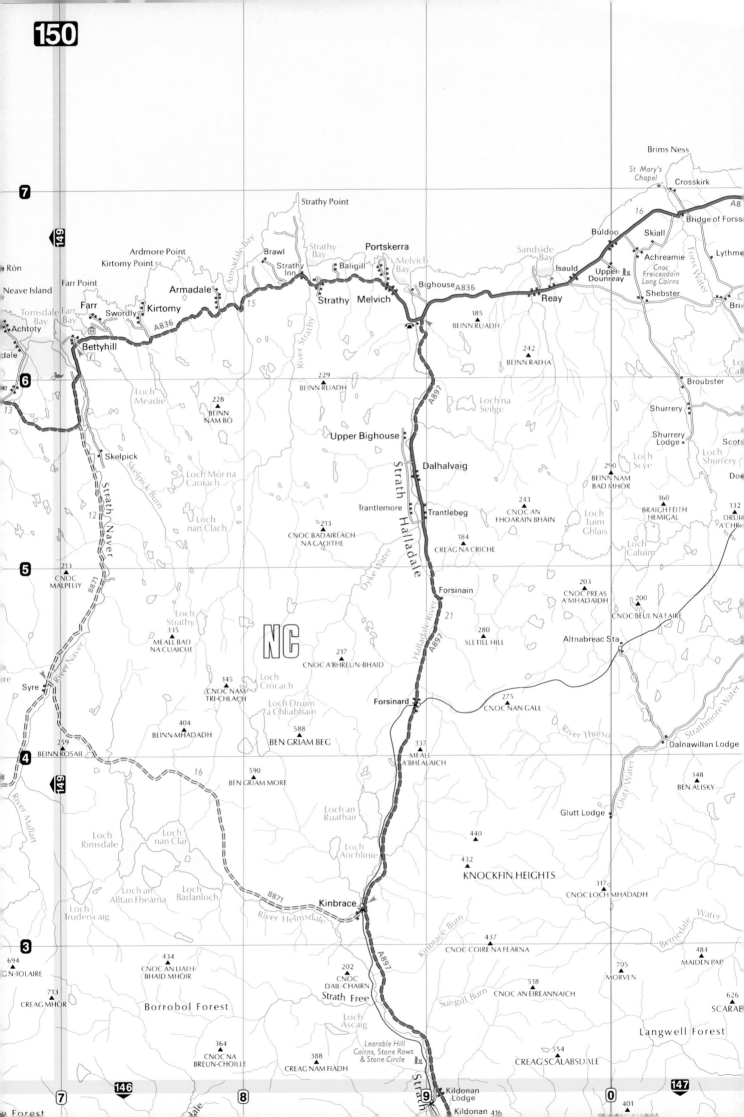

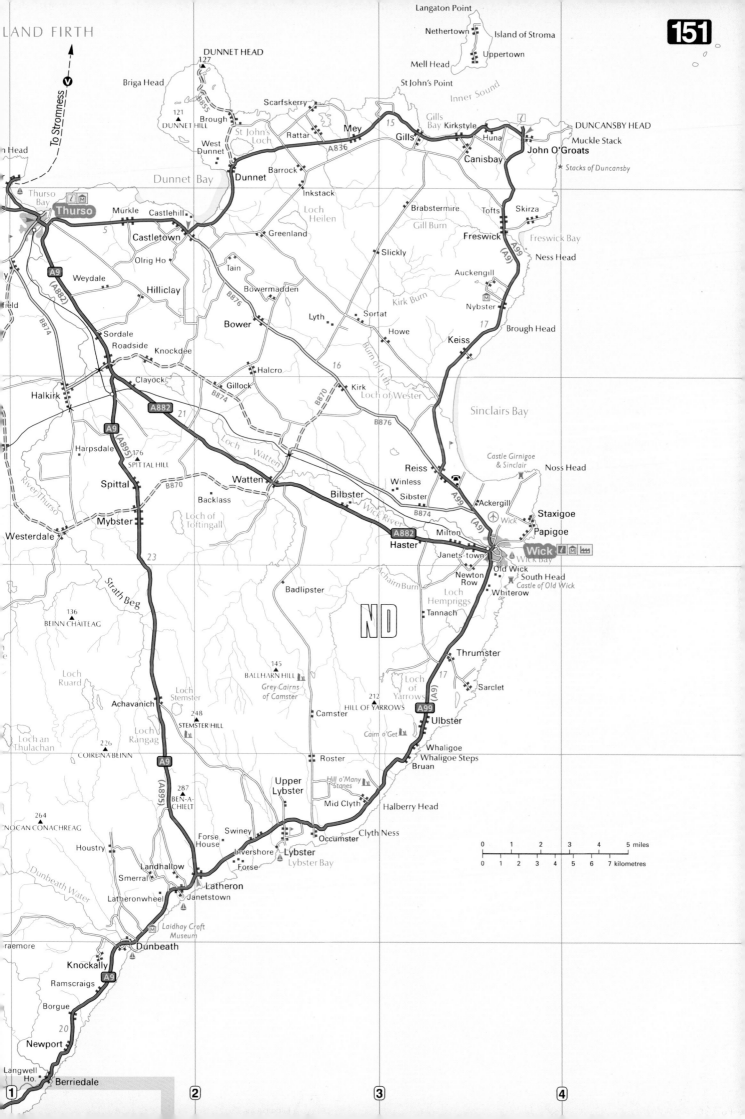

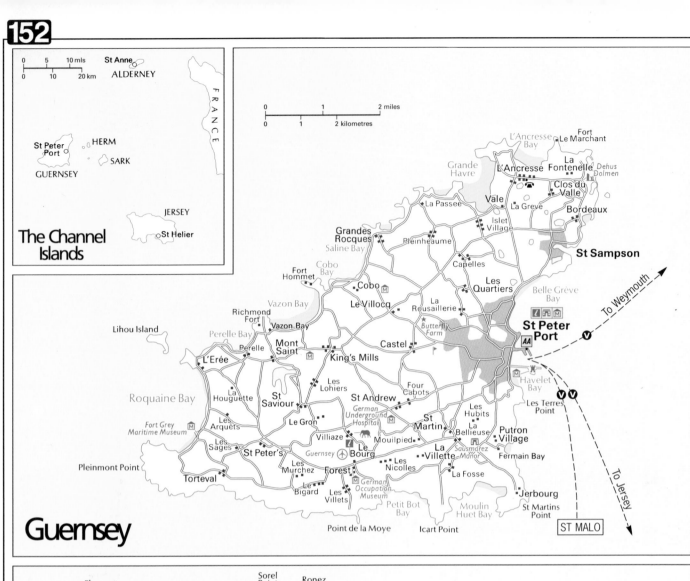

The Channel Islands

ALDERNEY
St Anne

FRANCE

HERM
St Peter
Port
SARK
GUERNSEY

JERSEY
St Helier

0 5 10 mls
0 10 20 km

Guernsey

2 miles / 2 kilometres

Fort Le Marchant
L'Ancresse Bay
Grande Havre
L'Ancresse
La Fontenelle
Dehus Dolmen
Clos du Valle
Vale
La Greve
Bordeaux
La Passee
Islet Village
St Sampson
Grandes Rocques
Pleinheaume
Capelles
Les Quartiers
Saline Bay
Cobo Bay
Fort Hommet
Cobo
La Rousaillerie
Belle Grève Bay
Richmond Fort
Le Villocq
Butterfly Farm
St Peter Port
Vazon Bay
Castel
To Weymouth
Perelle Bay
Mont Saint
King's Mills
AA
Perelle
L'Erée
Les Lohiers
Havelet Bay
Lihou Island
La Houguette
St Saviour
St Andrew
Four Cabots
Les Terres Point
Roquaine Bay
Le Gron
German Underground Hospital
Les Hubits
Fort Grey Maritime Museum
Les Arquets
Villiaze
Le Bourg
St Martin
La Bellieuse
Putron Village
Les Sages
St Peter's
Guernsey
Moulpied
La Villette
Sausmarez Manor
Fermain Bay
Pleinmont Point
Les Murchez
Forest
Les Nicolles
La Fosse
Le Bigard
Les Villets
German Occupation Museum
Jerbourg
Torteval
Petit Bot Bay
Moulin Huet Bay
St Martins Point
Point de la Moye
Icart Point
To Jersey
ST MALO

Jersey

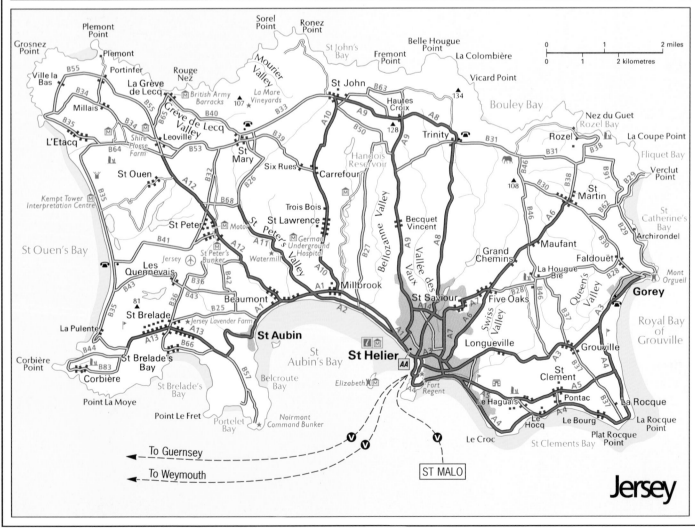

Grosnez Point
Plemont Point
Sorel Point
Ronez Point
Belle Hougue Point
Plemont
St John's Bay
Fremont Point
La Colombière
Ville la Bas
Portinfer
Rouge Nez
Mourier Valley
Vicard Point
B55
La Grève de Lecq
B34
British Army Barracks
La Mare Vineyards
Bouley Bay
Millais
B55
Grève de Lecq Valley
107
St John
B63
Nez du Guet
B35
B40
Hautes Croix
Rozel Bay
L'Etacq
Leoville
B65
B39
A10
A9
128
Trinity
B31
Rozel
La Coupe Point
Shire Horse Farm
B53
St Mary
B50
A8
B38
Fliquet Bay
B64
B32
Six Rues
Carrefour
Hanois Reservoir
B46
Verclut Point
St Ouen
B26
B31
St Martin
B91
B29
St Catherine's Bay
Kempt Tower Interpretation Centre
B68
Trois Bois
108
B30
B38
Archirondel
St Peter
St Lawrence
Bellozanne Valley
B46
A6
B62
B41
Motor
German Underground Hospital
Becquet Vincent
Maufant
Faldouët
St Ouen's Bay
Jersey Bunker
St Peter's Valley
B27
A8
Grand Chemins
La Hougue Bie
Mont Orgueil
Les Quennevais
St Peter's Bunker
Watermill
Vallée des Vaux
A6
B28
B46
Queen's Valley
B28
Gorey
B36
B42
A11
A10
St Saviour
Five Oaks
A3
Beaumont
A1
Millbrook
A14
Swiss Valley
A6
A1
Grouville
Royal Bay of Grouville
81
B36
B43
B25
A2
Longueville
A7
B31
St Brelade
Jersey Lavender Farm
St Aubin
St Helier
A5
St Clement
A4
La Pulente
A13
A13
AA
A4
La Rocque
Corbière Point
B66
St Aubin's Bay
St
Aubin's Bay
Fort Regent
Le Haguais
Pontac
La Rocque Point
B44
B83
Elizabeth
A5
Corbière
St Brelade's Bay
Belcroute Bay
A4
Le Hocq
Le Bourg
Plat Rocque Point
Point La Moye
St Brelade's Bay
Noirmont Command Bunker
Le Croc
St Clements Bay
Point Le Fret
Portelet Bay
To Guernsey
To Weymouth
ST MALO

The Isle of Man

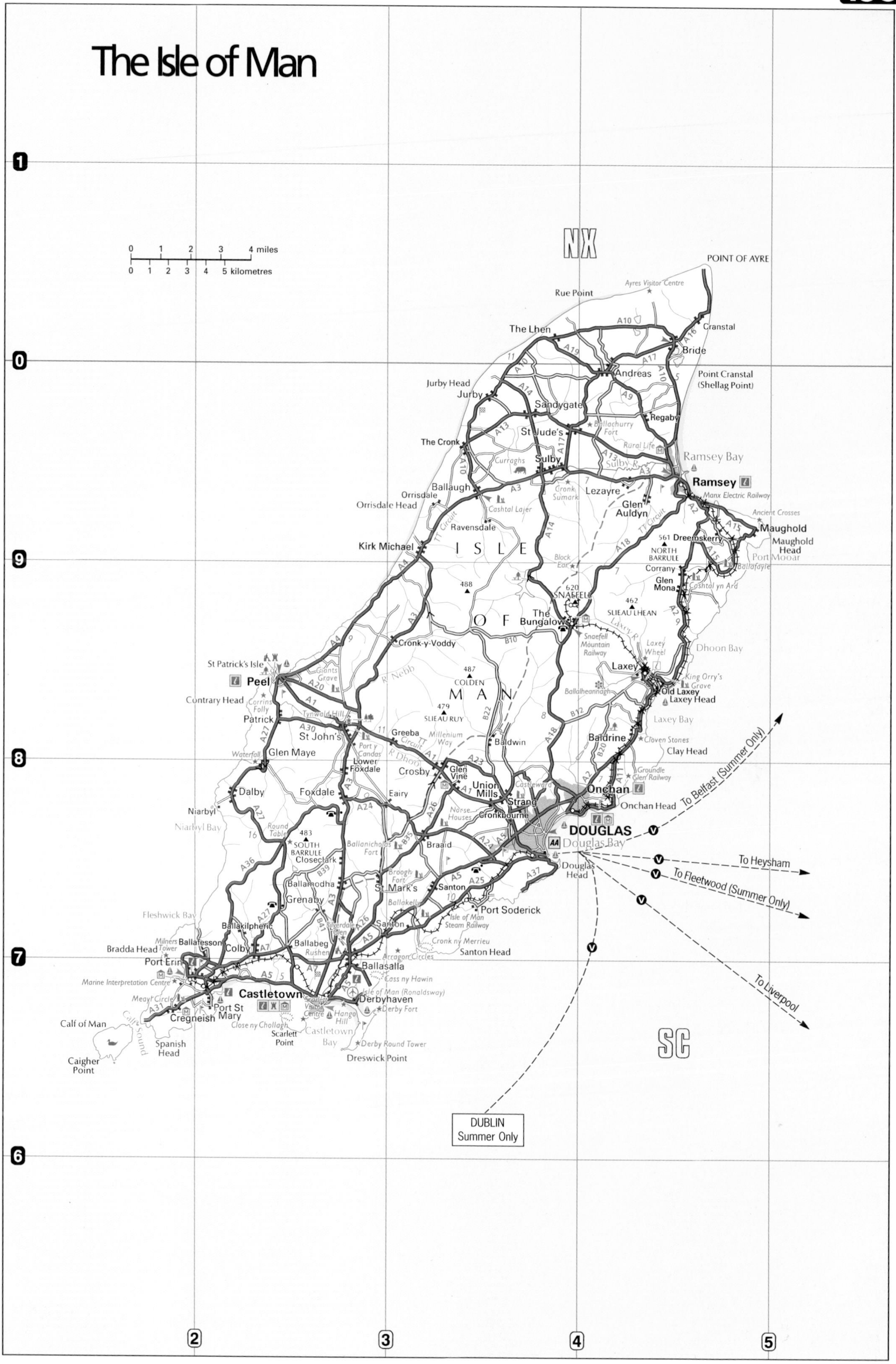

0 1 2 3 4 miles
0 1 2 3 4 5 kilometres

NX

POINT OF AYRE

Ayres Visitor Centre

Rue Point

The Lhen

Cranstal
Bride

A10

A19

A17 A16

A14

Jurby Head
Jurby

Sandygate

Andreas

Point Cranstal
(Shellag Point)

A9

A10

Ballachurry
Fort

Regaby

St Jude's

The Cronk

Sulby

Rural Life

Ramsey Bay

A13

Ballaugh

A3

Currraghs

Cronk
Sumark

Sulby R.

Ramsey

Manx Electric Railway

Orrisdale

Orrisdale Head

Lezayre

Glen
Auldyn

A2

Ancient Crosses

Cashtal Lajer

ISLE

Maughold

Ravensdale

A14

A18

561 Dreemskerry

Maughold
Head

Kirk Michael

Block
Eary

NORTH
BARRULE

Port Mooar

Corrany

Ballafayle

TT Circuit

488

620
SNAEFELL

7

Glen
Mona

Cashtal yn Ard

OF

Cronk-y-Voddy

B10

The
Bungalow

462
SLIEAU LHEAN

Dhoon Bay

Snaefell
Mountain
Railway

Laxey
Wheel

Laxey R.

R. Neb

487

COLDEN

MAN

Giants'
Grave

Laxey

King Orry's
Grave

Ballalheannagh

St Patrick's Isle

A4

A20

Peel

479
SLIEAU RUY

B22

A18

Old Laxey
Laxey Head

Contrary Head

Corrins
Folly
Tower

Patrick

A1

Tynwald Hill

Greeba

Millenium
Way

Baldwin

Baldrine

B20

Laxey Bay

Clay Head

Cloven Stones

St John's

11

Port y
Candas

Groudle
Glen Railway

Glen Maye

Waterfall

Lower
Foxdale

Crosby

R. Dhoo

Glen
Vine

A23

Union
Mills

A2

Castleward

To Belfast (Summer Only)

Dalby

Niarbyl

Niarbyl Bay

Foxdale

A24

Eairy

A26

Norse
Houses

Strang
Cronkbourne

Onchan

Onchan Head

DOUGLAS

Douglas Bay

To Heysham

16

Round
Table

483
SOUTH
BARRULE
Closeclark

Ballanichallan
Fort

Braaid

A5
A25

A2

AA

V

To Fleetwood (Summer Only)

A36

A27

Ballamodha

Brough
Fort

St Mark's

Santon

A37

Douglas
Head

V

To Liverpool

Grenaby

Ballakelly

Port Soderick

Fleshwick Bay

Ballakilpheric

B41

Silverdale

Santon

Isle of Man
Steam Railway

Isle of Man (Ronaldsway)

Cronk ny Merrieu

Santon Head

Bradda Head

Milners
Tower

Ballafesson
Colby

Ballabeg
Rushen

A5

Arragon Circles

Cass ny Hawin

V

Port Erin

A7

Ballasalla

Marine Interpretation Centre

Meayl Circle

A3

Castletown

Derbyhaven
Derby Fort

Cregneish

Port St
Mary

Close ny Chollagh

Hango
Hill

Castletown
Bay

Calf of Man

Calf Sound

Spanish
Head

Scarlett
Point

Derby Round Tower

SC

Caigher
Point

Dreswick Point

DUBLIN
Summer Only

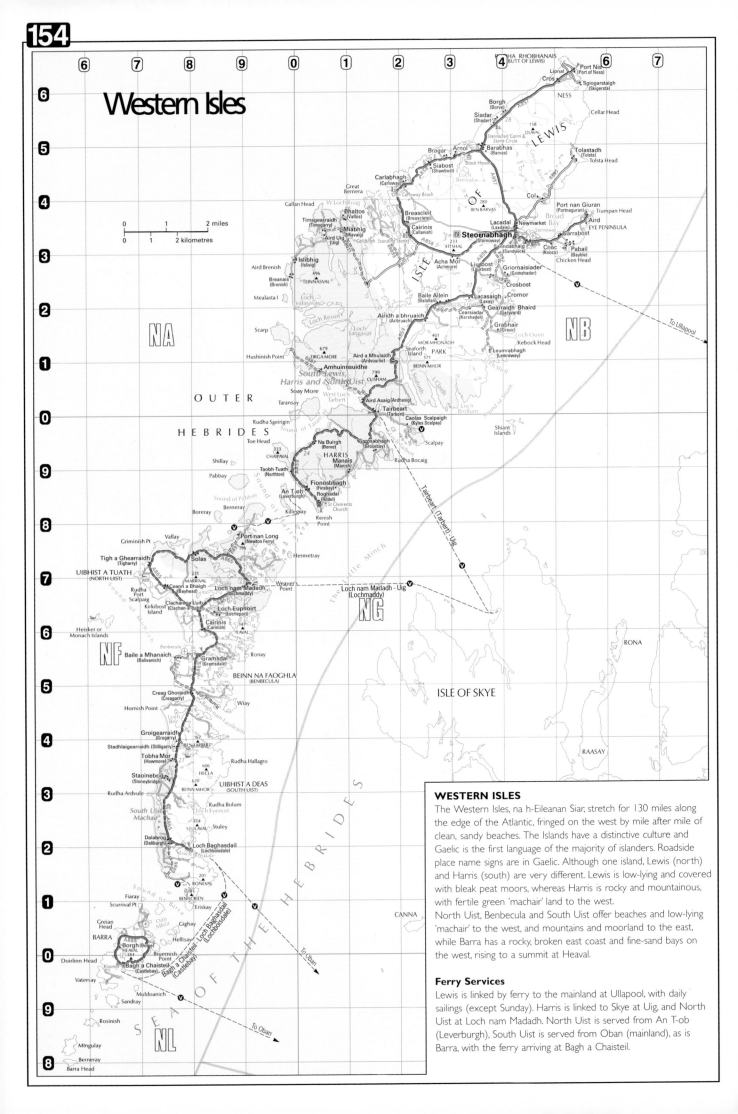

Western Isles

WESTERN ISLES

The Western Isles, na h-Eileanan Siar, stretch for 130 miles along the edge of the Atlantic, fringed on the west by mile after mile of clean, sandy beaches. The Islands have a distinctive culture and Gaelic is the first language of the majority of islanders. Roadside place name signs are in Gaelic. Although one island, Lewis (north) and Harris (south) are very different. Lewis is low-lying and covered with bleak peat moors, whereas Harris is rocky and mountainous, with fertile green 'machair' land to the west.

North Uist, Benbecula and South Uist offer beaches and low-lying 'machair' to the west, and mountains and moorland to the east, while Barra has a rocky, broken east coast and fine-sand bays on the west, rising to a summit at Heaval.

Ferry Services

Lewis is linked by ferry to the mainland at Ullapool, with daily sailings (except Sunday). Harris is linked to Skye at Uig, and North Uist at Loch nam Madadh. North Uist is served from An T-ob (Leverburgh), South Uist is served from Oban (mainland), as is Barra, with the ferry arriving at Bagh a Chaisteil.

Scottish Islands

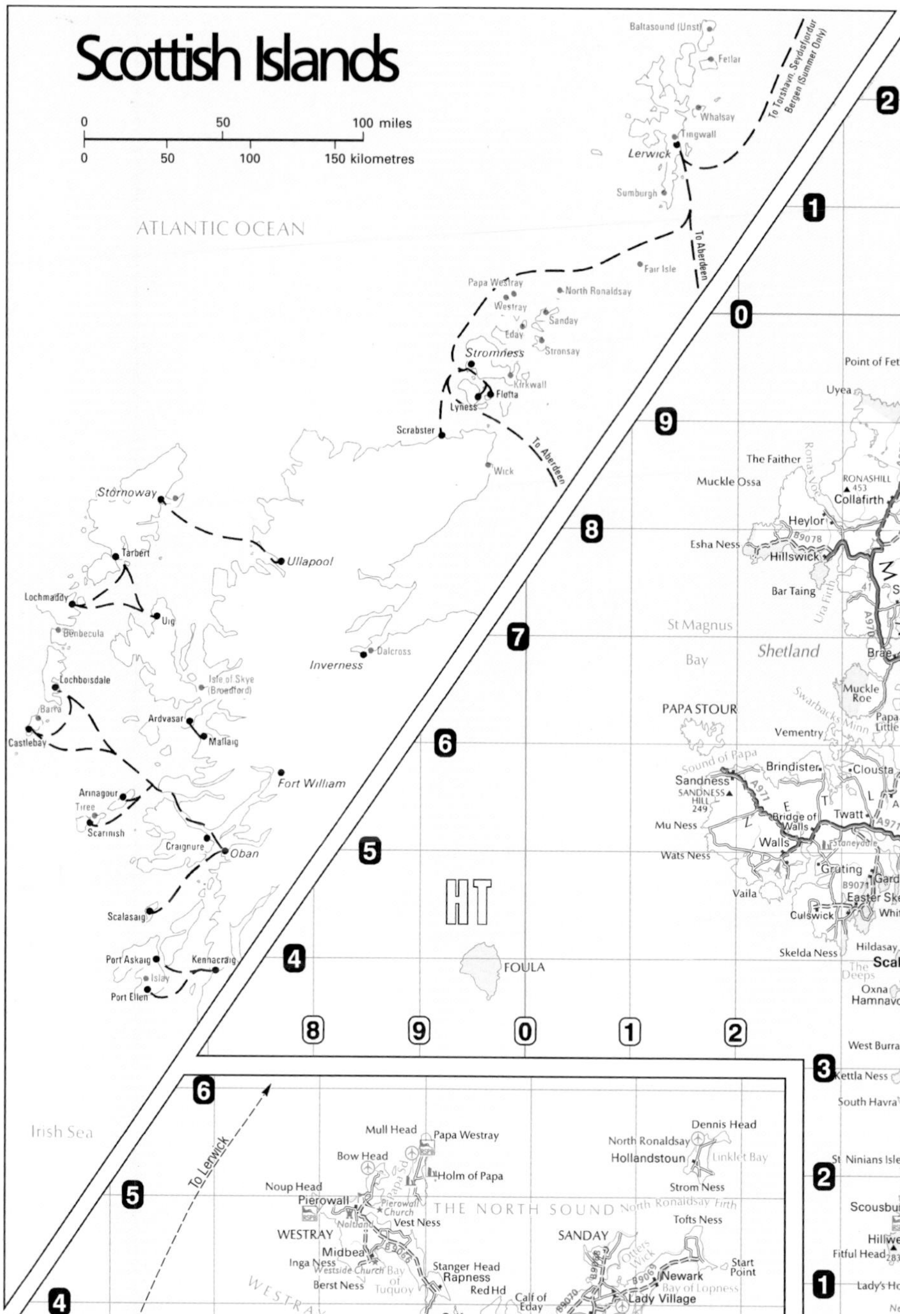

0   50   100 miles
0   50   100   150 kilometres

ATLANTIC OCEAN

Baltasound (Unst)
Fetlar
Whalsay
Tingwall
Lerwick
Sumburgh
Fair Isle

To Torshavn Seydisfjordur Bergen (Summer Only)

To Aberdeen

Papa Westray
Westray
North Ronaldsay
Eday
Sanday
Stromness
Stronsay
Kirkwall
Fletta
Lyness
Scrabster
To Aberdeen
Wick

Stornoway
Tarbert
Ullapool
Lochmaddy
Uig
Benbecula
Isle of Skye (Broadford)
Dalcross
Inverness
Lochboisdale
Ardvasar
Barra
Mallaig
Castlebay
Arinagour
Tiree
Fort William
Scarinish
Oban
Craignure
Scalasaig
Port Askaig
Islay
Kennacraig
Port Ellen

Irish Sea

HT
FOULA

Shetland Islands

HP
Muckle Flugga
HERMA NESS
The Noup
LIBBERS HILL 171
Burrafirth
Lamba Ness
Norwick
Haroldswick
UNST
Baltasound
Balta
Loch of Cliff
Gloup Holm
Bluemull Sound
Cullivoe
Belmont
Uyeasound
Ness of Ramnageo
Gutcher
Linga
Uyea
Tressa Ness
Ramna Stacks
Nev Sellafirth
of Stuis
Brough Lodge
Strandburgh Ness
Point of Fethaland
Whale Firth
Hascosay
FETLAR
Uyea
Isbister
Horra
Mid Yell
Vatsetter
The Faither
West Sandwick
YELL
Otterswick
Colgrave Sound
The Snap
Muckle Ossa
Collafirth
Ollaberry
Ulsta
Burravoe
Rams Ness
Heylor
Sullom Voe
Toft
Copister
Esha Ness
Hillswick
Sullom
Mossbank
Lunna Ness
Bar Taing
Hamnavoe
Lunna
OUT SKERRIES
Brae
Flora Ness
St Magnus
Bay
Muckle Roe
Voe
Laxo
Vidlin
Brough
Skaw Taing
Shetland
PAPA STOUR
Vementry
Papa Little
Gonfirth
WHALSAY
Brindister
Clousta
Catfirth
Symbister
Sandness
Aith
Neap
Brettabister
Twatt
South Nesting Bay
Moul of Eswick
Walls
Heglibister
Girlsta
Mu Ness
Tresta
TÖRSHAVN HANTSHOLM Summer Only
Wats Ness
Gruting
Garderhouse
Vaila
Easter Skeld
Whiteness
BERGEN Summer Only
Culswick
Score Head
Gunnista
Skelda Ness
Hildasay
BRESSAY
LERWICK
Scalloway
Isle of Noss
Oxna
Hamnavoe
Kirkabister
West Burra
Bard Ness
Fladdabister
HU
Kettla Ness
Clift Hills
Helli Ness
South Havra
Heswick
Stove
Mousa
St Ninians Isle
Sandwick
Scousburgh
Boddam
Hilliwell
Fitful Head
Tolob
Lady's Holm
SUMBURGH HEAD
Ness of Burgi
Jarlshof
Sumburgh
To Stromness
To Aberdeen

0   1   2 miles
0   1   2 kilometres

Orkney Islands

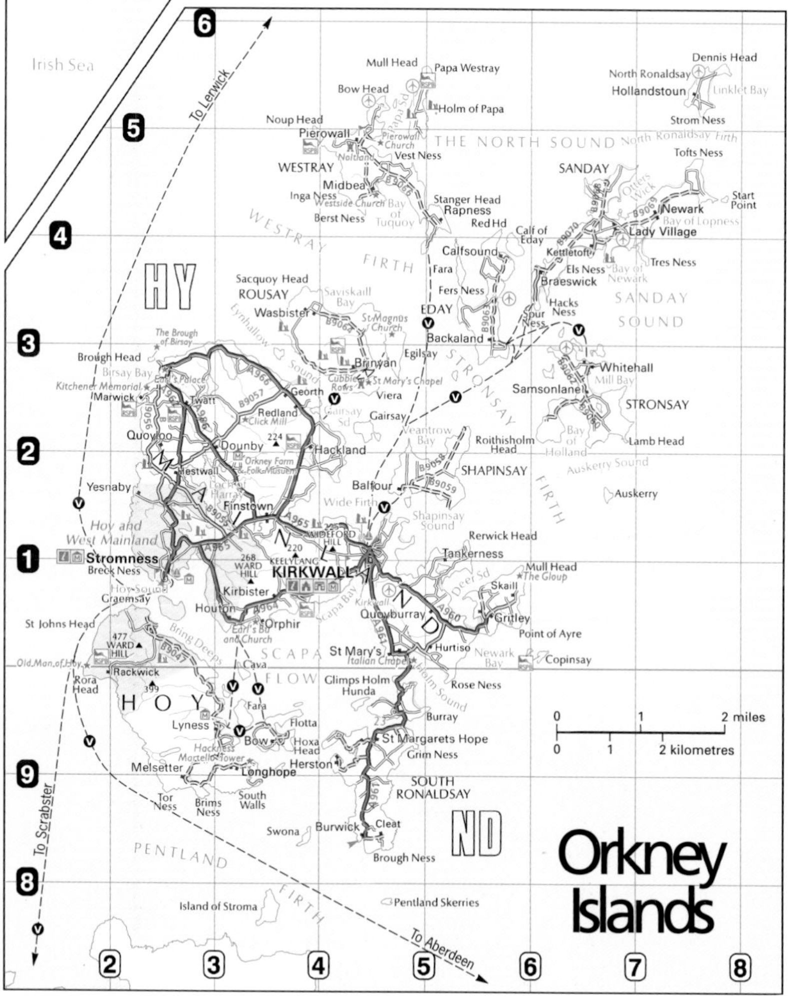

To Lerwick
Dennis Head
Papa Westray
Bow Head
Mull Head
Holm of Papa
North Ronaldsay
Hollandstoun
Linklet Bay
Noup Head
Pierowall Church
Strom Ness
WESTRAY
Vest Ness
THE NORTH SOUND
Tofts Ness
Inga Ness
Midbea
North Ronaldsay Firth
Westside Church
Stanger Head
SANDAY
Berst Ness
Rapness
Calf of Eday
Start Point
Sacquoy Head
Calfsound
Newark
ROUSAY
Fara
Kettletoft
Lady Village
Savskaill Bay
St Magnus Church
Kili Holm
Els Ness
Bay of Newark
Tres Ness
Wasbister
EDAY
Fers Ness
Hacks Ness
Brough Head
Gibbister
Backaland
SANDAY SOUND
Birsay
Egilsay
Quoyloo
Twatt
St Mary's Chapel
Whitehall
Redland
Gairsay
Samsonlanehill
Dounby
Viera
STRONSAY
Yesnaby
Hackland
Weantirow Bay
Lamb Head
Stromness
Finstown
Roithisholm Head
SHAPINSAY
Auskerry
Westmill
Balfour
Auskerry Sound
HOY
KIRKWALL
Wide Firth
Rerwick Head
Houton
Kirbister
Mull Head
The Gloup
St Johns Head
Orphir
Tankerness
Graemsay
Earl and Church
Skaill
Deer Sd
WARD HILL
St Mary's Italian Chapel
Queanburray
Grutly
Point of Ayre
Rora Head
Cava
Hurtiso
Newark Bay
Old Man of Hoy
Glimps Holm Hunda
Rose Ness
Lyness
Fara
Burray
Copinsay
Melsetter
Bow
Hoxa Head
St Margarets Hope
Grim Ness
Tor Ness
Longhope
Herston
Brims Ness
South Walls
SOUTH RONALDSAY
Swona
Burwick
Cleat
ND
Brough Ness
To Scrabster
PENTLAND FIRTH
Island of Stroma
Pentland Skerries
To Aberdeen

SHETLAND ISLANDS

The most northerly of all Britain's islands, this group numbers 100, though only 15 are inhabited. Most people live on the largest island, Mainland, on which Lerwick is the only town of importance. The scenery is magnificent, with unspoiled views, and the islands' northerly position means summer days have little or no darkness.

Ferry Services

The main service from the mainland is from Aberdeen to the island port of Lerwick. A service from Stromness (Orkney) to Lerwick is also available. During the summer months there are also services linking Shetland with Norway. Shetland Islands Council operates an inter-island service.

ORKNEY ISLANDS

Lying 20 miles north of the Scottish mainland, Orkney comprises 70 islands, of which 18 are inhabited, Mainland being the largest. Apart from Hoy, Orkney is generally green and flat, with few trees. The islands abound with prehistoric antiquities and rare birds. The climate is one of even temperatures and 'twilight' summer nights, but with violent winds at times.

Ferry Services

The main service is from Scrabster on the Caithness coast to the island port of Stromness. A service from Aberdeen to Stromness provides a link to Shetland at Lerwick. Inter-island services are also operated (advance reservations recommended).

Ireland

Bloody For[eland]
Gola Island
Aran Island
Dungloe
Gweebarra Bay
Rossan Point
Ardara
Glenti[es]
Glencolumbkille (Gleann Cholm Cille)
Malin More
Glencolumbkille Folk Museum
Carrick (An Charraig)
SLIEVE LEAGUE 601
Killybegs
Kilcar (Cill Charthaigh)
Dunki[neely]
St John's Point
Donegal Bay
Bundoran
Inishmurray
Kinlough
Cliffony
Grange
Lissadell
525 BENBULBEN
Drumcliff
Rosses Point
Sligo Bay
Parke's Castle
Strandhill
Sligo
Ballysadare
Dromahair
Colloney

Erris Head
Broad Haven
Downpatrick Head
Belmullet (Béal an Mhuirhead)
Bunnahowen
Ballycastle
Killala Bay
Easky
Dromore West
Enniscrone
Killala
Bangor Erris
Crossmolina
Ballina
Bunnyconnellan
Tobercurry
Charlestown
Carracastle
Ballaghaderreen
Inishkea
Duvillaun More
Blacksod Bay
SLIEVE-MORE 672
Keel
Achill Head
Achill Island
Mulrany
Newport
Castlebar
Turlough
Swinford
Knock International
Kilkelly
Frenchpark
NEPHIN 806
Foxford
Lough Conn
Lough Cullin
Lough Feeagh
OX MTS
Clare Island
Clew Bay
Westport
Louisburgh
Ballyhean
Balla
Knock
Loughglinn
Castlerea
Castleplunkett
Inishturk
Caher Island
CROAGH PATRICK 765
Partry
Lough Carra
Claremorris
Ballyhaunis
Ballinlough
Ballintober
Inishbofin
Inishshark
Cruagh
Letterfrack
Kylemore 730
Leenane
Clonbur (An Fhairche)
Lough Mask
Ballinrobe
Kilmaine
Neale
Ballindine
Dunmore
Ballymoe
Glenamaddy
Creggs
Roscommon
Fuerty
Clifden
682
Partry

1   2   3

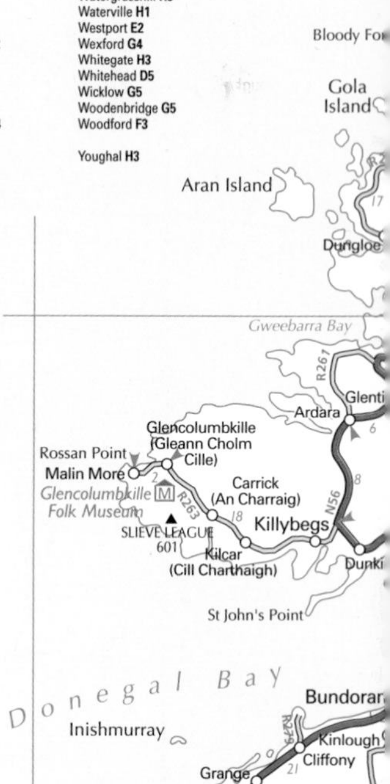

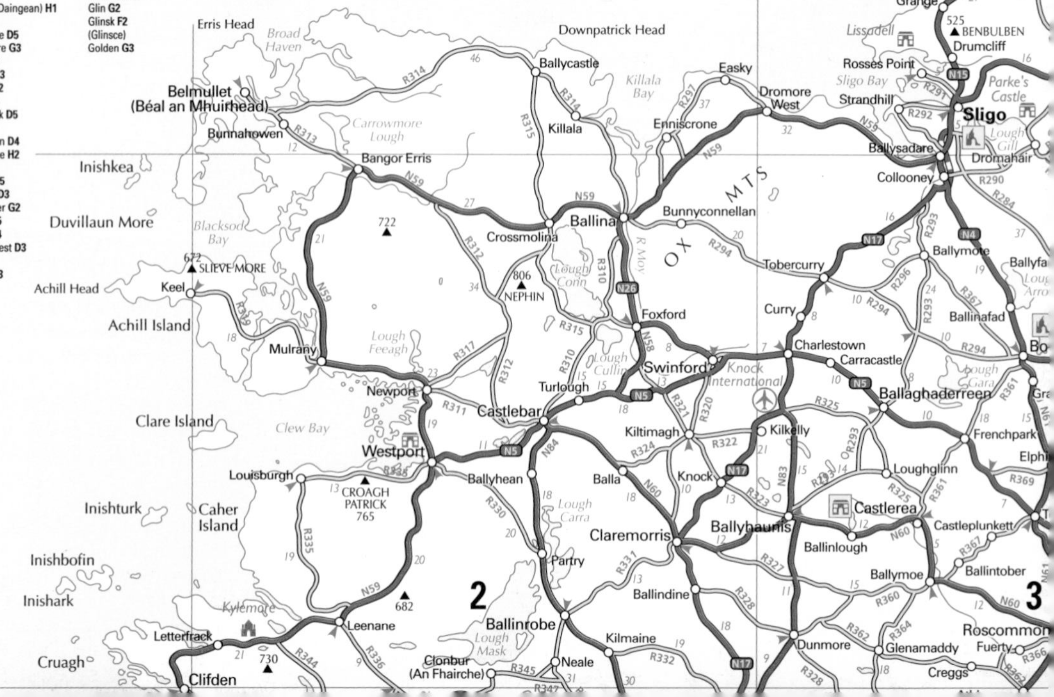

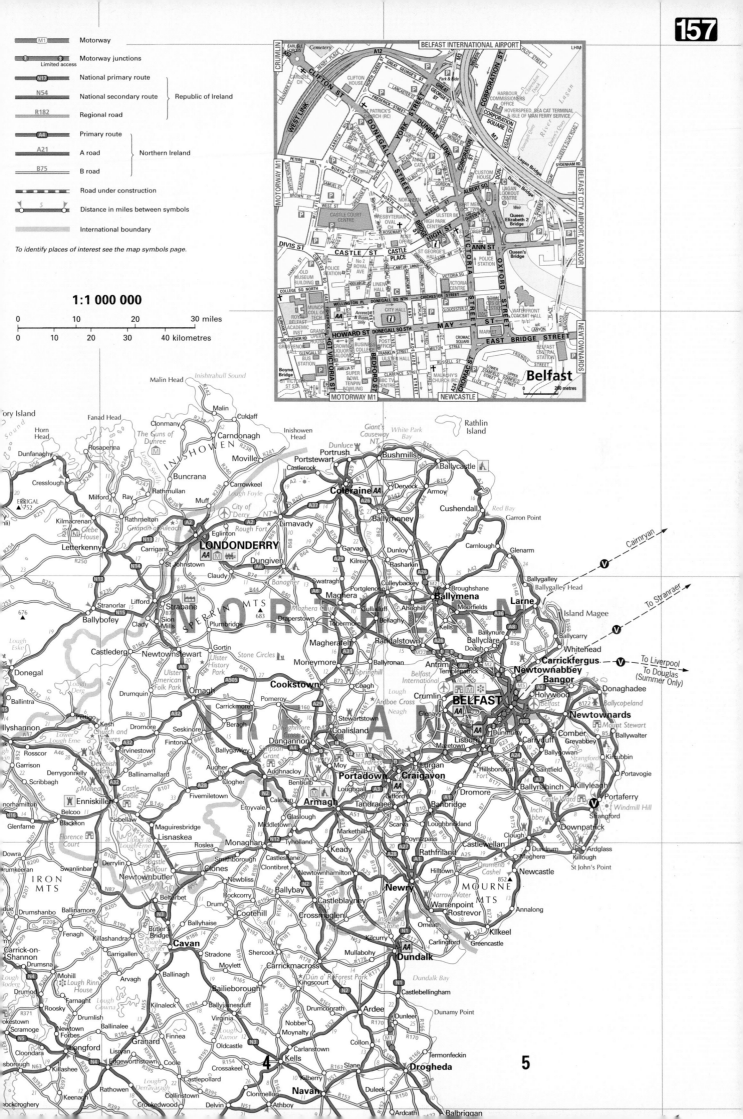

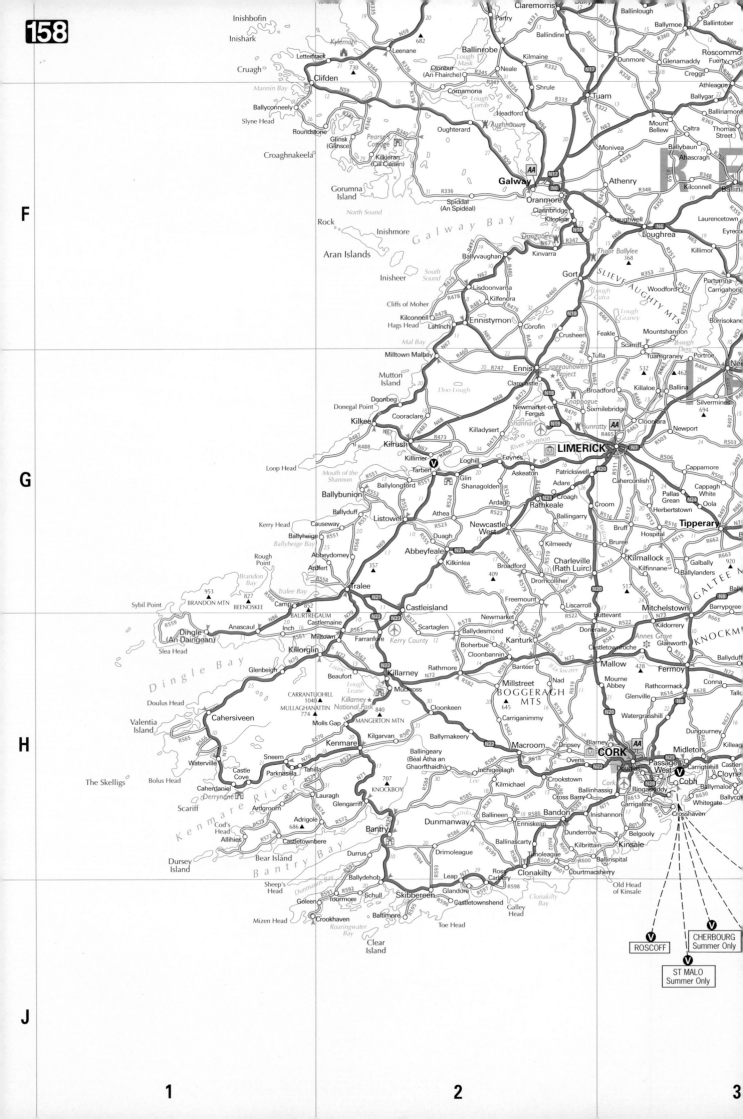

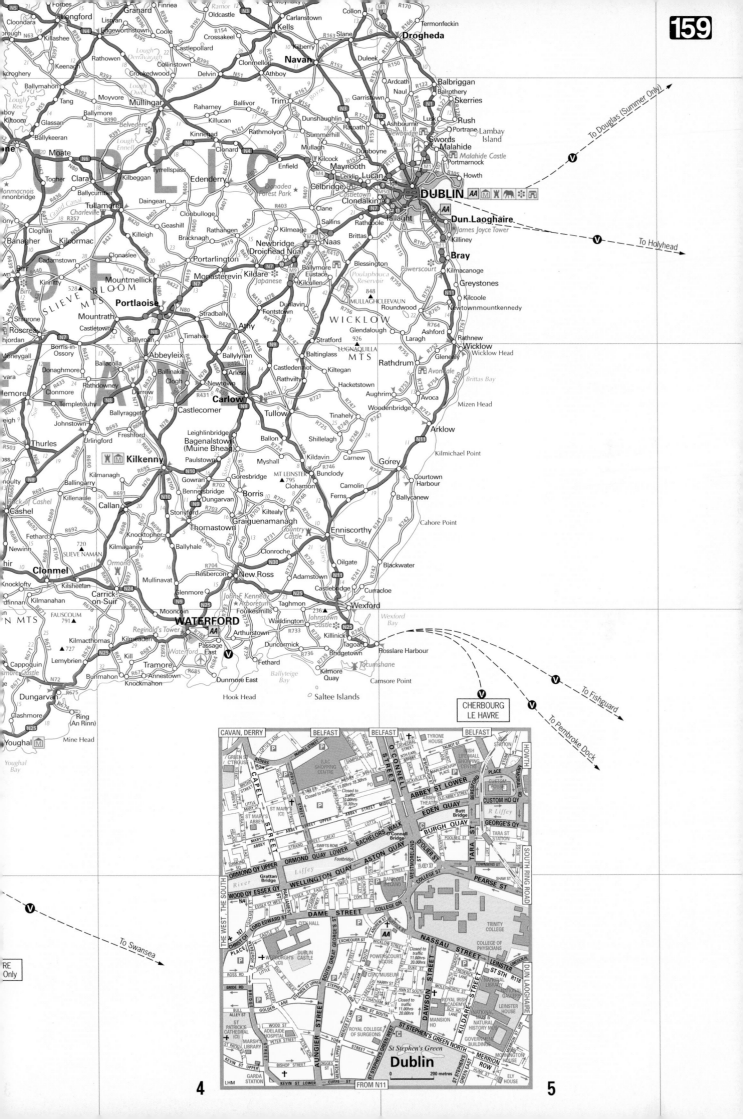

ports and airports

The following pages detail the major airports and seaports which help to provide a comprehensive domestic and international communications network. The maps indicate the approach roads into each complex and provide information on parking. Telephone numbers are provided for obtaining details on cost of parking and other travel information.

London Gatwick and London Heathrow are two of the busiest airports in the world, and many of the smaller airports listed below are constantly improving and expanding available services and destinations. The name of the airline concerned, or the flight number, must be known before aircraft arrivals and departures can be checked. Generally, no contact may be made with the passengers after they have cleared Customs on departure or before they have done so on arrival.

Always use the designated car parks. Your vehicle is liable to be removed if left unattended even for very short periods on any roads near the airport terminals. Facilities for travellers with disabilities are provided at the listed air and seaports, and in some cases parking concessions are available for Orange Badge holders. If special assistance is required the relevant airline or shipping company should be contacted.

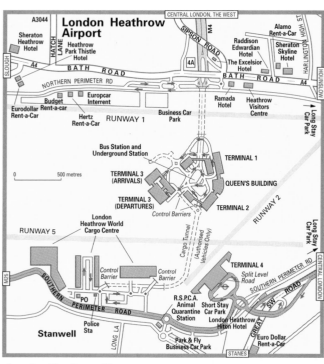

London Heathrow Airport – 16 miles west of London

Telephone: 0181 759 4321
Parking: Short-stay, long-stay and business parking available. For charge details tel: 0181 745 7160
Public Transport: Coach, bus and London Underground
There are several 4-star and 3-star hotels within easy reach of the airport, and car hire facilities are available

London Gatwick Airport – 35 miles south of London

Telephone: 01293 535353
Parking: Short-stay and long-stay parking available at both the North and South terminals. For charge details tel: 01293 502390 (short-stay) and either 0800 128128 or 01293 569222 (long-stay)
Public Transport: Coach, bus and rail. There are several 4-star and 3-star hotels within easy reach of the airport, and car hire facilities are available

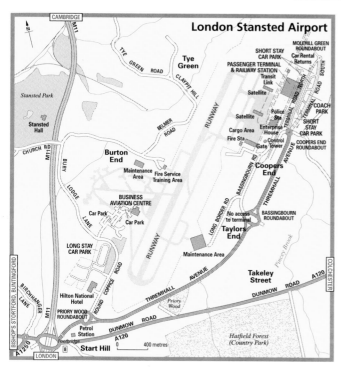

London Stansted Airport

London Stansted Airport – 38 miles north-east of London

Telephone: 01279 680500
Parking: Short-stay and long-stay open-air parking available. For charge details tel: 01279 662373
Public Transport: Coach, bus and a direct rail link to London on the 'Stansted Express'
There are several 4-star and 3-star hotels within easy reach of the airport, and car hire facilities are available

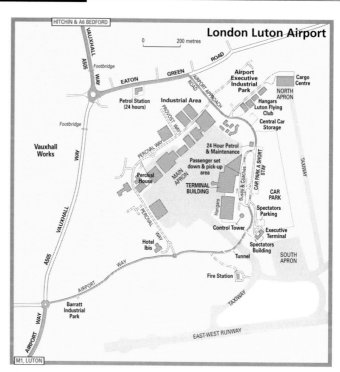

London Luton Airport

London Luton Airport – 35 miles north of London

Telephone: 01582 405100
Parking: Short-stay and long-stay open air parking available
Public Transport: Coach, bus and rail
There is one 2-star hotel at the airport and several 3-star hotels within easy reach of the airport. Car hire facilities are available

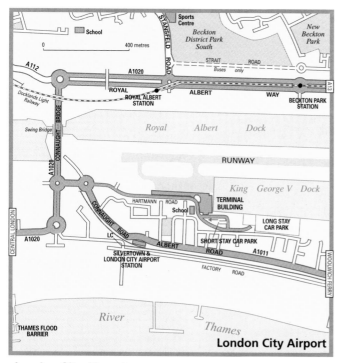

London City Airport

London City Airport – 7 miles east of London

Telephone: 0171 474 5555
Parking: Short-stay and long-stay parking available
Public Transport: 'Shuttlebus' service into London. Easy access to rail network and London Underground
There is a 4-star and 2-star hotel within easy reach of the airport, and car hire facilities are available

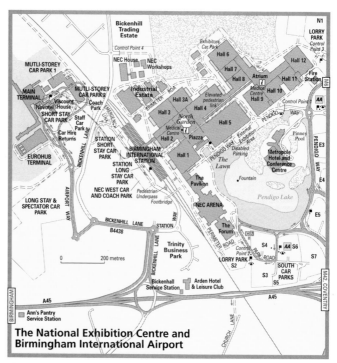

The National Exhibition Centre and Birmingham International Airport

Birmingham International Airport – 8 miles east of of Birmingham

Telephone: 0121 767 5511 (Main Terminal), 0121 767 7502 (Eurohub Terminal)
Parking: Short-stay and long-stay parking available
For charge details tel: 0121 767 7861
Public Transport: Bus service and shuttle-bus service to Birmingham International railway station and the NEC.
There are several 3-star hotels within easy reach of the airport, and car hire facilities are available

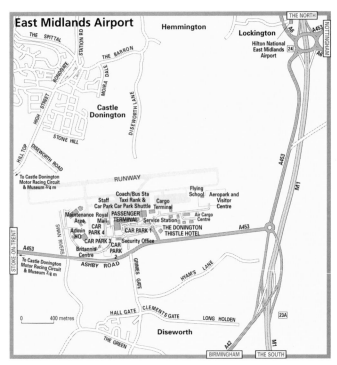

East Midlands Airport
15 miles southwest of Nottingham. Next to the M1 at junctions 23A and 24

Telephone: 01332 852852
Parking: Short-stay and long-stay parking available. For charge details tel:0800 128128
Public Transport: Bus and coach services to major towns and cities in the East Midlands
There are several 3-star hotels within easy reach of the airport, and car hire facilities are available

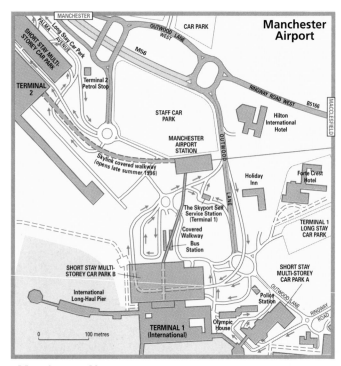

Manchester Airport – 10 miles south of Manchester

Telephone: 0161 489 3000
Parking: Short-stay and long-stay parking available.
Public Transport: Bus, coach and rail. Manchester airport railway station connects with the Rail network
There are several 4-star and 3-star hotels within easy reach of the airport, and car hire facilities are available

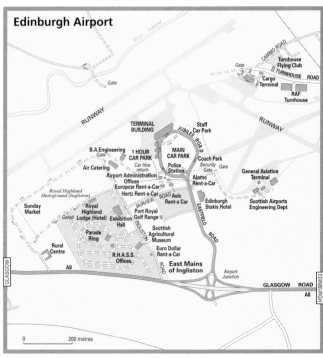

Edinburgh Airport – 7 miles west of Edinburgh

Telephone: 0131 333 1000
Parking: Open-air parking is available. For charge details tel: 0131 344 3197
Public Transport: Regular coach services operate between central Edinburgh and Glasgow
There is one 4-star are several 3-star hotels within easy reach of the airport, and car hire facilities are available

Glasgow Airport – 8 miles west of Glasgow

Telephone: 0141 887 1111
Parking: Short-stay and long-stay parking is available, mostly open-air. For charge details tel: 0141 889 2751
Public Transport: Regular coach services operate between central Glasgow and Edinburgh
There are several 3-star hotels within easy reach of the airport, and car hire facilities are available

major ports

Dover

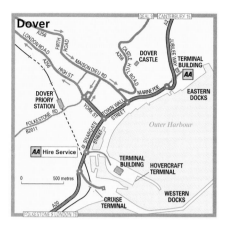

Pay-and-display parking available at the Dover Eastern Docks and at the Hoverport Terminal: for further information tel: 01304 240400
Other long-stay parking facilities are available with collection and delivery service: for charge details tel: 01304 203777, 208041 or 201227

Harwich International Port

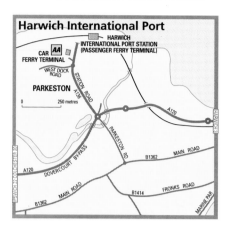

Open-air parking available at the terminal: for charge details tel: 01255 242000. Further parking 5 miles from Harwich International Port with collection and delivery service: for charge details tel: 01255 870217

Holyhead

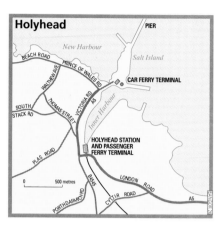

Open-air pay-and-display parking available close to the Passenger Terminal: for charge details tel: 01407 762304

Hull

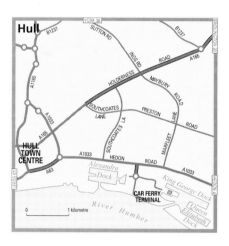

Free open-air parking at King George Dock (left at owners risk): tel: 01482 795141. Undercover parking available: for charge details tel: 01482 781021

Newhaven

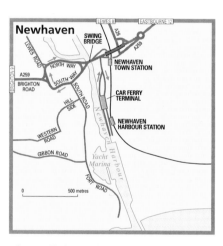

Open and limited parking within harbour complex: for charge details tel: 01273 514131

Plymouth

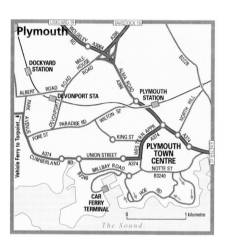

Free open-air parking available outside the terminal building: tel: 01752 252200 or 0990 360360

Poole

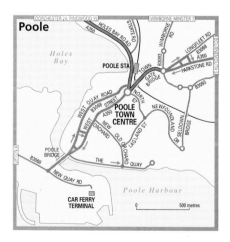

Free open-air parking for 300 vehicles available adjacent to ferry terminal: tel: 01202 685311

Portsmouth

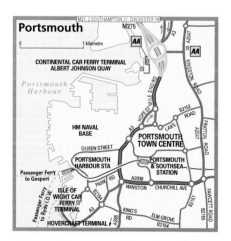

Lock-up parking spaces available at Albert Johnson Quay: for charge details tel: 01705 751261
Pay-and-display parking available opposite the Hovercraft Terminal. Mutli-storey parking is also available close to the Isle of Wight Passenger Ferry Terminal: for charge details tel: 01705 823153 or 812071

Southampton

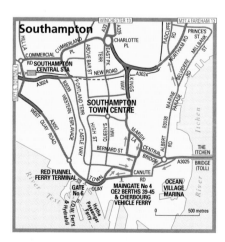

Covered or fenced compound parking for 1,600 vehicles within the Western Docks with a collection and delivery service: for charge details tel: 01703 228001/2/3

163

the Channel Tunnel

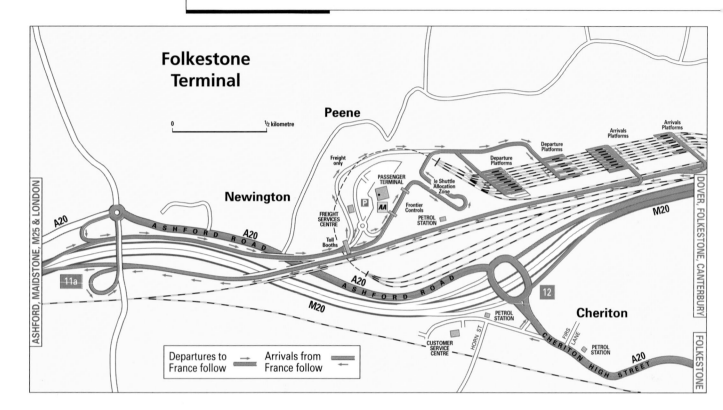

Services to Europe

The Le Shuttle service for cars, motorcycles, coaches, cars towing caravans and trailers, and HGV vehicles runs between terminals at Folkestone and Calais.

It takes just over one hour to travel from the M20 motorway in Kent, via the Channel tunnel to the A16 autoroute in France.

The high number of trains running every day means travellers are not required to make advance reservations - just turn up and go. Call Le Shuttle Customer Services Centre (tel: 0990 353535) for further information.

Trains run at 15-minute intervals at peak times with the journey in the tunnel from platform to platform taking just 35 minutes.

Travellers pass through British and French frontier controls on departure, saving time on the other side of the channel. Each terminal has tax-and-duty free shops, bureau de change, restaurants and a variety of shops. In Calais, the Cité de l'Europe contains further shops, restaurants, hotels and a hypermarket.

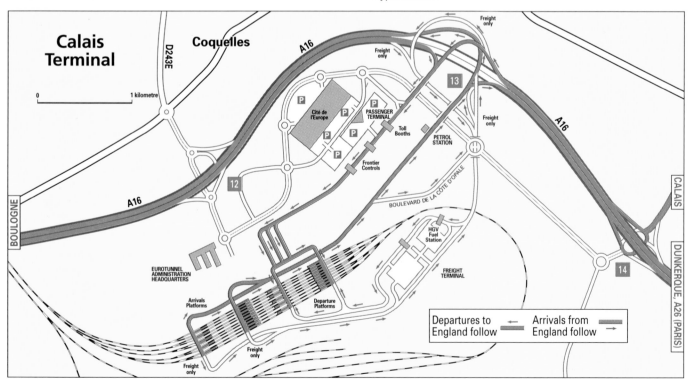

ferry routes

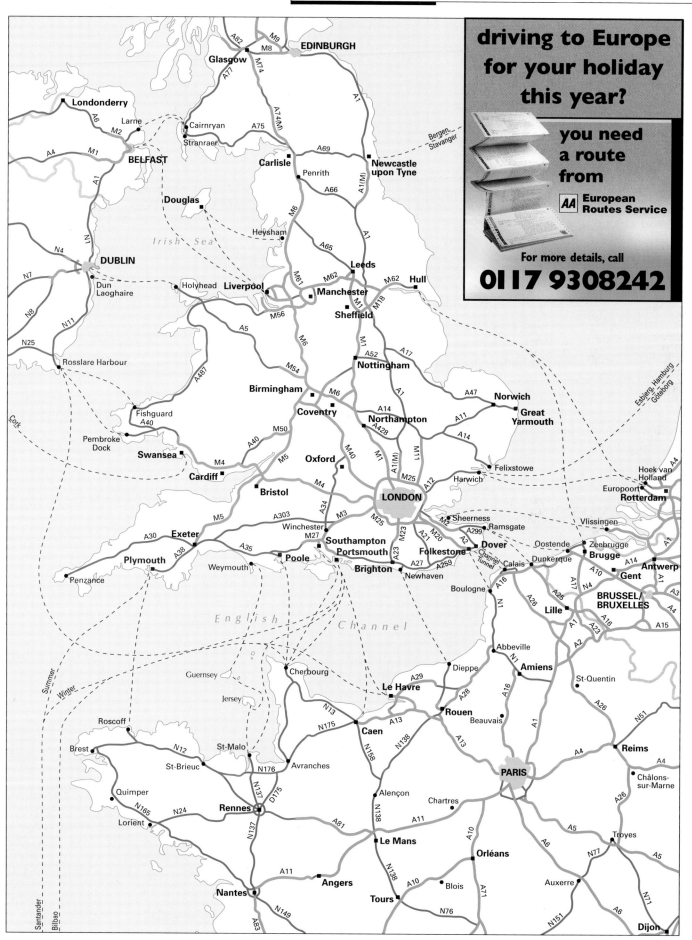

M25 London orbital motorway

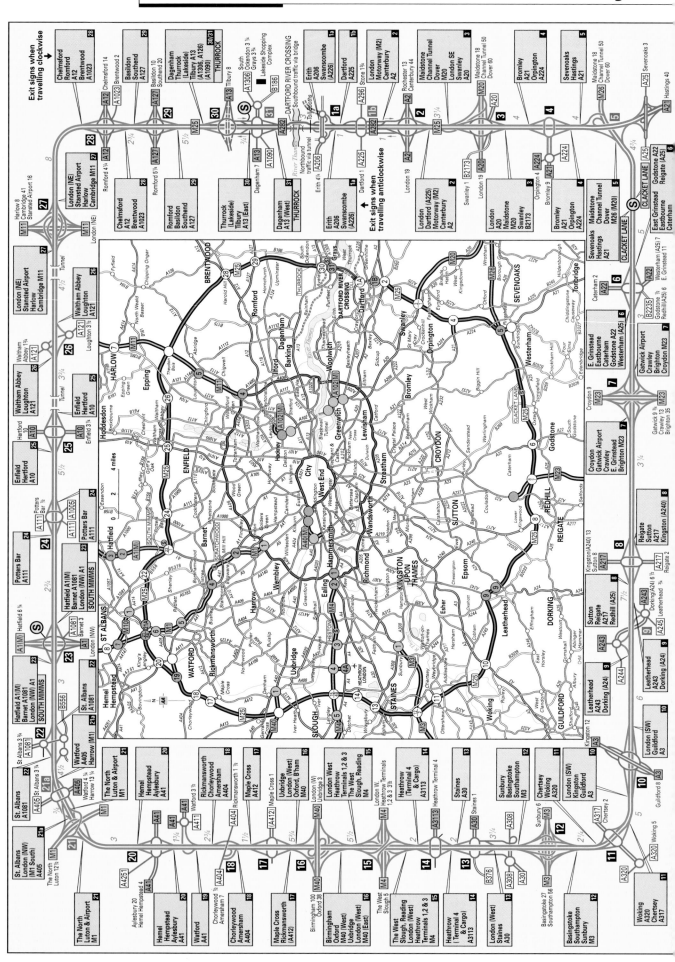

town plans

Inverness
Aberdeen
Dundee
Perth
St Andrews
Glasgow
Edinburgh
Belfast
Newcastle upon Tyne
Sunderland
Carlisle
Durham
Middlesbrough
Harrogate
York
Lancaster
Bradford
Leeds
Hull
Blackpool
Huddersfield
Liverpool
Manchester
Sheffield
DUBLIN
Llandudno
Chester
Lincoln
Hanley
Nottingham
Shrewsbury
Derby
Leicester
Norwich
Wolverhampton
Peterborough
Aberystwyth
Birmingham
Coventry
Northampton
Warwick
Cambridge
Worcester
Stratford-upon-Avon
Milton Keynes
Ipswich
Cheltenham
Luton
Gloucester
Oxford
Swansea
Swindon
Windsor
LONDON
Margate
Cardiff
Bristol
Reading
Ramsgate
Bath
Basingstoke
Maidstone
Canterbury
Andover
Guildford
Dover
Taunton
Salisbury
Winchester
Tunbridge Wells
Southampton
Brighton
Poole
Portsmouth
Eastbourne
Exeter
Bournemouth
Plymouth
Torquay

London

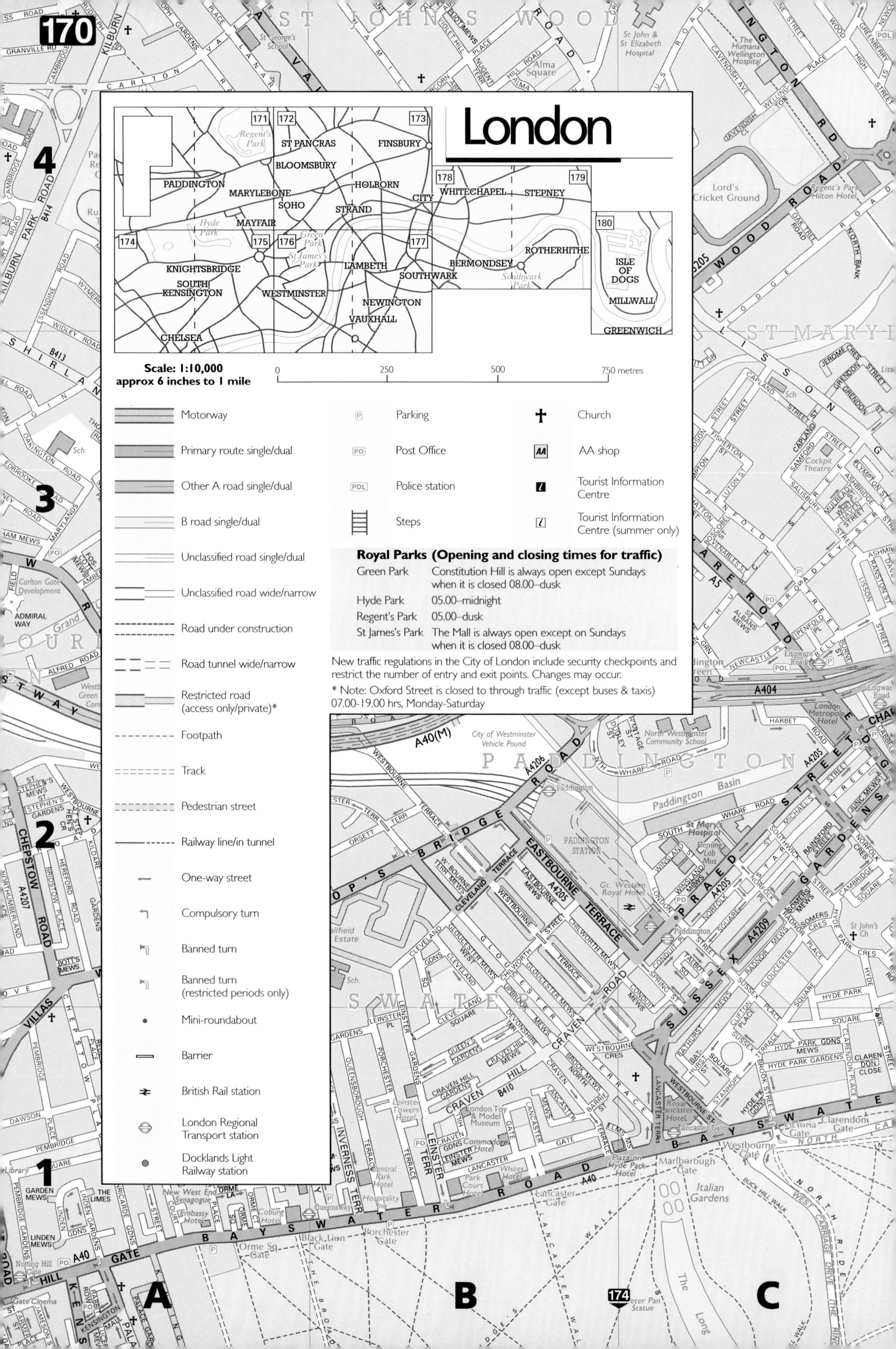

| 171 | 172 | | 173 |
Regent's Park | ST PANCRAS | FINSBURY |
| BLOOMSBURY |
PADDINGTON | | HOLBORN | 178 | WHITECHAPEL | STEPNEY | 179 |
MARYLEBONE | SOHO | CITY |
| STRAND | 180 |
Hyde Park | MAYFAIR | | ROTHERHITHE |
| 174 | 175 | 176 | 177 | BERMONDSEY |
Green Park | | ISLE |
St James's Park | | OF |
KNIGHTSBRIDGE | LAMBETH | SOUTHWARK | Southwark Park | DOGS |
SOUTH | WESTMINSTER | | MILLWALL |
KENSINGTON | | NEWINGTON |
| VAUXHALL | GREENWICH |
CHELSEA |

Scale: 1:10,000
approx 6 inches to 1 mile

0   250   500   750 metres

Motorway

Primary route single/dual

Other A road single/dual

B road single/dual

Unclassified road single/dual

Unclassified road wide/narrow

Road under construction

Road tunnel wide/narrow

Restricted road
(access only/private)*

- - - - - Footpath

········· Track

========= Pedestrian street

- - - - - Railway line/in tunnel

← One-way street

Compulsory turn

Banned turn

Banned turn
(restricted periods only)

• Mini-roundabout

Barrier

⇌ British Rail station

London Regional
Transport station

• Docklands Light
Railway station

P Parking

PO Post Office

POL Police station

Steps

✝ Church

AA AA shop

ℹ Tourist Information
Centre

ℹ Tourist Information
Centre (summer only)

Royal Parks (Opening and closing times for traffic)

Green Park   Constitution Hill is always open except Sundays
when it is closed 08.00–dusk

Hyde Park   05.00–midnight

Regent's Park   05.00–dusk

St James's Park   The Mall is always open except on Sundays
when it is closed 08.00–dusk

New traffic regulations in the City of London include security checkpoints and
restrict the number of entry and exit points. Changes may occur.

* Note: Oxford Street is closed to through traffic (except buses & taxis)
07.00–19.00 hrs, Monday-Saturday

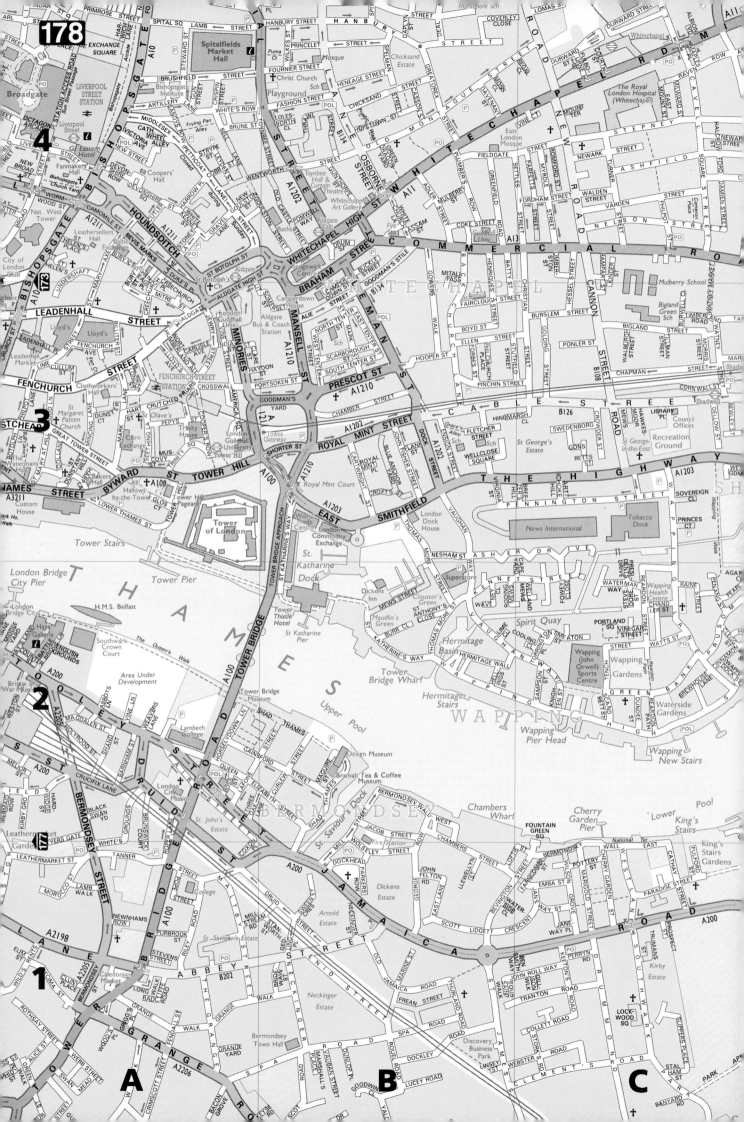

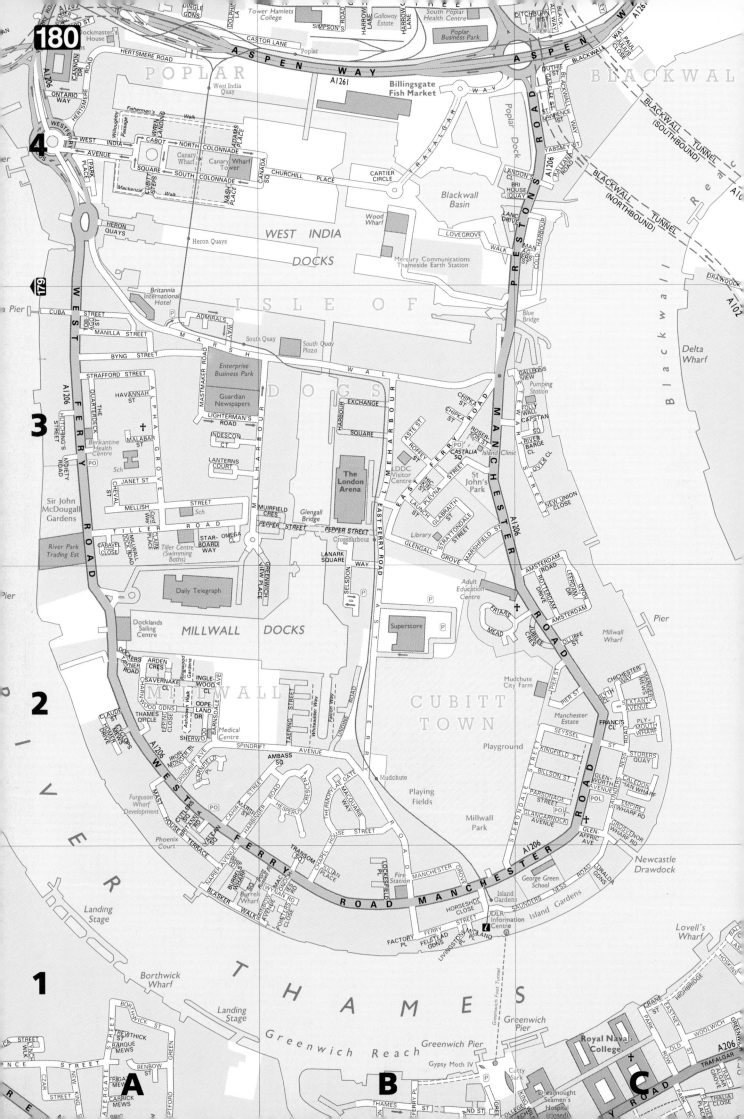

London street index

In the index the street names are listed in alphabetical order and written in full, but may be abbreviated on the map. Postal codes are listed where information is available. Each entry is followed by its map page number in bold type, and an arbitrary letter and grid reference number. For example, for Exhibition Road SW7 **174** C3, turn to page '**174**'. The letter 'C' refers to the grid square located at the bottom of the page; the figure '3' refers to the grid square located at the left-hand side of the page. Exhibition Road is found within the intersecting square. SW7 is the postcode. A proportion of street names and their references are also followed by the name of another street in italics. These entries do not appear on the map due to insufficient space but can be located adjacent to the name of the road in italics.

A

Abbey Orchard Street SW1 **176** B3
Abbey Street SE1 **178** A1
Abbots Gardens W8 **174** A3
St Mary's Place
Abbots Lane SE1 **178** A2
Abbots Walk W8 **174** A3
St Mary's Place
Abchurch Lane EC4 **173** F1
Aberdour Street SE1 **177** F2
Abingdon Road W8 **174** A3
Abingdon Street SW1 **176** B3
Abingdon Villas W8 **174** A3
Achilles Way W1 **175** E4
Ackroyd Drive E3 **179** F4
Acorn Walk SE16 **179** F2
Acton Street WC1 **172** C4
Adam And Eve Court W1 **171** E1
Oxford Street
Adam And Eve Mews W8 **174** A3
Adam Street WC2 **172** B1
Adam's Row W1 **171** E1
Adams Place E14 **180** A4
Addington Street SE1 **176** C3
Addle Hill EC4 **173** E1
Addle Street EC2 **173** E2
Adelaide Street WC2 **172** B1
William IV Street
Adelina Grove E1 **178** D4
Adeline Place WC1 **172** B2
Adelphi Terrace WC2 **172** B1
Adams Street
Adler Street E1 **178** B4
Admiral Place SE16 **179** E2
Admiral Way W9 **170** A3
Admirals Way E14 **180** A3
Adpar Street W2 **170** C3
Adrian Mews SW10 **174** A1
Agar Street WC2 **172** B1
Agatha Close E1 **178** C2
Agdon Street EC1 **173** D3
Agnes Street E14 **179** F4
Ainstey Street SE16 **179** D1
Brunel Road
Air Street W1 **172** A1
Alaska Street SE1 **176** C4
Albany Mews SE5 **177** E1
Albany Road SE5 **177** E1
Albany Street NW1 **171** F4
Albatross Way SE16 **179** D1
Albemarle Street W1 **171** F1
Albemarle Way EC1 **172** C3
Clerkenwell Road
Albert Court SW7 **174** C3
Albert Embankment SE1 **176** B1
Albert Gardens E1 **179** D3
Albert Hall Mansions SW7 **174** C3
Albert Mews W8 **174** B3
Albert Place W8 **174** B3
Alberta Street SE17 **177** D1
Albion Close W2 **171** D1
Albion Mews W2 **171** D1
Albion Place EC1 **173** D3
Albion Street SE16 **179** D1
Albion Street W2 **171** D1
Albion Way EC1 **173** E2
Albion Yard E1 **178** C4
Aldburgh Mews W1 **171** E2
Marylebone Lane
Aldenham Street NW1 **172** A4
Aldermanbury EC2 **173** E2
Aldermanbury Square EC2 **173** E2
Aldermanbury
Alderney Street SW1 **175** F2
Aldersgate Street EC1 **173** E3
Aldford Street W1 **171** E1
Aldgate EC3 **178** A3
Aldgate High Street EC3 **178** A3
Aldwych WC2 **172** C1
Alexander Place SW7 **174** C2
Alexander Square SW3 **174** C2
Alford Place N1 **173** E4
Alfred Mews W1 **172** A3
Alfred Place WC1 **172** A3
Alice Street SE1 **177** F3
Alie Street E1 **178** B3
All Hallows Lane EC4 **173** F1
All Soul's Place W1 **171** F2
Langham Street
Allen Street W8 **174** A3
Allington Street SW1 **175** F3
Allsop Place NW1 **171** D3
Alpha Grove E14 **180** A3
Alpha Place SW3 **175** D1
Alsace Road SE17 **177** F1
Alscot Road SE1 **178** B1
Alvey Street SE17 **177** F2
Ambassador Square E14 **180** B2
Ambergate Street SE17 **177** D1
Ambrosden Avenue SW1 **176** A3
Amelia Street SE17 **177** E2
Amen Corner EC4 **173** D2
Amen Court EC4 **173** D2
America Square EC3 **178** A3
America Street SE1 **177** E4
Amoy Place E14 **179** F3
Ampton Place WC1 **172** C4
Ampton Street WC1 **172** C4
Amsterdam Road E14 **180** C2
Amwell Street EC1 **172** C4
Anderson Street SW3 **175** D2
Andrew Borde Street WC2 **172** B2
Charing Cross Road
Angel Court EC2 **173** F2
Angel Court SW1 **176** A4
King Street
Angel Passage EC4 **173** F1
Angel Place SE1 **177** E4
Angel Street EC1 **173** E2
Ann Moss Way SE16 **179** D1
Ansdell Street W8 **174** A3
Antill Terrace E1 **179** D4
Apothecary Street EC4 **173** D2
New Bridge Street
Apple Tree Yard SW1 **172** A1
Appold Street EC2 **173** F3
Aquinas Street SE1 **177** D4
Arbour Square E1 **179** D4
Archangel Street SE16 **179** E1
Archer Street W1 **172** A1
Arden Crescent E14 **180** A2
Argent Street SE1 **177** E4
Loman Street
Argyle Square WC1 **172** B4
Argyle Street WC1 **172** B4
Argyle Walk WC1 **172** B4
Argyll Road W8 **174** A3
Argyll Street W1 **171** F2
Arlington Street SW1 **175** F4
Arlington Way EC1 **173** D4
Arne Street WC2 **172** B2
Arneway Street SW1 **176** A2
Arnside Street SE17 **177** E1
Arthur Street EC4 **173** F1
Artichoke Hill E1 **178** C3
Artillery Lane E1 **178** A4
Artillery Passage E1 **178** A4
Artillery Lane
Artillery Row SW1 **176** A3
Artizan Street E1 **178** A4
Harrow Place
Arundel Street WC2 **172** C1
Ashbridge Street NW8 **170** C3
Ashburn Gardens SW7 **174** B2
Ashburn Mews SW7 **174** B2
Ashburn Place SW7 **174** B2
Ashby Street EC1 **173** D4
Ashdown Walk E14 **180** A2
Asher Drive E1 **178** B3
Ashfield Street E1 **178** C4
Ashland Place W1 **170** E3
Ashley Place SW1 **175** F3
Ashmill Street NW1 **170** C3
Aske Street N1 **173** F4
Asolando Drive SE17 **177** E2
King & Queen Street
Aspen Way E14 **180** B4
Assam Street E1 **178** B4
Assembly Passage E1 **179** D4
Aste Street E14 **180** B3
Astell Street SW3 **175** D2
Aston Street E14 **179** E4
Astwood Mews SW7 **174** B2
Atherstone Mews SW7 **174** B2
Atterbury Street SW1 **176** B2
Attneave Street WC1 **172** C4
Auckland Street SE11 **176** C1
Augustus Street NW1 **171** F4
Aulton Place SE11 **177** D1
Austin Friars EC2 **173** F2
Austin Friars Square EC2 **173** F2
Austin Friars
Austral Street SE11 **177** D2
Ave Maria Lane EC4 **173** E2
Aveline Street SE11 **176** C1
Avery Row W1 **171** F1
Avis Square E1 **179** E4
Avon Place SE1 **177** E3
Avonmouth Street SE1 **177** E3
Aybrook Street W1 **171** E2
Aylesbury Road SE17 **177** F1
Aylesbury Street EC1 **173** D3
Aylesford Street SW1 **176** A1
Aylward Street E1 **179** D4
Ayres Street SE1 **177** E4

B

Babmaes Street SW1 **176** A4
Jermyn Street
Bacchus Walk N1 **173** F4
Bache's Street N1 **173** F4
Back Church Lane E1 **178** B4
Back Hill EC1 **173** D3
Bacon Grove SE1 **178** A1
Bainbridge Street WC1 **172** B2
Baker Street W1 & NW1 **171** D3
Baker's Mews W1 **171** E2
Baker's Row EC1 **173** F3
Baker's Yard EC1 **173** D3
Baker's Row
Bakers Hall Court EC3 **178** A3
Harp Lane
Balcombe Street NW1 **171** D3
Balderton Street W1 **171** E1
Baldwin Street EC1 **173** F4
Baldwin's Gardens EC1 **172** C3
Balfe Street N1 **172** B4
Balfour Mews W1 **171** E1
Balfour Place W1 **171** E1
Balfour Street SE17 **177** F2
Ballast Quay SE10 **180** C1
Balneil Gate SW1 **176** A1
Baltic Street EC1 **173** E3
Balvaird Place SW1 **176** B2
Bancroft Road E1 **176** C1
Bank End SE1 **177** E4
Bankside Jetty SE1 **173** E1
Banner Street EC1 **173** E3
Banyard Road SE16 **178** C1
Barbon Close WC1 **172** C3
Barge House Street SE1 **173** D1
Barkston Gardens SW5 **174** A2
Barleycorn Way E14 **179** F3
Barlow Place W1 **171** F1
Barlow Street SE17 **177** F2
Barnaby Place SW7 **174** C2
Barnardo Street E1 **179** D3
Barnby Street NW1 **172** A4
Barnes Street E14 **179** E4
Barnfield Place E14 **180** A2
Barnham Street SE1 **178** A2
Barnsdale Avenue E14 **180** A2
Baron's Place SE1 **177** D3
Barque Mews SE8 **180** A1
Barrett Street W1 **171** E2
Barrie Street W2 **170** B1
Barrow Hill Road NW8 **170** C4
St Johns Wood High Street
Barter Street WC1 **172** B2
Barth Lane EC2 **173** F2
Bartholomew Close EC1 **173** E2
Bartholomew Square EC1 **173** E3
Bartholomew Street SE1 **177** F2
Barton Street SW1 **176** B3
Basil Street SW3 **175** D3
Basinghall Avenue EC2 **173** E2
Basinghall Street EC2 **173** E2
Bastwick Street EC1 **173** E3
Bate Street E14 **179** F3
Bateman Street W1 **172** A2
Bateman's Buildings W1 **172** A2
Bath Court EC1 **172** C3
Warner Street
Bath Place N1 **173** F4
Bath Street EC1 **173** E4
Bath Terrace SE1 **177** E3
Bathurst Mews W2 **170** C1
Bathurst Street W2 **170** C1
Battle Bridge Lane SE1 **177** F4
Batty Street E1 **178** B4
Bayley Street WC1 **172** A2
Baylis Road SE1 **176** C3
Bayswater Road W2 **170** A1
Baythorne Street E3 **179** F4
Beaconsfield Road SE17 **177** F1
Beak Street W1 **172** A1
Bear Gardens SE1 **173** E1
Bear Lane SE1 **177** D4
Bear Street WC2 **172** B1
Cranbourn Street
Beatrice Place W8 **174** A2
Beauchamp Place SW3 **175** D3
Beauchamp Street EC1 **173** D3
Brooke Street
Beaufort Gardens SW3 **175** D3
Beaufort Street SW3 **174** B1
Beaumont Mews W1 **171** E2
Beaumont Place W1 **172** A3
Beaumont Street W1 **171** E3
Beccles Street E14 **179** F3
Beckway Street SE17 **177** F2
Bedale Street SE1 **177** E3
Borough High Street
Bedford Avenue WC1 **172** B2
Bedford Court WC2 **172** B1
Bedford Gardens W8 **174** A4
Bedford Place WC1 **172** B3
Bedford Row WC1 **172** C3
Bedford Square WC1 **172** B2
Bedford Street WC2 **172** B1
Bedford Way WC1 **172** B3
Bedfordbury WC2 **172** B1
Bedser Close SE11 **176** C1
Beech Street EC2 **173** E3
Beeston Place SW1 **175** F3
Bekesbourne Street E14 **171** E2
Marylebone Lane
Belgrave Mews North SW1 **175** E3
Belgrave Mews South SW1 **175** E3
Belgrave Mews West SW1 **175** E3
Belgrave Place SW1 **175** E3
Belgrave Road SW1 **175** F2
Belgrave Square SW1 **175** E3
Belgrave Street E1 **179** E3
Belgrove Street WC1 **172** B4
Bell Lane E1 **178** A4

C

London district index

District names are listed in alphabetical order and are referenced to the London district map on pages 168–169. Each entry is followed by its map page number, in bold type, plus a grid reference.

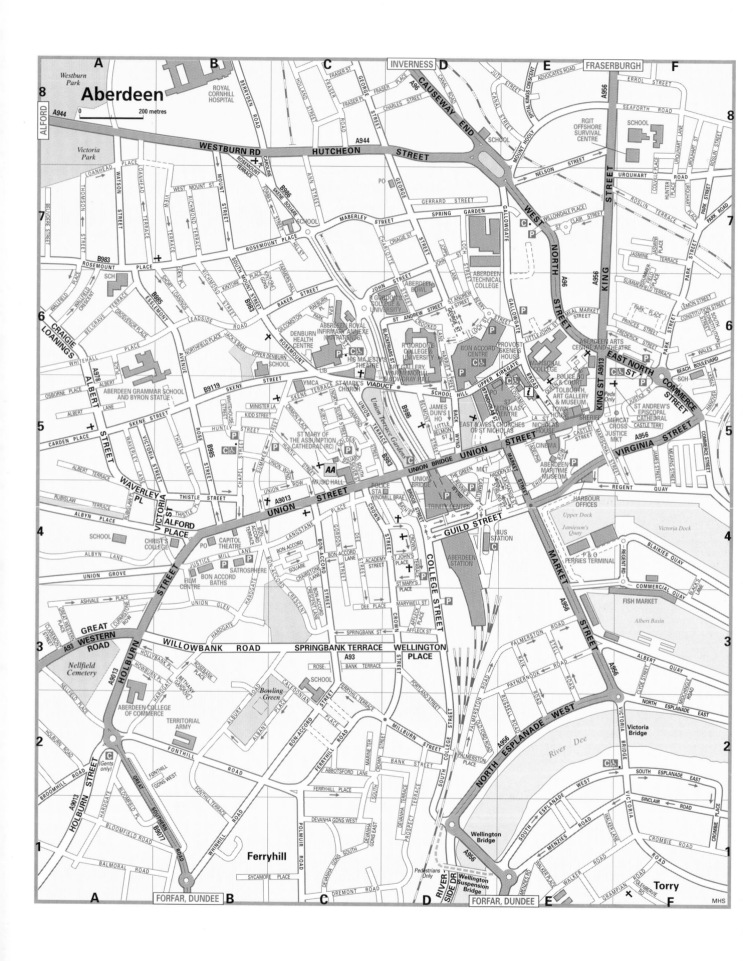

Aberdeen

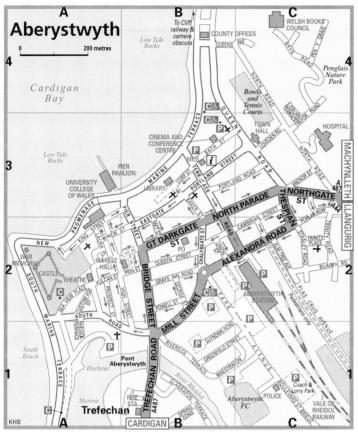

Aberystwyth

Aberystwyth is found on atlas page **43**,
grid reference SN**5881**

Baker Street	B3	Riverside Terrace	B1
Bath Steet	B3	Sea View Place	A2
Boulevard St Brieuc	C1	South Marine Terrace	A1-A2
Bridge Street	B1-B2	South Road	A2-B1
Bryn Road	C4	Spring Gardens	B1
Buarth Road	C2	Stanley Road	C2
Cambrian Street	C2-C3	Terrace Road	B3-C2
Chalybeate Street	B2	Thespian Street	C2-C3
Corporation Street	B3	Trefechan Road	B1
Custom House Street	A2	Trefor Road	C3-C4
Eastgate	B2-B3	Trinity Place	C2
Elmtree Avenue	C2	Trinity Road	C2-C3
George Street	B2	Union Street	B2
Glanrafon Terrace	B1	Vaenor Road	C3
Glyndwr Road	B1	Vulcan Street	A2
Grays Inn Road	B2		
Great Darkgate Street	B2		
Greenfield Street	B1-C1		
High Street	A2-B2		
King Street	A2-A3		
Laura Place	A2		
Lisburn Terrace	C3-C4		
Loveden Road	C3		
Maesyrafon	B1-C1		
Marine Terrace	B4-B3		
Market Street	B2		
Mill Street	B1-B2		
New Promenade	A2-B3		
New Street	A2-B2		
North Parade	B2-C3		
North Road	C3-C4		
Northgate Street	C3		
Park Avenue	B2-C1		
Pen y Graig	C4		
Pier Street	B2-B3		
Plas Crug Avenue	C1-C2		
Poplar Row	C2-C3		
Portland Road	B3-C3		
Portland Street	B3-C3		
Powell Street	B2		
Princess Street	B2		
Prospect Street	A2		
Queen Street	B2		
Queens Avenue	B4-C4		
Queens Road	B4-C3		
Rheidol Terrace	A1		

Aberdeen

Aberdeen is found on atlas page **135**,
grid reference NJ**9306**

Abbotsford Lane	C2	Broomhill Road	A1-A2
Academy Street	C4-D4	Caledonian Lane	C2
Advocates Road	E8	Caledonian Place	C3-C2
Affleck Place	D3	Canal Road	D8
Affleck Street	D3	Canal Street	D8-E8
Albany Place	B2-C2	Carden Place	A5
Albert Lane	A5	Carmelite Street	D4-D5
Albert Quay	F3-E3	Caroline Place	B7-B8-C7
Albert Place	A5-A6	Castle Street	E5
Albert Street	A5-A6	Castle Terrace	F5
Albert Terrace	A5	Causewayend	D8
Albury Road	B2-B3-C3	Chapel Street	B5-B4
Albyn Lane	A4-B4	Charles Street	C8-D8
Albyn Place	A4	Charlotte Street	D7-C7-D6
Alford Place	B4	Claremont Street	A3
Ann Street	C7-C8	Clyde Street	F2-F3
Ashvale Place	A3-B3	College Street	D4-D3
Back Wynd	D5	Colville Place	F7-F8
Baker Street	C6	Commerce Street	F5
Balmoral Road	A1-B1	Commercial Quay	F3-F4
Bank Street	D2	Constitution Street	F6
Bath Street	D4	Craibstone Lane	C4
Beach Boulevard	F6	Craigie Loanings	A6
Belgrave Terrace	A6	Craigie Street	D7
Belmont Street	D5	Crimon Place	C5
Belvidere Street	A7	Crombie Place	F1-F2
Berry Street	D6-E6	Crombie Road	F1
Berryden Road	B8	Crooked Lane	D6
Bethany Gardens	B2-B3	Crown Street	C4-D4-D3-D2
Blackfriars Street	D5-D6	Crown Terrace	D4
Black's Lane	F3-F4	Cuparstone Row	A3
Blaikies Quay	F4	Dee Place	C3-D3
Bloomfield Place	A2-A1-B1	Dee Street	C4-C3
Bloomfield Road	A1-B1	Deemont Road	C1-D1
Bon-Accord Crescent	B4-C4-C3	Devanha Gardens East	C1
Bon-Accord Crescent Lane	C3-C4	Devanha Gardens South	C1
Bon-Accord Lane	C4	Devanha Gardens West	C1
Bon-Accord Square	C4	Devanha Terrace	D1-D2
Bon-Accord Street	B2-C2-C3-C4	Diamond Street	C5
Bon-Accord Terrace	B4	Duff Street	F7
Bridge Street	D4	East North Street	E6-F6
Broad Street	E5	Eden Place	B6-B7

Erroll Street	F8	Justice Street	F5
Esslemont Avenue	A6-B6-B5	Justice Mill Lane	B4
Exchange Street	E5-E4	Jute Street	D8-E8
Farmers Hall	C7-C6	Kidd Street	B5-C5
Ferryhill Place	C2	King Street	E5-E6-E7-E8
Ferryhill Road	C2-D2	Kintore Gardens	B6-C6
Ferryhill Terrace	C3-C2	Kintore Place	B6-B7-C7
Flourmill Lane	E5	Langstane Place	C4
Fonthill Gardens West	A2-B2	Leadside Road	B6
Fonthill Road	A2-B2-C2	Lemon Street	F6
Fonthill Terrace	B1-B2	Little Belmont Street	D5
Forbes Street	B7-C7	Little John Street	E6
Fraser Place	C8-D8	Loanhead Place	A7
Fraser Road	C8	Loanhead Terrace	A7
Fraser Street	C8	Loch Street	D7-D6
Frederick Street	F6	Maberley Street	C7-D7
Gallowgate	E7-E6	Marischal Street	E5-F5-F4
George Street	C8-D8-D7-D6	Market Street	E5-E4-E3
Gerrard Street	D7	Marine Terrace	C2
Gilcomston Park	C6	Marywell Street	D3
Glenbervie Road	F1	Meal Market Street	E6
Golden Square	C5	Mearns Street	F5-F4
Gordon Street	C4-C3	Menzies Road	E1-F1-F2
Grampian Road	E1-F1	Midchingle Road	F2-F3
Great Southern Road	A1-A2-B1	Millburn Street	D2
Great Western Place	A3	Minister Lane	B5-C5
Great Western Road	A3	Mount Holly	E8
Grosvenor Place	A6	Mount Street	B7
Guild Street	D4-E4	Nellfield Place	A2-A3
Hadden Street	D5-E5	Nelson Street	E7-E8
Hanover Street	F6-F5	North Esplanade East	F2
Hardgate	A1-A2-B2-B3-B4	North Esplanade West	D1-E3
Harriet Street	D5-D6	North Silver Street	C5
Hill Street	C7	Northfield Place	B6
Holburn Road	A2	Old Ford Road	D2
Holburn Street	A1-A2-A3-B3-B4	Osborne Place	A5
Holland Street	C8	Oscar Road	F1
Hollybank Place	A3-B3	Palmerston Place	D2
Howburn Place	A3-B3	Palmerston Road	D2-D3-B3
Hunter Place	F7	Park Place	F6
Huntly Street	B5-C5-C4	Park Road	F7
Hutcheon Street	C8-D8	Park Street	F6-F7
Irvine Place	A2	Polmuir Road	C1-C2
Jack's Brae	B6	Portland Street	D3-D2
James Street	F5	Poynernook Road	D2-E2-E3
Jasmine Place	F7	Princes Street	F6
Jasmine Terrace	F7	Prospect Terrace	D1-D2
John Street	C6-D6-D7	Queen Street	E5-E6
Jopp's Lane	D7-D6	Raeburn Place	C6

Raik Road	E3-E2	Sycamore Place	B1-C1
Regent Road	F4	The Green	D5
Regent Quay	E4-F4	Thistle Lane	B5-B4
Rennies Wynd	D4	Thistle Place	B4
Richmond Street	B6-B7	Thistle Street	B4
Richmond Terrace	B7	Thomson Street	A7
Riverside Drive	D1	Union Bridge	D4-D5
Rose Street	B5-B4	Union Glen	B3
Rosebank Place	B3	Union Grove	A4-B4
Rosebank Terrace	C3-D3	Union Row	B4-C4
Rosemount Place	A7-B7-C7	Union Street	B4-C4-D4-D5-E5
Rosemount Terrace	B8-B7	Union Terrace	C5-D5
Rosemount Viaduct	B6-C6-C5	Union Wynd	B5-C5-C4
Roslin Street	F7-F8	Upper Denburn	B6-C6
Roslin Terrace	F7	Upper Kirkgate	D5-D6-E6
Rubislaw Place	A4	Urquhart Lane	F7-F8
Rubislaw Terrace	A4	Urquhart Place	F7
Ruby Lane	C5	Urquhart Road	F7
Russell Road	E2-E3	Urquhart Street	F8-F7
St Andrew Street	D6	Victoria Bridge	F2
St Clair Street	E7	Victoria Road	F2-F1
St John's Place	D4	Victoria Street	A5-B5-B4
St Mary's Place	D4	View Terrace	B7
St Nicholas Street	D5-E5	Virginia Street	E5-F5
School Hill	D5	Wales Street	F6
Seaforth Road	F8	Walker Lane	E1-F1
Ship Row	E4-E5	Walker Place	E1
Short Loanings	B6	Walker Road	E1-F1
Sinclair Road	F1-F2	Wallfield Crescent	A6
Skene Square	C6-C5	Wallfield Place	A6
Skene Street	A5-B5-C5	Watson Street	A7-A8
Skene Terrace	C5	Waverley Lane	A5-A4
South College Street	D3-D2-D1	Waverley Place	A4-B4
South Constitution Street	F6	Wellington Place	D3
South Crown Street	C1-C2-D2	Wellington Road	E1
South Esplanade East	F2	West Mount Street	B7
South Esplanade West	F2-F1-E2	West North Street	E7-E6
South Mount Street	B7-B6	Westburn Road	A8-B8
South Silver Street	C5	Whinhill Road	B1-B2
Spa Street	C6	Whitehall Place	A6-B6
Spital Kings Crescent	E8	Whitehouse Street	B5
Spring Garden	D7	Willowbank Road	B3-C3
Springbank Street	C3-D3	Willowdale Place	E7
Springbank Terrace	C3-D3	Windmill Brae	C4-D4
Stell Road	E3		
Stirling Street	D4-E4		
Summerfield Place	F6-F7	AA shop	C5
Summerfield Terrace	F6	19-20 Golden Square	
Summer Street	B4-B5-C5	Aberdeen AB9 1JN	

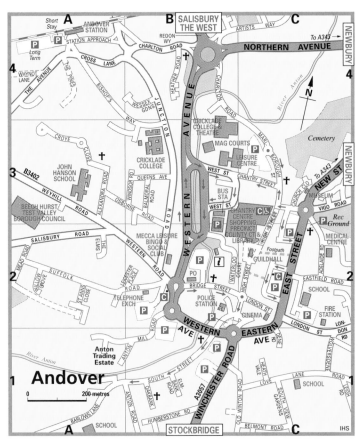

Andover

Andover is found on atlas page **23**,
grid reference SU**36**4**5**

Adelaide Road	C2-C3	The Elms	A2
Alexandra Road	A3	The Pines	A4
Anton Mill Road	A1-B1-B2	Vigo Road	C3
Anton Road	B1	Waterloo Court	B2
Artists Way	B4-C4	Wessex Gardens	B4
Balmoral Road	B3	Western Avenue	B1-B2-B3
Barlows Lane	A1	Western Road	A2-B2
Belmont Road	B1-C1	West Street	B2-B3
Bishop's Way	A4-B4-B3	Weyhill Road	A3
Bridge Street	B2	Whynot Lane	A4
Chantry Street	B3-C3	Winchester Road	B1
Charlton Road	B4-B3-C3	Windsor Road	B3
Church Close	C3	Willow Grove	A2
Cross Lane	A4	Wolversdene Road	C1
Croye Close	A3		
Dene Road	C1		
Eastfield Road	C2		
East Street	C2-C3		
Eastern Avenue	C1-C2		
Elmbank Road	B1		
Heath Vale	C1		
Heather Drive	B4		
High Street	B2-C2-C3		
Humberstone Road	B1		
Junction Road	B2-B3-B4		
Leicester Place	B2		
Leigh Road	C1		
London Road	C1		
London Street	C1		
Love Lane	C1-C2		
Marlborough Street	C3		
Mead Road	A2		
New Street	C3		
Northern Avenue	B4-C4		
Oak Bank Road	B1		
Old Winton Road	B1-C1		
Osborne Road	A3-B3		
Queens Avenue	B3		
Redon Way	B4		
St Anns Close	A2		
Salisbury Road	A2		
South Street	B1-B2		
Southview Gardens	C1		
Station Approach	A4		
Suffolk Road	A2-B2		
The Avenue	A4		

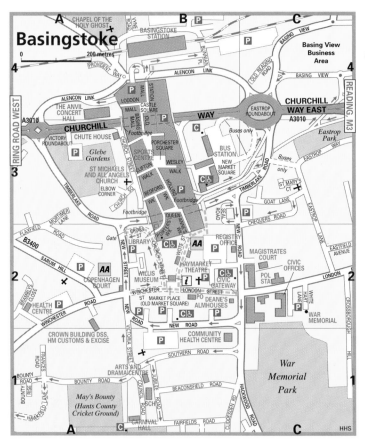

Basingstoke

Basingstoke is found on atlas page **24**,
grid reference SU**63**5**2**

Alencon Link	A4-C4
Basing View	C4
Beaconsfield Road	B1
Bounty Rise	A1
Bounty Road	A1
Bramblys Close	A2
Bunnian Place	B4
Chequers Road	B2-C3
Church Square	A2-B2
Church Street	A2-B2
Churchill Way	A3-B4
Churchill Way East	C4
Cliddesden Road	B1
Council Road	B1
Cross Street	A2-B2
Crossborough Hill	C1-C2
Eastrop Lane	C2-C3
Eastrop Way	C3
Elbow Corner	A3
Fairfields Road	B1
Flaxfield Road	B2
Frances Road	A1
Goat Lane	C3
Hackwood Road	B1-C1
Hawkfield Lane	A1
Jubilee Road	B1
London Road	C2
London Street	B2
Mortimer Lane	A2-A3
New Road	A2-B3
New Street	A2
Old Reading Road	C3
Provident Way	A4
Sarum Hill	A2
Seal Road	B1-B2
Southern Road	B1
St Mary's Court	C3
Timberlake Road	A3-C3
Victoria Street	A2-B1
Vyne Road	A4-B4
White Hart Lane	C2
Winchester Road	A2
Winchester Street	B2
Wote Street	B2

AA shop
21-23 Wote Street
Basingstoke RG21 1NE

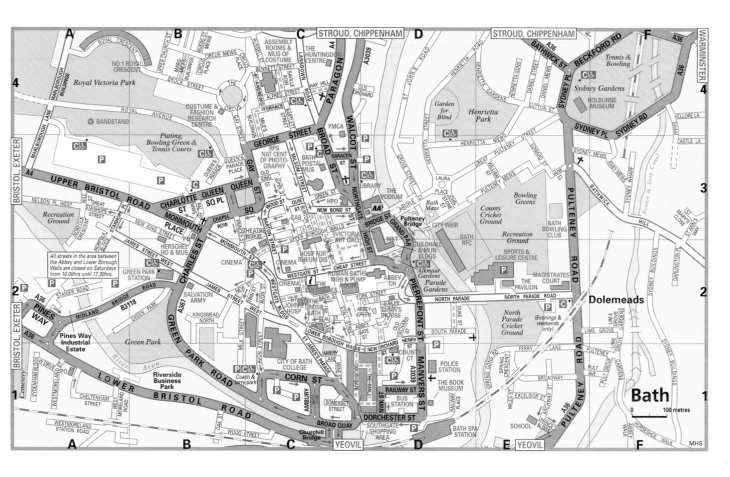

Bath

Bath is found on atlas page **22**,
grid reference ST**7464**

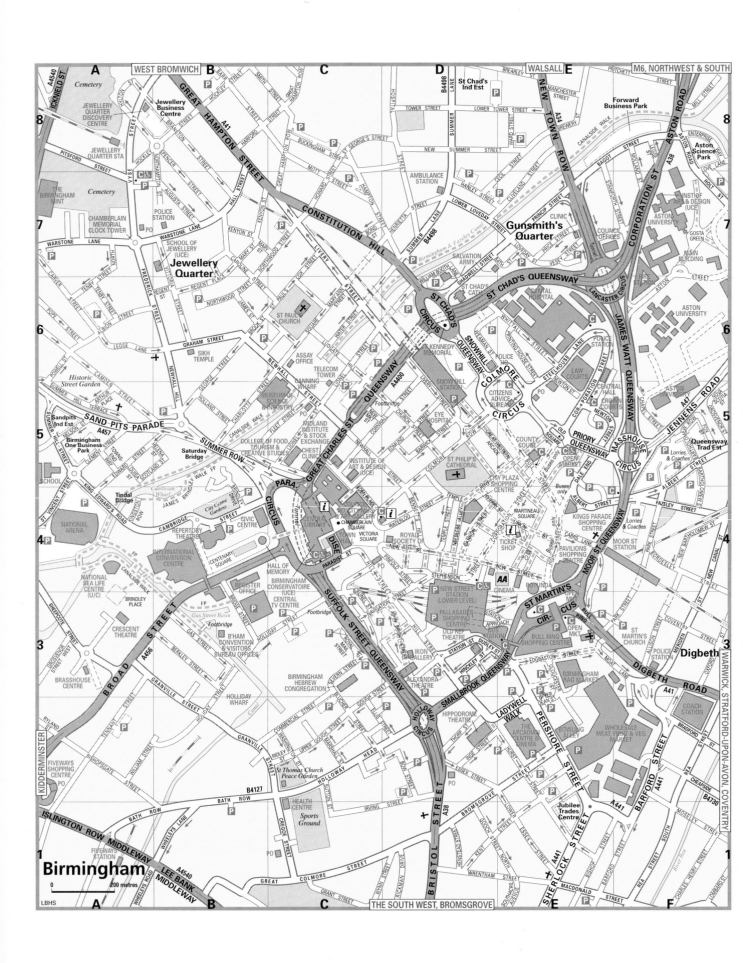

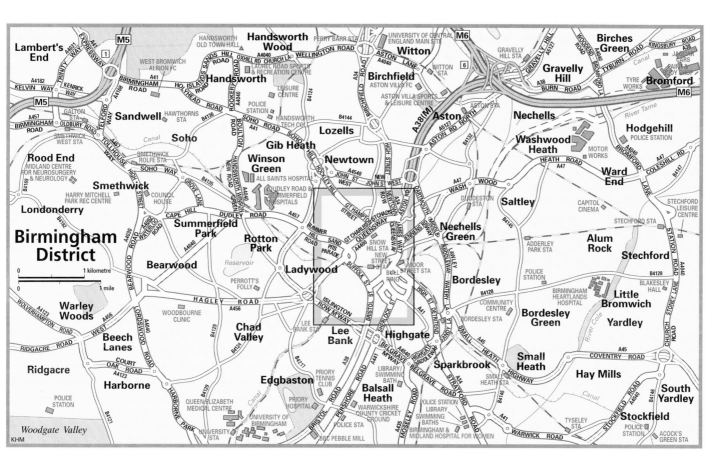

Birmingham

Birmingham is found on atlas page **61**,
grid reference SP**0786**

Albert St	E4-F4-F5	Cannon Street	D4	Gosta Green	F7	King Edwards Road	A5-A4	Old Square	E5	Summer Hill Terrace	A5
Albion Street	A6	Caroline Street	B7-B6-C6	Gough Street	C2-C3-D3	Kingston Row	A4	Oxford Street	D7	Summer Lane	D7-D8
Allison Street	F3-F4	Carrs Lane	E4	Graham Street	B6	Ladywell Walk	D2-E2-E3	Paradise Circus	B4-C4-C5-B5	Summer Row	B5
Arthur Place	A5	Carver Street	A7-A6	Grant Street	C1	Lancaster Circus	E7-E6-F6-F7	Paradise Street	C4	Sutton Street	C2-C1
Aston Road	F8-F7	Cecil Street	D7-E7-E8	Granville Street	A3-B3-B2-C2	Lee Bank Middleway	B1	Park Street	E3-F3-F4	Temple Row	D5-D4-E5
Aston Street	F6-F7	Chamberlain Square	C4	Great Charles Street	C5	Legge Lane	A6-B6	Pershore Street	E2	Temple Street	D4
Augusta Street	B7	Chapel Street	F5	Great Colmore Street	B1-C1-C2	Lionel Street	C5-C6-D6	Pinfold Street	C4-D4	Tenby Street	A7
Bagot Street	E7-E8-F8	Charles Henry Street	F1	Great Hampton Row	C7-C8	Livery Street	C7-C6-D6-D5	Pitsford Street	A7-A8	Tenby Street North	A6-A7
Barford Street	F2-F1-E1	Charlotte Street	B5-C6	Great Hampton Street	B8-B7	Louisa Street	A5	Pope Street	A7	Tennant Street	A1-A2-A3
Barr Street	B8-C8	Cherry Street	D4-E4	Great Western Arcade	D5-E5	Love Lane	F7-F8	Powell Street	A6	Thorp Street	D2
Bartholomew Row	F5	Church Street	D5	Grosvenor Street	F5	Loveday Street	E7	Price Street	E7	Tower Street	D8
Bartholomew Street	F4-F5	Clement Street	A5	Grosvenor Street West	A3	Lower Essex Street	D2-E2-E1	Princip Street	E7	Townsend Way	A5
Barwick Street	D5	Cliveland Street	D7-E7-E8	Hall Street	B7-B8	Lower Loveday Street	D7-E7	Printing House Street	E6	Union Street	E4
Bath Row	A1-B1-B2-C2	Coleshill Street	F5-F6	Hampton Street	D7-C7-C8	Lower Tower Street	D8-E8	Priory Queensway	E5	Upper Dean Street	E2-E3
Bath Street	D7-E7	Colmore Circus	D5-D6-E6-E5	Hanley Street	D7	Ludgate Hill	C6-C5	Pritchett Street	E8-F8	Upper Gough Street	C2
Bennett's Hill	D4	Colmore Row	C4-D4-D5	Harford Street	B8-C8	Macdonald Street	E1-F1	Queensway	C5-D6	Vesey Street	E7
Berkley Street	B3	Commercial Street	B2-C2-C3	Helena Street	A5-B5	Manchester Street	E8	Rea Street	F1-F2	Vittoria Street	B7-B6
Birchall Street	F1	Constitution Hill	C7-D7-D6	Henrietta Street	C7-D7	Marshall Street	C2	Rea Street South	F1	Vyse Street	A7-A8-B8
Bishop Street	E1	Cornwall Street	C5-D5-D6	Henstead Street	D1	Mary Ann Street	C6	Regent Place	B7-B6	Ward Street	E8
Bishopsgate Street	A2-A1-B1	Corporation Street	D4-E5-E6-F7	High Street	E4	Mary Street	B7-C7	Rickman Drive	D1	Warstone Lane	A7-B7
Blucher Street	C3-C2	Coventry Street	F3	Hill Street	C4-D3	Masshouse Circus	E5-F5	Ridley Street	C2	Washington Street	C2
Bond Street	C7	Cox Street	C6-C7	Hinckley Street	D3	Meriden Street	F3	Royal Mail Street	C3	Water Street	C6
Bordesley Street	F4	Cregoe Street	C1	Hockley Street	A8-B8	Mill Street	F8	St Chad's Circus	D6	Waterloo Street	C4-D4
Bow Street	D2	Dale End	E4-E5	Holland Street	B5	Moat Lane	E3-F3	St Chad's Queensway	D6-E6-E7	Weaman Street	E6-D6
Bradford Street	F2	Digbeth Road	F3	Holliday Street	A2-B2-B3-C3	Molland Street	F8-F7	St Martin's Circus	E4-E5	Wheeleys Lane	A1-B1
Branston Street	A8-B8-B7	Dudley Street	D3	Holloway Circus	D2	Moor Street Queensway	E4-F4	St Paul's Square	B6-C6	Wheeleys Road	A1
Brearley Street	D8-E8	Eden Place	C5-C4	Holloway Head	C2-D2	Moseley Street	F2-F1	St Vincent Street	A4-A5	Whittall Street	D6-E6
Brewery Street	E8	Edgbaston Street	E3	Hospital Street	D8-D7	Mott Street	C8-C7	Sand Pits Parade	A5-B5	William Booth Lane	D6-D7
Bridge Street	B3-B4	Edmund Street	C5-D5	Howard Street	C7-C8-D8	Navigation Street	C3-D3-D4	Severn Street	C3	William Street	A2-B2
Brindley Drive	B4-B5	Edward Street	A4-A5	Hurst Street	D2-E2-E1	Needless Alley	D4	Shadwell Street	D6-D7-E7	Wrentham Street	D1-E1
Brindley Place	A4	Ellis Street	C2-D2	Hylton Street	A8	Nelson Street	A5	Sheepcote Street	A4-A3	Wynn Street	C1-D1
Bristol Street	D1-D2	Enterprise Way	F8	Icknield Street	A8	New Bartholomew Street	F4	Sherlock Street	E1	
Broad Street	A2-A3-B3-B4-C4	Essex Street	D2	Inge Street	D2	New Canal Street	F4	Smallbrook Queensway	D2-D3-E3	
Bromsgrove Street	D1-D2-E2	Fazeley Street	F4	Irving Street	C1-D1-D2	New Street	C4-D4-E4	Smith Street	B8-C8	
Brook Street	B6	Fleet Street	B5-C5	Islington Row Middleway	A1	New Summer Street	D8-E8	Snowhill Queensway	D6	
Brunel Street	C3	Fox Street	F5	James Brindley Walk	A4-B4-B5	New Town Row	E8-E7	Spencer Street	B8-B7	
Buckingham Street	C8	Frederick Street	A7-A6-B6	James Street	B6	Newhall Hill	B6-B5	Staniforth Street	E8-E7-F7	
Bull Ring	E3-F3	Gas Street	B3	James Watt Queensway	F5-F6-E6	Newhall Street	B6-C6-C5-D5	Station Street	D3	
Bull Street	E5-E4	George Road	A1	Jennens Road	F5-F6	Newton Street	E5-E6	Steelhouse Lane	E5-E6	
Cambridge Street	A4-B4	George Street	B6-B5	John Bright Street	D3	Northampton Street	A8-B8-B7	Stephenson Street	D4	AA shop	D4
Camden Street	A6-A5	Gloucester Street	E3	Kent Street	D1-E1	Northwood Street	B6-B7-C7	Suffolk Street Queensway	C4-D2	134 New Street
Canalside Walk	B3-A4-A5-B5-C5	Gooch Street North	D1-E1	Kenyon Street	B7	Nova Scotia Street	F5	Summer Hill Street	A5	Birmingham B2 4NP

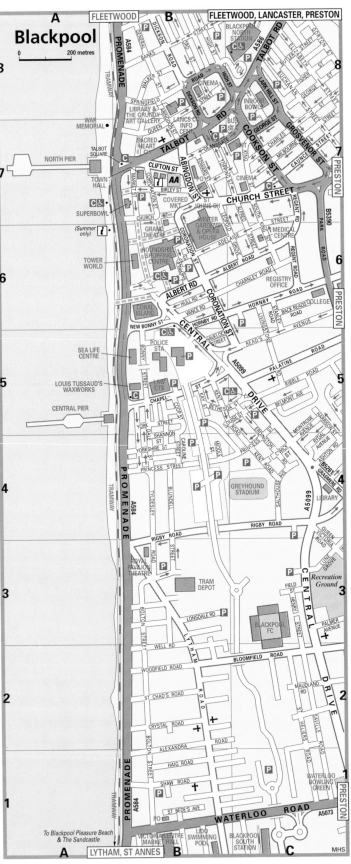

Blackpool

Blackpool is found on atlas page **80**, grid reference SD**3036**

Abingdon Street	B7-B8	Walker Street	B8
Adelaide Street	B6-C7	Waterloo Road	B1-C1
Albert Road	B6-C6	Well Road	B2-B3
Alexandra Road	B1-B2	Woodfield Road	B2
Alfred Street	C6-C7	York Street	B5
Ashton Road	C4	Yorkshire Street	B4
Back Reads Road	C6		
Banks Street	B8		
Belmont Avenue	C5		
Bethesda Street	B5-C5		
Birley Street	B7		
Bloomfield Road	B2-C3		
Blundell Street	B3-B4		
Bolton Street	B1-B3		
Bonny Street	B5		
Buchanan Street	C7-C8		
Butler Street	C8		
Caroline Street	B4		
Caunce Street	C7		
Central Drive	B6-C1		
Chadwick Street	C4		
Chapel Street	B5		
Charles Street	C7-C8		
Charnley Road	B6-C6		
Church Street	B7-C8		
Clifton Street	B7		
Cocker Street	B8		
Cookson Street	C7-C8		
Coop Street	B5		
Coronation Street	B7-C5		
Corporation Street	B7		
Crystal Road	B2		
Dale Street	B4-B5		
Deansgate	B7-C8		
Dickson Road	B7-B8		
Edward Street	B7		
Elizabeth Street	C8		
Erdington Road	C4-C5		
Field Street	C3		
Fisher Street	C8		
General Street	B8		
George Street	C7-C8		
Gorton Street	C8		
Grasmere Road	C4		
Haig Road	B1		
Harrison Street	C4-C5		
Havelock Street	B5		
Henry Street	C2-C3		
High Street	B8-C8		
Hornby Road	B6-C6		
Hull Street	B6		
Kay Street	B5		
Kent Road	B5-C4		
Keswick Road	C4		
King Street	C7		
Lark Hill Street	C8		
Leamington Road	C7		
Leopold Grove	B7-C6		
Livingstone Road	C5-C6		
Lonsdale Road	B3		
Lord Street	B8		
Louise Street	B5-C5		
Lune Grove	C3		
Lytham Road	B1-B3		
Market Street	B7		
Maudland Road	C2		
Middle Street	B4		
Milbourne Street	C7-C8		
Montrose Avenue	C4-C5		
New Bonny Street	B6		
North Promenade	B6-B8		
Palatine Road	C5		
Palmer Avenue	C3		
Park Road	C5-C7		
Peter Street	C7		
Princess Street	B4-C5		
Promenade	A1-B6		
Queen Street	B7-B8		
Queen Victoria Road	C4		
Read's Avenue	B5-C6		
Regent Road	C6-C7		
Ribble Road	C5		
Rigby Road	B3-C4		
Rydal Avenue	C4-C5		
Salthouse Avenue	C4		
Saville Road	C1-C2		
Shannon Street	B4-B5		
Shaw Road	B1		
Sheppard Street	B6		
South King Street	C6-C7		
Springfield Road	B8		
St Bede's Avenue	B1		
St Chad's Road	B2		
St Heliers Road	C1-C2		
Stanley Road	C5-C6		
Talbot Road	B7-C8		
Topping Street	B7-C7	AA shop	B7
Tyldesley Road	B3-B4	13 Clifton Street	
Vance Road	B6	Blackpool FY1 1JD	

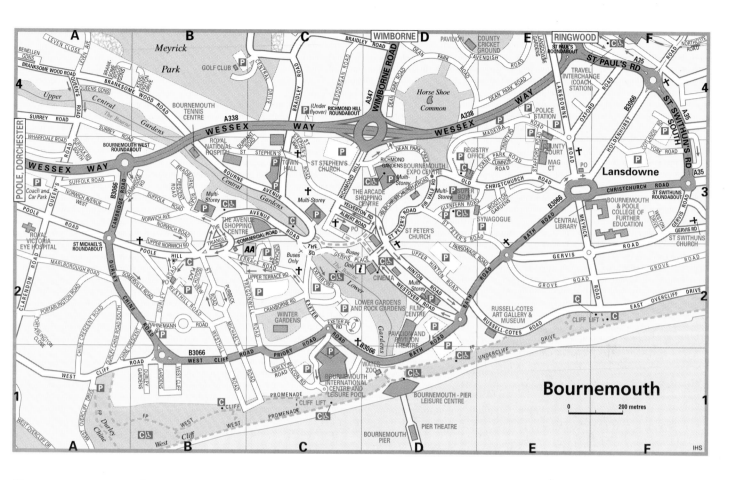

Bournemouth

Bournemouth is found on atlas page 12,
grid reference SZ0809

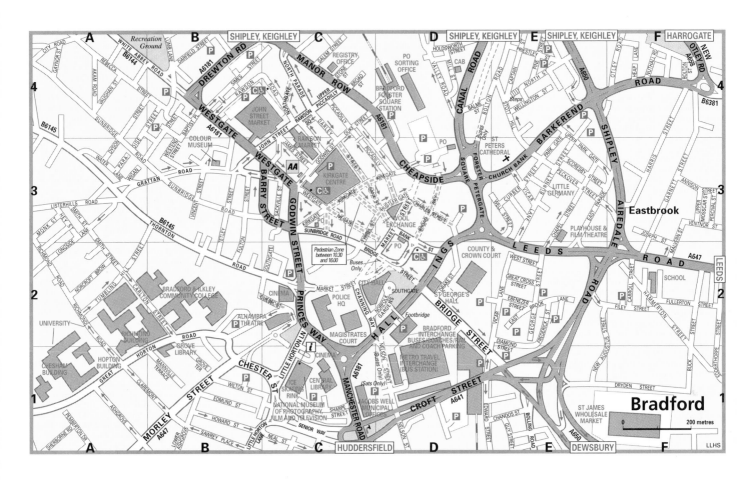

Bradford

Bradford is found on atlas page **82**,
grid reference SE1632

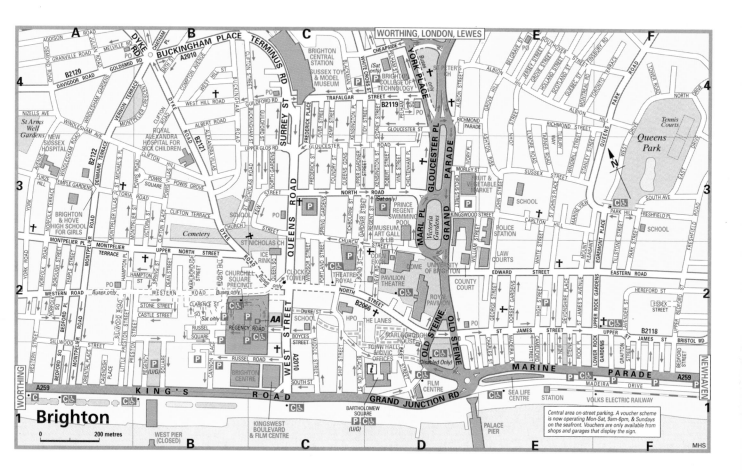

Brighton

Brighton is found on atlas page **15**,
grid reference TQ**31**04

Addison Road	A4	Devonshire Place	E2	John Street	E2-E3-E4	Park Street	F2-F3	Sydney Street	D3-D4
Albert Road	B4	Ditchling Road	D4	Julian Road	A4	Pelham Square	D4	Tarner Road	E3-E4
Albion Hill	D4-F4	Dorset Gardens	E2	Kemp Street	C3-C4	Pelham Street	D4	Temple Gardens	A3
Albion Street	D4	Duke Street	C2	Kensington Place	C3-C4	Portland Street	C2	Temple Street	A2
Alexandra Villas	B2-B3	Dyke Road	A4-C2	Kensington Street	D3	Powis Grove	B3	Terminus Road	C4
Ashton Rise	E3-E4	East Drive	F3-F4	Kew Street	C3	Powis Road	B3	Tichbourne Street	C3
Bath Street	B4	East Street	D1-D2	King's Road	A1-C1	Powis Square	B2	Tilbury Way	E3-E4
Bedford Place	A2	Eastern Road	F2	Kingswood Street	D3-E3	Powis Villas	B3	Tillstone Street	F2-F3
Bedford Square	A1-A2	Edward Street	D2-E2	Lavender Street	F2	Preston Street	A1-B2	Toronto Terrace	E4-F4
Bedford Street	F1-F2	Egremont Place	E2-F3	Little Preston Street	A1-A2	Prestonville Road	B4	Tower Road	F4
Belgrave Street	E4	Elmore Road	E3-E4	Lower Rock Gardens	E1-F2	Quebec Street	E4	Trafalgar Street	C4-D4
Black Lion Street	C1	Essex Street	F2	Madeira Place	E1-E2	Queen Square	C2	Upper Bedford Street	F2
Blackman Street	C4	Finsbury Road	E4-F4	Marine View	E3	Queens Park Road	E3-F4	Upper Gardner Street	C3
Bond Street	C2	Foundry Street	C3	Marlborough Place	D2-D3	Queens Road	C2-C4	Upper Gloucester Road	B3-C3
Borough Street	A2	Frederick Place	C3-C4	Marlborough Street	B2	Queens Gardens	C3	Upper North Street	B2
Boyces Street	C2	Frederick Street	C3	Melville Road	A4-B4	Regency Square	B1-B2	Upper Rock Gardens	E2-F2
Bristol Road	F2	Freshfield Place	F3	Middle Street	C1-C2	Regent Hill	B2	Upper Street	F2
Buckingham Place	B4	Freshfield Road	F2-F3	Montpelier Crescent	A4-B4	Regent Street	D3	Vernon Terrace	A4-B4
Buckingham Road	B3-B4	Furze Hill	A3	Montpelier Place	A2-A3	Richmond Parade	D4	Victoria Road	A3-B3
Buckingham Street	C3-C4	Gardner Street	C3	Montpelier Road	A1-A3	Richmond Street	E4	Victoria Street	B2-B3
Camelford Street	E1-E2	George Street	E2	Montpelier Street	A2-B3	Robert Street	D3	Vine Street	D3
Cannon Place	B1-B2	Gloucester Place	D3-D4	Montpelier Terrace	A2	Rock Place	E1-E2	West Drive	F3-F4
Carlton Hill	E3	Gloucester Road	C3-D3	Montpelier Villas	A2-A3	Russel Road	B1-C1	West Hill Road	B4
Castle Street	B2	Gloucester Street	D4	Montreal Road	E4	Russel Square	B2	West Hill Street	B4
Cavendish Place	A1	Goldsmid Road	A4-B4	Morley Street	D3	Scotland Street	E4	West Street	C1-C2
Charles Street	E1-E2	Grafton Street	F1-F2	Mount Pleasant	E2-E3	Ship Street	C1-C2	Western Road	A2-B2-C2
Chatham Place	B4	Grand Junction Road	C1-D1	New England Street	C4	Sillwood Road	A2	Western Street	A1-A2
Cheapside	C4-D4	Grand Parade	D2-D4	New Road	D2	Sillwood Street	A1-A2	White Street	E2-E3
Cheltenham Place	D3	Granville Road	A4	New Steine	E1-E2	South Avenue	F3	William Street	D2-D3
Church Street	B3-C3-D2	Grove Hill	E4	Nizells Avenue	A4	South Street	C1	Windledham Avenue	A3-A4
Circus Street	D3	Grove Street	E4	Norfolk Road	A2	Southover Street	E4-F4	York Avenue	A3-A4
Clarence Square	B2	Guildford Road	B4-C4	Norfolk Square	A2	Spring Gardens	C3	York Place	D4
Clarence Street	B2	Guildford Street	C3-C4	Norfolk Terrace	A3	Spring Street	B2	York Road	A2
Clifton Hill	A3-B3	Hampton Place	A2	North Drive	F4	St James's Avenue	E2		
Clifton Place	B2-B3	Hampton Street	A2-B2	North Gardens	C3	St James's Street	D2-E2		
Clifton Road	B3-B4	Hanover Street	D4-E4	North Road	C3-D3	St John's Place	E3		
Clifton Street	B4-C4	Hereford Street	F2	North Street	C2-D2	St Michael's Place	A3		
Clifton Terrace	B3	High Street	E2	Old Steine	D1-D2	St Nicholas Road	B3-C3		
Compton Avenue	B4	Holland Street	E4	Oriental Place	A1	Stanley Street	E3-E4		
Davigdor Road	A4	Ivory Place	D3	Osmond Road	A4	Stone Street	B2	AA shop	C2
Dean Street	B2	James Street	F2	Over Street	C3-C4	Surrey Street	C3-C4	10 Churchill Square	
Denmark Terrace	A3	Jersey Street	E4	Park Hill	F3	Sussex Street	E3	Brighton BN1 2EY	

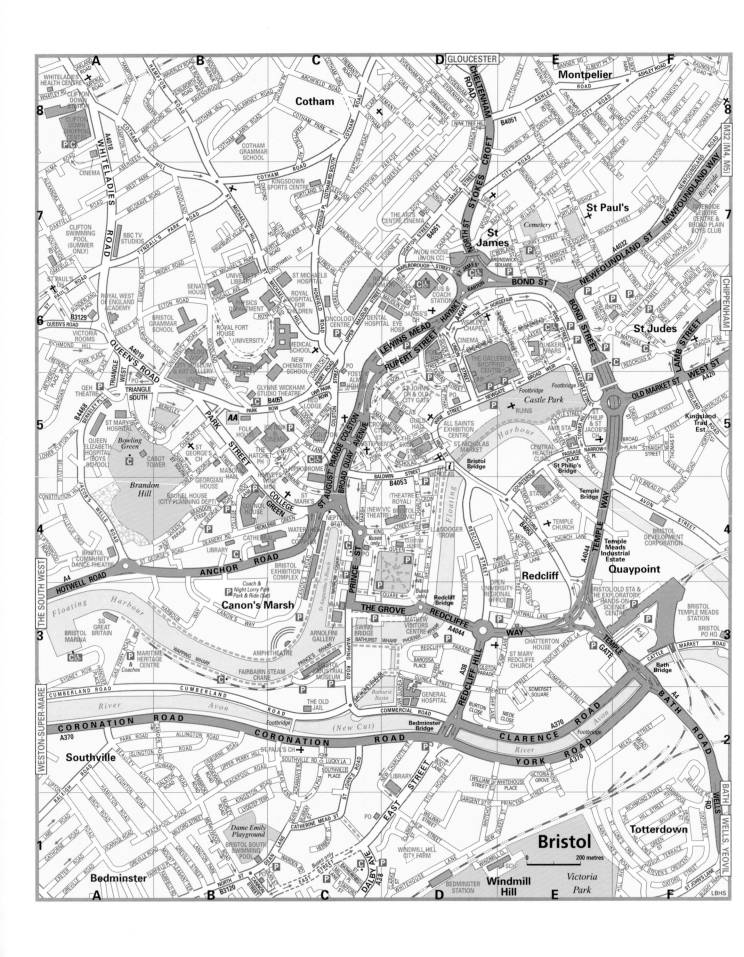

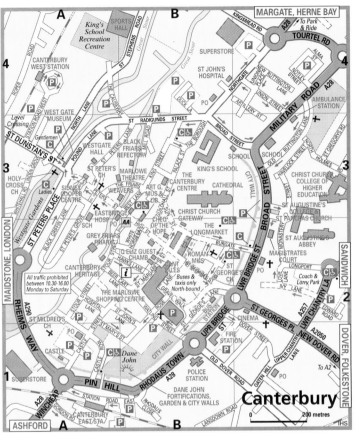

Canterbury

Canterbury is found on atlas page **29**, grid reference TR1457

Alma Street	C4	Lower Bridge Street	C2	St Georges Place	C1-C2
Artillery Street	B4-C3	Lower Chantry Lane	C1-C2	St Georges Street	B2
Beer Cart Lane	A2-B2	Military Road	C3-C4	St Gregory's Road	C3
Best Lane	B3	Mill Road	B3	St Margaret's Street	B2
Black Griffin Lane	A2-A3	Monastery Street	C2-C3	St Mary's Street	A2-B1
Broad Street	B3-C3-C2	New Dover Road	C1	St Peter's Grove	A2-A3
Burgate	B2-C2	New Ruttington Lane	C4	St Peters Lane	A3-B3
Castle Row	A1-A2	North Holmes Road	C3	St Peters Place	A2-A3
Castle Street	A1-A2	North Lane	A3-A4	St Peters Street	A3-B3
Dover Street	B2-C1	Northgate	B4-C4	St Radigunds Street	B3
Duck Lane	B4	Notley Street	C4	St Stephen's Road	A4-B4
Edward Road	C2	Oaten Hill	C1	Station Road East	A1-B1
Gordon Road	A1	Old Dover Road	B1-C1	Station Road West	A3-A4
Gravel Walk	B2	Old Ruttington Lane	C3-C4	Stour Street	A2-B2
Guildhall Street	B2-B3	Palace Street	B3	Sun Street	B2-B3
Havelock Street	C3	Pin Hill	A1-B1	The Borough	B3
Hawks Lane	A2-B2	Pound Lane	A3	The Causeway	A4-B4
High Street	B2-B3	Rheims Way	A1-A2	The Friars	A3-B3
Hospital Lane	A2	Rhodaus Close	B1	Tourtel Road	C4
Ivy Lane	C2	Rhodaus Town	B1	Union Place	C4
King Street	B3	Roper Road	A4	Upper Bridge Street	B1-B2
Kingsmead Road	B4-C4	Rose Lane	B1-B2	Upper Chantry Lane	C1
Lansdown Road	B1	Simmonds Road	A1	Watling Street	B1-B2
Linden Grove	A3	St Dunstan's Street	A3	White Horse Lane	B2
Love Lane	C2	St George's Lane	B1-B2	Whitehall Road	A2-A3
				Wincheap	A1

AA shop		B3
13 Best Lane		
Canterbury CT1 2JB		

Bristol

Bristol is found on atlas page **34**, grid reference ST5972

Abbotsford Road	A8-B8	Campbell Street	E8	Denbigh Street	E8	Horfield Road	C6-C7
Aberdeen Road	A7-A8-B8	Cannon Street	B1	Denmark Street	C5-C4	Horton Road	F5
Acraman's Road	C2	Canon's Road	C3-C4	Dighton Street	D7	Hotwell Road	A3-A4
Albert Park	F8	Canon's Way	B3	Dove Lane	F7	Houlton Street	F6-F7
Albert Park Place	E8	Canynge Street	E3	Dove Street	C7-D7-D8	Howard Road	A2-B2
Alexandra Road	A7	Castle Street	E5	Dove Street South	D7-D8	Imperial Road	A8
Alfred Hill	C7-C6	Catherine Mead Street	C1	Drummond Road	E8	Islington Road	A2-B2
Alfred Place	D3	Cattle Market Road	F3	East Street	C1-D1-D2	Jacob Street	F5
Allington Road	B2	Charles Street	D7	Edgeware Road	B2	Jacob's Wells Road	A4-A5
Alma Road	A7-A8	Charlotte Street	B5	Elmdale Road	A7-A6-B6	Jamaica Street	D7
Alpha Road	C1-C2	Charlotte Street South	B5	Elton Road	A6-B6	Jubilee Street	F5
Anchor Road	A4-B4-C4	Cheese Lane	E5	Eugene Street	C7-D7	Kingsdown Parade	C7-C8-D8
Archfield Road	C8	Cheltenham Road	D8	Eugene Street	F6	Kings Square	D7
Argyle Road	E7-E8	Church Lane	E4	Exeter Road	A1	King Street	C4-D4
Armada Place	D8	City Road	D7-E7-E8-F8	Fairfax Street	D5	Kingston Road	B1-B2
Ashley Road	E8-F8	Clare Road	C8-D8	Fairfield Place	A1-B1	Lamb Street	F5-F6
Avon Street	E4-F4	Clarence Road	D2-E2-E2-F3	Fairfield Road	A1	Langton Park	B1
Backfields	D7-E7	Clarke Street	D1	Franklyn Street	F8	Leighton Road	A1-A2
Badminton Road	F8	Clement Street	F7	Frederick Place	A6	Lewins Mead	C6-D6
Baldwin Street	C5-D5	Clevedon Terrace	C7	Fremantle Road	C8-D8	Lime Road	A1
Banner Road	E8	College Green	B4-C4-B4-B5	Fremantle Square	D8	Little Ann Street	F6
Barossa Place	D3	College Street	B4	Frog Lane	B4	Little George Street	F6
Barton Road	F4-F5	Colston Avenue	C5	Frogmore Street	C5	Little Paul Street	B7-C7
Bath Road	F2	Colston Parade	D3	Gas Ferry Road	A3	Lodge Street	C5
Bathurst Parade	C2-C3	Colston Street	C5-C6	Gathorpe Road	A1	Lower Castle Street	E5-E6
Beauley Road	A2-B1	Commercial Road	C2-D2	Gloucester Street	E7-E6	Lower Church Lane	C5-C6
Belgrave Road	A7-B7	Corn Street	C5-D5	Great Ann Street	F6	Lower Clifton Hill	A5
Bellevue	A4-A5	Coronation Road	A2-B2-C2-D2	Great George Street	B4-B5	Lower Guinea Street	D2-D3
Bellevue Crescent	A4	Cotham Grove	C8	Green Street	F1	Lower Maudlin Street	D6
Bellevue Road	F2	Cotham Hill	A8-B7	Greville Road	A1	Lower Park Row	C5
Berkeley Place	A5	Cotham Lawn Road	B8	Greville Street	B1	Lucky Lane	C2
Berkeley Square	A5-B5	Cotham Park	C8	Grosvenor Road	E8-F8	Ludlow Close	F8
Birch Road	A1-A2	Cotham Road	B7-C7-C8	Guinea Street	D2-D3	Lydstep Terrace	B1-B2
Bishop Street	E7	Cotham Road South	C7-C8	Gwyn Street	E8	Marlborough Hill	C7
Bond Street	D6-E6	Cotham Side	C8-D8	Halston Drive	F7-F8	Marlborough Street	D6-D7
Boot Lane	D2	Cotham Vale	B8	Hamilton Road	A1-A2	Marsh Street	C4
Bragg's Lane	F6	Cottage Place	C7	Hampton Lane	A8	Mead Rise	F2
Brandon Steep	B4	Countership	E4-E5	Hampton Park	A8	Mead Street	E2-F2
Brighton Street	E8	Crow Lane	D4	Hampton Road	B8	Mede Close	E2
Brigstocke Road	E7-E8	Cumberland Road	A2-B2-C2	Hanover Place	A3	Merchant Street	D6-E6-E5
Broadmead	D6-E6	Cumberland Street	D7-E7	Harbour Way	A3-B3	Meridian Place	A5-A6
Broad Plain	F5	Dalby Avenue	C1	Hatfield Avenue	C8	Merrywood Road	B1
Broad Quay	C4-C5	Dale Street	F6	Haymarket	D6	Midland Road	F5
Broad Street	C5-D5	Dalston Road	B2	Henry Street	F1	Milford Street	B1
Broad Weir	E5-E6	Dalrymple Road	E8	Hepburn Road	D8-E8	Mill Avenue	D4
Brunswick Street	E7	Davey Street	F8	Herbert Street	C1	Mill Lane	C1
Burnell Drive	E8-F8	David Street	F5	Highbury Villas	B7	Mitchell Court	E4
Burton Close	D2	Deanery Road	B4	High Street	D5	Mitchell Lane	E4
Bushy Park	F1	Dean Lane	B1-C1-C2	Hilll Avenue	F1	Montague Place	C7
Cambridge Street	F1	Dean Street	B1	Hill Street	B5	Moon Street	D7
Camden Road	A2	Dean Street	E7	Hill Street	F1	Morgan Street	F8

Morley Road	B1	Park Road	A2	Stokes Croft	D7-D8
Mount Pleasant Terrace	B1	Park Row	B5-C5	Straight Street	F5
Murray Street	C1	Park Street	B5	Stratton Street	E6
Myrtle Road	B7-C7	Passage Place	E5	Sunderland Place	A6
Narrow Place	E5	Pembroke Road	B2	Surrey Street	E7
Narrow Quay	C3-C4	Pembroke Street	E7	Sydenham Hill	D8
Nelson Street	C5-D5-D6	Penn Street	E6	Sydenham Lane	D8
New Charlotte Street	C2-D2	Pennywell Road	F6	Sydenham Road	D8
New Charlotte Road	F7-F8	Perry Road	C5-C6	Sydney Row	A3
Newfoundland Street	E6-E7-F7	Philip Street	D1	Temple Back	E4-E5
Newfoundland Way	F8	Picton Street	E8	Temple Gate	E3
Newgate	D5-E5	Pipe Lane	C5	Temple Street	E4
New Kingsley Road	F4-F5	Portland Square	E7	Temple Way	E3-E4-E5
New Queen Street	D1	Portland Street	C7	Terrell Street	C6-C7
New Street	F6	Portwall Lane	D3-E3	The Grove	C3-D3
New Thomas Street	F5	Prewett Street	D2-E3	The Horsefair	D6-E6
Nine Tree Hill	D8	Prince Street	C3-C4	The Pithay	D5
North Road	B1	Princess Street	D1-E1-E2	Thomas Street	F8
North Street	D7	Princes Street	E2	Three Queens Lane	D4-E4
Nugent Hill	D8	Priory Road	A6-B7	Tower Hill	E5
Oakfield Place	A6-A7	Pritchard Street	E7-E6	Trelawney Road	B8-C8
Oakfield Road	A7	Pump Lane	D3-E3	Trenchard Street	C5
Old Bread Street	F4	Pyle Hill Crescent	F1	Triangle South	A5
Old Market Street	F4	Quakers Friars	E5	Triangle West	A6
Osborne Road	B2	Queen Charlotte Street	D4	Tyndall Avenue	B6
Oxford Street	F1	Queen's Avenue	A6	Tyndall's Park Road	A7-B7
Oxford Street	B7	Queen's Parade	B4	Union Street	D5-D6
Park Place	A6	Queen's Road	A6-B6-B5	Unity Street	F5
		Queen Square	C3-C4-D4-E3	University Road	B6
		Queen Street	E5	Upper Byron Place	A5
		Raleigh Road	A1-A2	Upper Maudlin Street	C6
		Ravenswood Road	B8	Upper Perry Hill	B2
		Redcliff Backs	D4-D3	Upper York Street	D7-E7
		Redcliffe Parade	D3	Upton Road	A1-A2
		Redcliffe Way	D3-E3	Vicarage Road	A1
		Redcliff Hill	D2-D3	Victoria Grove	E2
		Redcliff Mead Lane	E3	Victoria Street	E4
		Redcliff Street	D3-D4	Victoria Walk	D8
		Redcross Street	F6	Wade Street	F6
		Richmond Hill	A6	Walker Street	C7
		Richmond Street	F1-F2	Wapping Road	C3
		River Street	F6	Warden Road	C1
		Royal Fort Road	B6-C6	Warwick Road	A8
		Rupert Street	C6-D6	Water Lane	E4
		Russ Street	F5	Waterloo Road	F5
		St Augustine's Parade	C4-C5	Waterloo Street	F5-F6
		St Catherines Place	C1	Wellington Avenue	E8
		St George's Road	A4-B4	Wellington Road	E6-F6-F7
		St James' Barton	D6	Wells Road	F1
		St John's Lane	F1	Welsh Back	D3-D4-D5
		St John's Road	C1-C2	West Park	A7
		St Luke's Crescent	E1-F1	West Street	F5-F6
		St Luke's Road	E2-E1-F1	Whatley Road	A8
		St Matthew's Road	C7-C8	Whitehouse Lane	C1-D1
		St Matthias Park	E6-F6	Whitehouse Place	D2-E2
		St Michael's Hill	B7-B6-C6	Whitehouse Street	D1-D2
		St Michael's Park	B6-B7	Whiteladies Road	A6-A7-A8
		St Nicholas Road	F8	Whitson Street	D6
		St Nicholas Street	C5-D5	Wilder Street	D7-E7
		St Paul's Road	A6-A7	William Street	D2
		St Paul's Street	E7	William Street	E8-F8
		St Thomas Street	D4-E4-E3	William Street	F1
		Sargent Street	D1	Willway Street	D1
		Ship Lane	D2	Wilson Place	F7
		Silver Street	D6	Wilson Street	E7-F7
		Small Street	C5-D5	Windmill Close	D1
		Somerset Square	E2	Windsor Terrace	F1
		Somerset Street	E2-E3	Wine Street	D5
		Somerset Street	C7-D7-D8	Woodland Road	B5-B6-B7
		Southleigh Road	A7	York Place	B4
		Southville Place	C2	York Road	D2-E2-F2
		Southville Road	C2	York Street	E6-E7
		Southwell Street	B6-C7	
		Springfield Road	D8	
		Spring Street	E2	
		Stackpool Road	A1-A2-B2	AA shop	B5
		Stafford Street	C1	Fanum House	
		Steven's Crescent	F1	26-32 Park Row	
		Stillhouse Lane	D1-D2	Bristol BS1 5LY	

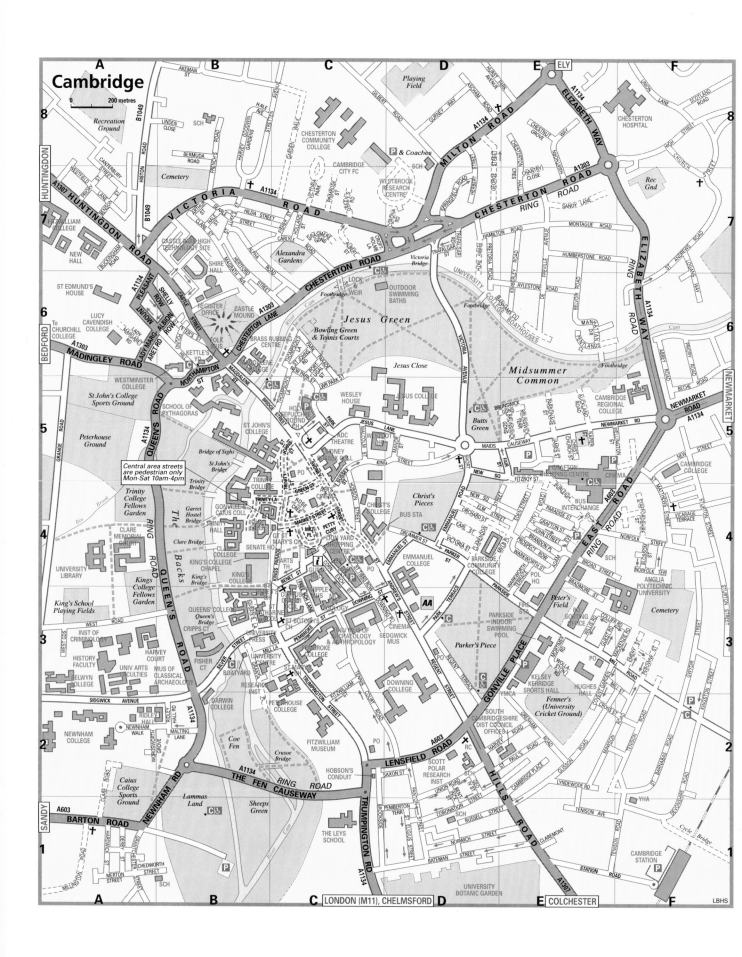

Cambridge

0   200 metres

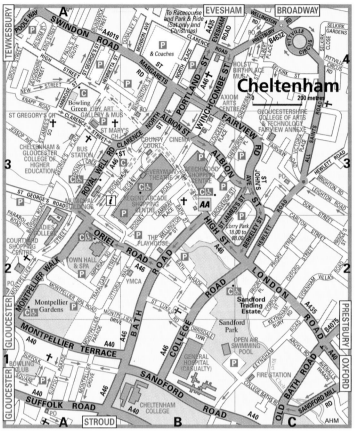

Cheltenham

Cheltenham is found on atlas page **35**,
grid reference SO**9422**

Albert Place	C4	Monson Avenue	B4	Suffolk Road	A1
Albert Road	C4	Montpellier Drive	A2-B1	Suffolk Square	A1
Albion Street	B3-C3	Montpellier Grove	A1	Swindon Road	A4-B4
All Saints Road	C3-C4	Montpellier Parade	A1-A2	Sydenham Villas Road	C2
Ambrose Street	A4	Montpellier Spa Road	A2	Trafalgar Street	A2-B2
Argyll Road	C1	Montpellier Street	A2-A3	Victoria Place	C3
Avenalls Parade	C1	Montpellier Terrace	A1-B1	Victoria Walk	A2-B2
Bath Parade	B2	Montpellier Walk	A2-A3	Wellington Road	C4
Bath Road	A1-B3	New Street	A4	Wellington Street	B2
Bath Street	B2-B3	North Place	B4	Winchcombe Street	B3-B4
Bayshill Road	A2-A3	North Street	B3-B4		
Bennington Street	B3-B4	Old Bath Road	C1		
Berkeley Street	C2-C3	Oriel Road	A2-B2		
Brighton Road	C3	Orrisdale Terrace	B1		
Brunswick Street	A4	Oxford Street	C2		
Cambray Place	B2-B3	Pitville Circus	C4		
Carlton Street	C2-C3	Pitville Circus Road	C4		
Christowe Lane	C1	Poole Way	A4		
Clarence Road	B4	Portland Street	B3-B4		
Clarence Street	A3-B3	Prestbury Road	C4		
College Baths Road	C1	Prince's Street	C2		
College Lawn	B1	Priory Place	C2		
College Road	B1-C2	Priory Street	C2		
Corpus Street	C2	Promenade	A3-B3		
Devonshire Street	A4	Regent Street	A3-B3		
Duke Street	C2-C3	Rodney Road	B2-B3		
Dunalley Street	B4	Royal Crescent	A3		
Evesham Road	B4	Royal Well Road	A3		
Fairview Road	B4-C3	Sandford Mill Road	C1		
Gloucester Place	B3	Sandford Road	B1-C1		
Great Norwood Street	A1	Selkirk Close	C4		
Grosvenor Street	B2-C3	Selkirk Gardens	C4		
Grove Street	A4	Selkirk Street	C4		
Henrietta Street	A4	Sherborne Place	B3-C3		
Hewlett Road	C2-C3	Sherborne Street	C3-C4		
High Street	A4-B3-B2	St George's Place	A3		
Imperial Square	A2	St George's Road	A3		
Jersey Avenue	C3	St George's Street	A4		
Jessop Avenue	A3	St James's Square	A3-A4		
Keynsham Road	B1-C2	St James's Street	B2-C3		
Keynshambury Road	C1-C2	St John's Avenue	C3		
King Street	A4	St Luke's Road	B1-B2		
Knapp Road	A4	St Margarets Road	B4		
Leighton Road	C3	St Paul's Road	B4	AA shop	B3
London Road	C1-C2	St Paul's Street South	A4	90 High Street	
Milsom Street	A4	Suffolk Parade	A1	Cheltenham GL50 1EG	

Cambridge

Cambridge is found on atlas page **53**,
grid reference TL**4558**

Abbey Road	F5-F6	Clare Road	A1-A2	Green Street	C4-C5	Malcolm Street	C5	Pound Hill	B6	The Fen Causeway	B2-C2
Adam and Eve Street	E4	Clare Street	B7	Green's Road	C7	Malting Lane	B2	Pretoria Road	D6-D7	Thomson's Lane	C5-C6
Akeman Street	B8	Claremont	E1	Gresham Road	E2	Manhatten Drive	E6	Primrose Street	C7	Trafalgar Road	D7
Albert Street	C7	Clarendon Street	D4-E4	Guest Road	E3	Manor Street	D5	Priory Road	F5-F6	Trafalgar Street	D7
Albion Row	B6	Collier Road	E3-F3	Gurney Way	D8	Market Place	C4	Priory Street	A7	Trinity Lane	B4-C4
Alpha Road	B7-B6-C6	Corn Exchange Street	C3-C4	Gwydir Street	F2-F3	Market Street	C4	Prospect Row	E4	Trinity Street	C4-C5
Arthur Street	B7	Corona Road	D7	Hale Avenue	B8	Mawson Road	E2-F2-F3	Queen's Lane	B3	Trumpington Street	C2-C3
Ascham Road	D8	Coronation Street	D1-D2	Hale Street	B7	Melbourne Place	D4-E4	Queens Road	B2-B4-A4-B5	Trumpington Road	C1-C2
Auckland Road	E5	Covent Garden	E2-E3	Hamilton Road	D7-E7	Merton Street	A1	Regent Street	D2-D3	Union Lane	F8
Aylestone Road	D6-E6	Cross Street	E2-F2	Hardwick Street	A1	Mill Lane	B3-C3	Regent Terrace	D2-D3	Union Road	D2
Banhams Close	D6-E6	De Freville Avenue	E6-E7	Harvey Goodwin Gardens	B7-B8	Mill Road	F2-F3-E3	Ridley Hall Road	B2	Vicarage Terrace	F4
Barton Road	A1	Derby Street	A1	Harvey Road	D2-E2	Mill Street	E3-F3-F2	Rose Crescent	C4	Victoria Avenue	D5-D6-D7
Bateman Street	C1-D1-E1	Devonshire Road	F1-F2	Hawthorn Way	E7-E8	Millington Road	A1	Russell Street	D1-E1	Victoria Park	C7-C8
Beche Road	F5-F6	Downing Place	C3-D3	Herbert Street	D7-D8	Milton Road	D7-D8-E8	Sandy Lane	E7	Victoria Road	A7-B7-C7-D7
Belvoir Road	E6-E7	Downing Street	C3-D3	Hertford Street	B7-B6-C6	Montague Road	E7-F7	Saxon Street	C2-D2	Victoria Street	D4
Benet Street	C4	Drummer Street	D4	High Street	F8	Mortimer Road	E3	Scotland Road	F8	Warkworth Street	E4
Benson Street	A7	Earl Street	D4	Hilda Street	B7-C7	Mount Pleasant	A6	Searle Street	B7-C7	Warkworth Terrrace	E3-E4
Bermuda Road	B8	East Road	E3-E4-F4-F5	Hills Road	E1-D2	Napier Street	E5	Shelly Row	A6-B6	Wellington Street	E5-F5
Blossom Street	F4	Eden Street	E4	Histon Road	A7-A8	New Park Street	C5-C6	Short Street	D5	West Gardens	A3
Bradmore Street	E3-E4	Elizabeth Way	E8-E7-F7-F6-F5	Hobson Street	C4-C5	New Square	D5-D4	Sidgwick Avenue	A2-B2	West Road	A3-B3
Brandon Place	E4	Elm Street	D4-E4	Holland Street	C7	New Street	F5	Silver Street	B3-C3	Westfield Lane	A7
Brentwick Street	D1-D2	Emerey Street	F3	Humberstone Road	E7-F7	Newmarket Road	E5-F5	Springfield Road	D7	Willis Road	E3
Bridge Street	B5-C5	Emmanuel Road	D4-D5	Huntingdon Road	A7	Newnham Road	A1-B1-B2	St Andrew's Street	D3-D4-C4	Wollaston Road	E3
Broad Street	E4-F4	Emmanuel Street	D4	Hurst Park Avenue	D8-E8	Newnham Walk	A2-B2	St Andrews Road	F6-F7	Wordworth Grove	A2
Brookside	C1-C2	Fair Street	E5	James Street	E5	Norfolk Street	E4-F4	St Barnabas Road	F2		
Brunswick Gardens	E5	Ferry Path	D6-D7	Jesus Lane	C5-D5	Norfolk Terrace	F4	St Eligius Street	D1		
Brunswick Terrace	E5	Fisher Street	C7	John Street	E4	Northampton Street	B5-B6	St John's Road	C6		
Buckingham Road	A7	Fitzroy Street	E5	Kimberley Road	E6-E7	Norwich Street	D1-E1	St John's Street	C5		
Burleigh Street	E4-E5	Fitzwilliam Street	C2-C3	King Street	D5-E5	Orchard Street	D4-E4	St Luke's Street	B7		
Cambridge Place	E2	Free School Lane	C3-C4	Kings Parade	C4	Panton Street	D1-D2	St Matthews Street	F4-F5		
Canterbury Street	A7-A8	French Road	B7-B8	Kingston Street	F2-F3	Paradise Street	E4	St Paul's Road	D2-E2		
Carlyle Road	B7-C7	Garden Walk	C7-C8	Lady Margaret Road	A6	Park Parade	C6	St Peter's Street	B6		
Castle Street	B6	George IV Street	D2	Lenfield Road	C2-D2	Park Street	C5	St Tibbs Row	C3-C4		
Chantry Close	E7	George Street	D7-D8	Linden Close	A8-B8	Park Terrace	D3-D4	Staffordshire Street	F4		
Chedworth Street	A1-B1	Gilbert Road	C8-D8	Logans Way	F6-F7	Parker Street	D4	Station Road	E1-F1		
Chesterton Hall Crescent	E7-E8	Glisson Road	E1-E2	Lower Park Street	C5-C6	Parkside	E3-D3-D4	Stretten Avenue	B7-B8-C8		
Chesterton Lane	B6-C6	Gonville Place	D2-D3-E3	Lyndewode Road	E2	Parsonage Street	E5	Sturton Street	F3-F4-F5		
Chesterton Road	E7-D7-C7-C6	Grafton Street	E4	Mackenzie Road	E3-F3	Pemberton Terrace	C1-D1	Sussex Street	C4-C5		
Chestnut Grove	E8	Grange Road	A3-A4-A5-A6	Madingley Road	A6-B6-B5	Pembroke Street	C3	Sydney Street	C4-C5	AA shop	D3
Christchurch Street	E5	Granta Place	B2-B3	Magdalene Street	B5-B6	Pentlands Close	E6	Tenison Avenue	E1	Janus House	
Church Street	F7-F8	Grantchester Street	A1	Magrath Avenue	B7-B6	Perowne Street	F3	Tenison Road	E1-F1-E2-F2	46-48 St Andrew's Street	
City Road	E4	Grasmere Gardens	C7	Maids Causeway	D5-E5	Portugal Street	C6	Tennis Court Road	C3-C2-D2	Cambridge CB2 3BH	

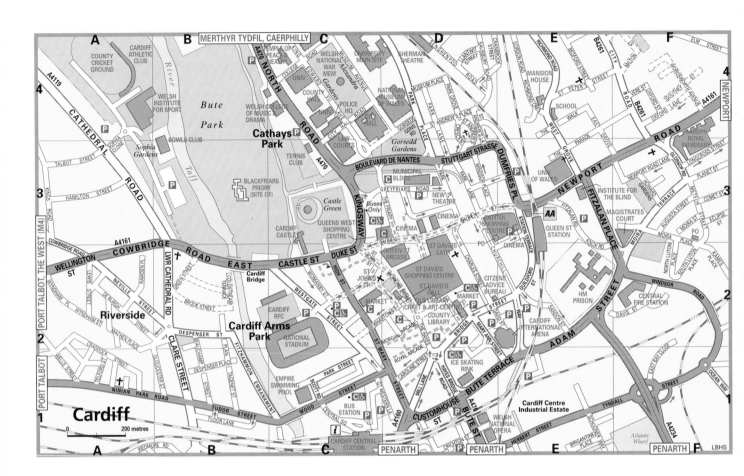

Cardiff

Cardiff is found on atlas page **33**,
grid reference ST**1876**

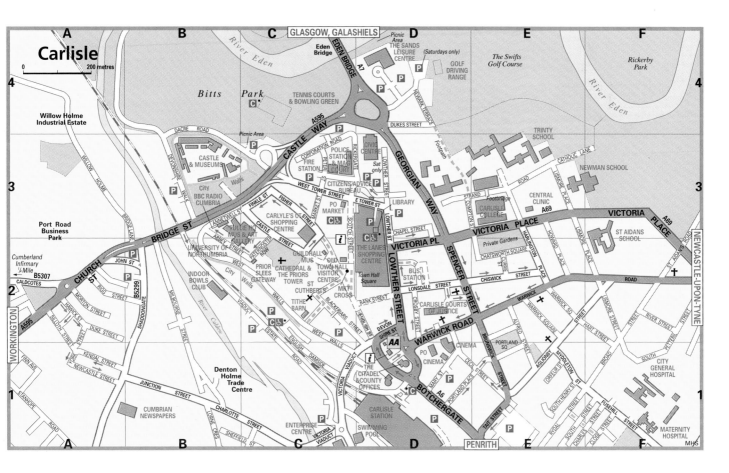

Carlisle

Carlisle is found on atlas page **93**,
grid reference NY**3956**

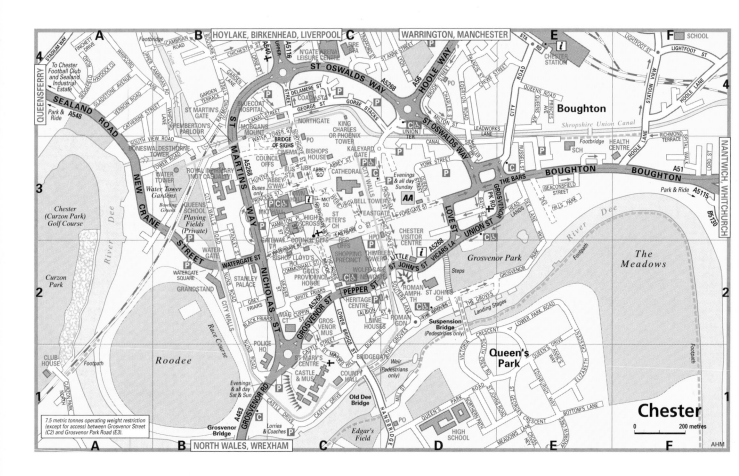

Chester

Chester is found on atlas page **71**,
grid reference SJ**4066**

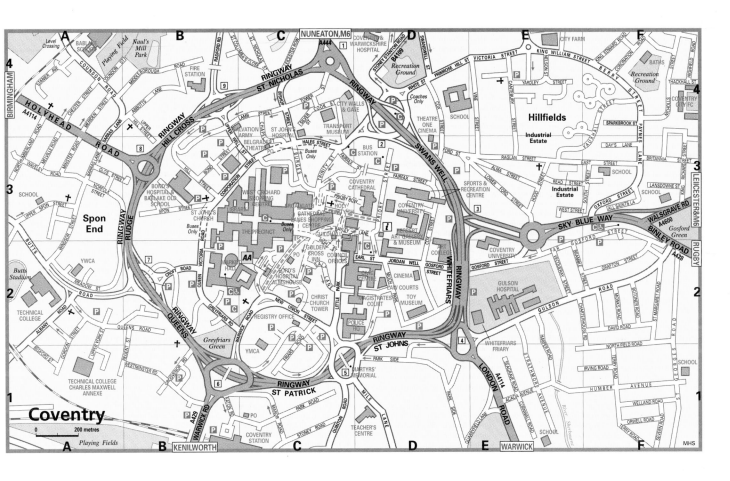

Coventry

Coventry is found on atlas page **61**,
grid reference SP**3378**

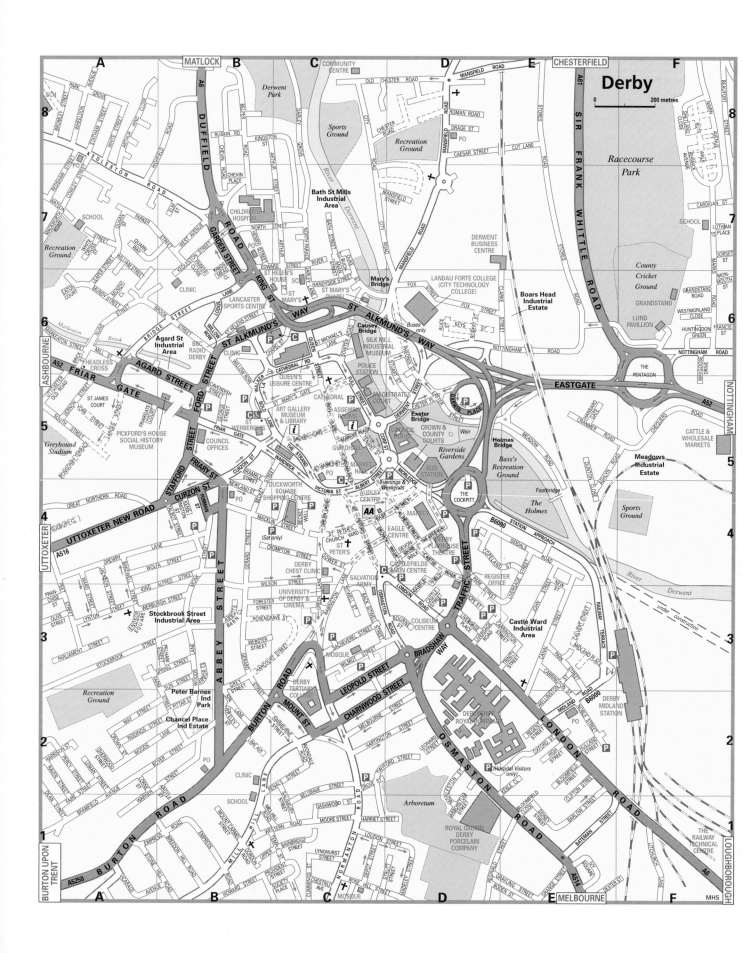

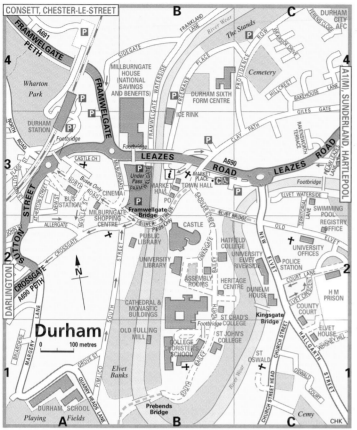

Durham

Durham is found on atlas page **96**,
grid reference NZ2742

Allergate	A2	Old Elvet	C2
Atherton Street	A2-A3	Oswald Court	C1
Bakehouse Lane	C4	Owengate	B2
Briardene	A1	Pelaw Leazes Lane	C3
Castle Church	A3	Pimlico South Street	A1-A2-B2
Church Street	C1	Providence Row	C3-C4
Church Street Head	C1	Quarry Heads Lane	A1
Clay Path	B3-C3	Ravensworth Terrace	C3
Court Lane	C2	Saddler Street	B2-B3
Crossgate	A2	Sidegate	A4-B4
Elvet Bridge	B3-C3-C2	Silver Street	B2-B3
Elvet Crescent	C2	South Bailey	B1
Elvet Waterside	C3	Sutton Street	A2-A3
Ferens Close	C4	Sutton Street	A3
Framwelgate	A3-A4	Territorial Lane	C2-C3
Framwelgate Peth	A4	Wearside Drive	C4
Framwelgate Waterside	B3-B4	Whinney Hill	C1
Frankland Lane	B4		
Freemans Place	B3-B4-C4		
Giles Gate	C3-C4		
Grove Street	A1		
Halgarth Street	C1		
Hilcrest	C4		
John Street	A2		
Leazes Road	B3-C3		
Margery Lane	A1-A2		
Milburngate	A3-B3		
Neville Street	A2-A3		
New Elvet	C2-C3		
New Street	A3		
North Bailey	B1-B2		
North Road	A3		

Derby

Derby is found on atlas page **62**,
grid reference SK3536

Abbey Street	B2-B3-B4	Bute Walk	F8-F7	Dorset Street	F7
Abbots Barn Close	B3	Caesar Street	D8	Drage Street	D8
Agard Street	A6-B6-B5	Calvert Street	E3	Drewry Lane	A4-B4
Albert Street	C4-C5-D5	Canal Street	E3-E4	Duke Street	C7-C6
Albion Street	D4	Cardigan Street	F7	Duffield Road	B8-B7
Alice Street	D6	Carrington Street	D3-E3	Dunton Close	E5-E4
Arbor Close	B3	Castle Field	D3-D4	Eastgate	E5
Arboretum Street	D1-D2	Castle Street	D3	East Street	C4-D4
Argyle Street	B2	Castle Walk	D4	Eaton Court	A6
Arthur Hind Close	A7-A8	Cathedral Road	B5-B6-C5-C6	Edward Street	B7-C7
Arthur Street	B8-C8-C7-C6	Cavendish Street	B5	Elm Street	B7
Ashlyn Road	E4-E5-F5	Chancel Street	B2	Empress Road	A1-B1
Avondale Road	C2	Chapel Street	C6	Endsor Square	A3
Babington Lane	C3-C4	Charnwood Street	C2-D2-D3	Exeter Place	D5
Back Sitwell Street	C3	Chester Road	C8-D8	Exeter Street	D5
Bainbridge Street	C1	Chequers Road	F5	Faire Street	A1-A2
Bakewell Street	A4-A3	Chestnut Avenue	C1	Farm Street	A3-B3-B2
Barlow Street	E1-E2	Chevin Place	B7	Ford Street	B5-B6
Bateman Street	E1	Chevin Road	B8-B7	Forester Street	B3-C3
Bath Street	C7	City Road	C8-C7-D7-D6	Forman Street	B4
Beaufort Street	F8-F7	Clarke Street	D6-E6	Fox Street	D6
Becket Street	B4-B5-C5	Clifton Street	E1-E2	Franchise Street	A3
Becket Well	C4	Copeland Street	D4-E4	Francis Street	F6
Belgrave Street	C1-C2	Corn Market	C5	Friar Gate	A6-A5-B5
Belper Road	B8-B7	Corporation Street	D5	Friargate Court	A5
Berwick Avenue	F8-F7	Cowley Street	A7-A8	Friary Street	B5
Bloomfield Close	E1	Cranmer Road	E5-F5	Full Street	C6-C5
Bloomfield Street	E2	Crompton Street	B4-C4	Garden Street	B6-B7
Boden Street	D1-E1	Crown Street	A2	George Street	B5
Bold Lane	B5-C5	Crown Walk	C4-D4	Gerard Street	B2-B3-B4
Bourne Street	D3	Cummings Street	C1	Gordon Road	B1
Boyer Street	A2-B2	Curzon Street	B4-B5	Gower Street	C4
Bradshaw Way	D3	Cut Lane	E8	Grandstand Road	A6
Bramble Street	B5	Darley Grove	C8-C7	Grange Street	E1
Bramfield Avenue	A1-A2	Darley Lane	C6-C7	Grayling Street	D1-E1
Breedon Hill Road	B1	Darwin Place	D5	Great Northern Road	A4
Brick Street	A6	Dashwood Street	C1	Green Lane	C3-C4
Bridge Street	A5-A6-B6	Dean Street	A2-A1	Grey Street	B3
Bromley Street	A8	Depot Street	C1	Grove Street	C2-D2
Brook Street	A6-B6	Derwent Street	D5-D6	Handyside Street	C6
Buchanan Street	C6-C7	Devonshire Walk	D4	Hansard Gate	E5
Burton Road	A1-B1-B2-C2-C3	Dexter Street	E1-F1	Harcourt Street	B3-C3

Harriet Street	C1-D1	Mundy Close	A6	Sowter Road	C6
Harrison Street	A2	Mundy Street	A6	Spa Lane	B2
Hartington Street	C2-D2	Nairn Avenue	F7-F8	Spring Street	B3
Henry Street	B7	New Street	E4	Stafford Street	B4-B5
Highfield Road	A7-A8-B8	Newland Street	B4	Statham Street	A8
High Street	E2	Noble Street	E2	Station Approach	D4-E4
Hope Street	D3	Normanton Road	C1-C2-C3	Stockbrook Street	A2-A3-B3
Howard Street	B1	North Parade	C7	Stone Hill Road	A1-B1
Hulland Street	E2	North Street	B7-C7	Stores Road	E6-E7-E8
Huntingdon Green	F6	Nottingham Road	D6-E6-F6	Strutt Street	D1
Iron Gate	C5	Nuns Street	A6	Stuart Street	D5-D6
Ivy Square	E1	Old Chester Road	C8-D8	Sudbury Close	A4
Jackson Street	A3-A4	Olive Street	A3	Sun Street	B3
John Street	E3-E4	Osmaston Road	E1-C4	Swinburne Street	C2
Keble Close	E2	Otter Street	C7-C8	Talbot Street	B4
Kedleston Road	A8-A7-B7	Oxford Street	E2	Temple Street	C1
Kedleston Street	B7	Parker Close	B6-B7	Tenant Street	C5
Kensington Street	B4	Parker Street	A7-B7	Theatre Walk	D4
Keys Street	D6	Park Grove	A8	The Cockpitt	D4
King Alfred Street	A3-B3-B4	Park Street	D4-D3-E3	The Pentagon	F5-F6
Kings Mead Close	B6	Parliament Street	A3	The Strand	C5
Kingston Street	B8-C8	Peet Street	A3-A4	Traffic Street	D3-D4
King Street	B6-C6	Pelham Street	B3	Trinity Street	E3
Kirk Street	D8	Percy Street	A2	Twyford Street	C2-D2
Larges Street	A5	Phoenix Street	D6	Upper Bainbridge Street	B1-C1
Leaper Street	A6-A7	Pittar Street	B2	Uttoxeter New Road	A4-B4
Leman Street	A2	Ponsonby Terrace	A5	Uttoxeter Old Road	A5
Leonard Street	D2	Provident Street	C1	Vicarage Avenue	A1-B1
Leopold Street	C2-C3-D3	Quarn Street	A7	Victoria Street	C4
Lime Avenue	B2-C2	Quarn Way	A7	Vernon Street	A5
Litchurch Lane	F1	Queen Street	C5-C6	Ward Street	A3-A4
Liversage Place	D3	Railway Terrace	E3-E4	Warner Street	A1-A2-B2
Liversage Road	D3	Raven Street	A1-A2	Wardwick	B5-C5-C4
Liversage Street	E3-E4	Redshaw Street	A7-A8	Watson Street	A7
Lodge Lane	B6	Regent Street	E2	Waygoose Drive	F5-F6
London Road	D4-D3-E3-E2-F2-F1	Reginald Street	D1-E1	Webster Street	B3-C3
Lorne Street	A2	Renals Street	B2-C2	Wellington Street	E2-E3
Lothian Place	F7	Riddings Street	A2	Werburgh Street	A3-B3
Loudon Street	C1-D1	River Street	C7	West Avenue	B7
Lower Eley Street	B2	Robert Street	D6	Western Road	B1-C1
Lyndhurst Street	C1	Roman Road	D8	Westmorland Close	F6
Lynton Street	B3	Rose Hill Street	C1-D1	Wheeldon Avenue	A8
Macklin Street	B4-C4	Rosengrave Street	B3-C3	White Street	A8
Mackworth Road	A7	Ruskin Road	B8	Whitecross Street	A8
Madeley Street	D1	St Alkmund's Way	B6-D5	William Street	A6-A7
Mansfield Road	D6-D7-D8-E8	St Helens Street	B6	Willow Row	B5-B6
Mansfield Street	C7-D7	St James Court	A5	Wilmot Street	C3-D3
May Street	A6	St James Street	C5	Wilson Street	B3-B4-C4
Markeaton Street	A6	St Marks Road	F6-F7	Wolfa Street	A4-B4
Market Place	C5	St Mary's Gate	B5-C5	Woods Lane	A2-B2-B3
Meadow Road	E5	St Michael's Lane	C6	Wood Street	D6
Melbourne Street	C2-D2	St Peter's Church Yard	C4	York Street	A5
Midland Place	E3	St Peter's Street	C4		
Midland Road	E2-E3	Sacheverel Street	C3		
Mill Hill Lane	B1-B2-C2	Sadler Gate	C5		
Mill Hill Road	B1-C1	Salisbury Street	C1-C2		
Mill Street	A6	Sherwood Street	A2		
Monk Street	B3-B4	Shetland Close	F8		
Monmouth Street	F6	Siddals Road	D4-E4		
Moore Street	C1	Sidney Street	E1		
Morledge	D4-D5	Sir Frank Whittle Road	F6-E6-E8		
Morleston Street	D1-D2	Sitwell Street	C3	AA shop	D4
Mount Street	C2	Society Place	C1	22 East Street	
Mount Carmel Street	B1	South Street	A5	Derby DE1 2AF	

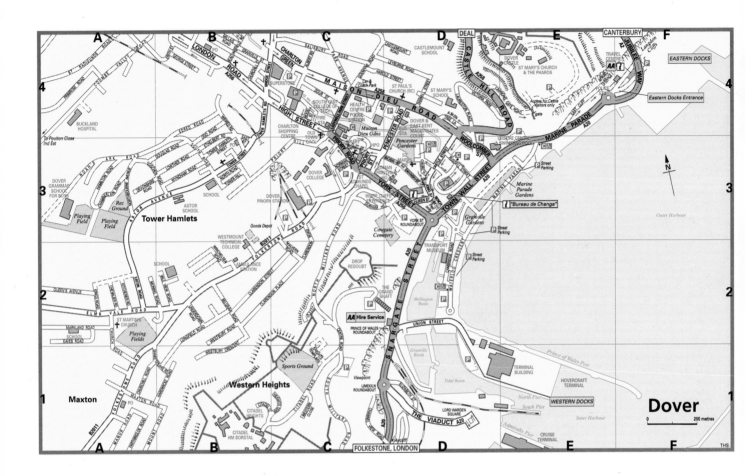

Dover

Dover is found on atlas page **29**,
grid reference TR3241

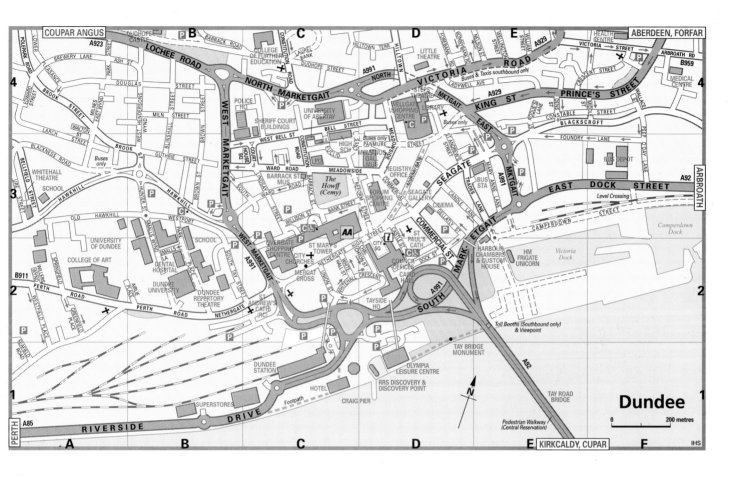

Dundee

Dundee is found on atlas page **126**,
grid reference NO**4030**

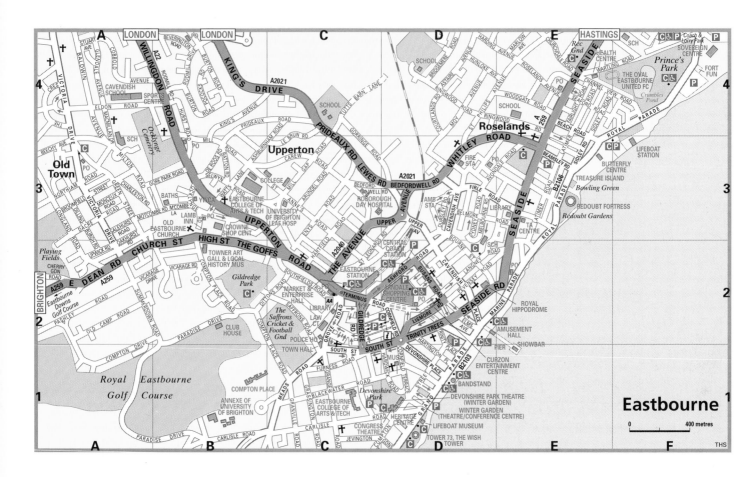

Eastbourne

Eastbourne is found on atlas page **16**,
grid reference TV**6199**

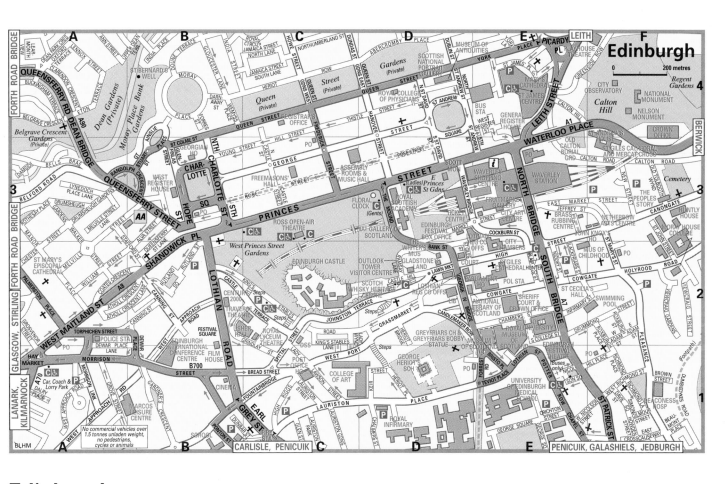

Edinburgh

Edinburgh is found on atlas page **117**,
grid reference NT**2573**

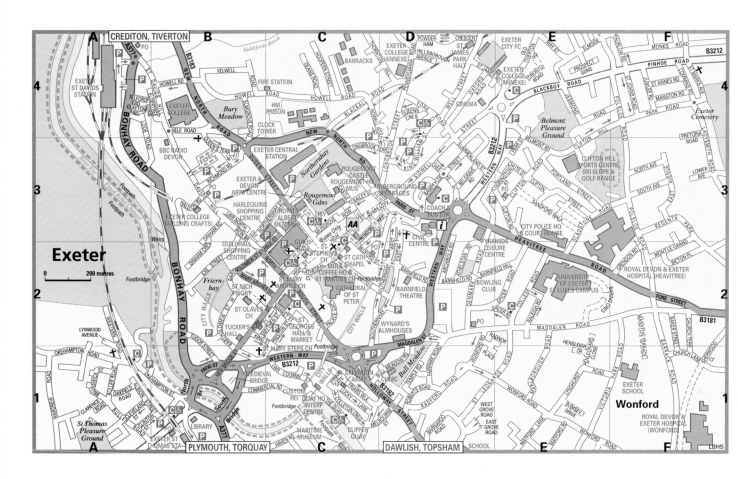

Exeter

Exeter is found on atlas page **9**,
grid reference SX**9292**

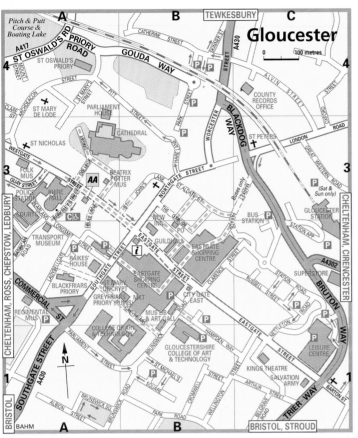

Gloucester

Gloucester is found on atlas page **35**, grid reference SO**8318**

Albion Street	AI	St Michael's Square	BI
Alvin Street	C3-C4	St Oswald's Road	A4
Archdeacon Street	A3-A4	Station Approach	C2
Arthur Street	CI	Station Road	C2
Barbican Road	A2	The Oxbode	B2-B3
Barton Street	CI	Trier Way	CI
Bearland	A3	Wellington Street	BI-CI
Belgrave Road	CI	Westgate Street	A3-B3
Berkeley Street	A3	Worcester Street	B3-B4
Blackdog Way	B4-C3		
Brunswick Road	AI-B2		
Brunswick Square	AI		
Bruton Way	CI-C3		
Bull Lane	A2-A3		
Catherine Street	B4		
Clare Street	A4		
Clarence Street	B2-C2		
College Street	A3		
Commercial Street	A2		
Cromwell Street	BI		
Eastgate Street	B2-CI		
Gouda Way	A4-B4		
Great Western Road	C3		
Greyfriars	A2-BI		
Hampden Way	B2-CI		
Hare Lane	B3		
Ladybellgate	A2		
London Road	C3		
Longsmit Street	A2-A3		
Market Parade	B2-C3		
Mount Street	A4		
Nettleton Road	CI-C2		
Northgate Street	B3		
Oxford Street	C3-C4		
Park Road	BI		
Park Street	B3-B4		
Parliament Street	AI-BI		
Pitt Street	A4-B3		
Priory Road	A4		
Quay Street	A3		
Russell Street	B2-C2		
Skinner Street	B4		
Southgate Street	AI-B2		
St Aldate Street	B3	AA shop	A3
St John's Lane	B3	51 Westgate Street	
St Mary's Street	A4	Gloucester GLI 2NW	

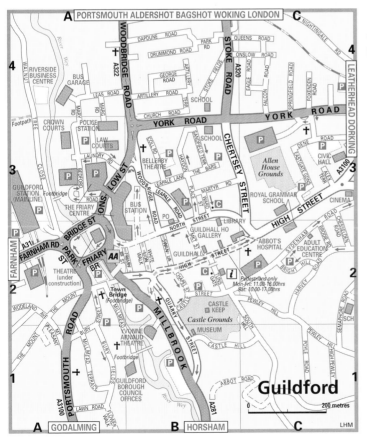

Guildford

Guildford is found on atlas page **25**, grid reference SU**9949**

Abbot Road	BI-CI	Nightingale Road	C4
Alex Terrace	C3	North Street	A2-B3
Artillery Road	B4	Onslow Road	B4-C4
Artillery Terrace	B4	Onslow Street	A3-B4
Bedford Road	A3	Park Road	B4
Bridge Street	A2-A3	Park Street	A2
Bright Hill	C2	Pewley Hill	B2-CI
Brodie Road	C2	Portsmouth Road	AI-A2
Bury Fields	AI	Poyle Road	CI
Bury Street	AI-A2	Quarry Street	A2-BI
Castle Hill	BI-CI	Queens Road	B4-C4
Castle Street	B2-C2	Sandfield Terrace	B3
Chapel Street	B2	Semaphore Road	CI-C2
Chertsey Street	B3-C2	South Hill	B2-CI
Chesselden Road	C2-C3	Springfield Road	C4
Church Road	B3-B4	Stoke Fields	B4
College Road	B3	Stoke Road	B4
Dapdune Road	B4	Swan Lane	B2
Dene Road	C3	Sydenham Road	C2-C3
Drummond Road	B4	The Bars	B3
Eagle Road	C4	The Mount	AI-A2
Eastgate Gardens	C3	Tunsgate	B2
Falcon Road	C4	Walnut Tree Close	A2-A4
Farnham Road	A2	Ward Street	B3
Flower Walk	AI	Whitelion Walk	B2
Foxenden Road	C4	Wodeland Ave	A2
Friary Bridge	A2	Woodbridge Road	B2-B3-B4-A4
Friary Street	A2-B2	York Road	B3-C4
George Road	B4		
Harvey Road	C2		
Haydon Place	B3		
High Pewley	CI		
High Street	B2-C3		
Laundry Road	A3		
Lawn Road	AI		
Leapale Lane	B3		
Leapale Road	B3		
Leas Road	A4		
Margaret Road	A3-A4		
Market Street	B2		
Martyr Road	B3		
Mary Road	A3-A4		
Millbrook	A2-BI		
Millmead	A2-BI	AA shop	A2
Millmead Terrace	AI	22 Friary Street	
Mount Pleasant	AI-A2	Guildford GUI 4EH	

215

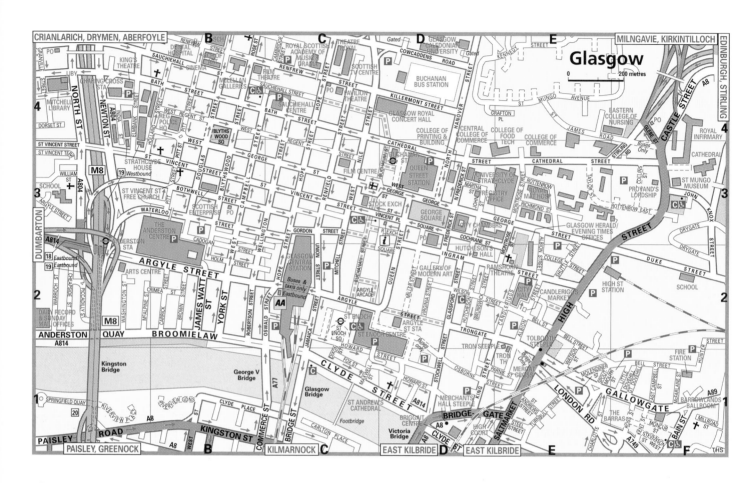

Glasgow

Glasgow is found on atlas page **115**,
grid reference NS**5865**

Albion Street	E1-E3	Fox Street	C1	North Street	A2-A4	Washington Street	A2
Anderston Quay	A2	Gallowgate	E1-F1	Osborne Street	C2-E1	Waterloo Street	A3-C3
Argyle Arcade	C2	George Square	D3	Oswald Street	B1-C2	Watson Street	E1-E2
Argyle Street	A2-D2	George Street	D3-E2	Paisley Road	A1-B1	Wellington Street	B2-C4
Argyle Street	A3	Glassford Street	D2	Parnie Street	D1-E1	West Campbell Street	B2-B4
Bain Street	F1	Gordon Street	C3	Piccadilly Street	A2	West George Street	B3-D3
Barrack Street	F1	Grafton Place	D4-E4	Pitt Street	B3-B4	West Nile Street	C3-C4
Bath Street	A4-C3	Granville Street	A4	Queen Street	D2-D3	West Regent Street	B4-C3
Bell Street	E2-F1	Great Doverhill	F1	Renfield Street	C3-C4	West Street	B1
Blythswood Street	B2-B4	Greendyke Street	E1	Renfrew Street	A4-C4	William Street	A3
Bothwell Street	A3-C3	High Street	E2-F3	Richmond Street	E3	Wilson Street	D2-E2
Bridge Street	C1	Holland Street	A3-B4	Riverview Gardens	B1	York Street	B2
Bridgegate	D1-E1	Holm Street	B2-C2	Riverview Place	A1		
Broomielaw	B2-C1	Hope Street	C2-C4	Robertson Street	B2		
Brown Street	B2	Howard Street	C2-D1	Rose Street	B4		
Brunswick Street	D2	Hunter Street	F1-F2	Ross Street	F1		
Buchanan Street	C2-C3	Hutcheson Street	D2	Rottenrow	E3		
Cadogan Street	B2-C2	India Street	A3-A4	Rottenrow East	E3-F3		
Cambridge Street	C4	Ingram Street	D2-E2	Royal Exchange Square	C1-D2		
Candleriggs	E2	Jamaica Street	C1-C2	Saltmarket	D1-E1		
Carlton Place	C1	James Watt Street	B2	Shuttle Street	E2		
Carrick Street	B2	John Knox Street	F2-F3	South Frederick Street	D2-D3		
Castle Street	F3-F4	John Street	D3	Spoutmouth Street	E1		
Cathedral Street	D3-F3	Kennedy Street	D4-F4	Springfield Quay	A1		
Centre Street	B1	Kent Street	F1	St Andrews Street	E1		
Charlotte Street	E1	Killermont Street	D4	St Enoch Square	C2		
Cheapside Street	A2	King Street	D1-D2	St James Road	E4-F3		
Clyde Place	B1	Kingston Street	B1-C1	St Mungo Avenue	D4-F4		
Clyde Street	C1-D1	Little Doverhill	F1	St Vincent Street	A3-C3		
Cochrane Street	D3-E2	London Road	E1	St Vincent Terrace	A3		
College Street	E2	Martha Street	D3	Steel Street	E1		
Collins Street	F3	Maxwell Street	C1	Stevenson Street West	F1		
Commerce Street	B1	McAlpine Street	A2	Stirling Road	E3-F4		
Cowcaddens Road	C4-D4	McFarlane Street	F1	Stockwell Street	D1-D2		
Crimea Street	A2-B2	Miller Street	D2-D3	Taylor Street	E3		
Dixon Street	C1	Millroad Street	F1	Trongate	D2-E2		
Dorset Street	A4	Mitchell Street	C2-C3	Turnbull Street	E1		
Douglas Street	B2-B4	Molendiner Street	E1	Union Street	C2		
Drygate	F2-F3	Montrose Street	E2-E3	Victoria Bridge	D1		
Duke Street	F2	Newton Street	A2-A4	Vincent Place	C3-D3	AA shop	C2
East Campbell Street	F1	North Frederick Street	D3	Virginia Street	D2	269 Argyle Street	
Elmbank Street	A3-A4	North Hanover Street	D3-D4	Warroch Street	A2	Glasgow G2 8DW	

216

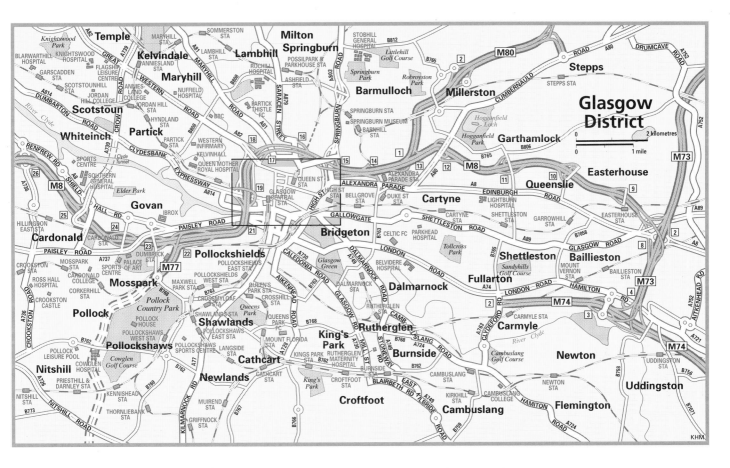

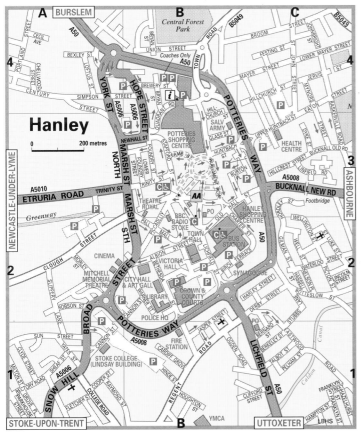

Hanley

Hanley is found on atlas page **72**,
grid reference SJ**8847**

Street	Grid	Street	Grid	Street	Grid
Albion Street	B2	Hillcrest Street	C3	Stafford Street	B3
Baskerville Road	C3-C4	Hinde Street	B1	Stubbs Lane	C1-C2
Berkeley Street	C1	Hope Street	B3-B4	Sun Street	A1
Bernard Street	C1-C2	Hordley Street	C3	Talbot Street	C1
Bethedsa Street	B2	Houghton Street	B1	Town Road	B4
Bexley Street	A4	Huntbach Street	B3-C3	Trinity Street	A3-B3
Birch Terrace	B2-C2	Jasper Street	B1-B2	Union Street	B4
Botteslow Street	C2	Jervis Street	C4	Upper Huntbach Street	C3-C4
Brewery Street	B4	Johnbright Street	C4	Warner Street	B2
Broad Street	A1-B2	Lamb Street	B3	Waterloo Street	C2
Broom Street	B4-C4	Lichfield Street	B2-C1	Well Street	C2
Bryan Street	B4	Lincoln Street	C2	Wellington Street	C2-C3
Bucknall New Road	C3	Linfield Road	C3	Yates Street	A1
Bucknall Old Road	C3	Loftus Street	A4	York Street	A3-A4
Bucknall Road	C3	Lower Foundry Street	B3		
Burton Place	B3-C3	Lower Mayer Street	C4		
Cannon Street	A1-B2	Marsh Street North	A3-B3		
Cardiff Grove	B1	Marsh Street South	B2-B3		
Cecil Avenue	A4	Mayer Street	B4-C4		
Century Street	A3-A4	Milton Street	A1		
Charter Street	B3-C2	Morley Street	A2		
Chellwood Street	A4	Mynors Street	C3-C4		
Clifford Street	C1	Nelson Place	C2		
Clough Street	A2-B3	Newhall Street	A3-B3		
Clyde Street	A1	Ogden Street	B1-C1		
College Street	A1	Old Hall Street	B2-C3		
Cooper Street	A1	Pall Mall	B2-B3		
Derby Street	C2	Parkhouse Street	A1		
Dyke Street	C3	Parliament Row	B3		
Eastwood Road	C1	Pelham Street	C1		
Eaton Street	C4	Piccadilly	B2-B3		
Etruria Road	A3	Picton Street	C2		
Festing Street	C4	Portland Street	A4		
Fletcher Street	A1	Potteris Way	A2-A4		
Foundry Street	B3	Quadrant Road	B3-B4		
Franklyn Street	C1	Raymond Street	A1-B1		
Gilman Street	C2	Rectory Road	A1		
Glass Street	B3	Regent Street	B1-C2		
Grove Place	A1	Robson Street	A2		
Hampton Street	C1	Sheaf Street	A1		
Harley Street	C2	Simpson Street	A4-B4		
Hassell Street	C2	Slippery Lane	A1-A2		
Hazelhurst Street	C1	Snow Hill	A1	AA shop	B3
Hillchurch Street	B3-B4	St John Street	C4	32-38 Stafford Street	
Hillchurch Street	C4	St Luke Street	C2	Hanley ST1 1JP	

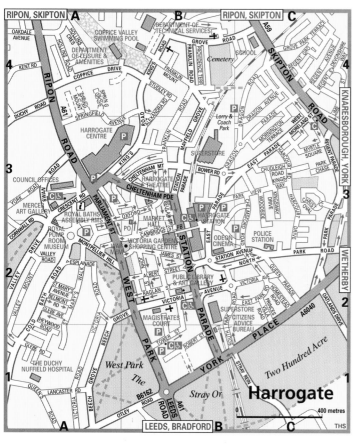

Harrogate

Harrogate is found on atlas page **82**,
grid reference SE**3054**

Albert Street	B2	Montpellier Hill	A2
Alexandra Road	B3-B4	Mornington Terrace	C3-C4
Beech Grove	A1-B2	Myrtle Square	C3
Belmont Road	A1	North Park Road	B2-C2
Beulah Street	B3	Oakdale Avenue	A4
Bower Road	B3	Oatlands Drive	C1-C2
Cambridge Street	B2	Otley Road	A1-B1
Chelmsford Road	C3-C4	Oxford Street	A3-B3
Cheltenham Mount	B3	Park Chase	C3
Cheltenham Parade	A3-B3	Park Parade	C2-C3
Christchurch Oval	C3	Park View Way	B3-C3
Chudleigh Road	C3	Parliament Street	A2-A3
Cold Bath Road	A1-A2	Princes Villa Road	C2
Coppice Drive	A4	Providence Terrace	B4
Cornwall Road	A2-A3	Queen Parade	C2
Crescent Road	A3	Queen's Road	A1
Devonshire Way	C4	Raglan Street	B2
Dragon Avenue	C3-C4	Regent Avenue	C4
Dragon Parade	C3-C4	Regent Grove	C4
Dragon Road	B3-C4	Regent Parade	C3
Duchy Road	A3-A4	Regent Street	C4
East Parade	B2-C3	Ripon Road	A3-A4
East Park Road	B2-C2	Robert Street	B1
Esplanade	A2	Skipton Road	C3-C4
Franklin Mount	B4	South Park Road	B1-B2
Franklin Road	B3-B4	Spring Grove	A4
Glebe Avenue	A2	Spring Mount	A4
Glebe Road	A1	Springfield Avenue	A3-B4
Grove Park Terrace	C4	St Mary's Avenue	A2
Grove Road	B4-C4	Station Avenue	B2-C2
Harcourt Drive	C2-C3	Station Parade	B1-B2-B3
Harcourt Road	C3	Stray Rein	B1-C1
Heywood Road	A1-A2	St Mary's Walk	A1-A2
Hollins Crescent	A4	Studley Road	B4
Hollins Road	A4	Swan Road	A3
Homestead Road	C2	Tower Street	B1-B2
James Street	B2	Valley Drive	A2
John Street	B2	Valley Mount	A1-A2
Kent Road	A4	Valley Road	A2
King's Road	A3-B4	Victoria Avenue	B2-C2
Kings Way	C3	Victoria Road	A1-A2
Kingsway Drive	C3	West Park	A2-B1
Lancaster Road	A1	Westmoreland Street	C3-C4
Leeds Road	B1	Woodside	C2-C3
Lime Street	C4	York Place	B1-C2
Mayfield Grove	B3-B4	York Road	A3

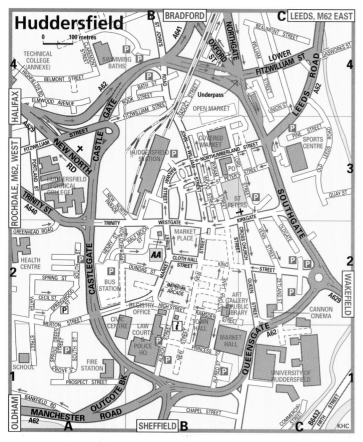

Huddersfield

Huddersfield is found on atlas page **82**,
grid reference SE**1416**

Albion Street	B1-B2	Pine Street	C3
Alfred Street	B1	Portland Street	A3
Bankfield Road	A1	Princess Street	B1
Bath Street	B4	Prospect Street	A1
Beaumont Street	C4	Quay Street	C3
Belmont Street	A4	Queen Street	C2
Byram Street	B3	Queensgate	B1-C2
Castlegate	B1-B4	Railway Street	B3
Cecil Street	A2	Ramsden Street	B2-C2
Chapel Street	B1	Rook Street	A4-B4
Claremont Street	A4	South Street	A1-A2
Cloth Hall Street	B2	Southgate	B4-C2
Commercial Street	C1	Spring Green Street	A1
Cross Church Street	C2	Spring Street	A2
Dundas Street	B2	Springwood Street	A2
Elmwood Avenue	A4	St John's Road	B4
Firth Street	C1	St Peter's Street	B3-C3
Fitzwilliam Street	A3-B4	Trinity Street	A2-A3
Gasworks Street	C4	Trinity Westgate	A2-B2
Greenhead Road	A2	Union Street	C4
Grove Street	A1	Upperhead Row	A2
Half Moon Street	B2	Venn Street	C2-C3
Henry Street	A2	Viaduct Street	B4
High Street	B2	Victoria Lane	B1-B2
Highfields Road	A4	Water Street	A1-A2
Imperial Arcade	B2	William Street	C4
John William Street	B3-B4	Wood Street	B3
King Street	B2-C2	Zetland Street	C2
Kirkgate	B2-C3		
Leeds Road	C3-C4		
Lord Street	B3-C3		
Lower Fitzwilliam Street	C4		
Manchester Road	A1-B1		
Market Street	A2-B2		
Merton Street	B1		
New North Parade	A3-B3		
New North Road	A3-A4		
New Street	B1-B2		
Northgate	B4-C4		
Northumberland Street	B3-C3		
Old Leeds Road	C3-C4		
Oldgate	C2-C3	AA shop	B2
Outcote Bridge	A1-B1	7 Cherry Tree Centre	
Oxford Street	B4	Market Street	
Park Drive South	A3	Huddersfield HD1 2ET	

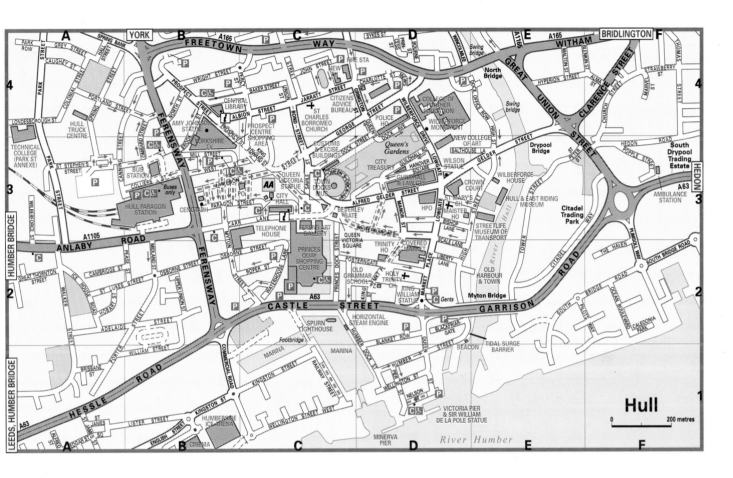

Hull

Hull is found on atlas page **85**,
grid reference TA**0829**

AA shop   C3
28 Paragon Street
Hull HU1 3NE

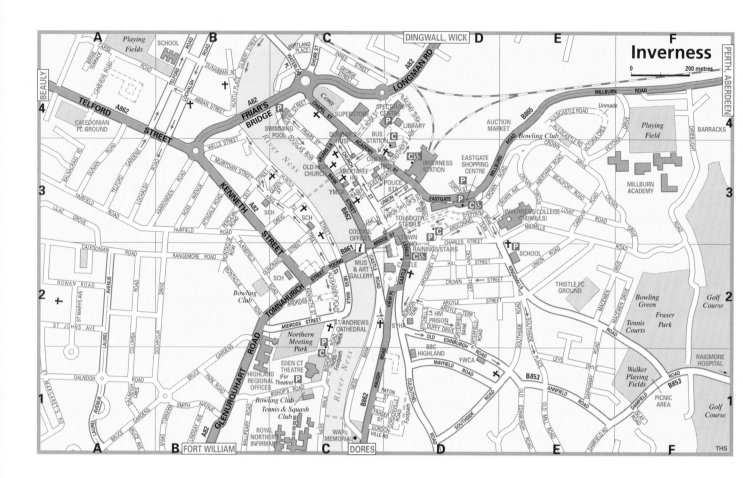

Inverness

Inverness is found on atlas page **140**,
grid reference NH**6645**

Abban Street	B4	Dalneigh Road	A1-B1	Longman Road	C4-D4	Victoria Crescent	E3-F4
Abertarff Road	E3	Damfield Road	E1-F1	Lovat Road	E3-F3	Victoria Drive	E3-F4
Academy Street	C4-D3	Darnaway Road	E1-E2	Macewen Drive	E2-F2	View Place	D2
Alexander Place	C2	Denny Street	D2	Maxwell Drive	B1	Waterloo Place	C4
Annfield Road	E1-F1	Diriebught Road	F1-F4	Mayfield Road	D1	Wells Street	B3-B4
Ardconnel Street	D2	Dochfour Drive	A1-B3	Midmills Road	E3-F2	Young Street	C2
Ardconnel Terrace	D3	Douglas Row	C3-C4	Millburn Road	D3-F4		
Ardross Place	C2	Duffy Drive	D2	Mitchell's Lane	D2		
Ardross Street	B2-C2	Dunabban Road	B4	Montague Row	B2-B3		
Argyle Street	D2-E2	Dunain Road	A3-A4	Muirtown Street	B3		
Argyle Terrace	D2	Duncraig Street	B2-C3	Ness Bank	C1-C2		
Attadale Road	B3	Eastgate	D3	Ness Walk	C1-C2		
Auldcastle Road	E3-F4	Eriskay Road	F1	Old Edinburgh Road	D2-E1		
Ballifeary Road	B1	Fairfield Road	A3-B3	Old Mill Road	E1		
Balnacraig Road	A3-A4	Forth Street	D3	Park Road	B1		
Bank Lane	C3	Fraser Street	C1-D1	Paton Street	C1-D1		
Bank Street	C3	Fraser Street	C3	Perceval Road	B3		
Baron Taylor's Street	D3	Friar's Bridge	B4-C4	Planefield Road	B3-C2		
Beaufort Road	E3	Friars Lane	C3-C4	Porterfield Bank	D2		
Birnie Terrace	A4	Friars Street	C3-C4	Portland Place	C4		
Bishop's Road	B1-C2	George Street	C4	Queen Street	B3-C3		
Bordon Terrace	D2	Gilbert Street	B4	Queensgate	C3-D3		
Bridge Street	C2-D3	Glebe Street	C4	Railway Terrace	D4		
Bruce Avenue	A1	Glenurquhart Road	B1-B2	Rangemore Road	B2		
Bruce Gardens	A1-B2	Gordonville Road	C1-D1	Rose Street	C4		
Caledonian Road	A3-B2	Greig Street	B3-C3	Ross Avenue	B3		
Cameron Road	A4	Harrowden Road	A3-B3	Rowan Road	A2		
Carse Road	A4-B4	Haugh Road	C1-D2	Shore Street	C4		
Castle Road	C2	Hill Street	D2-E2	Smith Avenue	B1		
Castle Street	D2-D3	Huntly Place	B4	Southside Place	E1-D2		
Cawdor Road	E3	Huntly Street	B4-C2	Southside Road	D1-E2		
Celt Street	B3	Inglis Street	D3	St Johns Avenue	A2		
Chapel Street	C4	Innes Street	C4-D4	St Margaret's Road	A1-A2		
Charles Street	D3	Islay Road	F1	St Marys Avenue	A2		
Church Street	C3-D3	Kenneth Street	B3-C2	Stephens Brae	D3		
Columba Road	A1-A2	King Street	B3-C2	Strother's Lane	D3-D4		
Crown Avenue	D3-E3	Kingsmills Road	D3-F1	Telford Gardens	A3-A4		
Crown Circus	E3	Laurel Avenue	A1-A2	Telford Road	A4-B4		
Crown Road	D3-F2	Leys Drive	E1-F1	Telford Street	A4-B3		
Crown Street	D2-E2	Lilac Grove	A3	Tomnahurich Street	B2-C2		
Culduthel Road	D1-D2	Lindsay Avenue	B1	Union Road	E2-E3		
Dalneigh Crescent	A1	Lochalsh Road	A3-B4	Union Street	C3-D3		

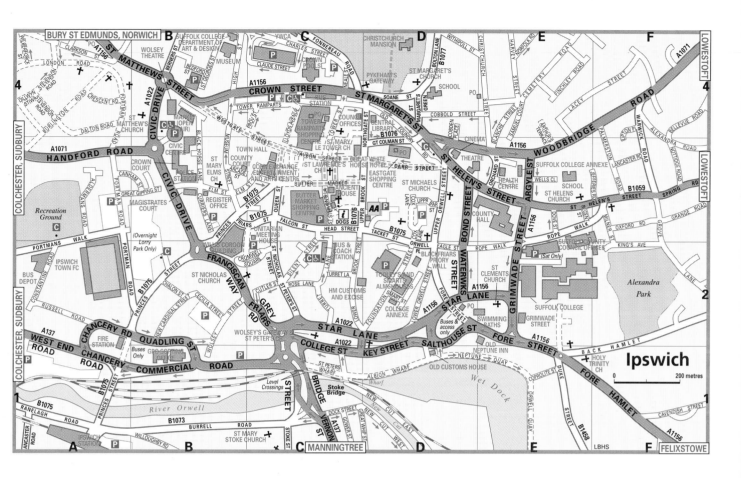

Ipswich

Ipswich is found on atlas page **54**,
grid reference TM1644

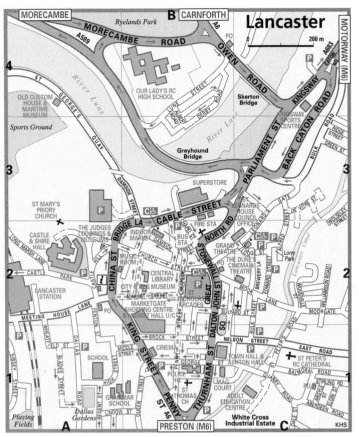

Lancaster

Lancaster is found on atlas page **87**, grid reference SD**4761**

Aberdeen Road	C1	Moorgate	C2
Albert Road	B3-B4	Morecambe Road	A4-B4
Alfred Street	C2-C3	Nelson Street	B1-C1
Argyle Street	C1	North Road	B2-B3
Back Caton Road	C3-C4	Owen Road	B4-C4
Balmoral Road	C1	Parliament Street	C3-C4
Blades Street	A1	Penny Street	B1-B2
Brewery Lane	C2	Quarry Road	C1
Bridge Lane	A2-B2	Queen Street	B1
Brock Street	B2	Regent Street	A1
Bulk Road	C3-C4	Ridge Street	C3
Bulk Street	C1-C2	Sibsey Street	A1
Cable Street	B2-B3	St George's Quay	A3-A4
Castle Hill	A2	St Leonard's Gate	B2-C3
Castle Park	A2	St Peter's Road	C1-C2
Caton Road	C4	Stirling Road	C1
Chapel Street	B2	Stonewall	B2
Cheapside	B2	Sulyard Street	B2-C2
China Street	A2	Thurnham Street	B1
Church Street	B2	Wheatfield Street	A1-A2
Dale Street	C1	Williamson Road	C2
Dallas Road	A1-A2	Wolseley Street	C2-C3
Dalton Square	B1-B2	Woodville Street	C2
Damside Street	A3-B3-B2		
De Vitre Street	C3		
Derby Road	B3-B4		
East Road	C1		
Edward Street	C2		
Elgin Street	C1		
Fenton Street	A1-A2		
George Street	B1-C1		
Great John Street	B2		
Green Street	C3		
High Street	A1		
King Street	A1-A2		
Kingsway	C4		
Lindow Street	A1-A2		
Lodge Street	C2		
Long Marsh Lane	A2		
Lune Street	B3-B4		
Main Way	C4		
Market Street	B2		
Meeting House Lane	A2		
Middle Street	A1-B1		
Moor Lane	B2-C2		

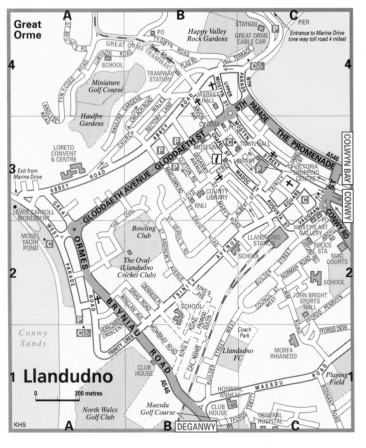

Llandudno

Llandudno is found on atlas page **69**, grid reference SH**7882**

Abbey Road	A3-C4	Rectory Lane	B3-B4
Albert Street	B2-C3	South Parade	B4-C3
Anglesey Road	A3-A4	St Andrew's Avenue	B2-B3
Argyll Road	C2	St Beuno's Road	A4
Arvon Avenue	B3-B4	St David's Road	B2-B3
Augusta Street	C2-C3	St Mary's Road	B3-C2
Bodnant Road	C1	St Seirol's Road	B2-B3
Bryniau Road	A2-B1	The Oval	A2-B3
Builder Street	C2	The Parade	C3
Builder Street West	B1-C2	Trinity Avenue	B1-C3
Cae Mawr	B1	Trinity Crescent	A1-B1
Chapel Street	B3	Trinity Square	C3
Church Walks	A3-B4	Ty-Gwyn Road	B4
Clifton Road	B3	Tyn-y-Coed Road	A4
Clonnel Street	C3	Upper Mostyn Street	B4
Conwy Road	C2-C3	Vaughan Street	C2-C3
Council Street West	C2	West Parade	A2-A3
Cwlach Road	B3-B4	Winllan Avenue	A2-B2
Cwm Road	C1-C2		
Deganwy Avenue	B3		
Denness Place	B2		
Dinas Road	B2		
Ffordd Dulyn	B1-B2		
Ffordd Dewi	C1		
Ffordd Penrhyn	C1-C2		
Ffordd Ysbyty	B1-C1		
Gloddaeth Avenue	A2-B3		
Gloddaeth Street	B3		
Great Ormes Road	A1-A3		
Haulfre Gardens	A3-B4		
Herkomer Crescent	A1-A2		
Hill Terrace	B4-C4		
King's Avenue	B2		
King's Road	B1-B2		
Lloyd Street	B3-C3		
Llwynon Road	A4-B4		
Madoc Street	B3-C3		
Maelgwn Road	B3		
Maesdu Road	B1-C1		
Mostyn Street	B3-C3		
Mowbray Road	B1		
Norman Road	C2		
North Parade	C4		
Oxford Road	C2		
Plas Road	B4		

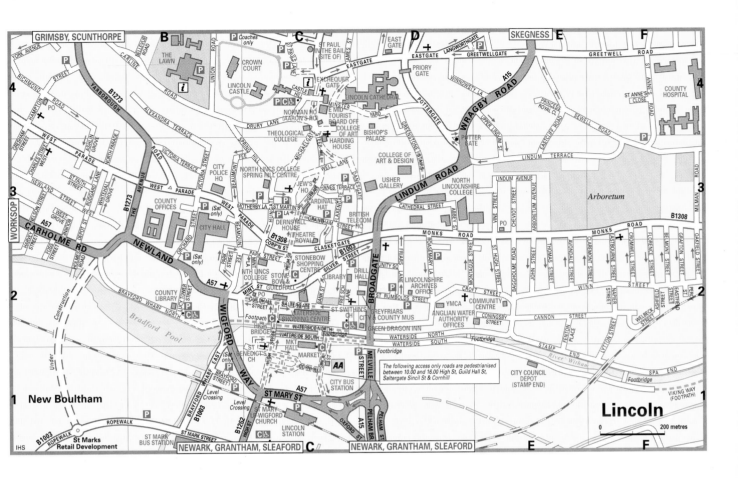

Lincoln

Lincoln is found on atlas page **76**,
grid reference SK**9771**

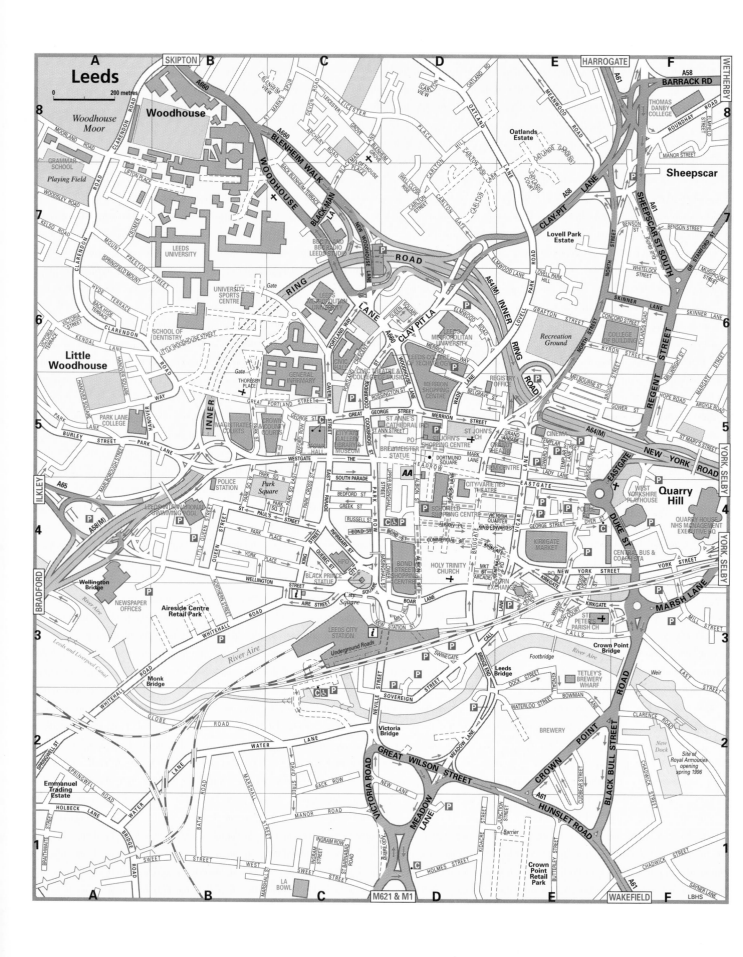

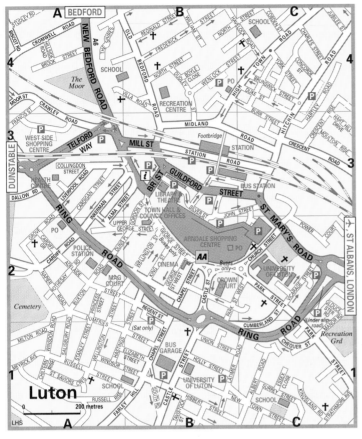

Luton

Luton is found on atlas page **38**,
grid reference TL**0921**

Adelaide Street	A2-B2	Hartley Road	C3-C4	Tavistock Street	B1
Albert Road	B1-C1	Hastings Street	A1-B2	Telford Way	A3
Alma Street	A2-B3	Havelock Road	B4-C4	The Shires	A4
Biscot Road	A4	Hibbert Street	B1	Union Street	B1
Boyle Close	B4	High Town Road	B3-C4	Upper George Street	A2-B2
Bridge Street	B3	Hillside Road	A4	Vicarage Street	C2
Brook Street	A4	Hitchin Road	C3-C4	Villa Road	A4-B4
Brunswick Street	C4	Holly Street	B1	Wellington Street	A1-B2
Burr Street	C3-C4	Inkerman Street	A2-A3	Wenlock Street	B4-C4
Buxton Road	A2	John Street	B2-C3	William Street	B4
Cardiff Grove	A2	Jubilee Street	C4	Windsor Street	A1-B1
Cardiff Road	A2	King Street	B2	Winsdon Road	A1-A2
Cardigan Street	A3	Kingsland Road	C1	York Street	C4
Castle Street	B1-B2	Latimer Road	B1-C1		
Chapel Street	B1-B2	Liverpool Road	A3		
Charles Street	C4	Manor Road	C1-C2		
Chequer Street	C1	Meyrick Avenue	A2		
Chiltern Rise	A1	Midland Road	D3-C3		
Church Street	B2-C2	Mill Street	B3		
Cobden Street	C4	Milton Road	A1		
Collingdon Street	A3	Moor Street	A4		
Concorde Street	C4	Moulton Rise	C3		
Crawley Green Road	C2	Napier Road	A2		
Crawley Road	A3-A4	New Bedford Street	A4-B3		
Crescent Rise	C3-C4	New Town Street	B1-C1		
Crescent Road	C3	North Street	B4-C4		
Cromwell Road	A4	Old Bedford Road	A4-B3		
Cumberland Street	C1-C2	Park Street	C1-C2		
Dallow Road	A3	Park Street West	B2-C2		
Dudley Street	B3-B4	Power Court	C2		
Duke Street	C3-C4	Princess Street	A2		
Dumfries Street	A2-B1	Regent Street	B1-B2		
Duns Place	A2-B2	Reginald Street	B4		
Dunstable Road	A4-C2	Rothesay Road	A2		
Elizabeth Street	A1-B1	Russell Rise	A1		
Essex Close	C1	Russell Street	A1-B1		
Farley Hill	A1-B1	Salisbury Road	A1-A2		
Francis Street	A3-A4	Silver Street	B3		
Frederick Street	B4	South Road	B1		
George Street	B2	St Mary's Road	C2-C3		
George Street West	B2	St Saviours Crescent	A1		
Gloucester Road	C2	Stanley Street	A1-A2		
Gordon Street	B2-B3	Station Road	B3-C3		
Grove Road	A2-A3	Strathmore Avenue	C1	AA shop	B2
Guildford Street	B3-C3	Studley Road	A4	45 George Street	
Hart Hill Drive	C3	Surrey Street	C1	Luton LU1 2AQ	

Leeds

Leeds is found on atlas page **82**,
grid reference SE**2932**

Aire Street	C3	Clay Pit Lane	D6-E7	Infirmary Street	C4	Mushroom Street	F6-F7	St Mary's Street	F5
Albion Place	D4	Commercial Street	D4	Ingram Row	C1	Neville Street	C2-D3	St Paul's Street	B4-C4
Albion Street	D3-D5	Concord Street	E6-F6	Ingram Street	C1	New Lane	C2-D1	Sweet Street	C1
Archery Road	C8	Cookridge Street	C5-D6	Inner Ring Road	B5-E5	New Station Street	C3-D3	Sweet Street West	A1-B1
Argyle Road	F5	Cromer Terrace	A7-B7	Junction Street	E1	New Woodhouse Lane	C6-C7	Swinegate	D3
Back Blenheim Terrace	C7-C8	Cross York Street	E3-E4	Kelso Road	A7	New York Road	E5-F5	Templar Lane	E5
Back Row	C1-C2	Crown Point Road	E2-F3	Kendal Lane	A6	New York Street	E4-F4	Templar Street	E5
Barrack Road	F8	Crown Street	E3	Kendal Street	E2-E3	North Street	E5-E7	The Calls	E3-F3
Bath Road	B1-B2	Cudbear Street	E1-E2	Kidacre Street	D1	Northern Street	B3-B4	The Headrow	C5-D4
Bedford Street	C4	David Street	C1-C2	King Edward Street	D4-E4	Oatland Court	E7	Thoresby Place	B5-B6
Belgrave Street	D4-E4	Devon Road	C8	King Street	C4	Oatland Lane	D8-E7	Upper Basinghall Street	D4-D5
Benson Street	F7	Dewsbury Road	D1	Kirkgate	D4-F3	Oatland Road	D8	Vicar Lane	E4-E5
Black Bull Street	E1-F2	Dock Street	E3	Lady Lane	E4-E5	Oatlands Gardens	E8	Victoria Quarter	D4-E4
Black Hyde Terrace	A6	Dortmund Square	D5	Lands Lane	D4	Oxford Row	C5	Victoria Road	C1-C2
Blackman Lane	C7-C8	Duke Street	E4-F3	Leicester Grove	C8	Park Cross Street	C4-C5	Victoria Street	A6
Blenheim Grove	C8-D8	Dyer Street	E4	Leicester Place	C8-D8	Park Lane	A5-B5	Victoria Terrace	A6
Blenheim View	B8-C8	East Parade	C4-C5	Leylands Road	F6	Park Place	B4-C4	Wade Lane	D5
Blenheim Walk	B8-D7	East Street	F2-F3	Lifton Place	A7-B7	Park Road	C4-C5	Water Lane	A1-C2
Boar Lane	D3-E4	Eastgate	E4-F5	Little Queen Street	B4	Park Square East	C4-C5	Waterloo Street	E2
Bond Street	C4-D4	Edward Street	E5	Little Woodhouse Street	B6	Park Square North	B5-C4	Well Close Rise	D7-D8
Bowman Street	E2	Elmfield Terrace	C8	Lofthouse Place	C7	Park Square South	C4	Wellington Street	A4-C3
Braithwaite Street	A1	Elmwood Lane	D7-E6	Lovell Park Hill	E6	Park Square West	B4-B5	Westgate	B5-C5
Bridge End	D3	Elmwood Road	D6	Lovell Park Road	D6-E7	Park Street	B5	Wharf Street	E3
Bridge Road	A1	George Street	C5	Lower Basinghall Street	D3-D4	Portland Crescent	C5-C6	Whitehall Road	A2-C3
Bridge Street	E4-E5-F6	George Street	E4	Manor Road	C1	Portland Way	C6	Whitelock Street	F6-F7
Briggate	D3-D5	Globe Road	A2-C2	Manor Street	F8	Quebec Street	C4	Woodhouse Lane	B8-D5
Burley Street	A5	Gower Street	E5-F5	Margate Street	F5-F6	Queen Square	D6	Woodsley Road	A7
Butterley Street	E1	Grafton Street	E6	Mark Lane	D5-E5	Queen Street	B4	York Place	B4-C4
Byron Street	E6-F6	Grand Arcade	E5	Market Street Arcade	D4	Regent Street	F5-F6	York Street	F4
Call Lane	D3-E3	Great George Street	C5-D5	Marlborough Street	A4-A5	Rossington Street	C5-D5		
Carlton Carr	D7-E8	Great Portland Street	B5-C5	Marsh Lane	F3-F4	Rossville Road	F7		
Carlton Gate	D7	Great Stamford Street	F6-F7	Marshall Street	B1-B2	Roundhay Road	F8		
Carlton Hill	D7-D8	Great Wilson Street	D2	Meadow Lane	D1-D2	Russell Street	C4		
Carlton Rise	D7-D8	Greek Street	C4	Meanwood Road	E7-E8	Sheepscar Street South	F6-F8		
Carlton Street	D7	Hanover Square	A5-A6	Melbourne Street	E5	Skinner Lane	E6-F6		
Carlton View	D8	Hanover Way	A5-B5	Merrion Street	D5-E5	South Parade	C4		
Caverley Street	B6-C5	High Court	E3	Merrion Way	D6	Sovereign Street	C2-D3		
Central Road	D3-E4	Holbeck Lane	A1	Mill Hill	D3	Springfield Mount	A7-B6		
Chadwick Street	F1-F2	Holmes Street	D1	Mill Street	F3-F4	Springwell Road	A1-A2		
City Square	C3-C4	Hope Road	F5	Millwright Street	F5-F6	St Ann Street	C5-D5	AA shop	B2
Clarence Road	F2	Hunslet Road	E1-F1	Moorland Road	A8-B7	St Barnabas Road	C1	95 The Headrow	
Clarendon Road	B5-B8	Hyde Terrace	A6	Mount Preston Street	A7-B6	St Mark's Spur	B8-C8	Leeds LS1 6LU	

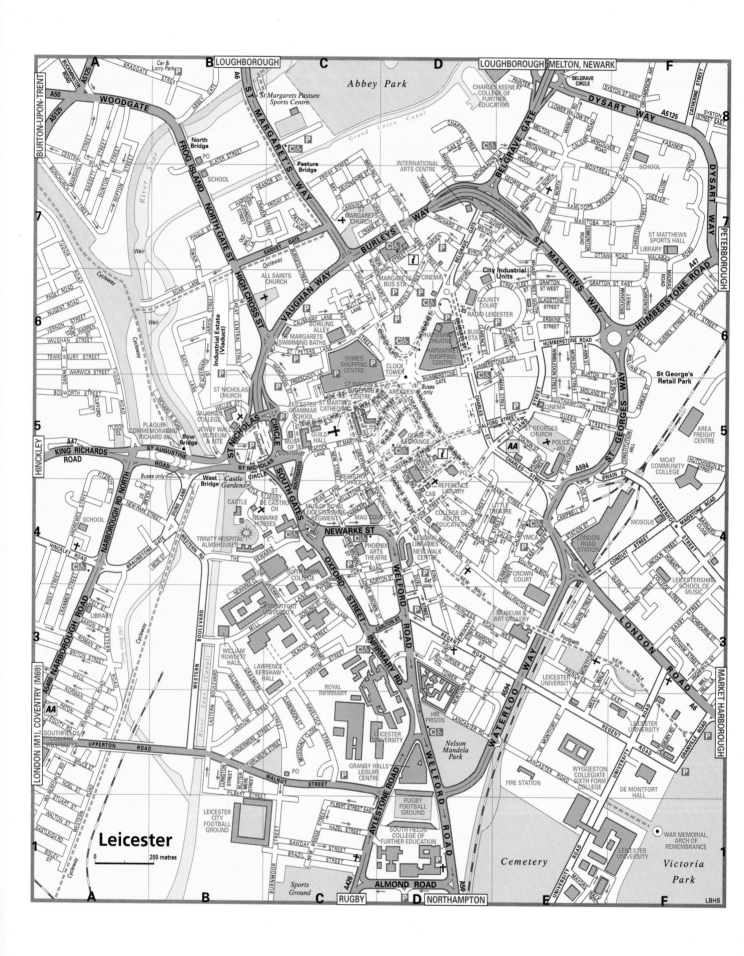

Leicester

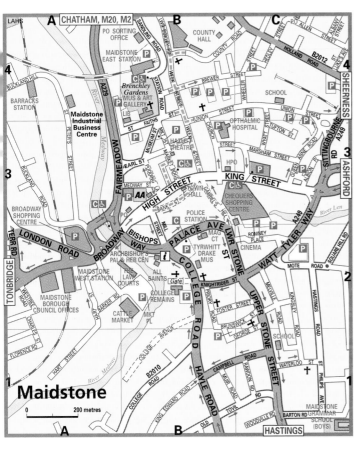

Maidstone

Maidstone

Maidstone is found on atlas page **28**, grid reference TQ**7555**

Albany Street	C4	Knightrider Street	B2-C2	Week Street	B3-B4
Albion Place	C3	London Road	A2-A3	Westree Road	A2
Allen Street	C4	Lower Boxley Road	B4	Wheeler Street	C4
Bank Street	B3	Market Buildings	B3	Woodville Road	C1
Barker Road	A2	Market Street	B3	Wyatt Street	C3-C4
Barker Street	A2	Marsham Street	C3		
Barton Road	C1	Medway Street	B3		
Bishops Way	B2	Melville Road	C1-C2		
Brewer Street	B4-C4	Mill Street	B2-B3		
Broadway	A2-B2	Mote Road	C2		
Brunswick Street	B2-C2	Muir Road	B1-C1		
Buckland Hill	A4	Museum Street	B3		
Buckland Road	A3	Old Tovil Road	B1-C1		
Campbell Road	B1-C1	Palace Avenue	B2-B3		
Charles Street	A1-A2	Priory Road	B2		
Church Street	B3-C3	Pudding Lane	B3		
College Avenue	B1-B2	Queen Anne Road	C3		
College Road	B1-B2	Rawdon Road	C1		
County Road	B4-C4	Romney Place	C2		
Earl Street	B3	Sandling Road	B4		
Fairmeadow	A3-A4	Sittingbourne Road	C3-C4		
Florence Road	A1	Square Hill Road	C2		
Foster Street	B2-C2	St Faiths Street	B3-B4		
Gabriel's Hill	B3	St Luke's Avenue	C4		
George Street	B1-C2	St Peter's Street	A3-A4		
Hart Street	A1-A2	St Philips Avenue	C1		
Hastings Road	C1-C2	Station Road	B4		
Hayle Road	B1	Terrace Road	A2		
Hedley Street	C4	Tonbridge Road	A2		
High Street	B3	Tufton Street	C3		
Holland Road	C4	Union Street	B3-C4		
Kingsley Road	C1-C2	Upper Stone Street	C1-C2	AA shop	B3
King Edward Road	B1	Waterloo Street	C1	26-27 High Street	
King Street	B3-B4	Watt Tyler Way	C2-C3	Maidstone ME14 1JF	

Leicester

Leicester is found on atlas page **62**, grid reference SK**5804**

Abbey Gate	B8	Calais Street	E4	Dunkirk Street	E4
Abbey Street	D7	Calgary Road	E8	Duns Lane	B4-B5
Albion Street	D4	Campbell Street	E4	Dunton Street	A7-A8
All Saints Road	B7	Cank Street	C5-D5	Dysart Way	F7-F8-E8
Almond Road	C1-D1	Canning Place	C7	East Bond Street	C6-D6
Andrewes Street	A4-A5	Carlton Street	C3-D3	East Street	E4
Archdeacon Lane	D7-D8-E8	Castle Street	B4-C4	Eastern Boulevard	B2-B3
Aylestone Road	C1-D2	Catherine Street	F8	Eastleigh Road	A1
Barnard Close	F4	Causeway Lane	C6	Edmonton Road	E7
Baron Street	E5-E6	Celt Street	A3	Equity Road	A2
Bassett Street	A7-A8	Central Road	A7-A8	Erskine Street	E6
Bath Lane	B5-B6	Chancery Street	C4	Filbert Street	B1-C1-B2-C2
Bay Street	C7	Charles Street	E4-D6-D5-E5	Filbert Street East	C1
Bede Street	A4-B4	Charlton Street	C3-D3	Fitzroy Street	A4-A5
Bedford Street North	E7	Charter Street	D8	Fleet Street	E6
Bedford Street South	D7-E7	Chatham Street	D4-D5	Fosse Road	A8
Belgrave Circle	E8	Cheapside	D5	Fox Street	E4
Belgrave Gate	D7-D8-E8	Chester Close	F7	Freeschool Lane	C5-C6
Bell Lane	F6	Christow Street	F7	Friar Lane	C5-C4
Belvoir Street	D4	Church Gate	C7-C6-D6	Friday Street	B7-C7-C8
Bisley Street	A1	Church Street	E5	Frog Island	B7-B8
Blackfriars Street	B5-B6	Clarence Street	D6	Gallowtree Gate	D5
Bonchurch Street	A7-A8	Clarendon Street	C2	Garden Street	D7
Bonners Lane	C4	Clifford Street	A5	Gas Street	D8
Bosworth Street	A5	Clyde Street	E6	Gateway Street	B4-C4-C3
Bowling Green Street	D5-D4	College Street	F4-F5	Gaul Street	A3-A2
Bradgate Street	A8-B8	Colton Street	E5	George Street	E7
Braunstone Gate	A4-B4	Conduit Street	E4-F4	Gladstone Street	E6
Brazil Street	C1	Coniston Street	B2	Glebe Street	F3-F4
Britannia Street	E8	Constitution Hill	F5	Gosling Street	C3
Briton Street	A3	Crafton Street	E6-F6	Gotham Street	F3
Brougham Street	F6	Crane Street	C7	Gower Street	E7-D7
Bruce Street	A2	Cranmer Street	A3-A4	Grafton Place	C7-D7
Brunswick Street	F6-F7	Craven Street	B7-C7	Grafton Street East	E6-F6
Burgess Street	C6-C7	Crescent Street	D3	Grafton Street West	E7
Burleys Way	C7-D7	Dannet Street	A5-A6	Graham Street	F6
Burnmoor Street	C1	Deacon Street	C3	Granby Street	D4-D5-E4
Burton Street	E6	De Montfort Street	E2-E3-F3	Grange Lane	C3
Butt Close Lane	C6	Devonshire Street	C7	Grange Street	F2-F3
Buttermere Street	B2	Dover Street	D4-E4	Granville Road	F2-F3
Byron Street	D6-D7-E6-E7	Dryden Street	D7-E7	Grasmere Street	B2-B3-C2-C1
Calais Hill	E4	Duke Street	D4-D3	Gravel Street	C6-D7
				Great Central Street	B6

Greyfriars	C5	Newarke Street	C4-D4	Southgates	C4-C5
Guildhall Lane	C5	Newbridge Street	C1	Sparkenhoe Street	F4-F5
Halford Street	D5-E5	New Park Street	A4-B4	Station Street	E4
Harding Street	B7	New Road	C7-D7	Stuart Street	A2
Havelock Street	C2-C3	New Street	C4-C5	Sussex Street	F6
Haymarket	D6	Newtown Street	D2-D3	Swain Street	E5-F5
Hazel Street	C1	New Walk	D4-E4-E3-F3	Swan Street	B6-B7
Heanor Street	B7-C7	Nicholas Street	E5-F5	Syston Street East	F8
High Cross Street	C5-B6-C6	Noel Street	A1-A2	Syston Street West	E8-F8
Highfield Street	F3	Northgate Street	B7	The Newarke	B4-C4
High Street	C5-D5	Norman Street	A2-A3	Taylor Road	F7-F8
Hinckley Road	A4	Norton Street	C4-D4	Tewkesbury Street	A6
Hobart Street	F4	Nugent Street	A6	The Gateway	B4-C3
Hoby Street	A6	Old Mill Lane	B7	Thames Street	D7
Horsefair Street	C5-D5	Orchardson Avenue	F8	Thirlemere Street	B2-C3
Hotel Street	C5	Orchard Street	D7	Tichbourne Street	F3
Humberstone Gate	D5-D6-E6	Ottawa Road	E7-F7	Tower Street	D2-D3
Humberstone Road	F6-E6	Oxford Street	C3-C4	Tudor Close	A5
Hutchinson Street	F5	Paget Road	A7	Tudor Road	A5-A6-A7
Infirmary Road	C3-C2-D3	Painter Street	E8	Turner Street	D3
Jarrom Street	B2-C2-C3	Paton Street	A2	Ullswater Street	B3-B2
Jarvis Street	B6	Peacock Lane	C5	University Road	E1-E2-F2-F3
Johnson Street	B7	Pingle Street	B7	Upper Brown Street	C4
Kamloops Crescent	E7-F7	Pocklingtons Walk	C4-D4	Upper King Street	D3
Kashmir Road	F8-F7	Prebend Street	F3-F4	Upperton Road	A2-B2
Kent Street	F6	Princess Road East	E3-F3-F2	Vancouver Road	E8-F8
King Richards Road	A5	Princess Road West	D3-E3	Vaughan Way	C6-C7
King Street	D3-D4	Queen Street	E5	Vaughan Street	A6
Lancaster Road	D3-E3-E2	Rawson Street	D3-E3	Vernon Street	A6
Latimer Street	A3-A4	Regent Road	D3-E3-E2-F2	Walnut Street	B2-C2-D2
Lee Street	E6-D6	Repton Street	A7-A8	Walton Street	A1
Lincoln Street	E6	Richard III Road	B5	Wanlip Road	E8
Little Holme Street	A4-B4	Ridley Street	A3-A4	Warren Street	A4
London Road	E4-F3-E3-F2	Roman Street	A3	Warwick Street	A5-A6
Lower Brown Street	C3-C4-D3	Rutland Street	D5-E5-E6	Waterloo Way	E2-E3-D2-E4
Lower Willow Street	E8	Rydal Street	B2	Watling Street	C7-C8
Madras Road	F6-F7	St Augustine Road	A5-B5	Welford Road	D1-D2-D3-D4
Maidstone Road	F4-F5	St George Street	E5	Welles Street	B5
Malabar Road	F7	St Georges Way	E5-F5-F6	Wellington Street	D4-E3-E4
Manitoba Road	E7-F7	St James Street	E6	Western Boulevard	B2-B3
Mansfield Street	D6-D7	St John Street	D8	Western Road	A1-A2-A3-A4-B4
Mantle Road	A6-A7	St Margaret's Way	B8-C8-C7	West Street	D2-D3-E3
Market Place	C5-D5	St Martins	C5	Wharf Street North	E7-E8
Market Street	D4-D5	St Matthews Way	E6-E7	Wharf Street South	E6-E7
Marshall Street	A7-A8	St Nicholas Circle	B5-C5	Wilberforce Road	A1-A2-A3
Mayors Walk	E1	St Peters Lane	C6	William Street	F6
Melton Street	E8	Salisbury Road	F2	Wilton Street	D7
Midland Street	E5	Samuel Street	F5	Wimbledon Street	E5-E6
Mill Hill Lane	F3	Sanvey Gate	B7-C7	Windermere Street	B2-C2
Mill Lane	B3-C3	Sawday Street	C1	Woodboy Street	E8-E7
Millstone Lane	C4	Saxby Street	F3-F4	Woodgate	A8-B8
Morledge Street	E5-E6	Saxon Street	A3	Yeoman Street	D6-E5-E6
Montreal Road	E7-E8-F7	Severn Street	F4	York Road	C4-D4
Mossdale Close	C2	Short Street	C6-D6		
Narborough Road	A2-A3-A4	Silver Street	C5-D5		
Narborough Road North	A3-A5	Slater Street	B8		
Navigation Street	D7-D8	Soar Lane	B6-B7	AA shop	E4
Nelson Street	E3	South Albion Street	E4	132 Charles Street	
Newarke Close	B3-B4	Southampton Street	E5	Leicester LE1 1NA	

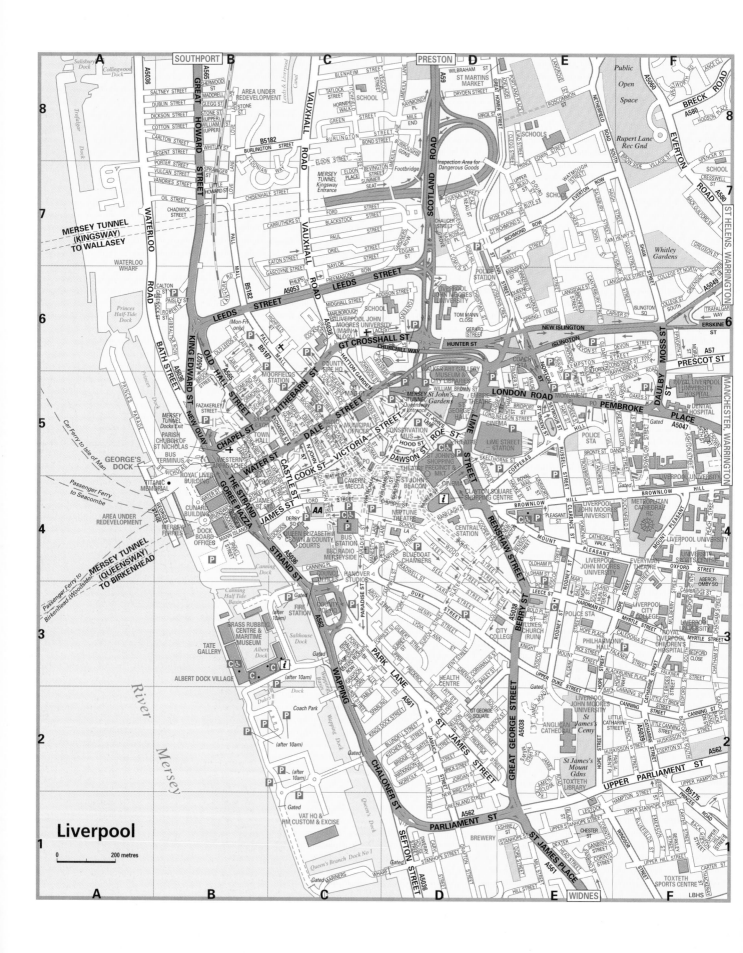

Liverpool

0   200 metres

LBHS

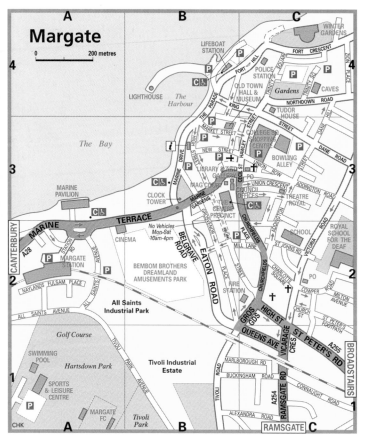

Margate

Margate is found on atlas page **29**, grid reference TR**3571**

Addington Road	C3	Fort Hill	B4-C4	Queens Avenue	CI
Addington Street	C2-C3	Fulsam Place	A2	Ramsgate Road	CI
Alexandra Road	BI-CI	Grosvenor Gardens	C2	St Johns Road	C2
All Saints Avenue	A2	Grosvenor Place	B2-B3	St Peter's Footpath	CI-C2
Belgrave Road	B2	Hawley Street	C3-C4	St Peter's Road	CI
Buckingham Road	BI-CI	High Street	B3-B2-C2	Station Road	A2
Cecil Street	C3	King Street	B4-C4-C3	The Parade	B4
Charlotte Square	C2	Marine Drive	B3	Tivoli Park Avenue	A2-AI-BI
Churchfields	C2	Marine Gardens	B3	Tivoli Road	BI
Churchfields Place	C2-C3	Marine Terrace	A2-A3-B3	Trinity Square	C4
Church Street	C2	Market Street	B3-C3	Union Crescent	C3
Connaught Road	CI	Marlborough Road	BI-CI	Union Row	C3
Cowper Road	C2	Mill Lane	B2-C2	Vicarage Crescent	CI
Dane Hill	C3-C4	Milton Avenue	C2	Victoria Road	C2-C3
Dane Road	C3	Naylands	A2	Zion Place	C4
Eaton Road	B2-B3	New Street	B3		
Fort Crescent	C4	Northdown Road	C4		

Liverpool

Liverpool is found on atlas page **78**, grid reference SJ**3490**

Addison Street	C6-D6	Brunswick Street	B4	Craven Street	E5-E6	Gradwell Street	D3-D4	Mile End	D8	Seymour Street	E5
Adelaide Place	E8	Burlington Street	B8-D8	Cresswell Street	F7	Grafton Street	DI	Mill Street	EI	Shaw Street	F6-F7
Ainsworth Street	E4-E5	Burroughs Gardens	D8	Cross Hall Street	C5-D5	Grayson Street	C3	Moira Street	F6	Shaws Alley	C3-D2
Alfred Mews	E2	Bute Street	E7	Crown Street	F5	Great Crosshall Street	C6-D6	Monument Place	E5	Sherwood Street	B8
Anson Place	F5	Caledonia Street	F3	Cunliffe Place	C5	Great George Street	EI-E3	Moorfields	C5	Simpson Street	D2
Anson Street	E5	Calton Street	B6	Dale Street	C5-D5	Great Homer Street	D7-D8	Moss Street	F6	Skelthorne Street	D5-E5
Argyle Street	C3-D3	Cambridge Street	F3	Dansie Street	E5-F5	Great Howard Street	B6-B8	Mount Pleasant	F4	Slater Street	D3-D4
Arrad Street	F3-F4	Campbell Street	D3-D4	Daulby Street	F5	Great Newton Street	F4-F5	Mount Pleasant Street	E4-F4	Soho Street	E7
Ashton Street	F4-F5	Canning Place	C4	Dawson Street	D5	Great Orford Street	F4	Mount Street	E3	South Hunter Street	E3
Ashwell Street	EI	Canning Street	E2-F2	Devon Street	E6-F6	Greek Street	E5	Mulberry Street	F3-F4	South John Street	C4-C5
Audley Street	E5-E6	Canterbury Street	E6	Dexter Street	EI	Green Street	C8-D8	Myrtle Street	F3	Sparling Street	C2-D2-D3
Back Canning Street	F2-F3	Carlton Street	A8-B8	Dickson Street	A8-B8	Greenland Street	DI-E2	Nash Grove	D7	Spencer Street	F8
Back Gibson Street	FI	Carpenters Row	C3	Douro Street	E7	Greenock Street	B6	Naylor Street	C6-D7	Spranger Street	B7
Back Guildford Street	F7	Carruthers Street	B7-C7	Dryden Street	D8	Greenside	F6	Nelson Street	D2	Springfield Street	E6-E7
Back Sandon Street	F2	Carter Street	FI	Dublin Street	A8-B8	Gregson Street	F7	Netherfield Road South	E8-F7	St Andrew Street	E4-E5
Bailey Street	D2-E3	Carver Street	E6-F6	Duckinfield Street	F4	Grenville Street South	D3-E2	New Bird Street	DI-D2	St Ann Street	D7-E6
Baltimore Street	E3-E4	Caryl Street	DI	Duke Street	C3-E3	Grosvenor Street	D7	New Islington	E6-F6	St Brides Street	F2-F3
Bath Street	A6-B5	Castle Street	C4-C5	Dwerry House Street	DI	Hackins Hey	C5	New Quay	B5	St James Place	EI
Baton Street	B7-C7	Catharine Street	F2-F3	Earle Street	B5-B6	Haigh Street	E7-F6	Newington	E4	St James Road	EI-E2
Bayhorse Lane	E5-F6	Cathedral Walk	E4	East Street	B6	Hampton Street	EI-F2	Norfolk Street	D2	St James Street	D2-E2
Beckwith Street	C3	Cazneau Street	D7	Eberle Street	C5	Hanover Street	C3-D4	North John Street	C5	St John's Lane	D5
Bedford Close	F3	Chadwick Street	B7	Edgar Street	D7	Hardman Street	E3	Norton Street	E5-E6	St Josephs Crescent	D6-E6
Bedford Street North	F3-F4	Chaloner Street	C2-DI	Edmund Street	B5	Harker Street	E6	Oakes Street	F5	St Nicholas Place	B5
Bedford Street South	F2-F3	Chapel Street	B5	Egerton Street	F2	Hart Street	E5	Oil Street	A7-B7	St Thomas Street	C5-D5
Benson Street	E4	Chatham Street	F3	Eldon Place	C7	Hatton Garden	C5-C6	Old Hall Street	B5-B6	St Vincent Street	E5
Berkley Street	FI-F2	Chaucer Street	D7	Eldon Street	C7-C8	Hawke Street	E4-E5	Old Leeds Street	B6	Stafford Street	E5-E6
Berry Street	E3	Cheapside	C5-C6	Eldonian Way	B8-C8	Head Street	EI	Oldham Place	E4	Stanhope Street	DI-EI
Bevington Street	C7-D7	Chester Street	EI	Elizabeth Street	F5	Henry Street	D3	Oldham Street	E4	Stanley Street	C4-C5
Birchfield Street	E6	Chisenhale Street	B7-C7	Emerson Street	FI	Highfield Street	B6-c6	Oriel Street	C7-D7	Stone Street	B8
Birkett Street	E7	Christian Street	D6	Epworth Street	F6	Hill Street	EI	Ormond Street	B5	Strand Street	B4-C4
Bixteth Street	B5-C5	Church Street	C4-D4	Erskine Street	F6	Hodson Place	F8	Oxford Street	F4	Suffolk Street	D3
Blackburne Place	E3-F3	Churchill Way	C6-D6	Everton Road	F7-F8	Hood Street	D5	Paisley Street	B6	Summer Seat	C7-D7
Blackstock Street	C7-D7	Clarence Street	E4	Everton Row	E7	Hope Place	E3	Pall Mall	B7-C7	Tabley Street	C2-D3
Blair Street	EI	Clegg Street	E7-E8	Exchange Street East	C5	Hope Street	E2-F4	Paradise Street	C3-C4	Tarleton Street	D4-D5
Blenheim Street	C8-D8	Cockspur Street	C6	Falkner Street	E3-F3	Hopeway	F3	Park Lane	C3-D2	Tatlock Street	C8
Bluefields Street	FI	College Street North	F6	Fazakerley Street	B5	Hornby Walk	C8	Parker Street	D4	Tempest Hey	C5
Blundell Street	C2-D2	College Street South	F6	Fenwick Street	B5-C4	Hotham Street	E5	Parliament Close	EI-D2	Temple Street	C5
Bold Place	E3	Colquitt Street	D3-E3	Finch Place	F6	Hunter Street	D6	Parliament Place	F2	Thackeray Street	FI
Bold Street	D4-E3	Comus Street	D6-D7	Fleet Street	D3-D4	Hurst Street	C2-C3	Parliament Street	DI-EI	The Strand	B4
Bolton Street	D4-D5	Constance Street	E6-F6	Flint Street	DI-D2	Huskisson Street	E2-F2	Parr Street	D3	Titchfield Street	C7-C8
Bond Street	C8-D8	Cook Street	C4-C5	Fontenoy Street	D6	Ilford Street	E5	Paul Street	C7-D7	Tithebarn Street	C5-C6
Breck Road	F8	Cookson Street	D2-E2	Ford Street	C7-D7	Iliad Street	E8	Peach Street	F5	Tom Mann Close	D6
Brick Street	D2	Cooper Street	D4-E4	Forrest Street	C3-D3	Irwell Street	B4	Pembroke Place	E5-F5	Trafalgar Way	F6
Bridgewater Street	D2	Copperas Hill	D4-E5	Fox Street	D8-E7	Islington	E6	Pembroke Street	F5	Trowbridge Street	E4-E5
Bridport Street	E5	Corinto Street	EI-FI	Fraser Street	E5-E6	Islington Square	F6	Percy Street	F2	Upper Beau Street	E7
Bronte Street	E5	Corn Hill	C3	Freemasons Row	C6-D7	Jamaica Street	DI-D2	Peter's Lane	C4-D4	Upper Duke Street	E2-E3
Brook Street	B5	Cornwall Street	D2	Gardners Row	D7	James Street	B4-C4	Philips Street	C6	Upper Frederick Street	D3-D2-E2
Brow Side	F7-F8	Corwallis Street	D3-E3	Gascoyne Street	B7-C6	John Street	E7	Pilgrim Street	E3	Upper Hampton Street	F2
Brownlow Hill	D4-F4	Cotton Street	A8-B8	George Street	B5	Johnson Street	C5-C6	Pitt Street	D2-D3	Upper Hill Street	FI
Brownlow Street	F4-F5	Covent Garden	B5	George's Dockway	B4	Jordan Street	D2	Pleasant Street	E4	Upper Parliament Street	EI-F2
				Gerard Street	D6	Juvenal Street	D7	Pomonia Street	D7	Upper Richmond Street	D7-E7
				Gibraltar Row	B6	Kempson Street	E6-F6	Porter Street	A7-B7	Upper Stanhope Street	EI-FI
				Gilbert Street	D3	Kent Street	D3	Portland Place	E8	Upper Stone Street	B8
				Gildart Street	E5-E6	Kinder Street	F6-F7	Pownhall Street	C3	Upper William Street	B8
				Gill Street	E5-F4	King Edward Street	B5-B6	Prescot Street	F6	Vandries Street	A7-B7
				Glegg Street	B8	Kings Dock Street	C2-D2	Prince Edwin Street	E7-E8	Vauxhall Road	C6-C8
				Gore Street	EI	Kitchen Street	D2	Princes Parade	A5-A6	Vernon Street	C5
				Goree Piazza	B4	Knight Street	E3	Princes Road	FI-F2	Vescock Street	C8-D8
						Lace Street	C6-D6	Princes Street	C5	Victoria Street	C5-D5
						Lance Close	F8	Pudsey Street	D5-E5	Village Street	F7-F8
						Langrove Street	E8	Queen Ann Street	E5	Virgil Street	D8
						Langsdale Street	E6-F6	Ranelagh Street	D4	Vulcan Street	A7-B7
						Lanyork Road	B6	Raymond Place	D8	Wakefield Street	E6
						Leece Street	E3	Redcross Street	B4-C4	Wapping	C2-C3
						Leeds Street	B6-D6	Regent Street	A8-B8	Water Street	B4-B5-C5
						Lestock Street	EI	Renshaw Street	D4-E4	Waterloo Road	A6-A8
						Lime Street	D4-D6	Rice Street	E3	Watkinson Street	D2
						Limekiln Lane	D7-D8	Richmond Row	D7-E7	Watmough Street	E7
						Little Catharine Street	F2	Roberts Street	B6	Webster Street	C6-D6
						Little Catharine Street	F2	Rodney Street	E3-E4	Wentworth Road	F8
						Little Howard Street	B7	Roe Street	D5	Whitechapel	C4-D5
						Little St Brides Street	F2	Rokeby Street	E7	Whitley Street	D8
						London Road	D5-E5-F5-F6	Roscoe Street	E3-E4	Wilbraham Street	D8
						Lord Nelson Street	D5-E5	Roscommon Street	E8	Wilde Street	E5
						Lord Street	C4	Rose Hill	D6-D7	William Brown Street	D5
						Love Lane	B7-B8	Rose Place	D7-E7	Williamson Street	C4-D5
						Lower Castle Street	C4-C5	Royal Mail Street	E4-E5	Windsor Street	EI-FI
						Lydia Ann Street	D3	Rumford Street	B5	Wood Street	D3-D4
						Maddrell Street	B8	Russell Street	E4-E5	York Street	D3
						Manesty's Lane	C4	Salisbury Street	E7-F6		
						Mann Island	B4	Saltney Street	A8-B8		
						Mansfield Street	E6-E7	Sanbino Street	EI		
						Mariners Wharf	CI-DI	Sandon Street	F2-F3	AA shop	
						Marlborough Street	C6	School Lane	C4-D4		C4
						Maryland Street	E4-E3-F3	Scotland Road	D6-D8		
						Matthews Street	C4-C5	Seel Street	D4-E3	Derby Square	
						Midghall Street	C6	Sefton Street	DI	Liverpool L2 IUF	

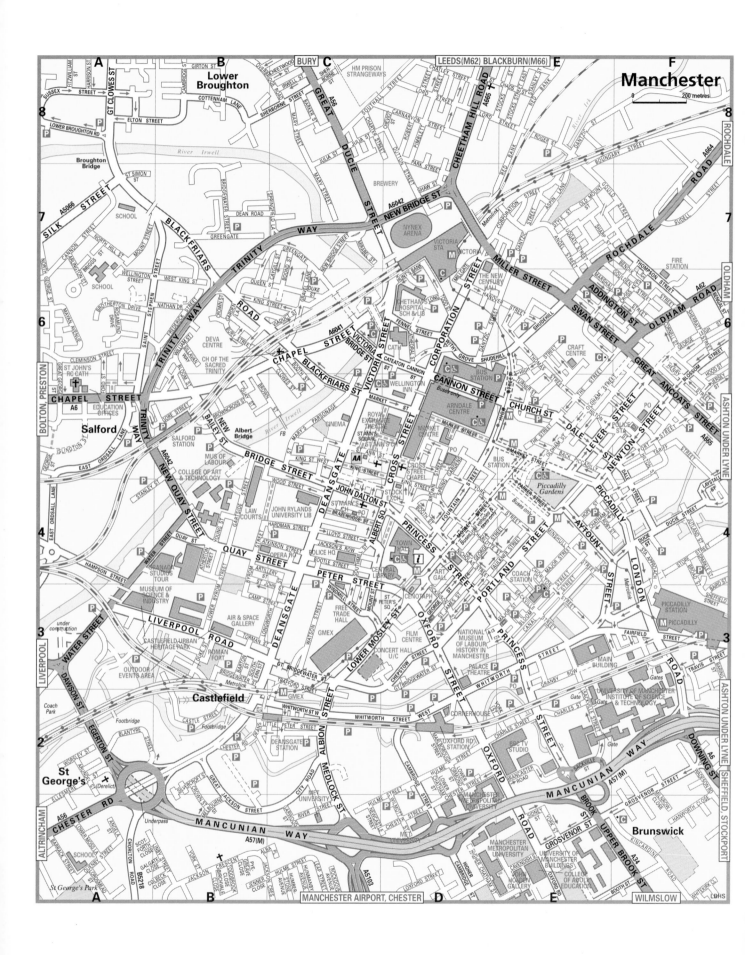

Manchester

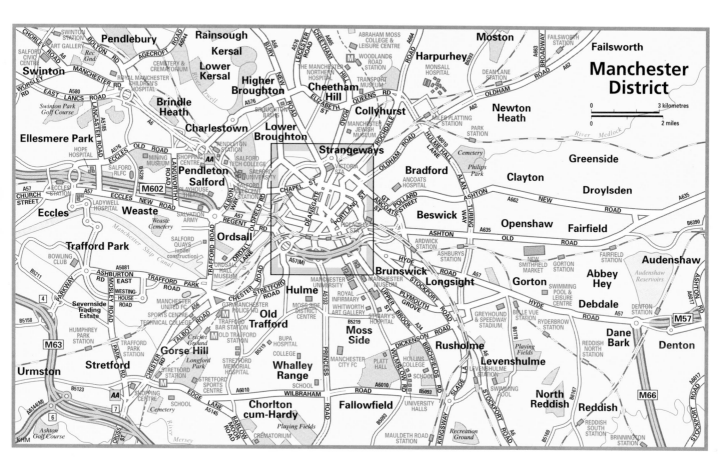

Manchester

Manchester is found on atlas page **79**,
grid reference SJ8497

Street	Grid		Street	Grid		Street	Grid		Street	Grid		Street	Grid
Addington Street	E6-F6		Camp Street	B3-C3		Ellesmere Street	A1-A2		King Street	C5-D5-D4		Pimblett Street	D8		Toddbrook Close	B1
Alba Place	B1-C1		Canal Street	E3-E4		Elton Street	A8-B8		King Street West	C5		Port Street	F5		Torman Street	B3-C3
Albert Square	C4-D4		Cannon Street	D5-D6		Fairfield Street	E3-F3		Laystall Street	F4-F5		Portland Street	D3-E4		Trafford Street	C2-C3
Albion Street	C2-C3		Carnarvon Street	C8-D8		Faulkner Street	D4-E4		Leap Street	C1		Princess Street	D4-E2		Travis Street	F3
Angel Street	E6-E7		Castle Street	B2-B3		Fennel Street	D6		Lever Street	E5-F5		Pyegreave Close	B1		Trinity Way	A5-C7
Angela Street	A1		Cateaton Street	D6		Fitzwilliam Street	A8		Linby Street	A1-B1		Quay Street	B4-C4		Turner Street	E5
Arlington Street	A6-A7		Cathedral Street	D6		Ford Street	A5-A6		Little Peter Street	B2-C2		Quay Street	B5		Upper Brook Street	E1-F1
Artillery Street	B4-C4		Cavendish Street	E1		Fountain Street	D4-D5		Liverpool Road	A3-B3		Queen Street	B6-C6		Viaduct Street	C6
Arundel Street	A1-A2		Caygill Street	B6-C7		Frederick Street	B6		Livesey Street	F8		Quenby Street	A1		Victoria Bridge Street	C6
Aspin Lane	E7		Chapel Street	A5-D6		Galgate Close	A1-B1		Lloyd Street	C4		Red Bank	D7-E8		Victoria Street	C5-D6
Atherton Street	B4		Charles Street	D2-E2		Garden Lane	B6		London Road	F2-F4		River Street	C1		Wadeson Road	F1-F2
Atkinson Street	B4-C4		Charlotte Street	D4-E4		Gartside Street	B4-B5		Long Millgate	D6-D7		Robert Street	D8		Watson Street	C3-C4
Aytoun Street	E3-E4		Charter Street	C8-D8		Garwood Street	C1		Longworth Street	B3-C4		Roby Street	E4-F4		Wellington Street	A6
Back Piccadilly	E5		Chatham Street	E4		George Leigh Street	F6		Lord Street	D8-E8		Rochdale Road	E6-F7		West King Street	B6
Baird Street	F3-F4		Chatley Street	D8		George Street	A5		Lordsmead Street	A1		Rockdove Avenue	C1		Whitekirk Close	F1
Baring Street	F3		Cheetham Hill Road	D7-D8		George Street	D3-D4-E4		Lower Broughton Road	A8		Roger Street	E8		Whitworth Street	D2-E3
Barker Street	C8		Cheetwood Street	B8-C8		Girton Street	B8		Lower Byrom Street	B3-B4		Rosamund Drive	A6		Whitworth Street West	C2-D2
Barrack Street	A1		Chepstow Street	D3		Gore Street	A5-B5		Lower Chatham Street	D1-D2		Sackville Street	E2-E4		William Street	B6
Barton Street	B3		Chester Road	B2		Gould Street	E8-F7		Lower Mosley Street	C3-D3		Saint Stephen Street	A5-B7		Wilmott Street	D1
Bendix Street	F6-F7		Chester Road	A1		Goulden Street	E7-F6		Lower Moss Lane	A1		Scotforth Close	A1		Windmill Street	C3
Bengal Street	F6		Chester Street	D1-D2		Granby Row	E3		Lower Ormond Street	D2		Sharp Street	E7		Withy Grove	D6
Birchvale Close	B1		Cheviot Street	D8		Gravel Lane	C6-C7		Loxford Street	D1		Shaw Street	D7		Wood Street	B5-C4
Blackfriars Road	A8-C6		Chorlton Road	A1		Great Ancoats Street	F5-F6		Ludgate Street	E7		Sheffield Street	F3		Worsley Street	A2
Blackfriars Street	C5-C6		Chorlton Street	E3-E4		Great Bridge Street	C3-D3		Major Street	D3-E4		Sherborne Street	B8-C8		York Street	B1
Blantyre Street	A2-B2		Church Street	E5		Great Ducie Street	C8-D6		Mancunian Way	B1-F2		Sherratt Street	F6		York Street	D2-E2
Bloom Street	B5-B6		City Road	C1-C2		Great George Street	A5-A6		Market Street	C5-E4		Shudehill	D6-E6		York Street	D5-E4
Bloom Street	E3-E4		Cleminson Street	A6		Great Gower Street	A8		Marlborough Street	D2		Sidney Street	E1		York Street	E1
Blossom Street	F5-F6		Clowes Street	C5-C6		Great Jackson Street	B1-B2		Marshall Street	E6-F6		Silk Street	A7		Young Street	B4
Boond Street	C6-C7		Colbeck Close	A1-B1		Greengate	B7-C7-C6		Mary Street	C7-C8		Sillavan Way	B6			
Booth Street	C5-C6		Cornell Street	F6		Grosvenor Street	E1-F2		Mayan Avenue	A6		Silvercroft Street	B1-B2			
Booth Street	D4		Corporation Street	D5-E7		Hanover Street	D6-E6		Medlock Street	C1-C2		Southall Street	C8-D8			
Booth Street	E1-F1		Cottenham Lane	B8		Hanworth Close	F1		Melbourne Street	B1		Southern Street	B3			
Bootle Street	C4		Cross Keys Street	E6-F6		Hardman Street	B4-C4		Miller Street	D7-E6		Southmill Street	C4			
Boundary Street	E8-F8		Cross Street	D4-D5		Harrison Street	A8		Milnrow Close	F1-F2		Sparkle Street	F4			
Brancaster Road	E2		Crown Street	B1-B2		Henry Street	F5-F6		Minchull Street	E4		Spring Gardens	D4-D5			
Brazenose Street	C4		Crown Street	B6		High Street	D5-E6		Mirabel Street	C7		Springfield Lane	B7-C7			
Bridge Street	B5-C4		Dale Street	E5-F4		Higher Cambridge Street	D1		Mosley Street	D4		St Ann Street	C5-D5			
Bridgewater Street	B3		Dantzic Street	D6-E7-E8		Higher Chatham Street	D1-E1		Mount Street	A7		St Chads Street	D8-E8			
Bridgewater Street	B7-B8		Dawson Street	A2-A3		Hilton Street	E5-F5		Mount Street	C3		St James Street	D3-D4			
Briggs Street	A6-A7		Dean Road	B7		Hood Street	F5-F6		Nathan Drive	B6		St John Street	B4-C3			
Broad Street	F3-F4		Deans Gate	B2		Hope Street	B5		New Bailey Street	B5		St Mary's Parsonage	C5			
Brook Street	E1-E2		Deansgate	B3-C5		Hulme Street	C1		New Bridge Street	C6-C7-D7		St Simon Street	A7			
Brotherton Drive	A6		Dickinson Street	D3-D4		Hulme Street	C1-D2		New Quay Street	A5-B4		Stanley Street	E8			
Brown Street	B5-C5		Downing Street	F2		Humberstone Avenue	C1		Newcastle Street	C1-D1		Stanley Street	A4-B5			
Brown Street	D4-D5		Duke Street	B3		Hunmanby Avenue	C1		Newton Street	E4-F5		Station Approach	F3-F4			
Browncross Street	B5		Duke Street	C6		Hunt's Bank	D6-D7		Nicholas Street	D4		Stocks Street	D8-E8			
Bury Street	B6-C6		Ducie Street	F4		Irwell Street	C8		North George Street	A6-A7		Stocks Street East	E8			
Byrom Street	B3-C4		Dutton Street	D7-D8		Islington Street	A5		North Hill Street	A7		Store Street	F3-F4			
Cambridge Street	B8		East Ordsall Lane	A4-A5		Jackson Crescent	B1-C1		Old Mount Street	E7		Style Street	E7			
Cambridge Street	D1-D2		Egerton Street	A2		Jackson's Row	C4		Oldham Road	F6		Sudell Street	F7			
						Jenner Close	B1		Oldham Street	E5-F7		Sussex Street	A8			
						Jersey Street	F5-F6		Overbridge Street	B8-C8		Swan Street	E6-F6			
						John Dalton Street	C4-D4		Oxford Street	D3-E1		Tariff Street	F5			
						Julia Street	C7-C8		Park Street	D7-D8		The Street	E5-F6			
						Jutland Street	F4		Parker Street	E4		Thomas Street	E5-E6			
						Kincardine Road	F1		Peter Street	C4-D3		Thompson Street	F6-F7			
						King Street	B6-C6		Piccadilly	E4-F4		Todd Street	D6-D7			

AA shop   C5
St Ann's House
St Ann's Place
Manchester M2 7LP

231

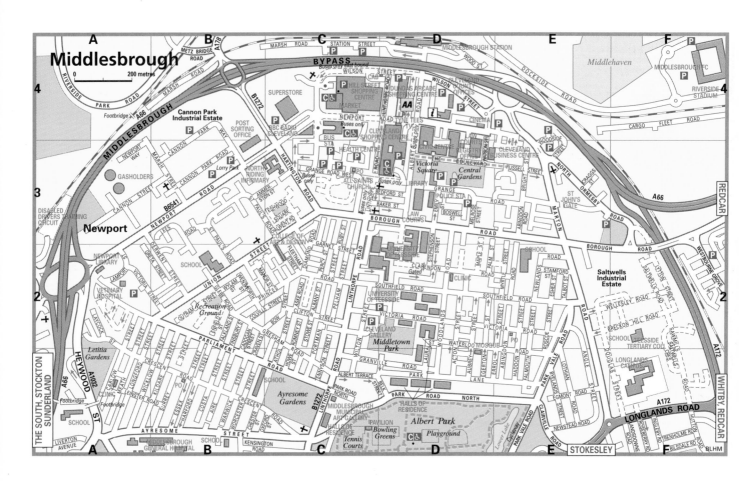

Middlesbrough

Middlesbrough is found on atlas page **97**, grid reference NZ**4919**

Abingdon Road	E1-E2-E3	Douglas Street	F1-E2	Maple Street	D2-D3	Tennyson Street	C1-C2
Acklam Road	A1	Egerton Street	D1-D2	Marsh Road	A4-B4-C4	The Boulevard	D3
Acton Street	D1-D2	Egmont Road	E1	Marsh Street	B3-B4	Trenholme Road	F1
Aire Street	B1	Emily Street	D3	Marton Road	E1-E4	Union Street	B2-C3
Albany Street	C2	Enfield Street	B2	Meath Street	A1-A2	Victoria Road	C2-E2
Albert Road	D3-D4	Errol Street	D1-E2	Melrose Street	D3	Victoria Street	A2-B2
Albert Terrace	C1	Esher Street	E2	Metz Bridge Road	B4	Warwick Street	B1
Alwent Road	C3	Eshwood Square	C3	Middlesbrough Bypass	A1-F1	Waterloo Road	D2-E1
Ammerston Street	B3-C3	Essex Street	B1-B2	Myrtle Street	E2-E3	Wellesley Road	E2-F2
Angle Street	E2-F1	Falkland Street	B2	Newlands Road	E2	Wentworth Street	B2
Aske Road	C2	Falmouth Street	E1-E2	Newport Road	A2-D4	Westbourne Grove	F2-F3
Athol Street	C1-C2	Finsbury Street	B2	Newport Way	A3	Wicklow Street	A1-B2
Aubrey Street	D1-D2	Fleetham Street	C2	Newstead Road	E1	Wilson Street	C4-D4
Ayresome Street	A1-C1	Garnet Street	C2-C3	North Ormesby Road	E3-F3	Wilton Street	C1-C2
Baker Street	C3-D3	Glebe Road	B2	Outram Street	B2	Wood Street	D4
Bedford Street	C3-D3	Grange Road	D3-E3	Oxford Street	B1-C1	Woodlands Road	D1-D3
Belk Street	C1-D1	Grange Road West	C3	Palm Street	D2-D3	Woodside Street	E3-E4
Bilsdale Road	F1	Granville Road	C1-D1	Park Lane	D1-E1	Worcester Street	B1
Borough Road	C3-F3	Gresham Road	B2-C1	Park Road North	C1-E1	Wylam Street	B2
Boswell Street	D3	Greta Street	A2-B2	Park Vale Road	E1-E2		
Bow Street	C2	Haddon Street	E1-E2	Parliament Road	A2-C1		
Breckon Hill Road	E2-F2	Harford Street	B1-B2	Pelham Street	C2-C3		
Bright Street	E3	Hartington Road	B4-C3	Percy Street	C2-C3		
Byelands Street	E1	Heywood Street	A1-A2	Portman Street	C1-C2		
Cadogan Street	B2	Howe Street	C1	Princes Road	B2-C2		
Cannon Park Road	B3	Hutton Road	F1	Riverside Park Road	A4		
Cannon Park Way	B3-B4	Ingleby Road	F1	Romney Street	C2		
Cannon Street	A3-B3	Kensington Road	B1-C1	Roscoe Street	D2		
Cargo Fleet Road	E4-F4	Kildare Street	A1-B2	Roseberry Road	F1		
Carlow Street	A1-A2	Lamport Street	A2	Roseberry Road	F1		
Chester Street	B1	Lansdowne Road	F1	Russell Street	E3		
Clairville Road	E1	Laura Street	D1-D2	Saltwells Road	F2		
Clarendon Road	D2-E2	Laycock Street	A2	Sawmills Crescent	F1-F2		
Clifton Street	C2	Lees Road	B3	Sawmills Road	F1-F2		
Colville Street	B2-C2	Leinster Road	A1-B1	Southfield Road	C2-E2		
Costa Street	B1-B2	Linthorpe Road	C1-D4	St Paul's Road	B2-B3		
Craggs Street	E3	Liverton Avenue	A1	Stamford Street	E2		
Craven Street	B1-B2	Longford Street	A1-B2	Station Street	C4-D4		
Crescent Road	A1-C1	Longlands Road	F1	Stephenson Street	D2-D3		
Derwent Street	A3-B2	Lothian Road	E1	Stowe Street	C2	AA shop	D4
Diamond Road	C2-C3	Lytton Street	F2	Surrey Street	B1-B2	17 Corporation Road	
Dockside Road	D4-F4	Manor Street	A2-C1	Talbot Street	E2	Middlesbrough TS1 1LS	

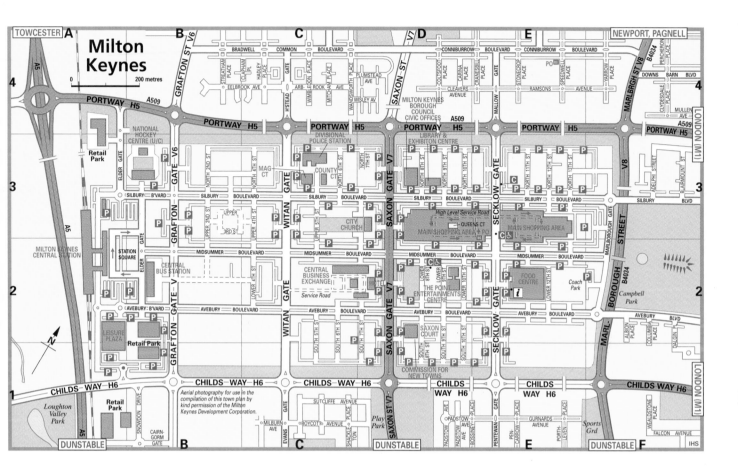

Milton Keynes

Milton Keynes is found on atlas page **38**, grid reference SP**8537**

Adelphi Place	A3	Marlborough Street	E4	Upper Fourth Street	C3-C2
Albion Place	F2	Marigold Place	C4	Upper Second Street	B3-B2
Arbrook Avenue	C4	Mayditch Place	B2-F2	Upper Third Street	B3-C3
Avebury Boulevard	A2-F2	Midsummer Boulevard	C1	Wandsworth Place	C4
Bayard Avenue	F4	Milburn Avenue	C4	Wealdstone Place	F1
Blairmount Street	F3	Mitcham Place	F4	Wimbledon Place	C4
Bossiney Place	E1	Mullen Avenue	D3	Wisley Avenue	D4
Boycott Avenue	C1-D1	North Eighth Street	E3	Witan Gate	C1-C3
Bradwell Common Blvd	B4-D4	North Eleventh Street	C3	Yarrow Place	F4
Brill Place	C4	North Fourth Street	D3		
Burnham Drive	F4	North Ninth Street	B3		
Byrony Place	D4	North Second Street	D3		
Carlina Place	A1-F1	North Seventh Street	C3		
Childs Way	D4-E4	North Sixth Street	D3		
Cleavers Avenue	C4	North Tenth Street	E3		
Clapham Place	F4	North Thirteenth Street	E3		
Clydesdale Place	C4	North Twelfth Street	D1		
Coleshill Place	D4	Padstow Avenue	E1		
Coltsfoot Place	F1-F2	Pencarrow Place	E1		
Columbia Place	D4-E4-F4	Pentewan Gate	F4		
Conniburrow Boulevard	E4	Percheron Place	D4		
Cranesbill Place	F1-F2	Plumstead Avenue	A4-F4		
Dalgin Place	C4	Portway	E4-F4		
Dorney Place	B4-C4	Ramsons Avenue	D1-D2-D3		
Eelbrook Avenue	A4-A3,B3-B2	Saxon Gate	D1,D4		
Elder Gate	C1	Saxon Street	E1-E2-E3		
Evans Gate	F1	Secklow Gate	C1		
Falcon Avenue	E4	Shackleton Place	A3-F3		
Fennel Drive	B1-B2-B3	Silbury Boulevard	B1		
Grafton Gate	B4	Snowdon Drive	D1-D2		
Grafton Street	E1	South Eighth Street	C1-C2		
Gurnards Avenue	C4	South Fifth Street	D1-D2		
Hadley Place	C4	South Ninth Street	C1-C2		
Hampstead Gate	D2	South Seventh Street	C1-C2		
Lower Eighth Street	C2	South Sixth Street	D1-D2		
Lower Fourth Street	D2	South Tenth Street	E4		
Lower Ninth Street	D2	Speedwell Place	A3-A2		
Lower Tenth Street	E2	Station Square	E4		
Lower Twelfth Street	E4	Stonecrop Place	B4		
Majoram Place	E4	Streatham Place	C1-D1		
Mallow Gate	F2-F3	Sutcliffe Avenue	C3-C2		
Marlborough Gate	F1-F4	Upper Fifth Street	C3-C2		

Newcastle upon Tyne

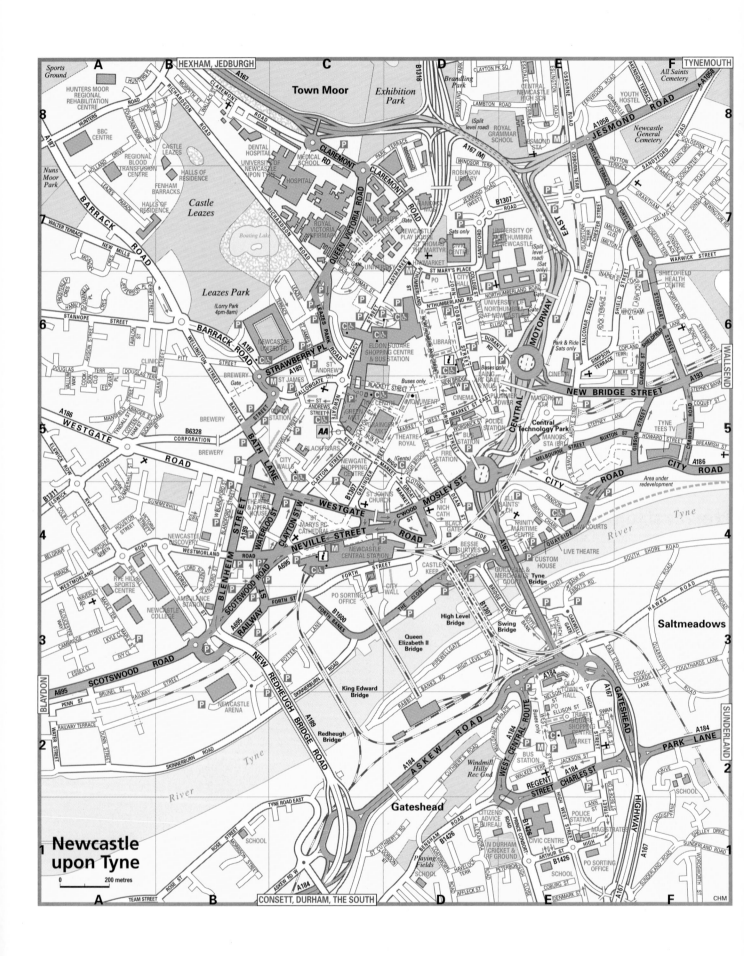

Newcastle
upon Tyne

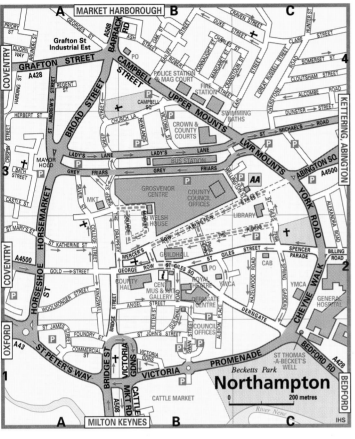

Northampton

Northampton is found on atlas page **49**, grid reference SP**7560**

Abington Square	C3	Horseshoe Street	A1-A2
Abington Street	B2-B3-C3	Hunter Street	C4
Albion Place	B1-B2	Kingswell	A1-A2
Alcombe Road	C4	Lady's Lane	A3-B3-C3
Alexandra Road	C2-C3	Lower Mounts	C3
Angel Street	B2	Margaret Street	B4
Arundel Street	A4	Market Square	B2
Ash Street	B4	Mayor Hold	A3
Bailiff Street	B4	Mercer's Row	B2
Barrack Road	A4-B4	Newlands	B3
Bath Street	A3	Oak Street	B4
Bedford Road	C1	Overstone Road	C3-C4
Billing Road	C2	Priory Street	A4
Bridge Street	A1-A2	Quorn Way	A4
Broad Street	A3-A4	Regent Street	A4
Campbell Street	A4-B4	Robert Street	B4
Castle Street	A3	Sheep Street	A3-A4
Cattlemarket Road	B1	Silver Street	A3
Charles Street	B4-C4	Somerset Street	C4
Cheyne Walk	C1-C2	Spencer Parade	C2
Church Lane	A3-B3-B4	Spring Gardens	C2
Clare Street	C4	St Andrew's Street	A3-A4
Cloutsham Street	C4	St Giles Square	B2
College Street	A2	St Giles Street	B2-C2
Commercial Street	A1	St Giles Terrace	C2-C3
Connaught Street	B4	St James Street	A1
Cranstoun Street	B4-C4	St John's Street	B1
Craven Street	B4-C4	St Katherine Street	A2
Crispin Street	A3	St Mary's Street	A2
Derngate	C1-C2-B2	St Michael's Road	C3
Duke Street	B4-C4	St Peter's Way	A1
Dunster Street	C3-C4	Swan Street	B1-B2
Earl Street	B3-C4	The Drapery	A2-B2
Fetter Street	B1-B2	The Riding	B2-C2
Foundry Street	A1	Upper Mounts	B3-B4
George Row	B2	Victoria Gardens	B1
Georges Street	A4	Victoria Promenade	B1-C1
Gold Street	A2	Victoria Street	B3-B4
Grafton Street	A4	Wellington Street	B3-C3
Great Russell Street	C4	Woolmonger Street	A2
Grey Friars	A3-B3-C3	York Road	C2-C3
Guildhall Road	B1-B2		
Harding Street	A4		
Hazelwood Road	C2	AA shop	C3
Herbert Street	A3	67 Abington Street	
Horsemarket	A2-A3	Northampton NN1 2BH	

Newcastle upon Tyne

Newcastle upon Tyne is found on atlas page **103**, grid reference NZ**2464**

Abbots Road	E3-E4	Clothmarket	D4-D5	George Street	B3-B4	Market Street East	D5	Queen Victoria Road	C7	Tower Street	E4-E5
Abinger Street	A5	Coatsworth Road	D1	Gibson Street	F5	Market Street West	D5	Rabbit Banks Road	C2-D3	Tyndall Street	A5
Akenside Terrace	F8	Coburg Street	E1	Gloucester Way	A3	Melbourne Street	E5	Railway Street	A2-B4	Tyne Road East	C1
Alexandra Road	D1	Colby Court	A4	Goldspink Lane	F8	Milk Market	E4	Railway Terrace	A2	Tyneside Road	A2
Ancrum Street	A8-B8	College Street	D6	Gordon Street	C1-D1	Mill Road	F2-F4	Regent Street	E1-E2	Vallum Way	A5-A6
Ann Street	E1	Collingwood Street	D4-D5	Grainger Street	C4-D5	Milton Place	E7-F7	Richardson Road	A8-C6	Victoria Street	A4
Argyle Street	E5	Cookson Close	A5-A6	Grantham Road	F7	Mitford Street	A2-B2	Rock Terrace	E6	Walker Terrace	E2
Arthur Street	E1	Copland Terrace	F6	Granville Road	E8-F8	Monday Crescent	A6-A7	Rose Street	B1	Wallace Street	B8
Askew Road	C1-E3	Coppice Way	F6	Grey Street	D4-D5	Morpeth Street	B8	Rosedale Terrace	F7	Walter Terrace	A7
Askew Road West	B1-C1	Coquet Street	F5	Groat Market	D4-D4	Morrison Street	B1	Rye Hill	A3-A4	Water Street	A2
Avison Street	A6	Corporation Street	A5-C5	Hamilton Crescent	A6	Moseley Street	D4-D5	Saint Thomas Street	C6-C7	Waterloo Street	B4-C4
Bank Road	E3-E4	Cottenham Street	A6	Havelock Terrace	D1	Mulgrave Terrace	D2-E2	Sandgate	E4	Warwick Street	F7
Barrack Road	A8-B6	Coulthards Lane	F3	Hawks Road	E3-F4	Napier Street	E6-F6	Sandyford Road	D7-F8	Waverley Road	A3
Bath Lane	B5-C4	Crawhall Road	F5	Haymarket	D6-D7	Nelson Street	E2-E3	Scotswood Road	A1-C4	Wellington Street	B5-B6
Belle Grove West	A8-B8	Dean Street	D4	Helmsley Road	F7-F8	Neville Street	C4	Shelley Drive	F1	West Blandford Street	B4
Belgrave Parade	A4	Denmark Street	E1	High Bridge	D5	New Bridge Street	E5-F6	Shield Street	E6-F7	West Central Route	E2-E3
Bensham Road	C1-D1	Derby Street	A6	High Level Road	D3	New Bridge Street West	D5	Shieldfield Lane	F6	West Street	E2
Bigg Market	C5-D5	Diana Street	B5-B6	High Street	E1-E3	New Mills	A7	Side	D4-E4	Westgate Road	A5-D4
Blackett Street	C5-D5	Dinsdale Place	F7	High Street West	E1-E2	New Redheugh Bridge Rd	B3-C1	Simpson Terrace	E6	Westmorland Road	A3-B4
Blackgate	D4	Dinsdale Road	F7	Hillgate	E3-E4	Newgate Street	C5	Skinnerburn Road	A2-C3	Windsor Terrace	D7-D8
Blandford Street	B3-B4	Doncaster Road	F7-F8	Holland Drive	A7-A8	Newington Road	F7	South Shore Road	E4-F4	Wordsworth Street	F1
Blenheim Street	B3-B5	Dorset Road	F3-F4	Hopper Street	E2	Northumberland Road	D6-E6	St Andrews Street	C5	Worswick Street	D5-E5
Bottle Bank	E3	Douglas Terrace	A5-A6	Houston Street	A4	Northumberland Street	D5-D7	St Ann's Street	F4-F5	Wrotham Place	F6
Brandling Park	D8	Dunn Street	A2	Howard Street	F5	Nun Street	C5	St Bede's Drive	E1-E2	York Street	A4-A5
Breamish Street	F5	Durant Road	D6-E6	Hunters Road	A8-B8	Oakwellgate	E3	St Cuthbert's Road	C1-D1-D2		
Bridge Street	D4-E3	East Street	E3-F3	Hutton Terrace	E8-F7	Osborne Road	E8	St James Street	C6		
Broad Chare	E4	Edward Place	A5-A6	Ivy Close	A3	Osborne Terrace	E7-E8	St Mary's Place	D6-D7		
Brunel Street	A2-A3	Ellison Street	D6-E6	Jackson Street	E2	Oystershell Lane	B5	St Mary's Street	F4		
Buckingham Street	A5-B5	Ellison Street	E2	Jefferson Place	A6	Pandon	E4	Stanhope Street	A6-B6		
Buxton Street	E5-F5	Elswick Road	A4-A5	Jesmond Road (West)	D7-E7	Park Lane	F2	Starbeck Avenue	F7-F8		
Byron Street	E6-E7	Elswick Row	A5	Jesmond Road	E7-F8	Park Terrace	C8-D8	Stepney Bank	F5		
Cambridge Street	A3	Elswick Street	A5	John Dobson Street	D5-D6	Penn Street	A2	Stepney Lane	E5-F5		
Central Motorway East	D5-E7	Eskdale Terrace	E8	Kelvin Grove	F8	Percy Street	C6	Stepney Road	F6		
Charles Street	E2	Eslington Road	E8	Kirkdale Green	A4	Peterborough Street	D1-E1	Stoddart Street	F5-F6		
Chester Street	E7	Essex Close	A3	Kyle Close	A3	Pilgrim Street	D5	Stowell Street	C5		
Church Street	E3	Falconar Street	E6	Lambton Road	D8-E8	Pipewellgate	D3-E3	Strawberry Place	B6-C6		
City Road	E5-F5	Fernwood Road	E8-F8	Leazes Park Road	C6	Pitt Street	B6	Summerhill Green	A4-B5		
Claremont Road	B8-D7	Forth Banks	C3	Leazes Terrace	C6	Portland Road	E8-F7-F6	Summerhill Street	A4-A5	AA shop	C5
Clarence Street	F5-F6	Forth Street	C3-D4	Lindisfarne Drive	F1-F2	Portland Terrace	E7-E8	Sunderland Road	F1	33-35 Whitecross Way	
Clayton Park Square	D8-E8	Fountain Row	A8	Mansfield Street	A5	Pottery Lane	C3	Swan Street	E2	Eldon Centre	
Clayton Street	C4-C5	Gallowgate	C5	Maple Street	A3	Prince Consort Road	E1	Team Street	A1-B1	Newcastle upon Tyne	
Clayton Street West	C4	Gateshead Highway	E3-F1	Maple Terrace	A3-A4	Quayside	E4-F4	The Close	C3-D4	NE1 7YN	

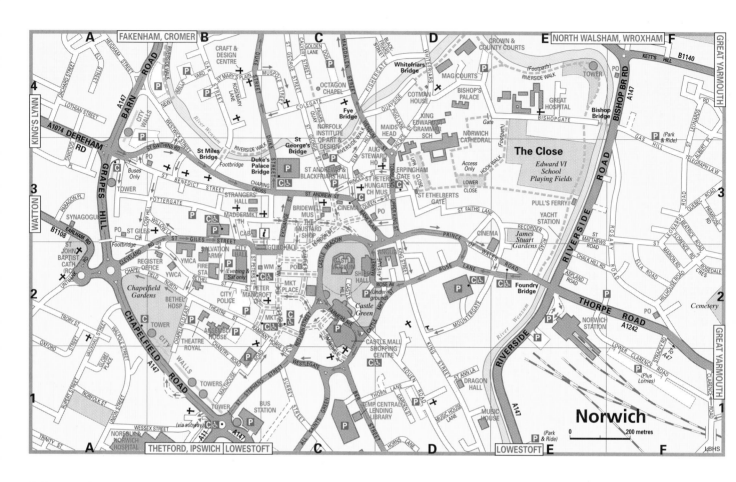

Norwich

Norwich is found on atlas page **67**,
grid reference TG**2308**

AA shop
Fanum House
126 Thorpe Road
Norwich NR1 1RL

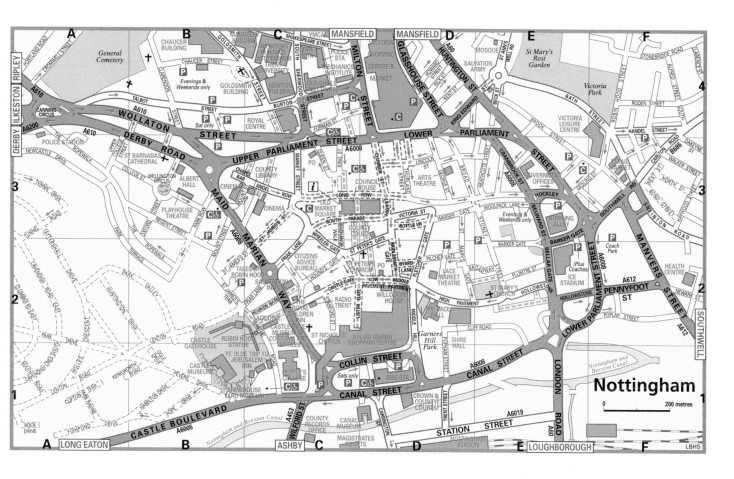

Nottingham

Nottingham is found on atlas page **62**,
grid reference SK**5739**

AA shop
484 Derby Road
Nottingham NG7 2GT

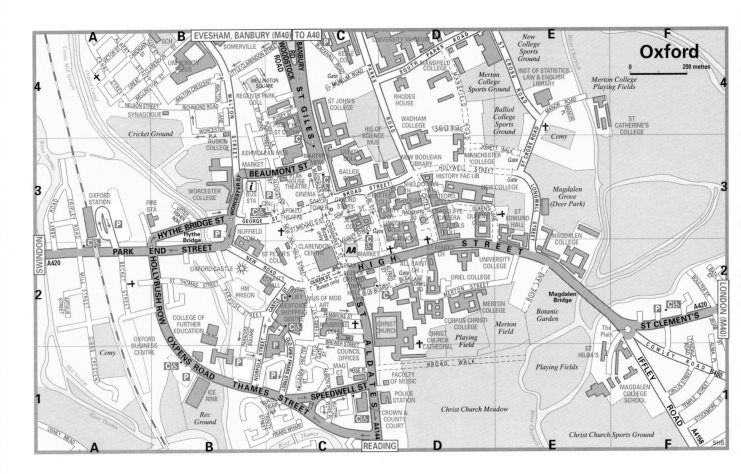

Oxford

Oxford is found on atlas page **37**,
grid reference SP5106

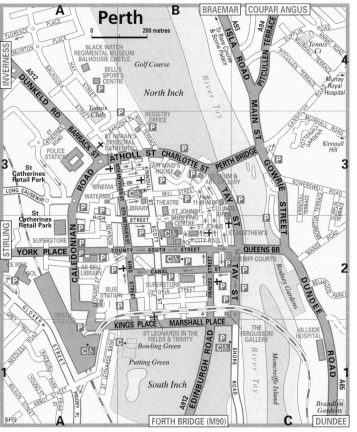

Perth

Perth is found on atlas page **126**,
grid reference NO**1123**

Abbot Street	A1
Annat Road	C4
Atholl Street	A3-B3
Balhousie Street	A3-A4
Barossa Place	A3-B3
Barrack Street	A3
Bellwood Park	C2
Bowerswell Road	C3
Brompton Terrace	C2-C3
Caledonian Road	A2-A3
Canal Street	B2
Charlotte Street	B3
County South Street	A2-B2
Dundee Road	C1-C2
Dunkeld Street	A3-A4
Dupplin Road	C4
Dupplin Terrace	C2-C3
Edinburgh Road	B1
Florence Place	A4
Friar Street	A1
Gannochy Road	C3-C4
Glover Street	A1-A2
Gowrie Street	C2-C3
Grey Street	A1-A2
Hay Street	A3-A4
High Street	A2-B2
Isla Road	B4-C4
King Street	B2
Kings Place	A1-B1
Kinnoull Street	B3
Kinnoull Terrace	C2-C3
Leonard Street	A2
Long Causeway	A3
Main Street	C3-C4
Manse Road	C2
Marshall Place	B1
Mill Street	B3
Muirhall Road	C3
Muirhall Terrace	C4
Muirton Place	A4
Needless Road	A1
Newrow	A2
North Methven Street	A3-B3
Perth Bridge	B3-C3
Pitcullen Terrace	C4
Potterhill Gardens	C3

Princes Street	B2
Priory Place	A1
Queen's Bridge	C2
Raeburn Park	A1
Rose Terrace	B3
Scott Street	B2
Shore Road	B1
South Methven Street	B2-B3
St Catherines Road	A3
St Leonards Bank	A1
Tay Street	B1-B3
Victoria Street	B2
Wilson Street	A1
York Place	A2
Young Street	A1

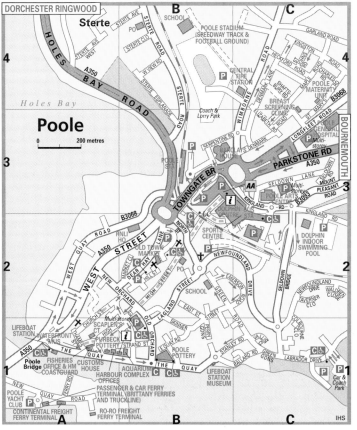

Poole

Poole is found on atlas page **11**,
grid reference SZ**0090**

Ballard Road	B1-C1
Charles Road	C4
Church Street	A1-A2
Colbourne Close	C2-C1
Dear Hay Lane	A2-B2
Denmark Lane	C3-C4
Denmark Road	C3
East Quay Road	B1
East Street	B2-B1
Elizabeth Road	C3-C4
Emerson Road	B2-C2
Ferry Road	A1
Garland Road	C4
Green Road	B2-C1
Hackford Road	C4
High Street	A1-B1-B2-B3
Hill Street	B2
Holes Bay Road	B3-B4-A4
Jolliffe Road	C4
Kingland Road	B2-B3-C3
Kingston Road	C4
Labrador Drive	B1
Lagland Street	B1-B2
Longfleet Road	C3-C4
Maple Road	C3-C4
Market Close	B2
Marnhull Road	C4
Mount Pleasant Road	C3
New Orchard	A2-B2
New Quay Road	A1
Newfoundland Drive	B2-C2-C1
North Street	B2
Old Orchard	B2-B1
Parkstone Road	C3
Perry Gardens	B1
St Johns Road	C4
St Mary's Road	C3-C4
Seldown Bridge	C1-C2
Seldown Lane	C3
Seldown Road	C3
Serpentine Road	B3-C3
Skinner Street	B1-B2
Stanley Road	B1-C1
Sterte Avenue	A4-B4
Sterte Avenue West	A4

Sterte Close	B3
Sterte Esplanade	B4-B3
Sterte Road	B4-B3
Strand Street	A1-B1
Taverner Close	C2
Thames Street	A1
The Quay	A1-B1
Towngate Bridge	B3
Vallis Close	C1
Waldren Close	C2
West Quay Road	A1-A2-B2-B3
West Street	A1-A2-B2
West View Road	B4
Wimborne Road	C4-C3

AA shop	B3
10 Falkland Square	
Poole BH15 1ER	

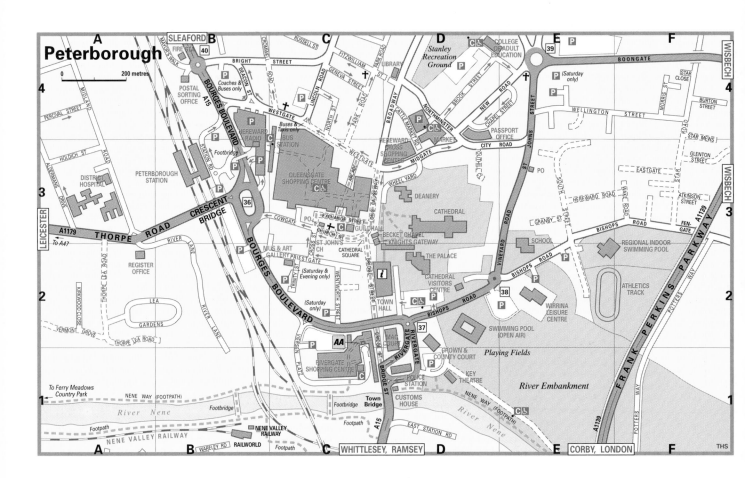

Peterborough

Peterborough is found on atlas page **64**,
grid reference TL1998

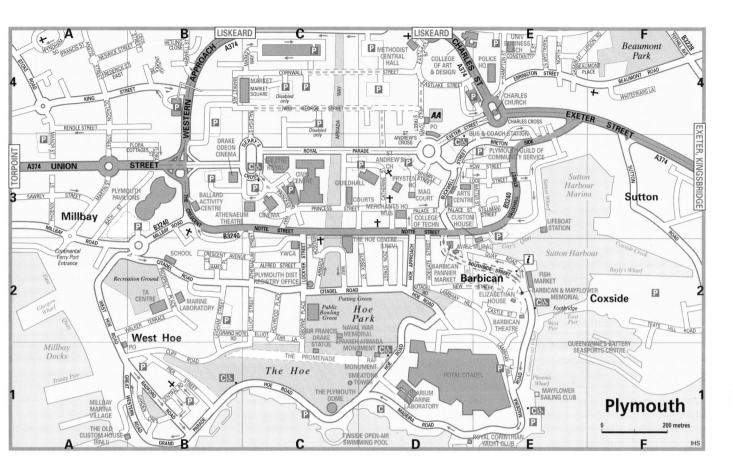

Plymouth

Plymouth is found on atlas page **6**,
grid reference SX**475**4

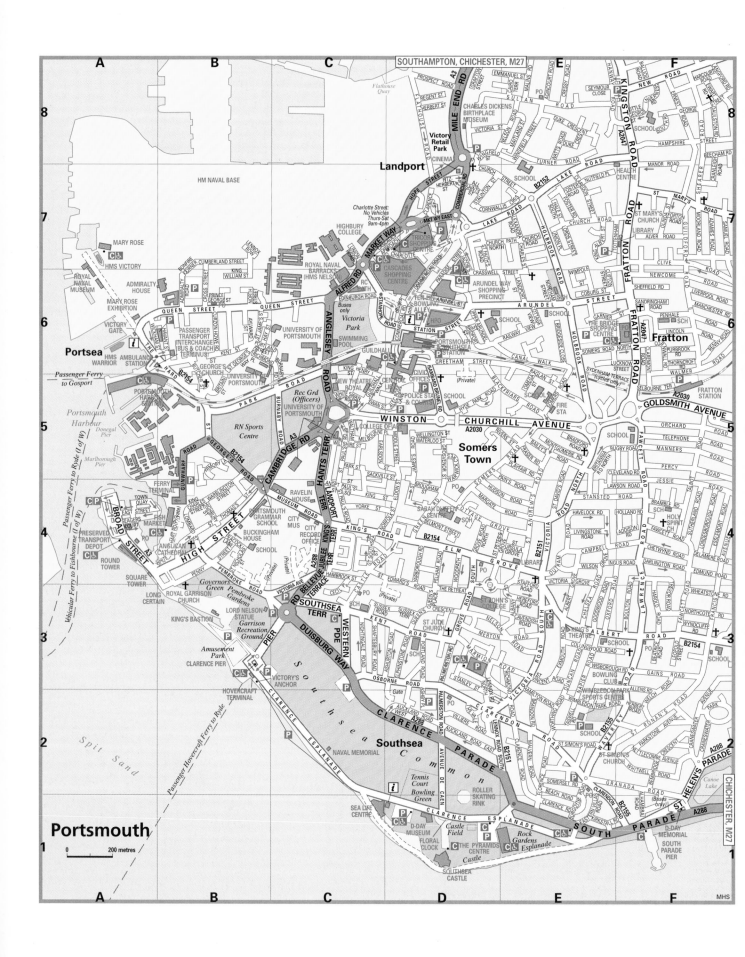

Portsmouth

0   200 metres

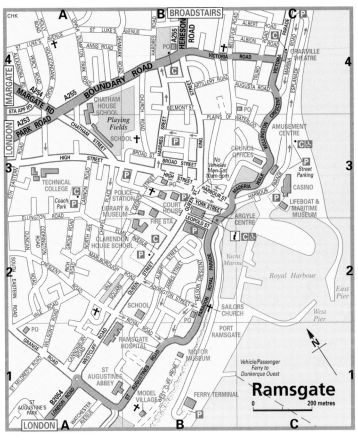

Ramsgate

Ramsgate is found on atlas page **29**,
grid reference TR**38**65

Addington Street	B2	High Street	A3-B3	Watchester Avenue	A1
Albert Road	C4	Hollicondane Road	A4	Wellington Crescent	C3-C4
Albert Street	B2	Holly Road	A4	West Cliff Promenade	B1
Albion Road	B4-C4	James Street	B2	Westcliff Road	A1-A2
Alexandra Road	A4	King Street	B3-B4	Willson's Road	A1-A2
Anns Road	A4	Leopold Street	B2-B3	York Street	B3
Artillery Road	B4	London Road	A1		
Augusta Road	B4-C4	Madeira Walk	B3-C3		
Bellevue Road	B4	Margate Road	A4		
Belmont Street	B4	Marina Road	C4		
Boundary Road	A4-B4	Marlborough Road	A2-B2		
Broad Street	B3	Nelson Crescent	B2		
Cannonbury Road	A1	North Avenue	A2		
Canon Road	A3	Paragon Royal Parade	B1-B2		
Chapel Place	A2-A3	Park Road	A3		
Chatham Street	A3	Percy Road	A4		
Church Road	B3-B4	Plains of Waterloo	B3-C3		
Codrington Road	A2	Queen Street	A2-B2-B3		
Crescent Road	A2	Richmond Road	A2		
Denmark Road	A4-B4	Royal Road	A2-B2-B1		
Duncan Road	A2	South Eastern Road	A2-A3		
Ellington Road	A2-A3	St Augustine's Park	A1		
Elms Avenue	A2-B2	St Augustines Road	A1-B1		
Esplanade	C3-C4	St Luke's Avenue	A4-B4		
George Street	B3	St Mildred's Road	A1		
Grange Road	A1	Station Approach Road	A4		
Grove Road	A2	Truro Road	C4		
Harbour Parade	B3-C3	Upper Dumpton Park Road	A4		
Harbour Street	B3	Vale Road	A1-A2		
Hardres Road	B4	Vale Square	A2-B2		
Hardres Street	B3-B4	Victoria Parade	C4		
Hereson Road	B4	Victoria Road	B4-C4		

Portsmouth

Portsmouth is found on atlas page **13**,
grid reference SU**64**00

Adames Road	F7	Campbell Road	E4-F4	Edmund Road	F4	Hereford Road	E3	Northam Street	E6	St Ursula Grove	E4
Addison Road	F4	Canal Walk	E5-E6	Eldon Street	D4-D5	High Street	B4	Northcote Road	F3	St Vincent Road	E3
Admiralty Road	B6	Cascades Approach	C7-D7	Elm Grove	D4-E4	Highbury Street	B4	Nuttfield Place	E7	Stafford Road	E3-E4
Agincourt Road	E8	Castle Road	C3-D4	Elphinstone Road	D3	Holbrook Road	E5-E7	Olinda Street	F7	Stanhope Road	C6-D6
Albany Road	E3-E4	Cavendish Road	E3	Emmanuel Street	D8-E8	Holland Road	F4	Omega Street	E5	Stanley Street	D3-E2
Albert Grove	E3-E4	Cecil Place	C3-C4	Ernest Road	F7-F8	Hope Street	D7	Orchard Road	F5	Stansted Road	E4-F4
Albert Road	E5-F3	Charles Street	E6-E7	Esslemont Road	F4	Hudson Road	D4-E4	Osborne Road	C3-D3	Station Street	D6
Alec Rose Lane	D5	Charlotte Street	D7	Ewart Road	F8	Hyde Park Road	D5	Outram Road	E4	Staunton Street	D7
Alexandra Road	E7	Chelsea Road	E3-E4	Exmouth Road	E3	Inglis Road	E4-F4	Oxford Road	E3-F4	Sultan Road	D8-E8
Alfred Road	C6	Chetwynd Road	F4	Fawcett Road	F3-F5	Inverness Road	F8	Pain's Road	E4	Sussex Road	C3-D3
Alhambra Road	F1-F2	Church Path North	D7-E7	Fitzherbert Street	D7	Isambard Brunel Road	D5-D6	Palmerston Road	D2-D3	Sussex Terrace	D3
All Saints Street	D7	Church Road	E7	Flathouse Road	D7-D8	Jacob's Street	D6-D7	Paradise Street	D6-D7	Sutherland Road	F4
Allens Road	F3	Church Street	D7-E7	Florence Road	E1-E2	Jessie Road	F4	Park Road	B5-C6	Swan Street	C5
Alver Road	F7	Claredon Street	E7	Forge Street	F8	Jubilee Terrace	C4	Park Street	C5	Sydenham Terrace	E6-F5
Anglesey Road	C5-C6	Claremont Road	F5-F6	Forton Road	F7	Kent Road	C3-D3	Parkstone Road	F2	Talbot Road	F4-F5
Armoury Lane	B5	Clarence Esplanade	B3-E1	Foster Road	E7	Kent Street	B6	Peacock Lane	B4	Taswell Road	E2
Arundel Street	D6-F6	Clarence Parade	C2-E1	Francis Avenue	F3-F4	King Albert Street	E7	Pembroke Road	B4-C3	Telephone Road	F5
Ashby Place	D2-D3	Clarence Road	E1-E2	Fraser Road	E5	King Charles Street	B4	Penhale Road	F6	The Hard	A6-B5
Ashurton Road	C3-D3	Clarence Street	D7	Fratton Road	F5-F7	King Henry Street	C5-C6	Penny Street	B3-B4	The Retreat	D3
Auckland Road East	D2	Clarendon Road	D2-F1	Fulham Road	D4	King Street	C4-D4	Percy Road	F4-F5	The Vale	D2
Auckland Road West	D2	Cleveland Road	E4-F5	Gains Road	F3	King William Street	B6-B7	Pier Road	B3-C3	Thorncroft Road	F6
Avenue De Caen	D1-D2	Clifton Street	E6-F6	Garnier Street	E6-F6	King's Road	C4-D4	Playfair Road	E4-E5	Tottenham Road	E7-F7
Aylward Street	B6	Clive Road	F6-F7	Goldsmith Avenue	F5	King's Terrace	C4	Portland Road	D3	Town Quay	A4
Bailey's Road	E5	Coburg Street	E6	Goodwood Road	E3-E4	Kingston Road	F7-F8	Portland Street	B6-C6	Trevor Road	F3-F4
Balliou Road	F8	Collingwood Road	E3-F3	Grafton Street	D8	Kirkstall Road	E1-F1	Prince George Street	B6	Turner Road	E8
Beach Road	E1-E2	Commercial Road	D6-D7	Granada Road	E2-F1	Lake Road	D7-E8	Prospect Road	D8	Union Place	E7
Beatrice Road	F3	Cornwall Road	F7	Great Southsea Road	C4	Landport Street	C4	Purbrook Road	F6	Union Road	C7
Beecham Road	F8	Cornwallis Crescent	D7-E7	Green Road	D4	Landport Street	E6	Queen Street	A6-C6	Upper Arundel Street	D6
Bellevue Terrace	C3-C4	Cottage Road	D4-E4	Greetham Street	D6-E6	Landport Terrace	C4	Queen's Crescent	D3	Victoria Avenue	B3-C4
Belmont Street	D4	Cottage View	E6	Grosvenor Street	D4-D5	Langford Road	F8	Queen's Place	D3	Victoria Grove	E4
Bembridge Crescent	F2	Craneswater Avenue	F2-F3	Grove Road North	D4	Lawrence Road	F3-F4	Raglan Street	E5-E6	Victoria Road North	E4-E5
Blackfriars Road	D6-E5	Craneswater Park	F2	Grove Road South	D3-D4	Lawson Road	E4-F4	Railway View	D6-E6	Victoria Road South	E2-E4
Bonfire Corner	B6-B7	Cranleigh Road	F7-F8	Guildford Road	F6-F7	Lennox Road North	D2-D3	Regent Road	D8	Victoria Street	D8-E8
Boulton Road	F3-F4	Craswell Street	D6-E6	Guildhall Walk	C5	Lennox Road South	D2-E2	Renny Road	F6	Villiers Road	D2
Bradford Road	E5	Cressy Road	E8	Gunwharf Road	B4-B5	Lennox Row	B7	Richmond Place	B6	Walmer Road	F5-F6
Bramble Road	F4	Cross Street	B6-B7	Hale Street South	E7	Leopold Street	F3	Richmond Road	E2-E3	Waltham Street	C5
Brandon Road	E2	Cumberland Street	B7	Hambrook Street	C4	Lincoln Road	F6	Rivers Street	D5-E5	Warblington Street	B4
Bridgeside Close	E6	Curzon Howe Road	B6	Hamilton Road	E2-E3	Little George Street	F8	Rugby Road	E5-F5	Warwick Crescent	D4-D5
Bridport Street	D6	Darlington Road	F4	Hampshire Street	F8	Liverpool Road	F6	Sackville Street	C5-D4	Waterloo Street	D5
Britain Street	B5	Daulston Road	F8	Hampshire Terrace	C4-C5	Livingstone Road	E4	Samuel Road	F7	Watts Road	E8
Britannia Road North	E5	Delamere Road	F4	Hanway Road	E8-F8	Lombard Street	B4	Sandringham Road	F6	Waverley Road	E2-F3
Broad Street	A4	Duisburg Way	C2-C3	Harcourt Road	F8	Londesborough Road	F4	Seagers Court	A4	Welch Road	F2-F3
Brougham Street	D4	Duke Crescent	E8	Harold Road	F3-F4	Lords Street	E7	Selbourne Terrace	F5	Wellington Street	D5
Burgoyne Road	E1-E2	Duncan Road	E3	Havant Street	B6	Lucknow Street	E6-F6	Seymour Close	E8	Western Parade	C3
Burnaby Road	C5-C6	Earlsdon Street	C4-D5	Havelock Road	E4	Maitland Street	E8	Shaftesbury Road	C3	Wheatstone Road	F3
Butcher Street	B5-B6	East Street	A4	Hay Street	B6	Mallins Road	E8	Shearer Road	F7-F8	White Hart Road	B4
Cairo Terrace	E8	Eastern Villas Road	E1-E2	Herbert Road	F2	Malvern Road	E2	Sheffield Road	F6	White Swan Road	C5
Cambridge Road	B4-C5	Edinburgh Road	C6	Herbert Street	D8	Manchester Road	F6	Somers Road	D4-E5	Whitwell Road	F2
						Manners Road	F5	Somers Road North	E6-F6	Wickham Street	A6-B6
						Manor Road	F7-F8	Somerset Road	E2	Wilson Grove	E4
						Margate Road	D4-E4	South Parade	E1-F1	Wiltshire Street	C5
						Market Way	C7-D7	South Road	F8	Wimbledon Park Road	E2
						Market Way East	D7	Southsea Terrace	C3	Wimpole Street	E6
						Marmion Road	D3-E3	St Andrew's Road	E4-E5	Wingfield Street	D8-E8
						Melbourne Place	C5-D5	St David's Road	E4-E5	Winston Churchill Avenue	C5-E5
						Merton Road	D3-E3	St Edward's Road	C4-D3	Wisborough Road	E3-F3
						Middle Street	D5	St Faith's Road	D7	Woodpath	D3-D4
						Mile End Road	D8	St George's Road	B4-B5	Worthing Road	E2
						Montgomerie Road	E5	St George's Way	B6	Wyndcliffe Road	F3
						Moorland Road	F7	St Helen's Parade	F1-F2	Yarborough Road	D4
						Museum Road	C4	St James's Road	D4-D5	Yorke Street	C4-D4
						Napier Road	E2-E3	St James's Street	B6		
						Nelson Road	D3-E3	St Mary's Road	F7	AA shop	
						Nelson Road	E8	St Nicholas Street	B4	12 London Road	
						Nettlecombe Avenue	F2	St Paul's Road	C4-C5	Portsmouth PO1 1NL	
						New Road	F8	St Paul's Square	C4		
						Newcome Road	F6	St Peter's Grove	E4	AA Port shop	
						Nightingale Road	C3	St Ronan's Road	F2	Wharf Road View	
						Norfolk Street	C4-D4	St Simon's Road	E2	Portsmouth PO2 8HB	
						North Street	B6	St Thomas's Street	B4		

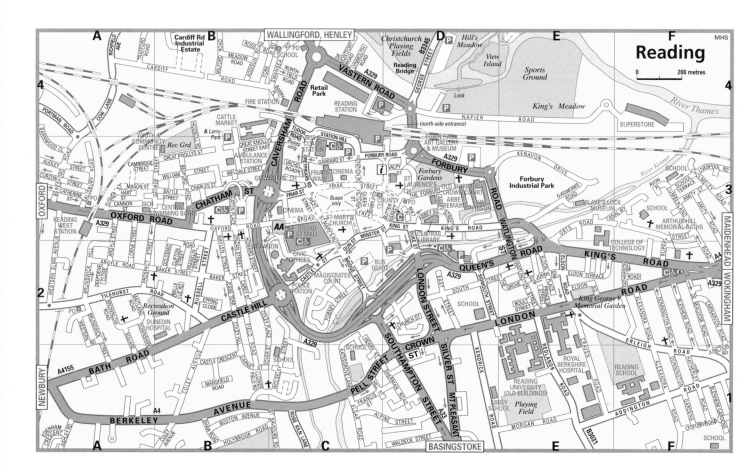

Reading

Reading is found on atlas page **24**,
grid reference SU**71**73

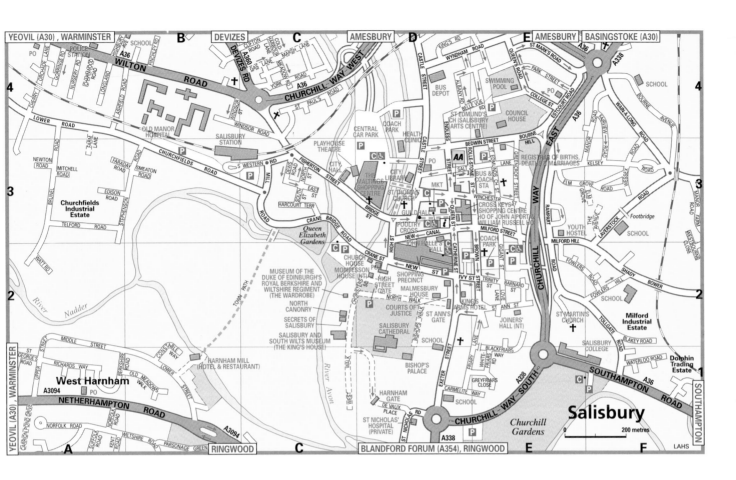

Salisbury

Salisbury is found on atlas page **23**,
grid reference SU1429

AA shop   D3
1 Winchester Street
Salisbury SP1 1HB

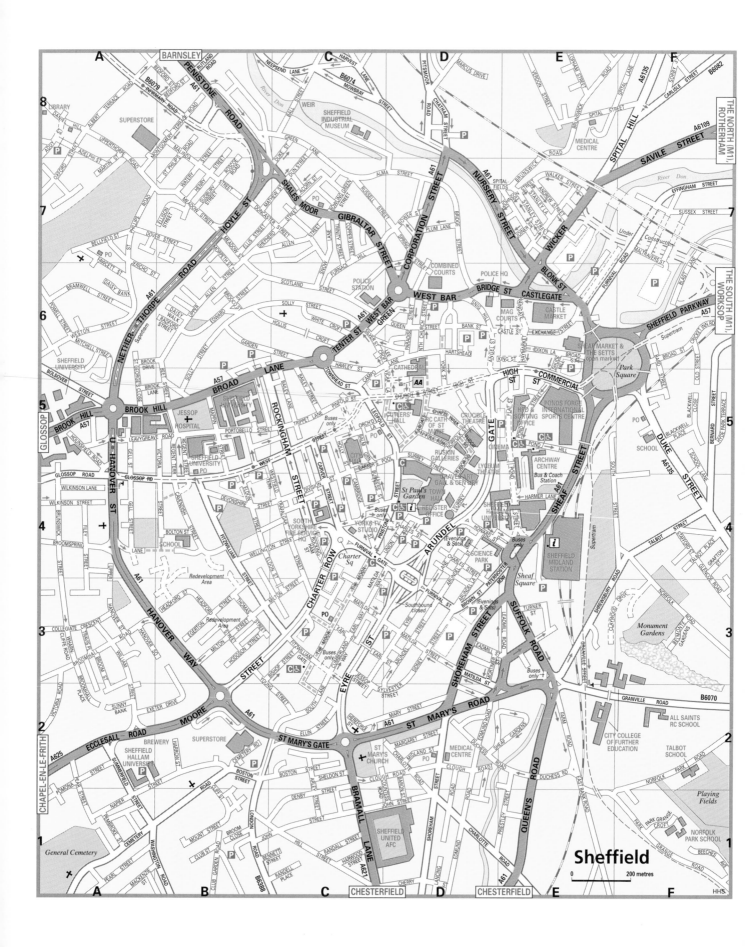

Sheffield

0   200 metres

246

HHS

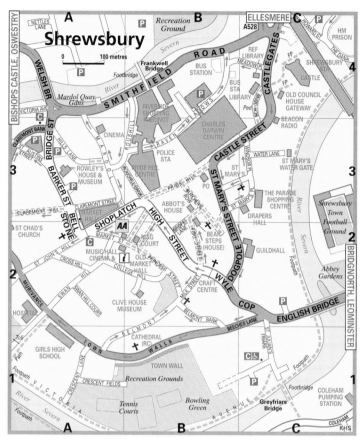

Shrewsbury

Shrewsbury is found on atlas page **59**,
grid reference SJ4912

Barker Street	A3	Roushill Bank	B3
Beeches Lane	B1-C2	School Gardens	C3-C4
Belmont	A1-B2	Shoplatch	A2-B3
Belmont Bank	B2	Smithfield Road	A4-C4
Bellstone	A2-A3	St Austins Street	A3
Bridge Street	A3	St John's Hill	A2
Butcher's Row	B3	St Julian's Friars	C1-C2
Castle Street	B3-C3	St Mary's Place	B3-C3
Castlegates	C4	St Mary's Street	B2-B3
Claremont Bank	A3	Swan Hill	A2
Claremont Hill	A3	Swan Hill Court	A2
Claremont Street	A3	The Dana	C4
Coleham	C1	Town Walls	A2-B1
College Hill	A2-B2	Victoria Avenue	A4
Crescent Fields	A1-B1	Water Lane	C3
Crescent Lane	A1	Welsh Bridge	A4
Cross Hill	A2	Windsor Place	C3
Dogpole	B2	Wyle Cop	B2-C2
English Bridge	C2		
Fish Street	B2-B3		
Grope Lane	B2-B3		
High Street	B2-B3		
Hills Lane	A3		
Howard Street	C4		
Mardol	A3-A4		
Market Street	A2		
Meadow Place	B4-C4		
Milk Street	B2		
Murivance	A2		
Nettles Lane	A4		
Pride Hill	B3		
Princess Street	B2	AA shop	A2
Raven Meadows	B3-B4	6 Market Street	
Roushill	A3-B4	Shrewsbury SY1 1LE	

Sheffield

Sheffield is found on atlas page **74**,
grid reference SK3587

Acorn Street	C7	Brook Lane	A5-B5	Doncaster Street	B7-C7
Adelphi Street	A7-A8	Broom Close	C1-B1	Dover Street	A7-B7
Addy Street	A8	Broom Street	A3-A2	Duchess Road	D2-E2
Albert Terrace Road	A8	Broomhall Place	A2-A3	Duke Street	C8
Allen Street	C7	Broomhall Road	A3	Duke Street	F4-F5
Alma Street	C7-D7	Broomspring Lane	A4-B4	Earl Street	C3-D3
Andrew Street	E7	Brown Street	D3	Earl Way	C3
Angel Street	D5-D6	Brunswick Street	A3-A4	East Bank Road	E1-E2
Arley Street	C1-C2	Brunswick Road	E7-E8	Ecclesall Road	A2-B2
Arundel Gate	D4-D5	Burgess Street	C4-C5	Edmund Road	D1-D2
Arundel Street	D3-D4	Cambridge Street	C4	Edward Street	B6
Bailey Lane	C5	Campo Lane	C5-D5-D6	Effingham Street	F7
Bailey Street	C5	Carlisle Street	F8	Egerton Street	B3
Ball Street	C8	Carver Street	C4-C5	Eldon Street	B4-C4
Balm Green	C5	Castle Street	D6-E6	Ellin Street	C2
Bank Street	D6	Castlegate	E6	Ellis Street	B7
Bard Street	F5-F6	Cavendish Street	B4	Ellison Street	B7
Barker's Pool	C4-C5-D5	Cemetery Road	A1-B1-B2	Eyre Street	C2-C3-D3-D4
Baron Street	D1-D2	Chapel Walk	D5	Exchange Street	E6
Bedford Street	B8	Charles Street	D4	Exeter Drive	A2-B2
Beeches Avenue	F1	Charlotte Road	D2-D1-E1	Eyre Lane	C3-D3
Beet Street	B5-B6	Charter Row	C3-C4	Fargate	D5
Belmonte Gardens	F3	Chatham Street	D7-D8	Farm Road	E2
Bennet Street	B1-C1	Cherry Street	D1	Fawcett Street	A6-A7
Bernard Street	F4-F5-F6	Church Street	C5-D5	Filey Street	A3-A4
Bishop Street	B2-C2	Claywood Drive	E3-F3	Fitzwilliam Gate	C3
Blackwell Close	F5	Cliff Street	B1	Fitzwilliam Street	B4-B3-C3
Blackwell Place	F5	Clough Road	C2-D2	Flat Street	E5
Blast Lane	F6-F7	Club Garden Road	B1	Furnace Hill	C6-C7
Blonk Street	E6	Club Street	B1	Furnival Gate	C4-D4
Bolton Street	B4	Collegiate Crescent	A3	Furnival Road	E6-F6-F7
Bolsover Street	A5	Commercial Street	E5	Furnival Street	D3
Boston Street	B2-C2	Copper Street	C7	Garden Street	B6-C6
Bower Street	C7-D7	Corporation Street	D6-D7	Gell Street	A4-A5
Bowling Green Street	C7	Countess Road	D1-D2	Gibraltar Street	D7-C7-D6
Bramall Lane	C1-C2	Cricket Inn Road	F6	Glencoe Road	F3-F4
Bramwell Street	A6	Cumberland Way	C3	Glossop Road	A4-B4
Bridge Street	D7-D6-E6	Daisy Bank	A6	Grafton Street	F4
Broad Lane	B5-C5-C6	Daisy Walk	B6	Granville Road	E2-F2
Broad Street	F6	Daniel Hill	A8	Granville Street	E3-E4
Brocco Street	B6	Denby Street	C1	Green Lane	B8-C8-C7
Brook Drive	A6-B6	Devonshire Street	B4-C4	Hanover Square	A3
Brook Hill	A5-B5	Division Street	C4	Hanover Way	A3-B3-B2

Harmer Lane	E4	Nursery Street	D7-E7-E6	Spring Street	D6-E7
Harrow Street	B2	Old Street	F6-F5	Stafford Street	F4
Hartshead	D6	Orchard Lane	C5	Stanley Lane	E7
Harvest Lane	C8	Oxford Street	A7-A8	Stanley Street	E7
Harwood Street	C1	Paradise Street	D6	Sudbury Street	F7
Hawley Street	C6-C5	Park Grange Croft	F1	Suffolk Road	E3
Haymarket	E6	Park Grange Road	E1-F1	Summerfield Street	A2-A1
Headford Street	B3	Park Square	E5-E6-F6-F5	Sunny Bank	A2
Henry Street	B7	Paternoster Row	D3-D4-E4	Surrey Place	D4
Hereford Street	C2	Pear Street	A1-A2	Surrey Street	D5
High Street	D5-E5	Pearl Street	A1	Sussex Street	F7
Hill Street	B1-C1	Pembroke Street	A1	Sylvester Street	C2-D2
Hodgson Street	B3	Penistone Road	B7-B8	Talbot Place	F4
Hollis Croft	B6-C6	Pinfold Street	C5	Talbot Street	F4
Holly Street	C4-C5	Pinstone Street	C4-D4-D5	Tenter Street	C6
Hounsfield Road	A5	Pitsmoor Road	D8	The Moor	C3-C4
Howard Street	D4-E4	Plum Lane	D7	Thomas Street	B3
Hoyle Street	B7	Pomona Street	A1-A2	Townhead Street	C5
Hyde Park Terrace	F5	Pond Hill	E5	Trippet Lane	C5
Infirmary Road	A8-B8	Pond Street	E5	Trafalgar Street	C3-C4
Jericho Street	A6-A7	Portobello Street	B5-C5	Travis Place	A3
Jessop Street	C2-C3	Powell Street	A6	Trinity Street	C7
John Street	B1-C1-D1	Priestley Street	D1-E1-E2	Tudor Square	D4-D5
Johnson Street	D7-E7	Queen Street	C6-D6	Turner Street	E3
Joiner Street	E7	Queen's Road	E1-E2	Union Street	C4-D4
King Street	D5-E5	Radford Street	B6	Upper Allen Street	B6
Lancing Road	D1	Randall Street	C1	Upper Hanover Street	A3-A4-A5
Leadmill Street	D3	Randall Place	C1	Upperthorpe Road	A7-A8
Leadmill Road	E3	Regent Street	B4-B5	Verdon Street	E8
Leavygreave Road	A5-B5	Regent Terrace	B4-B5	Vicar Lane	C5-D5
Lee Croft	C6	Rockingham Street	B5-C5-C4	Victoria Road	A2-A3
Leopold Street	C5-C6	Roscoe Road	B7	Victoria Street	B4-B5
London Road	B1-B2-C2	Russell Street	C7	Waingate	E6
Lopham Street	E8	Rutland Road	B8	Walker Street	E7
Mackenie Street	A1	St Georges Close	A5-A6	Washington Road	A1-B1
Maltravers Street	F6-F7	St Mary's Gate	C2	Watery Street	B7-B8
Mappin Street	B5	St Mary's Road	C2-D2-E2	Wellington Street	B4-C4
Marcus Drive	D8	St Philip's Road	A6-A7-B7-B8	West Bar	D6
Margaret Street	D2	Savile Street	E7-F7-F8	West Bar Green	C6-D6
Martin Street	A7-A8	School Lane	F5	West Street	B4-B5-C5
Mary Street	C2-D2	Scotland Street	B6-C6	Westtield Terrace	B4-C5
Mathew Street	B7-C7	Shales Moor	B7-C7	Weston Street	A5-A6
Matilda Street	C3-D3-D2	Sheaf Gardens	D2-E2	Wharncliffe Road	A3
Matilda Way	C3-C4	Sheaf Street	E4-E5	White Croft	C6
Meadow Street	B6-B7	Sheffield Parkway	F6	Wicker	E6-E7
Milton Street	B3-C3	Shepherd Street	B6-B7-C7	Wilkinson Lane	A4
Mitchell Street	A5-A6	Shoreham Street	D1-D2-E3	Wilkinson Street	A4
Montgomery Terrace Road		Shrewsbury Road	E3-E4-F3-F4	William Street	A2-A3
	A7-B8-A8	Shude Hill	E5-E6	York Street	D5-D6
Moore Street	B2-B3-C3	Sidney Street	D3	Young Street	B3-C2
Morpeth Street	B6-B7	Silver Street	C6		
Mount Street	B1	Snig Hill	D6		
Mowbray Street	C8-D8	Snow Lane	C6-C7		
Napier Street	A2-A1-B2	Solly Street	B5-B6-C6		
Neepsend Lane	B8-C8	Sorby Street	F8		
Netherthorpe Road	A5-A6-B6-B7	South Lane	C2		
Norfolk Park Road	E1-E2-F2	South Street	E4-E5		
Norfolk Road	F3-F4	Spitalfields	D7-E7		
Norfolk Row	D5	Spital Hill	E7-E8-F8		
Norfolk Street	D5	Spital Lane	F8	AA shop	D5
North Church Street	D6	Spital Street	E8-F8	5 St James Row,	
				Sheffield S1 1AY	

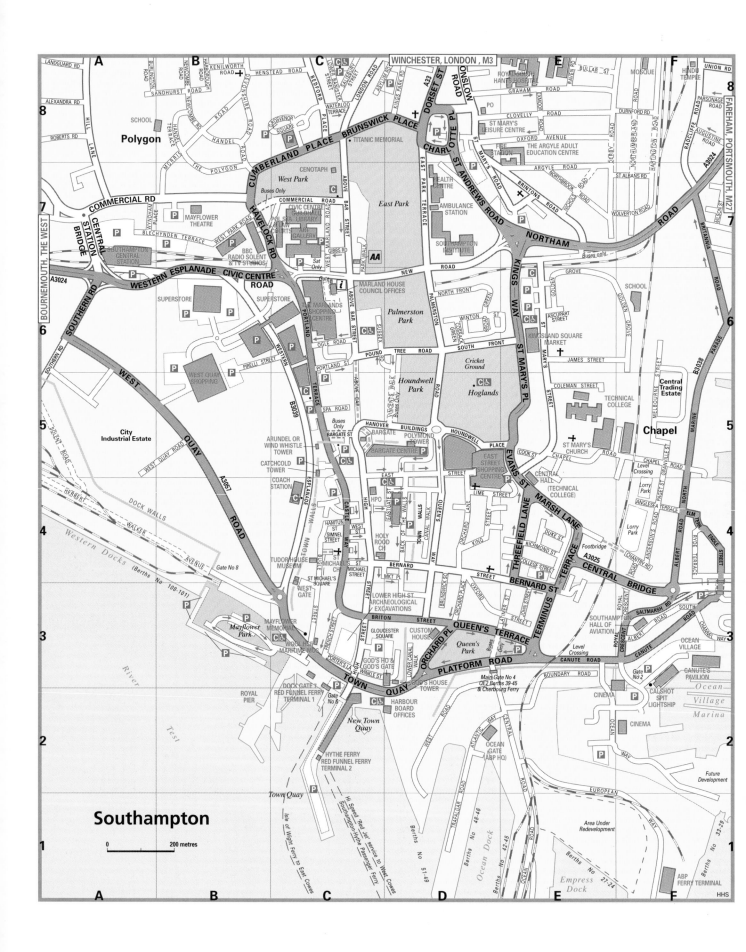

Southampton

0   200 metres

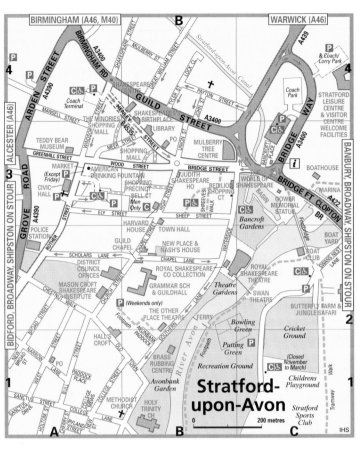

Stratford-upon-Avon

Stratford-upon-Avon is found on atlas page **48**,
grid reference SP**2055**

Arden Street	A4	Tyler Street	B4
Avonbank Paddock	B1-B2	Union Street	B3
Bancroft Place	C3	Waterside	B2-B3
Birmingham Road	A4	Wenlock Road	C4
Brewery Street	A4	West Street	A1-A2
Bridge Foot	C3	Windsor Street	A3-A4
Bridge Street	B3	Wood Street	A3-B3
Bridge Way	C3-C4		
Broad Street	A1-A2		
Bull Street	A1-A2		
Chapel Lane	B2-B3		
Cherry Street	A1		
Chestnut Walk	A2		
Church Street	A2-B2		
Clopton Bridge	C2-C3		
College Lane	A1-B1		
College Mews	A1		
College Street	A1-B1		
Ely Street	A3-B3		
Great William Street	B4		
Greenhill Street	A3		
Grove Road	A2-A3		
Guild Street	A4-B3		
Henley Street	A4-B3		
High Street	B3		
Holtom Street	A1		
Lock Close	B4		
Mansell Street	A3-A4		
Meer Street	A3-B3		
Mulberry Street	B4		
Narrow Lane	A1		
New Broad Street	A1		
New Street	A1		
Old Town	A2-B1		
Paddock Place	A1		
Payton Street	B4-C4		
Rother Street	A2-A3		
Ryland Street	A1		
Sanctus Drive	A1		
Sanctus Street	A1		
Scholars Lane	A2-B2		
Shakespeare Street	A4-B4		
Sheep Street	B3		
Shreeves Walk	B3		
Southern Lane	B1-B2		
Swans Nest Lane	C2		

Southampton

Southampton is found on atlas page **13**,
grid reference SU**4112**

Above Bar Street	C5-C6-C7-C8	Cumberland Place	B7 -C7-C8	Lower Banister Street	C8	Saltmarsh Road	F3
Albert Road North	F4	Derby Road	E7-E8-F8	Lower Canal Walk	D3	Sandhurst Road	A8-B8
Albert Road South	F3	Devonshire Road	B8	Marine Parade	F5-F6	Simnel Street	C4
Alexandra Road	A8	Dorset Street	D8	Market Place	D4	Solent Road	A4-A5
Altlantic Way	D2-E2	Duke Street	E4	Marsh Lane	E4	South Front	D6-E6
Anderson's Road	F4	Dunford Road	F8	Melbourne Street	F5-F6	Southern Road	A5-A6
Anglesea Terrace	F4	East Gate Street	D4	Michael Street	C4	Spa Road	C5
Argyle Road	E7	East Park Terrace	D7-D8	Morris Road	B7-B8	St Albans Road	F7
Ascupart Street	E6	East Street	C4-D4-D5	New Road	C7-D6-D7-E7	St Andrews Road	E7-D7-D8
Asylum Road	C8-D8	Elm Terrace	F4	Newcombe Road	B8	St Mary's Place	E5-E6
Augustine Road	F8	Endle Street	F4	Nichols Road	E7	St Mary's Road	E7-D7-D8
Back of the Walls	D3-D4	European Way	F1-E1-E2	North Front	D6	St Mary's Street	E5-E6-E7
Bargate Street	C5	Evans Street	E4-E5	Northam Road	E7-F7	St Michael's Square	C4
Bedford Place	C8	Exmoor Road	E8	Northbrook Road	E7	Sussex Road	C6-D6
Bernard Street	C4-D4-D3-E3	French Street	C3	Northumberland Road	F7-F8	Terminus Terrace	E3-E4
Blechynden Terrace	A7-B7	Gibbs Road	C7	Ocean Road	E1	The Polygon	B7-B8
Boundary Road	E2-E3	Gloucester Square	C3-D3	Ocean Way	F1-F2-E2-E3	Threefield Lane	E4
Brintons Road	E7-D7-D8	Golden Grove	E6-F6	Ogle Street	C6	Town Quay	C3-C2-D2
Britannia Road	F6-F7	Graham Road	D8-E8	Onslow Road	D8	Trafalgar Road	D1-D2
Briton Street	C3-D3	Granville Street	F4-F5	Orchard Lane	D4	Union Road	F8
Broad Green	D6	Grosvenor Square	C8	Orchard Place	D3-D4	Vincents Walk	D5-D6
Brunswick Place	C8-D8	Hamtun Street	C4	Oxford Avenue	D8-E8	Waterloo Terrace	C8
Brunswick Square	D3-D4	Handel Road	B7-B8	Oxford Street	E3-D3-D4	West Marland Road	B6-B7
Bugle Street	C3-C4	Handel Terrace	B8	Page Street	F4	West Park Road	B6
Bullar Street	E8	Hanover Buildings	C5-D5	Palmerston Road	D5-D6	West Quay Road	A6-C3
Burlington Road	A8-B8	Harborough Road	B8	Park Walk	C6-C7	West Road	D1-D2-D3
Canal Walk	D4	Hartington Road	F7-F8	Pasonage Road	F8	West Street	C4
Canute Road	E3-F3	Havelock Road	B7-C7	Pirelli Street	B6-E6	Western Esplanade	A6-C3
Castle Way	C4-C3	Henstead Road	B8-C8	Platform Road	D3-E3	Wilson Street	F7
Central Bridge	E4-F4-F3	Herbert Walker Avenue	A4-B3	Porter's Lane	C3	Winkle Street	C3
Central Road	E2	High Street	C3-C4-C5	Portland Street	C6	Winton Street	D6-E6
Central Station Bridge	A6-A7	Hill Lane	A7-A8	Portland Terrace	C6-C5	Wolverton Road	E7-F7
Channel Way	F3	Houndwell Place	D5-E5	Pound Tree Road	C6-D6	Wyndham Place	A7
Chantry Road	F4	James Street	E6-F6	Queen's Terrace	D3-E3		
Chapel Road	E5-F5	John Street	E3	Queens Way	D3-D4-D5		
Charlotte Place	D8	Kenilworth Road	B8	Radcliffe Road	F7-F8		
Civic Centre Road	B6-C6	King Street	D4	Raven Road	E8		
Clovelly Road	D8-E8	Kings Park Road	D8	Richmond Street	E4		
Coleman Street	E5	Kings Way	E6-E7	Roberts Road	A8		
College Street	E4	Languard Road	A8	Royal Cresent	F3		
Commercial Road	A7-B7-C7	Latimer Street	E3	Royal Cresent Road	F3-F4		
Cook Street	E5	Lime Street	D4-E4	Ryde Terrace	F4		
Cossack Green	D6	London Road	C8	Salisbury Street	C8		

AA shop   C7
126 Above Bar Street
Southampton SO9 1GY

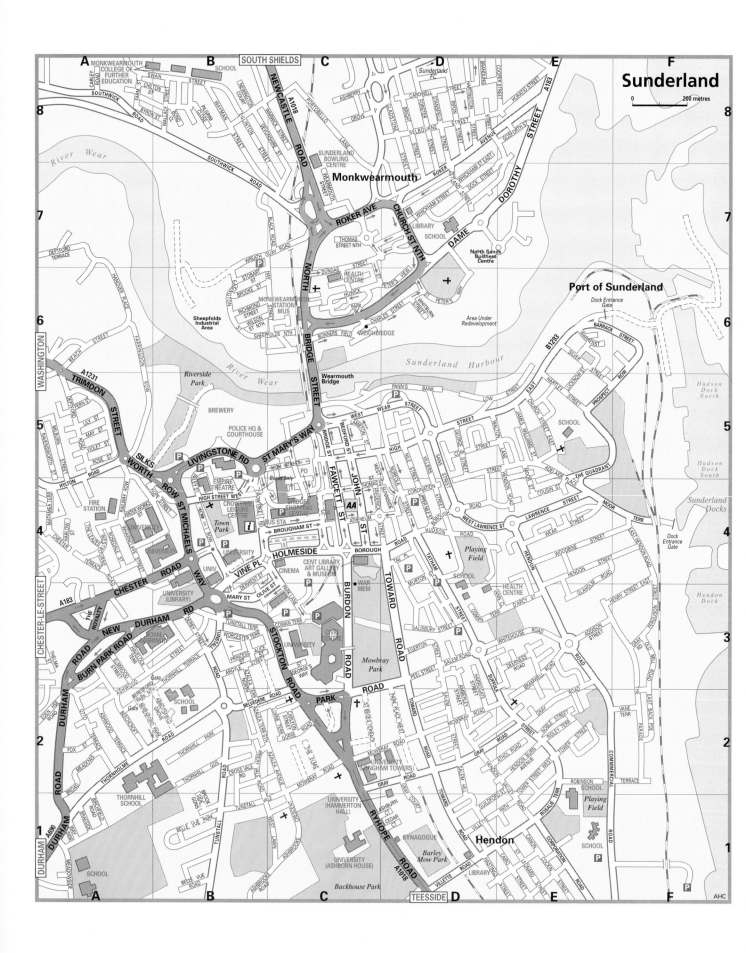

Sunderland

0   200 metres

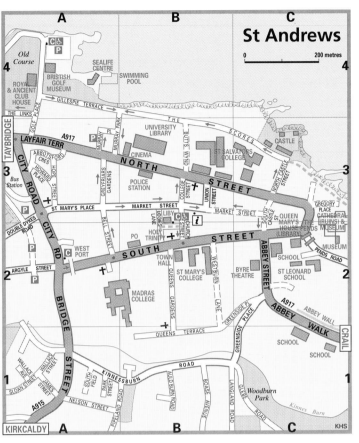

St Andrews

St Andrews is found on atlas page **127**, grid reference NO**5116**

Abbey Street	C2	Wallace Street	A1
Abbey Walk	C1-C2	Westburn Lane	B2
Abbotsford Crescent	A3		
Argyle Street	A2		
Auld Burn Road	B1		
Bell Street	A2-A3		
Boase Avenue	B1		
Bridge Street	A1-A2		
Butts Wynd	B3		
Church Street	B2-B3		
City Road	A2-A3		
College Street	B3		
Double Dykes Road	A2-A3		
Gillespie Terrace	A4		
Glebe Road	C1		
Golf Place	A3-A4		
Greenside Place	C1-C2		
Gregory Place	C3		
Greyfriars Gardens	A3		
Hope Street	A3		
Howard Place	A3		
James Street	A1		
Kinnessburn Road	A1-B1		
Langland Road	C1		
Layfair Terrace	A3		
Logies Lane	B2-B3		
Market Street	B3-C3		
Murray Park	A3-B4		
Murray Place	A3		
Nelson Street	A1		
North Castle Street	C3		
North Street	A3-C3		
Park Street	A1		
Pends Road	C2		
Pipeland Road	A1-B1		
Queens Gardens	B1-B2		
Queens Terrace	B1		
Sloan Street	A1		
South Castle Street	C2-C3		
South Street	A2-C2		
Southfield	A1		
St Mary's Place	A3		
The Links	A4		
The Scores	B4-C3		
Union Street	B3		
Wallace Avenue	A1		

Sunderland

Sunderland is found on atlas page **96**, grid reference NZ**3957**

Abbotsfield Grove	B2	Cedar Court	D1	Guildford Street	D1-E2	Old Mill Road	F3	The Elms	C2
Addison Street	E3	Charles Street	C6-D6	Gunton Street	B8-C7	Olive Street	B3-C4	The Leazes	A4
Adelaide Place	E4-E5	Chester Road	A3-B4	Hanover Place	A6-A7	Osman Terrace	D3-E3	The Parade	E3-F2
Alice Street	B3	Chester Terrace	A4	Hartington Street	D8	Otto Terrace	A2	The Quadrant	E5
Amberley Street	D2-D3	Chilton Street	A8-B8	Harlow Street	A4	Paley Street	B4-B5	The Royalty	A3
Ann Close	D3-E3	Church Street East	E5	Harrogate Street	D2-D3	Pann's Bank	C5-D5	Thelma Street	A3
Argyle Street	B3-C3	Commercial Road	E1-E2	Hartley Street	E5-E6	Park Lane	C3-C4	Thomas Street North	C7
Ashberry Grove	C8	Cooper Street	E8	Hastings Road	D1-E1	Park Place West	D2	Thornhill Gardens	B2
Ashbrooke Crescent	C1	Cork Street	D5-E5	Havelock Terrace	A3	Park Road	C2-D3	Thornhill Park	B2
Ashbrooke Road	B1-C1	Coronation Street	D4-E5	Hay Street	C6-C7	Peel Street	D3	Thornhill Terrace	B3
Ashburn Court	C1-C2	Corporation Road	E1	Hendon Burn Avenue	D2-E2	Pilgrim Close	B8	Thornholme Road	A1-B2
Ashwood Street	A2-B3	Cousin Street	E4	Hendon Road	E2-E5	Portobello Lane	C7-C8	Toward Road	D1-D4
Ashwood Terrace	A2	Cowan Terrace	C3	Hendon Street	E4-F4	Princess Street	B3	Tower Street	E2
Atheneum	C4-D4	Cross Vale Road	B2	Hendon Valley Road	D2-E1	Prospect Row	E5-F6	Tower Street West	E2
Athol Road	D2-E2	Crowtree Road	B4	Henry Street East	E3-F4	Railway Row	A4-A5	Trimdon Street	A5-A6
Azalea Avenue	C2	D'Arcy Street	E3	High Street	B5-D5	Ravensworth Street	A4-A5	Tunstall Road	B1-B3
Azalea Terrace North	B2-B3	Dame Dorothy Street	D6-E8	High Street West	B4	Richmond Street	B6	Tunstall Terrace	B3
Azalea Terrace South	B2	Deerness Road	E3	Holmside	C4	Ridley Terrace	E2	Tunstall Vale	B1-C2
Beach Street	A6	Deptford Road	A5	Hope Street	A4-B4	Ripon Street	D8	Upper Nile Street	D4
Bedford Street	C5	Deptford Terrace	A7	Horatio Street	E8	Robinson Terrace	E2-F2	Vane Terrace	F2
Beechcroft	A2	Derby Street	B3	Howick Park	C6	Roker Avenue	C7-E8	Villette Path	D1-E1
Belle Vue Park	B1	Derwent Street	B3-C3	Hudson Street	D4	Rosalie Terrace	E1-E2	Villette Road	D1-E1
Belvedere Road	B2-C3	Devonshire Street	B8-C7	Hylton Road	A4-A5	Rose Street	A5	Villiers Street	D4-D5
Beresford Park North	A2-B3	Dock Street	D7-E8	James Williams Street	E5	Rosedale Street	A4	Vine Place	B3-B4
Beresford Road	A2-B2	Dundas Street	C6-C7	John Street	C4-C5	Ryhope Road	C2-D1	Violet Street	A5
Birchfield Road	A1	Durham Road	A1-A3	Lambton Street	C5	Salem Hill	D2	Wallace Street	B8
Black Road	B7-C7	Easington Street	B6	Lawrence Street	E4	Salem Road	D3	Walton Lane	D5-E5
Bond Close	B8	East Back Poe	F2	Lily Street	A5	Salem Street	D2-D3	Warren Street	E6
Bonners Field	C6	East Barrack Street	D5-F6	Livingstone Road	B5	Salisbury Street	D3	Warwick Street	B8-C8
Borough Road	C4-E4	East Hendon Road	F4	Lorne Terrace	C2	Sans Street	D4-D5	Waterworks Street	A4
Braeside	A1	Eden House Road	A2	Low Row	B4	Selbourne Street	D8	Wayman Street	B8-C7
Bramwell Road	E2-E3	Egerton Street	D3	Low Street	D5-E5	Sheepfolds North	B6-C6	Wayside	A1
Brandling Street	D8	Elmwood Street	A3	Lucknow Street	E5-E6	Silksworth Row	A5-B4	Wear Street	E4
Bridge Street	C5	Farm Street	A8	Mary Street	B3	Silver Street	E5-E6	Wearmouth Street	C7
Briery Vale Road	B1-B2	Farringdon Row	A5-A6	Matamba Terrace	A4	Southwick Road	A8-C7	West Lawn	B1-C1
Bright Street	D7-D8	Fawcett Street	C4-C5	May Street	A5	St Bedes Terrace	C2	West Lawrence Street	D4-E4
Broad Meadows	A1-A2	Ferguson Street	F3	Meadowside	A1	St George's Way	C3	West Sunniside	C5-D4
Brooke Street	B6	Fern Street	A5	Milburn Street	A5	St Leonard Street	E1	West Wear Street	C5-D5
Brookside Gardens	B1-B2	Forster Street	D7-D8	Moor Street	E4-E5	St Mary's Way	B5-C5	Westbourne Road	A3-A4
Brougham Street	B4-C4	Fox Street	A2	Moor Terrace	E4-F4	St Michael's Way	B3-B4	Wharncliffe Street	A4
Burdon Road	C2-C4	Frederick Street	C4-D4	Mowbray Road	C2-E2	St Peter's View	C7-D7	Whickham Street	D7-D8
Burn Park Road	A3	George Street	D5	Murton Street	D3-D4	St Peter's Way	D6-D7	Whitburn Street	D6
Byron Street	A8-B8	Gladstone Street	D7-D8	New Durham Road	A3-B3	St Thomas Street	C4-D4	Whitehouse Road	D3-E3
Cairo Street	E1	Glaholm Road	E3-E4	Newington Court	B8	Stansfield Street	D7-D8	Wilson Street North	B6
Canon Cockin Street	E1	Gorse Road	C2	Nile Street	D4-D5	Stobart Street	B6-B7	Woodbine Street	E4-F4
Cardwell Street	D8	Gosforth Street	E8	Noble Street	E2	Stockton Road	B3-C2	Worcester Terrace	B3
Carley Road	A8	Gray Court	D1-D2	Norfolk Street	D4-D5	Swan Street	A8-B8	Wreath Quay Road	B6-C7
Carlyon Street	C2	Gray Road	C2-E3-F3	North Bridge Street	C5-C7	Tavistock Place	D4	Zetland Street	D7

AA shop	C4
49 Fawett Street	
Sunderland SR1 1RR	

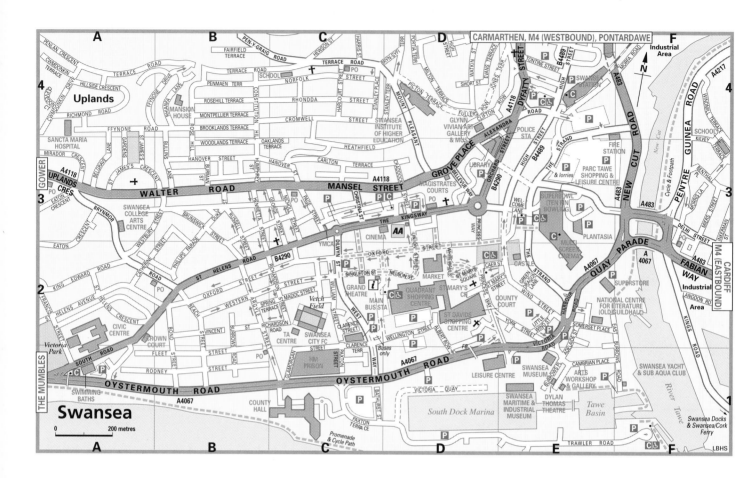

Swansea

Swansea is found on atlas page **32**,
grid reference SS**65**9**2**

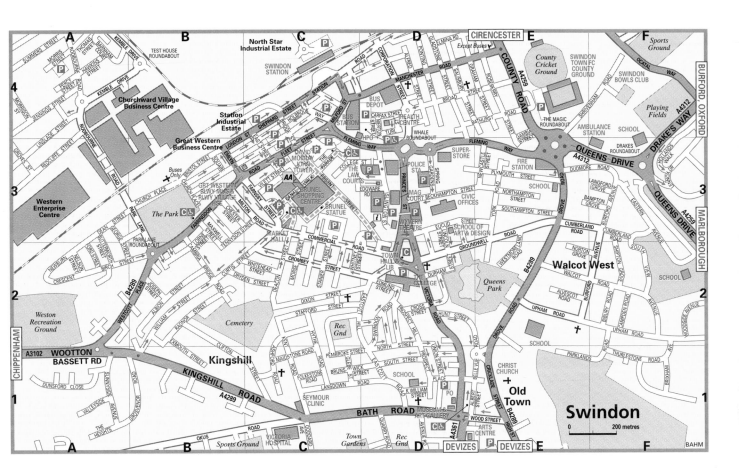

Swindon

Swindon is found on atlas page **36**,
grid reference SU1484

Albert Street	D1	Drove Road	E2-E3	King William Street	D1	Shipton Grove	F2
Albion Street	B2	Dryden Street	B2-C2	Langford Grove	F3	Shrivenham Road	E4-F4
Alfred Street	D4	Dudmore Road	E3-F3	Lansdown Road	C1-D1	South Street	D1
Alvescot Road	E2	Dunsford Close	A1	Lennox Drive	F3	South View Avenue	F2-F3
Ashford Road	C1-C2	Durham Street	D2	Linslade Street	A3-A4	Southampton Street	E3
Avenue Road	D1	East Street	C3-C4	Lincoln Street	D2-D3	Spring Gardens	D3
Bampton Grove	E3-F3	Eastcott Hill	D2-D3	London Street	B3-C4	Stafford Street	C2
Barnham Court	A4	Eastcott Road	D1	Lorne Street	B2-B3	Stanier Street	C2
Bath Road	C1-D1	Eastern Avenue	F2-F3	Maidstone Road	C1	Station Road	C4-D4
Bathurst Road	D4-E4	Edgware Road	C3-D3	Manchester Road	C4-E4	Summers Street	A4
Beckhampton Street	D3	Edmund Street	D2	Maxwell Street	B2-B3	Sunnyside Avenue	A1
Bellevue Road	D1-E2	Elmina Road	D4	Merton Street	D4	Swindon Road	D2
Bibury Road	F2	Emlyn Square	B3	Milford Street	C4	Tennyson Street	B2-C3
Birch Street	2-B2	Euclid Street	D3-E3	Milton Road	B3-C3	The Heights	A1
Bradford Road	D1	Exmouth Street	B1-B2	Morris Street	A4	The Parade	C3
Bridge Street	C3-C4	Farnsby Street	C3	Morrison Street	A4	Thomas Street	A4
Bristol Street	B3	Farringdon Road	B2-C3	Morse Street	C2-C2	Thurlestone Road	F1
Brixham Avenue	F1	Fleet Street	C3-C4	Nelson Street	A2	Turl Street	D4
Broad Street	D4-E4	Fleming Way	C4-E3	Newburn Crescent	A2	Union Street	D1
Brunswick Street	C1-D1	Folkestone Road	C1	Newcastle Street	E3	Upham Road	E2-F2
Burford Avenue	E2-F3	Ford Street	A2	North Street	D1	Valleyside	A1
Butterworth Street	A2-A3	Gambia Street	E3-E4	Northampton Street	E3	Victoria Road	D1-D2
Cambria Bridge Road	B2-B3	George Street	A2-A3	Norton Grove	E2-F2	Vilett Street	C3
Campden Road	F2	Gladstone Street	D4	Ocatal Way	F4	Walcot Road	E2-F2
Canal Walk	C3	Glebe Street	C1	Okus Road	B1-C1	Westcott Place	A2-B2
Carfax Street	D4	Goddard Avenue	C1	Park Lane	A3-B3	Westmoreland Road	E2-E3
Chester Street	B3	Graham Street	D4-E4	Parklands Road	E1-F2	Whitehead Street	B2-C2
Church Place	B3	Grosvenor Road	A1-B1	Pembroke Street	C1-D1	Whitney Street	C2-D3
Clifton Street	B2-C1	Groundwell Road	D2-E3	Percy Street	A4	William Street	B1-B2
College Street	C3-D3	Groves Street	A3	Plymouth Street	D3-E3	Wood Street	D1-E1
Commercial Road	C3-D2	Hawkins Street	A4	Ponting Street	D4	Woodside Avenue	F2
Corporation Street	D4	High Street	E1	Princes Street	D3	Wootton Bassett Road	A1
County Road	E4	Hollands Walk	F3-F4	Prospect Hill	D1-D2	York Road	E2-E3
Cricklade Street	E1	Holbrook Way	C4	Prospect Place	D1		
Crombey Street	C2-D2	Hunt Street	D2	Queens Drive	E3-F2		
Cross Street	D2	Hythe Road	C1-C2	Radnor Street	B1-B2		
Cumberland Road	E3-F2	Islington Street	D3	Redcliffe Street	A3-A4		
Curtis Street	B2-C3	Jennings Street	A4	Regent Street	C3-D3		
Deacon Street	C2-C3	Joseph Street	B2	Rodbourne Road	A3-A4	AA shop	C3
Dean Street	A2-A3	Kemble Drive	A4-B4	Roseberry Street	E3-E4	22 Canal Walk	
Dixon Street	C2-D2	Kent Road	C1-C2	Salisbury Street	D4-E4	Brunel Shopping Centre	
Drakes Drive	F3-F4	Kingshill Road	B1-C1	Sheppard Street	C4	Swindon SN1 1LD	

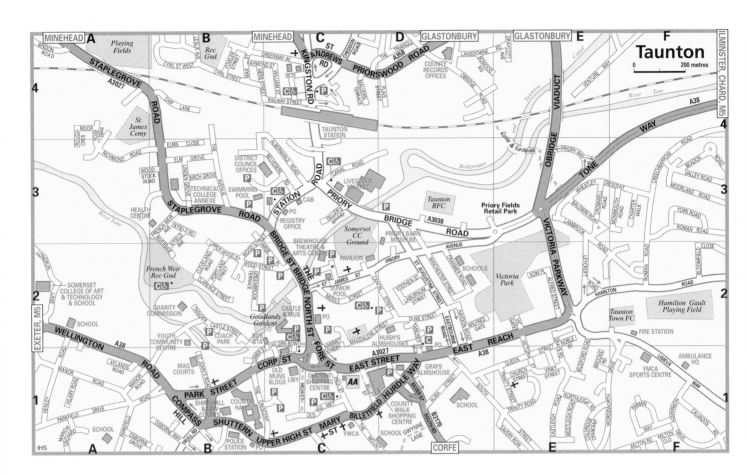

Taunton

Taunton is found on atlas page **20**,
grid reference ST**2224**

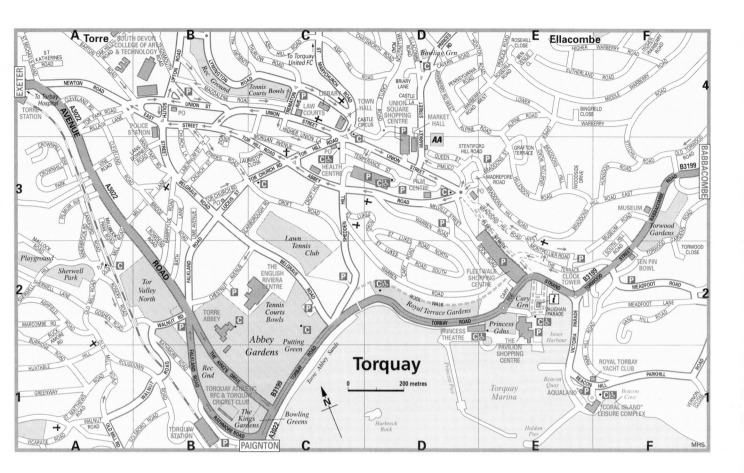

Torquay

Torquay is found on atlas page **7**,
grid reference SX**9164**

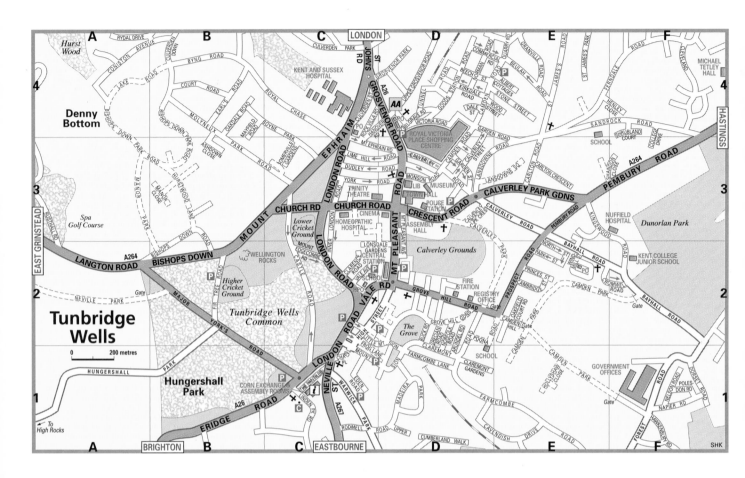

Tunbridge Wells

Tunbridge Wells is found on atlas page 16,
grid reference TQ5839

Albert Cottages	E4	Dale Street	D4	Major York's Road	A2-C1	The Pantiles	C1
Arundel Road	D1-D2	Dorset Road	F1	Manor Close	B3	Tunnel Road	D4
Ashdown Close	B3-B4	Dudley Road	C3-D3	Manor Park	A3-B2	Upper Cumberland Walk	D1
Bayhall Road	E3-F2	Earl's Road	B4	Mayfield Road	B3-B4	Upper Grosvenor Road	D4
Beech Street	D4	Eden Road	C1	Molyneux Park Road	B4-C3	Vale Avenue	C2
Belgrave Road	D4	Eridge Road	B1-C1	Monson Road	D3	Vale Road	C2-D2
Beulah Road	E4	Farmcombe Lane	D1	Mount Edgecombe Road	C2	Victoria Road	D4
Bishops Down	B2	Farmcombe Road	D1-E1	Mount Ephraim Road	C3-D3	Warwick Park	C1
Bishops Down Lane	A2-B2	Ferndale Road	E4-F4	Mount Ephraim	B2-C4	Windmill Street	E2
Bishops Down Park Road	A4-B4	Fir Tree Road	B2	Mount Pleasant Avenue	D2-D3	Wood Street	D4-E4
Boyne Park	B4-C3	Forest Road	F1-F2	Mount Pleasant Road	D2-D3	York Road	C3-D3
Buck Road	D2	Frog Lane	C2-D1	Mount Sion	C1-D1		
Byng Road	B4	Garden Road	D4-E3	Napier Road	F1		
Calverley Park	D2-D3	Garden Street	D3	Nelson Road	F1		
Calverley Park Crescent	D3	Goods Station Road	D4	Neville Park	A2-B2		
Calverley Park Gardens	D3-E3	Granville Road	E4	Neville Street	C1		
Calverley Road	D3	Grecian Road	D2	Norfolk Road	D1-D2		
Calverley Street	D3	Grosvenor Park	C4-D4	Norman Road	D4		
Cambridge Street	E2	Grosvenor Road	C4-D3	North Street	E2		
Camden Hill	E2	Grove Hill Gardens	D2	Oakdale Road	B4		
Camden Park	F1-E1-E2	Grove Hill Road	D2-E2	Oakfield Court Road	E2		
Camden Road	D3-E4	Hanover Road	C3-D4	Park Street	E2		
Carlton Crescent	E3	Hawkenbury Road	F1	Pembury Road	E3-F4		
Carlton Road	E3	Henley Close	E4-F4	Polesdon Road	F1		
Castle Road	C1-C3	High Street	C2-D2	Poona Road	D2-E2		
Cavendish Drive	D1-E1	Holyshaw Close	E1	Princes Street	E2		
Chapel Place	C1	Hungershall Park	A1-B2	Prospect Road	E2-E3		
Church Road	C3-C4	Hurstwood Lane	B3	Quarry Road	E4		
Claremont Gardens	D1	Inner London Road	C2-C3	Rock Villa Road	C3-C4		
Claremont Road	D1-D2	Kingswood Road	E3-F2	Rodmell Road	C1-D1		
Clarence Road	C2	Kirkdale Road	D4	Royal Chase	B4-C3		
Cleveland	F4	Lake Road	A4-B4	Rusthall Road	A2-A3		
College Drive	F3-F4	Langton Road	A2-A3	Rydal Drive	A4		
Commercial Road	D4-E4	Lansdowne Road	D3-E4	Sandrock Road	E4-F4		
Coniston Avenue	A4-B4	Lansdowne Square	D3-E3	Shandon Close	E3-F3		
Court Road	B4	Lime Hill Road	C3-D3	Shrubland Court	F4		
Crescent Road	D3	Linden Park Road	C1	Somerville Gardens	C3		
Cromwell Road	E2-F2	Little Mount Sion	C2-D1	St James's Park	E4		
Culverden Down	B4	London Road	C1-C4	St James's Road	E4	AA shop	D4
Culverden Park	C4	Lonsdale Gardens	C2-D2	St John's Road	C4	2 Upper Grosvenor Road	
Culverden Street	C4	Madeira Park	D1	Stone Street	D4-E4	Tunbridge Wells TN1 2EN	

Warwick

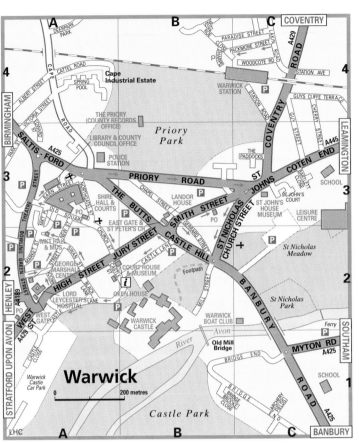

Warwick is found on atlas page **48**,
grid reference SP**2865**

Albert Street	A4	St John's Court	C3
Archery Fields	C1	St Johns	C3
Banbury Road	B2-C1	St Nicholas Church St	B2-C3
Barn Street	A3	Station Avenue	C4
Bartlett Close	C3	Station Road	C4
Black Lane	A2	Swan Street	A2
Bowling Green Street	A2	The Butts	A3-B2
Bridge Brooke Close	B1-C1	The Paddocks	C3
Bridge End	B1-C1	Theatre Street	A3
Brook Street	A2	Victoria Street	A3-A4
Cape Road	A3-A4	Vine Street	B4
Castle Close	A1	West Street	A1-A2
Castle Hill	B2	Woodcote Road	C4
Castle Lane	A2-B2		
Castle Street	A2-B2		
Cattel Road	A4		
Chapel Street	B3		
Cherry Street	C3-C4		
Church Street	A2		
Coten End	C3		
Coventry Road	C3-C4		
Deerpark Park	A4		
Edward Street	A3-A4		
Gerrard Street	B2-B3		
Guy Street	C3-C4		
Guys Cliffe Terrace	C4		
High Street	A2		
Jury Street	A2-B2		
Lakin Road	C4		
Market Place	A3		
Market Street	A2		
Mill Street	B2		
Myton Road	C1		
New Street	A2-A3		
Northgate Street	A3		
Old Square	A3		
Packmore Street	B4-C4		
Paradise Street	B4-C4		
Park Street	A3		
Priory Road	A3-C3		
Roe Close	B4		
Saltisford	A3-A4		
Sharpe Close	B4		
Smith Street	B2-C3		
Spring Pool	A4		

Windsor

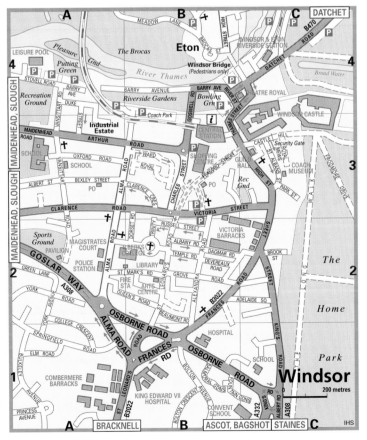

Windsor is found on atlas page **26**,
grid reference SU**9576**

Adelaide Square	B2-C2	Royal Mews	C3
Albany Road	B2	Royal Ward	B3
Albert Road	C1	Russell Street	B2
Albert Street	A3	Sheet Street	C2-C3
Alexandra Road	B1-B3	Springfield Road	A1-A2
Alma Road	B1-B3	St Albans Street	C3
Arthur Road	A3-B3	St Leonard's Road	A1-B3
Balmoral Gardens	B1	St Mark's Road	A2-B2
Barry Avenue	A4-B4	Stovell Road	A4
Beaumont Road	B2	Temple Road	B2
Bexley Street	A3	Thames Street	B3-C4
Bolton Avenue	B1	The Long Walk	C1-C3
Bolton Crescent	B1	Trinity Place	B2-B3
Brocas Street	B4	Vansittart Road	A2-A4
Brook Street	C2	Victoria Street	B3-C3
Bulkeley Avenue	A1	York Avenue	A1-A2
Castle Hill	C3	York Road	A2
Charles Street	B3		
Clarence Crescent	B3		
Clarence Road	A3-B3		
College Crescent	A1-A2		
Dagmar Road	B2		
Datchet Road	B4-C4		
Devereaux Road	B2		
Dorset Road	B2-B3		
Duke Street	A3-A4		
Elm Road	A1		
Fountain Gardens	B1-C1		
Frances Road	B1-C2		
Frogmore Drive	C2-C3		
Goslar Way	A2		
Goswell Road	B3-B4		
Green Lane	A2		
Grove Road	B2		
High Street	B4		
High Street	C3		
King's Road	C1-C2		
Maidenhead Road	A3		
Meadow Lane	A4-B4		
Osborne Road	A2-C1		
Oxford Road	A3		
Park Street	C3		
Peascod Street	B3		
Princess Avenue	A1		
Queen's Road	A2-B2		
River Street	B4		

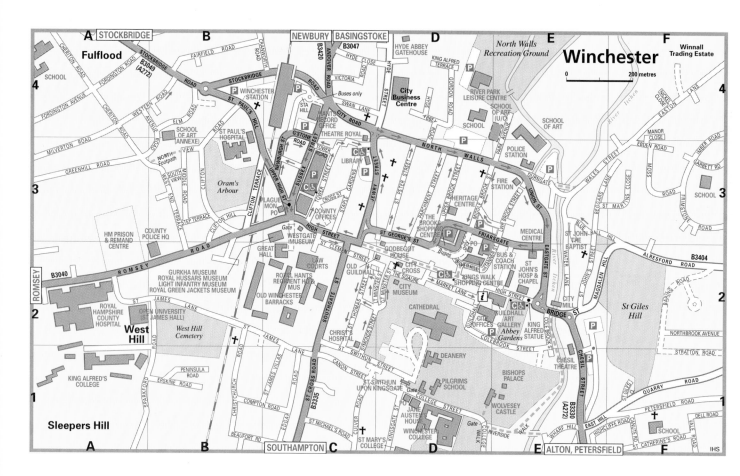

Winchester

Winchester is found on atlas page **24**,
grid reference SU**4829**

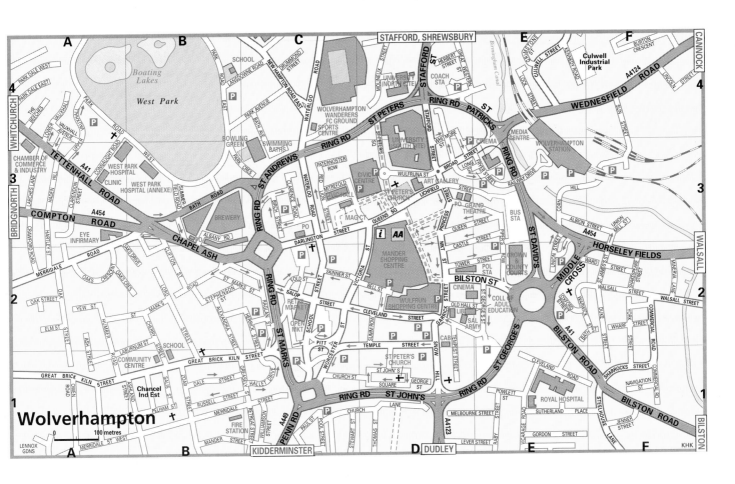

Wolverhampton

Wolverhampton is found on atlas page **60**,
grid reference SO**91**98

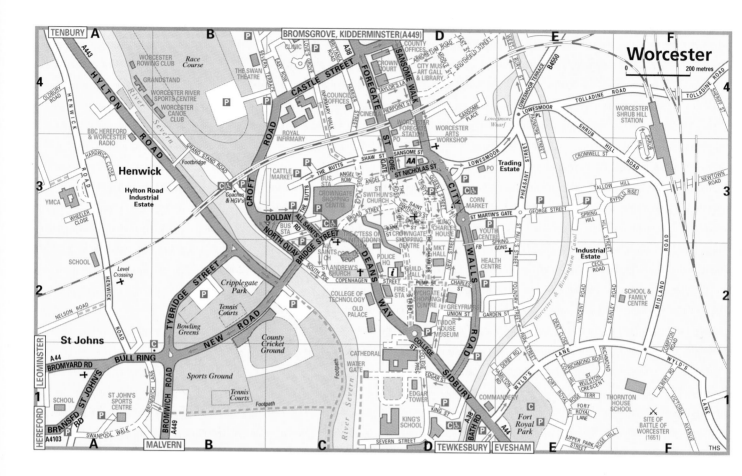

Worcester

Worcester is found on atlas page **47**,
grid reference SO**8554**

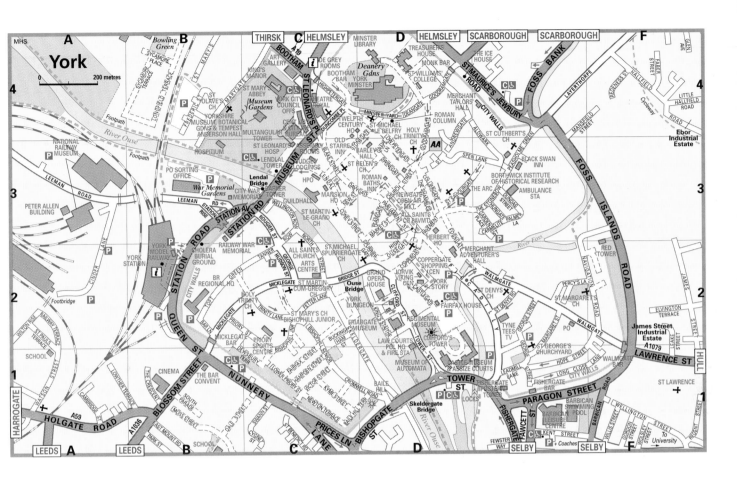

York

York is found on atlas page **83**,
grid reference SE**60**5**1**

index

Each place name entry in this index is identified by its County, County Borough or Council Area name. These are shown in *italics*.

A list of the abbreviated forms used is shown on the left.

To locate a place name in the atlas turn to the map page indicated in bold type in the index and use the 4-figure grid reference.

For example, **Hythe** *Kent* **29** TR**1634** is found on page 29.

The two letters 'TR' refer to the National Grid.

To pinpoint our example the first bold figure **'1'** is found along the bottom edge of the page.

The following figure '6' indicates how many imaginary tenths to move east of the line **'1'**.

The next bold figure **'3'** is found up the left-hand side of the page.

The last figure '4' shows how many imaginary tenths to move north of the line **'3'**. You will locate Hythe where these two lines intersect.

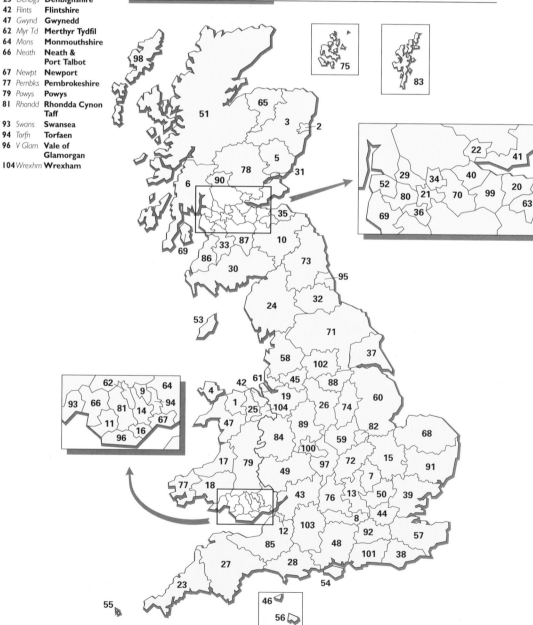

A

Alyth Astwick

Alyth P & K	126	NO2448
Amber Hill Lincs	76	TF2346
Amber Row Derbys	74	SK3856
Ambergate Derbys	74	SK3451
Amberley Gloucs	35	SO8501
Amberley W Susx	14	TQ0213
Ambirstone E Susx	16	TQ5911
Amble Nthumb	103	NU2604
Amblecote W Mids	60	SO8985
Ambler Thorn W York	82	SE0929
Ambleside Cumb	87	NY3704
Ambleston Pembks	30	SN0025
Ambrosden Oxon	37	SP6019
Amcotts Lincs	84	SE8514
America Cambs	53	TL4378
Amersham Bucks	26	SU9597
Amersham on the Hill Bucks	26	SU9798
Amerton Staffs	73	SJ9927
Amesbury Wilts	23	SU1541
Amhuinnsuidhe W Isls	154	NB0408
Amington Staffs	61	SK2304
Amisfield Town D & G	100	NY0082
Amlwch Angles	68	SH4492
Ammanford Carmth	32	SN6212
Amotherby N York	90	SE7473
Ampfield Hants	13	SU4023
Ampleforth N York	90	SE5878
Ampney Crucis Gloucs	36	SP0601
Ampney St Mary Gloucs	36	SP0802
Ampney St Peter Gloucs	36	SP0801
Amport Hants	23	SU3044
Ampthill Beds	38	TL0337
Ampton Suffk	54	TL8671
Amroth Pembks	31	SN1608
Amulree P & K	125	NN8936
Amwell Herts	39	TL1613
An T-ob W Isls	154	NG0286
Anaheilt Highld	130	NM8162
Ancaster Lincs	63	SK9843
Anchor Shrops	58	SO1785
Ancroft Nthumb	111	NT9945
Ancrum Border	110	NT6224
Ancton W Susx	14	SU9800
Anderby Lincs	77	TF5275
Andersea Somset	21	ST3333
Andersfield Somset	20	ST2434
Anderson Dorset	11	SY8897
Anderton Ches	79	SJ6475
Anderton Cnwll	6	SX4351
Andover Hants	23	SU3645
Andoversford Gloucs	35	SP0219
Andreas IOM	153	SC4199
Anelog Gwynd	56	SH1527
Anerley Gt Lon	27	TQ3369
Anfield Mersyd	78	SJ3692
Angarrack Cnwll	2	SW5838
Angarrick Cnwll	3	SW7937
Angelbank Shrops	46	SO5776
Angersleigh Somset	20	ST1918
Angerton Cumb	93	NY2257
Angle Pembks	30	SM8603
Angmering W Susx	14	TQ0604
Angram N York	88	SD8899
Angram N York	83	SE5248
Angrouse Cnwll	2	SW6619
Anick Nthumb	102	NY9465
Ankerville Highld	147	NH8174
Ankle Hill Leics	63	SK7518
Anlaby E R Yk	84	TA0328
Anmer Norfk	65	TF7429
Anmore Hants	13	SU6611
Anna Valley Hants	23	SU3543
Annan D & G	101	NY1966
Annaside Cumb	86	SD0986
Annat Ag & B	122	NN0322
Annat Highld	138	NG8954
Annathill N Lans	116	NS7270
Annbank S Ayrs	106	NS4023
Annesley Notts	75	SK5053
Annesley Woodhouse Notts	75	SK4953
Annfield Plain Dur	96	NZ1651
Anniesland C Glas	115	NS5368
Annitsford T & W	103	NZ2674
Annscroft Shrops	59	SJ4507
Ansdell Lancs	80	SD3428
Ansford Somset	21	ST6433
Ansley Warwks	61	SP3091
Anslow Staffs	73	SK2125
Anslow Gate Staffs	73	SK1924
Anslow Lees Staffs	73	SK2024
Ansteadbrook Surrey	14	SU9332
Anstey Hants	24	SU7240
Anstey Herts	39	TL4033
Anstey Leics	62	SK5508
Anstruther Fife	127	NO5703
Ansty W Susx	15	TQ2923
Ansty Warwks	61	SP4083
Ansty Wilts	22	ST9526
Ansty Cross Dorset	11	ST7603
Anthill Common Hants	13	SU6312
Anthony's Surrey	26	TQ0161
Anthorn Cumb	93	NY1958
Antingham Norfk	67	TG2533
Anton's Gowt Lincs	77	TF3047
Antony Cnwll	5	SX4054
Antrobus Ches	79	SJ6480
Antron Cnwll	2	SW6327
Anvil Corner Devon	18	SS3704
Anvil Green Kent	29	TR1049
Anwick Lincs	76	TF1150
Anwoth D & G	99	NX5856
Aperfield Gt Lon	27	TQ4158
Apes Dale H & W	60	SO9972
Apethorpe Nhants	51	TL0295
Apeton Staffs	72	SJ8518
Apley Lincs	76	TF1075
Apperknowle Derbys	74	SK3878
Apperley Gloucs	47	SO8628
Apperley Bridge W York	82	SE1937
Apperley Dene Nthumb	95	NZ0558
Appersett N York	88	SD8690
Appin Ag & B	122	NM9346
Appleby Lincs	84	SE9514
Appleby Magna Leics	61	SK3109
Appleby Parva Leics	61	SK3008
Appleby Street Herts	39	TL3304
Appleby-in-Westmorland Cumb	94	NY6820
Applecross Highld	137	NG7144
Appledore Devon	18	SS4630
Appledore Devon	9	ST0614
Appledore Kent	17	TQ9529
Appledore Heath Kent	17	TQ9530
Appleford Oxon	37	SU5293
Applegarth Town D & G	100	NY1084
Applehaigh S York	83	SE3512
Appleshaw Hants	23	SU3048
Applethwaite Cumb	93	NY2625
Appleton Ches	78	SJ5186
Appleton Ches	79	SJ6184
Appleton Oxon	37	SP4401
Appleton Roebuck N York	83	SE5542
Appleton Thorn Ches	79	SJ6383
Appleton Wiske N York	89	NZ3804
Appleton-le-Moors N York	90	SE7387
Appleton-le-Street N York	90	SE7373
Appletreehall Border	109	NT5117
Appletreewick N York	88	SE0560
Appley Somset	20	ST0721
Appley Bridge Lancs	78	SD5209
Apse Heath IOW	13	SZ5683
Apsley End Beds	38	TL1232
Apsley Heath Warwks	61	SP0970
Apuldram W Susx	14	SU8403
Arabella Highld	147	NH8076
Arbirlot Angus	127	NO6040
Arboll Highld	147	NH8781
Arborfield Berks	24	SU7567
Arborfield Cross Berks	24	SU7666
Arbourthorne S York	74	SK3785
Arbroath Angus	127	NO6441
Arbuthnott Abers	135	NO8074
Arcadia Kent	28	TQ8836
Archddu Carmth	32	SN4401
Archdeacon Newton Dur	96	NZ2517
Archencarroch D & Cb	115	NS4182
Archiestown Moray	141	NJ2244
Archirondel Jersey	152	JS0000
Arclid Green Ches	72	SJ7861
Ardaily Ag & B	104	NR6450
Ardalanish Ag & B	121	NM3619
Ardanaiseig Hotel Ag & B	123	NN0824
Ardarroch Ag & B	114	NS2494
Ardarroch Highld	137	NG8339
Ardbeg Ag & B	104	NR4146
Ardbeg Ag & B	114	NS0766
Ardbeg Ag & B	114	NS1583
Ardcharnich Highld	145	NH1788
Ardchiavaig Ag & B	121	NM3818
Ardchonnel Ag & B	122	NM9812
Ardchullarie More Stirlg	124	NN5813
Arddleen Powys	58	SJ2616
Ardechive Highld	131	NN1490
Ardeer N Ayrs	106	NS2740
Ardeley Herts	39	TL3027
Ardelve Highld	138	NG8627
Arden Ag & B	115	NS3684
Ardens Grafton Warwks	48	SP1154
Ardentallen Ag & B	122	NM8324
Ardentinny Ag & B	114	NS1887
Ardentraive Ag & B	114	NS0374
Ardeonaig Hotel Stirlg	124	NN6735
Ardersier Highld	140	NH7855
Ardessie Highld	145	NH0689
Ardfern Ag & B	122	NM8004
Ardgay Highld	146	NH5990
Ardgour Highld	130	NN0163
Ardgowan Inver	114	NS2073
Ardhallow Ag & B	114	NS1674
Ardhasig W Isls	154	NB1202
Ardheslaig Highld	137	NG7855
Ardindrean Highld	145	NH1588
Ardingly W Susx	15	TQ3429
Ardington Oxon	36	SU4388
Ardington Wick Oxon	36	SU4389
Ardlamont Ag & B	114	NR9865
Ardleigh Essex	41	TM0529
Ardleigh Heath Essex	41	TM0430
Ardler P & K	126	NO2642
Ardley Oxon	49	SP5427
Ardley End Essex	39	TL5214
Ardlui Ag & B	123	NN3115
Ardlussa Ag & B	113	NR6487
Ardmaddy Ag & B	123	NN0837
Ardmair Highld	145	NH1097
Ardmaleish Ag & B	114	NS0768
Ardminish Ag & B	104	NR6448
Ardmolich Highld	129	NM7172
Ardmore Ag & B	115	NS3178
Ardmore Highld	146	NH7086
Ardnadam Ag & B	114	NS1780
Ardnagrask Highld	139	NH5249
Ardnarff Highld	138	NG8935
Ardnastang Highld	130	NM8061
Ardno Ag & B	123	NN1508
Ardochy Lodge Hotel Highld	131	NH2002
Ardpatrick Ag & B	113	NR7559
Ardrishaig Ag & B	113	NR8585
Ardross Highld	146	NH6174
Ardrossan N Ayrs	106	NS2342
Ardsley S York	83	SE3805
Ardsley East W York	82	SE3025
Ardslignish Highld	121	NM5661
Ardtalla Ag & B	112	NR4654
Ardtoe Highld	129	NM6270
Arduaine Ag & B	122	NM7910
Ardvasar Highld	129	NG6303
Ardvorlich P & K	124	NN6322
Ardvourlie W Isls	154	NB1810
Ardwell D & G	98	NX1045
Ardwick Gt Man	79	SJ8597
Areley Kings H & W	60	SO7970
Arevegaig Highld	129	NM6568
Arford Hants	14	SU8236
Argoed Caerph	33	ST1799
Argoed Shrops	59	SJ3220
Argoed Mill Powys	45	SN9963
Argos Hill E Susx	16	TQ5728
Aribrauch W Isls	154	NB2417
Aridhglas Ag & B	120	NM3123
Arileod Ag & B	120	NM1655
Arinagour Ag & B	120	NM2257
Ariogan Ag & B	122	NM8627
Arisaig Highld	129	NM6586
Arisaig House Highld	129	NM6984
Arkendale N York	89	SE3861
Arkesden Essex	39	TL4834
Arkholme Lancs	87	SD5871
Arkle Town N York	88	NZ0001
Arkleby Cumb	92	NY1439
Arkleton D & G	101	NY3791
Arkley Gt Lon	26	TQ2295
Arksey S York	83	SE5807
Arkwright Derbys	74	SK4270
Arle Gloucs	47	SO9223
Arlecdon Cumb	92	NY0418
Arlescote Warwks	48	SP3848
Arlesey Beds	39	TL1936
Arleston Shrops	60	SJ6609
Arley Ches	79	SJ6680
Arley Warwks	61	SP2890
Arlingham Gloucs	35	SO7010
Arlington Devon	19	SS6140
Arlington E Susx	16	TQ5407
Arlington Gloucs	36	SP1006
Arlington Beccott Devon	19	SS6241
Armadale Highld	150	NC7864
Armadale Highld	129	NG6303
Armadale W Loth	116	NS9368
Armaside Cumb	92	NY1527
Armathwaite Cumb	94	NY5046
Arminghall Norfk	67	TG2504
Armitage Staffs	73	SK0715
Armitage Bridge W York	82	SE1313
Armley W York	82	SE2833
Armscote Warwks	48	SP2444
Armshead Staffs	72	SJ9348
Armston Nhants	51	TL0685
Armthorpe S York	83	SE6204
Arnabost Ag & B	120	NM2159
Arnaby Cumb	86	SD1884
Arncliffe N York	88	SD9371
Arncliffe Cote N York	88	SD9470
Arncroach Fife	127	NO5105
Arndilly House Moray	141	NJ2847
Arne Dorset	11	SY9788
Arnesby Leics	50	SP6192
Arnfield Derbys	79	SK0197
Arngask P & K	126	NO1410
Arnicle Ag & B	105	NR7138
Arnisdale Highld	130	NG8410
Arnish Highld	137	NG5948
Arniston Mdloth	118	NT3362
Arnol W Isls	154	NB3148
Arnold E R Yk	85	TA1241
Arnold Notts	62	SK5845
Arnprior Stirlg	116	NS6194
Arnside Cumb	87	SD4578
Aros Ag & B	121	NM5645
Arowry Wrexhm	71	SJ4639
Arrad Foot Cumb	86	SD3080
Arram E R Yk	84	TA0344
Arrathorne N York	89	SE2093
Arreton IOW	13	SZ5386
Arrina Highld	137	NG7458
Arrington Cambs	52	TL3250
Arrochar Ag & B	123	NN2904
Arrow Warwks	48	SP0856
Arrowfield Top H & W	61	SP0374
Arscott Shrops	59	SJ4307
Artafallie Highld	140	NH6349
Arthington W York	82	SE2644
Arthingworth Nhants	50	SP7581
Arthog Gwynd	57	SH6414
Arthrath Abers	143	NJ9636
Arthursdale W York	83	SE3737
Artrochie Abers	143	NK0031
Arundel W Susx	14	TQ0106
Asby Cumb	92	NY0620
Ascog Ag & B	114	NS1062
Ascot Berks	25	SU9268
Ascott Warwks	48	SP3234
Ascott Earl Oxon	36	SP3018
Ascott-under-Wychwood Oxon	36	SP3018
Asenby N York	89	SE3975
Asfordby Leics	63	SK7019
Asfordby Hill Leics	63	SK7219
Asgarby Lincs	64	TF1145
Asgarby Lincs	77	TF3366
Ash Devon	19	SS5208
Ash Devon	7	SX8349
Ash Dorset	11	ST8610
Ash Kent	27	TQ6064
Ash Kent	29	TR2858
Ash Somset	20	ST2822
Ash Somset	21	ST4720
Ash Surrey	25	SU9051
Ash Green Surrey	25	SU9049
Ash Green Warwks	61	SP3384
Ash Magna Shrops	71	SJ5739
Ash Mill Devon	19	SS7823
Ash Parva Shrops	71	SJ5739
Ash Priors Somset	20	ST1529
Ash Street Suffk	54	TM0146
Ash Thomas Devon	9	ST0010
Ash Vale Surrey	25	SU8951
Ashampstead Berks	37	SU5676
Ashampstead Green Berks	37	SU5677
Ashbocking Suffk	54	TM1754
Ashbocking Green Suffk	54	TM1854
Ashbourne Derbys	73	SK1746
Ashbourne Green Derbys	73	SK1948
Ashbrittle Somset	20	ST0521
Ashburnham Place E Susx	16	TQ6814
Ashburton Devon	7	SX7570
Ashbury Devon	5	SX5098
Ashbury Oxon	36	SU2685
Ashby Lincs	84	SE8908
Ashby by Partney Lincs	77	TF4266
Ashby cum Fenby Lincs	77	TA2500
Ashby de la Launde Lincs	76	TF0555
Ashby Folville Leics	63	SK7012
Ashby Magna Leics	50	SP5690
Ashby Parva Leics	50	SP5288
Ashby Puerorum Lincs	77	TF3271
Ashby St Ledgers Nhants	50	SP5768
Ashby St Mary Norfk	67	TG3202
Ashby-de-la-Zouch Leics	62	SK3516
Ashchurch Gloucs	47	SO9233
Ashcombe Devon	9	SX9179
Ashcombe Somset	21	ST3361
Ashcott Somset	21	ST4336
Ashdon Essex	53	TL5842
Ashe Hants	24	SU5350
Asheldham Essex	41	TL9701
Ashen Essex	53	TL7442
Ashendon Bucks	37	SP7014
Asheridge Bucks	38	SP9304
Ashfield H & W	46	SO5923
Ashfield Hants	12	SU3619
Ashfield Stirlg	124	NN7803
Ashfield Suffk	55	TM2062
Ashfield Green Suffk	53	TL7655
Ashfield Green Suffk	55	TM2573
Ashfields Shrops	72	SJ7026
Ashfold Crossways W Susx	15	TQ2328
Ashford Devon	19	SS5335
Ashford Devon	7	SX6948
Ashford Kent	28	TR0142
Ashford Surrey	26	TQ0771
Ashford Bowdler Shrops	46	SO5170
Ashford Carbonel Shrops	46	SO5270
Ashford Hill Hants	24	SU5562
Ashford in the Water Derbys	74	SK1969
Ashgill S Lans	116	NS7850
Ashill Devon	9	ST0811
Ashill Norfk	66	TF8804
Ashill Somset	10	ST3217
Ashingdon Essex	40	TQ8693
Ashington Dorset	11	SZ0098
Ashington Nthumb	103	NZ2687
Ashington Somset	21	ST5621
Ashington W Susx	15	TQ1315
Ashkirk Border	109	NT4722
Ashlett Hants	13	SU4603
Ashleworth Gloucs	47	SO8125
Ashleworth Quay Gloucs	47	SO8125
Ashley Cambs	53	TL6961
Ashley Ches	79	SJ7784
Ashley Devon	19	SS6511
Ashley Dorset	12	SU1304
Ashley Gloucs	35	ST9394
Ashley Hants	23	SU3831
Ashley Hants	12	SZ2595
Ashley Kent	29	TR3048
Ashley Nhants	50	SP7990
Ashley Staffs	72	SJ7636
Ashley Wilts	22	ST8268
Ashley Green Bucks	38	SP9705
Ashley Heath Dorset	12	SU1204
Ashley Moor H & W	46	SO4767
Ashmansworth Hants	24	SU4157
Ashmansworthy Devon	18	SS3418
Ashmead Green Gloucs	35	ST7699
Ashmill Devon	5	SX3995
Ashmore Dorset	11	ST9117
Ashmore Green Berks	24	SU5069
Ashorne Warwks	48	SP3057
Ashover Derbys	74	SK3463
Ashover Hay Derbys	74	SK3460
Ashow Warwks	61	SP3170
Ashperton H & W	47	SO6441
Ashprington Devon	7	SX8157
Ashreigney Devon	19	SS6313
Ashridge Park Herts	38	SP9912
Ashtead Surrey	26	TQ1857
Ashton Cambs	64	TF1005
Ashton Ches	71	SJ5069
Ashton Cnwll	2	SW6028
Ashton Cnwll	5	SX3868
Ashton Devon	8	SX8584
Ashton H & W	46	SO5164
Ashton Hants	13	SU5419
Ashton Inver	114	NS2377
Ashton Nhants	49	SP7649
Ashton Nhants	51	TL0588
Ashton Somset	21	ST4149
Ashton Common Wilts	22	ST8958
Ashton Hill Wilts	22	ST9057
Ashton Keynes Wilts	36	SU0494
Ashton under Hill H & W	47	SO9937
Ashton upon Mersey Gt Man	79	SJ7892
Ashton Watering Somset	21	ST5369
Ashton-in-Makerfield Gt Man	78	SJ5798
Ashton-under-Lyne Gt Man	79	SJ9399
Ashurst Hants	12	SU3310
Ashurst Kent	16	TQ5138
Ashurst W Susx	15	TQ1715
Ashurst Wood W Susx	15	TQ4136
Ashwater Devon	5	SX3895
Ashwell Herts	39	TL2639
Ashwell Rutlnd	63	SK8613
Ashwell Somset	10	ST3616
Ashwell End Herts	39	TL2540
Ashwellthorpe Norfk	66	TM1497
Ashwick Somset	21	ST6348
Ashwicken Norfk	65	TF7018
Ashwood Staffs	60	SO8688
Askam in Furness Cumb	86	SD2177
Aske Hall N York	89	NZ1703
Askern S York	83	SE5613
Askerswell Dorset	10	SY5292
Askett Bucks	38	SP8105
Askham Cumb	94	NY5123
Askham Notts	75	SK7374
Askham Bryan N York	83	SE5548
Askham Richard N York	83	SE5347
Asknish Ag & B	114	NR9391
Askrigg N York	88	SD9491
Askwith N York	82	SE1648
Aslackby Lincs	64	TF0830
Aslacton Norfk	54	TM1590
Aslockton Notts	63	SK7440
Asney Somset	21	ST4636
Aspall Suffk	54	TM1664
Aspatria Cumb	92	NY1441
Aspenden Herts	39	TL3528
Asperton Lincs	64	TF2637
Aspley Staffs	72	SJ8133
Aspley Guise Beds	38	SP9335
Aspley Heath Beds	38	SP9334
Aspull Gt Man	78	SD6108
Aspull Common Gt Man	79	SJ6498
Asselby E R Yk	84	SE7127
Asserby Lincs	77	TF4977
Asserby Turn Lincs	77	TF4777
Assington Suffk	54	TL9338
Assington Green Suffk	53	TL7751
Astbury Ches	72	SJ8461
Astcote Nhants	49	SP6753
Asterby Lincs	77	TF2679
Asterley Shrops	59	SJ3707
Asterton Shrops	59	SO3991
Asthall Oxon	36	SP2811
Asthall Leigh Oxon	36	SP3013
Astle Highld	146	NH7391
Astley Gt Man	79	SD7000
Astley H & W	47	SO7867
Astley Shrops	59	SJ5218
Astley W York	83	SE3828
Astley Warwks	61	SP3189
Astley Abbots Shrops	60	SO7096
Astley Bridge Gt Man	81	SD7111
Astley Cross H & W	47	SO8069
Astley Green Gt Man	79	SJ7099
Astley Town H & W	47	SO7968
Aston Berks	37	SU7884
Aston Ches	71	SJ5578
Aston Ches	71	SJ6146
Aston Derbys	74	SK1783
Aston Flints	71	SJ3067
Aston H & W	46	SO4662
Aston H & W	46	SO4671
Aston Herts	39	TL2722
Aston Oxon	36	SP3403
Aston S York	75	SK4685
Aston Shrops	59	SJ5328
Aston Shrops	59	SJ6109
Aston Shrops	60	SO8093
Aston Staffs	72	SJ7541
Aston Staffs	72	SJ8923
Aston Staffs	72	SJ9130
Aston W Mids	61	SP0888
Aston Abbotts Bucks	38	SP8420
Aston Botterell Shrops	59	SO6384
Aston Cantlow Warwks	48	SP1460
Aston Clinton Bucks	38	SP8812
Aston Crews H & W	47	SO6723
Aston Cross Gloucs	47	SO9433
Aston End Herts	39	TL2724
Aston Fields H & W	47	SO9669
Aston Flamville Leics	50	SP4692
Aston Heath Ches	71	SJ5678
Aston Ingham H & W	47	SO6823
Aston juxta Mondrum Ches	72	SJ6456
Aston le Walls Nhants	49	SP4950
Aston Magna Gloucs	48	SP1935
Aston Munslow Shrops	59	SO5186
Aston on Clun Shrops	59	SO3981
Aston Pigott Shrops	59	SJ3305
Aston Rogers Shrops	59	SJ3406
Aston Rowant Oxon	37	SU7299
Aston Sandford Bucks	37	SP7507
Aston Somerville H & W	48	SP0438
Aston Subedge Gloucs	48	SP1441
Aston Tirrold Oxon	37	SU5586
Aston Upthorpe Oxon	37	SU5586
Aston-Eyre Shrops	59	SO6594
Aston-upon-Trent Derbys	62	SK4129
Astonlane Shrops	59	SO6494
Astrop Nhants	49	SP5036
Astrope Herts	38	SP8914
Astwick Beds	39	TL2138

Astwith Barkston

Astwith Derbys 75 SK4464
Astwood Bucks 38 SP9547
Astwood H & W 47 SO9365
Astwood Bank H & W 48 SP0462
Aswarby Lincs 64 TF0639
Aswardby Lincs 77 TF3770
Atch Lench H & W 48 SP0350
Atcham Shrops 59 SJ5409
Athelhampton Dorset 11 SY7694
Athelington Suffk 55 TM2171
Athelney Somset 21 ST3428
Athelstaneford E Loth 118 NT5377
Atherfield Green IOW 13 SZ4679
Atherington Devon 19 SS5922
Atherington W Susx 14 TQ0000
Atherstone Somset 10 ST3816
Atherstone Warwks 61 SP3097
Atherstone on Stour Warwks 48 SP2051
Atherton Gt Man 79 SD6703
Atley Hill N York 89 NZ2802
Atlow Derbys 73 SK2248
Attadale Highld 138 NG9238
Attenborough Notts 62 SK5034
Atterby Lincs 76 SK9792
Attercliffe S York 74 SK3788
Atterley Shrops 59 SO6397
Atterton Leics 61 SP3598
Attleborough Norfk 66 TM0495
Attleborough Warwks 61 SP3790
Attlebridge Norfk 66 TG1216
Attleton Green Suffk 53 TL7454
Atwick E R Yk 85 TA1850
Atworth Wilts 22 ST8565
Auberrow H & W 46 SO4947
Aubourn Lincs 76 SK9262
Auchedly Abers 143 NJ8933
Auchenblae Abers 135 NO7279
Auchenbowie Stirlg 116 NS7987
Auchencairn D & G 92 NX7951
Auchencairn D & G 100 NX9884
Auchencairn N Ayrs 105 NS0427
Auchencrow Border 119 NT8560
Auchendinny Mdloth 117 NT2561
Auchengray S Lans 117 NS9954
Auchenhalrig Moray 141 NJ3761
Auchenheath S Lans 108 NS8043
Auchenhessnane D & G 100 NX8096
Auchenlochan Ag & B 114 NR9772
Auchenmade N Ayrs 115 NS3548
Auchenmalg D & G 98 NX2352
Auchentibber S Lans 116 NS6755
Auchentiber N Ayrs 115 NS3647
Auchentroig Stirlg 115 NS5493
Auchindrean Highld 145 NH1980
Auchininna Abers 142 NJ6546
Auchinleck E Ayrs 107 NS5521
Auchinloch N Lans 116 NS6570
Auchinstarry N Lans 116 NS7176
Auchintore Highld 130 NN0972
Auchiries Abers 143 NK0737
Auchlee Abers 135 NO8996
Auchleven Abers 142 NJ6224
Auchlochan S Lans 107 NS7937
Auchlossan Abers 134 NJ5601
Auchlyne Stirlg 124 NN5129
Auchmillan E Ayrs 107 NS5129
Auchmithie Angus 127 NO6743
Auchmuirbridge Fife 126 NO2101
Auchnacree Angus 134 NO4663
Auchnagatt Abers 143 NJ9241
Auchnarrow Moray 141 NJ2023
Auchnotteroch D & G 98 NW9960
Auchroisk Moray 141 NJ3351
Auchronie Angus 134 NO4480
Auchterarder P & K 125 NN9412
Auchteraw Highld 131 NH3507
Auchterblair Highld 140 NH9222
Auchtercairn Highld 144 NG8077
Auchterderran Fife 117 NT2195
Auchterhouse Angus 126 NO3337
Auchterless Abers 142 NJ7141
Auchtermuchty Fife 126 NO2311
Auchterneed Highld 139 NH4959
Auchtertool Fife 117 NT2190
Auchtertyre Highld 138 NG8427
Auchtoo Stirlg 124 NN5520
Auckengill Highld 151 ND3663
Auckley S York 75 SE6400
Audenshaw Gt Man 79 SJ9197
Audlem Ches 72 SJ6543
Audley Staffs 72 SJ7950
Audley End Essex 39 TL5337
Audley End Essex 54 TL8137
Audley End Suffk 54 TL8553
Audmore Staffs 72 SJ8321
Audnam W Mids 60 SO8986
Aughertree Cumb 93 NY2538
Aughton Lancs 78 SD3905
Aughton Lancs 87 SD5567
Aughton E R Yk 84 SE7038
Aughton S York 75 SK4586
Aughton Wilts 23 SU2356
Aughton Park Lancs 78 SD4006
Auldallan Angus 134 NO3158
Auldearn Highld 140 NH9255
Aulden H & W 46 SO4654
Auldgirth D & G 100 NX9186
Auldhouse S Lans 116 NS6250
Ault a' chruinn Highld 138 NG9420
Ault Hucknall Derbys 75 SK4665
Aultbea Highld 144 NG8789
Aultgrishin Highld 144 NG7485
Aultguish Inn Highld 145 NH3570
Aultmore Moray 142 NJ4053
Aultnagoire Highld 139 NH5423
Aultnamain Inn Highld 146 NH6681
Aunby Lincs 64 TF0214
Aunk Devon 9 ST0400
Aunsby Lincs 64 TF0438
Aust Gloucs 34 ST5788
Austendike Lincs 64 TF2821
Austerfield S York 75 SK6694
Austerlands Gt Man 79 SD9505
Austhorpe W York 83 SE3733
Austonley W York 82 SE1107
Austrey Warwks 61 SK2906
Austwick N York 88 SD7668
Authorpe Lincs 77 TF3980
Authorpe Row Lincs 77 TF5373
Avebury Wilts 36 SU1069
Avebury Trusloe Wilts 36 SU0969
Aveley Essex 27 TQ5680
Avening Gloucs 35 ST8898
Averham Notts 75 SK7654
Aveton Gifford Devon 7 SX6947
Aviemore Highld 132 NH8913
Avington Berks 23 SU3767
Avoch Highld 140 NH7055
Avon Dorset 12 SZ1498
Avon Dassett Warwks 49 SP4150
Avonbridge Falk 116 NS9172
Avonmouth Bristl 34 ST5178
Avonwick Devon 7 SX7158
Awbridge Hants 12 SU3224
Awkley Gloucs 34 ST5985
Awliscombe Devon 9 ST1301
Awre Gloucs 35 SO7008
Awsworth Notts 62 SK4844
Axborough H & W 60 SO8579
Axbridge Somset 21 ST4354
Axford Hants 24 SU6043
Axford Wilts 36 SU2370
Axminster Devon 10 SY2998
Axmouth Devon 10 SY2591
Axton Flints 70 SJ1080
Aycliffe Dur 96 NZ2822
Aydon Nthumb 103 NZ0065
Aylburton Gloucs 34 SO6101
Ayle Cumb 94 NY7149
Aylebridge Cnwll 18 SS2103
Aylesbeare Devon 9 SY0392
Aylesbury Bucks 38 SP8213
Aylesby Lincs 85 TA2007
Aylesford Kent 28 TQ7359
Aylesham Kent 29 TR2452
Aylestone Leics 50 SK5700
Aylestone Park Leics 50 SK5800
Aylmerton Norfk 66 TG1839
Aylsham Norfk 67 TG1926
Aylton Gloucs 47 SO6537
Aylworth Gloucs 36 SP1021
Aymestrey H & W 46 SO4265
Aynho Nhants 49 SP5133
Ayot Green Herts 39 TL2214
Ayot St Lawrence Herts 39 TL1916
Ayot St Peter Herts 39 TL2115
Ayr S Ayrs 106 NS3321
Aysgarth N York 88 SE0088
Ayshford Devon 9 ST0415
Ayside Cumb 87 SD3983
Ayston Rutlnd 51 SK8600
Aythorpe Roding Essex 40 TL5815
Ayton Border 119 NT9260
Azerley N York 89 SE2574

B

Babbacombe Devon 7 SX9265
Babbington Notts 62 SK4943
Babbinswood Shrops 59 SJ3329
Babbs Green Herts 39 TL3916
Babcary Somset 21 ST5628
Babel Carmth 44 SN8235
Babel Green Suffk 53 TL7348
Babell Flints 70 SJ1573
Babeny Devon 7 SX6775
Babington Somset 22 ST7051
Bablock Hythe Oxon 36 SP4304
Babraham Cambs 53 TL5150
Babworth Notts 75 SK6880
Bachau Angles 68 SH4383
Bache Shrops 59 SO4681
Bacheldre Powys 58 SO2492
Bachelor's Bump E Susx 17 TQ8412
Back o' th' Brook Staffs 73 SK0751
Back of Keppoch Highld 129 NM6587
Back Street Suffk 53 TL7458
Backaland Ork 155 HY5630
Backbarrow Cumb 87 SD3584
Backe Carmth 31 SN2615
Backfolds Abers 143 NK0252
Backford Ches 71 SJ3971
Backford Cross Ches 71 SJ3873
Backies Highld 147 NC8302
Backlass Highld 151 ND2053
Backwell Somset 21 ST4968
Backworth T & W 103 NZ3072
Bacon's End W Mids 61 SP1888
Baconsthorpe Norfk 66 TG1236
Bacton H & W 46 SO3732
Bacton Norfk 67 TG3433
Bacton Suffk 54 TM0567
Bacton Green Suffk 54 TM0365
Bacup Lancs 81 SD8622
Badachro Highld 137 NG7873
Badbury Wilts 36 SU1980
Badby Nhants 49 SP5658
Badcall Highld 148 NC1541
Badcall Highld 148 NC2455
Badcaul Highld 144 NH0291
Baddeley Edge Staffs 72 SJ9150
Baddeley Green Staffs 72 SJ9151
Baddesley Clinton Warwks 61 SP2070
Baddesley Ensor Warwks 61 SP2798
Baddidarroch Highld 145 NC0822
Baddinsgill Border 117 NT1254
Badenscoth Abers 142 NJ6938
Badenyon Abers 141 NJ3319
Badgall Cnwll 5 SX2486
Badgeney Cambs 65 TL4397
Badger Shrops 60 SO7699
Badger's Cross Cnwll 2 SW4833
Badgers Mount Kent 27 TQ4962
Badgeworth Gloucs 35 SO9019
Badgworth Somset 21 ST3952
Badharlick Cnwll 5 SX2686
Badicaul Highld 137 NG7529
Badingham Suffk 55 TM3068
Badlesmere Kent 28 TR0153
Badlieu Border 108 NT0518
Badlipster Highld 151 ND2448
Badluachrach Highld 144 NG9994
Badninish Highld 147 NH7594
Badrallach Highld 145 NH0691
Badsey H & W 48 SP0743
Badshot Lea Surrey 25 SU8648
Badsworth W York 83 SE4614
Badwell Ash Suffk 54 TL9868
Badwell Green Suffk 54 TM0169
Bag Enderby Lincs 77 TF3571
Bagber Dorset 11 ST7513
Bagby N York 89 SE4680
Bagendon Gloucs 35 SP0106
Bagginswood Shrops 60 SO6881
Baggrow Cumb 93 NY1741
Bagh a Chaisteil W Isls 154 NL6698
Bagham Kent 29 TR0753
Bagillt Flints 70 SJ2175
Baginton Warwks 61 SP3474
Baglan Neath 32 SS7492
Bagley Shrops 59 SJ4027
Bagley Somset 21 ST4645
Bagley W York 82 SE2235
Bagmore Hants 24 SU6544
Bagnall Staffs 72 SJ9250
Bagnor Berks 24 SU4569
Bagot Shrops 46 SO5873
Bagshot Surrey 25 SU9063
Bagshot Wilts 23 SU3165
Bagstone Gloucs 35 ST6987
Bagthorpe Notts 75 SK4651
Bagworth Leics 62 SK4408
Bagwy Llydiart H & W 46 SO4426
Baildon W York 82 SE1539
Baildon Green W York 82 SE1439
Baile a Mhanaich W Isls 154 NF7755
Baile Ailein W Isls 154 NB2920
Baile Mor Ag & B 120 NM2824
Bailey Green Hants 13 SU6627
Baileyhead Cumb 101 NY5179
Bailiff Bridge W York 82 SE1425
Baillieston C Glas 116 NS6764
Bailrigg Lancs 87 SD4858
Bainbridge N York 88 SD9390
Bainshole Abers 142 NJ6035
Bainton Cambs 64 TF0906
Bainton E R Yk 84 SE9652
Bainton Oxon 49 SP5827
Baintown Fife 126 NO3503
Bairnkine Border 110 NT6515
Baker Street Essex 40 TQ6381
Baker's End Herts 39 TL3917
Bakewell Derbys 74 SK2168
Bala Gwynd 58 SH9235
Balallan W Isls 154 NB2920
Balbeg Highld 139 NH4431
Balbeggie P & K 126 NO1629
Balblair Highld 139 NH5145
Balblair Highld 140 NH7066
Balby S York 75 SE5600
Balcary D & G 92 NX8149
Balchraggan Highld 139 NH5343
Balchrick Highld 148 NC1960
Balcombe W Susx 15 TQ3130
Balcombe Lane W Susx 15 TQ3132
Balcomie Links Fife 127 NO6209
Baldersby N York 89 SE3578
Baldersby St James N York 89 SE3676
Balderstone Gt Man 79 SD9010
Balderstone Lancs 81 SD6332
Balderton Notts 75 SK8151
Baldhu Cnwll 3 SW7743
Baldinnie Fife 127 NO4211
Baldinnies P & K 125 NO0216
Baldock Herts 39 TL2434
Baldovie Dund C 127 NO4533
Baldrine IOM 153 SC4281
Baldslow E Susx 17 TQ8013
Baldwin IOM 153 SC3581
Baldwin's Gate Staffs 72 SJ7939
Baldwin's Hill Surrey 15 TQ3839
Baldwinholme Cumb 93 NY3351
Bale Norfk 66 TG0136
Baledgarno P & K 126 NO2730
Balemartine Ag & B 120 NL9841
Balerno C Edin 117 NT1666
Balfarg Fife 126 NO2803
Balfield Angus 134 NO5468
Balfour Ork 155 HY4716
Balfron Stirlg 115 NS5489
Balgaveny Abers 142 NJ6540
Balgavies Angus 127 NO5451
Balgonar Fife 117 NT0293
Balgowan D & G 98 NX1142
Balgowan Highld 132 NN6494
Balgown Highld 136 NG3868
Balgracie D & G 98 NW9860
Balgray Angus 126 NO4038
Balgray S Lans 108 NS8824
Balham Gt Lon 27 TQ2873
Balhary P & K 126 NO2646
Balholmie P & K 126 NO1436
Baligill Highld 150 NC8565
Balintore Angus 133 NO2859
Balintore Highld 147 NH8675
Balintraid Highld 146 NH7370
Balivanich W Isls 154 NF7755
Balk N York 89 SE4780
Balkeerie Angus 126 NO3244
Balkholme E R Yk 84 SE7828
Ball Shrops 59 SJ3026
Ball Green Staffs 72 SJ8952
Ball Haye Green Staffs 72 SJ9856
Ball Hill Hants 24 SU4163
Ball's Green Gloucs 35 ST8699
Ballabeg IOM 153 SC2570
Ballachulish Highld 130 NN0858
Ballafesson IOM 153 SC2070
Ballakilpheric IOM 153 SC2271
Ballamodha IOM 153 SC2773
Ballanlay Ag & B 114 NS0462
Ballantrae S Ayrs 98 NX0882
Ballards Gore Essex 40 TQ9092
Ballards Green Warwks 61 SP2791
Ballasalla IOM 153 SC2870
Ballater Abers 134 NO3695
Ballaugh IOM 153 SC3493
Ballchraggan Highld 147 NH7675
Ballechin P & K 125 NN9353
Ballencrieff E Loth 118 NT4878
Ballevullin Ag & B 120 NL9546
Ballidon Derbys 73 SK2054
Balliekine N Ayrs 105 NR8739
Balliemore Ag & B 114 NS1099
Balligmorrie S Ayrs 106 NX2290
Ballimore Ag & B 114 NR9283
Ballimore Stirlg 124 NN5317
Ballindalloch Moray 141 NJ1636
Ballindean P & K 126 NO2529
Ballingdon Essex 54 TL8640
Ballinger Common Bucks 38 SP9103
Ballingham H & W 46 SO5731
Ballingry Fife 117 NT1797
Ballinluig P & K 125 NN9752
Ballinshoe Angus 126 NO4153
Ballintuim P & K 126 NO1055
Balloch D & Cb 115 NS3982
Balloch Highld 140 NH7247
Balloch N Lans 116 NS7374
Balloch P & K 125 NN8419
Balloch S Ayrs 106 NX3295
Ballochroy Ag & B 113 NR7352
Ballogie Abers 134 NO5795
Balls Cross W Susx 14 SU9826
Balls Green E Susx 16 TQ4936
Ballygown Ag & B 121 NM4343
Ballygrant Ag & B 112 NR3966
Ballyhaugh Ag & B 120 NM1758
Ballymenoch Ag & B 115 NS3086
Ballymichael N Ayrs 105 NR9231
Balmacara Highld 137 NG8028
Balmaclellan D & G 99 NX6579
Balmae D & G 99 NX6844
Balmaha Stirlg 115 NS4290
Balmalcolm Fife 126 NO3208
Balmangan D & G 99 NX6445
Balmedie Abers 143 NJ9618
Balmer Heath Shrops 59 SJ4434
Balmerino Fife 126 NO3524
Balmerlawn Hants 12 SU3003
Balmore E Duns 115 NS5973
Balmuchy Highld 147 NH8678
Balmuir Angus 127 NO5648
Balmule Fife 117 NT2088
Balmullo Fife 127 NO4220
Balnacoil Lodge Highld 147 NC8011
Balnacroft Abers 133 NO2894
Balnafoich Highld 140 NH6835
Balnaguard P & K 125 NN9451
Balnahard Ag & B 121 NM4534
Balnahard Ag & B 112 NR4199
Balnain Highld 139 NH4430
Balnakeil Highld 149 NC3968
Balnapaling Highld 147 NH7969
Balne N York 83 SE5918
Balquharn P & K 125 NO0235
Balquhidder Stirlg 124 NN5320
Balsall Common W Mids 61 SP2376
Balsall Heath W Mids 61 SP0784
Balsall Street W Mids 61 SP2276
Balscote Oxon 48 SP3942
Balsham Cambs 53 TL5850
Baltasound Shet 155 HP6208
Balterley Staffs 72 SJ7650
Balterley Green Staffs 72 SJ7650
Baltersan D & G 99 NX4261
Baltonsborough Somset 21 ST5434
Balvarran P & K 133 NO0761
Balvicar Ag & B 122 NM7616
Balvraid Highld 129 NG8416
Balvraid Highld 140 NH8231
Balwest Cnwll 2 SW5930
Bamber Bridge Lancs 81 SD5625
Bamber's Green Essex 40 TL5722
Bamburgh Nthumb 111 NU1734
Bamff P & K 126 NO2251
Bamford Derbys 74 SK2083
Bamford Gt Man 81 SD8612
Bampton Cumb 94 NY5118
Bampton Devon 20 SS9522
Bampton Oxon 36 SP3103
Bampton Grange Cumb 94 NY5218
Banavie Highld 130 NN1177
Banbury Oxon 49 SP4540
Banc-y-ffordd Carmth 31 SN4037
Bancffosfelem Carmth 32 SN4811
Banchory Abers 135 NO6995
Banchory-Devenick Abers 135 NJ9002
Bancycapel Carmth 31 SN4214
Bancyfelin Carmth 31 SN3218
Bandirran P & K 126 NO2030
Bandrake Head Cumb 86 SD3187
Banff Abers 142 NJ6863
Bangor Gwynd 69 SH5772
Bangor's Green Lancs 78 SD3709
Bangor-is-y-coed Wrexhm 71 SJ3845
Bangors Cnwll 18 SX2099
Bangrove Suffk 54 TL9372
Banham Norfk 54 TM0687
Bank Hants 12 SU2807
Bank Ground Cumb 86 SD3196
Bank Newton N York 81 SD9053
Bank Street H & W 47 SO6362
Bank Top Lancs 78 SD5207
Bank Top W York 82 SE1024
Bankend D & G 100 NY0268
Bankfoot P & K 125 NO0635
Bankglen E Ayrs 107 NS5912
Bankhead Aber C 135 NJ9009
Bankhead N Ayrs 106 NS3739
Bankhead S Lans 116 NS9844
Banknock Falk 116 NS7779
Banks Cumb 101 NY5664
Banks Lancs 80 SD3920
Banks Green H & W 47 SO9967
Bankshill D & G 101 NY1982
Banningham Norfk 67 TG2129
Bannister Green Essex 40 TL6920
Bannockburn Stirlg 116 NS8190
Banstead Surrey 27 TQ2559
Bantham Devon 7 SX6643
Banton N Lans 116 NS7480
Banwell Somset 21 ST3959
Bapchild Kent 28 TQ9263
Bapton Wilts 22 ST9938
Bar Hill Cambs 52 TL3863
Barabhas W Isls 154 NB3649
Barassie S Ayrs 106 NS3232
Barbaraville Highld 146 NH7472
Barber Booth Derbys 74 SK1184
Barber Green Cumb 87 SD3982
Barbieston S Ayrs 107 NS4317
Barbon Cumb 87 SD6282
Barbridge Ches 71 SJ6156
Barbrook Devon 19 SS7147
Barby Nhants 50 SP5470
Barcaldine Ag & B 122 NM9641
Barcheston Warwks 48 SP2639
Barclose Cumb 101 NY4462
Barcombe E Susx 15 TQ4114
Barcombe Cross E Susx 15 TQ4115
Barcroft W York 82 SE0437
Barden N York 89 SE1493
Barden Park Kent 16 TQ5746
Bardfield End Green Essex 40 TL6231
Bardfield Saling Essex 40 TL6826
Bardney Lincs 76 TF1269
Bardon Leics 62 SK4412
Bardon Mill Nthumb 102 NY7764
Bardowie E Duns 115 NS5873
Bardown E Susx 16 TQ6629
Bardrainney Inver 115 NS3373
Bardsea Cumb 86 SD3074
Bardsey W York 83 SE3643
Bardsley Gt Man 79 SD9201
Bardwell Suffk 54 TL9473
Bare Lancs 87 SD4564
Bareppa Cnwll 3 SW7729
Barewood H & W 46 SO3856
Barfad D & G 98 NX3266
Barford Norfk 66 TG1107
Barford Warwks 48 SP2760
Barford St John Oxon 49 SP4433
Barford St Martin Wilts 23 SU0531
Barford St Michael Oxon 49 SP4332
Barfrestone Kent 29 TR2650
Bargate Derbys 62 SK3546
Bargeddie N Lans 116 NS6964
Bargoed Caerph 33 ST1599
Bargrennan D & G 98 NX3577
Barham Cambs 52 TL1375
Barham Kent 29 TR2050
Barham Suffk 54 TM1451
Barholm Lincs 64 TF0810
Barkby Leics 63 SK6309
Barkby Thorpe Leics 63 SK6309
Barkers Green Shrops 59 SJ5228
Barkestone-le-Vale Leics 63 SK7734
Barkham Berks 25 SU7766
Barking Gt Lon 27 TQ4484
Barking Suffk 54 TM0753
Barking Tye Suffk 54 TM0652
Barkingside Gt Lon 27 TQ4489
Barkisland W York 82 SE0519
Barkla Shop Cnwll 3 SW7350
Barkston Lincs 63 SK9341

Barkston Ash

Berkhamsted

Barkston Ash N York	83	SE4936
Barkway Herts	39	TL3835
Barlanark C Glas	116	NS6664
Barlaston Staffs	72	SJ8938
Barlavington W Susx	14	SU9716
Barlborough Derbys	75	SK4777
Barlby N York	83	SE6333
Barlestone Leics	62	SK4205
Barley Herts	39	TL4038
Barley Lancs	81	SD8240
Barley Hole S York	74	SK3697
Barleycroft End Herts	39	TL4327
Barleythorpe Rutlnd	63	SK8409
Barling Essex	40	TQ9389
Barlings Lincs	76	TF0774
Barlochan D & G	92	NX8157
Barlow Derbys	74	SK3474
Barlow N York	83	SE6428
Barlow T & W	96	NZ1561
Barmby Moor E R Yk	84	SE7748
Barmby on the Marsh E R Yk	83	SE6928
Barmer Norfk	66	TF8133
Barming Heath Kent	28	TQ7255
Barmollack Ag & B	105	NR8043
Barmouth Gwynd	57	SH6116
Barmpton Dur	96	NZ3118
Barmston E R Yk	91	TA1659
Barnaby Green Suffk	55	TM4780
Barnacarry Ag & B	114	NS0094
Barnack Cambs	64	TF0705
Barnacle Warwks	61	SP3884
Barnard Castle Dur	95	NZ0516
Barnard Gate Oxon	36	SP4010
Barnardiston Suffk	53	TL7148
Barnbarroch D & G	92	NX8456
Barnburgh S York	83	SE4803
Barnby Suffk	55	TM4789
Barnby Dun S York	83	SE6109
Barnby in the Willows Notts	76	SK8552
Barnby Moor Notts	75	SK6684
Barncorkrie D & G	98	NX0935
Barnes Gt Lon	26	TQ2276
Barnes Street Kent	16	TQ6447
Barnet Gt Lon	26	TQ2496
Barnet Gate Gt Lon	26	TQ2195
Barnetby le Wold Lincs	84	TA0509
Barney Norfk	66	TF9932
Barnham Suffk	54	TL8779
Barnham W Susx	14	SU9503
Barnham Broom Norfk	66	TG0807
Barnhead Angus	135	NO6657
Barnhill Ches	71	SJ4854
Barnhill Dund C	127	NO4731
Barnhill Moray	141	NJ1457
Barnhills D & G	98	NW9871
Barningham Dur	89	NZ0810
Barningham Suffk	54	TL9676
Barnoldby le Beck Lincs	85	TA2303
Barnoldswick Lancs	81	SD8746
Barns Green W Susx	14	TQ1226
Barnsdale Bar N York	83	SE5014
Barnsley Gloucs	36	SP0704
Barnsley S York	83	SE3406
Barnsley Shrops	60	SO7592
Barnsole Kent	29	TR2756
Barnstaple Devon	19	SS5633
Barnston Essex	40	TL6419
Barnston Mersyd	78	SJ2783
Barnstone Notts	63	SK7335
Barnt Green H & W	60	SP0173
Barnton C Edin	117	NT1874
Barnton Ches	71	SJ6375
Barnwell All Saints Nhants	51	TL0484
Barnwell St Andrew Nhants	51	TL0584
Barnwood Gloucs	35	SO8518
Baron's Cross H & W	46	SO4758
Barons Wood Devon	8	SS7003
Baronwood Cumb	94	NY5143
Barr S Ayrs	106	NX2794
Barrachan D & G	99	NX3649
Barrapoll Ag & B	120	NL9442
Barras Cumb	88	NY8312
Barrasford Nthumb	102	NY9173
Barrets Green Ches	71	SJ5859
Barrhead E Rens	115	NS4958
Barrhill S Ayrs	98	NX2382
Barrington Cambs	52	TL3849
Barrington Somset	10	ST3818
Barripper Cnwll	2	SW6338
Barrmill N Ayrs	115	NS3651
Barrnacarry Bay Ag & B	122	NM8122
Barrock Highld	151	ND2570
Barrow Gloucs	47	SO8824
Barrow Lancs	81	SD7338
Barrow Rutlnd	63	SK8815
Barrow Shrops	59	SJ6500
Barrow Somset	22	ST7231
Barrow Suffk	53	TL7663
Barrow Bridge Gt Man	81	SD6811
Barrow Burn Nthumb	110	NT8610
Barrow Gurney Somset	21	ST5268
Barrow Haven Lincs	84	TA0622
Barrow Hill Derbys	74	SK4275
Barrow Island Cumb	86	SD1968
Barrow Nook Lancs	78	SD4402
Barrow Street Wilts	22	ST8330
Barrow upon Soar Leics	62	SK5717
Barrow upon Trent Derbys	62	SK3528
Barrow Vale Somset	21	ST6460
Barrow's Green Ches	78	SJ5287
Barrow's Green Ches	72	SJ6857
Barrow-in-Furness Cumb	86	SD2068
Barrow-upon-Humber Lincs	84	TA0620
Barroway Drove Norfk	65	TF5703
Barrowby Lincs	63	SK8736
Barrowden Rutlnd	51	SK9400
Barrowford Lancs	81	SD8539
Barry Angus	127	NO5334
Barry V Glam	20	ST1268
Barry Island V Glam	20	ST1166
Barsby Leics	63	SK6911
Barsham Suffk	55	TM3989
Barston W Mids	61	SP2078
Bartestree H & W	46	SO5640
Barthol Chapel Abers	143	NJ8133
Bartholomew Green Essex	40	TL7221
Barthomley Ches	72	SJ7652
Bartley Hants	12	SU3012
Bartley Green W Mids	60	SP0081
Bartlow Cambs	53	TL5845
Barton Cambs	52	TL4055
Barton Ches	71	SJ4454
Barton Cumb	94	NY4826
Barton Devon	7	SX9167
Barton Gloucs	48	SP0925
Barton H & W	46	SO2957
Barton Lancs	78	SD3509
Barton Lancs	80	SD5137
Barton N York	89	NZ2208
Barton Oxon	37	SP5507
Barton Warwks	48	SP1051
Barton Bendish Norfk	65	TF7105
Barton End Gloucs	35	ST8498
Barton Green Staffs	73	SK1717
Barton Hartshorn Bucks	49	SP6430
Barton in Fabis Notts	62	SK5132
Barton in the Beans Leics	62	SK3906
Barton Mills Suffk	53	TL7173
Barton on Sea Hants	12	SZ2393
Barton Seagrave Nhants	51	SP8877
Barton St David Somset	21	ST5432
Barton Stacey Hants	24	SU4341
Barton Town Devon	19	SS6840
Barton Turf Norfk	67	TG3522
Barton upon Irwell Gt Man	79	SJ7697
Barton Waterside Lincs	84	TA0222
Barton-le-Clay Beds	38	TL0830
Barton-le-Street N York	90	SE7274
Barton-le-Willows N York	90	SE7163
Barton-on-the-Heath Warwks	48	SP2532
Barton-under-Needwood Staffs	73	SK1818
Barton-upon-Humber Lincs	84	TA0221
Barugh S York	82	SE3108
Barugh Green S York	82	SE3107
Barvas W Isls	154	NB3649
Barway Cambs	53	TL5575
Barwell Leics	50	SP4496
Barwick Devon	8	SS5907
Barwick Herts	39	TL3819
Barwick Somset	10	ST5513
Barwick in Elmet W York	83	SE4037
Baschurch Shrops	59	SJ4221
Bascote Warwks	48	SP4063
Bascote Heath Warwks	48	SP3962
Base Green Suffk	54	TM0163
Basford Green Staffs	72	SJ9851
Bashall Eaves Lancs	81	SD6943
Bashall Town Lancs	81	SD7142
Bashley Hants	12	SZ2496
Basildon Berks	37	SU6078
Basildon Essex	40	TQ7189
Basingstoke Hants	24	SU6352
Baslow Derbys	74	SK2572
Bason Bridge Somset	21	ST3446
Bassaleg Newpt	34	ST2786
Bassendean Border	110	NT6245
Bassenthwaite Cumb	93	NY2332
Bassett Hants	13	SU4216
Bassingbourn Cambs	39	TL3343
Bassingfield Notts	62	SK6137
Bassingham Lincs	76	SK9060
Bassingthorpe Lincs	63	SK9628
Bassus Green Herts	39	TL3025
Basted Kent	27	TQ6055
Baston Lincs	64	TF1113
Bastwick Norfk	67	TG4217
Batch Somset	21	ST3255
Batchworth Herts	26	TQ0694
Batchworth Heath Herts	26	TQ0792
Batcombe Dorset	10	ST6103
Batcombe Somset	22	ST6938
Bate Heath Ches	79	SJ6879
Batford Herts	38	TL1415
Bath Somset	22	ST7464
Bath Side Essex	41	TM2532
Bathampton Somset	22	ST7766
Bathealton Somset	20	ST0823
Batheaston Somset	22	ST7767
Bathford Somset	22	ST7866
Bathgate W Loth	117	NS9768
Bathley Notts	75	SK7759
Bathpool Cnwll	5	SX2874
Bathpool Somset	20	ST2526
Bathville W Loth	116	NS9367
Bathway Somset	21	ST5952
Batley W York	82	SE2224
Batsford Gloucs	48	SP1833
Batson Devon	7	SX7339
Batt's Corner Surrey	25	SU8140
Battersby N York	90	NZ5907
Battersea Gt Lon	27	TQ2776
Battisborough Cross Devon	6	SX5948
Battisford Suffk	54	TM0554
Battisford Tye Suffk	54	TM0354
Battle E Susx	17	TQ7515
Battle Powys	45	SO0130
Battleborough Somset	21	ST3450
Battledown Gloucs	35	SO9621
Battledykes Angus	127	NO4555
Battlefield Shrops	59	SJ5117
Battlesbridge Essex	40	TQ7894
Battlesden Beds	38	SP9628
Battleton Somset	20	SS9127
Battlies Green Suffk	54	TL9064
Battramsley Cross Hants	12	SZ3198
Battyeford W York	82	SE1920
Baughton H & W	47	SO8841
Baughurst Hants	24	SU5860
Baulds Abers	134	NO6093
Baulking Oxon	36	SU3191
Baumber Lincs	76	TF2274
Baunton Gloucs	35	SP0104
Baveney Wood Shrops	60	SO6979
Baverstock Wilts	23	SU0332
Bawburgh Norfk	66	TG1508
Bawdeswell Norfk	66	TG0420
Bawdrip Somset	21	ST3439
Bawdsey Suffk	55	TM3440
Bawtry S York	75	SK6493
Baxenden Lancs	81	SD7726
Baxter's Green Suffk	53	TL7557
Baxterley Warwks	61	SP2896
Bay Horse Lancs	80	SD4952
Bayble W Isls	154	NB5231
Baybridge Hants	13	SU5223
Baybridge Nthumb	95	NY9550
Baycliff Cumb	86	SD2872
Baydon Wilts	36	SU2878
Bayford Herts	39	TL3108
Bayford Somset	22	ST7229
Bayhead W Isls	154	NF7468
Bayley's Hill Kent	27	TQ5151
Baylham Suffk	54	TM1051
Baynard's Green Oxon	49	SP5429
Baysdale Abbey N York	90	NZ6206
Baysham H & W	46	SO5727
Bayston Hill Shrops	59	SJ4808
Baythorne End Essex	53	TL7242
Bayton H & W	60	SO6973
Bayton Common H & W	60	SO7173
Bayworth Oxon	37	SP4901
Beach Gloucs	35	ST7071
Beachampton Bucks	49	SP7736
Beachamwell Norfk	65	TF7505
Beachborough Kent	29	TR1638
Beachley Gloucs	34	ST5591
Beacon Devon	9	ST1805
Beacon End Essex	40	TL9524
Beacon Hill E Susx	16	TQ5030
Beacon Hill Kent	17	TQ8232
Beacon Hill Notts	75	SK8153
Beacon Hill Surrey	14	SU8736
Beacon's Bottom Bucks	37	SU7895
Beaconsfield Bucks	26	SU9490
Beacontree Gt Lon	27	TQ4786
Beadlam N York	90	SE6584
Beadlow Beds	38	TL1038
Beadnell Nthumb	111	NU2229
Beaford Devon	19	SS5515
Beal N York	83	SE5325
Beal Nthumb	111	NU0642
Bealbury Cnwll	5	SX3766
Bealsmill Cnwll	5	SX3576
Beam Hill Staffs	73	SK2325
Beamhurst Staffs	73	SK0536
Beaminster Dorset	10	ST4701
Beamish Dur	96	NZ2253
Beamsley N York	82	SE0752
Bean Kent	27	TQ5872
Beanacre Wilts	22	ST9066
Beanley Nthumb	111	NU0818
Beardon Devon	5	SX5184
Beardwood Lancs	81	SD6629
Beare Devon	9	SS9901
Beare Green Surrey	15	TQ1742
Bearley Warwks	48	SP1860
Bearley Cross Warwks	48	SP1761
Bearpark Dur	96	NZ2343
Bearsden D & Cb	115	NS5372
Bearstead Kent	28	TQ8055
Bearstone Shrops	72	SJ7239
Bearwood W Mids	60	SP0286
Beatley Heath Herts	27	TQ2599
Beattock D & G	108	NT0802
Beauchamp Roding Essex	40	TL5809
Beauchief S York	74	SK3381
Beaudesert Warwks	48	SP1565
Beaufort Blae G	33	SO1611
Beaulieu Hants	12	SU3802
Beauly Highld	139	NH5246
Beaumaris Angles	69	SH6076
Beaumont Cumb	93	NY3459
Beaumont Essex	41	TM1624
Beaumont Jersey	152	JS0000
Beaumont Hill Dur	96	NZ2918
Beausale Warwks	61	SP2470
Beauworth Hants	13	SU5726
Beaver Kent	28	TR0040
Beaver Green Kent	28	TR0041
Beaworthy Devon	18	SX4699
Beazley End Essex	40	TL7429
Bebington Mersyd	78	SJ3383
Bebside Nthumb	103	NZ2781
Beccles Suffk	55	TM4289
Becconsall Lancs	80	SD4523
Beck Foot Cumb	87	SD6196
Beck Hole N York	90	NZ8202
Beck Row Suffk	53	TL6977
Beck Side Cumb	86	SD2382
Beck Side Cumb	87	SD3780
Beckbury Shrops	60	SJ7601
Beckenham Gt Lon	27	TQ3769
Beckering Lincs	76	TF1280
Beckermet Cumb	86	NY0106
Beckett End Norfk	65	TL7798
Beckfoot Cumb	92	NY0949
Beckfoot Cumb	86	NY1600
Beckfoot Cumb	86	SD1989
Beckford H & W	47	SO9736
Beckhampton Wilts	23	SU0868
Beckingham Lincs	76	SK8753
Beckingham Notts	75	SK7789
Beckington Somset	22	ST8051
Beckjay Shrops	46	SO3977
Beckley E Susx	17	TQ8523
Beckley Hants	12	SZ2296
Beckley Oxon	37	SP5611
Becks W York	82	SE0345
Beckside Cumb	87	SD6187
Beckton Gt Lon	27	TQ4381
Beckwithshaw N York	82	SE2653
Becquet Vincent Jersey	152	JS0000
Bedale N York	89	SE2688
Bedburn Dur	95	NZ0931
Bedchester Dorset	11	ST8517
Beddau Rhondd	33	ST0585
Beddgelert Gwynd	69	SH5948
Beddingham E Susx	16	TQ4407
Beddington Gt Lon	27	TQ3065
Beddington Corner Gt Lon	27	TQ2866
Bedfield Suffk	55	TM2166
Bedfield Little Green Suffk	55	TM2365
Bedford Beds	38	TL0449
Bedgebury Cross Kent	17	TQ7134
Bedham W Susx	14	TQ0122
Bedhampton Hants	13	SU7006
Bedingfield Suffk	54	TM1768
Bedingfield Green Suffk	54	TM1866
Bedingfield Street Suffk	54	TM1768
Bedlam N York	89	SE2661
Bedlam Lane Kent	28	TQ8845
Bedlington Nthumb	103	NZ2681
Bedlinog Myr Td	33	SO0901
Bedminster Bristl	34	ST5871
Bedminster Down Bristl	34	ST5770
Bedmond Herts	38	TL0903
Bednall Staffs	72	SJ9517
Bedrule Border	110	NT6017
Bedstone Shrops	46	SO3676
Bedwas Caerph	33	ST1789
Bedwellty Caerph	33	SO1600
Bedworth Warwks	61	SP3687
Bedworth Woodlands Warwks	61	SP3487
Beeby Leics	63	SK6608
Beech Hants	24	SU6938
Beech Staffs	72	SJ8538
Beech Hill Berks	24	SU6964
Beechingstoke Wilts	23	SU0859
Beedon Berks	37	SU4878
Beedon Hill Berks	37	SU4877
Beeford E R Yk	85	TA1253
Beeley Derbys	74	SK2667
Beelsby Lincs	85	TA2001
Beenham Berks	24	SU5868
Beenham's Heath Berks	25	SU8375
Beer Devon	9	SY2289
Beer Somset	21	ST4031
Beer Hackett Dorset	10	ST6011
Beercrocombe Somset	21	ST3220
Beesands Devon	7	SX8140
Beesby Lincs	77	TF4680
Beeson Devon	7	SX8140
Beeston Beds	52	TL1648
Beeston Ches	71	SJ5358
Beeston Norfk	66	TF9015
Beeston Notts	62	SK5236
Beeston W York	82	SE2830
Beeston Regis Norfk	66	TG1642
Beeswing D & G	100	NX8969
Beetham Cumb	87	SD4979
Beetham Somset	10	ST2712
Beetley Norfk	66	TF9718
Began Cardif	34	ST2283
Begbroke Oxon	37	SP4614
Begdale Cambs	65	TF4506
Begelly Pembks	31	SN1107
Beggar's Bush Powys	46	SO2664
Beggarinton Hill W York	82	SE2724
Beguildy Powys	45	SO1979
Beighton Norfk	67	TG3808
Beighton S York	75	SK4483
Beighton Hill Derbys	73	SK2951
Bein Inn P & K	126	NO1513
Beith N Ayrs	115	NS3553
Bekesbourne Kent	29	TR1955
Bekesbourne Hill Kent	29	TR1856
Belaugh Norfk	67	TG2818
Belbroughton H & W	60	SO9277
Belchalwell Dorset	11	ST7909
Belchalwell Street Dorset	11	ST7909
Belchamp Otten Essex	54	TL8041
Belchamp St Paul Essex	53	TL7942
Belchamp Walter Essex	54	TL8240
Belchford Lincs	77	TF2975
Belford Nthumb	111	NU1034
Belgrave Leics	62	SK5906
Belhelvie Abers	143	NJ9417
Belhinnie Abers	142	NJ4627
Bell Bar Herts	39	TL2505
Bell Busk N York	81	SD9056
Bell End H & W	60	SO9477
Bell Heath H & W	60	SO9477
Bell Hill Hants	13	SU7324
Bell o' th'Hill Ches	71	SJ5245
Bellabeg Abers	134	NJ3513
Bellanoch Ag & B	113	NR7992
Bellasize E R Yk	84	SE8227
Bellaty Angus	133	NO2359
Belle Vue Cumb	93	NY3756
Belle Vue W York	83	SE3419
Belleau Lincs	77	TF4078
Bellerby N York	89	SE1192
Bellever Devon	8	SX6577
Bellfield S Lans	108	NS8234
Bellfield S Lans	108	NS9620
Bellimoor H & W	46	SO3840
Bellingdon Bucks	38	SP9405
Bellingham Nthumb	102	NY8383
Belloch Ag & B	105	NR6737
Bellochantuy Ag & B	104	NR6632
Bellows Cross Dorset	12	SU0613
Bells Cross Suffk	54	TM1552
Bells Yew Green E Susx	16	TQ6135
Bellshill N Lans	116	NS7360
Bellshill Nthumb	111	NU1230
Bellside N Lans	116	NS8058
Bellsquarry W Loth	117	NT0465
Belluton Somset	21	ST6164
Belmesthorpe Rutlnd	64	TF0410
Belmont Gt Lon	27	TQ2562
Belmont Lancs	81	SD6715
Belmont S Ayrs	106	NS3419
Belmont Shet	155	HP5600
Belnacraig Abers	141	NJ3716
Belowda Cnwll	4	SW9661
Belper Derbys	62	SK3447
Belper Lane End Derbys	74	SK3349
Belph Derbys	75	SK5475
Belsay Nthumb	103	NZ0978
Belsay Castle Nthumb	103	NZ0878
Belses Border	110	NT5725
Belsford Devon	7	SX7659
Belsize Herts	26	TL0300
Belstead Suffk	54	TM1241
Belstone Devon	8	SX6293
Belthorn Lancs	81	SD7124
Beltinge Kent	29	TR1967
Beltingham Nthumb	102	NY7863
Beltoft Lincs	84	SE8006
Belton Leics	62	SK4420
Belton Lincs	84	SE7806
Belton Lincs	63	SK9339
Belton Norfk	67	TG4802
Belton Rutlnd	63	SK8101
Beltring Kent	28	TQ6747
Belvedere Gt Lon	27	TQ4978
Belvoir Leics	63	SK8133
Bembridge IOW	13	SZ6488
Bemersley Green Staffs	72	SJ8854
Bemerton Wilts	23	SU1230
Bempton E R Yk	91	TA1972
Ben Rhydding W York	82	SE1347
Benacre Suffk	55	TM5184
Benbuie D & G	107	NX7196
Benderloch Ag & B	122	NM9038
Benenden Kent	17	TQ8033
Benfield D & G	99	NX3763
Benfieldside Dur	95	NZ0952
Bengates Norfk	67	TG3027
Bengeworth H & W	48	SP0443
Benhall Green Suffk	55	TM3961
Benhall Street Suffk	55	TM3561
Benholm Abers	135	NO8069
Beningbrough N York	90	SE5257
Benington Herts	39	TL2923
Benington Lincs	77	TF3946
Benllech Angles	68	SH5182
Benmore Ag & B	114	NS1385
Bennacott Cnwll	5	SX2992
Bennan N Ayrs	105	NR9921
Bennet Head Cumb	93	NY4423
Bennetland E R Yk	84	SE8228
Bennett End Bucks	37	SU7897
Bennington Sea End Lincs	65	TF4145
Benniworth Lincs	76	TF2081
Benny Cnwll	4	SX1192
Benover Kent	28	TQ7048
Benson Oxon	37	SU6291
Bentfield Green Essex	39	TL5025
Benthall Shrops	60	SJ6602
Bentham Gloucs	35	SO9116
Benthoul Aber C	135	NJ8003
Bentlawn Shrops	59	SJ3301
Bentley E R Yk	84	TA0136
Bentley Hants	25	SU7844
Bentley S York	83	SE5605
Bentley Suffk	54	TM1138
Bentley Warwks	61	SP2895
Bentley Heath W Mids	61	SP1675
Benton Devon	19	SS6536
Bentpath D & G	101	NY3190
Bentwichen Devon	19	SS7333
Bentworth Hants	24	SU6640
Benvie Angus	126	NO3231
Benville Dorset	10	ST5303
Benwick Cambs	52	TL3490
Beoley H & W	48	SP0669
Beoraidbeg Highld	129	NM6793
Bepton W Susx	14	SU8618
Berden Essex	39	TL4629
Bere Alston Devon	6	SX4466
Bere Ferrers Devon	6	SX4563
Bere Regis Dorset	11	SY8494
Berea Pembks	30	SM7930
Berepper Cnwll	2	SW6523
Bergh Apton Norfk	67	TG3001
Berhill Somset	21	ST4436
Berinsfield Oxon	37	SU5795
Berkeley Gloucs	35	ST6899
Berkeley Heath Gloucs	35	ST6999
Berkeley Road Gloucs	35	SO7200
Berkhamsted Herts	38	SP9907

Berkley Blanefield

Berkley Somset	22	ST8049
Berkswell W Mids	61	SP2479
Bermondsey Gt Lon	27	TQ3479
Bernera Highld	129	NG8020
Bernice Ag & B	114	NS1391
Bernisdale Highld	136	NG4050
Berrick Prior Oxon	37	SU6294
Berrick Salome Oxon	37	SU6293
Berriedale Highld	147	ND1222
Berrier Cumb	93	NY3929
Berriew Powys	58	SJ1801
Berrington H & W	46	SO5767
Berrington Nthumb	111	NU0043
Berrington Shrops	59	SJ5206
Berrington Green H & W	46	SO5766
Berrow H & W	47	SO7934
Berrow Somset	20	ST2951
Berrow Green H & W	47	SO7458
Berry Brow W York	82	SE1314
Berry Cross Devon	18	SS4714
Berry Down Cross Devon	19	SS5743
Berry Hill Gloucs	34	SO5712
Berry Hill Pembks	30	SN0640
Berry Pomeroy Devon	7	SX8261
Berry's Green Gt Lon	27	TQ4359
Berryhillock Moray	142	NJ5054
Berryhillock Moray	142	NJ5060
Berrynarbor Devon	19	SS5646
Bersham Wrexhm	71	SJ3049
Berthengam Flints	70	SJ1179
Berwick E Susx	16	TQ5105
Berwick Bassett Wilts	36	SU0973
Berwick Hill Nthumb	103	NZ1775
Berwick St James Wilts	23	SU0739
Berwick St John Wilts	22	ST9422
Berwick St Leonard Wilts	22	ST9233
Berwick-upon-Tweed Nthumb	119	NT9953
Bescaby Leics	63	SK8126
Bescar Cumb	80	SD3913
Besford H & W	47	SO9144
Besford Shrops	59	SJ5525
Besom Hill Gt Man	79	SD9508
Bessacarr S York	75	SE6100
Bessels Leigh Oxon	37	SP4501
Besses o' th' Barn Gt Man	79	SD8005
Bessingby E R Yk	91	TA1566
Bessingham Norfk	66	TG1636
Bestbeech Hill E Susx	16	TQ6231
Besthorpe Norfk	66	TM0595
Besthorpe Notts	75	SK8264
Beswick E R Yk	84	TA0147
Betchcott Shrops	59	SO4398
Betchworth Surrey	26	TQ2150
Bethania Cardgn	43	SN5763
Bethania Gwynd	57	SH7044
Bethel Angles	68	SH3970
Bethel Gwynd	68	SH5265
Bethel Gwynd	70	SH9839
Bethel Powys	58	SJ1021
Bethersden Kent	28	TQ9240
Bethesda Gwynd	69	SH6266
Bethesda Pembks	31	SN0918
Bethlehem Carmth	44	SN6825
Bethnal Green Gt Lon	27	TQ3482
Betley Staffs	72	SJ7548
Betsham Kent	27	TQ6071
Betteshanger Kent	29	TR3152
Bettiscombe Dorset	10	ST3900
Bettisfield Wrexhm	59	SJ4635
Betton Shrops	72	SJ6936
Betton Strange Shrops	59	SJ5009
Bettws Newpt	34	ST2890
Bettws Bledrws Cardgn	44	SN5952
Bettws Cedewain Powys	58	SO1296
Bettws Evan Cardgn	42	SN3047
Bettws-Newydd Mons	34	SO3606
Bettyhill Highld	150	NC7061
Betws Brdgnd	33	SS9086
Betws Carmth	32	SN6311
Betws Garmon Gwynd	69	SH5357
Betws Gwerfil Goch Denbgs	70	SJ0346
Betws-y-coed A & C	69	SH7956
Betws-yn-Rhos A & C	69	SH9073
Beulah Cardgn	42	SN2846
Beulah Powys	45	SN9251
Bevendean E Susx	15	TQ3306
Bevercotes Notts	75	SK6972
Beverley E R Yk	84	TA0339
Beverstone Gloucs	35	ST8694
Bevington Gloucs	35	ST6596
Bewaldeth Cumb	93	NY2034
Bewcastle Cumb	101	NY5674
Bewdley H & W	60	SO7875
Bewerley N York	89	SE1565
Bewholme E R Yk	85	TA1649
Bewlbridge Kent	16	TQ6834
Bexhill E Susx	17	TQ7407
Bexley Gt Lon	27	TQ4973
Bexleyheath Gt Lon	27	TQ4875
Bexleyhill W Susx	14	SU9125
Bexon Kent	28	TQ8959
Bexwell Norfk	65	TF6303
Beyton Suffk	54	TL9363
Beyton Green Suffk	54	TL9363
Bhaltos W Isls	154	NB0936
Bibstone Gloucs	35	ST6991
Bibury Gloucs	36	SP1106
Bicester Oxon	49	SP5823
Bickenhill W Mids	61	SP1882
Bicker Lincs	64	TF2237
Bicker Bar Lincs	64	TF2438
Bicker Gauntlet Lincs	64	TF2139
Bickershaw Gt Man	79	SD6201
Bickerstaffe Lancs	78	SD4404
Bickerton Ches	71	SJ5052
Bickerton Devon	7	SX8139
Bickerton N York	83	SE4550
Bickerton Nthumb	103	NT9900
Bickford Staffs	60	SJ8814
Bickington Devon	19	SS5332
Bickington Devon	7	SX8072
Bickleigh Devon	9	SS9407
Bickleigh Devon	6	SX5262
Bickleton Devon	19	SS5030
Bickley Ches	71	SJ5348
Bickley Gt Lon	27	TQ4268
Bickley H & W	47	SO6371
Bickley N York	91	SE9191
Bickley Moss Ches	71	SJ5448
Bicknacre Essex	40	TL7802
Bicknoller Somset	20	ST1139
Bicknor Kent	28	TQ8658
Bickton Hants	12	SU1412
Bicton H & W	46	SO4764
Bicton Shrops	59	SJ4415
Bicton Shrops	59	SO2983
Bidborough Kent	16	TQ5643
Bidden Hants	24	SU7049
Biddenden Kent	28	TQ8538
Biddenden Green Kent	28	TQ8842
Biddenham Beds	38	TL0250
Biddestone Wilts	35	ST8673
Biddisham Somset	21	ST3853
Biddlesden Bucks	49	SP6340
Biddlestone Nthumb	111	NT9508
Biddulph Staffs	72	SJ8858
Biddulph Moor Staffs	72	SJ9058
Bideford Devon	18	SS4526
Bidford-on-Avon Warwks	48	SP1052
Bidston Mersyd	78	SJ2890
Bielby E R Yk	84	SE7843
Bieldside Aber C	135	NJ8702
Bierley IOW	13	SZ5078
Bierton Bucks	38	SP8415
Big Balcraig D & G	99	NX3843
Big Carlae D & G	107	NX6597
Big Sand Highld	144	NG7578
Bigbury Devon	7	SX6646
Bigbury-on-Sea Devon	7	SX6544
Bigby Lincs	84	TA0507
Biggar Cumb	86	SD1966
Biggar S Lans	108	NT0437
Biggin Derbys	74	SK1559
Biggin Derbys	73	SK2549
Biggin N York	83	SE5434
Biggin Hill Gt Lon	27	TQ4159
Biggleswade Beds	39	TL1944
Bigholms D & G	101	NY3180
Bighouse Highld	150	NC8964
Bighton Hants	24	SU6134
Bigland Hall Cumb	87	SD3583
Biglands Cumb	93	NY2553
Bignor W Susx	14	SU9814
Bigrigg Cumb	92	NY0013
Bilborough Notts	62	SK5241
Bilbrook Somset	20	ST0341
Bilbrook Staffs	60	SJ8703
Bilbrough N York	83	SE5346
Bilbster Highld	151	ND2853
Bildershaw Dur	96	NZ2024
Bildeston Suffk	54	TL9949
Billacott Cnwll	5	SX2690
Billericay Essex	40	TQ6794
Billesdon Leics	63	SK7202
Billesley Warwks	48	SP1456
Billingborough Lincs	64	TF1133
Billinge Mersyd	78	SD5200
Billingford Norfk	66	TG0120
Billingford Norfk	54	TM1678
Billingham Dur	97	NZ4624
Billinghay Lincs	76	TF1554
Billingley S York	83	SE4304
Billingshurst W Susx	14	TQ0825
Billingsley Shrops	60	SO7085
Billington Beds	38	SP9422
Billington Lancs	81	SD7235
Billington Staffs	72	SJ8820
Billockby Norfk	67	TG4313
Billy Row Dur	96	NZ1637
Bilsborrow Lancs	80	SD5139
Bilsby Lincs	77	TF4776
Bilsham W Susx	14	SU9702
Bilsington Kent	17	TR0434
Bilsthorpe Notts	75	SK6460
Bilsthorpe Moor Notts	75	SK6560
Bilston Mdloth	117	NT2664
Bilston W Mids	60	SO9596
Bilstone Leics	62	SK3605
Bilting Kent	28	TR0549
Bilton E R Yk	85	TA1632
Bilton N York	83	SE4749
Bilton N York	89	SE3157
Bilton Nthumb	111	NU2210
Bilton Warwks	50	SP4873
Bilton Banks Nthumb	111	NU2010
Binbrook Lincs	76	TF2093
Binchester Blocks Dur	96	NZ2232
Bincombe Dorset	11	SY6884
Binegar Somset	21	ST6149
Bines Green W Susx	15	TQ1817
Binfield Berks	25	SU8471
Binfield Heath Oxon	37	SU7477
Bingfield Nthumb	102	NY9772
Bingham Notts	63	SK7039
Bingham's Melcombe Dorset	11	ST7702
Bingley W York	82	SE1039
Bings Shrops	59	SJ5318
Binham Norfk	66	TF9839
Binley Hants	24	SU4253
Binley W Mids	61	SP3778
Binnegar Dorset	11	SY8887
Binniehill Falk	116	NS8572
Binns Farm Moray	141	NJ3164
Binscombe Surrey	25	SU9645
Binsey Oxon	37	SP4907
Binstead Hants	25	SU7740
Binstead IOW	13	SZ5892
Binsted W Susx	14	SU9806
Binton Warwks	48	SP1454
Bintree Norfk	66	TG0123
Binweston Shrops	59	SJ3004
Birch Essex	40	TL9419
Birch Gt Man	79	SD8507
Birch Close Dorset	11	ST8803
Birch Cross Staffs	73	SK1230
Birch Green Essex	40	TL9418
Birch Green H & W	47	SO8645
Birch Green Herts	39	TL2911
Birch Heath Ches	71	SJ5461
Birch Hill Ches	71	SJ5173
Birch Vale Derbys	74	SK0286
Birch Wood Somset	9	ST2414
Bircham Newton Norfk	65	TF7733
Bircham Tofts Norfk	65	TF7732
Birchanger Essex	39	TL5122
Birchburn N Ayrs	105	NR9129
Birchencliffe W York	82	SE1218
Bircher H & W	46	SO4765
Birchfield W Mids	61	SP0790
Birchgrove Cardif	33	ST1679
Birchgrove E Susx	15	TQ4029
Birchgrove Swans	32	SS7098
Birchington Kent	29	TR3069
Birchley Heath Warwks	61	SP2894
Birchmoor Green Beds	38	SP9534
Birchover Derbys	74	SK2362
Birchyfield H & W	47	SO6453
Bircotes Notts	75	SK6391
Bird End W Mids	60	SP0194
Bird Street Suffk	54	TM0052
Birdbrook Essex	53	TL7041
Birdforth N York	90	SE4875
Birdham W Susx	14	SU8200
Birdingbury Warwks	50	SP4368
Birdlip Gloucs	35	SO9214
Birdoswald Cumb	102	NY6166
Birds Edge W York	82	SE2007
Birds Green Essex	40	TL5808
Birdsall N York	90	SE8165
Birdsgreen Shrops	60	SO7785
Birdsmoorgate Dorset	10	ST3900
Birdwell S York	83	SE3401
Birdwood Gloucs	35	SO7418
Birgham Border	110	NT7939
Birichin Highld	147	NH7592
Birkacre Lancs	81	SD5714
Birkby N York	89	NZ3202
Birkdale Mersyd	80	SD3214
Birkenbog Abers	142	NJ5365
Birkenhead Mersyd	78	SJ3288
Birkenhills Abers	142	NJ7445
Birkenshaw W York	82	SE2028
Birkhall Abers	134	NO3493
Birkhill Angus	126	NO3534
Birkhill D & G	109	NT2015
Birkholme Lincs	63	SK9623
Birkin N York	83	SE5326
Birks W York	82	SE2626
Birkshaw Nthumb	102	NY7765
Birley H & W	46	SO4553
Birley Carr S York	74	SK3392
Birling Kent	28	TQ6860
Birling Nthumb	111	NU2406
Birling Gap E Susx	16	TV5596
Birlingham H & W	47	SO9343
Birmingham W Mids	61	SP0786
Birnam P & K	125	NO0341
Birness Abers	143	NJ9933
Birse Abers	134	NO5697
Birsemore Abers	134	NO5297
Birstall Leics	62	SK5909
Birstall W York	82	SE2225
Birstwith N York	89	SE2359
Birthorpe Lincs	64	TF1033
Birtley H & W	46	SO3669
Birtley Nthumb	102	NY8778
Birtley T & W	96	NZ2756
Birts Street H & W	47	SO7836
Bisbrooke Rutlnd	51	SP8899
Biscathorpe Lincs	76	TF2284
Biscovey Cnwll	3	SX0552
Bish Mill Devon	19	SS7425
Bisham Berks	26	SU8485
Bishampton H & W	47	SO9951
Bishop Auckland Dur	96	NZ2028
Bishop Burton E R Yk	84	SE9839
Bishop Middleham Dur	96	NZ3231
Bishop Monkton N York	89	SE3266
Bishop Norton Lincs	76	SK9892
Bishop Sutton Somset	21	ST5859
Bishop Thornton N York	89	SE2563
Bishop Wilton E R Yk	84	SE7955
Bishop's Castle Shrops	59	SO3288
Bishop's Cleeve Gloucs	47	SO9627
Bishop's Frome H & W	47	SO6648
Bishop's Green Essex	40	TL6217
Bishop's Green Hants	24	SU5063
Bishop's Itchington Warwks	48	SP3857
Bishop's Norton Gloucs	47	SO8424
Bishop's Nympton Devon	19	SS7523
Bishop's Offley Staffs	72	SJ7729
Bishop's Stortford Herts	39	TL4821
Bishop's Sutton Hants	24	SU6032
Bishop's Tachbrook Warwks	48	SP3161
Bishop's Tawton Devon	19	SS5729
Bishop's Waltham Hants	13	SU5517
Bishop's Wood Staffs	60	SJ8309
Bishop`s Caundle Dorset	11	ST6913
Bishopbridge Lincs	76	TF0391
Bishopbriggs E Duns	116	NS6070
Bishopmill Moray	141	NJ2163
Bishops Cannings Wilts	23	SU0364
Bishops Gate Surrey	25	SU9871
Bishops Hull Somset	20	ST2024
Bishops Lydeard Somset	20	ST1729
Bishopsbourne Kent	29	TR1852
Bishopsteignton Devon	7	SX9073
Bishopstoke Hants	13	SU4619
Bishopston Swans	32	SS5789
Bishopstone Bucks	38	SP8010
Bishopstone E Susx	16	TQ4701
Bishopstone H & W	46	SO4143
Bishopstone Kent	26	TQ2068
Bishopstone Wilts	23	SU0625
Bishopstone Wilts	36	SU2483
Bishopstrow Wilts	22	ST8943
Bishopswood Somset	10	ST2612
Bishopsworth Bristl	21	ST5768
Bishopthorpe N York	83	SE5947
Bishopton Dur	96	NZ3621
Bishopton Rens	115	NS4371
Bishopton Warwks	48	SP1956
Bishton Newpt	34	ST3887
Bishton Staffs	73	SK0220
Bisley Gloucs	35	SO9005
Bisley Surrey	25	SU9559
Bisley Camp Surrey	25	SU9357
Bispham Lancs	80	SD3140
Bispham Green Lancs	80	SD4813
Bissoe Cnwll	3	SW7741
Bisterne Hants	12	SU1401
Bitchet Green Kent	27	TQ5654
Bitchfield Lincs	63	SK9828
Bittadon Devon	19	SS5441
Bittaford Devon	7	SX6656
Bittering Norfk	66	TF9417
Bitterley Shrops	46	SO5677
Bitterne Hants	13	SU4513
Bitteswell Leics	50	SP5385
Bitton Gloucs	35	ST6869
Bix Oxon	37	SU7284
Blaby Leics	50	SP5697
Black Bourton Oxon	36	SP2804
Black Callerton T & W	103	NZ1769
Black Car Norfk	66	TM0995
Black Corner W Susx	15	TQ2939
Black Corries Highld	123	NN2956
Black Crofts Ag & B	122	NM9234
Black Cross Cnwll	4	SW9060
Black Dog Devon	19	SS8009
Black Heddon Nthumb	103	NZ0775
Black Lane Gt Man	79	SD7708
Black Lane Ends Lancs	81	SD9243
Black Moor W York	82	SE2939
Black Notley Essex	40	TL7620
Black Street Suffk	55	TM5186
Black Tar Pembks	30	SM9909
Black Torrington Devon	18	SS4605
Blackadder Border	119	NT8452
Blackawton Devon	7	SX8051
Blackbank Warwks	61	SP3586
Blackbeck Cumb	86	NY0207
Blackborough Devon	9	ST0909
Blackborough End Norfk	65	TF6615
Blackboys E Susx	16	TQ5220
Blackbrook Derbys	62	SK3347
Blackbrook Staffs	72	SJ7638
Blackbrook Surrey	15	TQ1846
Blackburn Abers	135	NJ8212
Blackburn Lancs	81	SD6827
Blackburn W Loth	117	NS9865
Blackcraig E Ayrs	107	NS6308
Blackden Heath Ches	79	SJ7871
Blackdog Abers	135	NJ9513
Blackdown Devon	5	SX5079
Blackdown Dorset	10	ST3903
Blackdyke Cumb	92	NY1452
Blackenall Heath W Mids	60	SK0002
Blacker S York	83	SE3309
Blacker Hill S York	83	SE3602
Blackfen Gt Lon	27	TQ4674
Blackfield Hants	13	SU4402
Blackford Cumb	101	NY3961
Blackford P & K	125	NN8908
Blackford Somset	21	ST4147
Blackford Somset	21	ST6526
Blackford Bridge Gt Man	79	SD8007
Blackfordby Leics	62	SK3217
Blackgang IOW	13	SZ4876
Blackhall C Edin	117	NT1975
Blackhall Dur	97	NZ4638
Blackhall Colliery Dur	97	NZ4539
Blackhaugh Border	109	NT4238
Blackheath Essex	40	TM0021
Blackheath Gt Lon	27	TQ3876
Blackheath Suffk	55	TM4274
Blackheath Surrey	14	TQ0346
Blackheath W Mids	60	SO9786
Blackhill Abers	143	NK0039
Blackhill Abers	143	NK0755
Blackhill Abers	143	NK0843
Blackhill Dur	95	NZ0851
Blackhill of Clackriach Abers	143	NJ9246
Blackhorse Devon	9	SX9893
Blackhorse Hill E Susx	17	TQ7714
Blackjack Lincs	64	TF2639
Blackland Somset	19	SS8336
Blackland Wilts	22	SU0168
Blacklaw D & G	108	NT0408
Blackley Gt Man	79	SD8502
Blacklunans P & K	133	NO1460
Blackmarstone H & W	46	SO5038
Blackmill Brdgnd	33	SS9386
Blackmoor Hants	14	SU7733
Blackmoor Somset	21	ST4661
Blackmoorfoot W York	82	SE0913
Blackmore Essex	40	TL6001
Blackmore End Essex	40	TL7430
Blackmore End Herts	39	TL1716
Blackness Falk	117	NT0579
Blacknest Berks	25	SU9568
Blacknest Hants	25	SU7941
Blacko Lancs	81	SD8541
Blackpill Swans	32	SS6190
Blackpool Devon	7	SX8547
Blackpool Devon	7	SX8174
Blackpool Lancs	80	SD3036
Blackpool Gate Cumb	101	NY5377
Blackridge W Loth	116	NS8967
Blackrock Cnwll	2	SW6534
Blackrock Mons	33	SO2112
Blackrock Mons	34	ST5188
Blackrod Gt Man	78	SD6110
Blacksboat Moray	141	NJ1838
Blackshaw D & G	100	NY0465
Blackshaw Head W York	82	SD9527
Blacksmith's Green Suffk	54	TM1465
Blacksnape Lancs	81	SD7121
Blackstone W Susx	15	TQ2316
Blackthorn Oxon	37	SP6219
Blackthorpe Suffk	54	TL9063
Blacktoft E R Yk	84	SE8324
Blacktop Aber C	135	NJ8604
Blackwall Derbys	73	SK2548
Blackwater Cnwll	3	SW7346
Blackwater Hants	25	SU8459
Blackwater IOW	13	SZ5086
Blackwater Somset	10	ST2615
Blackwaterfoot N Ayrs	105	NR9028
Blackwell Cumb	93	NY4053
Blackwell Derbys	74	SK1272
Blackwell Derbys	75	SK4458
Blackwell Dur	89	NZ2713
Blackwell H & W	60	SO9972
Blackwell Warwks	48	SP2443
Blackwellsend Green Gloucs	47	SO7825
Blackwood Caerph	33	ST1797
Blackwood D & G	100	NX9087
Blackwood S Lans	116	NS7844
Blackwood Hill Staffs	72	SJ9255
Blacon Ches	71	SJ3868
Bladbean Kent	29	TR1847
Bladnoch D & G	99	NX4254
Bladon Oxon	37	SP4514
Bladon Somset	21	ST4220
Blaen Dyryn Powys	45	SN9336
Blaen-y-Coed Carmth	31	SN3427
Blaen-y-cwm Blae G	33	SO1311
Blaen-y-cwm Rhondd	33	SS9298
Blaenannerch Cardgn	42	SN2448
Blaenau Ffestiniog Gwynd	57	SH7045
Blaenavon Torfn	34	SO2508
Blaenffos Pembks	31	SN1937
Blaengarw Brdgnd	33	SS9092
Blaengeuffardd Cardgn	43	SN6480
Blaengwrach Neath	33	SN8605
Blaengwynfi Neath	33	SS8996
Blaenllechau Rhondd	33	ST0097
Blaenpennal Cardgn	43	SN6264
Blaenplwyf Cardgn	43	SN5775
Blaenporth Cardgn	42	SN2648
Blaenrhondda Rhondd	33	SS9299
Blaenwaun Carmth	31	SN2327
Blaenycwm Cardgn	43	SN8275
Blagdon Devon	7	SX8561
Blagdon Somset	20	ST2118
Blagdon Somset	21	ST5059
Blagdon Hill Somset	9	ST2117
Blagill Cumb	94	NY7347
Blaguegate Lancs	78	SD4506
Blaich Highld	130	NN0376
Blain Highld	129	NM6769
Blaina Blae G	33	SO2008
Blair Atholl P & K	132	NN8665
Blair Drummond Stirlg	116	NS7399
Blairgowrie P & K	126	NO1745
Blairingone P & K	117	NS9896
Blairlogie Stirlg	116	NS8396
Blairmore Ag & B	114	NS1983
Blairmore Highld	148	NC1959
Blairnamarrow Moray	141	NJ2015
Blairs Ferry Ag & B	114	NR9869
Blaisdon Gloucs	35	SO7017
Blake End Essex	40	TL7023
Blakebrook H & W	60	SO8276
Blakedown H & W	60	SO8878
Blakeley Lane Staffs	72	SJ9746
Blakemere Ches	71	SJ5571
Blakemere H & W	46	SO3641
Blakemore Devon	7	SX7660
Blakeney Gloucs	35	SO6707
Blakeney Norfk	66	TG0243
Blakenhall Ches	72	SJ7247
Blakenhall W Mids	60	SO9197
Blakeshall H & W	60	SO8381
Blakesley Nhants	49	SP6250
Blanchland Nthumb	95	NY9650
Bland Hill N York	82	SE2053
Blandford Camp Dorset	11	ST9107
Blandford Forum Dorset	11	ST8806
Blandford St Mary Dorset	11	ST8805
Blanefield Stirlg	115	NS5479

Bradley Green
Brokerswood

Bradley Green *Somset* 20 ST2538
Bradley Green *Warwks* 61 SK2800
Bradley in the Moors *Staffs* 73 SK0541
Bradley Stoke *Gloucs* 34 ST6181
Bradmore *Notts* 62 SK5830
Bradney *Somset* 21 ST3338
Bradninch *Devon* 19 SS6133
Bradninch *Devon* 9 SS9904
Bradnop *Staffs* 73 SK0155
Bradnor Green *H & W* 46 SO2957
Bradpole *Dorset* 10 SY4894
Bradshaw *Gt Man* 81 SD7312
Bradshaw *W York* 82 SE0514
Bradshaw *W York* 82 SE0729
Bradstone *Devon* 5 SX3880
Bradwall Green *Ches* 72 SJ7563
Bradwell *Bucks* 38 SP8340
Bradwell *Derbys* 74 SK1781
Bradwell *Devon* 19 SS5042
Bradwell *Essex* 40 TL8122
Bradwell *Norfk* 67 TG5003
Bradwell Waterside *Essex* 41 TL9907
Bradwell-on-Sea *Essex* 41 TM0006
Bradworthy *Devon* 18 SS3214
Brae *Highld* 140 NH6662
Brae *Shet* 155 HU3568
Brae Roy Lodge *Highld* 131 NN3391
Braeface *Falk* 116 NS7880
Braegrum *P & K* 125 NO0025
Braehead *Angus* 127 NO6952
Braehead *D & G* 99 NX4152
Braehead *S Lans* 117 NS9550
Braelangwell Lodge *Highld* 146 NH5192
Braemar *Abers* 133 NO1591
Braemore *Highld* 150 ND0829
Braemore *Highld* 145 NH2079
Braes of Coul *Angus* 133 NO2857
Braes of Enzie *Moray* 142 NJ3957
Braeside *Inver* 114 NS2374
Braeswick *Ork* 155 HY6137
Braevallich *Ag & B* 122 NM9507
Brafferton *Dur* 96 NZ2921
Brafferton *N York* 89 SE4370
Brafield-on-the-Green *Nhants* 51 SP8258
Bragar *W Isls* 154 NB2947
Bragbury End *Herts* 39 TL2621
Braidwood *S Lans* 116 NS8448
Brailsford *Derbys* 73 SK2541
Brailsford Green *Derbys* 73 SK2541
Brain's Green *Gloucs* 35 SO6609
Braintree *Essex* 40 TL7523
Braiseworth *Suffk* 54 TM1371
Braishfield *Hants* 23 SU3725
Braithwaite *Cumb* 93 NY2323
Braithwaite *W York* 82 SE0341
Braithwell *S York* 75 SK5394
Braken Hill *W York* 83 SE4216
Bramber *W Susx* 15 TQ1810
Brambridge *Hants* 13 SU4721
Bramcote *Notts* 62 SK5037
Bramcote *Warwks* 61 SP4088
Bramdean *Hants* 24 SU6128
Bramerton *Norfk* 67 TG2904
Bramfield *Herts* 39 TL2915
Bramfield *Suffk* 55 TM3973
Bramford *Suffk* 54 TM1246
Bramhall *Gt Man* 79 SJ8984
Bramham *W York* 83 SE4242
Bramhope *W York* 82 SE2543
Bramley *Derbys* 74 SK4079
Bramley *Hants* 24 SU6458
Bramley *S York* 75 SK4892
Bramley *Surrey* 25 TQ0044
Bramley *W York* 82 SE2435
Bramley Corner *Hants* 24 SU6359
Bramley Green *Hants* 24 SU6658
Bramley Head *N York* 89 SE1258
Bramling *Kent* 29 TR2256
Brampford Speke *Devon* 9 SX9298
Brampton *Cambs* 52 TL2170
Brampton *Cumb* 101 NY5361
Brampton *Cumb* 94 NY6723
Brampton *Lincs* 76 SK8479
Brampton *Norfk* 67 TG2223
Brampton *S York* 83 SE4101
Brampton *Suffk* 55 TM4381
Brampton Abbotts *H & W* 46 SO6026
Brampton Ash *Nhants* 50 SP7987
Brampton Bryan *H & W* 46 SO3772
Brampton-en-le-Morthen *S York* 75 SK4887
Bramshall *Staffs* 73 SK0532
Bramshaw *Hants* 12 SU2615
Bramshill *Hants* 24 SU7461
Bramshott *Hants* 14 SU8432
Bramwell *Somset* 21 ST4329
Bran End *Essex* 40 TL6525
Branault *Highld* 128 NM5269
Brancaster *Norfk* 65 TF7743
Brancaster Staithe *Norfk* 66 TF7944
Brancepeth *Dur* 96 NZ2237
Branch End *Nthumb* 103 NZ0661
Branchill *Moray* 141 NJ0852
Brand End *Lincs* 64 TF3745
Brand Green *Gloucs* 47 SO7328
Branderburgh *Moray* 141 NJ2371
Brandesburton *E R Yk* 85 TA1147
Brandeston *Suffk* 55 TM2460
Brandis Corner *Devon* 18 SS4104
Brandiston *Norfk* 66 TG1421
Brandon *Dur* 96 NZ2340
Brandon *Lincs* 76 SK9048
Brandon *Nthumb* 111 NU0417
Brandon *Suffk* 53 TL7886
Brandon *Warwks* 50 SP4176
Brandon Bank *Cambs* 53 TL6288
Brandon Creek *Norfk* 65 TL6091
Brandon Parva *Norfk* 66 TG0708
Brandsby *N York* 90 SE5872
Brandy Wharf *Lincs* 76 TF0196
Brane *Cnwll* 2 SW4028
Branksome *Dorset* 12 SZ0492
Branksome Park *Dorset* 12 SZ0590
Bransbury *Hants* 24 SU4242
Bransby *Lincs* 76 SK8978
Branscombe *Devon* 9 SY1988
Bransford *H & W* 47 SO7952
Bransgore *Hants* 12 SZ1897
Bransholme *E R Yk* 85 TA1033
Bransley *Shrops* 47 SO6575
Branson's Cross *H & W* 61 SP0970
Branston *Leics* 63 SK8129
Branston *Lincs* 76 TF0166
Branston *Staffs* 73 SK2221
Branston Booths *Lincs* 76 TF0668
Branstone *IOW* 13 SZ5583
Brant Broughton *Lincs* 76 SK9154
Brantham *Suffk* 54 TM1034
Branthwaite *Cumb* 92 NY0525
Branthwaite *Cumb* 93 NY2937
Brantingham *E R Yk* 84 SE9429
Branton *Nthumb* 111 NU0416
Branton *S York* 83 SE6401
Branton Green *N York* 89 SE4362
Branxton *Nthumb* 110 NT8937
Brassey Green *Ches* 71 SJ5260
Brassington *Derbys* 73 SK2254
Brasted *Kent* 27 TQ4755
Brasted Chart *Kent* 27 TQ4653
Brathens *Abers* 135 NO6798
Bratoft *Lincs* 77 TF4764
Brattleby *Lincs* 76 SK9481
Bratton *Shrops* 59 SJ6413
Bratton *Somset* 20 SS9446
Bratton *Wilts* 22 ST9152
Bratton Clovelly *Devon* 5 SX4691
Bratton Fleming *Devon* 19 SS6437
Bratton Seymour *Somset* 22 ST6729
Braughing *Herts* 39 TL3925
Braughing Friars *Herts* 39 TL4124
Braunston *Lincs* 63 SK8306
Braunston *Nhants* 50 SP5466
Braunstone *Leics* 62 SK5502
Braunton *Devon* 18 SS4836
Brawby *N York* 90 SE7378
Brawdy *Pembks* 30 SM8524
Brawl *Highld* 150 NC8166
Braworth *N York* 90 NZ5007
Bray *Berks* 26 SU9079
Bray Shop *Cnwll* 5 SX3374
Bray's Hill *E Susx* 16 TQ6714
Braybrooke *Nhants* 50 SP7684
Braydon *Wilts* 36 SU0488
Braydon Brook *Wilts* 35 ST9891
Braydon Side *Wilts* 35 SU0185
Brayford *Devon* 19 SS6834
Braystones *Cumb* 86 NY0106
Braythorn *N York* 82 SE2449
Brayton *N York* 83 SE6030
Braywick *Berks* 26 SU8979
Braywoodside *Berks* 26 SU8775
Brazacott *Cnwll* 5 SX2691
Breach *Kent* 28 TQ8465
Breach *Kent* 29 TR1947
Breachwood Green *Herts* 39 TL1522
Breaden Heath *Shrops* 59 SJ4436
Breadsall *Derbys* 62 SK3639
Breadstone *Gloucs* 35 SO7000
Breadward *H & W* 46 SO2854
Breage *Cnwll* 2 SW6128
Breakachy *Highld* 139 NH4644
Bream *Gloucs* 34 SO6005
Breamore *Hants* 12 SU1517
Brean *Somset* 20 ST2956
Breanais *W Isls* 154 NA9925
Brearley *W York* 82 SE0225
Brearton *N York* 89 SE3261
Breascleit *W Isls* 154 NB2135
Breasclete *W Isls* 154 NB2135
Breaston *Derbys* 62 SK4533
Brechfa *Carmth* 44 SN5230
Brechin *Angus* 134 NO6060
Breckles *Norfk* 66 TL9594
Breckonside *D & G* 100 NX8489
Brecon *Powys* 45 SO0428
Bredbury *Gt Man* 79 SJ9291
Brede *E Susx* 17 TQ8218
Bredenbury *H & W* 46 SO6056
Bredfield *Suffk* 55 TM2653
Bredgar *Kent* 28 TQ8860
Bredhurst *Kent* 28 TQ7962
Bredon *H & W* 47 SO9236
Bredon's Hardwick *H & W* 47 SO9135
Bredon's Norton *H & W* 47 SO9339
Bredwardine *H & W* 46 SO3344
Breedon on the Hill *Leics* 62 SK4022
Breich *W Loth* 117 NS9560
Breightmet *Gt Man* 79 SD7409
Breighton *E R Yk* 84 SE7033
Breinton *H & W* 46 SO4739
Bremhill *Wilts* 35 ST9773
Bremridge *Devon* 19 SS6929
Brenchley *Kent* 28 TQ6741
Brendon *Devon* 18 SS3607
Brendon *Devon* 19 SS7748
Brendon Hill *Somset* 20 ST0234
Brenfield *Ag & B* 113 NR8482
Brenish *W Isls* 154 NA9925
Brenkley *T & W* 103 NZ2175
Brent Eleigh *Suffk* 54 TL9448
Brent Knoll *Somset* 21 ST3350
Brent Mill *Devon* 7 SX6959
Brent Pelham *Herts* 39 TL4330
Brentford *Gt Lon* 26 TQ1777
Brentingby *Leics* 63 SK7818
Brentwood *Essex* 27 TQ5993
Brenzett *Kent* 17 TR0027
Brenzett Green *Kent* 17 TR0128
Brereton *Staffs* 73 SK0516
Brereton Green *Ches* 72 SJ7764
Brereton Heath *Ches* 72 SJ8065
Brereton Hill *Staffs* 73 SK0515
Bressingham *Norfk* 54 TM0780
Bressingham Common *Norfk* 54 TM0981
Bretby *Derbys* 73 SK2922
Bretford *Warwks* 50 SP4377
Bretforton *H & W* 48 SP0944
Bretherdale Head *Cumb* 87 NY5705
Bretherton *Lancs* 80 SD4720
Brettabister *Shet* 155 HU4857
Brettenham *Norfk* 54 TL9383
Brettenham *Suffk* 54 TL9654
Bretton *Derbys* 74 SK2078
Bretton *Flints* 71 SJ3563
Brewer Street *Surrey* 27 TQ3251
Brewers End *Essex* 39 TL5521
Brewood *Staffs* 60 SJ8808
Briantspuddle *Dorset* 11 SY8193
Brick End *Essex* 40 TL5725
Brick Houses *S York* 74 SK3081
Brickendon *Herts* 39 TL3208
Bricket Wood *Herts* 26 TL1202
Brickkiln Green *Essex* 40 TL7331
Bricklehampton *H & W* 47 SO9742
Bride *IOM* 153 NX4401
Bridekirk *Cumb* 92 NY1133
Bridell *Pembks* 31 SN1742
Bridestowe *Devon* 5 SX5189
Brideswell *Abers* 142 NJ5738
Bridford *Devon* 8 SX8186
Bridge *Cnwll* 2 SW6744
Bridge *Kent* 29 TR1854
Bridge End *Beds* 38 TL0050
Bridge End *Cumb* 93 NY3748
Bridge End *Cumb* 86 SD1884
Bridge End *Devon* 7 SX6946
Bridge End *Dur* 95 NZ0236
Bridge End *Essex* 40 TL6731
Bridge End *Lincs* 64 TF1436
Bridge End *Nthumb* 102 NY8965
Bridge End *Surrey* 26 TQ0756
Bridge Green *Essex* 39 TL4636
Bridge Hewick *N York* 89 SE3370
Bridge of Alford *Abers* 142 NJ5617
Bridge of Allan *Stirlg* 116 NS7997
Bridge of Avon *Moray* 141 NJ1835
Bridge of Avon *Moray* 141 NJ1520
Bridge of Balgie *P & K* 124 NN5746
Bridge of Brewlands *Angus* 133 NO1961
Bridge of Brown *Highld* 141 NJ1120
Bridge of Cally *P & K* 126 NO1351
Bridge of Canny *Abers* 135 NO6597
Bridge of Craigisla *Angus* 126 NO2553
Bridge of Dee *D & G* 99 NX7359
Bridge of Don *Aber C* 135 NJ9409
Bridge of Dulsie *Highld* 140 NH9341
Bridge of Dye *Abers* 135 NO6586
Bridge of Earn *P & K* 126 NO1318
Bridge of Ericht *P & K* 131 NN5258
Bridge of Feugh *Abers* 135 NO7094
Bridge of Forss *Highld* 150 ND0368
Bridge of Gairn *Abers* 134 NO3597
Bridge of Gaur *P & K* 124 NN5056
Bridge of Marnoch *Abers* 142 NJ5950
Bridge of Orchy *Ag & B* 123 NN2939
Bridge of Tilt *P & K* 132 NN8765
Bridge of Tynet *Moray* 141 NJ3861
Bridge of Walls *Shet* 155 HU2752
Bridge of Weir *Rens* 115 NS3965
Bridge of Westfield *Highld* 150 ND0664
Bridge Reeve *Devon* 19 SS6613
Bridge Sollers *H & W* 46 SO4142
Bridge Street *Suffk* 54 TL8749
Bridge Trafford *Ches* 71 SJ4571
Bridge Yate *Gloucs* 35 ST6872
Bridgefoot *Cumb* 92 NY0529
Bridgehampton *Somset* 21 ST5624
Bridgehill *Dur* 95 NZ0951
Bridgehouse Gate *N York* 89 SE1565
Bridgemary *Hants* 13 SU5803
Bridgend *Abers* 142 NJ5135
Bridgend *Ag & B* 112 NR3362
Bridgend *Angus* 134 NO5368
Bridgend *Border* 109 NT5235
Bridgend *Brdgnd* 33 SS9079
Bridgend *Cardgn* 42 SN1745
Bridgend *Cumb* 93 NY4014
Bridgend *D & G* 108 NT0708
Bridgend *Devon* 6 SX5548
Bridgend *Fife* 126 NO3911
Bridgend *Moray* 141 NJ3731
Bridgend *P & K* 126 NO1224
Bridgend *W Loth* 117 NT0475
Bridgend of Lintrathen *Angus* 126 NO2854
Bridgerule *Devon* 18 SS2702
Bridges *Shrops* 59 SO3996
Bridgetown *Devon* 5 SX3389
Bridgetown *Somset* 20 SS9233
Bridgham *Norfk* 54 TL9685
Bridgnorth *Shrops* 60 SO7193
Bridgtown *Staffs* 60 SJ9808
Bridgwater *Somset* 20 ST2937
Bridlington *E R Yk* 91 TA1866
Bridport *Dorset* 10 SY4692
Bridstow *H & W* 46 SO5824
Brierfield *Lancs* 81 SD8436
Brierley *Gloucs* 35 SO6215
Brierley *H & W* 46 SO4955
Brierley *W York* 83 SE4010
Brierley Hill *W Mids* 60 SO9186
Brierton *Dur* 97 NZ4730
Briery *Cumb* 93 NY2824
Brig o'Turk *Stirlg* 124 NN5306
Brigg *Lincs* 84 TA0007
Briggate *Norfk* 67 TG3127
Briggswath *N York* 90 NZ8608
Brigham *Cumb* 92 NY0830
Brigham *Cumb* 93 NY2823
Brigham *E R Yk* 85 TA0753
Brighouse *W York* 82 SE1422
Brighstone *IOW* 13 SZ4282
Brightgate *Derbys* 74 SK2659
Brighthampton *Oxon* 36 SP3803
Brightholmlee *Derbys* 74 SK2895
Brightley *Devon* 8 SX6097
Brightling *E Susx* 16 TQ6820
Brightlingsea *Essex* 41 TM0817
Brighton *Cnwll* 3 SW9054
Brighton *E Susx* 15 TQ3104
Brighton le Sands *Mersyd* 78 SJ3098
Brightons *Falk* 116 NS9277
Brightor *Cnwll* 5 SX3561
Brightwalton *Berks* 36 SU4279
Brightwalton Green *Berks* 36 SU4278
Brightwalton Holt *Berks* 36 SU4377
Brightwell *Oxon* 37 SU5790
Brightwell *Suffk* 55 TM2543
Brightwell Baldwin *Oxon* 37 SU6595
Brightwell Upperton *Oxon* 37 SU6594
Brignall *Dur* 95 NZ0712
Brigsley *Lincs* 85 TA2501
Brigsteer *Cumb* 87 SD4889
Brigstock *Nhants* 51 SP9485
Brill *Bucks* 37 SP6513
Brill *Cnwll* 3 SW7229
Brilley *H & W* 46 SO2648
Brimfield *H & W* 46 SO5267
Brimfield Cross *H & W* 46 SO5368
Brimington *Derbys* 74 SK4073
Brimley *Devon* 8 SX8077
Brimpsfield *Gloucs* 35 SO9312
Brimpton *Berks* 24 SU5564
Brimscombe *Gloucs* 35 SO8702
Brimstage *Mersyd* 78 SJ3082
Brincliffe *S York* 74 SK3284
Brind *E R Yk* 84 SE7430
Brindham *Somset* 21 ST5139
Brindister *Shet* 155 HU2857
Brindle *Lancs* 81 SD5924
Brineton *Staffs* 60 SJ8013
Bringhurst *Leics* 51 SP8492
Brington *Cambs* 51 TL0875
Briningham *Norfk* 66 TG0434
Brinkely *Notts* 75 SK7153
Brinkhill *Lincs* 77 TF3773
Brinkley *Cambs* 53 TL6354
Brinklow *Warwks* 50 SP4379
Brinkworth *Wilts* 35 SU0184
Brinscall *Lancs* 81 SD6221
Brinscombe *Somset* 21 ST4251
Brinsea *Somset* 21 ST4461
Brinsley *Notts* 75 SK4548
Brinsop *H & W* 46 SO4444
Brinsworth *S York* 74 SK4289
Brinton *Norfk* 66 TG0335
Brinyan *Ork* 155 HY4327
Brisco *Cumb* 93 NY4252
Brisley *Norfk* 66 TF9421
Brislington *Bristl* 35 ST6270
Brissenden Green *Kent* 28 TQ9439
Bristol *Bristl* 34 ST5972
Briston *Norfk* 66 TG0632
Brisworthy *Devon* 6 SX5665
Britannia *Lancs* 81 SD8821
Britford *Wilts* 23 SU1627
Brithdir *Caerph* 33 SO1401
Brithdir *Gwynd* 57 SH7618
British *Torfn* 34 SO2503
British Legion Village *Kent* 28 TQ7257
Briton Ferry *Neath* 32 SS7394
Britwell Salome *Oxon* 37 SU6792
Brixham *Devon* 7 SX9255
Brixton *Devon* 6 SX5552
Brixton *Gt Lon* 27 TQ3175
Brixton Deverill *Wilts* 22 ST8638
Brixworth *Nhants* 50 SP7470
Brize Norton *Oxon* 36 SP2907
Broad Alley *H & W* 47 SO8867
Broad Blunsdon *Wilts* 36 SU1491
Broad Campden *Gloucs* 48 SP1537
Broad Carr *W York* 82 SE0919
Broad Chalke *Wilts* 23 SU0325
Broad Clough *Lancs* 81 SD8623
Broad Ford *Kent* 28 TQ7139
Broad Green *Cambs* 53 TL6859
Broad Green *Cambs* 53 TL6860
Broad Green *Essex* 40 TL8823
Broad Green *H & W* 47 SO7756
Broad Green *H & W* 60 SO9970
Broad Green *Suffk* 53 TL7859
Broad Haven *Pembks* 30 SM8613
Broad Hill *Cambs* 53 TL5976
Broad Hinton *Wilts* 36 SU1075
Broad Laying *Hants* 24 SU4362
Broad Marston *H & W* 48 SP1446
Broad Meadow *Staffs* 72 SJ8348
Broad Oak *Cumb* 86 SD1194
Broad Oak *E Susx* 17 TQ8219
Broad Oak *E Susx* 16 TQ6022
Broad Oak *H & W* 34 SO4821
Broad Oak *Hants* 24 SU7551
Broad Oak *Kent* 29 TR1761
Broad Oak *Mersyd* 78 SJ5395
Broad Road *Suffk* 55 TM2676
Broad Street *E Susx* 17 TQ8616
Broad Street *Essex* 39 TL5516
Broad Street *Kent* 28 TQ7672
Broad Street *Kent* 28 TQ8356
Broad Street *Wilts* 23 SU1059
Broad Street Green *Essex* 40 TL8509
Broad Town *Wilts* 36 SU0977
Broad's Green *Essex* 40 TL6912
Broadbottom *Gt Man* 79 SJ9993
Broadbridge *W Susx* 14 SU8105
Broadbridge Heath *W Susx* 15 TQ1431
Broadclyst *Devon* 9 SX9897
Broadfield *Inver* 115 NS3373
Broadfield *Pembks* 31 SN1303
Broadford *Highld* 129 NG6423
Broadford Bridge *W Susx* 14 TQ0921
Broadgairhill *Border* 109 NT2010
Broadgate *Lincs* 64 TF3610
Broadgrass Green *Suffk* 54 TL9663
Broadhaugh *Border* 119 NT8655
Broadheath *Gt Man* 79 SJ7689
Broadheath *H & W* 47 SO6665
Broadhembury *Devon* 9 ST1004
Broadhempston *Devon* 7 SX8066
Broadholme *Notts* 76 SK8874
Broadland Row *E Susx* 17 TQ8319
Broadlay *Carmth* 31 SN3709
Broadley *Gt Man* 81 SD8816
Broadley *Moray* 142 NJ3961
Broadley Common *Essex* 39 TL4207
Broadmayne *Dorset* 11 SY7286
Broadmere *Hants* 24 SU6247
Broadmoor *Gloucs* 35 SO6415
Broadmoor *Pembks* 31 SN0906
Broadnymett *Devon* 8 SS7001
Broadoak *Dorset* 10 SY4396
Broadoak *Gloucs* 35 SO6912
Broadoak *Wrexhm* 71 SJ3658
Broadstairs *Kent* 29 TR3967
Broadstone *Dorset* 11 SZ0095
Broadstone *Mons* 34 SO5102
Broadstone *Shrops* 59 SO5489
Broadwas *H & W* 47 SO7555
Broadwater *Herts* 39 TL2422
Broadwater *W Susx* 15 TQ1404
Broadwaters *H & W* 60 SO8477
Broadway *Carmth* 31 SN2910
Broadway *Carmth* 31 SN3808
Broadway *H & W* 48 SP0937
Broadway *Pembks* 30 SM8713
Broadway *Somset* 10 ST3215
Broadway *Suffk* 55 TM3979
Broadwell *Gloucs* 34 SO5811
Broadwell *Gloucs* 48 SP2027
Broadwell *Oxon* 36 SP2504
Broadwell *Warwks* 50 SP4565
Broadwey *Dorset* 11 SY6683
Broadwindsor *Dorset* 10 ST4302
Broadwood Kelly *Devon* 8 SS6106
Broadwoodwidger *Devon* 5 SX4189
Brobury *H & W* 46 SO3444
Brochel *Highld* 137 NG5846
Brock *Lancs* 80 SD5140
Brock's Green *Hants* 24 SU5061
Brockamin *H & W* 47 SO7753
Brockbridge *Hants* 13 SU6118
Brockdish *Norfk* 55 TM2179
Brockencote *H & W* 60 SO8873
Brockenhurst *Hants* 12 SU3002
Brocketsbrae *S Lans* 108 NS8239
Brockford Green *Suffk* 54 TM1265
Brockford Street *Suffk* 54 TM1167
Brockhall *Nhants* 49 SP6362
Brockham *Surrey* 15 TQ1949
Brockhampton *Gloucs* 47 SO9326
Brockhampton *Gloucs* 36 SP0322
Brockhampton *H & W* 46 SO5931
Brockhampton Green *Dorset* 11 ST7106
Brockholes *W York* 82 SE1510
Brockhurst *Derbys* 74 SK3364
Brockhurst *Warwks* 50 SP4683
Brocklebank *Cumb* 93 NY3042
Brocklesby *Lincs* 85 TA1311
Brockley *Somset* 21 ST4666
Brockley *Suffk* 54 TL8371
Brockley Green *Suffk* 53 TL7247
Brockley Green *Suffk* 54 TL8254
Brockleymoor *Cumb* 94 NY4937
Brockmoor *W Mids* 60 SO9088
Brockscombe *Devon* 5 SX4695
Brockton *Shrops* 59 SJ3104
Brockton *Shrops* 60 SJ7103
Brockton *Shrops* 59 SO3285
Brockton *Shrops* 59 SO5794
Brockton *Staffs* 72 SJ8131
Brockweir *Gloucs* 34 SO5401
Brockwood Park *Hants* 13 SU6226
Brockworth *Gloucs* 35 SO8916
Brocton *Cnwll* 4 SX0168
Brocton *Staffs* 72 SJ9619
Brodick *N Ayrs* 105 NS0135
Brodie *Moray* 140 NH9757
Brodsworth *S York* 83 SE5007
Brogaig *Highld* 136 NG4767
Brogborough *Beds* 38 SP9638
Broken Cross *Ches* 79 SJ6873
Broken Cross *Ches* 79 SJ8973
Brokenborough *Wilts* 35 ST9189
Brokerswood *Wilts* 22 ST8352

C

Carndu
Chelworth Lower Green

Carndu *Highld*	138	NG8827
Carnduff *S Lans*	116	NS6646
Carne *Cnwll*	3	SW7724
Carne *Cnwll*	3	SW9138
Carne *Cnwll*	4	SW9558
Carnell *E Ayrs*	107	NS4731
Carnewas *Cnwll*	4	SW8569
Carnforth *Lancs*	87	SD4970
Carnhedryn *Pembks*	30	SM8027
Carnhell Green *Cnwll*	2	SW6137
Carnie *Abers*	135	NJ8005
Carnkie *Cnwll*	2	SW7134
Carnkiet *Cnwll*	3	SW7852
Carno *Powys*	58	SN9696
Carnoch *Highld*	130	NM8696
Carnock *Fife*	117	NT0489
Carnon Downs *Cnwll*	3	SW7940
Carnousie *Abers*	142	NJ6650
Carnoustie *Angus*	127	NO5534
Carnwath *S Lans*	117	NS9846
Carnyorth *Cnwll*	2	SW3733
Carol Green *W Mids*	61	SP2577
Carpalla *Cnwll*	3	SW9654
Carperby *N York*	88	SE0089
Carr *Gt Man*	81	SD7816
Carr *S York*	75	SK5090
Carr Gate *W York*	82	SE3123
Carr Shield *Nthumb*	95	NY8047
Carr Vale *Derbys*	75	SK4669
Carradale *Ag & B*	105	NR8138
Carrbridge *Highld*	140	NH9022
Carrbrook *Gt Man*	79	SD9800
Carrefour *Jersey*	152	JS0000
Carreglefn *Angles*	68	SH3889
Carrhouse *Lincs*	84	SE7706
Carrick *Ag & B*	114	NR9086
Carrick Castle *Ag & B*	114	NS1994
Carriden *Falk*	117	NT0181
Carrington *Gt Man*	79	SJ7492
Carrington *Lincs*	77	TF3155
Carrington *Mdloth*	117	NT3160
Carrismerry *Cnwll*	4	SX0158
Carrog *A & C*	69	SH7647
Carrog *Denbgs*	70	SJ1043
Carron *Falk*	116	NS8882
Carron *Moray*	141	NJ2241
Carron Bridge *Stirlg*	116	NS7483
Carronbridge *D & G*	100	NX8698
Carronshore *Falk*	116	NS8983
Carrow Hill *Mons*	34	ST4390
Carruth House *Inver*	115	NS3566
Carrutherstown *D & G*	100	NY1071
Carrville *Dur*	96	NZ3043
Carrycoats Hall *Nthumb*	102	NY9279
Carsaig *Ag & B*	121	NM5421
Carscreugh *D & G*	98	NX2260
Carse Gray *Angus*	127	NO4553
Carseriggan *D & G*	98	NX3167
Carsethorn *D & G*	92	NX9959
Carshalton *Gt Lon*	27	TQ2764
Carsington *Derbys*	73	SK2553
Carskey *Ag & B*	104	NR6508
Carsluith *D & G*	99	NX4854
Carsphairn *D & G*	107	NX5693
Carstairs *S Lans*	116	NS9345
Carstairs Junction *S Lans*	117	NS9545
Carswell Marsh *Oxon*	36	SU3299
Carter's Clay *Hants*	23	SU3024
Carters Green *Essex*	39	TL5110
Carterton *Oxon*	36	SP2806
Carterway Heads *Dur*	95	NZ0451
Carthew *Cnwll*	3	SX0056
Carthorpe *N York*	89	SE3083
Cartington *Nthumb*	103	NU0204
Cartland *S Lans*	116	NS8646
Cartledge *Derbys*	74	SK3276
Cartmel *Cumb*	87	SD3878
Cartmel Fell *Cumb*	87	SD4188
Carway *Carmth*	32	SN4606
Carwinley *Cumb*	101	NY4072
Cashe's Green *Gloucs*	35	SO8205
Cashmoor *Dorset*	11	ST9713
Cassington *Oxon*	37	SP4511
Cassop Colliery *Dur*	96	NZ3438
Castell *A & C*	69	SH7669
Castell-y-bwch *Torfn*	34	ST2792
Casterton *Lancs*	87	SD6279
Castle *Cnwll*	4	SX0958
Castle Acre *Norfk*	66	TF8115
Castle Ashby *Nhants*	51	SP8659
Castle Bolton *N York*	88	SE0391
Castle Bromwich *W Mids*	61	SP1489
Castle Bytham *Lincs*	63	SK9818
Castle Caereinion *Powys*	58	SJ1605
Castle Camps *Cambs*	53	TL6242
Castle Carrock *Cumb*	94	NY5455
Castle Cary *Somset*	21	ST6432
Castle Combe *Wilts*	35	ST8477
Castle Donington *Leics*	62	SK4427
Castle Douglas *D & G*	99	NX7662
Castle Eaton *Wilts*	36	SU1496
Castle Eden *Dur*	96	NZ4238
Castle End *Cambs*	64	TF1208
Castle Frome *H & W*	47	SO6645
Castle Gate *Cnwll*	2	SW4934
Castle Green *Cumb*	87	SD5392
Castle Green *Surrey*	25	SU9761
Castle Gresley *Derbys*	73	SK2717
Castle Hedingham *Essex*	53	TL7835
Castle Hill *Kent*	28	TQ6942
Castle Hill *Suffk*	54	TM1446
Castle Kennedy *D & G*	98	NX1159
Castle Lachlan *Ag & B*	114	NS0195
Castle Morris *Pembks*	30	SM9031
Castle O'er *D & G*	101	NY2492
Castle Pulverbatch *Shrops*	59	SJ4202
Castle Rising *Norfk*	65	TF6624
Castle Street *W York*	82	SD9524
Castle Stuart *Highld*	140	NH7449
Castlebay *W Isls*	154	NL6698
Castlebythe *Pembks*	30	SN0229
Castlecary *Falk*	116	NS7878
Castlecraig *Highld*	147	NH8269
Castlecroft *Staffs*	60	SO8598
Castlecroft *W Mids*	60	SO8797
Castleford *W York*	83	SE4225
Castlehill *Border*	109	NT2135
Castlehill *D & Cb*	115	NS3875
Castlehill *Highld*	151	ND1968
Castlemartin *Pembks*	30	SR9198
Castlemorton *H & W*	47	SO7937
Castleside *Dur*	95	NZ0748
Castlethorpe *Bucks*	38	SP8044
Castlethorpe *Lincs*	84	SE9807
Castleton *Border*	101	NY5189
Castleton *Derbys*	74	SK1582
Castleton *Gt Man*	79	SD8810
Castleton *N York*	90	NZ6807
Castleton *Newpt*	34	ST2583
Castletown *Dorset*	11	SY6874
Castletown *Highld*	151	ND1967
Castletown *IOM*	153	SC2667
Castletown *T & W*	96	NZ3658
Castley *N York*	82	SE2646
Caston *Norfk*	66	TL9597
Castor *Cambs*	64	TL1298
Caswell Bay *Swans*	32	SS5987
Cat and Fiddle *Ches*	79	SK0072
Cat's Ash *Newpt*	34	ST3790
Catacol *N Ayrs*	105	NR9149
Catbrook *Mons*	34	SO5102
Catch *Flints*	70	SJ2070
Catchall *Cnwll*	2	SW4228
Catchem's Corner *W Mids*	61	SP2576
Catchgate *Dur*	96	NZ1652
Catcliffe *S York*	74	SK4288
Catcomb *Wilts*	35	SU0076
Catcott *Somset*	21	ST3939
Catcott Burtle *Somset*	21	ST4043
Catel *Guern*	152	GN0000
Caterham *Surrey*	27	TQ3455
Catfield *Norfk*	67	TG3821
Catfield Common *Norfk*	67	TG4021
Catfirth *Shet*	155	HU4354
Catford *Gt Lon*	27	TQ3773
Catforth *Lancs*	80	SD4735
Cathcart *C Glas*	115	NS5860
Cathedine *Powys*	45	SO1425
Catherine Slack *W York*	82	SE0928
Catherine-de-Barnes *W Mids*	61	SP1780
Catherington *Hants*	13	SU6914
Catherston Leweston *Dorset*	10	SY3694
Catherton *Shrops*	47	SO6578
Cathpair *Border*	118	NT4646
Catisfield *Hants*	13	SU5506
Catley Lane Head *Gt Man*	81	SD8715
Catley Southfield *H & W*	47	SO6844
Catlodge *Highld*	132	NN6392
Catlow *Lancs*	81	SD8836
Catlowdy *Cumb*	101	NY4576
Catmere End *Essex*	39	TL4939
Catmore *Berks*	37	SU4580
Caton *Devon*	7	SX7872
Caton *Lancs*	87	SD5364
Caton Green *Lancs*	87	SD5565
Cator Court *Devon*	8	SX6877
Catrine *E Ayrs*	107	NS5225
Catsfield *E Susx*	17	TQ7213
Catsfield Stream *E Susx*	17	TQ7113
Catsgore *Somset*	21	ST5025
Catsham *Somset*	21	ST5533
Catshill *H & W*	60	SO9573
Catstree *Shrops*	60	SO7496
Cattadale *Ag & B*	105	NR6710
Cattal *N York*	83	SE4454
Cattawade *Suffk*	41	TM1033
Catterall *Lancs*	80	SD4942
Catteralslane *Shrops*	71	SJ5640
Catterick *N York*	89	SE2397
Catterick Bridge *N York*	89	SE2299
Catterick Garrison *N York*	89	SE1897
Catterlen *Cumb*	94	NY4833
Catterline *Abers*	135	NO8678
Catterton *N York*	83	SE5145
Catteshall *Surrey*	25	SU9844
Catthorpe *Leics*	50	SP5578
Cattishall *Suffk*	54	TL8865
Cattistock *Dorset*	10	SY5999
Catton *Cumb*	95	NY8257
Catton *N York*	89	SE3678
Catton *Norfk*	67	TG2312
Catwick *E R Yk*	85	TA1345
Catworth *Cambs*	51	TL0873
Caudle Green *Gloucs*	35	SO9410
Caulcott *Beds*	38	TL0042
Caulcott *Oxon*	49	SP5024
Cauldcots *Angus*	127	NO6547
Cauldhame *Stirlg*	116	NS6493
Cauldmill *Border*	109	NT5315
Cauldon *Staffs*	73	SK0749
Cauldon Lowe *Staffs*	73	SK0747
Cauldwell *Derbys*	73	SK2517
Caulkerbush *D & G*	92	NX9257
Caulside *D & G*	101	NY4480
Caundle Marsh *Dorset*	11	ST6713
Caunsall *H & W*	60	SO8581
Caunton *Notts*	75	SK7460
Causeway *Hants*	13	SU7422
Causeway End *Cumb*	87	SD4885
Causeway End *D & G*	99	NX4260
Causeway End *Essex*	40	TL6819
Causewayend *S Lans*	108	NT0336
Causewayhead *Cumb*	92	NY1253
Causewayhead *Stirlg*	116	NS8095
Causey Park *Nthumb*	103	NZ1794
Causey Park Bridge *Nthumb*	103	NZ1894
Causeyend *Abers*	143	NJ9419
Cavendish *Suffk*	54	TL8046
Cavenham *Suffk*	53	TL7670
Caversfield *Oxon*	49	SP5825
Caversham *Berks*	24	SU7274
Caverswall *Staffs*	72	SJ9542
Caverton Mill *Border*	110	NT7425
Cavil *E R Yk*	84	SE7730
Cawdor *Highld*	140	NH8450
Cawkwell *Lincs*	77	TF2879
Cawood *N York*	83	SE5737
Cawsand *Cnwll*	6	SX4350
Cawston *Norfk*	66	TG1323
Cawston *Warwks*	50	SP4773
Cawthorn *N York*	90	SE7788
Cawthorne *S York*	82	SE2808
Caxton *Cambs*	52	TL3058
Caxton End *Cambs*	52	TL2759
Caxton End *Cambs*	52	TL3157
Caxton Gibbet *Cambs*	52	TL2960
Caynham *Shrops*	46	SO5573
Caythorpe *Lincs*	76	SK9348
Caythorpe *Notts*	63	SK6845
Cayton *N York*	91	TA0583
Ceann a Bhaigh *W Isls*	154	NF7468
Ceannacroc Lodge *Highld*	131	NH2211
Cearsiadar *W Isls*	154	NB3320
Ceciliford *Mons*	34	SO5003
Cefn *Newpt*	34	ST2788
Cefn Berain *A & C*	70	SH9969
Cefn Byrle *Powys*	33	SN8311
Cefn Canel *Powys*	58	SJ2331
Cefn Coch *Powys*	58	SJ1026
Cefn Cribwr *Brdgnd*	33	SS8582
Cefn Cross *Brdgnd*	33	SS8682
Cefn Mably *Caerph*	34	ST2283
Cefn-brith *A & C*	70	SH9350
Cefn-bryn-brain *Carmth*	32	SN7413
Cefn-coed-y-cymmer *Myr Td*	33	SO0308
Cefn-ddwysarn *Gwynd*	70	SH9638
Cefn-Einion *Shrops*	58	SO2886
Cefn-mawr *Wrexhm*	70	SJ2842
Cefn-y-bedd *Wrexhm*	71	SJ3156
Cefn-y-pant *Carmth*	31	SN1925
Cefneithin *Carmth*	32	SN5513
Cefngorwydd *Powys*	45	SN9045
Cefnpennar *Rhondd*	33	SO0300
Ceint *Angles*	68	SH4875
Cellan *Cardgn*	44	SN6149
Cellardyke *Fife*	127	NO5704
Cellarhead *Staffs*	72	SJ9547
Cellerton *Cumb*	94	NY4925
Celynen *Caerph*	33	ST2195
Cemaes *Angles*	68	SH3793
Cemmaes *Powys*	57	SH8406
Cemmaes Road *Powys*	57	SH8104
Cenarth *Cardgn*	31	SN2641
Cerbyd *Pembks*	30	SM8227
Ceres *Fife*	126	NO4011
Cerne Abbas *Dorset*	11	ST6601
Cerney Wick *Gloucs*	36	SU0796
Cerrigceinwen *Angles*	68	SH4274
Cerrigydrudion *A & C*	70	SH9548
Cess *Norfk*	67	TG4417
Ceunant *Gwynd*	69	SH5361
Chaceley *Gloucs*	47	SO8530
Chacewater *Cnwll*	3	SW7544
Chackmore *Bucks*	49	SP6835
Chacombe *Nhants*	49	SP4944
Chadbury *H & W*	47	SP0146
Chadderton *Gt Man*	79	SD9005
Chadderton Fold *Gt Man*	79	SD9006
Chaddesden *Derbys*	62	SK3836
Chaddesley Corbett *H & W*	60	SO8973
Chaddlehanger *Devon*	5	SX4678
Chaddleworth *Berks*	36	SU4178
Chadlington *Oxon*	36	SP3321
Chadshunt *Warwks*	48	SP3453
Chadwell *Leics*	63	SK7824
Chadwell *Shrops*	60	SJ7814
Chadwell End *Beds*	51	TL0865
Chadwell Heath *Gt Lon*	27	TQ4888
Chadwell St Mary *Essex*	40	TQ6478
Chadwick *H & W*	47	SO8369
Chadwick End *W Mids*	61	SP2073
Chadwick Green *Mersyd*	78	SJ5299
Chaffcombe *Somset*	10	ST3510
Chafford Hundred *Essex*	40	TQ6079
Chagford *Devon*	8	SX7087
Chailey *E Susx*	15	TQ3919
Chainbridge *Cambs*	27	TL4200
Chainhurst *Kent*	28	TQ7248
Chalbury Common *Dorset*	12	SU0206
Chaldon *Surrey*	27	TQ3155
Chaldon Herring or East Chaldon *Dorset*	11	SY7983
Chale *IOW*	13	SZ4877
Chale Green *IOW*	13	SZ4879
Chalfont Common *Bucks*	26	TQ0092
Chalfont St Giles *Bucks*	26	SU9893
Chalfont St Peter *Bucks*	26	TQ0090
Chalford *Gloucs*	35	SO8903
Chalford *Oxon*	37	SP7200
Chalford *Wilts*	22	ST8650
Chalgrave *Beds*	38	TL0127
Chalgrove *Oxon*	37	SU6396
Chalk *Kent*	28	TQ6773
Chalk End *Essex*	40	TL6310
Chalkhouse Green *Berks*	37	SU7178
Chalkway *Somset*	10	ST3707
Chalkwell *Kent*	28	TQ8963
Challaborough *Devon*	7	SX6544
Challacombe *Devon*	19	SS6940
Challoch *D & G*	99	NX3867
Challock Lees *Kent*	28	TR0050
Chalmington *Dorset*	10	ST5900
Chalton *Beds*	38	TL0326
Chalton *Beds*	52	TL1450
Chalton *Hants*	13	SU7315
Chalvey *Berks*	26	SU9679
Chalvington *E Susx*	16	TQ5109
Chambers Green *Kent*	28	TQ9243
Chandler's Cross *Herts*	26	TQ0698
Chandler's Ford *Hants*	13	SU4319
Chandlers Cross *H & W*	47	SO7738
Channel's End *Beds*	51	TL1056
Chantry *Somset*	22	ST7146
Chantry *Suffk*	54	TM1443
Chapel *Cumb*	93	NY2231
Chapel *Fife*	117	NT2593
Chapel Allerton *Somset*	21	ST4050
Chapel Allerton *W York*	82	SE3037
Chapel Amble *Cnwll*	4	SW9975
Chapel Brampton *Nhants*	50	SP7266
Chapel Chorlton *Staffs*	72	SJ8137
Chapel Cross *E Susx*	16	TQ6120
Chapel End *Beds*	38	TL0542
Chapel End *Beds*	51	TL1058
Chapel End *Cambs*	52	TL1282
Chapel End *Warwks*	61	SP3393
Chapel Field *Gt Man*	79	SD7906
Chapel Green *Warwks*	61	SP2785
Chapel Green *Warwks*	49	SP4660
Chapel Haddlesey *N York*	83	SE5826
Chapel Hill *Abers*	143	NK0635
Chapel Hill *Lincs*	76	TF2054
Chapel Hill *Mons*	59	SO5399
Chapel Hill *N York*	83	SE3446
Chapel Lawn *Shrops*	46	SO3176
Chapel le Dale *N York*	88	SD7377
Chapel Leigh *Somset*	20	ST1229
Chapel Milton *Derbys*	74	SK0581
Chapel of Garioch *Abers*	142	NJ7124
Chapel Rossan *D & G*	98	NX1044
Chapel Row *Berks*	24	SU5769
Chapel Row *E Susx*	16	TQ6312
Chapel Row *Essex*	40	TL7900
Chapel St Leonards *Lincs*	77	TF5672
Chapel Stile *Cumb*	86	NY3205
Chapel Town *Cnwll*	3	SW8855
Chapel-en-le-Frith *Derbys*	74	SK0580
Chapelbridge *Cambs*	64	TL2993
Chapelend Way *Essex*	53	TL7039
Chapelgate *Lincs*	65	TF4124
Chapelhall *N Lans*	116	NS7862
Chapelhope *Border*	109	NT2318
Chapelknowe *D & G*	101	NY3173
Chapels *Cumb*	86	SD2383
Chapelton *Angus*	127	NO6247
Chapelton *Devon*	19	SS5726
Chapelton *S Lans*	116	NS6848
Chapeltown *Lancs*	81	SD7315
Chapeltown *Moray*	141	NJ2320
Chapeltown *S York*	74	SK3596
Chapmans Well *Devon*	5	SX3593
Chapmanslade *Wilts*	22	ST8247
Chapmore End *Herts*	39	TL3216
Chappel *Essex*	40	TL8928
Charaton *Cnwll*	5	SX3069
Chard *Somset*	10	ST3208
Chard Junction *Somset*	10	ST3404
Chardleigh Green *Somset*	10	ST3110
Chardstock *Devon*	10	ST3004
Charfield *Gloucs*	35	ST7292
Chargrove *Gloucs*	35	SO9219
Charing *Kent*	28	TQ9549
Charing Heath *Kent*	28	TQ9249
Charing Hill *Kent*	28	TQ9550
Charingworth *Gloucs*	48	SP1939
Charlbury *Oxon*	36	SP3519
Charlcombe *Somset*	22	ST7467
Charlcutt *Wilts*	35	ST9875
Charlecote *Warwks*	48	SP2656
Charles *Devon*	19	SS6832
Charles Tye *Suffk*	54	TM0252
Charleshill *Surrey*	25	SU8944
Charleston *Angus*	126	NO3845
Charlestown *Aber C*	135	NJ9300
Charlestown *Cnwll*	3	SX0351
Charlestown *Derbys*	74	SK0392
Charlestown *Dorset*	11	SY6579
Charlestown *Fife*	117	NT0683
Charlestown *Gt Man*	79	SD8100
Charlestown *Highld*	144	NG8174
Charlestown *Highld*	140	NH6448
Charlestown *W York*	82	SD9726
Charlestown *W York*	82	SE1638
Charlesworth *Derbys*	79	SK0092
Charlinch *Somset*	20	ST2338
Charlton *Gt Lon*	27	TQ4178
Charlton *H & W*	60	SO8371
Charlton *H & W*	47	SP0045
Charlton *Hants*	23	SU3547
Charlton *Herts*	39	TL1728
Charlton *Nhants*	49	SP5335
Charlton *Nthumb*	102	NY8184
Charlton *Oxon*	36	SU4088
Charlton *Shrops*	59	SJ5911
Charlton *Somset*	20	ST2926
Charlton *Somset*	21	ST6343
Charlton *Somset*	22	ST6852
Charlton *W Susx*	14	SU8812
Charlton *Wilts*	22	ST9022
Charlton *Wilts*	35	ST9588
Charlton *Wilts*	23	SU1156
Charlton Abbots *Gloucs*	48	SP0324
Charlton Adam *Somset*	21	ST5328
Charlton Hill *Shrops*	59	SJ5807
Charlton Horethorne *Somset*	22	ST6623
Charlton Kings *Gloucs*	35	SO9621
Charlton Mackrell *Somset*	21	ST5328
Charlton Marshall *Dorset*	11	ST9004
Charlton Musgrove *Somset*	22	ST7229
Charlton on the Hill *Dorset*	11	ST8903
Charlton-all-Saints *Wilts*	23	SU1723
Charlton-on-Otmoor *Oxon*	37	SP5616
Charlwood *Hants*	24	SU6731
Charlwood *Surrey*	15	TQ2441
Charminster *Dorset*	11	SY6792
Charmouth *Dorset*	10	SY3693
Charndon *Bucks*	49	SP6724
Charney Bassett *Oxon*	36	SU3894
Charnock Green *Lancs*	81	SD5516
Charnock Richard *Lancs*	81	SD5515
Charsfield *Suffk*	55	TM2556
Chart Corner *Kent*	28	TQ7950
Chart Hill *Kent*	28	TQ7949
Chart Sutton *Kent*	28	TQ8049
Charter Alley *Hants*	24	SU5958
Charterhall *Border*	110	NT7647
Charterhouse *Somset*	21	ST4955
Chartershall *Stirlg*	116	NS7990
Charterville Allotments *Oxon*	36	SP3110
Chartham *Kent*	29	TR1054
Chartham Hatch *Kent*	29	TR1056
Charton *Surrey*	26	TQ0869
Chartridge *Bucks*	38	SP9303
Chartway Street *Kent*	28	TQ8350
Charwelton *Nhants*	49	SP5356
Chase Terrace *Staffs*	61	SK0309
Chasetown *Staffs*	61	SK0408
Chastleton *Oxon*	48	SP2429
Chasty *Devon*	18	SS3402
Chatburn *Lancs*	81	SD7644
Chatcull *Staffs*	72	SJ7934
Chatham *Caerph*	33	ST2188
Chatham *Kent*	28	TQ7567
Chatham Green *Essex*	40	TL7115
Chathill *Nthumb*	111	NU1827
Chatley *H & W*	47	SO8561
Chattenden *Kent*	28	TQ7572
Chatter End *Essex*	39	TL4725
Chatteris *Cambs*	52	TL3985
Chatterton *Lancs*	81	SD7918
Chattisham *Suffk*	54	TM0942
Chatto *Border*	110	NT7717
Chatton *Nthumb*	111	NU0528
Chaul End *Beds*	38	TL0521
Chawleigh *Devon*	19	SS7112
Chawley *Oxon*	37	SP4604
Chawston *Beds*	52	TL1556
Chawton *Hants*	24	SU7037
Chaxhill *Gloucs*	35	SO7414
Chazey Heath *Oxon*	37	SU6977
Cheadle *Gt Man*	79	SJ8688
Cheadle *Staffs*	73	SK0043
Cheadle Heath *Gt Man*	79	SJ8789
Cheadle Hulme *Gt Man*	79	SJ8786
Cheam *Gt Lon*	26	TQ2463
Cheapside *Berks*	25	SU9469
Chearsley *Bucks*	37	SP7110
Chebsey *Staffs*	72	SJ8528
Checkendon *Oxon*	37	SU6683
Checkley *Ches*	72	SJ7346
Checkley *Staffs*	73	SK0237
Checkley Green *Ches*	72	SJ7245
Chedburgh *Suffk*	53	TL7957
Cheddar *Somset*	21	ST4553
Cheddington *Bucks*	38	SP9217
Cheddleton *Staffs*	72	SJ9752
Cheddleton Heath *Staffs*	72	SJ9853
Cheddon Fitzpaine *Somset*	20	ST2427
Chedglow *Wilts*	35	ST9493
Chedgrave *Norfk*	67	TM3699
Chedington *Dorset*	10	ST4805
Chediston *Suffk*	55	TM3577
Chediston Green *Suffk*	55	TM3578
Chedworth *Gloucs*	36	SP0512
Chedzoy *Somset*	21	ST3437
Cheesden *Gt Man*	81	SD8216
Cheeseman's Green *Kent*	28	TR0338
Cheetham Hill *Gt Man*	79	SD8401
Cheetwood *Gt Man*	79	SJ8399
Cheldon *Devon*	19	SS7313
Chelford *Ches*	79	SJ8174
Chellaston *Derbys*	62	SK3730
Chellington *Beds*	51	SP9555
Chelmarsh *Shrops*	60	SO7288
Chelmick *Shrops*	59	SO4791
Chelmondiston *Suffk*	55	TM2037
Chelmorton *Derbys*	74	SK1169
Chelmsford *Essex*	40	TL7007
Chelmsley Wood *W Mids*	61	SP1887
Chelsea *Gt Lon*	27	TQ2778
Chelsfield *Gt Lon*	27	TQ4864
Chelsham *Surrey*	27	TQ3758
Chelston *Somset*	20	ST1521
Chelsworth *Suffk*	54	TL9748
Cheltenham *Gloucs*	35	SO9422
Chelveston *Nhants*	51	SP9969
Chelvey *Somset*	21	ST4668
Chelwood *Somset*	21	ST6361
Chelwood Common *E Susx*	15	TQ4128
Chelwood Gate *E Susx*	15	TQ4130
Chelworth *Wilts*	35	ST9694
Chelworth Lower Green *Wilts*	36	SU0892

Clopton
Corndon

Clopton Suffk 55 TM2253
Clopton Corner Suffk 55 TM2254
Clopton Green Suffk 53 TL7655
Clopton Green Suffk 54 TL9759
Clos du Valle Guern 152 GN0000
Closeburn D & G 100 NX8992
Closeburnmill D & G 100 NX9094
Closeclark IOM 153 SC2775
Closworth Somset 10 ST5610
Clothall Herts 39 TL2731
Clotton Ches 71 SJ5264
Cloudesley Bush Warwks 50 SP4686
Clough Gt Man 79 SD9408
Clough Foot W York 81 SD9123
Clough Head N York 82 SE0918
Cloughton N York 91 TA0194
Cloughton Newlands N York 91 TA0096
Clousta Shet 155 HU3057
Clova Angus 134 NO3273
Clovelly Devon 18 SS3124
Clovenfords Border 109 NT4536
Clovulin Highld 130 NN0063
Clow Bridge Lancs 81 SD8228
Clowne Derbys 75 SK4875
Clows Top H & W 60 SO7172
Cloy Wrexhm 71 SJ3943
Cluanie Inn Highld 130 NH0711
Cluanie Lodge Highld 130 NH0910
Clubworthy Cnwll 5 SX2792
Clugston D & G 98 NX3557
Clun Shrops 59 SO3080
Clunas Highld 140 NH8846
Clunbury Shrops 59 SO3780
Clune Highld 140 NH7925
Clunes Highld 131 NN1988
Clungunford Shrops 46 SO3978
Clunie Abers 142 NJ6350
Clunie P & K 126 NO1043
Clunton Shrops 59 SO3381
Clutton Ches 71 SJ4654
Clutton Somset 21 ST6259
Clutton Hill Somset 21 ST6359
Clwt-y-bont Gwynd 69 SH5762
Clydach Mons 34 SO2213
Clydach Swans 32 SN6800
Clydach Vale Rhondd 33 SS9792
Clydebank D & Cb 115 NS4970
Clydey Pembks 31 SN2535
Clyffe Pypard Wilts 36 SU0777
Clynder Ag & B 114 NS2484
Clynderwen Carmth 31 SN1219
Clyne Neath 32 SN8000
Clynnog-fawr Gwynd 68 SH4149
Clyro Powys 45 SO2143
Clyst Honiton Devon 9 SX9893
Clyst Hydon Devon 9 ST0301
Clyst St George Devon 9 SX9888
Clyst St Lawrence Devon 9 ST0200
Clyst St Mary Devon 9 SX9791
Cnoc W Isls 154 NB4931
Cnwch Coch Cardgn 43 SN6774
Coad's Green Cnwll 5 SX2976
Coal Aston Derbys 74 SK3679
Coal Pool W Mids 60 SP0199
Coal Street Suffk 55 TM2371
Coalbrookdale Shrops 60 SJ6604
Coalbrookvale Blae G 33 SO1909
Coalburn S Lans 108 NS8134
Coalburns T & W 96 NZ1260
Coalcleugh Nthumb 95 NY8045
Coaley Gloucs 35 SO7701
Coalfell Cumb 94 NY5959
Coalhill Essex 40 TQ7597
Coalmoor Shrops 60 SJ6607
Coalpit Heath Gloucs 35 ST6780
Coalpit Hill Staffs 72 SJ8253
Coalport Shrops 60 SJ6902
Coalsnaughton Clacks 116 NS9195
Coaltown of Balgonie Fife 117 NT2999
Coaltown of Wemyss Fife 118 NT3295
Coalville Leics 62 SK4214
Coanwood Nthumb 94 NY6859
Coat Somset 21 ST4520
Coatbridge N Lans 116 NS7365
Coatdyke N Lans 116 NS7465
Coate Wilts 23 SU0462
Coate Wilts 36 SU1882
Coates Cambs 64 TL3097
Coates Gloucs 35 SO9701
Coates Lincs 75 SK8181
Coates Lincs 76 SK9083
Coates W Susx 14 SU9917
Coatham N York 97 NZ5925
Coatham Mundeville Dur 96 NZ2820
Cobbaton Devon 19 SS6126
Coberley Gloucs 35 SO9616
Cobhall Common H & W 46 SO4535
Cobham Kent 28 TQ6768
Cobham Surrey 26 TQ1060
Coblers Green Essex 40 TL6819
Cobley Dorset 12 SU0220
Cobnash H & W 46 SO4560
Cobo Guern 152 GN0000
Cobridge Staffs 72 SJ8747
Coburby Abers 143 NJ9164
Cock Alley Derbys 74 SK4170
Cock Bank Wrexhm 71 SJ3545
Cock Bevington Warwks 48 SP0552
Cock Bridge Abers 133 NJ2509
Cock Clarks Essex 40 TL8102
Cock End Suffk 53 TL7253
Cock Green Essex 40 TL6919
Cock Marling E Susx 17 TQ8718
Cock Street Kent 28 TQ7850
Cockayne N York 90 SE6198
Cockayne Hatley Beds 52 TL2649
Cockburnspath Border 119 NT7770
Cockenzie and Port Seton E Loth 118 NT4075
Cocker Bar Lancs 80 SD5022
Cocker Brook Lancs 81 SD7425
Cockerdale W York 82 SE2329
Cockerham Lancs 80 SD4651
Cockermouth Cumb 92 NY1230
Cockernhoe Green Herts 38 TL1223
Cockett Swans 32 SS6394
Cockfield Dur 96 NZ1224
Cockfield Suffk 54 TL9054
Cockfosters Gt Lon 27 TQ2796
Cocking W Susx 14 SU8717
Cocking Causeway W Susx 14 SU8819
Cockington Devon 7 SX8963
Cocklake Somset 21 ST4449
Cockle Park Nthumb 103 NZ2091
Cockley Beck Cumb 86 NY2501
Cockley Cley Norfk 66 TF7904
Cockpole Green Berks 37 SU7981
Cocks Cnwll 3 SW7652
Cockshutford Shrops 59 SO5885
Cockshutt Shrops 59 SJ4328
Cockthorpe Norfk 66 TF9842
Cockwells Cnwll 2 SW5234
Cockwood Devon 9 SX9780
Cockwood Somset 20 ST2242
Cockyard Derbys 74 SK0479
Cockyard H & W 46 SO4133
Coddenham Suffk 54 TM1354
Coddington Ches 71 SJ4555
Coddington H & W 47 SO7142
Coddington Notts 76 SK8354
Codford St Mary Wilts 22 ST9739
Codford St Peter Wilts 22 ST9639
Codicote Herts 39 TL2118
Codmore Hill W Susx 14 TQ0520
Codnor Derbys 74 SK4149
Codrington Gloucs 35 ST7278
Codsall Staffs 60 SJ8603
Codsall Wood Staffs 60 SJ8404
Coed Morgan Mons 34 SO3511
Coed Talon Flints 70 SJ2659
Coed Ystumgwern Gwynd 57 SH5824
Coed-y-Bryn Cardgn 42 SN3545
Coed-y-caerau Newpt 34 ST3891
Coed-y-paen Mons 34 ST3398
Coed-yr-ynys Powys 33 SO1520
Coedana Angles 68 SH4382
Coedely Rhondd 33 ST0285
Coedkernew Newpt 34 ST2783
Coedpoeth Wrexhm 70 SJ2851
Coedway Powys 59 SJ3315
Coelbren Powys 33 SN8511
Coffinswell Devon 7 SX8968
Coffle End Beds 51 TL0159
Cofton Hackett H & W 60 SP0075
Cogan V Glam 33 ST1771
Cogenhoe Nhants 51 SP8260
Cogges Oxon 36 SP3609
Coggeshall Essex 40 TL8522
Coggin's Mill E Susx 16 TQ5927
Coignafearn Highld 140 NH7018
Coilacriech Abers 134 NO3296
Coilantogle Stirlg 124 NN5907
Coillore Highld 136 NG3537
Coiltry Highld 131 NH3506
Coity Brdgnd 33 SS9281
Col W Isls 154 NB4739
Colaboll Highld 146 NC5610
Colan Cnwll 4 SW8661
Colaton Raleigh Devon 9 SY0787
Colbost Highld 136 NG2148
Colburn N York 89 SE1999
Colbury Hants 12 SU3410
Colby Cumb 94 NY6620
Colby IOM 153 SC2370
Colby Norfk 67 TG2231
Colchester Essex 41 TL9925
Cold Ash Berks 24 SU5169
Cold Ashby Nhants 50 SP6576
Cold Ashton Gloucs 35 ST7572
Cold Aston Gloucs 36 SP1219
Cold Blow Pembks 31 SN1212
Cold Brayfield Bucks 38 SP9252
Cold Cotes N York 88 SD7171
Cold Green H & W 47 SO6842
Cold Hanworth Lincs 76 TF0383
Cold Harbour Herts 38 TL1415
Cold Harbour Oxon 37 SU6379
Cold Harbour Wilts 22 ST8645
Cold Hatton Shrops 59 SJ6221
Cold Hatton Heath Shrops 59 SJ6321
Cold Hesledon Dur 96 NZ4146
Cold Hiendley W York 83 SE3714
Cold Higham Nhants 49 SP6653
Cold Kirby N York 90 SE5384
Cold Newton Leics 63 SK7106
Cold Northcott Cnwll 5 SX2086
Cold Norton Essex 40 TL8500
Cold Overton Leics 63 SK8010
Cold Weston Shrops 59 SO5583
Coldbackie Highld 149 NC6160
Coldbeck Cumb 88 NY7204
Coldean E Susx 15 TQ3308
Coldeast Devon 7 SX8174
Colden W York 82 SD9628
Colden Common Hants 13 SU4822
Coldfair Green Suffk 55 TM4360
Coldham Cambs 65 TF4303
Coldharbour Cnwll 3 SW7548
Coldharbour Devon 9 ST0612
Coldharbour Gloucs 34 SO5503
Coldharbour Surrey 15 TQ1443
Coldingham Border 119 NT9065
Coldmeece Staffs 72 SJ8532
Coldred Kent 29 TR2747
Coldridge Devon 8 SS6907
Coldstream Border 110 NT8439
Coldwaltham W Susx 14 TQ0216
Coldwell H & W 46 SO4235
Cole Somset 22 ST6733
Cole End Warwks 61 SP2089
Cole Green Herts 39 TL2811
Cole Green Herts 39 TL4330
Cole Henley Hants 24 SU4651
Cole's Cross Devon 7 SX7746
Colebatch Shrops 59 SO3187
Colebrook Devon 9 ST0006
Colebrook Devon 6 SX5457
Colebrooke Devon 8 SX7699
Coleby Lincs 84 SE8919
Coleby Lincs 76 SK9760
Coleford Devon 8 SS7701
Coleford Gloucs 34 SO5710
Coleford Somset 22 ST6848
Coleford Water Somset 20 ST1133
Colegate End Norfk 55 TM1987
Colehill Dorset 12 SU0201
Coleman Green Herts 39 TL1812
Coleman's Hatch E Susx 16 TQ4433
Colemere Shrops 59 SJ4332
Colemore Hants 24 SU7030
Colemore Green Shrops 60 SO7197
Colenden P & K 126 NO1029
Coleorton Leics 62 SK4017
Colerne Wilts 35 ST8271
Coles Cross Dorset 10 ST3902
Coles Green Suffk 54 TM1041
Colesbourne Gloucs 35 SP0013
Colesden Beds 52 TL1255
Coleshill Bucks 26 SU9495
Coleshill Oxon 36 SU2393
Coleshill Warwks 61 SP2089
Colestocks Devon 9 ST0900
Coley Somset 21 ST5855
Colgate W Susx 15 TQ2332
Colgrain Ag & B 115 NS3280
Colinsburgh Fife 127 NO4703
Colinton C Edin 117 NT2168
Colintraive Ag & B 114 NS0374
Colkirk Norfk 66 TF9126
Collace P & K 126 NO2032
Collafirth Shet 155 HU3482
Collaton Devon 7 SX7139
Collaton Devon 7 SX7952
Collaton St Mary Devon 7 SX8660
College Green Somset 21 ST5736
College of Roseisle Moray 141 NJ1466
College Town Berks 25 SU8560
Collessie Fife 126 NO2813
Colleton Mills Devon 19 SS6615
Collier Row Gt Lon 27 TQ5091
Collier Street Kent 28 TQ7145
Collier's End Herts 39 TL3720
Collier's Green Kent 17 TQ7822
Colliers Green Kent 28 TQ7538
Colliery Row T & W 96 NZ3249
Collieston Abers 143 NK0328
Collin D & G 100 NY0276
Collingbourne Ducis Wilts 23 SU2453
Collingbourne Kingston Wilts 23 SU2355
Collingham W York 83 SE3945
Collington H & W 47 SO6460
Collingtree Nhants 49 SP7555
Collins Green Ches 78 SJ5594
Collins Green H & W 47 SO7457
Colliston Angus 127 NO6045
Colliton Devon 9 ST0804
Collyweston Nhants 63 SK9902
Colmonell S Ayrs 98 NX1485
Colmworth Beds 51 TL1058
Coln Rogers Gloucs 36 SP0809
Coln St Aldwyns Gloucs 36 SP1405
Coln St Dennis Gloucs 36 SP0810
Colnbrook Berks 26 TQ0277
Colne Cambs 52 TL3775
Colne Lancs 81 SD8939
Colne Bridge W York 82 SE1720
Colne Edge Lancs 81 SD8841
Colne Engaine Essex 40 TL8430
Colney Norfk 66 TG1807
Colney Heath Herts 39 TL2005
Colney Street Herts 26 TL1502
Colpy Abers 142 NJ6432
Colquhar Border 109 NT3341
Colquite Cnwll 4 SX0570
Colscott Devon 18 SS3614
Colsterdale N York 89 SE1381
Colsterworth Lincs 63 SK9324
Colston Bassett Notts 63 SK7033
Colt Hill Hants 24 SU7551
Colt's Hill Kent 16 TQ6443
Coltfield Moray 141 NJ1163
Coltishall Norfk 67 TG2719
Colton Cumb 86 SD3185
Colton N York 83 SE5444
Colton Norfk 66 TG1009
Colton Staffs 73 SK0420
Colton W York 83 SE3732
Columbjohn Devon 9 SX9699
Colva Powys 45 SO1952
Colvend D & G 92 NX8654
Colwall H & W 47 SO7542
Colwell Nthumb 102 NY9575
Colwich Staffs 73 SK0121
Colwick Notts 62 SK6140
Colwinston V Glam 33 SS9375
Colworth W Susx 14 SU9103
Colwyn Bay A & C 69 SH8578
Colyford Devon 10 SY2592
Colyton Devon 9 SY2494
Combe Berks 23 SU3760
Combe Devon 7 SX7238
Combe Devon 7 SX8448
Combe H & W 46 SO3463
Combe Oxon 36 SP4116
Combe Almer Dorset 11 SY9597
Combe Common Surrey 14 SU9436
Combe Fishacre Devon 7 SX8465
Combe Florey Somset 20 ST1531
Combe Hay Somset 22 ST7359
Combe Martin Devon 19 SS5846
Combe Moor H & W 46 SO3663
Combe Raleigh Devon 9 ST1502
Combe St Nicholas Somset 10 ST3011
Combeinteignhead Devon 7 SX9071
Comberbach Ches 79 SJ6477
Comberford Staffs 61 SK1907
Comberton Cambs 52 TL3856
Comberton H & W 46 SO4968
Combpyne Devon 10 SY2892
Combridge Staffs 73 SK0937
Combrook Warwks 48 SP3051
Combs Derbys 74 SK0478
Combs Suffk 54 TM0456
Combs Ford Suffk 54 TM0457
Combwich Somset 20 ST2542
Comers Abers 135 NJ6707
Comhampton H & W 47 SO8367
Commercial Pembks 31 SN1416
Commercial End Cambs 53 TL5563
Commins Coch Powys 57 SH8402
Common Edge Lancs 80 SD3232
Common End Cumb 92 NY0022
Common Moor Cnwll 5 SX2469
Common Platt Wilts 36 SU1186
Common Side Derbys 74 SK3375
Common The Wilts 23 SU2432
Commondale N York 90 NZ6610
Commonside Ches 71 SJ5473
Commonside Derbys 73 SK2441
Commonwood Shrops 59 SJ4828
Commonwood Wrexhm 71 SJ3753
Compass Somset 20 ST2934
Compstall Gt Man 79 SJ9690
Compstonend D & G 99 NX6652
Compton Berks 37 SU5280
Compton Devon 7 SX8664
Compton Hants 23 SU3529
Compton Hants 13 SU4625
Compton Staffs 60 SO8284
Compton Surrey 25 SU9546
Compton W Susx 14 SU7714
Compton Wilts 23 SU1351
Compton Abbas Dorset 22 ST8618
Compton Abdale Gloucs 36 SP0516
Compton Bassett Wilts 36 SU0372
Compton Beauchamp Oxon 36 SU2786
Compton Bishop Somset 21 ST3955
Compton Chamberlayne Wilts 23 SU0229
Compton Dando Somset 21 ST6464
Compton Dundon Somset 21 ST4932
Compton Durville Somset 10 ST4117
Compton Greenfield Gloucs 34 ST5681
Compton Martin Somset 21 ST5457
Compton Pauncefoot Somset 21 ST6426
Compton Valence Dorset 10 SY5993
Compton Verney Warwks 48 SP3152
Comrie Fife 117 NT0289
Comrie P & K 124 NN7722
Conaglen House Highld 130 NN0268
Conchra Highld 138 NG8827
Concraigie P & K 125 NO0944
Conder Green Lancs 80 SD4556
Conderton H & W 47 SO9637
Condicote Gloucs 48 SP1528
Condorrat N Lans 116 NS7373
Condover Shrops 59 SJ4905
Coney Hill Gloucs 35 SO8517
Coney Weston Suffk 54 TL9578
Coneyhurst Common W Susx 14 TQ1023
Coneysthorpe N York 90 SE7171
Conford Hants 14 SU8233
Congdon's Shop Cnwll 5 SX2878
Congerstone Leics 62 SK3605
Congham Norfk 65 TF7123
Conghurst Kent 17 TQ7628
Congl-y-wal Gwynd 57 SH7044
Congleton Ches 72 SJ8562
Congresbury Somset 21 ST4363
Congreve Staffs 60 SJ9013
Conheath D & G 100 NX9969
Conicavel Moray 140 NH9853
Coningsby Lincs 76 TF2257
Conington Cambs 52 TL1885
Conington Cambs 52 TL3266
Conisbrough S York 75 SK5098
Conisholme Lincs 77 TF4095
Coniston Cumb 86 SD3097
Coniston E R Yk 85 TA1535
Coniston Cold N York 81 SD9054
Conistone N York 88 SD9867
Connah's Quay Flints 71 SJ2969
Connel Ag & B 122 NM9134
Connel Park E Ayrs 107 NS6012
Connor Downs Cnwll 2 SW5939
Conon Bridge Highld 139 NH5455
Cononley N York 82 SD9846
Consall Staffs 72 SJ9848
Consett Dur 95 NZ1051
Constable Burton N York 89 SE1690
Constable Lee Lancs 81 SD8123
Constantine Cnwll 3 SW7329
Constantine Bay Cnwll 4 SW8774
Contin Highld 139 NH4556
Conwy A & C 69 SH7877
Conyer Kent 28 TQ9664
Conyer's Green Suffk 54 TL8867
Cooden E Susx 17 TQ7107
Cook's Green Essex 41 TM1818
Cookbury Devon 18 SS4006
Cookbury Wick Devon 18 SS3905
Cookham Berks 26 SU8985
Cookham Dean Berks 26 SU8685
Cookham Rise Berks 26 SU8885
Cookhill Warwks 48 SP0558
Cookley H & W 60 SO8480
Cookley Suffk 55 TM3475
Cookley Green Oxon 37 SU6990
Cookney Abers 135 NO8693
Cooks Green Suffk 54 TL9753
Cooksbridge E Susx 15 TQ4013
Cooksey Green H & W 47 SO9069
Cookshill Staffs 72 SJ9443
Cooksland Cnwll 4 SX0867
Cooksmill Green Essex 40 TL6306
Cookson Green Ches 71 SJ5774
Cookson's Green Dur 96 NZ2933
Coolham W Susx 14 TQ1122
Cooling Kent 28 TQ7575
Cooling Street Kent 28 TQ7474
Coombe Cnwll 2 SW6242
Coombe Cnwll 3 SW8340
Coombe Devon 8 SX8384
Coombe Devon 7 SX9373
Coombe Devon 9 SY1091
Coombe Gloucs 35 ST7694
Coombe Hants 13 SU6620
Coombe Wilts 23 SU1450
Coombe Bissett Wilts 23 SU1026
Coombe Cellars Devon 7 SX9072
Coombe Cross Hants 13 SU6620
Coombe End Somset 20 ST0329
Coombe Hill Gloucs 47 SO8826
Coombe Keynes Dorset 11 SY8484
Coombe Pafford Devon 7 SX9166
Coombe Street Somset 22 ST7631
Coombes W Susx 15 TQ1808
Coombeswood W Mids 60 SO9785
Cooper Street Kent 29 TR3060
Cooper Turning Gt Man 79 SD6308
Cooper's Corner Kent 16 TQ4849
Cooperhill Moray 141 NH9953
Coopers Green E Susx 16 TQ4723
Coopers Green Herts 39 TL1909
Coopersale Common Essex 27 TL4702
Coopersale Street Essex 27 TL4701
Cootham W Susx 14 TQ0714
Cop Street Kent 27 TQ2959
Copdock Suffk 54 TM1242
Copford Green Essex 40 TL9222
Copgrove N York 89 SE3463
Copister Shet 155 HU4879
Cople Beds 38 TL1048
Copley Dur 95 NZ0825
Copley Gt Man 79 SJ9798
Copley W York 82 SE0822
Coplow Dale Derbys 74 SK1679
Copmanthorpe N York 83 SE5646
Copmere End Staffs 72 SJ8029
Copp Lancs 80 SD4239
Coppathorne Cnwll 18 SS2000
Coppenhall Staffs 72 SJ9019
Coppenhall Moss Ches 72 SJ7058
Copperhouse Cnwll 2 SW5637
Coppicegate Shrops 60 SO7379
Coppingford Cambs 52 TL1679
Coppins Corner Kent 28 TQ9448
Copplestone Devon 8 SS7702
Coppull Lancs 81 SD5614
Coppull Moor Lancs 81 SD5512
Copsale W Susx 15 TQ1724
Copster Green Lancs 81 SD6733
Copston Magna Warwks 50 SP4588
Copt Heath W Mids 61 SP1777
Copt Hewick N York 89 SE3471
Copthall Green Essex 27 TL4201
Copthorne Cnwll 5 SX2692
Copthorne W Susx 15 TQ3139
Copy's Green Norfk 66 TF9439
Copythorne Hants 12 SU3014
Coram Street Suffk 54 TM0042
Corbets Tay Gt Lon 27 TQ5685
Corbiere Jersey 152 JS0000
Corbridge Nthumb 103 NY9964
Corby Nhants 51 SP8988
Corby Glen Lincs 63 TF0024
Corby Hill Cumb 94 NY4857
Cordon N Ayrs 105 NS0230
Cordwell Derbys 74 SK3176
Coreley Shrops 46 SO6173
Cores End Bucks 26 SU9087
Corfe Somset 20 ST2319
Corfe Castle Dorset 11 SY9681
Corfe Mullen Dorset 11 SY9896
Corfton Shrops 59 SO4985
Corgarff Abers 133 NJ2708
Corhampton Hants 13 SU6120
Corks Pond Kent 28 TQ6540
Corley Warwks 61 SP3085
Corley Ash Warwks 61 SP2986
Corley Moor Warwks 61 SP2884
Cormuir Angus 134 NO3066
Cornard Tye Suffk 54 TL9041
Corndon Devon 8 SX6985

Corner Row

Cross Green

Corner Row *Lancs*	80	SD4134
Corney *Cumb*	86	SD1191
Cornforth *Dur*	96	NZ3134
Cornhill *Abers*	142	NJ5858
Cornhill-on-Tweed *Nthumb*	110	NT8639
Cornholme *W York*	81	SD9126
Cornish Hall End *Essex*	53	TL6836
Cornoigmore *Ag & B*	120	NL9846
Cornriggs *Dur*	95	NY8441
Cornsay *Dur*	96	NZ1443
Cornsay Colliery *Dur*	96	NZ1643
Corntown *Highld*	139	NH5556
Corntown *V Glam*	33	SS9177
Cornwell *Oxon*	48	SP2727
Cornwood *Devon*	6	SX6059
Cornworthy *Devon*	7	SX8255
Corpach *Highld*	130	NN0976
Corpusty *Norfk*	66	TG1129
Corrachree *Abers*	134	NJ4604
Corran *Cnwll*	3	SW9946
Corran *Highld*	130	NG8409
Corran *Highld*	130	NN0263
Corrany *IOM*	153	SC4589
Corrie *D & G*	101	NY2086
Corrie *N Ayrs*	105	NS0242
Corriecravie *N Ayrs*	105	NR9223
Corriegills *N Ayrs*	105	NS0335
Corriegour Lodge Hotel *Highld*	131	NN2692
Corriemoille *Highld*	139	NH3663
Corrimony *Highld*	139	NH3730
Corringham *Essex*	40	TQ7083
Corringham *Lincs*	76	SK8691
Corris *Gwynd*	57	SH7508
Corris Uchaf *Gwynd*	57	SH7408
Corrow *Ag & B*	114	NN1800
Corry *Highld*	137	NG6424
Cors-y-Gedol *Gwynd*	57	SH6022
Corscombe *Devon*	8	SX6296
Corscombe *Dorset*	10	ST5105
Corse *Gloucs*	47	SO7826
Corse Lawn *Gloucs*	47	SO8330
Corsham *Wilts*	35	ST8770
Corsindae *Abers*	135	NJ6808
Corsley *Wilts*	22	ST8246
Corsley Heath *Wilts*	22	ST8245
Corsock *D & G*	99	NX7675
Corston *Somset*	22	ST6965
Corston *Wilts*	35	ST9283
Corstorphine *C Edin*	117	NT1972
Cortachy *Angus*	134	NO3959
Corton *Suffk*	67	TM5497
Corton *Wilts*	22	ST9340
Corton Denham *Somset*	21	ST6322
Coruanan Lodge *Highld*	130	NN0668
Corwen *Denbgs*	70	SJ0743
Coryates *Dorset*	10	SY6285
Coryton *Devon*	5	SX4583
Coryton *Essex*	40	TQ7382
Cosby *Leics*	50	SP5495
Coseley *W Mids*	60	SO9494
Cosford *Shrops*	60	SJ8005
Cosgrove *Nhants*	38	SP7942
Cosham *Hants*	13	SU6505
Cosheston *Pembks*	30	SN0003
Coshieville *P & K*	124	NN7749
Cossall *Notts*	62	SK4842
Cossall Marsh *Notts*	62	SK4842
Cossington *Leics*	62	SK6013
Cossington *Somset*	21	ST3540
Costallack *Cnwll*	2	SW4525
Costessey *Norfk*	66	TG1711
Costock *Notts*	62	SK5726
Coston *Leics*	63	SK8422
Coston *Norfk*	66	TG0506
Cote *Oxon*	36	SP3502
Cote *Somset*	21	ST3444
Cotebrook *Ches*	71	SJ5765
Cotehill *Cumb*	93	NY4650
Cotes *Cumb*	87	SD4886
Cotes *Leics*	62	SK5520
Cotes *Staffs*	72	SJ8434
Cotes Heath *Staffs*	72	SJ8334
Cotesbach *Leics*	50	SP5382
Cotgrave *Notts*	63	SK6435
Cotham *Notts*	63	SK7947
Cothelstone *Somset*	20	ST1831
Cotherstone *Dur*	95	NZ0119
Cothill *Oxon*	37	SU4699
Cotleigh *Devon*	9	ST2002
Cotmanhay *Derbys*	62	SK4543
Coton *Cambs*	52	TL4058
Coton *Nhants*	50	SP6771
Coton *Shrops*	59	SJ5334
Coton *Staffs*	72	SJ8120
Coton *Staffs*	72	SJ9731
Coton *Staffs*	61	SK1804
Coton Clanford *Staffs*	72	SJ8723
Coton Hayes *Staffs*	72	SJ9832
Coton Hill *Shrops*	59	SJ4813
Coton in the Clay *Staffs*	73	SK1628
Coton in the Elms *Derbys*	73	SK2415
Coton Park *Derbys*	73	SK2617
Cott *Devon*	7	SX7861
Cottage End *Hants*	24	SU4143
Cottam *E R Yk*	91	SE9964
Cottam *Lancs*	80	SD5032
Cottam *Notts*	75	SK8179
Cottenham *Cambs*	53	TL4467
Cotterdale *N York*	88	SD8393
Cottered *Herts*	39	TL3129
Cotteridge *W Mids*	61	SP0480
Cotterstock *Nhants*	51	TL0490
Cottesbrooke *Nhants*	50	SP7173
Cottesmore *Rutlnd*	63	SK9013
Cottingham *E R Yk*	84	TA0432
Cottingham *Nhants*	51	SP8490
Cottingley *W York*	82	SE1137
Cottisford *Oxon*	49	SP5831
Cottivett *Cnwll*	5	SX3662
Cotton *Suffk*	54	TM0666
Cotton End *Beds*	38	TL0845
Cotton Tree *Lancs*	81	SD9039
Cottown *Abers*	142	NJ5026
Cottown *Abers*	142	NJ7615
Cottown of Gight *Abers*	143	NJ8140
Cottrell *V Glam*	33	ST0774
Cotts *Devon*	6	SX4365
Cotwall *Shrops*	59	SJ6017
Cotwalton *Staffs*	72	SJ9234
Couch's Mill *Cnwll*	4	SX1459
Coughton *H & W*	34	SO5921
Coughton *Warwks*	48	SP0860
Coulaghailtro *Ag & B*	113	NR7165
Coulags *Highld*	138	NG9645
Coulderton *Cumb*	86	NX9808
Coull *Abers*	134	NJ5102
Coulport *Ag & B*	114	NS2187
Coulsdon *Gt Lon*	27	TQ2959
Coulston *Wilts*	22	ST9554
Coulter *S Lans*	108	NT0234
Coultershaw Bridge *W Susx*	14	SU9719
Coultings *Somset*	20	ST2241
Coulton *N York*	90	SE6373
Coultra *Fife*	126	NO3523
Cound *Shrops*	59	SJ5505
Coundlane *Shrops*	59	SJ5705
Coundon *Dur*	96	NZ2329
Coundon Grange *Dur*	96	NZ2228
Countersett *N York*	88	SD9187
Countess *Wilts*	23	SU1542
Countess Cross *Essex*	40	TL8631
Countess Wear *Devon*	9	SX9489
Countesthorpe *Leics*	50	SP5895
Countisbury *Devon*	19	SS7449
Coup Green *Lancs*	81	SD5927
Coupar Angus *P & K*	126	NO2239
Coupland *Cumb*	94	NY7118
Coupland *Nthumb*	110	NT9330
Cour *Ag & B*	105	NR8248
Courance *D & G*	100	NY0590
Court Henry *Carmth*	32	SN5522
Court-at-Street *Kent*	17	TR0935
Courteachan *Highld*	129	NM6897
Courteenhall *Nhants*	49	SP7653
Courtsend *Essex*	41	TR0293
Courtway *Somset*	20	ST2033
Cousland *Mdloth*	118	NT3768
Cousley Wood *E Susx*	16	TQ6533
Cove *Aber C*	135	NJ9501
Cove *Ag & B*	114	NS2282
Cove *Border*	119	NT7771
Cove *Devon*	20	SS9619
Cove *Hants*	25	SU8555
Cove *Highld*	144	NG8191
Cove Bottom *Suffk*	55	TM4979
Covehithe *Suffk*	55	TM5282
Coven *Staffs*	60	SJ9106
Coven Lawn *Staffs*	60	SJ9005
Coveney *Cambs*	53	TL4882
Covenham St Bartholomew *Lincs*	77	TF3394
Covenham St Mary *Lincs*	77	TF3394
Coventry *W Mids*	61	SP3378
Coverack *Cnwll*	3	SW7818
Coverack Bridges *Cnwll*	2	SW6630
Coverham *N York*	89	SE1086
Covington *Cambs*	51	TL0570
Covington *S Lans*	108	NS9739
Cow Green *Suffk*	54	TM0565
Cow Honeybourne *H & W*	48	SP1143
Cowan Bridge *Lancs*	87	SD6376
Cowbeech *E Susx*	16	TQ6114
Cowbit *Lincs*	64	TF2518
Cowbridge *V Glam*	33	SS9974
Cowdale *Derbys*	74	SK0771
Cowden *Kent*	16	TQ4640
Cowden Pound *Kent*	16	TQ4642
Cowden Station *Kent*	16	TQ4741
Cowdenbeath *Fife*	117	NT1691
Cowers Lane *Derbys*	73	SK3046
Cowes *IOW*	13	SZ4996
Cowesby *N York*	89	SE4689
Cowesfield Green *Wilts*	23	SU2523
Cowfold *W Susx*	15	TQ2122
Cowgill *Cumb*	88	SD7586
Cowhill *Gloucs*	34	ST6091
Cowie *Stirlg*	116	NS8389
Cowley *Derbys*	74	SK3376
Cowley *Devon*	9	SX9095
Cowley *Gloucs*	35	SO9614
Cowley *Gt Lon*	26	TQ0582
Cowley *Oxon*	37	SP5304
Cowley *Oxon*	49	SP6628
Cowling *Lancs*	81	SD5917
Cowling *N York*	82	SD9643
Cowling *N York*	89	SE2387
Cowlinge *Suffk*	53	TL7154
Cowmes *W York*	82	SE1815
Cowpe *Lancs*	81	SD8320
Cowpen *Nthumb*	103	NZ2981
Cowpen Bewley *Dur*	97	NZ4824
Cowplain *Hants*	13	SU6810
Cowshill *Dur*	95	NY8540
Cowslip Green *Somset*	21	ST4861
Cowthorpe *N York*	83	SE4252
Cox Common *Suffk*	55	TM4082
Coxall *Shrops*	46	SO3774
Coxbank *Ches*	72	SJ6541
Coxbench *Derbys*	62	SK3743
Coxbridge *Somset*	21	ST5436
Coxford *Cnwll*	4	SX1696
Coxford *Norfk*	66	TF8529
Coxgreen *Staffs*	60	SO8086
Coxheath *Kent*	28	TQ7451
Coxhoe *Dur*	96	NZ3136
Coxley *Somset*	21	ST5343
Coxley *W York*	82	SE2717
Coxley Wick *Somset*	21	ST5243
Coxpark *Cnwll*	5	SX4072
Coxtie Green *Essex*	27	TQ5696
Coxwold *N York*	90	SE5377
Coychurch *Brdgnd*	33	SS9379
Coylton *S Ayrs*	107	NS4219
Coylumbridge *Highld*	132	NH9111
Coytrahen *Brdgnd*	33	SS8885
Crab Orchard *Dorset*	12	SU0806
Crabbs Cross *H & W*	48	SP0465
Crabtree *W Susx*	15	TQ2125
Crabtree Green *Wrexhm*	71	SJ3344
Crackenthorpe *Cumb*	94	NY6622
Crackington Haven *Cnwll*	4	SX1496
Crackley *Staffs*	72	SJ8350
Crackley *Warwks*	61	SP2973
Crackleybank *Shrops*	60	SJ7611
Crackpot *N York*	88	SD9796
Cracoe *N York*	88	SD9760
Craddock *Devon*	9	ST0812
Cradle End *Herts*	39	TL4521
Cradley *H & W*	47	SO7347
Cradley *W Mids*	60	SO9485
Cradoc *Powys*	45	SO0130
Crafthole *Cnwll*	5	SX3654
Crafton *Bucks*	38	SP8819
Crag Foot *Lancs*	87	SD4873
Cragg Hill *W York*	82	SE2437
Cragg Vale *W York*	82	SE0023
Craggan *Highld*	141	NJ0226
Craghead *Dur*	96	NZ2150
Crai *Powys*	45	SN8924
Craibstone *Moray*	142	NJ4959
Craichie *Angus*	127	NO5047
Craig *Angus*	127	NO6956
Craig Llangiwg *Neath*	32	SN7204
Craig Penllyn *V Glam*	33	SS9777
Craig's End *Essex*	53	TL7137
Craig-y-Duke *Neath*	32	SN7002
Craig-y-nos *Powys*	33	SN8415
Craigbank *E Ayrs*	107	NS5911
Craigburn *Border*	117	NT2354
Craigcefnparc *Swans*	32	SN6702
Craigcleuch *D & G*	101	NY3486
Craigdam *Abers*	143	NJ8430
Craigdarroch *D & G*	107	NX7391
Craigdhu *Ag & B*	122	NM8205
Craigearn *Abers*	142	NJ7214
Craigellachie *Moray*	141	NJ2844
Craigend *P & K*	126	NO1120
Craigend *Rens*	115	NS4670
Craigendoran *Ag & B*	115	NS3181
Craighlaw *D & G*	98	NX3061
Craighouse *Ag & B*	113	NR5267
Craigie *P & K*	126	NO1143
Craigie *S Ayrs*	107	NS4232
Craigiefold *Abers*	143	NJ9165
Craigley *D & G*	99	NX7658
Craiglockhart *C Edin*	117	NT2271
Craiglug *Moray*	141	NJ3355
Craigmillar *C Edin*	117	NT3071
Craigmorloch *N Lans*	116	NS7475
Craignant *Shrops*	58	SJ2535
Craigneston *D & G*	107	NX7587
Craigneuk *N Lans*	116	NS7765
Craigneuk *N Lans*	116	NS7756
Craignure *Ag & B*	122	NM7236
Craigo *Angus*	135	NO6864
Craigrothie *Fife*	126	NO3810
Craigruie *Stirlg*	124	NN4920
Craigton *Aber C*	135	NJ8301
Craigton *Angus*	127	NO5138
Craigton *E Rens*	115	NS4954
Craigton of Airlie *Angus*	126	NO3250
Crail *Fife*	127	NO6107
Crailing *Border*	110	NT6824
Crakehall *N York*	89	SE2489
Crakehill *N York*	89	SE4273
Crakemarsh *Staffs*	73	SK0936
Crambe *N York*	90	SE7364
Cramlington *Nthumb*	103	NZ2676
Cramond *C Edin*	117	NT1976
Cramond Bridge *C Edin*	117	NT1775
Cranage *Ches*	79	SJ7568
Cranberry *Staffs*	72	SJ8235
Cranborne *Dorset*	12	SU0513
Cranbrook *Kent*	28	TQ7736
Cranbrook Common *Kent*	28	TQ7838
Crane Moor *S York*	82	SE3001
Crane's Corner *Norfk*	66	TF9113
Cranfield *Beds*	38	SP9542
Cranford *Devon*	18	SS3421
Cranford *Gt Lon*	26	TQ1076
Cranford St Andrew *Nhants*	51	SP9277
Cranford St John *Nhants*	51	SP9276
Cranham *Gloucs*	35	SO8913
Cranham *Gt Lon*	27	TQ5787
Cranhill *Warwks*	48	SP1253
Crank *Mersyd*	78	SJ5099
Cranleigh *Surrey*	14	TQ0539
Cranmer Green *Suffk*	54	TM0171
Cranmore *IOW*	13	SZ3990
Cranmore *Somset*	22	ST6643
Cranoe *Leics*	50	SP7695
Cransford *Suffk*	55	TM3164
Cranshaws *Border*	118	NT6861
Cranstal *IOM*	153	NX4602
Cranswick *E R Yk*	84	TA0252
Crantock *Cnwll*	4	SW7960
Cranwell *Lincs*	76	TF0349
Cranwich *Norfk*	65	TL7794
Cranworth *Norfk*	66	TF9804
Craobh Haven *Ag & B*	122	NM7907
Crapstone *Devon*	6	SX5067
Crarae *Ag & B*	114	NR9897
Crask Inn *Highld*	149	NC5224
Crask of Aigas *Highld*	139	NH4642
Craster *Nthumb*	111	NU2519
Craswall *H & W*	46	SO2735
Crateford *Staffs*	60	SJ9009
Cratfield *Suffk*	55	TM3175
Crathes *Abers*	135	NO7596
Crathie *Abers*	133	NO2695
Crathie *Highld*	132	NN5793
Crathorne *N York*	89	NZ4407
Craven Arms *Shrops*	59	SO4382
Crawcrook *T & W*	103	NZ1363
Crawford *Lancs*	78	SD4902
Crawford *S Lans*	108	NS9520
Crawfordjohn *S Lans*	108	NS8823
Crawick *D & G*	107	NS7811
Crawley *Hants*	24	SU4235
Crawley *Oxon*	36	SP3412
Crawley *W Susx*	15	TQ2636
Crawley Down *W Susx*	15	TQ3437
Crawley Side *Dur*	95	NY9940
Crawshawbooth *Lancs*	81	SD8125
Crawton *Abers*	135	NO8779
Crawton *N York*	90	SE6476
Craxe's Green *Essex*	40	TL9419
Cray *N York*	88	SD9479
Cray's Pond *Oxon*	37	SU6380
Crayford *Gt Lon*	27	TQ5175
Crayke *N York*	90	SE5670
Craymere Beck *Norfk*	66	TG0631
Crays Hill *Essex*	40	TQ7192
Craythorne *Staffs*	73	SK2426
Craze Lowman *Devon*	9	SS9814
Crazies Hill *Oxon*	37	SU7980
Creacombe *Devon*	18	SS3219
Creag Ghoraidh *W Isls*	154	NF7948
Creagan Inn *Ag & B*	122	NM9744
Creagorry *W Isls*	154	NF7948
Creaguaineach Lodge *Highld*	131	NN3068
Creamore Bank *Shrops*	59	SJ5130
Creaton *Nhants*	50	SP7071
Creca *D & G*	101	NY2270
Credenhill *H & W*	46	SO4543
Crediton *Devon*	8	SS8300
Creebank *D & G*	98	NX3477
Creebridge *D & G*	99	NX4165
Creech Heathfield *Somset*	20	ST2727
Creech St Michael *Somset*	20	ST2725
Creed *Cnwll*	3	SW9347
Creedy Park *Devon*	8	SS8301
Creekmouth *Gt Lon*	27	TQ4581
Creeting St Mary *Suffk*	54	TM0956
Creeton *Lincs*	64	TF0120
Creetown *D & G*	99	NX4759
Creggans Inn *Ag & B*	123	NN0902
Cregneash *IOM*	153	SC1867
Cregrina *Powys*	45	SO1252
Creich *Fife*	126	NO3221
Creigiau *Cardif*	33	ST0781
Crelly *Cnwll*	2	SW6732
Cremyll *Cnwll*	6	SX4553
Cressage *Shrops*	59	SJ5904
Cressbrook *Derbys*	74	SK1673
Cresselly *Pembks*	30	SN0606
Cressex *Bucks*	26	SU8492
Cressing *Essex*	40	TL7920
Cresswell *Nthumb*	103	NZ2993
Cresswell *Pembks*	30	SN0506
Cresswell *Staffs*	72	SJ9739
Creswell *Derbys*	75	SK5274
Creswell Green *Staffs*	61	SK0710
Cretingham *Suffk*	55	TM2260
Cretshengan *Ag & B*	113	NR7166
Crew Green *Powys*	59	SJ3215
Crewe *Ches*	71	SJ4253
Crewe *Ches*	72	SJ7056
Crewe Green *Ches*	72	SJ7255
Crewkerne *Somset*	10	ST4409
Crews Hill *H & W*	35	SO6722
Crews Hill Station *Herts*	27	TL3000
Crewton *Derbys*	62	SK3733
Crianlarich *Stirlg*	123	NN3825
Cribbs Causeway *Gloucs*	34	ST5780
Cribyn *Cardgn*	44	SN5250
Criccieth *Gwynd*	56	SH4938
Crich *Derbys*	74	SK3454
Crich Carr *Derbys*	74	SK3354
Crich Common *Derbys*	74	SK3553
Crichton *Mdloth*	118	NT3862
Crick *Mons*	34	ST4890
Crick *Nhants*	50	SP5872
Crickadarn *Powys*	45	SO0942
Cricket St Thomas *Somset*	10	ST3708
Crickheath *Shrops*	59	SJ2922
Crickhowell *Powys*	33	SO2118
Cricklade *Wilts*	36	SU0993
Cricklewood *Gt Lon*	26	TQ2385
Cridling Stubbs *N York*	83	SE5221
Crieff *P & K*	125	NN8621
Criggan *Cnwll*	4	SX0160
Criggion *Powys*	59	SJ2915
Crigglestone *W York*	82	SE3116
Crimble *Gt Man*	81	SD8611
Crimond *Abers*	143	NK0556
Crimonmogate *Abers*	143	NK0358
Crimplesham *Norfk*	65	TF6503
Crimscote *Warwks*	48	SP2347
Crinan *Ag & B*	113	NR7894
Crindledyke *N Lans*	116	NS8356
Cringleford *Norfk*	67	TG1905
Cringles *N York*	82	SE0448
Crinow *Pembks*	31	SN1214
Cripp's Corner *E Susx*	17	TQ7721
Cripplesease *Cnwll*	2	SW5036
Cripplestyle *Dorset*	12	SU0812
Crizeley *H & W*	46	SO4532
Croachy *Highld*	140	NH6527
Croanford *Cnwll*	4	SX0371
Crochmare House *D & G*	100	NX8977
Crock Street *Somset*	10	ST3213
Crockenhill *Kent*	27	TQ5067
Crocker End *Oxon*	37	SU7086
Crocker's Ash *H & W*	34	SO5316
Crockerhill *W Susx*	14	SU9206
Crockernwell *Devon*	8	SX7592
Crockerton *Wilts*	22	ST8642
Crocketford *D & G*	100	NX8372
Crockey Hill *N York*	83	SE6246
Crockham Hill *Kent*	27	TQ4450
Crockhurst Street *Kent*	16	TQ6245
Crockleford Heath *Essex*	41	TM0426
Croes-goch *Pembks*	30	SM8330
Croes-lan *Cardgn*	42	SN3844
Croes-y-mwyalch *Torfn*	34	ST3092
Croes-y-pant *Mons*	34	SO3104
Croeserw *Neath*	33	SS8795
Croesor *Gwynd*	57	SH6344
Croesyceiliog *Carmth*	31	SN4016
Croesyceiliog *Torfn*	34	ST3096
Croft *Ches*	79	SJ6393
Croft *Devon*	5	SX5296
Croft *Leics*	50	SP5195
Croft *Lincs*	77	TF5061
Croft Michael *Cnwll*	2	SW6637
Croft-on-Tees *Dur*	89	NZ2809
Croftamie *Stirlg*	115	NS4785
Crofton *Cumb*	93	NY3050
Crofton *Devon*	9	SX9680
Crofton *W York*	83	SE3817
Crofton *Wilts*	23	SU2562
Crofts *D & G*	99	NX7365
Crofts *Moray*	141	NJ2850
Crofts Bank *Gt Man*	79	SJ7695
Crofts of Dipple *Moray*	141	NJ3259
Crofts of Savoch *Abers*	143	NK0460
Crofty *Swans*	32	SS5294
Crogen *Gwynd*	58	SJ0036
Croggan *Ag & B*	122	NM7027
Croglin *Cumb*	94	NY5747
Crogo *D & G*	99	NX7576
Croik *Highld*	146	NH4591
Cromarty *Highld*	140	NH7867
Crombie *Fife*	117	NT0584
Cromdale *Highld*	141	NJ0728
Cromer *Herts*	39	TL2928
Cromer *Norfk*	67	TG2242
Cromford *Derbys*	73	SK2956
Cromhall *Gloucs*	35	ST6990
Cromhall Common *Gloucs*	35	ST6989
Cromor *W Isls*	154	NB4021
Crompton Fold *Gt Man*	79	SD9409
Cromwell *Notts*	75	SK7961
Cronberry *E Ayrs*	107	NS6022
Crondall *Hants*	25	SU7948
Cronk-y-Voddy *IOM*	153	SC3085
Cronkbourne *IOM*	153	SC3677
Cronton *Mersyd*	78	SJ4988
Crook *Cumb*	87	SD4695
Crook *Dur*	96	NZ1635
Crook Inn *Border*	108	NT1026
Crook of Devon *P & K*	117	NO0400
Crookdake *Cumb*	93	NY1943
Crooke *Gt Man*	78	SD5507
Crooked End *Gloucs*	35	SO6217
Crooked Holme *Cumb*	101	NY5161
Crooked Soley *Wilts*	36	SU3172
Crookedholm *E Ayrs*	107	NS4537
Crookes *S York*	74	SK3287
Crookhall *Dur*	95	NZ1150
Crookham *Berks*	24	SU5464
Crookham *Nthumb*	110	NT9138
Crookham Village *Hants*	25	SU7952
Crooklands *Cumb*	87	SD5383
Cropper *Derbys*	73	SK2335
Cropredy *Oxon*	49	SP4646
Cropston *Leics*	62	SK5510
Cropthorne *H & W*	47	SO9945
Cropton *N York*	90	SE7589
Cropwell Bishop *Notts*	63	SK6835
Cropwell Butler *Notts*	63	SK6837
Cros *W Isls*	154	NB5061
Crosbie *N Ayrs*	114	NS2149
Crosbost *W Isls*	154	NB3924
Crosby *Cumb*	92	NY0738
Crosby *IOM*	153	SC3279
Crosby *Lincs*	84	SE8912
Crosby *Mersyd*	78	SJ3198
Crosby Garret *Cumb*	88	NY7209
Crosby Ravensworth *Cumb*	94	NY6214
Crosby Villa *Cumb*	92	NY0939
Croscombe *Somset*	21	ST5944
Crosemere *Shrops*	59	SJ4329
Cross *Somset*	21	ST4154
Cross Ash *Mons*	34	SO4019
Cross Bush *W Susx*	14	TQ0306
Cross Coombe *Cnwll*	3	SW7251
Cross End *Beds*	51	TL0658
Cross End *Essex*	54	TL8534
Cross Flatts *W York*	82	SE1040
Cross Gates *W York*	83	SE3534
Cross Green *Devon*	5	SX3888

Cross Green

Daybrook

Cross Green *Staffs* 60 SJ9105
Cross Green *Suffk* 54 TL8353
Cross Green *Suffk* 54 TL8955
Cross Green *Suffk* 54 TL9852
Cross Hands *Carmth* 32 SN5612
Cross Hands *Pembks* 31 SN0712
Cross Hill *Derbys* 74 SK4148
Cross Hills *N York* 82 SE0145
Cross Houses *Shrops* 59 SJ5307
Cross Houses *Shrops* 60 SO6991
Cross in Hand *E Susx* 16 TQ5521
Cross Inn *Cardgn* 42 SN3957
Cross Inn *Cardgn* 43 SN5464
Cross Inn *Pembks* 31 SN1005
Cross Inn *Rhondd* 33 ST0582
Cross Keys *Wilts* 35 ST8771
Cross Lane *IOW* 13 SZ5089
Cross Lane Head *Shrops* 60 SO7195
Cross Lanes *Cnwll* 2 SW6921
Cross Lanes *Cnwll* 3 SW7642
Cross Lanes *N York* 90 SE5364
Cross Lanes *Wrexhm* 71 SJ3746
Cross o' th' hands *Derbys* 73 SK2846
Cross Oak *Powys* 45 SO1023
Cross of Jackston *Abers* 142 NJ7432
Cross Roads *Powys* 45 SN9756
Cross Street *Suffk* 54 TM1876
Cross Town *Ches* 79 SJ7578
Cross Ways *Dorset* 11 SY7788
Cross-at-Hand *Kent* 28 TQ7846
Crossaig *Ag & B* 113 NR8351
Crossapoll *Ag & B* 120 NL9943
Crosscanonby *Cumb* 92 NY0739
Crossdale Street *Norfk* 67 TG2239
Crossens *Mersyd* 80 SD3720
Crossford *Fife* 117 NT0786
Crossford *S Lans* 116 NS8246
Crossgate *Cnwll* 5 SX3488
Crossgate *Lincs* 64 TF2426
Crossgate *Staffs* 72 SJ9437
Crossgatehall *E Loth* 118 NT3669
Crossgates *E Ayrs* 115 NS3744
Crossgates *Fife* 117 NT1488
Crossgates *N York* 91 TA0284
Crossgates *Powys* 45 SO0864
Crossgill *Lancs* 87 SD5563
Crosshands *Carmth* 31 SN1923
Crosshands *E Ayrs* 107 NS4830
Crosshill *Fife* 117 NT1796
Crosshill *S Ayrs* 106 NS3206
Crosshouse *E Ayrs* 106 NS3938
Crosskeys *Ag & B* 115 NS3385
Crosskeys *Caerph* 34 ST2292
Crosskirk *Highld* 150 ND0369
Crossland Edge *W York* 82 SE1012
Crossland Hill *W York* 82 SE1114
Crosslands *Cumb* 87 SD3489
Crosslanes *Shrops* 59 SJ3218
Crosslee *Border* 109 NT3018
Crosslee *Rens* 115 NS4066
Crossley *W York* 82 SE2021
Crossmichael *D & G* 99 NX7366
Crosspost *W Susx* 15 TQ2522
Crossroads *Abers* 134 NJ5607
Crossroads *Abers* 135 NO7594
Crosston *Angus* 127 NO5256
Crossway *Mons* 34 SO4419
Crossway *Pembks* 31 SN1542
Crossway *Powys* 45 SO0558
Crossway Green *H & W* 47 SO8468
Crossway Green *Mons* 34 ST5294
Crosswell *Pembks* 31 SN1236
Crosthwaite *Cumb* 87 SD4391
Croston *Lancs* 80 SD4818
Crostwick *Norfk* 67 TG2515
Crostwight *Norfk* 67 TG3429
Crouch *Kent* 28 TR0558
Crouch *Kent* 27 TQ6155
Crouch End *Gt Lon* 27 TQ3088
Crouch Hill *Dorset* 11 ST7010
Croucheston *Wilts* 23 SU0625
Crough House Green *Kent* 16 TQ4346
Croughton *Nhants* 49 SP5433
Crovie *Abers* 143 NJ8065
Crow *Hants* 12 SU1604
Crow Edge *S York* 82 SE1804
Crow End *Cambs* 52 TL3257
Crow Green *Essex* 27 TQ5796
Crow Hill *H & W* 47 SO6326
Crow's Green *Essex* 40 TL6926
Crow's Nest *Cnwll* 5 SX2669
Crowan *Cnwll* 2 SW6434
Crowborough *E Susx* 16 TQ5131
Crowborough Town *E Susx* 16 TQ5031
Crowcombe *Somset* 20 ST1436
Crowdecote *Derbys* 74 SK1065
Crowden *Derbys* 74 SK0699
Crowden *Devon* 18 SX4999
Crowdhill *Hants* 13 SU4920
Crowdleham *Kent* 27 TQ5659
Crowell *Oxon* 37 SU7499
Crowfield *Nhants* 49 SP6141
Crowfield *Suffk* 54 TM1457
Crowfield Green *Suffk* 54 TM1458
Crowgate Street *Norfk* 67 TG3121
Crowhill *E Loth* 119 NT7374
Crowhole *Derbys* 74 SK3375
Crowhurst *E Susx* 17 TQ7512
Crowhurst *Surrey* 15 TQ3847
Crowhurst Lane End *Surrey* 15 TQ3747
Crowland *Lincs* 64 TF2410
Crowland *Suffk* 54 TM0170
Crowlas *Cnwll* 2 SW5133
Crowle *H & W* 47 SO9256
Crowle *Lincs* 84 SE7712
Crowle Green *H & W* 47 SO9156
Crowmarsh Gifford *Oxon* 37 SU6189
Crown Corner *Suffk* 55 TM2570
Crownhill *Devon* 6 SX4858
Crownpits *Surrey* 25 SU9743
Crownthorpe *Norfk* 66 TG0803
Crowntown *Cnwll* 2 SW6330
Crows-an-Wra *Cnwll* 2 SW3927
Crowshill *Norfk* 66 TF9506
Crowsnest *Shrops* 59 SJ3601
Crowthorne *Berks* 25 SU8464
Crowton *Ches* 71 SJ5774
Croxall *Staffs* 61 SK1913
Croxby *Lincs* 76 TF1898
Croxdale *Dur* 96 NZ2636
Croxden *Staffs* 73 SK0639
Croxley Green *Herts* 26 TQ0795
Croxton *Cambs* 52 TL2460
Croxton *Lincs* 85 TA0912
Croxton *Norfk* 66 TF9831
Croxton *Norfk* 54 TL8786
Croxton *Staffs* 72 SJ7832
Croxton Green *Ches* 71 SJ5552
Croxton Kerrial *Leics* 63 SK8329
Croxtonbank *Staffs* 72 SJ7832
Croy *Highld* 140 NH7949
Croy *N Lans* 116 NS7275
Croyde *Devon* 18 SS4439
Croyde Bay *Devon* 18 SS4339
Croydon *Cambs* 52 TL3149
Croydon *Gt Lon* 27 TQ3265
Crubenmore *Highld* 132 NN6790
Cruckmeole *Shrops* 59 SJ4309
Cruckton *Shrops* 59 SJ4310
Cruden Bay *Abers* 143 NK0836
Crudgington *Shrops* 59 SJ6318
Crudwell *Wilts* 35 ST9593
Crug *Powys* 45 SO1972
Crug-y-byddar *Powys* 58 SO1682
Crugmeer *Cnwll* 4 SW9076
Crugybar *Carmth* 44 SN6537
Crumlin *Caerph* 33 ST2197
Crumplehorn *Cnwll* 5 SX2051
Crumpsall *Gt Man* 79 SD8402
Crundale *Kent* 29 TR0749
Crundale *Pembks* 30 SM9718
Crunwear *Pembks* 31 SN1810
Cruwys Morchard *Devon* 19 SS8712
Crux Easton *Hants* 24 SU4256
Cruxton *Dorset* 10 SY6096
Crwbin *Carmth* 32 SN4713
Cryers Hill *Bucks* 26 SU8796
Crymmych *Pembks* 31 SN1834
Crynant *Neath* 32 SN7904
Crystal Palace *Gt Lon* 27 TQ3371
Cuaig *Highld* 137 NG7057
Cuan Ferry Village *Ag & B* 122 NM7514
Cubbington *Warwks* 48 SP3468
Cubert *Cnwll* 4 SW7857
Cubley *S York* 82 SE2401
Cublington *Bucks* 38 SP8422
Cublington *H & W* 46 SO4038
Cuckfield *W Susx* 15 TQ3025
Cucklington *Somset* 22 ST7527
Cuckney *Notts* 75 SK5671
Cuckold's Green *Kent* 28 TQ8276
Cuckoo Bridge *Lincs* 64 TF2020
Cuckoo's Corner *Hants* 24 SU7441
Cuckoo's Nest *Ches* 71 SJ3860
Cuddesdon *Oxon* 37 SP5903
Cuddington *Bucks* 37 SP7311
Cuddington *Ches* 71 SJ5971
Cuddington Heath *Ches* 71 SJ4746
Cuddy Hill *Lancs* 80 SD4937
Cudham *Gt Lon* 27 TQ4459
Cudliptown *Devon* 5 SX5279
Cudnell *Dorset* 12 SZ0696
Cudworth *S York* 83 SE3808
Cudworth *Somset* 10 ST3810
Cudworth Common *S York* 83 SE4007
Cuerden Green *Lancs* 81 SD5525
Cuerdley Cross *Ches* 78 SJ5486
Cufaude *Hants* 24 SU6557
Cuffley *Herts* 39 TL3003
Cuil *Highld* 122 NM9855
Culbokie *Highld* 140 NH6059
Culbone *Somset* 19 SS8448
Culburnie *Highld* 139 NH4941
Culcabock *Highld* 140 NH6844
Culcharry *Highld* 140 NH8650
Culcheth *Ches* 79 SJ6694
Culdrain *Abers* 142 NJ5134
Culford *Suffk* 54 TL8370
Culgaith *Cumb* 94 NY6029
Culham *Oxon* 37 SU5095
Culkein *Highld* 148 NC0333
Culkein Drumbeg *Highld* 148 NC1133
Culkerton *Gloucs* 35 ST9395
Cullen *Moray* 142 NJ5167
Cullercoats *T & W* 103 NZ3570
Cullerlie *Abers* 135 NJ7603
Cullicudden *Highld* 140 NH6463
Cullingworth *W York* 82 SE0636
Cullipool *Ag & B* 122 NM7413
Cullivoe *Shet* 155 HP5402
Culloden *Highld* 140 NH7246
Cullompton *Devon* 9 ST0207
Culm Davy *Devon* 9 ST1215
Culmington *Shrops* 59 SO4982
Culmstock *Devon* 9 ST1013
Culnacraig *Highld* 145 NC0603
Culnaightrie *D & G* 92 NX7750
Culnaknock *Highld* 137 NG5162
Culpho *Suffk* 55 TM2149
Culrain *Highld* 146 NH5794
Culross *Fife* 117 NS9886
Culroy *S Ayrs* 106 NS3114
Culsalmond *Abers* 142 NJ6532
Culscadden *D & G* 99 NX4748
Culshabbin *D & G* 98 NX3051
Culswick *Shet* 155 HU2745
Cultercullen *Abers* 143 NJ9223
Cults *Aber C* 135 NJ8903
Culverstone Green *Kent* 27 TQ6362
Culverthorpe *Lincs* 64 TF0240
Culworth *Nhants* 49 SP5446
Cum brwyno *Cardgn* 43 SN7180
Cumbernauld *N Lans* 116 NS7674
Cumbernauld Village *N Lans* 116 NS7676
Cumberworth *Lincs* 77 TF5073
Cumdivock *Cumb* 93 NY3448
Cuminestown *Abers* 143 NJ8050
Cumledge *Border* 119 NT7956
Cummersdale *Cumb* 93 NY3953
Cummertrees *D & G* 100 NY1366
Cummingston *Moray* 141 NJ1368
Cumnock *E Ayrs* 107 NS5620
Cumnor *Oxon* 37 SP4504
Cumrew *Cumb* 94 NY5550
Cumwhinton *Cumb* 93 NY4552
Cumwhitton *Cumb* 94 NY5052
Cundall *N York* 89 SE4272
Cunninghamhead *N Ayrs* 106 NS3741
Cupar *Fife* 126 NO3714
Cupar Muir *Fife* 126 NO3613
Cupernham *Hants* 23 SU3622
Curbar *Derbys* 74 SK2574
Curbridge *Hants* 13 SU5211
Curbridge *Oxon* 36 SP3308
Curdridge *Hants* 13 SU5213
Curdworth *Warwks* 61 SP1792
Curland *Somset* 10 ST2717
Curridge *Berks* 24 SU4972
Currie *C Edin* 117 NT1867
Curry Mallet *Somset* 21 ST3221
Curry Rivel *Somset* 21 ST3925
Curteis Corner *Kent* 28 TQ8539
Curtisden Green *Kent* 28 TQ7440
Curtisknowle *Devon* 7 SX7353
Cury *Cnwll* 2 SW6721
Cusgarne *Cnwll* 3 SW7540
Cushnie *Abers* 134 NJ5211
Cushuish *Somset* 20 ST1930
Cusop *H & W* 46 SO2441
Cutcloy *D & G* 99 NX4534
Cutcombe *Somset* 20 SS9339
Cutgate *Gt Man* 81 SD8614
Cuthill *Highld* 147 NH7587
Cutiau *Gwynd* 57 SH6317
Cutler's Green *Essex* 40 TL5930
Cutmadoc *Cnwll* 4 SX0963
Cutmere *Cnwll* 5 SX3260
Cutnall Green *H & W* 47 SO8868
Cutsdean *Gloucs* 48 SP0830
Cutsyke *W York* 83 SE4224
Cutthorpe *Derbys* 74 SK3473
Cuxham *Oxon* 37 SU6695
Cuxton *Kent* 28 TQ7066
Cuxwold *Lincs* 85 TA1701
Cwm *Blae G* 33 SO1805
Cwm *Denbgs* 70 SJ0677
Cwm Capel *Carmth* 32 SN4502
Cwm Dulais *Swans* 32 SN6103
Cwm Irfon *Powys* 45 SN8549
Cwm Morgan *Carmth* 31 SN2934
Cwm Penmachno *A & C* 69 SH7547
Cwm-bach *Carmth* 32 SN4801
Cwm-celyn *Blae G* 33 SO2008
Cwm-Cewydd *Gwynd* 57 SH8713
Cwm-cou *Cardgn* 31 SN2942
Cwm-Crownon *Powys* 33 SO1419
Cwm-Ifor *Carmth* 44 SN6625
Cwm-Llinau *Powys* 57 SH8408
Cwm-y-glo *Carmth* 32 SN5513
Cwm-y-glo *Gwynd* 69 SH5562
Cwmafan *Neath* 32 SS7791
Cwmaman *Rhondd* 33 ST0099
Cwmann *Carmth* 44 SN5847
Cwmavon *Torfn* 34 SO2706
Cwmbach *Carmth* 31 SN2526
Cwmbach *Powys* 45 SO1639
Cwmbach *Rhondd* 33 SO0201
Cwmbach Llechrhyd *Powys* 45 SO0254
Cwmbelan *Powys* 58 SN9481
Cwmbran *Torfn* 34 ST2994
Cwmcarn *Caerph* 34 ST2293
Cwmcarvan *Mons* 34 SO4707
Cwmdare *Rhondd* 33 SN9803
Cwmdu *Carmth* 44 SN6330
Cwmdu *Powys* 45 SO1823
Cwmdu *Swans* 32 SS6494
Cwmduad *Carmth* 31 SN3731
Cwmdwr *Carmth* 44 SN7132
Cwmergyr *Cardgn* 43 SN7982
Cwmfelin *Brdgnd* 33 SS8589
Cwmfelin *Myr Td* 33 SO0901
Cwmfelin Boeth *Carmth* 31 SN1919
Cwmfelin Mynach *Carmth* 31 SN2224
Cwmfelinfach *Caerph* 33 ST1891
Cwmffrwd *Carmth* 31 SN4217
Cwmgiedd *Powys* 32 SN7911
Cwmgorse *Carmth* 32 SN7010
Cwmgwili *Carmth* 32 SN5710
Cwmgwrach *Neath* 33 SN8604
Cwmhiraeth *Carmth* 31 SN3437
Cwmisfael *Carmth* 32 SN4915
Cwmllynfell *Neath* 32 SN7412
Cwmparc *Rhondd* 33 SS9495
Cwmpengraig *Carmth* 31 SN3536
Cwmpennar *Rhondd* 33 SO0300
Cwmrhos *Powys* 45 SO1824
Cwmrhydyceirw *Swans* 32 SS6699
Cwmsychbant *Cardgn* 44 SN4746
Cwmtillery *Blae G* 33 SO2105
Cwmyoy *Mons* 46 SO2923
Cwmystwyth *Cardgn* 43 SN7874
Cwrt *Gwynd* 32 SN6800
Cwrt-newydd *Cardgn* 44 SN4947
Cwrt-y-gollen *Powys* 34 SO2317
Cyfronydd *Powys* 58 SJ1408
Cylibebyll *Neath* 32 SN7404
Cymer *Neath* 33 SS8695
Cymmer *Rhondd* 33 ST0290
Cynghordy *Carmth* 44 SN8040
Cynheidre *Carmth* 32 SN4907
Cynonville *Neath* 33 SS8395
Cynwyd *Denbgs* 70 SJ0541
Cynwyl Elfed *Carmth* 31 SN3727

D

Daccombe *Devon* 7 SX9068
Dacre *Cumb* 93 NY4526
Dacre *N York* 89 SE1960
Dacre Banks *N York* 89 SE1962
Daddry Shield *Dur* 95 NY8937
Dadford *Bucks* 49 SP6638
Dadlington *Leics* 61 SP4097
Dafen *Carmth* 32 SN5201
Daffy Green *Norfk* 66 TF9609
Dagenham *Gt Lon* 27 TQ5084
Daglingworth *Gloucs* 35 SO9905
Dagnall *Bucks* 38 SP9916
Dagworth *Suffk* 54 TM0361
Dailly *S Ayrs* 106 NS2701
Dainton *Devon* 7 SX8566
Dairsie *Fife* 126 NO4117
Daisy Hill *Gt Man* 79 SD6504
Daisy Hill *W York* 82 SE2728
Dalabrog *W Isls* 154 NF7521
Dalavich *Ag & B* 122 NM9612
Dalbeattie *D & G* 100 NX8361
Dalbury *Derbys* 73 SK2634
Dalby *IOM* 153 SC2178
Dalby *Lincs* 77 TF4169
Dalby *N York* 90 SE6371
Dalcapon *P & K* 125 NN9754
Dalchalm *Highld* 147 NC9105
Dalchreichart *Highld* 131 NH2812
Dalchruin *P & K* 124 NN7116
Dalcrue *P & K* 125 NO0427
Dalderby *Lincs* 77 TF2565
Daldtich *Devon* 9 SY0483
Dale *Cumb* 94 NY5443
Dale *Derbys* 62 SK4338
Dale *Pembks* 30 SM8005
Dale Bottom *Cumb* 93 NY2921
Dale End *Derbys* 74 SK2161
Dale End *N York* 82 SD9645
Dale Hill *E Susx* 16 TQ7030
Dalehouse *N York* 97 NZ7717
Dalgarven *N Ayrs* 115 NS2846
Dalgety Bay *Fife* 117 NT1683
Dalgig *E Ayrs* 107 NS5512
Dalginross *P & K* 124 NN7721
Dalguise *P & K* 125 NN9847
Dalhalvaig *Highld* 150 NC8954
Dalham *Suffk* 53 TL7261
Daliburgh *W Isls* 154 NF7521
Dalkeith *Mdloth* 118 NT3367
Dallas *Moray* 141 NJ1252
Dallinghoo *Suffk* 55 TM2655
Dallington *E Susx* 16 TQ6519
Dallington *Nhants* 49 SP7362
Dallow *N York* 89 SE1971
Dalmally *Ag & B* 123 NN1627
Dalmary *Stirlg* 115 NS5195
Dalmellington *E Ayrs* 107 NS4705
Dalmeny *C Edin* 117 NT1477
Dalmigavie *Highld* 140 NH7319
Dalmigavie Lodge *Highld* 140 NH7523
Dalmore *Highld* 140 NH6668
Dalmuir *D & Cb* 115 NS4871
Dalnabreck *Highld* 129 NM7069
Dalnacardoch *P & K* 132 NN7270
Dalnahaitnach *Highld* 140 NH8519
Dalnaspidal *P & K* 132 NN6473
Dalnawillan Lodge *Highld* 150 ND0340
Daloist *P & K* 124 NN7857
Dalquhairn *S Ayrs* 106 NX3296
Dalreavoch Lodge *Highld* 147 NC7508
Dalry *N Ayrs* 115 NS2949
Dalrymple *E Ayrs* 106 NS3514
Dalserf *S Lans* 116 NS7950
Dalsmeran *Ag & B* 104 NR6413
Dalston *Cumb* 93 NY3650
Dalston *Gt Lon* 27 TQ3384
Dalswinton *D & G* 100 NX9385
Dalton *Cumb* 87 SD5476
Dalton *D & G* 100 NY1173
Dalton *Lancs* 78 SD4908
Dalton *N York* 89 NZ1108
Dalton *N York* 89 SE4376
Dalton *Nthumb* 103 NZ1172
Dalton *S York* 75 SK4594
Dalton Magna *S York* 75 SK4692
Dalton Parva *S York* 75 SK4593
Dalton Piercy *Dur* 97 NZ4631
Dalton-in-Furness *Cumb* 86 SD2274
Dalton-le-Dale *Dur* 96 NZ4048
Dalton-on-Tees *N York* 89 NZ2907
Dalveen *D & G* 108 NS8806
Dalveich *Stirlg* 124 NN6124
Dalwhinnie *Highld* 132 NN6384
Dalwood *Devon* 9 ST2400
Dam Green *Norfk* 54 TM0485
Damask Green *Herts* 39 TL2529
Damerham *Hants* 12 SU1016
Damgate *Norfk* 67 TG4009
Dan's Castle *Dur* 95 NZ1139
Dan-y-Parc *Powys* 34 SO2217
Danaway *Kent* 28 TQ8663
Danbury *Essex* 40 TL7805
Danby *N York* 90 NZ7008
Danby Bottom *N York* 90 NZ6904
Danby Wiske *N York* 89 SE3398
Dandaleith *Moray* 141 NJ2846
Danderhall *Mdloth* 117 NT3069
Dane End *Herts* 39 TL3321
Dane Hills *Leics* 62 SK5604
Dane Street *Kent* 28 TR0552
Danebridge *Ches* 72 SJ9665
Danegate *E Susx* 16 TQ5633
Danehill *E Susx* 15 TQ4027
Danemoor Green *Norfk* 66 TG0505
Danesford *Shrops* 60 SO7391
Danesmoor *Derbys* 74 SK4063
Daniel's Water *Kent* 28 TQ9541
Danshillock *Abers* 142 NJ7157
Danskine *E Loth* 118 NT5667
Danthorpe *E R Yk* 85 TA2532
Danzey Green *Warwks* 48 SP1269
Dapple Heath *Staffs* 73 SK0425
Darby Green *Hants* 25 SU8360
Darcy Lever *Gt Man* 79 SD7308
Daren-felen *Mons* 34 SO2212
Darenth *Kent* 27 TQ5671
Daresbury *Ches* 78 SJ5882
Darfield *S York* 83 SE4104
Dargate *Kent* 29 TR0861
Darite *Cnwll* 5 SX2569
Darland *Kent* 28 TQ7865
Darland *Wrexhm* 71 SJ3757
Darlaston *Staffs* 72 SJ8835
Darlaston *W Mids* 60 SO9796
Darlaston Green *W Mids* 60 SO9797
Darley *N York* 89 SE2059
Darley Abbey *Derbys* 62 SK3538
Darley Bridge *Derbys* 74 SK2661
Darley Dale *Derbys* 74 SK2663
Darley Green *Warwks* 61 SP1874
Darley Head *N York* 89 SE1959
Darleyhall *Herts* 38 TL1422
Darlingscott *Warwks* 48 SP2342
Darlington *Dur* 89 NZ2814
Darliston *Shrops* 59 SJ5733
Darlton *Notts* 75 SK7773
Darnford *Staffs* 61 SK1308
Darnick *Border* 109 NT5334
Darowen *Powys* 57 SH8201
Darra *Abers* 142 NJ7447
Darracott *Cnwll* 18 SS2811
Darracott *Devon* 18 SS2317
Darracott *Devon* 18 SS4739
Darras Hall *Nthumb* 103 NZ1570
Darrington *W York* 83 SE4820
Darsham *Suffk* 55 TM4169
Darshill *Somset* 21 ST6144
Dartford *Kent* 27 TQ5474
Dartington *Devon* 7 SX7862
Dartmeet *Devon* 7 SX6773
Dartmouth *Devon* 7 SX8751
Darton *S York* 82 SE3110
Darvel *E Ayrs* 107 NS5637
Darwell Hole *E Susx* 16 TQ6919
Darwen *Lancs* 81 SD6922
Datchet *Berks* 26 SU9877
Datchworth *Herts* 39 TL2619
Datchworth Green *Herts* 39 TL2718
Daubhill *Gt Man* 79 SD7007
Dauntsey *Wilts* 35 ST9782
Dauntsey Green *Wilts* 35 ST9981
Dava *Highld* 141 NJ0038
Davenham *Ches* 79 SJ6571
Davenport *Gt Man* 79 SJ9088
Davenport Green *Ches* 79 SJ8379
Davenport Green *Gt Man* 79 SJ8086
Daventry *Nhants* 49 SP5762
David Street *Kent* 27 TQ6464
Davidson's Mains *C Edin* 117 NT2175
Davidstow *Cnwll* 4 SX1587
Davington *D & G* 109 NT2302
Davington Hill *Kent* 28 TR0161
Daviot *Abers* 142 NJ7428
Daviot *Highld* 140 NH7239
Daviot House *Highld* 140 NH7240
Davis's Town *E Susx* 16 TQ5217
Davoch of Grange *Moray* 142 NJ4751
Davyhulme *Gt Man* 79 SJ7595
Daw End *W Mids* 61 SK0300
Daw's House *Cnwll* 5 SX3182
Dawesgreen *Surrey* 15 TQ2147
Dawley *Shrops* 60 SJ6808
Dawlish *Devon* 9 SX9576
Dawlish Warren *Devon* 9 SX9778
Dawn *A & C* 69 SH8672
Daws Green *Somset* 20 ST1921
Daws Heath *Essex* 40 TQ8188
Dawsmere *Lincs* 65 TF4430
Day Green *Ches* 72 SJ7757
Daybrook *Notts* 62 SK5744

Dayhills Drumelzier

Dayhills Staffs	72	SJ9532
Dayhouse Bank H & W	60	SO9678
Daylesford Gloucs	48	SP2425
Ddol Flints	70	SJ1471
Ddol-Cownwy Powys	58	SJ0117
Deal Kent	29	TR3752
Dean Cumb	92	NY0725
Dean Devon	19	SS6245
Dean Devon	19	SS7048
Dean Devon	7	SX7364
Dean Dorset	11	ST9715
Dean Hants	24	SU4431
Dean Hants	13	SU5619
Dean Lancs	81	SD8525
Dean Oxon	36	SP3422
Dean Somset	22	ST6743
Dean Bottom Kent	27	TQ5868
Dean Court Oxon	37	SP4705
Dean End Dorset	11	ST9717
Dean Head S York	74	SE2600
Dean Prior Devon	7	SX7363
Dean Row Ches	79	SJ8781
Dean Street Kent	28	TQ7453
Deanburnhaugh Border	109	NT3911
Deancombe Devon	7	SX7264
Deane Gt Man	79	SD6907
Deane Hants	24	SU5450
Deanhead W York	82	SE0415
Deanland Dorset	22	ST9918
Deanlane End W Susx	13	SU7412
Deanraw Nthumb	102	NY8162
Deans W Loth	117	NT0369
Deanscales Cumb	92	NY0926
Deanshanger Nhants	49	SP7639
Deanshaugh Moray	141	NJ3550
Deanston Stirlg	116	NN7101
Dearham Cumb	92	NY0736
Dearnley Gt Man	81	SD9215
Debach Suffk	55	TM2454
Debden Essex	53	TL5533
Debden Essex	27	TQ4496
Debden Green Essex	40	TL5831
Debenham Suffk	54	TM1763
Deblin's Green H & W	47	SO8148
Dechmont W Loth	117	NT0370
Dechmont Road W Loth	117	NT0269
Deddington Oxon	49	SP4631
Dedham Essex	41	TM0533
Dedham Heath Essex	41	TM0531
Dedworth Berks	26	SU9476
Deene Nhants	51	SP9492
Deenethorpe Nhants	51	SP9591
Deepcar S York	74	SK2897
Deepcut Surrey	25	SU9057
Deepdale Cumb	88	SD7184
Deepdale N York	88	SD8979
Deeping Gate Lincs	64	TF1509
Deeping St James Lincs	64	TF1609
Deeping St Nicholas Lincs	64	TF2115
Deerhurst Gloucs	47	SO8730
Deerhurst Walton Gloucs	47	SO8828
Deerton Street Kent	28	TQ9762
Defford H & W	47	SO9143
Defynnog Powys	45	SN9227
Deganwy A & C	69	SH7779
Degnish Ag & B	122	NM7812
Deighton N York	89	NZ3801
Deighton N York	83	SE6244
Deighton W York	82	SE1519
Deiniolen Gwynd	69	SH5763
Delabole Cnwll	4	SX0683
Delamere Ches	71	SJ5668
Delfrigs Abers	143	NJ9620
Dell Quay W Susx	14	SU8302
Delley Devon	19	SS5424
Delliefure Highld	141	NJ0730
Delly End Oxon	36	SP3513
Delmonden Green Kent	17	TQ7330
Delnashaugh Inn Moray	141	NJ1835
Delny Highld	146	NH7372
Delph Gt Man	82	SD9807
Delves Dur	95	NZ1149
Delvine P & K	126	NO1240
Dembleby Lincs	64	TF0437
Demelza Cnwll	4	SW9763
Denaby S York	75	SK4899
Denaby Main S York	75	SK4999
Denbies Surrey	26	TQ1450
Denbigh Denbgs	70	SJ0566
Denbrae Fife	126	NO3818
Denbury Devon	7	SX8268
Denby Derbys	62	SK3946
Denby Bottles Derbys	62	SK3846
Denby Dale W York	82	SE2208
Denchworth Oxon	36	SU3891
Dendron Cumb	86	SD2470
Denel End Beds	38	TL0335
Denfield P & K	125	NN9517
Denford Nhants	51	SP9976
Dengie Essex	41	TL9802
Denham Bucks	26	TQ0487
Denham Suffk	53	TL7561
Denham Suffk	55	TM1974
Denham End Suffk	53	TL7663
Denham Green Bucks	26	TQ0488
Denham Green Suffk	55	TM1974
Denhead Abers	143	NJ9952
Denhead Fife	127	NO4613
Denhead of Gray Dund C	126	NO3531
Denholm Border	110	NT5718
Denholme W York	82	SE0734
Denholme Clough W York	82	SE0732
Denio Gwynd	56	SH3635
Denmead Hants	13	SU6512
Denmore Aber C	135	NJ9411
Denne Park W Susx	15	TQ1628
Dennington Suffk	55	TM2867
Denny Falk	116	NS8082
Dennyloanhead Falk	116	NS8080
Denshaw Gt Man	82	SD9710
Denside Abers	135	NO8095
Densole Kent	29	TR2141
Denston Suffk	53	TL7652
Denstone Staffs	73	SK0940
Denstroude Kent	29	TR1061
Dent Cumb	87	SD7086
Dent-de-Lion Kent	29	TR3269
Denton Cambs	52	TL1587
Denton Dur	96	NZ2118
Denton E Susx	16	TQ4502
Denton Gt Man	79	SJ9295
Denton Kent	28	TQ6673
Denton Kent	29	TR2147
Denton Lincs	63	SK8632
Denton N York	82	SE1448
Denton Nhants	51	SP8358
Denton Norfk	55	TM2788
Denton Oxon	37	SP5902
Denver Norfk	65	TF6001
Denwick Nthumb	111	NU2014
Deopham Norfk	66	TG0400
Deopham Green Norfk	66	TM0499
Depden Suffk	53	TL7857
Depden Green Suffk	53	TL7756
Deptford Gt Lon	27	TQ3777
Deptford Wilts	22	SU0138
Derby Derbys	62	SK3536
Derby Devon	19	SS5633
Derbyhaven IOM	153	SC2867
Derculich P & K	125	NN8852
Deri Caerph	33	SO1201
Derril Devon	18	SS3003
Derringstone Kent	29	TR2049
Derrington Staffs	72	SJ8922
Derriton Devon	18	SS3303
Derry Hill Wilts	35	ST9670
Derrythorpe Lincs	84	SE8208
Dersingham Norfk	65	TF6830
Dervaig Ag & B	121	NM4352
Derwen Denbgs	70	SJ0750
Derwen Fawr Carmth	44	SN5722
Derwenlas Powys	57	SN7298
Derwydd Carmth	32	SN6117
Desborough Nhants	51	SP8083
Desford Leics	62	SK4703
Deskford Moray	142	NJ5061
Detchant Nthumb	111	NU0836
Detling Kent	28	TQ7958
Deuxhill Shrops	60	SO6987
Devauden Mons	34	ST4898
Devil's Bridge Cardgn	43	SN7376
Deviock Cnwll	5	SX3155
Devitts Green Warwks	61	SP2790
Devizes Wilts	22	SU0061
Devonport Devon	6	SX4554
Devonside Clacks	116	NS9196
Devoran Cnwll	3	SW7939
Dewarton Mdloth	118	NT3763
Dewlish Dorset	11	SY7798
Dewsbury W York	82	SE2421
Dewsbury Moor W York	82	SE2321
Deytheur Powys	58	SJ2317
Dial Somset	21	ST5366
Dial Green W Susx	14	SU9227
Dial Post W Susx	15	TQ1519
Dibberford Dorset	10	ST4504
Dibden Hants	13	SU4008
Dibden Purlieu Hants	13	SU4106
Dickens Heath W Mids	61	SP1176
Dickleburgh Norfk	54	TM1682
Didbrook Gloucs	48	SP0531
Didcot Oxon	37	SU5290
Diddington Cambs	52	TL1965
Diddlebury Shrops	59	SO5085
Didley H & W	46	SO4532
Didling W Susx	14	SU8318
Didmarton Gloucs	35	ST8287
Didsbury Gt Man	79	SJ8491
Didworthy Devon	7	SX6862
Digby Lincs	76	TF0854
Digg Highld	136	NG4668
Diggle Gt Man	82	SE0007
Digmoor Lancs	78	SD4905
Digswell Herts	39	TL2415
Digswell Water Herts	39	TL2514
Dihewyd Cardgn	44	SN4855
Dilham Norfk	67	TG3325
Dilhorne Staffs	72	SJ9743
Dillington Cambs	52	TL1365
Dilston Nthumb	102	NY9763
Dilton Wilts	22	ST8548
Dilton Marsh Wilts	22	ST8449
Dilwyn H & W	46	SO4154
Dimple Derbys	74	SK2960
Dimple Gt Man	81	SD7015
Dinas Carmth	31	SN2730
Dinas Cnwll	4	SW9274
Dinas Gwynd	56	SH2735
Dinas Pembks	30	SN0138
Dinas Rhondd	33	ST0091
Dinas Dinlle Gwynd	68	SH4356
Dinas Powys V Glam	33	ST1571
Dinas-Mawddwy Gwynd	57	SH8515
Dinder Somset	21	ST5744
Dinedor H & W	46	SO5336
Dingestow Mons	34	SO4510
Dingle Mersyd	78	SJ3687
Dingleden Kent	17	TQ8131
Dingley Nhants	50	SP7787
Dingwall Highld	139	NH5458
Dinham Mons	34	ST4792
Dinmael A & C	70	SJ0044
Dinnet Abers	134	NO4598
Dinnington S York	75	SK5285
Dinnington Somset	10	ST4012
Dinnington T & W	103	NZ2073
Dinorwic Gwynd	69	SH5961
Dinton Bucks	37	SP7610
Dinton Wilts	22	SU0131
Dinwoodie D & G	100	NY1190
Dinworthy Devon	18	SS3015
Dipford Somset	20	ST2021
Dipley Hants	24	SU7457
Dippen Ag & B	105	NR7937
Dippen N Ayrs	105	NS0422
Dippenhall Surrey	25	SU8146
Dippermill Devon	18	SS4406
Dippertown Devon	5	SX4284
Dipple Moray	141	NJ3258
Dipple S Ayrs	106	NS2002
Diptford Devon	7	SX7256
Dipton Dur	96	NZ1554
Diptonmill Nthumb	102	NY9361
Dirleton E Loth	118	NT5184
Dirt Pot Nthumb	95	NY8545
Discoed Powys	46	SO2764
Diseworth Leics	62	SK4524
Dishforth N York	89	SE3873
Disley Ches	79	SJ9784
Diss Norfk	54	TM1180
Disserth Powys	45	SO0358
Distington Cumb	92	NY0023
Ditchampton Wilts	23	SU0831
Ditchburn Nthumb	111	NU1320
Ditcheat Somset	21	ST6236
Ditchingham Norfk	67	TM3391
Ditchley Oxon	36	SP3820
Ditchling E Susx	15	TQ3215
Ditherington Shrops	59	SJ5014
Ditteridge Wilts	35	ST8169
Dittisham Devon	7	SX8655
Ditton Ches	78	SJ4986
Ditton Kent	28	TQ7158
Ditton Green Cambs	53	TL6558
Ditton Priors Shrops	59	SO6089
Dixton Gloucs	47	SO9830
Dixton Mons	34	SO5113
Dizzard Cnwll	4	SX1698
Dobcross Gt Man	82	SD9906
Dobroyd Castle W York	81	SD9323
Dobwalls Cnwll	5	SX2165
Doccombe Devon	8	SX7786
Dochgarroch Highld	140	NH6140
Dockenfield Surrey	25	SU8240
Docker Lancs	87	SD5774
Docking Norfk	65	TF7636
Docklow H & W	46	SO5657
Dockray Cumb	93	NY2649
Dockray Cumb	93	NY3921
Dod's Leigh Staffs	73	SK0134
Dodbrooke Devon	7	SX7444
Dodd's Green Ches	71	SJ6043
Doddinghurst Essex	27	TQ5999
Doddington Cambs	52	TL4090
Doddington Kent	28	TQ9357
Doddington Lincs	76	SK8970
Doddington Nthumb	111	NT9932
Doddington Shrops	46	SO6176
Doddiscombsleigh Devon	8	SX8586
Doddshill Norfk	65	TF6930
Doddy Cross Cnwll	5	SX3062
Dodford H & W	60	SO9373
Dodford Nhants	49	SP6160
Dodington Gloucs	35	ST7580
Dodington Somset	20	ST1740
Dodleston Ches	71	SJ3661
Dodscott Devon	19	SS5419
Dodside E Rens	115	NS5053
Dodworth S York	82	SE3105
Dodworth Bottom S York	83	SE3204
Dodworth Green S York	82	SE3004
Doe Bank W Mids	61	SP1197
Doe Lea Derbys	75	SK4666
Dog Village Devon	9	SX9896
Dogdyke Lincs	76	TF2055
Dogley Lane W York	82	SE1813
Dogmersfield Hants	25	SU7852
Dogridge Wilts	36	SU0887
Dogsthorpe Cambs	64	TF1901
Dol-for Powys	57	SH8106
Dol-gran Carmth	31	SN4334
Dolanacothi Carmth	44	SN6640
Dolanog Powys	58	SJ0612
Dolau Powys	45	SO1467
Dolbenmaen Gwynd	56	SH5043
Doley Shrops	72	SJ7429
Dolfor Powys	58	SO1087
Dolgarrog A & C	69	SH7767
Dolgellau Gwynd	57	SH7217
Dolgoch Gwynd	57	SH6504
Doll Highld	147	NC8803
Dollar Clacks	117	NS9698
Dollarfield Clacks	117	NS9697
Dolley Green Powys	46	SO2865
Dollwen Cardgn	43	SN6881
Dolphin Flints	70	SJ1973
Dolphinholme Lancs	80	SD5253
Dolphinton S Lans	117	NT1046
Dolton Devon	19	SS5712
Dolwen A & C	69	SH8874
Dolwyddelan A & C	69	SH7352
Dolybont Cardgn	43	SN6288
Dolyhir Powys	46	SO2457
Domgay Powys	58	SJ2818
Donaldson's Lodge Nthumb	110	NT8741
Doncaster S York	83	SE5703
Doncaster Carr S York	83	SE5801
Donehill Devon	8	SX7277
Donhead St Andrew Wilts	22	ST9124
Donhead St Mary Wilts	22	ST9024
Donibristle Fife	117	NT1688
Doniford Somset	20	ST0842
Donington Lincs	64	TF2035
Donington on Bain Lincs	76	TF2382
Donington Southing Lincs	64	TF2034
Donisthorpe Leics	61	SK3113
Donkey Street Kent	17	TR1032
Donkey Town Surrey	25	SU9360
Donnington Berks	24	SU4668
Donnington Gloucs	48	SP1928
Donnington H & W	47	SO7034
Donnington Shrops	59	SJ5708
Donnington Shrops	60	SJ7114
Donnington W Susx	14	SU8501
Donnington Wood Shrops	60	SJ7012
Donyatt Somset	10	ST3314
Doomsday Green W Susx	15	TQ1929
Doonfoot S Ayrs	106	NS3219
Doonholm S Ayrs	106	NS3317
Dorback Lodge Highld	141	NJ0716
Dorchester Dorset	11	SY6990
Dorchester Oxon	37	SU5794
Dordon Warwks	61	SK2500
Dore S York	74	SK3181
Dores Highld	140	NH5934
Dorking Surrey	15	TQ1649
Dorking Tye Suffk	54	TL9236
Dormans Land Surrey	15	TQ4041
Dormans Park Surrey	15	TQ3940
Dormington H & W	46	SO5840
Dormston H & W	47	SO9857
Dorn Gloucs	48	SP2034
Dorney Berks	26	SU9378
Dornie Highld	138	NG8826
Dornoch Highld	147	NH7989
Dornock D & G	101	NY2366
Dorrery Highld	150	ND0754
Dorridge W Mids	61	SP1775
Dorrington Lincs	76	TF0852
Dorrington Shrops	59	SJ4702
Dorrington Shrops	72	SJ7340
Dorsington Warwks	48	SP1349
Dorstone H & W	46	SO3141
Dorton Bucks	37	SP6814
Dosthill Staffs	61	SP2199
Dottery Dorset	10	SY4595
Doublebois Cnwll	5	SX1964
Dougarie N Ayrs	105	NR8837
Doughton Gloucs	35	ST8791
Douglas IOM	153	SC3775
Douglas S Lans	108	NS8330
Douglas and Angus Dund C	127	NO4233
Douglas Castle S Lans	108	NS8431
Douglas Pier Ag & B	114	NS1999
Douglas Water S Lans	108	NS8736
Douglas West S Lans	108	NS8231
Douglastown Angus	126	NO4147
Doulting Somset	21	ST6443
Dounby Ork	155	HY2920
Doune Highld	146	NC4400
Doune Stirlg	116	NN7201
Dounepark S Ayrs	106	NX1897
Dounie Highld	146	NH5690
Dousland Devon	6	SX5369
Dovaston Shrops	59	SJ3521
Dove Green Notts	75	SK4652
Dove Holes Derbys	74	SK0777
Dovenby Cumb	92	NY0933
Dover Gt Man	78	SD6000
Dover Kent	29	TR3241
Dovercourt Essex	41	TM2431
Doverdale H & W	47	SO8666
Doveridge Derbys	73	SK1133
Doversgreen Surrey	15	TQ2548
Dowally P & K	125	NO0048
Dowbridge Lancs	80	SD4331
Dowdeswell Gloucs	35	SP0019
Dowlais Myr Td	33	SO0607
Dowland Devon	19	SS5610
Dowlish Ford Somset	10	ST3513
Dowlish Wake Somset	10	ST3712
Down Ampney Gloucs	36	SU0996
Down Hatherley Gloucs	35	SO8622
Down St Mary Devon	8	SS7404
Down Thomas Devon	6	SX5050
Downacarey Devon	5	SX3790
Downderry Cnwll	5	SX3154
Downe Gt Lon	27	TQ4361
Downend Berks	37	SU4775
Downend Gloucs	35	ST6577
Downend Gloucs	35	ST8398
Downend IOW	13	SZ5387
Downfield Dund C	126	NO3932
Downgate Cnwll	5	SX2871
Downgate Cnwll	5	SX3672
Downham Cambs	53	TL5284
Downham Essex	40	TQ7296
Downham Gt Lon	27	TQ3871
Downham Lancs	81	SD7844
Downham Nthumb	110	NT8633
Downham Market Norfk	65	TF6103
Downhead Somset	21	ST5625
Downhead Somset	22	ST6945
Downhill Cnwll	4	SW8669
Downhill P & K	125	NO0930
Downholland Cross Lancs	78	SD3606
Downholme N York	89	SE1197
Downies Abers	135	NO9294
Downing Flints	70	SJ1578
Downley Bucks	26	SU8495
Downside Somset	21	ST6244
Downside Somset	21	ST6450
Downside Surrey	26	TQ1057
Downton Hants	12	SZ2693
Downton Wilts	12	SU1821
Downton on the Rock H & W	46	SO4273
Dowsby Lincs	64	TF1129
Dowsdale Lincs	64	TF2810
Dowsland Green Essex	40	TL8724
Doxey Staffs	72	SJ8923
Doxford Nthumb	111	NU1823
Doynton Gloucs	35	ST7274
Draethen Caerph	34	ST2287
Draffan S Lans	116	NS7945
Dragonby Lincs	84	SE9014
Dragons Green W Susx	15	TQ1423
Drakeholes Notts	75	SK7090
Drakelow H & W	60	SO8180
Drakemyre N Ayrs	115	NS2950
Drakes Broughton H & W	47	SO9248
Drakes Cross H & W	61	SP0876
Drakewalls Cnwll	6	SX4270
Draughton N York	82	SE0352
Draughton Nhants	50	SP7676
Drax N York	83	SE6726
Drax Hales N York	83	SE6725
Draycot Foliat Wilts	36	SU1777
Draycote Warwks	50	SP4470
Draycott Derbys	62	SK4433
Draycott Gloucs	48	SP1835
Draycott H & W	47	SO8548
Draycott Shrops	60	SO8093
Draycott Somset	21	ST4751
Draycott Somset	21	ST5521
Draycott in the Clay Staffs	73	SK1528
Draycott in the Moors Staffs	72	SJ9840
Drayford Devon	19	SS7813
Draynes Cnwll	5	SX2169
Drayton H & W	60	SO9075
Drayton Hants	13	SU6705
Drayton Leics	51	SP8392
Drayton Lincs	64	TF2439
Drayton Norfk	66	TG1813
Drayton Oxon	49	SP4241
Drayton Oxon	37	SU4894
Drayton Somset	21	ST4024
Drayton Bassett Staffs	61	SK1900
Drayton Beauchamp Bucks	38	SP9011
Drayton Parslow Bucks	38	SP8328
Drayton St Leonard Oxon	37	SU5996
Drebley N York	88	SE0559
Dreemskerry IOM	153	SC4791
Dreen Hill Pembks	30	SM9214
Drefach Cardgn	44	SN4945
Drefach Carmth	31	SN3538
Drefach Carmth	32	SN5213
Drefelin Carmth	31	SN3637
Dreghorn N Ayrs	106	NS3538
Drellingore Kent	29	TR2441
Drem E Loth	118	NT5079
Dresden Staffs	72	SJ9142
Drewsteignton Devon	8	SX7391
Driby Lincs	77	TF3874
Driffield E R Yk	91	TA0257
Driffield Gloucs	36	SU0799
Driffield Cross Roads Gloucs	36	SU0698
Drift Cnwll	2	SW4328
Drigg Cumb	86	SD0699
Drighlington W York	82	SE2228
Drimnin Highld	121	NM5554
Drimpton Dorset	10	ST4104
Drimsallie Highld	130	NM9578
Dringhoe E R Yk	85	TA1454
Dringhouses N York	83	SE5849
Drinkstone Suffk	54	TL9561
Drinkstone Green Suffk	54	TL9660
Drinsey Nook Notts	76	SK8773
Drive End Dorset	10	ST5808
Driver's End Herts	39	TL2220
Drointon Staffs	73	SK0226
Droitwich H & W	47	SO8963
Dron P & K	126	NO1416
Dronfield Derbys	74	SK3578
Dronfield Woodhouse Derbys	74	SK3378
Drongan E Ayrs	107	NS4418
Dronley Angus	126	NO3435
Droop Dorset	11	ST7508
Dropping Well S York	74	SK3994
Droxford Hants	13	SU6018
Droylsden Gt Man	79	SJ9097
Druid Denbgs	70	SJ0443
Druids Heath W Mids	61	SK0502
Druidston Pembks	30	SM8616
Druimachoish Highld	123	NN1246
Druimarbin Highld	130	NN0770
Druimdrishaig Ag & B	113	NR7370
Druimindarroch Highld	129	NM6884
Drum Ag & B	114	NR9276
Drum P & K	117	NO0400
Drumalbin S Lans	108	NS9038
Drumbeg Highld	148	NC1232
Drumblade Abers	142	NJ5840
Drumblair House Abers	142	NJ6343
Drumbreddon D & G	98	NX0843
Drumbuie Highld	137	NG7730
Drumburgh Cumb	93	NY2659
Drumburn D & G	92	NX8854
Drumchapel C Glas	115	NS5270
Drumchastle P & K	132	NN6858
Drumclog S Lans	107	NS6438
Drumeldrie Fife	127	NO4403
Drumelzier Border	108	NT1334

Drumfearn

East Pennar

Drumfearn *Highld* 129 NG6716
Drumfrennie *Abers* 135 NO7298
Drumguish *Highld* 132 NH7900
Drumhead *Abers* 134 NO6092
Drumin *Moray* 141 NJ1830
Drumjohn *D & G* 107 NX5297
Drumlamford *S Ayrs* 98 NX2876
Drumlasie *Abers* 135 NJ6405
Drumleaning *Cumb* 93 NY2751
Drumlemble *Ag & B* 104 NR6619
Drumlithie *Abers* 135 NO7880
Drummoddie *D & G* 99 NX3845
Drummore *D & G* 98 NX1336
Drummore *D & G* 100 NX9074
Drummuir *Moray* 141 NJ3843
Drumnadrochit *Highld* 139 NH5030
Drumnagorrach *Moray* 142 NJ5252
Drumpark *D & G* 100 NX8779
Drumrunie Lodge *Highld* 145 NC1604
Drumshang *S Ayrs* 106 NS2514
Drumuie *Highld* 136 NG4546
Drumuillie *Highld* 140 NH9420
Drumvaich *Stirlg* 124 NN6704
Drunzie *P & K* 126 NO1308
Druridge *Nthumb* 103 NZ2796
Drury *Flints* 71 SJ2964
Dry Doddington *Lincs* 63 SK8546
Dry Drayton *Cambs* 52 TL3861
Dry Sandford *Oxon* 37 SP4600
Dry Street *Essex* 40 TQ6986
Drybeck *Cumb* 94 NY6615
Drybridge *Moray* 142 NJ4362
Drybridge *N Ayrs* 106 NS3536
Drybrook *Gloucs* 35 SO6417
Dryburgh *Border* 110 NT5932
Dryhope *Border* 109 NT2624
Drym *Cnwll* 2 SW6133
Drymen *Stirlg* 115 NS4788
Drymuir *Abers* 143 NJ9046
Drynoch *Highld* 136 NG4031
Dryslwyn *Carmth* 32 SN5520
Dryton *Shrops* 59 SJ5905
Dubford *Abers* 143 NJ7963
Dublin *Suffk* 54 TM1669
Duchally *Highld* 145 NC3817
Duck End *Beds* 38 TL0544
Duck End *Cambs* 52 TL2464
Duck End *Essex* 40 TL6526
Duck's Cross *Beds* 52 TL1156
Duckend Green *Essex* 40 TL7223
Duckington *Ches* 71 SJ4851
Ducklington *Oxon* 36 SP3507
Duddingston *C Edin* 117 NT2872
Duddington *Nhants* 51 SK9800
Duddlestone *Somset* 20 ST2321
Duddleswell *E Susx* 16 TQ4628
Duddlewick *Shrops* 59 SO6583
Duddo *Nthumb* 110 NT9342
Duddon *Ches* 71 SJ5164
Duddon Bridge *Cumb* 86 SD1988
Dudleston *Shrops* 71 SJ3438
Dudleston Heath *Shrops* 59 SJ3736
Dudley *T & W* 103 NZ2573
Dudley *W Mids* 60 SO9490
Dudley Hill *W York* 82 SE1830
Dudley Port *W Mids* 60 SO9691
Dudnill *Shrops* 47 SO6474
Dudsbury *Dorset* 12 SZ0798
Dudswell *Herts* 38 SP9609
Duffield *Derbys* 62 SK3443
Duffryn *Neath* 33 SS8495
Dufftown *Moray* 141 NJ3240
Duffus *Moray* 141 NJ1668
Dufton *Cumb* 94 NY6825
Duggleby *N York* 90 SE8767
Duirinish *Highld* 137 NG7831
Duisdalemore *Highld* 129 NG7013
Duisky *Highld* 130 NN0076
Duke Street *Suffk* 54 TM0742
Dukestown *Blae G* 33 SO1410
Dukinfield *Gt Man* 79 SJ9397
Dulas *Angles* 68 SH4789
Dulcote *Somset* 21 ST5644
Dulford *Devon* 9 ST0706
Dull *P & K* 125 NN8049
Dullatur *N Lans* 116 NS7476
Dullingham *Cambs* 53 TL6357
Dullingham Ley *Cambs* 53 TL6456
Dulnain Bridge *Highld* 141 NH9925
Duloe *Beds* 52 TL1560
Duloe *Cnwll* 5 SX2358
Dulverton *Somset* 20 SS9127
Dulwich *Gt Lon* 27 TQ3373
Dumbarton *D & Cb* 115 NS3975
Dumbleton *Gloucs* 47 SP0135
Dumfries *D & G* 100 NX9776
Dumgoyne *Stirlg* 115 NS5283
Dummer *Hants* 24 SU5846
Dumpton *Kent* 29 TR3966
Dun *Angus* 135 NO6659
Dunalastair *P & K* 132 NN7158
Dunan *Ag & B* 114 NS1571
Dunan *Highld* 137 NG5828
Dunan *P & K* 124 NN4757
Dunaverty *Ag & B* 105 NR6807
Dunball *Somset* 21 ST3141
Dunbar *E Loth* 118 NT6778
Dunbeath *Highld* 151 ND1629
Dunbeg *Ag & B* 122 NM8833
Dunblane *Stirlg* 116 NN7801
Dunbog *Fife* 126 NO2817
Dunbridge *Hants* 23 SU3226
Duncanston *Highld* 139 NH5856
Duncanstone *Abers* 142 NJ5726
Dunchideock *Devon* 9 SX8787
Dunchurch *Warwks* 50 SP4871
Duncote *Nhants* 49 SP6750
Duncow *D & G* 100 NX9683
Duncrievie *P & K* 126 NO1309
Duncton *W Susx* 14 SU9617
Dundee *Dund C* 126 NO4030
Dundon *Somset* 21 ST4832
Dundonald *S Ayrs* 106 NS3634
Dundonnell *Highld* 145 NH0987
Dundraw *Cumb* 93 NY2149
Dundreggan *Highld* 131 NH3214
Dundrennan *D & G* 99 NX7447
Dundry *Somset* 21 ST5666
Dunecht *Abers* 135 NJ7509
Dunfermline *Fife* 117 NT0987
Dunfield *Gloucs* 36 SU1497
Dunford Bridge *S York* 82 SE1502
Dungate *Kent* 28 TQ9159
Dungavel *S Lans* 107 NS6537
Dunge *Wilts* 22 ST8954
Dunglass *E Loth* 119 NT7671
Dungworth *S York* 74 SK2789
Dunham *Notts* 75 SK8074
Dunham Town *Gt Man* 79 SJ7387
Dunham Woodhouses *Gt Man* 79 SJ7287
Dunham-on-the-Hill *Ches* 71 SJ4772
Dunhampstead *H & W* 47 SO9160
Dunhampton *H & W* 47 SO8466
Dunholme *Lincs* 76 TF0279
Dunino *Fife* 127 NO5311
Dunipace *Falk* 116 NS8083
Dunk's Green *Kent* 27 TQ6152
Dunkeld *P & K* 125 NO0242
Dunkerton *Somset* 22 ST7159
Dunkeswell *Devon* 9 ST1407
Dunkeswick *W York* 82 SE3047
Dunkirk *Ches* 71 SJ3872
Dunkirk *Gloucs* 35 ST7885
Dunkirk *Kent* 29 TR0759
Dunkirk *Staffs* 72 SJ8152
Dunkirk *Wilts* 22 ST9962
Dunlappie *Angus* 134 NO5867
Dunley *H & W* 47 SO7869
Dunley *Hants* 24 SU4553
Dunlop *E Ayrs* 115 NS4049
Dunmaglass *Highld* 140 NH5922
Dunmere *Cnwll* 4 SX0467
Dunmore *Ag & B* 113 NR7961
Dunmore *Falk* 116 NS8989
Dunn Street *Kent* 28 TQ7961
Dunnet *Highld* 151 ND2171
Dunnichen *Angus* 127 NO5048
Dunning *P & K* 125 NO0114
Dunnington *E R Yk* 85 TA1551
Dunnington *N York* 83 SE6652
Dunnington *Warwks* 48 SP0654
Dunnockshaw *Lancs* 81 SD8127
Dunoon *Ag & B* 114 NS1776
Dunphail *Moray* 141 NJ0048
Dunragit *D & G* 98 NX1557
Duns *Border* 119 NT7853
Duns Tew *Oxon* 49 SP4528
Dunsa *Derbys* 74 SK2470
Dunsby *Lincs* 64 TF1026
Dunscar *Gt Man* 81 SD7113
Dunscore *D & G* 100 NX8684
Dunscroft *S York* 83 SE6409
Dunsdale *N York* 97 NZ6019
Dunsden Green *Oxon* 37 SU7377
Dunsdon *Devon* 18 SS3008
Dunsfold *Surrey* 14 TQ0035
Dunsford *Devon* 8 SX8189
Dunshelt *Fife* 126 NO2410
Dunshillock *Abers* 143 NJ9848
Dunsill *Notts* 75 SK4661
Dunsley *N York* 90 NZ8511
Dunsley *Staffs* 60 SO8583
Dunsmore *Bucks* 38 SP8605
Dunsop Bridge *Lancs* 81 SD6649
Dunstable *Beds* 38 TL0122
Dunstall *Staffs* 73 SK1820
Dunstall Common *H & W* 47 SO8843
Dunstall Green *Suffk* 53 TL7460
Dunstan *Nthumb* 111 NU2419
Dunstan Steads *Nthumb* 111 NU2422
Dunster *Somset* 20 SS9943
Dunston *Lincs* 76 TF0662
Dunston *Norfk* 67 TG2202
Dunston *Staffs* 72 SJ9217
Dunston *T & W* 96 NZ2362
Dunston Heath *Staffs* 72 SJ9017
Dunstone *Devon* 6 SX5951
Dunstone *Devon* 7 SX7175
Dunsville *S York* 83 SE6407
Dunswell *E R Yk* 85 TA0735
Dunsyre *S Lans* 117 NT0748
Dunterton *Devon* 5 SX3779
Dunthrop *Oxon* 48 SP3528
Duntisbourne Abbots *Gloucs* 35 SO9607
Duntisbourne Rouse *Gloucs* 35 SO9805
Duntish *Dorset* 11 ST6906
Duntocher *D & Cb* 115 NS4872
Dunton *Beds* 39 TL2344
Dunton *Bucks* 38 SP8224
Dunton *Norfk* 66 TF8830
Dunton Bassett *Leics* 50 SP5490
Dunton Green *Kent* 27 TQ5157
Dunton Wayletts *Essex* 40 TQ6590
Duntulm *Highld* 136 NG4174
Dunure *S Ayrs* 106 NS2515
Dunvant *Swans* 32 SS5993
Dunvegan *Highld* 136 NG2547
Dunwich *Suffk* 55 TM4770
Dunwood *Staffs* 72 SJ9455
Durdar *Cumb* 93 NY4051
Durgan *Cnwll* 3 SW7727
Durham *Dur* 96 NZ2742
Durisdeer *D & G* 108 NS8903
Durisdeermill *D & G* 108 NS8804
Durkar *W York* 82 SE3116
Durleigh *Somset* 20 ST2736
Durley *Hants* 13 SU5116
Durley *Wilts* 23 SU2364
Durley Street *Hants* 13 SU5217
Durlock *Kent* 29 TR2757
Durlock *Kent* 29 TR3164
Durlow Common *Gloucs* 47 SO6339
Durmgley *Angus* 127 NO4250
Durn *Gt Man* 82 SD9416
Durness *Highld* 149 NC4068
Duror *Highld* 122 NM9955
Durran *Ag & B* 122 NM9607
Durrington *W Susx* 14 TQ1105
Durrington *Wilts* 23 SU1544
Durris *Abers* 135 NO7796
Dursley *Gloucs* 35 ST7598
Dursley Cross *Gloucs* 35 SO6920
Durston *Somset* 20 ST2928
Durweston *Dorset* 11 ST8508
Duston *Nhants* 49 SP7261
Duthil *Highld* 140 NH9324
Dutlas *Powys* 45 SO2177
Dutson *Cnwll* 5 SX3485
Dutton *Ches* 71 SJ5779
Duxford *Cambs* 53 TL4846
Duxford *Oxon* 36 SP3600
Dwygyfylchi *A & C* 69 SH7376
Dwyran *Angles* 68 SH4465
Dyce *Aber C* 135 NJ8812
Dye House *Nthumb* 95 NY9358
Dyer's End *Essex* 53 TL7238
Dyfatty *Carmth* 32 SN4401
Dyffryn *Brdgnd* 33 SS8593
Dyffryn *Myr Td* 33 SO0603
Dyffryn *V Glam* 33 ST0971
Dyffryn Ardudwy *Gwynd* 57 SH5823
Dyffryn Castell *Cardgn* 43 SN7782
Dyffryn Cellwen *Neath* 33 SN8510
Dyke *Devon* 18 SS3123
Dyke *Lincs* 64 TF1022
Dyke *Moray* 140 NH9858
Dykehead *Angus* 126 NO2453
Dykehead *Angus* 134 NO3859
Dykehead *N Lans* 116 NS8759
Dykehead *Stirlg* 115 NS5997
Dykelands *Abers* 135 NO7068
Dykends *Angus* 133 NO2557
Dykeside *Abers* 142 NJ7243
Dylife *Powys* 43 SN8694
Dymchurch *Kent* 17 TR1029
Dymock *Gloucs* 47 SO7031
Dyrham *Gloucs* 35 ST7475
Dysart *Fife* 117 NT3093
Dyserth *Denbgs* 70 SJ0578

E

Eachway *H & W* 60 SO9876
Eachwick *Nthumb* 103 NZ1171
Eagland Hill *Lancs* 80 SD4345
Eagle *Lincs* 76 SK8766
Eagle Barnsdale *Lincs* 76 SK8865
Eagle Manor *Lincs* 76 SK8868
Eaglescliffe *Dur* 96 NZ4215
Eaglesfield *Cumb* 92 NY0928
Eaglesfield *D & G* 101 NY2374
Eaglesham *E Rens* 115 NS5751
Eagley *Gt Man* 81 SD7112
Eairy *IOM* 153 SC2977
Eakring *Notts* 75 SK6762
Ealand *Lincs* 84 SE7811
Ealing *Gt Lon* 26 TQ1780
Eals *Nthumb* 94 NY6756
Eamont Bridge *Cumb* 94 NY5228
Earby *Lancs* 81 SD9046
Earcroft *Lancs* 81 SD6823
Eardington *Shrops* 60 SO7290
Eardisland *H & W* 46 SO4158
Eardisley *H & W* 46 SO3149
Eardiston *H & W* 47 SO6968
Eardiston *Shrops* 59 SJ3725
Earith *Cambs* 52 TL3875
Earl Shilton *Leics* 50 SP4697
Earl Soham *Suffk* 55 TM2363
Earl Sterndale *Derbys* 74 SK0966
Earl Stonham *Suffk* 54 TM1059
Earl's Croome *H & W* 47 SO8642
Earl's Down *E Susx* 16 TQ6419
Earl's Green *Suffk* 54 TM0366
Earle *Nthumb* 111 NT9826
Earlestown *Mersyd* 78 SJ5795
Earley *Berks* 24 SU7472
Earlham *Norfk* 67 TG1908
Earlish *Highld* 136 NG3861
Earls Barton *Nhants* 51 SP8563
Earls Colne *Essex* 40 TL8528
Earls Common *H & W* 47 SO9559
Earlsditton *Shrops* 47 SO6275
Earlsdon *W Mids* 61 SP3278
Earlsferry *Fife* 118 NO4800
Earlsfield *Gt Lon* 27 TQ2573
Earlsford *Abers* 143 NJ8334
Earlsheaton *W York* 82 SE2621
Earlston *Border* 110 NT5738
Earlston *E Ayrs* 106 NS4035
Earlswood *Surrey* 15 TQ2749
Earlswood *Warwks* 61 SP1174
Earlswood Common *Mons* 34 ST4594
Earnley *W Susx* 14 SZ8196
Earnshaw Bridge *Lancs* 80 SD5222
Earsdon *Nthumb* 103 NZ1993
Earsdon *T & W* 103 NZ3272
Earsham *Norfk* 55 TM3288
Earswick *N York* 90 SE6157
Eartham *W Susx* 14 SU9309
Earthcott *Gloucs* 35 ST6585
Easby *N York* 90 NZ5708
Easdale *Ag & B* 122 NM7417
Easebourne *W Susx* 14 SU9023
Easenhall *Warwks* 50 SP4679
Eashing *Surrey* 25 SU9443
Easington *Bucks* 37 SP6810
Easington *Dur* 96 NZ4143
Easington *E R Yk* 85 TA3919
Easington *N York* 97 NZ7417
Easington *Nthumb* 111 NU1234
Easington *Oxon* 37 SU6697
Easington Colliery *Dur* 96 NZ4344
Easington Lane *T & W* 96 NZ3646
Easingwold *N York* 90 SE5269
Easole Street *Kent* 29 TR2652
Eassie and Nevay *Angus* 126 NO3344
East Aberthaw *V Glam* 20 ST0366
East Allington *Devon* 7 SX7748
East Anstey *Devon* 19 SS8626
East Anton *Hants* 23 SU3747
East Appleton *N York* 89 SE2395
East Ashey *IOW* 13 SZ5888
East Ashling *W Susx* 14 SU8107
East Aston *Hants* 24 SU4445
East Ayton *N York* 91 SE9985
East Balsdon *Cnwll* 5 SX2898
East Bank *Blae G* 33 SO2105
East Barkwith *Lincs* 76 TF1681
East Barming *Kent* 28 TQ7254
East Barnby *N York* 90 NZ8212
East Barnet *Gt Lon* 27 TQ2795
East Barns *E Loth* 119 NT7176
East Barsham *Norfk* 66 TF9133
East Beckham *Norfk* 66 TG1639
East Bedfont *Gt Lon* 26 TQ0873
East Bergholt *Suffk* 54 TM0734
East Bierley *W York* 82 SE1929
East Bilney *Norfk* 66 TF9519
East Blatchington *E Susx* 16 TQ4800
East Bloxworth *Dorset* 11 SY8894
East Boldon *T & W* 96 NZ3661
East Boldre *Hants* 12 SU3700
East Bolton *Nthumb* 111 NU1216
East Bower *Somset* 21 ST3237
East Bradenham *Norfk* 66 TF9308
East Brent *Somset* 21 ST3451
East Bridgford *Notts* 63 SK6943
East Briscoe *Dur* 95 NY9719
East Buckland *Devon* 19 SS6831
East Budleigh *Devon* 9 SY0684
East Burnham *Bucks* 26 SU9584
East Burton *Dorset* 11 SY8287
East Butsfield *Dur* 95 NZ1145
East Butterwick *Lincs* 84 SE8306
East Calder *W Loth* 117 NT0867
East Carleton *Norfk* 66 TG1701
East Carlton *Nhants* 51 SP8389
East Carlton *W York* 82 SE2143
East Challow *Oxon* 36 SU3888
East Charleton *Devon* 7 SX7642
East Chelborough *Dorset* 10 ST5505
East Chevington *Nthumb* 103 NZ2699
East Chiltington *E Susx* 15 TQ3715
East Chinnock *Somset* 10 ST4913
East Chisenbury *Wilts* 23 SU1452
East Cholderton *Hants* 23 SU2945
East Clandon *Surrey* 26 TQ0651
East Claydon *Bucks* 49 SP7325
East Clevedon *Somset* 34 ST4171
East Coker *Somset* 10 ST5412
East Combe *Somset* 20 ST1631
East Compton *Somset* 21 ST6141
East Cornworthy *Devon* 7 SX8455
East Cote *Cumb* 92 NY1255
East Cottingwith *E R Yk* 84 SE7042
East Cowes *IOW* 13 SZ5095
East Cowick *E R Yk* 83 SE6620
East Cowton *N York* 89 NZ3003
East Cramlington *Nthumb* 103 NZ2776
East Cranmore *Somset* 22 ST6743
East Creech *Dorset* 11 SY9382
East Curthwaite *Cumb* 93 NY3348
East Dean *E Susx* 16 TV5598
East Dean *Gloucs* 35 SO6520
East Dean *Hants* 23 SU2726
East Dean *W Susx* 14 SU9012
East Dereham *Norfk* 66 TF9913
East Down *Devon* 19 SS6041
East Drayton *Notts* 75 SK7775
East Dulwich *Gt Lon* 27 TQ3375
East Dundry *Somset* 21 ST5766
East Ella *E R Yk* 84 TA0529
East End *Beds* 38 SP9642
East End *Beds* 51 TL1055
East End *Bucks* 38 SP9344
East End *E R Yk* 85 TA1931
East End *E R Yk* 85 TA2927
East End *Essex* 39 TL4210
East End *Hants* 24 SU4161
East End *Hants* 12 SZ3696
East End *Herts* 39 TL4527
East End *Kent* 17 TQ8335
East End *Kent* 28 TQ9673
East End *Oxon* 36 SP3915
East End *Somset* 34 ST4770
East End *Somset* 22 ST6746
East Everleigh *Wilts* 23 SU2053
East Farleigh *Kent* 28 TQ7353
East Farndon *Nhants* 50 SP7184
East Ferry *Lincs* 75 SK8199
East Firsby *Lincs* 76 TF0085
East Fortune *E Loth* 118 NT5479
East Garforth *W York* 83 SE4133
East Garston *Berks* 36 SU3576
East Ginge *Oxon* 37 SU4486
East Goscote *Leics* 63 SK6413
East Grafton *Wilts* 23 SU2560
East Grange *Moray* 141 NJ0961
East Green *Suffk* 55 TM4065
East Grimstead *Wilts* 23 SU2227
East Grinstead *W Susx* 15 TQ3938
East Guldeford *E Susx* 17 TQ9321
East Haddon *Nhants* 50 SP6668
East Hagbourne *Oxon* 37 SU5288
East Halton *Lincs* 85 TA1319
East Ham *Gt Lon* 27 TQ4283
East Hanney *Oxon* 36 SU4193
East Hanningfield *Essex* 40 TL7701
East Hardwick *W York* 83 SE4618
East Harling *Norfk* 54 TL9986
East Harlsey *N York* 89 SE4299
East Harnham *Wilts* 23 SU1428
East Harptree *Somset* 21 ST5655
East Hartburn *Dur* 96 NZ4217
East Hartford *Nthumb* 103 NZ2679
East Harting *W Susx* 14 SU7919
East Hatch *Wilts* 22 ST9228
East Hatley *Cambs* 52 TL2850
East Hauxwell *N York* 89 SE1693
East Haven *Angus* 127 NO5836
East Heath *Berks* 25 SU7967
East Heckington *Lincs* 64 TF1944
East Hedleyhope *Dur* 96 NZ1540
East Helmsdale *Highld* 147 ND0315
East Hendred *Oxon* 37 SU4588
East Heslerton *N York* 91 SE9276
East Hewish *Somset* 21 ST4064
East Hoathly *E Susx* 16 TQ5216
East Holme *Dorset* 11 SY8986
East Holywell *T & W* 103 NZ3073
East Horndon *Essex* 40 TQ6389
East Horrington *Somset* 21 ST5846
East Horsley *Surrey* 26 TQ0952
East Horton *Nthumb* 111 NU0330
East Howe *Dorset* 12 SZ0795
East Huntington *N York* 83 SE6155
East Huntspill *Somset* 21 ST3445
East Hyde *Beds* 38 TL1217
East Ilkerton *Devon* 19 SS7147
East Ilsley *Berks* 37 SU4980
East Keal *Lincs* 77 TF3863
East Kennett *Wilts* 23 SU1167
East Keswick *W York* 83 SE3644
East Kilbride *S Lans* 116 NS6354
East Kimber *Devon* 5 SX4998
East Kirkby *Lincs* 77 TF3362
East Knighton *Dorset* 11 SY8185
East Knowstone *Devon* 19 SS8423
East Knoyle *Wilts* 22 ST8830
East Kyloe *Nthumb* 111 NU0639
East Lambrook *Somset* 10 ST4318
East Langdon *Kent* 29 TR3346
East Langton *Leics* 50 SP7292
East Laroch *Highld* 130 NN0858
East Lavant *W Susx* 14 SU8608
East Lavington *W Susx* 14 SU9416
East Layton *N York* 89 NZ1609
East Leake *Notts* 62 SK5526
East Learmouth *Nthumb* 110 NT8637
East Leigh *Devon* 8 SS6905
East Leigh *Devon* 7 SX6852
East Leigh *Devon* 7 SX7657
East Lexham *Norfk* 66 TF8517
East Linton *E Loth* 118 NT5977
East Liss *Hants* 14 SU7827
East Lockinge *Oxon* 36 SU4287
East Lound *Lincs* 75 SK7899
East Lulworth *Dorset* 11 SY8682
East Lutton *N York* 91 SE9469
East Lydeard *Somset* 20 ST1829
East Lydford *Somset* 21 ST5731
East Malling *Kent* 28 TQ7056
East Malling Heath *Kent* 28 TQ6955
East Marden *W Susx* 14 SU8014
East Markham *Notts* 75 SK7373
East Martin *Hants* 12 SU0719
East Marton *N York* 81 SD9050
East Meon *Hants* 13 SU6822
East Mere *Devon* 9 SS9916
East Mersea *Essex* 41 TM0414
East Molesey *Surrey* 26 TQ1467
East Morden *Dorset* 11 SY9194
East Morton *D & G* 108 NS8800
East Morton *W York* 82 SE0942
East Ness *N York* 90 SE6978
East Newton *E R Yk* 85 TA2638
East Norton *Leics* 50 SK7800
East Oakley *Hants* 24 SU5749
East Ogwell *Devon* 7 SX8370
East Orchard *Dorset* 11 ST8317
East Ord *Nthumb* 119 NT9751
East Panson *Devon* 5 SX3692
East Parley *Dorset* 12 SZ1097
East Peckham *Kent* 28 TQ6648
East Pennar *Pembks* 30 SM9602

East Pennard

Erskine

East Pennard *Somset* 21 ST5937
East Perry *Cambs* 52 TL1566
East Portlemouth *Devon* 7 SX7538
East Prawle *Devon* 7 SX7836
East Preston *W Susx* 14 TQ0602
East Pulham *Dorset* 11 ST7209
East Putford *Devon* 18 SS3616
East Quantoxhead *Somset* 20 ST1343
East Rainham *Kent* 28 TQ8267
East Rainton *T & W* 96 NZ3347
East Ravendale *Lincs* 76 TF2399
East Raynham *Norfk* 66 TF8825
East Rigton *W York* 83 SE3743
East Rolstone *Somset* 21 ST3962
East Rounton *N York* 89 NZ4203
East Rudham *Norfk* 66 TF8228
East Runton *Norfk* 67 TG1942
East Ruston *Norfk* 67 TG3427
East Saltoun *E Loth* 118 NT4767
East Scrafton *N York* 89 SE0884
East Sheen *Gt Lon* 26 TQ2075
East Shefford *Berks* 36 SU3874
East Sleekburn *Nthumb* 103 NZ2883
East Somerton *Norfk* 67 TG4719
East Stockwith *Lincs* 75 SK7894
East Stoke *Dorset* 11 SY8686
East Stoke *Notts* 75 SK7549
East Stour *Dorset* 22 ST8022
East Stourmouth *Kent* 29 TR2662
East Stowford *Devon* 19 SS6326
East Stratton *Hants* 24 SU5440
East Studdal *Kent* 29 TR3149
East Sutton *Kent* 28 TQ8349
East Taphouse *Cnwll* 4 SX1863
East Thirston *Nthumb* 89 NZ1900
East Tilbury *Essex* 28 TQ6877
East Tisted *Hants* 24 SU7032
East Torrington *Lincs* 76 TF1483
East Tuddenham *Norfk* 66 TG0711
East Tytherley *Hants* 23 SU2929
East Tytherton *Wilts* 35 ST9674
East Village *Devon* 8 SS8405
East Wall *Shrops* 59 SO5293
East Walton *Norfk* 65 TF7416
East Water *Somset* 21 ST5350
East Week *Devon* 8 SX6692
East Wellow *Hants* 12 SU3020
East Wemyss *Fife* 118 NT3497
East Whitburn *W Loth* 117 NS9665
East Wickham *Gt Lon* 27 TQ4677
East Williamston *Pembks* 31 SN0904
East Winch *Norfk* 65 TF6916
East Winterslow *Wilts* 23 SU2434
East Wittering *W Susx* 14 SZ7997
East Witton *N York* 89 SE1486
East Woodburn *Nthumb* 102 NY9086
East Woodhay *Hants* 24 SU4061
East Woodlands *Somset* 22 ST7944
East Worldham *Hants* 24 SU7538
East Wretham *Norfk* 54 TL9190
East Youlstone *Devon* 18 SS2715
East-the-Water *Devon* 18 SS4526
Eastbourne *Dur* 89 NZ3013
Eastbourne *E Susx* 16 TV6199
Eastbridge *Suffk* 55 TM4566
Eastbrook *V Glam* 33 ST1671
Eastburn *W York* 82 SE0144
Eastbury *Berks* 36 SU3477
Eastbury *Herts* 26 TQ1092
Eastby *N York* 82 SE0154
Eastchurch *Kent* 28 TQ9871
Eastcombe *Gloucs* 35 SO8904
Eastcote *Gt Lon* 26 TQ1088
Eastcote *Nhants* 49 SP6853
Eastcote *W Mids* 61 SP1979
Eastcott *Cnwll* 18 SS2515
Eastcott *Wilts* 23 SU0255
Eastcourt *Wilts* 35 ST9792
Eastcourt *Wilts* 23 SU2361
Eastdown *Devon* 7 SX8249
Eastend *Essex* 40 TQ9492
Eastend *S Lans* 108 NS9537
Easter Balmoral *Abers* 133 NO2694
Easter Compton *Gloucs* 34 ST5782
Easter Dalziel *Highld* 140 NH7550
Easter Howgate *Mdloth* 117 NT2463
Easter Kinkell *Highld* 139 NH5755
Easter Moniack *Highld* 139 NH5543
Easter Ord *Abers* 135 NJ8304
Easter Pitkierie *Fife* 127 NO5606
Easter Skeld *Shet* 155 HU3144
Easter Softlaw *Border* 110 NT7532
Eastergate *W Susx* 14 SU9405
Easterhouse *C Glas* 116 NS6865
Eastern Green *W Mids* 61 SP2879
Easterton *Wilts* 23 SU0254
Eastertown *Somset* 21 ST3454
Eastfield *N Lans* 116 NS8964
Eastfield *N York* 91 TA0484
Eastgate *Dur* 95 NY9538
Eastgate *Lincs* 64 TF1019
Eastgate *Norfk* 66 TG1423
Eastham *Mersyd* 78 SJ3680
Eastham Ferry *Mersyd* 78 SJ3681
Easthampstead *Berks* 25 SU8667
Easthampton *H & W* 46 SO4063
Easthope *Shrops* 59 SO5695
Easthorpe *Essex* 40 TL9121
Easthorpe *Notts* 75 SK7053
Eastington *Devon* 19 SS7408
Eastington *Gloucs* 36 SP1213
Eastington *Gloucs* 35 SO7705
Eastlands *D & G* 100 NX8172
Eastleach Martin *Gloucs* 36 SP2004
Eastleach Turville *Gloucs* 36 SP1905
Eastleigh *Devon* 18 SS4827
Eastleigh *Hants* 13 SU4519
Eastling *Kent* 28 TQ9656
Eastly End *Surrey* 26 TQ0368
Eastmoor *Norfk* 65 TF7303
Eastney *Hants* 13 SZ6698
Eastnor *H & W* 47 SO7237
Eastoft *Lincs* 84 SE8016
Easton *Berks* 24 SU4172
Easton *Cambs* 52 TL1371
Easton *Cumb* 93 NY2759
Easton *Devon* 8 SX7289
Easton *Dorset* 11 SY6971
Easton *Hants* 24 SU5132
Easton *IOW* 12 SZ3486
Easton *Lincs* 63 SK9326
Easton *Norfk* 66 TG1310
Easton *Somset* 21 ST5147
Easton *Suffk* 55 TM2858
Easton *Wilts* 35 ST8970
Easton Grey *Wilts* 35 ST8887
Easton Maudit *Nhants* 51 SP8858
Easton on the Hill *Nhants* 64 TF0104
Easton Royal *Wilts* 23 SU2060
Easton-in-Gordano *Somset* 34 ST5175
Eastpeek *Devon* 5 SX3494
Eastrea *Cambs* 64 TL2997
Eastriggs *D & G* 101 NY2466
Eastrington *E R Yk* 84 SE7929
Eastrop *Wilts* 36 SU2092
Eastry *Kent* 29 TR3054
Eastshaw *W Susx* 14 SU8724
Eastville *Lincs* 77 TF4056
Eastwell *Leics* 63 SK7728
Eastwick *Herts* 39 TL4311
Eastwood *Essex* 40 TQ8688
Eastwood *Notts* 62 SK4646
Eastwood *W York* 82 SD9726
Eastwood End *Cambs* 65 TL4292
Eathorpe *Warwks* 48 SP3969
Eaton *Ches* 71 SJ5763
Eaton *Ches* 72 SJ8765
Eaton *Leics* 63 SK7928
Eaton *Norfk* 67 TG2006
Eaton *Notts* 75 SK7077
Eaton *Oxon* 37 SP4403
Eaton *Shrops* 59 SO3789
Eaton *Shrops* 59 SO5089
Eaton Bishop *H & W* 46 SO4439
Eaton Bray *Beds* 38 SP9720
Eaton Constantine *Shrops* 59 SJ5906
Eaton Ford *Beds* 52 TL1759
Eaton Green *Beds* 38 SP9621
Eaton Hastings *Oxon* 36 SU2598
Eaton Mascott *Shrops* 59 SJ5305
Eaton Socon *Cambs* 52 TL1759
Eaton upon Tern *Shrops* 72 SJ6523
Eaves Brow *Ches* 79 SJ6393
Eaves Green *W Mids* 61 SP2682
Ebberston *N York* 91 SE8982
Ebbesborne Wake *Wilts* 22 ST9924
Ebbw Vale *Blae G* 33 SO1609
Ebchester *Dur* 95 NZ1055
Ebdon *Somset* 21 ST3664
Ebford *Devon* 9 SX9887
Ebley *Gloucs* 35 SO8205
Ebnal *Ches* 71 SJ4948
Ebnall *H & W* 46 SO4758
Ebrington *Gloucs* 48 SP1840
Ebsworthy Town *Devon* 5 SX5090
Ecchinswell *Hants* 24 SU4959
Ecclaw *Border* 119 NT7568
Ecclefechan *D & G* 101 NY1974
Eccles *Border* 110 NT7641
Eccles *Gt Man* 79 SJ7798
Eccles *Kent* 28 TQ7360
Eccles Green *H & W* 46 SO3748
Eccles on Sea *Norfk* 67 TG4128
Eccles Road *Norfk* 54 TM0189
Ecclesall *S York* 74 SK3284
Ecclesfield *S York* 74 SK3593
Eccleshall *Staffs* 72 SJ8329
Eccleshill *W York* 82 SE1736
Ecclesmachan *W Loth* 117 NT0573
Eccleston *Ches* 71 SJ4162
Eccleston *Lancs* 80 SD5217
Eccleston *Mersyd* 78 SJ4895
Eccleston Green *Lancs* 80 SD5216
Echt *Abers* 135 NJ7405
Eckford *Border* 110 NT7026
Eckington *Derbys* 75 SK4379
Eckington *H & W* 47 SO9241
Ecton *Nhants* 51 SP8263
Ecton *Staffs* 74 SK0958
Edale *Derbys* 74 SK1285
Edburton *W Susx* 15 TQ2311
Edderside *Cumb* 92 NY1045
Edderton *Highld* 146 NH7084
Eddington *Kent* 29 TR1867
Eddleston *Border* 117 NT2447
Eddlewood *S Lans* 116 NS7153
Eden Mount *Cumb* 87 SD4077
Eden Park *Gt Lon* 27 TQ3667
Edenbridge *Kent* 16 TQ4446
Edenfield *Lancs* 81 SD8019
Edenhall *Cumb* 94 NY5632
Edenham *Lincs* 64 TF0621
Edensor *Derbys* 74 SK2469
Edentaggart *Ag & B* 115 NS3293
Edenthorpe *S York* 83 SE6206
Edern *Gwynd* 56 SH2739
Edgarley *Somset* 21 ST5238
Edgbaston *W Mids* 61 SP0684
Edgcombe *Cnwll* 2 SW7133
Edgcott *Bucks* 37 SP6722
Edgcott *Somset* 19 SS8438
Edge *Gloucs* 35 SO8409
Edge *Shrops* 59 SJ3908
Edge End *Gloucs* 34 SO5913
Edge Green *Ches* 71 SJ4851
Edgebolton *Shrops* 59 SJ5721
Edgefield *Norfk* 66 TG0934
Edgefield Green *Norfk* 66 TG0934
Edgefold *Gt Man* 79 SD7005
Edgehill *Warwks* 48 SP3747
Edgerley *Shrops* 59 SJ3518
Edgerton *W York* 82 SE1317
Edgeside *Lancs* 81 SD8322
Edgeworth *Gloucs* 35 SO9406
Edgeworthy *Devon* 19 SS8413
Edgiock *H & W* 48 SP0461
Edgmond *Shrops* 72 SJ7119
Edgmond Marsh *Shrops* 72 SJ7120
Edgton *Shrops* 59 SO3885
Edgware *Gt Lon* 26 TQ1991
Edgworth *Lancs* 81 SD7416
Edial *Staffs* 61 SK0808
Edinample *Stirlg* 124 NN6022
Edinbane *Highld* 136 NG3451
Edinburgh *C Edin* 117 NT2573
Edingale *Staffs* 61 SK2111
Edingham *D & G* 100 NX8363
Edingley *Notts* 75 SK6655
Edingthorpe *Norfk* 67 TG3132
Edingthorpe Green *Norfk* 67 TG3031
Edington *Border* 119 NT8955
Edington *Nthumb* 103 NZ1582
Edington *Somset* 21 ST3839
Edington *Wilts* 22 ST9253
Edington Burtle *Somset* 21 ST3943
Edingworth *Somset* 21 ST3653
Edith Weston *Rutlnd* 63 SK9205
Edithmead *Somset* 21 ST3249
Edlesborough *Bucks* 38 SP9719
Edlingham *Nthumb* 111 NU1109
Edlington *Lincs* 76 TF2371
Edmond Castle *Cumb* 94 NY4958
Edmondsham *Dorset* 12 SU0611
Edmondsley *Dur* 96 NZ2349
Edmondthorpe *Leics* 63 SK8517
Edmonton *Cnwll* 4 SW9672
Edmonton *Gt Lon* 27 TQ3492
Edmundbyers *Dur* 95 NZ0150
Ednam *Border* 110 NT7337
Ednaston *Derbys* 73 SK2341
Edradynate *P & K* 125 NN8751
Edrom *Border* 119 NT8255
Edstaston *Shrops* 59 SJ5132
Edstone *Warwks* 48 SP1861
Edvin Loach *H & W* 47 SO6658
Edwalton *Notts* 62 SK5935
Edwardstone *Suffk* 54 TL9442
Edwardsville *Myr Td* 33 ST0896
Edwinsford *Carmth* 44 SN6334
Edwinstowe *Notts* 75 SK6266
Edworth *Beds* 39 TL2241
Edwyn Ralph *H & W* 47 SO6457
Edzell *Angus* 134 NO6068
Efail Isaf *Rhondd* 33 ST0884
Efail-fach *Neath* 32 SS7895
Efail-rhyd *Powys* 58 SJ1626
Efailnewydd *Gwynd* 56 SH3535
Efailwen *Carmth* 31 SN1325
Efenechtyd *Denbgs* 70 SJ1155
Effgill *D & G* 101 NY3092
Effingham *Surrey* 26 TQ1153
Efflinch *Staffs* 73 SK1816
Efford *Devon* 9 SS8901
Egbury *Hants* 24 SU4352
Egdean *W Susx* 14 SU9920
Egerton *Gt Man* 81 SD7014
Egerton *Kent* 28 TQ9147
Egg Buckland *Devon* 6 SX5057
Eggesford *Devon* 19 SS6811
Eggington *Beds* 38 SP9525
Egginton *Derbys* 73 SK2628
Egglescliffe *Dur* 89 NZ4113
Eggleston *Dur* 95 NY9923
Egham *Surrey* 25 TQ0071
Egham Wick *Surrey* 25 SU9870
Eginswell *Devon* 7 SX8866
Egleton *Rutlnd* 63 SK8707
Eglingham *Nthumb* 111 NU1019
Egloshayle *Cnwll* 4 SX0072
Egloskerry *Cnwll* 5 SX2786
Eglwys Cross *Wrexhm* 71 SJ4740
Eglwys-Brewis *V Glam* 20 ST0068
Eglwysbach *A & C* 69 SH8070
Eglwysfach *Cardgn* 43 SN6996
Eglwyswrw *Pembks* 31 SN1438
Egmanton *Notts* 75 SK7368
Egremont *Cumb* 86 NY0110
Egremont *Mersyd* 78 SJ3192
Egton *N York* 90 NZ8006
Egton Bridge *N York* 90 NZ8004
Eight and Forty *E R Yk* 84 SE8529
Eight Ash Green *Essex* 40 TL9425
Eilanreach *Highld* 129 NG8018
Elan Village *Powys* 45 SN9364
Elberton *Gloucs* 34 ST6088
Elbridge *W Susx* 14 SU9101
Elburton *Devon* 6 SX5353
Elcombe *Wilts* 36 SU1280
Elcot *Berks* 36 SU3969
Elder Street *Essex* 53 TL5734
Eldernell *Cambs* 64 TL3298
Eldersfield *H & W* 47 SO7931
Elderslie *Rens* 115 NS4463
Eldmire *N York* 89 SE4274
Eldon *Dur* 96 NZ2328
Eldwick *W York* 82 SE1240
Elfhill *Abers* 135 NO8085
Elford *Nthumb* 111 NU1831
Elford *Staffs* 61 SK1810
Elgin *Moray* 141 NJ2162
Elgol *Highld* 128 NG5213
Elham *Kent* 29 TR1744
Elie *Fife* 118 NO4900
Elilaw *Nthumb* 111 NT9708
Elim *Angles* 68 SH3584
Eling *Hants* 12 SU3612
Elishaw *Nthumb* 102 NY8595
Elkesley *Notts* 75 SK6975
Elkstone *Gloucs* 35 SO9612
Ella *Abers* 142 NJ6459
Ellanbeich *Ag & B* 122 NM7417
Elland *W York* 82 SE1120
Elland Lower Edge *W York* 82 SE1221
Ellary *Ag & B* 113 NR7376
Ellastone *Staffs* 73 SK1143
Ellel *Lancs* 80 SD4856
Ellemford *Border* 119 NT7260
Ellen's Green *Surrey* 14 TQ0935
Ellenborough *Cumb* 92 NY0435
Ellenbrook *Gt Man* 79 SD7201
Ellenhall *Staffs* 72 SJ8426
Ellerbeck *N York* 89 SE4396
Ellerby *N York* 90 NZ7914
Ellerdine Heath *Shrops* 59 SJ6122
Ellerhayes *Devon* 9 SS9702
Elleric *Ag & B* 123 NN0448
Ellerker *E R Yk* 84 SE9229
Ellers *N York* 82 SE0043
Ellerton *N York* 89 SE2598
Ellerton *E R Yk* 84 SE7039
Ellerton *Shrops* 72 SJ7125
Ellesborough *Bucks* 38 SP8306
Ellesmere *Shrops* 59 SJ3934
Ellesmere Port *Ches* 71 SJ4076
Ellicombe *Somset* 20 SS9844
Ellingham *Hants* 12 SU1408
Ellingham *Norfk* 67 TM3592
Ellingham *Nthumb* 111 NU1725
Ellingstring *N York* 89 SE1783
Ellington *Cambs* 52 TL1671
Ellington *Nthumb* 103 NZ2791
Ellington Thorpe *Cambs* 52 TL1670
Elliots Green *Somset* 22 ST7945
Ellisfield *Hants* 24 SU6446
Ellishader *Highld* 137 NG5065
Ellistown *Leics* 62 SK4310
Ellon *Abers* 143 NJ9530
Ellonby *Cumb* 93 NY4235
Ellough *Suffk* 55 TM4486
Elloughton *E R Yk* 84 SE9428
Ellwood *Gloucs* 34 SO5908
Elm *Cambs* 65 TF4707
Elm Green *Essex* 40 TL7705
Elm Grove *Norfk* 67 TG4803
Elm Park *Gt Lon* 27 TQ5385
Elmbridge *H & W* 47 SO9068
Elmdon *Essex* 39 TL4639
Elmdon *W Mids* 61 SP1783
Elmdon Heath *W Mids* 61 SP1680
Elmer *W Susx* 14 SU9800
Elmer's Green *Lancs* 78 SD5006
Elmers End *Gt Lon* 27 TQ3668
Elmesthorpe *Leics* 50 SP4696
Elmhurst *Staffs* 61 SK1112
Elmley Castle *H & W* 47 SO9841
Elmley Lovett *H & W* 47 SO8769
Elmore *Gloucs* 35 SO7815
Elmore Back *Gloucs* 35 SO7616
Elms Green *H & W* 47 SO7266
Elmscott *Devon* 18 SS2321
Elmsett *Suffk* 54 TM0546
Elmstead Heath *Essex* 41 TM0622
Elmstead Market *Essex* 41 TM0624
Elmstead Row *Essex* 41 TM0621
Elmsted Court *Kent* 29 TR1144
Elmstone *Kent* 29 TR2660
Elmstone Hardwicke *Gloucs* 47 SO9125
Elmswell *E R Yk* 91 SE9958
Elmswell *Suffk* 54 TL9964
Elmton *Derbys* 75 SK5073
Elphin *Highld* 145 NC2111
Elphinstone *E Loth* 118 NT3970
Elrick *Abers* 135 NJ8106
Elrig *D & G* 98 NX3248
Elrington *Nthumb* 102 NY8563
Elsdon *Nthumb* 102 NY9393
Elsecar *S York* 74 SK3899
Elsenham *Essex* 39 TL5326
Elsfield *Oxon* 37 SP5410
Elsham *Lincs* 84 TA0312
Elsick House *Abers* 135 NO8894
Elsing *Norfk* 66 TG0516
Elslack *N York* 81 SD9349
Elson *Hants* 13 SU6002
Elson *Shrops* 59 SJ3735
Elsrickle *S Lans* 108 NT0643
Elstead *Surrey* 25 SU9043
Elsted *W Susx* 14 SU8119
Elsthorpe *Lincs* 64 TF0623
Elstob *Dur* 96 NZ3323
Elston *Lancs* 81 SD5932
Elston *Notts* 63 SK7647
Elston *Wilts* 23 SU0644
Elstone *Devon* 19 SS6716
Elstow *Beds* 38 TL0546
Elstree *Herts* 26 TQ1795
Elstronwick *E R Yk* 85 TA2232
Elswick *Lancs* 80 SD4238
Elswick *T & W* 103 NZ2263
Elsworth *Cambs* 52 TL3163
Elterwater *Cumb* 86 NY3204
Eltham *Gt Lon* 27 TQ4274
Eltisley *Cambs* 52 TL2759
Elton *Cambs* 51 TL0893
Elton *Ches* 71 SJ4575
Elton *Derbys* 74 SK2260
Elton *Dur* 96 NZ4017
Elton *Gloucs* 35 SO7014
Elton *Gt Man* 81 SD7911
Elton *H & W* 46 SO4570
Elton *Notts* 63 SK7638
Elton Green *Ches* 71 SJ4574
Eltringham *Nthumb* 103 NZ0762
Elvanfoot *S Lans* 108 NS9517
Elvaston *Derbys* 62 SK4032
Elveden *Suffk* 54 TL8280
Elvetham Hall *Hants* 25 SU7856
Elvingston *E Loth* 118 NT4674
Elvington *Kent* 29 TR2750
Elvington *N York* 84 SE7047
Elwell *Devon* 19 SS6631
Elwick *Dur* 97 NZ4532
Elwick *Nthumb* 111 NU1136
Elworth *Ches* 72 SJ7361
Elworthy *Somset* 20 ST0834
Ely *Cambs* 53 TL5480
Ely *Cardif* 33 ST1476
Emberton *Bucks* 38 SP8849
Embleton *Cumb* 92 NY1629
Embleton *Dur* 96 NZ4129
Embleton *Nthumb* 111 NU2322
Embo *Highld* 147 NH8192
Embo Street *Highld* 147 NH8091
Emborough *Somset* 21 ST6151
Embsay *N York* 82 SE0053
Emery Down *Hants* 12 SU2808
Emley *W York* 82 SE2413
Emley Moor *W York* 82 SE2313
Emmbrook *Berks* 25 SU8069
Emmer Green *Berks* 37 SU7276
Emmett Carr *Derbys* 75 SK4577
Emmington *Oxon* 37 SP7402
Emneth *Cambs* 65 TF4807
Emneth Hungate *Norfk* 65 TF5107
Empingham *Rutlnd* 63 SK9408
Empshott *Hants* 24 SU7531
Empshott Green *Hants* 24 SU7431
Emsworth *Hants* 13 SU7406
Enborne *Berks* 24 SU4365
Enborne Row *Hants* 24 SU4463
Enchmarsh *Shrops* 59 SO5096
Enderby *Leics* 50 SP5399
Endmoor *Cumb* 87 SD5384
Endon *Staffs* 72 SJ9253
Endon Bank *Staffs* 72 SJ9253
Enfield *Gt Lon* 27 TQ3597
Enfield Lock *Gt Lon* 27 TQ3698
Enfield Wash *Gt Lon* 27 TQ3598
Enford *Wilts* 23 SU1351
Engine Common *Gloucs* 35 ST6984
England's Gate *H & W* 46 SO5451
Englefield *Berks* 24 SU6272
Englefield Green *Surrey* 25 SU9971
Englesea-brook *Ches* 72 SJ7551
English Bicknor *Gloucs* 34 SO5815
English Frankton *Shrops* 59 SJ4529
Englishcombe *Somset* 22 ST7162
Engollan *Cnwll* 4 SW8670
Enham-Alamein *Hants* 23 SU3649
Enmore *Somset* 20 ST2435
Enmore Green *Dorset* 22 ST8523
Ennerdale Bridge *Cumb* 92 NY0615
Enniscaven *Cnwll* 4 SW9659
Enochdhu *P & K* 133 NO0662
Ensay *Ag & B* 121 NM3648
Ensbury *Dorset* 12 SZ0896
Ensdon *Shrops* 59 SJ4017
Ensis *Devon* 19 SS5626
Enson *Staffs* 72 SJ9328
Enstone *Oxon* 48 SP3724
Enterkinfoot *D & G* 108 NS8504
Enterpen *N York* 89 NZ4605
Enville *Staffs* 60 SO8286
Enys *Cnwll* 3 SW7836
Epney *Gloucs* 35 SO7611
Epperstone *Notts* 75 SK6548
Epping *Essex* 27 TL4502
Epping Green *Essex* 39 TL4305
Epping Green *Herts* 39 TL2906
Epping Upland *Essex* 39 TL4404
Eppleby *N York* 89 NZ1713
Eppleworth *E R Yk* 84 TA0131
Epsom *Surrey* 26 TQ2160
Epwell *Oxon* 48 SP3540
Epworth *Lincs* 84 SE7803
Epworth Turbary *Lincs* 84 SE7603
Erbistock *Wrexhm* 71 SJ3541
Erdington *W Mids* 61 SP1191
Eridge Green *E Susx* 16 TQ5535
Eridge Station *E Susx* 16 TQ5434
Erines *Ag & B* 113 NR8575
Erisey *Cnwll* 2 SW7117
Eriska *Ag & B* 122 NM9043
Eriswell *Suffk* 53 TL7278
Erith *Gt Lon* 27 TQ5177
Erlestoke *Wilts* 22 ST9653
Ermington *Devon* 6 SX6353
Erpingham *Norfk* 67 TG1931
Erriottwood *Kent* 28 TQ9459
Errogie *Highld* 139 NH5622
Errol *P & K* 126 NO2422
Erskine *Rens* 115 NS4770

Ervie
Firsby

Ervie *D & G* 98 NX0067
Erwarton *Suffk* 55 TM2234
Erwood *Powys* 45 SO0942
Eryholme *N York* 89 NZ3208
Eryrys *Denbgs* 70 SJ2057
Escalls *Cnwll* 2 SW3627
Escomb *Dur* 96 NZ1830
Escott *Somset* 20 ST0937
Escrick *N York* 83 SE6242
Esgair *Cardgn* 43 SN5868
Esgair *Carmth* 31 SN3728
Esgairgeiliog *Powys* 57 SH7606
Esgerdawe *Carmth* 44 SN6140
Esgyryn *A & C* 69 SH8078
Esh *Dur* 96 NZ1944
Esh Winning *Dur* 96 NZ1942
Esher *Surrey* 26 TQ1364
Esholt *W York* 82 SE1840
Eshott *Nthumb* 103 NZ2097
Eshton *N York* 81 SD9356
Eskadale *Highld* 139 NH4540
Eskbank *Mdloth* 118 NT3266
Eskdale Green *Cumb* 86 NY1400
Eskdalemuir *D & G* 101 NY2597
Eskett *Cumb* 92 NY0516
Eskham *Lincs* 77 TF3698
Eskholme *S York* 83 SE6317
Esperley Lane Ends *Dur* 96 NZ1324
Esprick *Lancs* 80 SD4036
Essendine *Rutlnd* 64 TF0412
Essendon *Herts* 39 TL2708
Essich *Highld* 140 NH6439
Essington *Staffs* 60 SJ9603
Esslemont *Abers* 143 NJ9229
Eston *N York* 97 NZ5418
Etal *Nthumb* 110 NT9339
Etchilhampton *Wilts* 23 SU0460
Etchingham *E Susx* 17 TQ7126
Etchinghill *Kent* 29 TR1639
Etchinghill *Staffs* 73 SK0218
Etchingwood *E Susx* 16 TQ5022
Etherdwick *E R Yk* 85 TA2337
Etling Green *Norfk* 66 TG0113
Etloe *Gloucs* 35 SO6806
Eton *Berks* 26 SU9677
Eton Wick *Berks* 26 SU9478
Etruria *Staffs* 72 SJ8647
Etteridge *Highld* 132 NN6892
Ettersgill *Dur* 95 NY8829
Ettiley Heath *Ches* 72 SJ7360
Ettingshall *W Mids* 60 SO9396
Ettington *Warwks* 48 SP2749
Etton *Cambs* 64 TF1406
Etton *E R Yk* 84 SE9743
Ettrick *Border* 109 NT2714
Ettrick Hill *Border* 109 NT2514
Ettrickbridge *Border* 109 NT3824
Etwall *Derbys* 73 SK2631
Eudon George *Shrops* 60 SO6888
Euston *Suffk* 54 TL8979
Euximoor Drove *Cambs* 65 TL4898
Euxton *Lancs* 81 SD5519
Evancoyd *Powys* 46 SO2663
Evanton *Highld* 140 NH6066
Evedon *Lincs* 76 TF0947
Evelith *Shrops* 60 SJ7405
Evelix *Highld* 147 NH7790
Evenjobb *Powys* 46 SO2662
Evenley *Oxon* 49 SP5834
Evenlode *Gloucs* 48 SP2129
Evenwood *Dur* 96 NZ1524
Evenwood Gate *Dur* 96 NZ1624
Evercreech *Somset* 21 ST6438
Everingham *E R Yk* 84 SE8042
Everleigh *Wilts* 23 SU2053
Everley *N York* 91 SE9788
Eversfield *Devon* 5 SX4792
Eversholt *Beds* 38 SP9833
Evershot *Dorset* 10 ST5704
Eversley *Hants* 25 SU7762
Eversley Cross *Hants* 25 SU7961
Everthorpe *E R Yk* 84 SE9031
Everton *Beds* 52 TL2051
Everton *Hants* 12 SZ2894
Everton *Mersyd* 78 SJ3491
Everton *Notts* 75 SK6990
Evertown *D & G* 101 NY3576
Evesbatch *H & W* 47 SO6948
Evesham *H & W* 48 SP0344
Evington *Leics* 62 SK6203
Ewden Village *S York* 74 SK2796
Ewdness *Shrops* 60 SO7396
Ewell *Surrey* 26 TQ2262
Ewell Minnis *Kent* 29 TR2643
Ewelme *Oxon* 37 SU6491
Ewen *Gloucs* 35 SU0097
Ewenny *V Glam* 33 SS9077
Ewerby *Lincs* 76 TF1247
Ewerby Thorpe *Lincs* 76 TF1347
Ewesley *Nthumb* 103 NZ0591
Ewhurst *Surrey* 14 TQ0940
Ewhurst Green *E Susx* 17 TQ7924
Ewhurst Green *Surrey* 14 TQ0939
Ewloe *Flints* 71 SJ3066
Ewloe Green *Flints* 71 SJ2966
Ewood *Lancs* 81 SD6725
Ewood Bridge *Lancs* 81 SD7920
Eworthy *Devon* 5 SX4495
Ewshot *Hants* 25 SU8149
Ewyas Harold *H & W* 46 SO3828
Exbourne *Devon* 8 SS6002
Exbury *Hants* 13 SU4200
Exceat *E Susx* 16 TV5199
Exebridge *Somset* 20 SS9324
Exelby *N York* 89 SE2987
Exeter *Devon* 9 SX9292
Exford *Somset* 19 SS8538
Exfordsgreen *Shrops* 59 SJ4505
Exhall *Warwks* 48 SP1055
Exhall *Warwks* 61 SP3485
Exlade Street *Oxon* 37 SU6581
Exley Head *W York* 82 SE0440
Exminster *Devon* 9 SX9487
Exmouth *Devon* 9 SY0081
Exning *Suffk* 53 TL6265
Exted *Kent* 29 TR1744
Exton *Devon* 9 SX9886
Exton *Hants* 13 SU6120
Exton *Rutlnd* 63 SK9211
Exton *Somset* 20 SS9233
Exwick *Devon* 9 SX9093
Eyam *Derbys* 74 SK2176
Eydon *Nhants* 49 SP5449
Eye *Cambs* 64 TF2202
Eye *H & W* 46 SO4964
Eye *Suffk* 54 TM1473
Eye Green *Cambs* 64 TF2303
Eye Kettleby *Leics* 63 SK7316
Eyemouth *Border* 119 NT9464
Eyeworth *Beds* 52 TL2545
Eyhorne Street *Kent* 28 TQ8354
Eyke *Suffk* 55 TM3151
Eynesbury *Beds* 52 TL1859
Eynsford *Kent* 27 TQ5465
Eynsham *Oxon* 36 SP4309
Eype *Dorset* 10 SY4491
Eyre *Highld* 136 NG4153
Eythorne *Kent* 29 TR2849
Eyton *H & W* 46 SO4761
Eyton *Shrops* 59 SJ3714
Eyton *Shrops* 59 SJ4422
Eyton *Shrops* 59 SO3787
Eyton *Wrexhm* 71 SJ3544
Eyton on Severn *Shrops* 59 SJ5806
Eyton upon the Weald Moor *Shrops* 72 SJ6515

F

Faccombe *Hants* 23 SU3857
Faceby *N York* 90 NZ4903
Fachwen *Powys* 58 SJ0316
Facit *Lancs* 81 SD8819
Fackley *Notts* 75 SK4761
Faddiley *Ches* 71 SJ5852
Fadmoor *N York* 90 SE6789
Faerdre *Swans* 32 SN6901
Fagwyr *Swans* 32 SN6702
Faifley *D & Cb* 115 NS4973
Failand *Somset* 34 ST5171
Failford *S Ayrs* 107 NS4626
Failsworth *Gt Man* 79 SD8901
Fair Oak *Hants* 13 SU4918
Fair Oak Green *Hants* 24 SU6660
Fairbourne *Gwynd* 57 SH6113
Fairburn *N York* 83 SE4727
Fairfield *Derbys* 74 SK0673
Fairfield *H & W* 60 SO9475
Fairfield *Kent* 17 TQ9626
Fairford *Gloucs* 36 SP1501
Fairford Park *Gloucs* 36 SP1501
Fairgirth *D & G* 92 NX8756
Fairhaven *Lancs* 80 SD3227
Fairlie *N Ayrs* 114 NS2054
Fairlight *E Susx* 17 TQ8511
Fairmile *Devon* 9 SY0897
Fairmile *Surrey* 26 TQ1161
Fairnilee *Border* 109 NT4532
Fairoak *Staffs* 72 SJ7632
Fairseat *Kent* 27 TQ6261
Fairstead *Essex* 40 TL7616
Fairwarp *E Susx* 16 TQ4626
Fairwater *Cardif* 33 ST1477
Fairy Cross *Devon* 18 SS4024
Fakenham *Norfk* 66 TF9229
Fakenham Magna *Suffk* 54 TL9176
Fala *Mdloth* 118 NT4460
Fala Dam *Mdloth* 118 NT4361
Falcondale *Cardgn* 44 SN5649
Falcut *Nhants* 49 SP5942
Faldingworth *Lincs* 76 TF0684
Faldouet *Jersey* 152 JS0000
Falfield *Gloucs* 35 ST6893
Falkenham *Suffk* 55 TM2939
Falkirk *Falk* 116 NS8880
Falkland *Fife* 126 NO2507
Fallgate *Derbys* 74 SK3561
Fallin *Stirlg* 116 NS8391
Falloden *Nthumb* 111 NU1922
Fallowfield *Gt Man* 79 SJ8593
Fallowfield *Nthumb* 102 NY9268
Falls of Blarghour *Ag & B* 122 NM9913
Falmer *E Susx* 15 TQ3508
Falmouth *Cnwll* 3 SW8032
Falnash *Border* 109 NT3905
Falsgrave *N York* 91 TA0288
Falstone *Nthumb* 102 NY7287
Fanagmore *Highld* 148 NC1749
Fancott *Beds* 38 TL0127
Fanellan *Highld* 139 NH4942
Fangdale Beck *N York* 90 SE5694
Fangfoss *E R Yk* 84 SE7653
Fanmore *Ag & B* 121 NM4144
Fannich Lodge *Highld* 139 NH2266
Fans *Border* 110 NT6140
Far Bletchley *Bucks* 38 SP8533
Far Cotton *Nhants* 49 SP7559
Far End *Cumb* 86 SD3098
Far Forest *H & W* 60 SO7275
Far Green *Gloucs* 35 SO7700
Far Moor *Gt Man* 78 SD5204
Far Oakridge *Gloucs* 35 SO9203
Far Sawrey *Cumb* 87 SD3795
Far Thorpe *Lincs* 77 TF2674
Farcet *Cambs* 64 TL2094
Farden *Shrops* 46 SO5775
Fareham *Hants* 13 SU5606
Farewell *Staffs* 61 SK0811
Farforth *Lincs* 77 TF3178
Faringdon *Oxon* 36 SU2895
Farington *Lancs* 80 SD5325
Farkhill *P & K* 125 NO0435
Farlam *Cumb* 94 NY5558
Farleigh *Devon* 7 SX7553
Farleigh *Somset* 21 ST5069
Farleigh *Surrey* 27 TQ3760
Farleigh Hungerford *Somset* 22 ST8057
Farleigh Wallop *Hants* 24 SU6247
Farlesthorpe *Lincs* 77 TF4774
Farleton *Cumb* 87 SD5380
Farleton *Lancs* 87 SD5767
Farley *Derbys* 74 SK2962
Farley *Staffs* 73 SK0644
Farley *Wilts* 23 SU2229
Farley Green *Suffk* 53 TL7353
Farley Green *Surrey* 14 TQ0545
Farley Hill *Berks* 24 SU7464
Farleys End *Gloucs* 35 SO7614
Farlington *N York* 90 SE6167
Farlow *Shrops* 59 SO6380
Farm Town *Leics* 62 SK3916
Farmborough *Somset* 22 ST6660
Farmbridge End *Essex* 40 TL6211
Farmcote *Gloucs* 48 SP0628
Farmcote *Shrops* 60 SO7791
Farmers *Carmth* 44 SN6444
Farmington *Gloucs* 36 SP1315
Farmoor *Oxon* 37 SP4506
Farms Common *Cnwll* 2 SW6734
Farmtown *Moray* 142 NJ5051
Farnachty *Moray* 142 NJ4261
Farnah Green *Derbys* 62 SK3347
Farnborough *Berks* 36 SU4381
Farnborough *Gt Lon* 27 TQ4464
Farnborough *Hants* 25 SU8753
Farnborough *Warwks* 49 SP4349
Farnborough Park *Hants* 25 SU8755
Farnborough Street *Hants* 25 SU8756
Farncombe *Surrey* 25 SU9744
Farndish *Beds* 51 SP9263
Farndon *Ches* 71 SJ4154
Farndon *Notts* 75 SK7651
Farnell *Angus* 127 NO6255
Farnham *Dorset* 11 ST9515
Farnham *Essex* 39 TL4724
Farnham *N York* 89 SE3460
Farnham *Suffk* 55 TM3660
Farnham *Surrey* 25 SU8346
Farnham Common *Bucks* 26 SU9585
Farnham Green *Essex* 39 TL4625
Farnham Royal *Bucks* 26 SU9583
Farningham *Kent* 27 TQ5467
Farnley *N York* 82 SE2148
Farnley *W York* 82 SE2532
Farnley Tyas *W York* 82 SE1612
Farnsfield *Notts* 75 SK6456
Farnworth *Ches* 78 SJ5187
Farnworth *Gt Man* 79 SD7306
Farr *Highld* 150 NC7163
Farr *Highld* 140 NH6833
Farr *Highld* 132 NH8203
Farraline *Highld* 139 NH5621
Farringdon *Devon* 9 SY0191
Farrington Gurney *Somset* 21 ST6355
Farsley *W York* 82 SE2135
Farther Howegreen *Essex* 40 TL8401
Farthing Green *Kent* 28 TQ8146
Farthing Street *Gt Lon* 27 TQ4262
Farthinghoe *Nhants* 49 SP5339
Farthingloe *Kent* 29 TR2940
Farthingstone *Nhants* 49 SP6154
Fartown *W York* 82 SE1518
Fartown *W York* 82 SE2233
Farway Street *Devon* 9 SY1895
Fasnacloich *Ag & B* 122 NN0247
Fasnakyle *Highld* 139 NH3128
Fassfern *Highld* 130 NN0278
Fatfield *T & W* 96 NZ2954
Faugh *Cumb* 94 NY5154
Fauld *Staffs* 73 SK1728
Fauldhouse *W Loth* 116 NS9360
Faulkbourne *Essex* 40 TL7917
Faulkland *Somset* 22 ST7354
Fauls *Shrops* 59 SJ5832
Faversham *Kent* 28 TR0161
Fawdington *N York* 89 SE4372
Fawdon *Nthumb* 111 NU0315
Fawfieldhead *Staffs* 74 SK0763
Fawkham Green *Kent* 27 TQ5865
Fawler *Oxon* 36 SP3717
Fawley *Berks* 36 SU3981
Fawley *Bucks* 37 SU7586
Fawley *Hants* 13 SU4503
Fawley Chapel *H & W* 46 SO5929
Fawnog *Flints* 70 SJ2466
Fawsley *Nhants* 49 SP5656
Faxfleet *E R Yk* 84 SE8624
Faygate *W Susx* 15 TQ2134
Fazakerley *Mersyd* 78 SJ3796
Fazeley *Staffs* 61 SK2001
Fearby *N York* 89 SE1981
Fearn *Highld* 147 NH8378
Fearnan *P & K* 124 NN7244
Fearnbeg *Highld* 137 NG7359
Fearnhead *Ches* 79 SJ6390
Fearnmore *Highld* 137 NG7260
Fearnoch *Ag & B* 114 NR9279
Featherstone *Staffs* 60 SJ9305
Featherstone *W York* 83 SE4221
Feckenham *H & W* 47 SP0162
Feering *Essex* 40 TL8720
Feetham *N York* 88 SD9898
Feizor *N York* 88 SD7867
Felbridge *Surrey* 15 TQ3739
Felbrigg *Norfk* 67 TG2039
Felcourt *Surrey* 15 TQ3841
Felday *Surrey* 14 TQ1144
Felden *Herts* 38 TL0404
Felin Fach *Cardgn* 44 SN5355
Felin gwm Isaf *Carmth* 44 SN5023
Felin gwm Uchaf *Carmth* 44 SN5024
Felin-newydd *Powys* 45 SO1135
Felindre *Cardgn* 44 SN5555
Felindre *Carmth* 32 SN5521
Felindre *Carmth* 44 SN7027
Felindre *Carmth* 31 SN3538
Felindre *Powys* 58 SO1681
Felindre *Powys* 45 SO1723
Felindre *Swans* 32 SN6302
Felindre Farchog *Pembks* 31 SN1039
Felinfach *Powys* 45 SO0933
Felinfoel *Carmth* 32 SN5102
Felixkirk *N York* 89 SE4684
Felixstowe *Suffk* 55 TM3034
Felixstoweferry *Suffk* 55 TM3237
Felkington *Nthumb* 110 NT9444
Felkirk *W York* 83 SE3812
Fell Foot *Cumb* 86 NY2903
Fell Lane *W York* 82 SE0440
Fell Side *Cumb* 93 NY3037
Felling *T & W* 96 NZ2762
Felmersham *Beds* 51 SP9957
Felmingham *Norfk* 67 TG2529
Felpham *W Susx* 14 SZ9499
Felsham *Suffk* 54 TL9457
Felsted *Essex* 40 TL6720
Feltham *Gt Lon* 26 TQ1073
Felthamhill *Gt Lon* 26 TQ0971
Felthorpe *Norfk* 66 TG1618
Felton *H & W* 46 SO5748
Felton *Nthumb* 103 NU1800
Felton *Somset* 21 ST5265
Felton Butler *Shrops* 59 SJ3917
Feltwell *Norfk* 53 TL7190
Fen Ditton *Cambs* 53 TL4860
Fen Drayton *Cambs* 52 TL3368
Fen End *Lincs* 64 TF2420
Fen End *W Mids* 61 SP2274
Fen Street *Norfk* 66 TL9895
Fen Street *Suffk* 54 TM1862
Fenay Bridge *W York* 82 SE1815
Fence *Lancs* 81 SD8237
Fence *S York* 75 SK4485
Fencehouses *T & W* 96 NZ3250
Fencote *N York* 89 SE2893
Fencott *Oxon* 37 SP5716
Fendike Corner *Lincs* 77 TF4560
Fenham *Nthumb* 111 NU0840
Fenham *T & W* 103 NZ2265
Feniscliffe *Lancs* 81 SD6526
Feniscowles *Lancs* 81 SD6425
Feniton *Devon* 9 SY1099
Fenn Green *Shrops* 60 SO7783
Fenn Street *Kent* 28 TQ7975
Fenny Bentley *Derbys* 73 SK1749
Fenny Bridges *Devon* 9 SY1198
Fenny Compton *Warwks* 49 SP4152
Fenny Drayton *Leics* 61 SP3596
Fenny Stratford *Bucks* 38 SP8734
Fenrother *Nthumb* 103 NZ1792
Fenstanton *Cambs* 52 TL3168
Fenstead End *Suffk* 54 TL8050
Fenton *Cambs* 52 TL3279
Fenton *Cumb* 94 NY5056
Fenton *Lincs* 76 SK8476
Fenton *Lincs* 76 SK8751
Fenton *Notts* 75 SK7982
Fenton *Nthumb* 111 NT9733
Fenton *Staffs* 72 SJ8944
Fenton Barns *E Loth* 118 NT5181
Fenwick *E Ayrs* 107 NS4643
Fenwick *Nthumb* 111 NU0640
Fenwick *Nthumb* 103 NZ0572
Fenwick *S York* 83 SE5916
Feock *Cnwll* 3 SW8238
Feolin Ferry *Ag & B* 112 NR4469
Fergushill *N Ayrs* 106 NS3343
Feriniquarrie *Highld* 136 NG1750
Fermain Bay *Guern* 152 GN0000
Fern *Angus* 134 NO4861
Ferndale *Rhondd* 33 SS9996
Ferndown *Dorset* 12 SU0700
Ferness *Moray* 140 NH9645
Fernham *Oxon* 36 SU2991
Fernhill Heath *H & W* 47 SO8759
Fernhurst *W Susx* 14 SU8928
Fernie *Fife* 126 NO3115
Ferniegair *S Lans* 116 NS7354
Fernilea *Highld* 136 NG3732
Fernilee *Derbys* 79 SK0178
Ferny Common *H & W* 46 SO3651
Ferrensby *N York* 89 SE3760
Ferriby Sluice *Lincs* 84 SE9720
Ferrindonald *Highld* 129 NG6608
Ferring *W Susx* 14 TQ0902
Ferry Point *Highld* 146 NH7385
Ferrybridge *W York* 83 SE4824
Ferryden *Angus* 127 NO7156
Ferryhill *Dur* 96 NZ2832
Ferryside *Carmth* 31 SN3610
Ferrytown *Highld* 146 NH7387
Fersfield *Norfk* 54 TM0683
Fersit *Highld* 131 NN3577
Feshiebridge *Highld* 132 NH8504
Fetcham *Surrey* 26 TQ1455
Fetterangus *Abers* 143 NJ9850
Fettercairn *Abers* 135 NO6573
Fewcott *Oxon* 49 SP5428
Fewston *N York* 82 SE1954
Ffair Rhos *Cardgn* 43 SN7368
Ffairfach *Carmth* 32 SN6321
Ffald-y-Brenin *Carmth* 44 SN6344
Ffawyddog *Powys* 33 SO2018
Ffestiniog *Gwynd* 57 SH7042
Ffordd-Las *Denbgs* 70 SJ1264
Fforest *Carmth* 32 SN5704
Fforest *Mons* 34 SO2820
Fforest Fach *Swans* 32 SS6295
Fforest Goch *Neath* 32 SN7401
Ffostrasol *Cardgn* 42 SN3747
Ffrith *Flints* 70 SJ2855
Ffynnon-Oer *Cardgn* 44 SN5353
Ffynnongroew *Flints* 70 SJ1382
Ffynonddewi *Cardgn* 42 SN3852
Fiag Lodge *Highld* 149 NC4528
Fickleshole *Surrey* 27 TQ3860
Fiddes *Abers* 135 NO8080
Fiddington *Gloucs* 47 SO9231
Fiddington *Somset* 20 ST2140
Fiddleford *Dorset* 11 ST8013
Fiddlers Green *Cnwll* 3 SW8155
Fiddlers Hamlet *Essex* 27 TL4701
Field *Staffs* 73 SK0233
Field Broughton *Cumb* 87 SD3881
Field Dalling *Norfk* 66 TG0038
Field Head *Leics* 62 SK4909
Fieldhead *Cumb* 93 NY4539
Fife Keith *Moray* 142 NJ4250
Fifehead Magdalen *Dorset* 22 ST7821
Fifehead Neville *Dorset* 11 ST7610
Fifehead St Quinton *Dorset* 11 ST7710
Fifield *Berks* 26 SU9076
Fifield *Oxon* 36 SP2418
Fifield *Wilts* 23 SU1450
Figheldean *Wilts* 23 SU1547
Filands *Wilts* 35 ST9388
Filby *Norfk* 67 TG4613
Filey *N York* 91 TA1180
Filgrave *Bucks* 38 SP8648
Filkins *Oxon* 36 SP2304
Filleigh *Devon* 19 SS6627
Filleigh *Devon* 19 SS7410
Fillingham *Lincs* 76 SK9485
Fillongley *Warwks* 61 SP2887
Filmore Hill *Hants* 13 SU6627
Filton *Gloucs* 34 ST6079
Fimber *E R Yk* 91 SE8960
Finavon *Angus* 127 NO4956
Fincham *Norfk* 65 TF6806
Finchampstead *Berks* 25 SU7963
Fincharn *Ag & B* 122 NM9003
Finchdean *Hants* 13 SU7312
Finchingfield *Essex* 40 TL6832
Finchley *Gt Lon* 27 TQ2690
Findern *Derbys* 73 SK3030
Findhorn *Moray* 141 NJ0364
Findhorn Bridge *Highld* 140 NH8027
Findo Gask *P & K* 125 NO0019
Findochty *Moray* 142 NJ4667
Findon *Abers* 135 NO9397
Findon *W Susx* 14 TQ1208
Findon Mains *Highld* 140 NH6060
Findrack House *Abers* 134 NJ6004
Finedon *Nhants* 51 SP9172
Fingal Street *Suffk* 55 TM2169
Fingask *P & K* 126 NO1619
Fingest *Bucks* 37 SU7791
Finghall *N York* 89 SE1889
Fingland *Cumb* 93 NY2557
Fingland *D & G* 107 NS7517
Finglesham *Kent* 29 TR3353
Fingringhoe *Essex* 41 TM0220
Finkle Green *Essex* 53 TL7040
Finkle Street *S York* 74 SK3099
Finlarig *Stirlg* 124 NN5733
Finmere *Oxon* 49 SP6332
Finnart *P & K* 124 NN5157
Finningham *Suffk* 54 TM0669
Finningley *S York* 75 SK6799
Finsbay *W Isls* 154 NG0786
Finstall *H & W* 60 SO9770
Finsthwaite *Cumb* 87 SD3687
Finstock *Oxon* 36 SP3616
Finstown *Ork* 155 HY3513
Fintry *Abers* 142 NJ7554
Fintry *Stirlg* 116 NS6186
Finzean *Abers* 134 NO5993
Fionnphort *Ag & B* 120 NM3023
Fionnsbhagh *W Isls* 154 NG0786
Fir Tree *Dur* 96 NZ1434
Firbank *Cumb* 87 SD6293
Firbeck *S York* 75 SK5688
Firby *N York* 89 SE2686
Firby *N York* 90 SE7466
Firgrove *Gt Man* 81 SD9113
Firsby *Lincs* 77 TF4562

G

Greygarth

Hardsough

Greygarth N York 89 SE1872
Greylake Somset 21 ST3833
Greyrigg D & G 100 NY0888
Greys Green Oxon 37 SU7182
Greysouthen Cumb 92 NY0729
Greystoke Cumb 93 NY4430
Greystone Angus 127 NO5343
Greywell Hants 24 SU7151
Gribb Dorset 10 ST3703
Gribthorpe E R Yk 84 SE7635
Griff Warwks 61 SP3689
Griffithstown Torfn 34 ST2998
Griffydam Leics 62 SK4118
Griggs Green Hants 14 SU8231
Grimeford Village Lancs 81 SD6112
Grimesthorpe S York 74 SK3689
Grimethorpe S York 83 SE4109
Grimley H & W 47 SO8360
Grimmet S Ayrs 106 NS3210
Grimoldby Lincs 77 TF3988
Grimpo Shrops 59 SJ3526
Grimsargh Lancs 81 SD5834
Grimsby Lincs 85 TA2710
Grimscote Nhants 49 SP6553
Grimscott Cnwll 18 SS2606
Grimshader W Isls 154 NB4025
Grimshaw Lancs 81 SD7024
Grimshaw Green Lancs 80 SD4912
Grimsthorpe Lincs 64 TF0422
Grimston E R Yk 85 TA2735
Grimston Leics 63 SK6821
Grimston Norfk 65 TF7222
Grimston Hill Notts 75 SK6865
Grimstone Dorset 10 SY6394
Grimstone End Suffk 54 TL9368
Grinacombe Moor Devon 5 SX4191
Grindale E R Yk 91 TA1271
Grindle Shrops 60 SJ7503
Grindleford Derbys 74 SK2477
Grindleton Lancs 81 SD7545
Grindley Brook Shrops 71 SJ5242
Grindlow Derbys 74 SK1877
Grindon Dur 96 NZ3925
Grindon Nthumb 110 NT9144
Grindon Staffs 73 SK0854
Grindon Hill Nthumb 102 NY8268
Grindonrigg Nthumb 110 NT9243
Gringley on the Hill Notts 75 SK7390
Grinsdale Cumb 93 NY3758
Grinshill Shrops 59 SJ5223
Grinton N York 88 SE0498
Griomaisiader W Isls 154 NB4025
Grishipoll Ag & B 120 NM1859
Grisling Common E Susx 16 TQ4322
Gristhorpe N York 91 TA0981
Griston Norfk 66 TL9499
Gritley Ork 155 HY5504
Grittenham Wilts 36 SU0382
Grittleton Wilts 35 ST8580
Grizebeck Cumb 86 SD2384
Grizedale Cumb 86 SD3394
Groby Leics 62 SK5207
Groes A & C 70 SJ0064
Groes-faen Rhondd 33 ST0680
Groes-Wen Caerph 33 ST1286
Groesffordd Gwynd 56 SH2739
Groesffordd Marli Denbgs 70 SJ0073
Groesllwyd Powys 58 SJ2111
Groeslon Gwynd 68 SH4755
Groeslon Gwynd 68 SH5260
Grogarry W Isls 154 NF7739
Grogport Ag & B 105 NR8144
Groigearraidh W Isls 154 NF7739
Gromford Suffk 55 TM3858
Gronant Flints 70 SJ0983
Groombridge E Susx 16 TQ5337
Grosebay W Isls 154 NG1593
Grosmont Mons 46 SO4024
Grosmont N York 90 NZ8305
Groton Suffk 54 TL9641
Grotton Gt Man 79 SD9604
Grouville Jersey 152 JS0000
Grove Bucks 38 SP9122
Grove Dorset 11 SY6972
Grove Kent 29 TR2362
Grove Notts 75 SK7479
Grove Oxon 36 SU4090
Grove Pembks 30 SM9900
Grove Green Kent 28 TQ7856
Grove Park Gt Lon 27 TQ4072
Grove Vale W Mids 61 SP0394
Grovenhurst Kent 28 TQ7140
Grovesend Gloucs 35 ST6589
Grovesend Swans 32 SN5900
Grubb Street Kent 27 TQ5869
Gruinard Highld 144 NG9489
Gruinart Ag & B 112 NR2966
Grula Highld 136 NG3826
Gruline Ag & B 121 NM5440
Grumbla Cnwll 2 SW4029
Grundisburgh Suffk 55 TM2251
Gruting Shet 155 HU2749
Gualachulain Highld 123 NN1145
Guanockgate Lincs 64 TF3710
Guardbridge Fife 127 NO4518
Guarlford H & W 47 SO8145
Guay P & K 125 NN9948
Guestling Green E Susx 17 TQ8513
Guestling Thorn E Susx 17 TQ8516
Guestwick Norfk 66 TG0626
Guide Lancs 81 SD7025
Guide Bridge Gt Man 79 SJ9297
Guide Post Nthumb 103 NZ2585
Guilden Down Shrops 59 SO3082
Guilden Morden Cambs 39 TL2744
Guilden Sutton Ches 71 SJ4468
Guildford Surrey 25 SU9949
Guildstead Kent 28 TQ8262
Guildtown P & K 126 NO1331
Guilsborough Nhants 50 SP6772
Guilsfield Powys 58 SJ2211
Guilton Kent 29 TR2858
Guiltreehill S Ayrs 106 NS3610
Guineaford Devon 19 SS5537
Guisborough N York 97 NZ6015
Guiseley W York 82 SE1942
Guist Norfk 66 TG0025
Guiting Power Gloucs 48 SP0924
Gullane E Loth 118 NT4882
Gulling Green Suffk 54 TL8256
Gulval Cnwll 2 SW4831
Gulworthy Devon 6 SX4572
Gumfreston Pembks 31 SN1001
Gumley Leics 50 SP6889
Gummow's Shop Cnwll 4 SW8657
Gun Green Kent 17 TQ7731
Gun Hill E Susx 16 TQ5614
Gun Hill Warwks 61 SP2889
Gunby Lincs 63 SK9121
Gunby Lincs 77 TF4666
Gunby E R Yk 84 SE7035
Gundleton Hants 24 SU6133
Gunn Devon 19 SS6333
Gunnerside N York 88 SD9598
Gunnerton Nthumb 102 NY9074
Gunness Lincs 84 SE8411
Gunnislake Cnwll 6 SX4371
Gunnista Shet 155 HU5043
Gunthorpe Cambs 64 TF1802
Gunthorpe Norfk 66 TG0134
Gunthorpe Notts 63 SK6844
Gunton Suffk 67 TM5395
Gunville IOW 13 SZ4788
Gunwalloe Cnwll 2 SW6522
Gupworthy Somset 20 SS9734
Gurnard IOW 13 SZ4795
Gurnett Ches 79 SJ9271
Gurney Slade Somset 21 ST6249
Gurnos Powys 32 SN7709
Gushmere Kent 28 TR0457
Gussage All Saints Dorset 11 SU0010
Gussage St Andrew Dorset 11 ST9714
Gussage St Michael Dorset 11 ST9811
Guston Kent 29 TR3244
Gutcher Shet 155 HU5499
Guthrie Angus 127 NO5650
Guy's Marsh Dorset 22 ST8420
Guyhirn Cambs 65 TF4003
Guyhirn Gull Cambs 65 TF3904
Guyzance Nthumb 103 NU2103
Gwaenysgor Flints 70 SJ0781
Gwalchmai Angles 68 SH3876
Gwastadnant Gwynd 69 SH6157
Gwaun-Cae-Gurwen Carmth 32 SN6911
Gwbert on Sea Cardgn 42 SN1650
Gwealavellan Cnwll 2 SW6041
Gwealeath Cnwll 2 SW6922
Gweek Cnwll 2 SW7026
Gwehelog Mons 34 SO3804
Gwenddwr Powys 45 SO0643
Gwendreath Cnwll 3 SW7217
Gwennap Cnwll 3 SW7340
Gwenter Cnwll 3 SW7417
Gwernaffield Flints 70 SJ2065
Gwernesney Mons 34 SO4101
Gwernogle Carmth 44 SN5333
Gwernymynydd Flints 70 SJ2162
Gwersyllt Wrexhm 71 SJ3153
Gwespyr Flints 70 SJ1183
Gwindra Cnwll 3 SW9552
Gwinear Cnwll 2 SW5937
Gwithian Cnwll 2 SW5841
Gwredog Angles 68 SH4085
Gwrhay Caerph 33 ST1899
Gwyddelwern Denbgs 70 SJ0746
Gwyddgrug Carmth 44 SN4635
Gwynfryn Wrexhm 70 SJ2552
Gwystre Powys 45 SO0665
Gwytherin A & C 69 SH8761
Gyfelia Wrexhm 71 SJ3245
Gyrn-goch Gwynd 68 SH4048

H

Habberley H & W 60 SO8177
Habberley Shrops 59 SJ3903
Habergham Lancs 81 SD8033
Habertoft Lincs 77 TF5069
Habin W Susx 14 SU8022
Habrough Lincs 85 TA1413
Hacconby Lincs 64 TF1025
Haceby Lincs 64 TF0236
Hacheston Suffk 55 TM3059
Hack Green Ches 72 SJ6448
Hackbridge Gt Lon 27 TQ2865
Hackenthorpe S York 74 SK4183
Hackford Norfk 66 TG0502
Hackforth N York 89 SE2492
Hackland Ork 155 HY3920
Hackleton Nhants 51 SP8055
Hacklinge Kent 29 TR3454
Hackman's Gate H & W 60 SO8978
Hackness N York 91 SE9790
Hackness Somset 21 ST3345
Hackney Gt Lon 27 TQ3484
Hackthorn Lincs 76 SK9982
Hackthorpe Cumb 94 NY5423
Hacton Gt Lon 27 TQ5585
Hadden Border 110 NT7836
Haddenham Bucks 37 SP7308
Haddenham Cambs 53 TL4675
Haddington E Loth 118 NT5173
Haddington Lincs 76 SK9162
Haddiscoe Norfk 67 TM4497
Haddo Abers 143 NJ8337
Haddon Cambs 64 TL1392
Hade Edge W York 82 SE1404
Hadfield Derbys 74 SK0296
Hadham Cross Herts 39 TL4218
Hadham Ford Herts 39 TL4321
Hadleigh Essex 40 TQ8187
Hadleigh Suffk 54 TM0242
Hadleigh Heath Suffk 54 TL9941
Hadley H & W 47 SO8564
Hadley Shrops 60 SJ6711
Hadley End Staffs 73 SK1320
Hadley Wood Gt Lon 27 TQ2698
Hadlow Kent 27 TQ6350
Hadlow Down E Susx 16 TQ5324
Hadnall Shrops 59 SJ5220
Hadstock Essex 53 TL5644
Hadzor H & W 47 SO9162
Haffenden Quarter Kent 28 TQ8840
Hafod-y-bwch Wrexhm 71 SJ3147
Hafod-y-coed Blae G 34 SO2200
Hafodunos A & C 69 SH8666
Hafodyrynys Caerph 34 ST2298
Haggate Lancs 81 SD8735
Haggbeck Cumb 101 NY4773
Haggerston Nthumb 111 NU0443
Haggington Hill Devon 19 SS5547
Haggs Falk 116 NS7879
Hagley H & W 46 SO5641
Hagley W Mids 60 SO9180
Hagmore Green Suffk 54 TL9539
Hagnaby Lincs 77 TF3462
Hagnaby Lincs 77 TF4879
Hagworthingham Lincs 77 TF3469
Haigh Gt Man 78 SD6009
Haighton Green Lancs 81 SD5634
Hail Weston Cambs 52 TL1662
Haile Cumb 86 NY0308
Hailes Gloucs 48 SP0430
Hailey Herts 39 TL3710
Hailey Oxon 37 SU6485
Hailey Oxon 36 SP3512
Hailsham E Susx 16 TQ5909
Hainault Gt Lon 27 TQ4591
Haine Kent 29 TR3566
Hainford Norfk 67 TG2218
Hainton Lincs 76 TF1884
Hainworth W York 82 SE0638
Haisthorpe E R Yk 91 TA1264
Hakin Pembks 30 SM8905
Halam Notts 75 SK6754
Halbeath Fife 117 NT1288
Halberton Devon 9 ST0112
Halcro Highld 151 ND2360
Hale Ches 78 SJ4782
Hale Cumb 87 SD5078
Hale Gt Man 79 SJ7786
Hale Hants 12 SU1818
Hale Somset 22 ST7427
Hale Surrey 25 SU8448
Hale Bank Ches 78 SJ4784
Hale Green E Susx 16 TQ5514
Hale Nook Lancs 80 SD3944
Hale Street Kent 28 TQ6749
Halebarns Gt Man 79 SJ7985
Hales Norfk 67 TM3797
Hales Staffs 72 SJ7134
Hales Green Derbys 73 SK1841
Hales Place Kent 29 TR1459
Halesgate Lincs 64 TF3226
Halesowen W Mids 60 SO9683
Halesworth Suffk 55 TM3877
Halewood Mersyd 78 SJ4585
Halford Devon 7 SX8174
Halford Shrops 59 SO4383
Halford Warwks 48 SP2645
Halfpenny Cumb 87 SD5387
Halfpenny Green Staffs 60 SO8291
Halfpenny Houses N York 89 SE2284
Halfway Berks 24 SU4068
Halfway Carmth 44 SN6430
Halfway Carmth 44 SN8232
Halfway S York 75 SK4381
Halfway Bridge W Susx 14 SU9321
Halfway House Shrops 59 SJ3411
Halfway Houses Kent 28 TQ9372
Halifax W York 82 SE0925
Halistra Highld 136 NG2459
Halkirk Highld 151 ND1359
Halkyn Flints 70 SJ2171
Hall E Rens 115 NS4154
Hall Cliffe W York 82 SE2918
Hall Cross Lancs 80 SD4230
Hall Dunnerdale Cumb 86 SD2195
Hall End Beds 38 TL0045
Hall End Beds 38 TL0737
Hall End W Mids 60 SP0092
Hall Glen Falk 116 NS8978
Hall Green W Mids 61 SP1181
Hall's Green Essex 39 TL4108
Hall's Green Herts 39 TL2728
Hallam Fields Derbys 62 SK4739
Halland E Susx 16 TQ4916
Hallaton Leics 50 SP7896
Hallatrow Somset 21 ST6357
Hallbankgate Cumb 94 NY5859
Hallbeck Cumb 87 SD6288
Hallen Gloucs 34 ST5580
Hallfield Gate Derbys 74 SK3958
Hallgarth Dur 96 NZ3243
Hallin Highld 136 NG2558
Halling Kent 28 TQ7063
Hallington Lincs 77 TF3085
Hallington Nthumb 102 NY9875
Halliwell Gt Man 79 SD6910
Halloughton Notts 75 SK6951
Hallow H & W 47 SO8258
Hallow Heath H & W 47 SO8259
Hallrule Border 110 NT5914
Hallsands Devon 7 SX8138
Hallthwaites Cumb 86 SD1885
Halltoft End Lincs 64 TF3645
Hallworthy Cnwll 4 SX1787
Hallyne Border 109 NT1940
Halmer End Staffs 72 SJ7948
Halmond's Frome H & W 47 SO6747
Halnaker W Susx 14 SU9007
Halsall Lancs 78 SD3710
Halse Nhants 49 SP5640
Halse Somset 20 ST1428
Halsetown Cnwll 2 SW5038
Halsham E R Yk 85 TA2727
Halsinger Devon 19 SS5138
Halstead Essex 40 TL8130
Halstead Kent 27 TQ4861
Halstead Leics 63 SK7505
Halstock Dorset 10 ST5308
Halsway Somset 20 ST1337
Haltcliff Bridge Cumb 93 NY3636
Haltham Lincs 77 TF2463
Halton Bucks 38 SP8710
Halton Ches 78 SJ5481
Halton Lancs 87 SD5064
Halton Nthumb 103 NY9967
Halton W York 83 SE3533
Halton Wrexhm 71 SJ3039
Halton East N York 82 SE0454
Halton Fenside Lincs 77 TF4263
Halton Gill N York 88 SD8776
Halton Green Lancs 87 SD5165
Halton Holegate Lincs 77 TF4165
Halton Lea Gate Nthumb 94 NY6458
Halton Quay Cnwll 5 SX4165
Halton Shields Nthumb 103 NZ0168
Halton West N York 81 SD8454
Haltwhistle Nthumb 102 NY7064
Halvergate Norfk 67 TG4106
Halwell Devon 7 SX7753
Halwill Devon 18 SX4299
Halwill Junction Devon 18 SS4400
Ham Devon 9 ST2301
Ham Gloucs 35 SO9721
Ham Gloucs 35 ST6898
Ham Gt Lon 26 TQ1772
Ham Kent 29 TR3254
Ham Somset 20 ST2825
Ham Somset 22 ST6748
Ham Wilts 23 SU3262
Ham Common Dorset 22 ST8125
Ham Green H & W 47 SO7544
Ham Green H & W 47 SP0163
Ham Green Kent 28 TQ8468
Ham Green Kent 17 TQ8926
Ham Green Somset 34 ST5375
Ham Hill Kent 28 TQ6960
Ham Street Somset 21 ST5534
Hamble-le-Rice Hants 13 SU4806
Hambleden Bucks 37 SU7886
Hambledon Hants 13 SU6414
Hambledon Surrey 25 SU9638
Hambleton Lancs 80 SD3742
Hambleton N York 83 SE5530
Hambleton Moss Side Lancs 80 SD3842
Hambridge Somset 21 ST3921
Hambridge Somset 21 ST5936
Hambrook Gloucs 35 ST6478
Hambrook W Susx 14 SU7806
Hamels Herts 39 TL3724
Hameringham Lincs 77 TF3167
Hamerton Cambs 52 TL1379
Hamilton S Lans 116 NS7255
Hamlet Dorset 10 ST5908
Hamlins E Susx 16 TQ5908
Hammerpot W Susx 14 TQ0605
Hammersmith Gt Lon 26 TQ2378
Hammerwich Staffs 61 SK0707
Hammerwood E Susx 16 TQ4339
Hammond Street Herts 39 TL3304
Hammoon Dorset 11 ST8114
Hamnavoe Shet 155 HU3735
Hamnavoe Shet 155 HU4971
Hampden Park E Susx 16 TQ6002
Hampden Row Bucks 26 SP8501
Hamperden End Essex 40 TL5730
Hampnett Gloucs 36 SP0915
Hampole S York 83 SE5010
Hampreston Dorset 12 SZ0598
Hampsfield Cumb 87 SD4080
Hampson Green Lancs 80 SD4954
Hampstead Gt Lon 27 TQ2685
Hampstead Norrey's Berks 37 SU5276
Hampsthwaite N York 89 SE2559
Hampt Cnwll 5 SX3874
Hampton Devon 10 SY2696
Hampton Gt Lon 26 TQ1369
Hampton H & W 48 SP0243
Hampton Kent 29 TR1568
Hampton Shrops 60 SO7486
Hampton Wilts 36 SU1892
Hampton Bishop H & W 46 SO5637
Hampton Green Ches 71 SJ5149
Hampton Heath Ches 71 SJ5049
Hampton in Arden W Mids 61 SP2080
Hampton Loade Shrops 60 SO7486
Hampton Lovett H & W 47 SO8865
Hampton Lucy Warwks 48 SP2557
Hampton on the Hill Warwks 48 SP2564
Hampton Poyle Oxon 37 SP5015
Hampton Wick Gt Lon 26 TQ1769
Hamptworth Wilts 12 SU2419
Hamrow Norfk 66 TF9124
Hamsey E Susx 15 TQ4012
Hamsey Green Gt Lon 27 TQ3559
Hamstall Ridware Staffs 73 SK1019
Hamstead IOW 13 SZ4091
Hamstead W Mids 61 SP0592
Hamstead Marshall Berks 24 SU4165
Hamsterley Dur 95 NZ1156
Hamsterley Dur 96 NZ1231
Hamstreet Kent 17 TR0033
Hamwood Somset 21 ST3756
Hamworthy Dorset 11 SY9991
Hanbury H & W 47 SO9664
Hanbury Staffs 73 SK1727
Hanby Lincs 64 TF0231
Hanchet End Suffk 53 TL6446
Hanchurch Staffs 72 SJ8441
Hand and Pen Devon 9 SY0495
Hand Green Ches 71 SJ5460
Handale N York 97 NZ7215
Handbridge Ches 71 SJ4065
Handcross W Susx 15 TQ2629
Handforth Ches 79 SJ8583
Handley Ches 71 SJ4657
Handley Derbys 74 SK3761
Handley Green Essex 40 TL6501
Handsacre Staffs 73 SK0915
Handsworth S York 74 SK4186
Handsworth W Mids 61 SP0489
Handy Cross Bucks 26 SU8590
Hanford Dorset 11 ST8411
Hanford Staffs 72 SJ8741
Hanging Langford Wilts 23 SU0337
Hangleton E Susx 15 TQ2607
Hangleton W Susx 14 TQ0803
Hanham Gloucs 35 ST6472
Hankelow Ches 72 SJ6645
Hankerton Wilts 35 ST9790
Hankham E Susx 16 TQ6105
Hanley Staffs 72 SJ8847
Hanley Castle H & W 47 SO8442
Hanley Child H & W 47 SO6565
Hanley Swan H & W 47 SO8142
Hanley William H & W 47 SO6766
Hanlith N York 88 SD8961
Hanmer Wrexhm 71 SJ4539
Hannaford Devon 19 SS6029
Hannah Lincs 77 TF4979
Hannington Hants 24 SU5355
Hannington Nhants 51 SP8170
Hannington Wilts 36 SU1793
Hannington Wick Wilts 36 SU1795
Hanscombe End Beds 38 TL1133
Hanslope Bucks 38 SP8046
Hanthorpe Lincs 64 TF0823
Hanwell Gt Lon 26 TQ1579
Hanwell Oxon 49 SP4343
Hanworth Gt Lon 26 TQ1271
Hanworth Norfk 67 TG1935
Happendon S Lans 108 NS8533
Happisburgh Norfk 67 TG3831
Happisburgh Common Norfk 67 TG3728
Hapsford Ches 71 SJ4774
Hapton Lancs 81 SD7931
Hapton Norfk 66 TM1796
Harberton Devon 7 SX7758
Harbertonford Devon 7 SX7856
Harbledown Kent 29 TR1357
Harborne W Mids 60 SP0284
Harborough Magna Warwks 50 SP4879
Harbottle Nthumb 102 NT9304
Harbourneford Devon 7 SX7162
Harbours Hill H & W 47 SO9565
Harbridge Hants 12 SU1410
Harbridge Green Hants 12 SU1410
Harbury Warwks 48 SP3759
Harby Leics 63 SK7431
Harby Notts 76 SK8770
Harcombe Devon 9 SX8881
Harcombe Devon 9 SY1590
Harcombe Bottom Devon 10 SY3395
Harden W Mids 60 SK0100
Harden W York 82 SE0838
Hardenhuish Wilts 35 ST9174
Hardgate Abers 135 NJ7901
Hardgate D & Cb 115 NS5072
Hardgate D & G 100 NX8167
Hardgate N York 89 SE2662
Hardham W Susx 14 TQ0317
Hardhorn Lancs 80 SD3537
Hardingham Norfk 66 TG0403
Hardingstone Nhants 49 SP7657
Hardington Somset 22 ST7452
Hardington Mandeville Somset 10 ST5111
Hardington Marsh Somset 10 ST5009
Hardington Moor Somset 10 ST5112
Hardisworthy Devon 18 SS2320
Hardley Hants 13 SU4205
Hardley Street Norfk 67 TG3701
Hardmead Bucks 38 SP9347
Hardraw N York 88 SD8691
Hardsough Lancs 81 SD7920

285

Hulme

Keeston

Hulme Staffs 72 SJ9345
Hulme End Staffs 74 SK1059
Hulme Walfield Ches 72 SJ8465
Hulse Heath Ches 79 SJ7283
Hulton Lane Ends Gt Man 79 SD6905
Hulver Street Norfk 66 TF9311
Hulver Street Suffk 55 TM4686
Hulverstone IOW 13 SZ3984
Humber Devon 7 SX8975
Humberston Lincs 85 TA3105
Humberstone Leics 63 SK6305
Humberton N York 89 SE4168
Humbie E Loth 118 NT4662
Humbleton E R Yk 85 TA2234
Humbleton Nthumb 111 NT9728
Humby Lincs 63 TF0032
Hume Border 110 NT7041
Humshaugh Nthumb 102 NY9171
Huna Highld 151 ND3573
Huncoat Lancs 81 SD7730
Huncote Leics 50 SP5197
Hundalee Border 110 NT6418
Hundall Derbys 74 SK3876
Hunderthwaite Dur 95 NY9821
Hundle Houses Lincs 77 TF2453
Hundleby Lincs 77 TF3966
Hundleton Pembks 30 SM9600
Hundon Suffk 53 TL7348
Hundred Acres Hants 13 SU5911
Hundred End Lancs 80 SD4122
Hundred House Powys 45 SO1154
Hundred The H & W 46 SO5264
Hungarton Leics 63 SK6907
Hungate End Bucks 38 SP7946
Hunger Hill Lancs 80 SD5411
Hungerford Berks 23 SU3368
Hungerford Hants 12 SU1612
Hungerford Somset 20 ST0440
Hungerford Newtown Berks 36 SU3571
Hungerstone H & W 46 SO4435
Hungerton Lincs 63 SK8729
Hungryhatton Shrops 72 SJ6626
Hunmanby N York 91 TA0977
Hunningham Warwks 48 SP3767
Hunnington H & W 60 SO9681
Hunny Hill IOW 13 SZ4990
Hunsdon Herts 39 TL4114
Hunsingore N York 83 SE4253
Hunslet W York 82 SE3130
Hunsonby Cumb 94 NY5835
Hunstanton Norfk 65 TF6740
Hunstanworth Dur 95 NY9448
Hunston Suffk 54 TL9768
Hunston W Susx 14 SU8601
Hunston Green Suffk 54 TL9866
Hunstrete Somset 21 ST6462
Hunsworth W York 82 SE1827
Hunt End H & W 48 SP0364
Hunt's Corner Norfk 54 TM0588
Hunt's Cross Mersyd 78 SJ4385
Hunter's Inn Devon 19 SS6548
Hunters Quay Ag & B 114 NS1879
Hunterston Ches 72 SJ6946
Huntham Somset 21 ST3426
Hunthill Lodge Angus 134 NO4771
Huntingdon Cambs 52 TL2471
Huntingdon H & W 46 SO2553
Huntingfield Suffk 55 TM3374
Huntingford Dorset 22 ST8030
Huntington E Loth 118 NT4874
Huntington H & W 46 SO4841
Huntington N York 83 SE6156
Huntington Staffs 60 SJ9712
Huntley Gloucs 35 SO7219
Huntly Abers 142 NJ5339
Hunton Hants 24 SU4840
Hunton Kent 28 TQ7149
Hunton N York 89 SE1892
Hunton Bridge Herts 26 TL0800
Hunts Green Bucks 38 SP8903
Hunts Green Warwks 61 SP1897
Huntscott Somset 20 SS9144
Huntsham Devon 20 ST0020
Huntshaw Devon 19 SS5023
Huntshaw Cross Devon 19 SS5222
Huntspill Somset 21 ST3145
Huntstile Somset 20 ST2633
Huntworth Somset 21 ST3134
Hunwick Dur 96 NZ1832
Hunworth Norfk 66 TG0635
Hurcott Somset 10 ST3916
Hurdcott Wilts 23 SU1733
Hurdsfield Ches 79 SJ9274
Hurley Berks 37 SU8283
Hurley Warwks 61 SP2495
Hurley Bottom Berks 37 SU8283
Hurley Common Warwks 61 SP2496
Hurlford E Ayrs 107 NS4536
Hurlston Green Lancs 80 SD3911
Hurn Dorset 12 SZ1296
Hurn's End Lincs 77 TF4249
Hursley Hants 13 SU4225
Hurst Berks 25 SU7973
Hurst Dorset 11 SY7990
Hurst N York 88 NZ0402
Hurst Somset 10 ST4518
Hurst Green E Susx 17 TQ7327
Hurst Green Essex 41 TM0916
Hurst Green Lancs 81 SD6838
Hurst Green Surrey 27 TQ3951
Hurst Hill W Mids 60 SO9393
Hurst Wickham W Susx 15 TQ2816
Hurstbourne Priors Hants 24 SU4346
Hurstbourne Tarrant Hants 23 SU3853
Hurstley H & W 46 SO3548
Hurstpierpoint W Susx 15 TQ2716
Hurstway Common H & W 46 SO2949
Hurstwood Lancs 81 SD8831
Hurtiso Ork 155 HY5001
Hurtmore Surrey 25 SU9445
Hurworth Burn Dur 96 NZ4033
Hurworth-on-Tees Dur 89 NZ3009
Hury Dur 95 NY9519
Husbands Bosworth Leics 50 SP6484
Husborne Crawley Beds 38 SP9635
Husthwaite N York 90 SE5175
Hut Green N York 83 SE5623
Hutcherleigh Devon 7 SX7850
Huthwaite N York 90 NZ4801
Huthwaite Notts 75 SK4659
Huttoft Lincs 77 TF5176
Hutton Border 119 NT9053
Hutton Cumb 93 NY4326
Hutton E R Yk 84 TA0253
Hutton Essex 40 TQ6395
Hutton Lancs 80 SD4926
Hutton Somset 21 ST3558
Hutton Bonville N York 89 NZ3300
Hutton Buscel N York 91 SE9784
Hutton Conyers N York 89 SE3273
Hutton Cranswick E R Yk 84 TA0252
Hutton End Cumb 93 NY4538
Hutton Hall N York 90 NZ6014
Hutton Hang N York 89 SE1788
Hutton Henry Dur 96 NZ4236
Hutton Lowcross N York 90 NZ5914
Hutton Magna Dur 89 NZ1212
Hutton Mulgrave N York 90 NZ8309
Hutton Roof Cumb 93 NY3734
Hutton Roof Cumb 87 SD5677
Hutton Rudby N York 89 NZ4606
Hutton Sessay N York 89 SE4776
Hutton Wandesley N York 83 SE5050
Hutton-le-Hole N York 90 SE7090
Huxham Devon 9 SX9497
Huxham Green Somset 21 ST5936
Huxley Ches 71 SJ5061
Huyton Mersyd 78 SJ4490
Hycemoor Cumb 86 SD0989
Hyde Gloucs 35 SO8801
Hyde Gt Man 79 SJ9494
Hyde Hants 12 SU1612
Hyde End Berks 24 SU7266
Hyde Heath Bucks 26 SP9300
Hyde Lea Staffs 72 SJ9120
Hyde Park Corner Somset 20 ST2832
Hydestile Surrey 25 SU9640
Hykeham Moor Lincs 76 SK9366
Hylands Essex 40 TL6704
Hyndford Bridge S Lans 108 NS9141
Hynish Ag & B 120 NL9839
Hyssington Powys 59 SO3194
Hystfield Gloucs 35 ST6695
Hythe Hants 13 SU4207
Hythe Kent 29 TR1634
Hythe Somset 21 ST4452
Hythe End Berks 26 TQ0172
Hyton Cumb 86 SD0987

I

Ibberton Dorset 11 ST7807
Ible Derbys 74 SK2457
Ibsley Hants 12 SU1509
Ibstock Leics 62 SK4009
Ibstone Bucks 37 SU7593
Ibthorpe Hants 23 SU3753
Iburndale N York 90 NZ8707
Ibworth Hants 24 SU5654
Icelton Somset 21 ST3765
Ickburgh Norfk 66 TL8195
Ickenham Gt Lon 26 TQ0786
Ickford Bucks 37 SP6407
Ickham Kent 29 TR2258
Ickleford Herts 39 TL1831
Icklesham E Susx 17 TQ8716
Ickleton Cambs 39 TL4943
Icklingham Suffk 53 TL7772
Ickornshaw N York 82 SD9642
Ickwell Green Beds 52 TL1545
Icomb Gloucs 36 SP2122
Idbury Oxon 36 SP2319
Iddesleigh Devon 19 SS5708
Ide Devon 9 SX8990
Ide Hill Kent 27 TQ4851
Ideford Devon 9 SX8977
Iden E Susx 17 TQ9123
Iden Green Kent 28 TQ7437
Iden Green Kent 17 TQ8031
Idle W York 82 SE1737
Idless Cnwll 3 SW8147
Idlicote Warwks 48 SP2844
Idmiston Wilts 23 SU1937
Idridgehay Derbys 73 SK2849
Idrigill Highld 136 NG3863
Idstone Oxon 36 SU2584
Iffley Oxon 37 SP5203
Ifield W Susx 15 TQ2537
Ifold W Susx 14 TQ0231
Iford Dorset 12 SZ1393
Iford E Susx 15 TQ4007
Ifton Mons 34 ST4688
Ifton Heath Shrops 59 SJ3237
Ightam Kent 27 TQ5956
Ightfield Shrops 71 SJ5938
Iken Suffk 55 TM4155
Ilam Staffs 73 SK1350
Ilchester Somset 21 ST5222
Ilderton Nthumb 111 NU0121
Ilford Gt Lon 27 TQ4486
Ilford Somset 10 ST3617
Ilfracombe Devon 19 SS5247
Ilkeston Derbys 62 SK4641
Ilketshall St Andrew Suffk 55 TM3887
Ilketshall St Margaret Suffk 55 TM3485
Ilkley W York 82 SE1147
Illand Cnwll 5 SX2878
Illey W Mids 60 SO9881
Illidge Green Ches 72 SJ7963
Illingworth W York 82 SE0728
Illogan Cnwll 2 SW6743
Illston on the Hill Leics 50 SP7099
Ilmer Bucks 37 SP7605
Ilmington Warwks 48 SP2143
Ilminster Somset 10 ST3614
Ilsington Dorset 11 SY7592
Ilsington Devon 7 SX7875
Ilston Swans 32 SS5590
Ilton N York 89 SE1978
Ilton Somset 10 ST3517
Imachar N Ayrs 105 NR8640
Immingham Lincs 85 TA1814
Immingham Dock Lincs 85 TA1916
Impington Cambs 53 TL4463
Ince Ches 71 SJ4576
Ince Blundell Mersyd 78 SD3203
Ince-in-Makerfield Gt Man 78 SD5904
Inchbae Lodge Hotel Highld 146 NH4069
Inchbare Angus 134 NO6065
Inchberry Moray 141 NJ3055
Inchinnan Rens 115 NS4769
Inchlaggan Highld 131 NH1701
Inchmichael P & K 126 NO2425
Inchnacardoch Hotel Highld 131 NH3810
Inchnadamph Highld 145 NC2521
Inchture P & K 126 NO2728
Inchvuilt Highld 139 NH2438
Inchyra P & K 126 NO1820
Indian Queens Cnwll 4 SW9159
Ingate Place Suffk 55 TM4288
Ingatestone Essex 40 TQ6499
Ingbirchworth S York 82 SE2205
Ingerthorpe N York 89 SE2866
Ingestre Staffs 72 SJ9724
Ingham Lincs 76 SK9483
Ingham Norfk 67 TG3926
Ingham Suffk 54 TL8570
Ingham Corner Norfk 67 TG3927
Ingleborough Norfk 65 TF4715
Ingleby Derbys 62 SK3426
Ingleby Arncliffe N York 89 NZ4400
Ingleby Barwick N York 89 NZ4414
Ingleby Cross N York 89 NZ4500
Ingleby Greenhow N York 90 NZ5706
Ingleigh Green Devon 8 SS6007
Inglesbatch Somset 22 ST7061
Inglesham Wilts 36 SU2098
Ingleston D & G 99 NX6048
Ingleston D & G 100 NX9865
Ingleton Dur 96 NZ1720
Ingleton N York 87 SD6972
Inglewhite Lancs 80 SD5439
Ingmire Hall Cumb 87 SD6391
Ingoe Nthumb 103 NZ0374
Ingoldisthorpe Norfk 65 TF6832
Ingoldmells Lincs 77 TF5668
Ingoldsby Lincs 64 TF0129
Ingram Nthumb 111 NU0115
Ingrave Essex 40 TQ6291
Ingrow W York 82 SE0539
Ings Cumb 87 SD4498
Ingst Gloucs 34 ST5887
Ingthorpe Lincs 63 SK9908
Ingworth Norfk 67 TG1929
Inkberrow H & W 47 SP0157
Inkerman Dur 95 NZ1139
Inkhorn Abers 143 NJ9239
Inkpen Berks 23 SU3664
Inkstack Highld 151 ND2570
Inmarsh Wilts 22 ST9460
Innellan Ag & B 114 NS1570
Innerleithen Border 109 NT3336
Innerleven Fife 118 NO3700
Innermessan D & G 98 NX0862
Innerwick E Loth 119 NT7273
Innesmill Moray 141 NJ2863
Insch Abers 142 NJ6228
Insh Highld 132 NH8101
Inskip Lancs 80 SD4637
Inskip Moss Side Lancs 80 SD4539
Instow Devon 18 SS4730
Insworke Cnwll 6 SX4252
Intake S York 74 SK3884
Inver Abers 133 NO2293
Inver Highld 147 NH8682
Inver P & K 125 NO0142
Inver-boyndie Abers 142 NJ6664
Inverailort Highld 129 NM7681
Inveralligin Highld 138 NG8457
Inverallochy Abers 143 NK0365
Inveran Highld 146 NH5797
Inveraray Ag & B 123 NN0908
Inverarish Highld 137 NG5535
Inverarity Angus 127 NO4544
Inverarnan Stirlg 123 NN3118
Inverasdale Highld 144 NG8284
Inveravon Falk 117 NS9579
Inverawe Ag & B 122 NN0231
Inverbeg Ag & B 115 NS3497
Inverbervie Abers 135 NO8272
Inverbroom Highld 145 NH1883
Invercreran House Hotel Ag & B 122 NN0146
Inverdruie Highld 132 NH8911
Inveresk E Loth 118 NT3471
Inveresragan Ag & B 122 NM9835
Inverey Abers 133 NO0889
Inverfarigaig Highld 139 NH5123
Inverfolia Ag & B 122 NM9544
Invergarry Highld 131 NH3001
Invergeldie P & K 124 NN7327
Invergloy Highld 131 NN2288
Invergordon Highld 140 NH7068
Invergowrie P & K 126 NO3430
Inverguseran Highld 129 NG7407
Inverhadden P & K 124 NN6757
Inverherive Hotel Stirlg 123 NN3626
Inverie Highld 129 NG7600
Inverinan Ag & B 122 NM9917
Inverinate Highld 138 NG9221
Inverkeilor Angus 127 NO6649
Inverkeithing Fife 117 NT1383
Inverkeithny Abers 142 NJ6247
Inverkip Inver 114 NS2072
Inverkirkaig Highld 145 NC0719
Inverlael Highld 145 NH1885
Inverlair Highld 131 NN3479
Inverliever Lodge Ag & B 122 NM8905
Inverlochy Ag & B 123 NN1927
Invermarkie Abers 142 NJ4239
Invermoriston Highld 139 NH4216
Inverness Highld 140 NH6645
Invernoaden Ag & B 114 NS1297
Inveroran Hotel Ag & B 123 NN2741
Inverquharity Angus 134 NO4057
Inverquhomery Abers 143 NK0146
Inverroy Highld 131 NN2581
Inversanda Highld 130 NM9459
Invershiel Highld 138 NG9319
Invershin Highld 146 NH5796
Invershore Highld 151 ND2435
Inversnaid Hotel Stirlg 123 NN3308
Inverugie Abers 143 NK0948
Inveruglas Ag & B 123 NN3109
Inveruglass Highld 132 NH8000
Inverurie Abers 142 NJ7721
Inwardleigh Devon 8 SX5699
Inworth Essex 40 TL8717
Iping W Susx 14 SU8522
Ipplepen Devon 7 SX8366
Ipsden Oxon 37 SU6285
Ipstones Staffs 73 SK0149
Ipswich Suffk 54 TM1644
Irby Mersyd 78 SJ2584
Irby in the Marsh Lincs 77 TF4663
Irby upon Humber Lincs 85 TA1904
Irchester Nhants 51 SP9265
Ireby Cumb 93 NY2338
Ireby Lancs 87 SD6575
Ireland Beds 38 TL1341
Ireleth Cumb 86 SD2277
Ireshopeburn Dur 95 NY8638
Ireton Wood Derbys 73 SK2847
Irlam Gt Man 79 SJ7294
Irnham Lincs 64 TF0226
Iron Acton Gloucs 35 ST6783
Iron Bridge Cambs 65 TL4898
Iron Cross Warwks 48 SP0552
Ironbridge Shrops 60 SJ6703
Ironmacannie D & G 99 NX6675
Irons Bottom Surrey 15 TQ2446
Ironville Derbys 75 SK4351
Irstead Norfk 67 TG3620
Irthington Cumb 101 NY4961
Irthlingborough Nhants 51 SP9470
Irton N York 91 TA0184
Irvine N Ayrs 106 NS3238
Isauld Highld 150 NC9865
Isbister Shet 155 HU3790
Isfield E Susx 16 TQ4417
Isham Nhants 51 SP8873
Isington Hants 25 SU7842
Islandpool H & W 60 SO8780
Isle Abbotts Somset 21 ST3520
Isle Brewers Somset 21 ST3621
Isle of Dogs Gt Lon 27 TQ3779
Isle of Whithorn D & G 99 NX4736
Isleham Cambs 53 TL6474
Isleornsay Highld 129 NG7012
Islesteps D & G 100 NX9672
Islet Village Guern 152 GN0000
Isley Walton Leics 62 SK4224
Islibhig W Isls 154 NB0029
Islington Gt Lon 27 TQ3184
Islip Nhants 51 SP9879
Islip Oxon 37 SP5214
Islivig W Isls 154 NB0029
Isombridge Shrops 59 SJ6113
Istead Rise Kent 27 TQ6370
Itchen Abbas Hants 24 SU5333
Itchen Stoke Hants 24 SU5532
Itchingfield W Susx 15 TQ1328
Itchington Gloucs 35 ST6587
Itteringham Norfk 66 TG1430
Itton Devon 8 SX6899
Itton Mons 34 ST4995
Ivegill Cumb 93 NY4143
Ivelet N York 88 SD9398
Iver Bucks 26 TQ0381
Iver Heath Bucks 26 TQ0283
Iveston Dur 96 NZ1350
Ivinghoe Bucks 38 SP9416
Ivinghoe Aston Bucks 38 SP9517
Ivington H & W 46 SO4756
Ivington Green H & W 46 SO4656
Ivy Cross Dorset 22 ST8623
Ivy Hatch Kent 27 TQ5854
Ivy Todd Norfk 66 TF8909
Ivybridge Devon 6 SX6356
Ivychurch Kent 17 TR0327
Iwade Kent 28 TQ9067
Iwerne Courtney or
Shroton Dorset 11 ST8512
Iwerne Minster Dorset 11 ST8614
Ixworth Suffk 54 TL9370
Ixworth Thorpe Suffk 54 TL9173

J

Jack Green Lancs 81 SD5925
Jack Hill N York 82 SE1951
Jack's Bush Hants 23 SU2636
Jack-in-the-Green Devon 9 SY0195
Jacksdale Notts 75 SK4451
Jackson Bridge W York 82 SE1607
Jackton S Lans 115 NS5952
Jacobs Well Surrey 25 TQ0053
Jacobstow Cnwll 5 SX1995
Jacobstowe Devon 8 SS5801
Jameston Pembks 30 SS0598
Jamestown D & Cb 115 NS3981
Jamestown Highld 139 NH4756
Janets-town Highld 151 ND3551
Janetstown Highld 151 ND1932
Jardine Hall D & G 100 NY1088
Jarrow T & W 103 NZ3364
Jarvis Brook E Susx 16 TQ5329
Jasper's Green Essex 40 TL7226
Jawcraig Falk 116 NS8475
Jaywick Essex 41 TM1413
Jealott's Hill Berks 25 SU8673
Jeater Houses N York 89 SE4394
Jedburgh Border 110 NT6420
Jeffreston Pembks 31 SN0906
Jemimaville Highld 140 NH7165
Jerbourg Guern 152 GN0000
Jerusalem Lincs 76 SK9170
Jesmond T & W 103 NZ2566
Jevington E Susx 16 TQ5601
Jingle Street Mons 34 SO4710
Jockey End Herts 38 TL0413
Jodrell Bank Ches 79 SJ7970
John O'Groats Highld 151 ND3872
John's Cross E Susx 17 TQ7421
Johnby Cumb 93 NY4332
Johnshaven Abers 135 NO7967
Johnson's Street Norfk 67 TG3717
Johnston Carmth 31 SN3919
Johnston Pembks 30 SM9310
Johnstone D & G 109 NT2400
Johnstone Rens 115 NS4263
Johnstonebridge D & G 100 NY1092
Johnstown Wrexhm 71 SJ3046
Joppa C Edin 118 NT3173
Joppa Cardgn 43 SN5666
Joppa S Ayrs 106 NS4119
Jordans Bucks 26 SU9791
Jordanston Pembks 30 SM9132
Jordanthorpe S York 74 SK3580
Joyden's Wood Kent 27 TQ5072
Jubilee Corner Kent 28 TQ8447
Jump S York 83 SE3801
Jumper's Town E Susx 16 TQ4632
Juniper Green C Edin 117 NT1968
Jurby IOM 153 SC3598
Jurston Devon 8 SX6984

K

Kaber Cumb 88 NY7911
Kames Ag & B 114 NR9771
Kames E Ayrs 107 NS6926
Kea Cnwll 3 SW8142
Keadby Lincs 84 SE8311
Keal Cotes Lincs 77 TF3660
Kearby Town End N York 83 SE3447
Kearsley Gt Man 79 SD7504
Kearsley Nthumb 103 NZ0275
Kearsney Kent 29 TR2844
Kearstwick Cumb 87 SD6079
Kearton N York 88 SD9998
Keasden N York 88 SD7266
Keason Cnwll 5 SX3168
Keaton Devon 7 SX6454
Keckwick Ches 78 SJ5783
Keddington Lincs 77 TF3488
Keddington Corner Lincs 77 TF3589
Kedington Suffk 53 TL7046
Kedleston Derbys 73 SK3040
Keelby Lincs 85 TA1610
Keele Staffs 72 SJ8045
Keele University Staffs 72 SJ8144
Keeley Green Beds 38 TL0046
Keelham W York 82 SE0732
Keeston Pembks 30 SM9019

Kinrossie Langrigg

Kinrossie P & K 126 NO1832
Kinsbourne Green Herts 38 TL1016
Kinsey Heath Ches 72 SJ6642
Kinsham H & W 46 SO3665
Kinsham H & W 47 SO9335
Kinsley W York 83 SE4114
Kinson Dorset 12 SZ0796
Kintbury Berks 23 SU3866
Kintessack Moray 141 NJ0060
Kintillo P & K 126 NO1317
Kinton H & W 46 SO4174
Kinton Shrops 59 SJ3719
Kintore Abers 143 NJ7916
Kintour Ag & B 112 NR4551
Kintra Ag & B 120 NM3125
Kintraw Ag & B 122 NM8204
Kinveachy Highld 140 NH9018
Kinver Staffs 60 SO8483
Kiplin E R Yk 89 SE2897
Kippax W York 83 SE4130
Kippen Stirlg 116 NS6494
Kippford or Scaur D & G 92 NX8354
Kipping's Cross Kent 16 TQ6440
Kirbister Ork 155 HY3607
Kirby Bedon Norfk 67 TG2705
Kirby Bellars Leics 63 SK7117
Kirby Cane Norfk 67 TM3794
Kirby Corner W Mids 61 SP2976
Kirby Cross Essex 41 TM2120
Kirby Fields Leics 62 SK5203
Kirby Grindalythe N York 91 SE9067
Kirby Hill N York 89 NZ1406
Kirby Hill N York 89 SE3968
Kirby Knowle N York 89 SE4687
Kirby le Soken Essex 41 TM2121
Kirby Misperton N York 90 SE7779
Kirby Muxloe Leics 62 SK5104
Kirby Row Norfk 67 TM3792
Kirby Sigston N York 89 SE4194
Kirby Underdale E R Yk 90 SE8058
Kirby Wiske N York 89 SE3784
Kirconnel D & G 100 NX9868
Kirdford W Susx 14 TQ0126
Kirk Highld 151 ND2859
Kirk Bramwith S York 83 SE6211
Kirk Deighton N York 83 SE3950
Kirk Ella E R Yk 84 TA0129
Kirk Hallam Derbys 62 SK4540
Kirk Hammerton N York 83 SE4655
Kirk Ireton Derbys 73 SK2650
Kirk Langley Derbys 73 SK2838
Kirk Merrington Dur 96 NZ2631
Kirk Michael IOM 153 SC3190
Kirk of Shotts N Lans 116 NS8462
Kirk Sandall S York 83 SE6108
Kirk Smeaton N York 83 SE5216
Kirk Yetholm Border 110 NT8228
Kirkabister Shet 155 HU4938
Kirkandrews D & G 99 NX6048
Kirkandrews upon Eden Cumb 93 NY3558
Kirkbampton Cumb 93 NY3056
Kirkbean D & G 92 NX9759
Kirkbride Cumb 93 NY2256
Kirkbridge N York 89 SE2590
Kirkbuddo Angus 127 NO5043
Kirkburn Border 109 NT2938
Kirkburn E R Yk 84 SE9855
Kirkburton W York 82 SE1912
Kirkby Lincs 76 TF0592
Kirkby Mersyd 78 SJ4099
Kirkby N York 90 NZ5305
Kirkby Fleetham N York 89 SE2894
Kirkby Green Lincs 76 TF0857
Kirkby Hall N York 89 SE2795
Kirkby in Ashfield Notts 75 SK4856
Kirkby la Thorpe Lincs 76 TF0946
Kirkby Lonsdale Cumb 87 SD6178
Kirkby Malham N York 88 SD8960
Kirkby Mallory Leics 50 SK4500
Kirkby Malzeard N York 89 SE2374
Kirkby Mills N York 90 SE7085
Kirkby on Bain Lincs 77 TF2462
Kirkby Overblow N York 83 SE3249
Kirkby Stephen Cumb 88 NY7708
Kirkby Thore Cumb 94 NY6325
Kirkby Underwood Lincs 64 TF0727
Kirkby Wharf N York 83 SE5041
Kirkby Woodhouse Notts 75 SK4954
Kirkby-in-Furness Cumb 86 SD2282
Kirkbymoorside N York 90 SE6986
Kirkcaldy Fife 117 NT2892
Kirkcambeck Cumb 101 NY5368
Kirkchrist D & G 99 NX6751
Kirkcolm D & G 98 NX0268
Kirkconnel D & G 107 NS7311
Kirkconnell D & G 99 NX6760
Kirkcowan D & G 98 NX3260
Kirkcudbright D & G 99 NX6850
Kirkdale Mersyd 78 SJ3493
Kirkfieldbank S Lans 108 NS8643
Kirkgunzeon D & G 100 NX8666
Kirkham Lancs 80 SD4232
Kirkham N York 90 SE7365
Kirkhamgate W York 82 SE2922
Kirkharle Nthumb 103 NZ0182
Kirkhaugh Nthumb 94 NY6949
Kirkheaton Nthumb 103 NZ0177
Kirkheaton W York 82 SE1818
Kirkhill Highld 139 NH5545
Kirkhope S Lans 108 NS9606
Kirkhouse Cumb 94 NY5759
Kirkhouse Green S York 83 SE6213
Kirkibost Highld 129 NG5518
Kirkinch P & K 126 NO3044
Kirkinner D & G 99 NX4251
Kirkintilloch E Duns 116 NS6573
Kirkland Cumb 92 NY0718
Kirkland Cumb 93 NY2648
Kirkland Cumb 94 NY6432
Kirkland D & G 107 NS7213
Kirkland D & G 99 NX4356
Kirkland D & G 100 NX8190
Kirkland D & G 100 NY0389
Kirkland Guards Cumb 93 NY1840
Kirkleatham N York 97 NZ5921
Kirklevington N York 89 NZ4309
Kirkley Suffk 67 TM5391
Kirklington N York 89 SE3181
Kirklington Notts 75 SK6757
Kirklinton Cumb 101 NY4367
Kirkliston C Edin 117 NT1274
Kirkmabreck D & G 99 NX4856
Kirkmaiden D & G 98 NX1236
Kirkmichael P & K 133 NO0759
Kirkmichael S Ayrs 106 NS3408
Kirkmuirhill S Lans 107 NS7842
Kirknewton Nthumb 110 NT9130
Kirknewton W Loth 117 NT1166
Kirkney Abers 142 NJ5132
Kirkoswald Cumb 94 NY5541
Kirkoswald S Ayrs 106 NS2407
Kirkpatrick D & G 100 NX9090
Kirkpatrick Durham D & G 100 NX7870
Kirkpatrick-Fleming D & G 101 NY2770
Kirksanton Cumb 86 SD1380
Kirkstall W York 82 SE2635
Kirkstead Lincs 76 TF1762
Kirkstile Abers 142 NJ5235
Kirkstile D & G 101 NY3690
Kirkstone Pass Inn Cumb 87 NY4007
Kirkstyle Highld 151 ND3472
Kirkthorpe W York 83 SE3621
Kirkton Abers 142 NJ6425
Kirkton Abers 143 NJ8243
Kirkton D & G 100 NX9781
Kirkton Fife 126 NO3625
Kirkton Highld 137 NG8227
Kirkton Highld 138 NG9141
Kirkton P & K 125 NN9618
Kirkton Manor Border 109 NT2238
Kirkton of Airlie Angus 126 NO3151
Kirkton of Auchterhouse Angus 126 NO3438
Kirkton of Barevan Highld 140 NH8347
Kirkton of Collace P & K 126 NO1931
Kirkton of Glenbuchat Abers 141 NJ3715
Kirkton of Logie Buchan Abers 143 NJ9829
Kirkton of Menmuir Angus 134 NO5364
Kirkton of Monikie Angus 127 NO5138
Kirkton of Rayne Abers 142 NJ6930
Kirkton of Skene Abers 135 NJ8007
Kirkton of Strathmartine Angus 126 NO3735
Kirkton of Tealing Angus 126 NO4038
Kirktown Abers 143 NJ9965
Kirktown Abers 143 NK0852
Kirktown of Bourtie Abers 143 NJ8025
Kirktown of Fetteresso Abers 135 NO8486
Kirktown of Mortlach Moray 141 NJ3138
Kirktown of Slains Abers 143 NK0329
Kirkwall Ork 155 HY4411
Kirkwhelpington Nthumb 103 NY9984
Kirmington Lincs 85 TA1011
Kirmond le Mire Lincs 76 TF1892
Kirn Ag & B 114 NS1878
Kirriemuir Angus 126 NO3853
Kirstead Green Norfk 67 TM2997
Kirtlebridge D & G 101 NY2372
Kirtling Cambs 53 TL6857
Kirtling Green Suffk 53 TL6855
Kirtlington Oxon 37 SP4919
Kirtomy Highld 150 NC7463
Kirton Abers 134 NJ6113
Kirton Lincs 64 TF3038
Kirton Notts 75 SK6969
Kirton Suffk 55 TM2740
Kirton End Lincs 64 TF2940
Kirton Holme Lincs 64 TF2642
Kirton in Lindsey Lincs 76 SK9398
Kirtonhill D & Cb 115 NS3875
Kirwaugh D & G 99 NX4054
Kishorn Highld 138 NG8440
Kislingbury Nhants 49 SP6959
Kite Green Warwks 48 SP1666
Kitebrook Warwks 48 SP2431
Kites Hardwick Warwks 50 SP4768
Kitleigh Cnwll 18 SX2499
Kitt Green Gt Man 78 SD5405
Kittisford Somset 20 ST0822
Kittle Swans 32 SS5789
Kitts Green W Mids 61 SP1587
Kittybrewster Aber C 135 NJ9207
Kitwood Hants 24 SU6633
Kivernoll H & W 46 SO4632
Kiveton Park S York 75 SK4982
Knaith Lincs 75 SK8284
Knaith Park Lincs 76 SK8485
Knap Corner Dorset 22 ST8023
Knaphill Surrey 25 SU9658
Knaplock Somset 19 SS8633
Knapp Somset 20 ST3025
Knapp Hill Hants 13 SU4023
Knapthorpe Notts 75 SK7458
Knapton N York 83 SE5652
Knapton N York 90 SE8876
Knapton Norfk 67 TG3034
Knapton Green H & W 46 SO4452
Knapwell Cambs 52 TL3362
Knaresborough N York 89 SE3557
Knarsdale Nthumb 94 NY6754
Knaven Abers 143 NJ8943
Knayton N York 89 SE4387
Knebworth Herts 39 TL2520
Knedlington E R Yk 84 SE7327
Kneesall Notts 75 SK7064
Kneesworth Cambs 39 TL3444
Kneeton Notts 63 SK7146
Knelston Swans 32 SS4688
Knenhall Staffs 72 SJ9237
Knettishall Suffk 54 TL9780
Knightacott Devon 19 SS6539
Knightcote Warwks 48 SP4054
Knightley Staffs 72 SJ8125
Knightley Dale Staffs 72 SJ8123
Knighton Devon 6 SX5349
Knighton Dorset 10 ST6111
Knighton Dorset 12 SZ0497
Knighton Leics 62 SK6001
Knighton Powys 46 SO2872
Knighton Somset 20 ST1944
Knighton Staffs 72 SJ7240
Knighton Staffs 72 SJ7527
Knighton Wilts 36 SU2971
Knighton on Teme H & W 47 SO6369
Knightsbridge Gloucs 47 SO8926
Knightsmill Cnwll 4 SX0780
Knightwick H & W 47 SO7356
Knill H & W 46 SO2960
Knipton Leics 63 SK8231
Knitsley Dur 95 NZ1048
Kniveton Derbys 73 SK2050
Knock Cumb 94 NY6727
Knock Highld 129 NG6709
Knock Moray 142 NJ5452
Knock W Isls 154 NB4931
Knock Castle N Ayrs 114 NS1963
Knockally Highld 151 ND1429
Knockan Highld 145 NC2110
Knockando Moray 141 NJ1941
Knockbain Highld 139 NH5543
Knockbain Highld 140 NH6256
Knockdee Highld 151 ND1760
Knockdown Wilts 35 ST8388
Knockeen S Ayrs 106 NX3195
Knockenkelly N Ayrs 105 NS0427
Knockentiber E Ayrs 106 NS4039
Knockespock House Abers 142 NJ5423
Knockhall Kent 27 TQ5974
Knockholt Kent 27 TQ4658
Knockholt Pound Kent 27 TQ4859
Knockin Shrops 59 SJ3322
Knockinlaw E Ayrs 107 NS4239
Knockmill Kent 27 TQ5761
Knocknain D & G 98 NW9764
Knocksheen D & G 99 NX5882
Knockvennie Smithy D & G 99 NX7571
Knodishall Suffk 55 TM4262
Knole Somset 21 ST4825
Knole Park Gloucs 34 ST5983
Knolls Green Ches 79 SJ8079
Knolton Wrexhm 71 SJ3739
Knook Wilts 22 ST9341
Knossington Leics 63 SK8008
Knott End-on-Sea Lancs 80 SD3548
Knotting Beds 51 TL0063
Knotting Green Beds 51 TL0062
Knottingley W York 83 SE5023
Knotty Green Bucks 26 SU9392
Knowbury Shrops 46 SO5775
Knowe D & G 98 NX3171
Knowehead D & G 107 NX6090
Knoweside S Ayrs 106 NS2512
Knowl Green Essex 53 TL7841
Knowl Hill Berks 37 SU8279
Knowle Bristl 34 ST6070
Knowle Devon 18 SS4938
Knowle Devon 8 SS7801
Knowle Devon 9 ST0007
Knowle Devon 9 SY0582
Knowle Shrops 46 SO5973
Knowle Somset 20 SS9643
Knowle W Mids 61 SP1876
Knowle Cross Devon 9 SY0397
Knowle Green Lancs 81 SD6338
Knowle Hill Surrey 25 SU9966
Knowle St Giles Somset 10 ST3411
Knowlefield Cumb 93 NY4057
Knowlton Dorset 12 SU0209
Knowlton Kent 29 TR2853
Knowsley Mersyd 78 SJ4395
Knowstone Devon 19 SS8323
Knox N York 89 SE2957
Knox Bridge Kent 28 TQ7840
Knucklas Powys 46 SO2574
Knuston Nhants 51 SP9266
Knutsford Ches 79 SJ7578
Knutton Staffs 72 SJ8347
Knypersley Staffs 72 SJ8856
Krumlin W York 82 SE0518
Kuggar Cnwll 3 SW7216
Kyle of Lochalsh Highld 137 NG7627
Kyleakin Highld 137 NG7526
Kylerhea Highld 129 NG7820
Kyles Scalpay W Isls 154 NG2198
Kylesku Highld 148 NC2233
Kylesmorar Highld 129 NM8093
Kylestrome Highld 148 NC2234
Kyloe Nthumb 111 NU0540
Kynaston H & W 47 SO6435
Kynaston Shrops 59 SJ3520
Kynnersley Shrops 72 SJ6716
Kyre Green H & W 46 SO6162
Kyre Park H & W 47 SO6263
Kyrewood H & W 46 SO5967
Kyrle Somset 20 ST0522

L

L'Ancresse Guern 152 GN0000
L'Eree Guern 152 GN0000
L'Etacq Jersey 152 JS0000
La Beilleuse Guern 152 GN0000
La Fontenelle Guern 152 GN0000
La Fosse Guern 152 GN0000
La Greve Guern 152 GN0000
La Greve de Lecq Jersey 152 JS0000
La Hougue Bie Jersey 152 JS0000
La Houguette Guern 152 GN0000
La Passee Guern 152 GN0000
La Pulente Jersey 152 JS0000
La Rocque Jersey 152 JS0000
La Rousaillerie Guern 152 GN0000
La Villette Guern 152 GN0000
Labbacott Devon 18 SS4021
Lacadal W Isls 154 NB4234
Lacasaigh W Isls 154 NB3321
Laceby Lincs 85 TA2106
Lacey Green Bucks 37 SP8200
Lach Dennis Ches 79 SJ7071
Lackenby N York 97 NZ5619
Lackford Suffk 53 TL7970
Lackford Green Suffk 53 TL7970
Lacock Wilts 22 ST9168
Ladbroke Warwks 49 SP4158
Ladderedge Staffs 72 SJ9654
Laddingford Kent 28 TQ6948
Lade Bank Lincs 77 TF3954
Ladock Cnwll 3 SW8950
Lady Hall Cumb 86 SD1986
Lady Village Ork 155 HY6841
Lady's Green Suffk 53 TL7559
Ladybank Fife 126 NO3009
Ladycross Cnwll 5 SX3188
Ladygill S Lans 108 NS9428
Ladykirk Border 110 NT8847
Ladykirk Ho Border 110 NT8845
Ladyridge H & W 46 SO5931
Ladywood H & W 47 SO8661
Ladywood W Mids 61 SP0586
Lag D & G 100 NX8786
Laga Highld 121 NM6361
Lagavulin Ag & B 104 NR4045
Lagg N Ayrs 105 NR9521
Laggan Highld 131 NN2997
Laggan Highld 132 NN6194
Laggan S Ayrs 98 NX0982
Laid Highld 149 NC4159
Laide Highld 144 NG9091
Laig Highld 128 NM4687
Laigh Church E Ayrs 115 NS4647
Laigh Fenwick E Ayrs 107 NS4542
Laigh Glenmuir E Ayrs 107 NS6120
Laighstonehall S Lans 116 NS7054
Laindon Essex 40 TQ6889
Lairg Highld 146 NC5806
Laisterdyke W York 82 SE1932
Laithes Cumb 93 NY4633
Lake Devon 19 SS5531
Lake Devon 5 SX5289
Lake Dorset 11 SY9990
Lake IOW 13 SZ5883
Lake Wilts 23 SU1339
Lake Side Cumb 87 SD3787
Lakenheath Suffk 53 TL7182
Laker's Green Surrey 14 TQ0335
Lakesend Norfk 65 TL5196
Lakley Lanes Bucks 38 SP8250
Laleham Surrey 26 TQ0568
Laleston Brdgnd 33 SS8779
Lamancha Border 117 NT2052
Lamanva Cnwll 3 SW7631
Lamarsh Essex 54 TL8835
Lamas Norfk 67 TG2423
Lamb Roe Lancs 81 SD7337
Lambden Border 110 NT7443
Lamberhurst Kent 28 TQ6736
Lamberhurst Down Kent 16 TQ6735
Lamberton Border 119 NT9658
Lambeth Gt Lon 27 TQ3178
Lambfair Green Suffk 53 TL7153
Lambley Notts 63 SK6345
Lambley Nthumb 94 NY6658
Lambourn Berks 36 SU3278
Lambourne End Essex 27 TQ4794
Lambs Green W Susx 15 TQ2136
Lambston Pembks 30 SM9016
Lamerton Devon 5 SX4577
Lamesley T & W 96 NZ2557
Lamington S Lans 108 NS9731
Lamlash N Ayrs 105 NS0231
Lamonby Cumb 93 NY4036
Lamorick Cnwll 4 SX0364
Lamorna Cnwll 2 SW4424
Lamorran Cnwll 3 SW8741
Lampen Cnwll 4 SX1867
Lampeter Cardgn 44 SN5747
Lampeter Velfrey Pembks 31 SN1514
Lamphey Pembks 30 SN0100
Lamplugh Cumb 92 NY0820
Lamport Nhants 50 SP7574
Lamyatt Somset 21 ST6536
Lana Devon 18 SS3007
Lana Devon 5 SX3496
Lanark S Lans 108 NS8843
Lanarth Cnwll 3 SW7621
Lancaster Lancs 87 SD4761
Lancaut Gloucs 34 ST5396
Lanchester Dur 96 NZ1647
Lancing W Susx 15 TQ1804
Land-hallow Highld 151 ND1833
Landbeach Cambs 53 TL4765
Landcross Devon 18 SS4523
Landerberry Abers 135 NJ7404
Landewednack Cnwll 2 SW7012
Landford Wilts 12 SU2519
Landimore Swans 32 SS4692
Landkey Devon 19 SS6031
Landkey Town Devon 19 SS5931
Landore Swans 32 SS6695
Landrake Cnwll 5 SX3760
Lands End Cnwll 2 SW3425
Landscove Devon 7 SX7766
Landshipping Pembks 30 SN0211
Landue Cnwll 5 SX3579
Landulph Cnwll 6 SX4361
Landwade Suffk 53 TL6268
Landywood Staffs 60 SJ9805
Lane Cnwll 4 SW8260
Lane Bottom Lancs 81 SD8735
Lane End Bucks 37 SU8091
Lane End Ches 79 SJ6890
Lane End Cnwll 4 SX0369
Lane End Hants 13 SU5525
Lane End Kent 27 TQ5671
Lane End Lancs 81 SD8747
Lane End Wilts 22 ST8145
Lane End Waberthwaite Cumb 86 SD1093
Lane Ends Derbys 73 SK2334
Lane Ends Dur 96 NZ1833
Lane Ends Lancs 81 SD7930
Lane Ends N York 82 SD9743
Lane Green Staffs 60 SJ8703
Lane Head Dur 89 NZ1211
Lane Head Gt Man 79 SJ6296
Lane Head W Mids 35 SO9700
Lane Heads Lancs 80 SD4339
Lane Side Lancs 81 SD7922
Laneast Cnwll 5 SX2283
Laneham Notts 75 SK8076
Lanehead Dur 95 NY8441
Lanehead Nthumb 102 NY7985
Laneshaw Bridge Lancs 81 SD9240
Langaford Devon 18 SX4199
Langaller Somset 20 ST2626
Langar Notts 63 SK7234
Langbank Rens 115 NS3873
Langbar N York 82 SE0951
Langbaurgh N York 90 NZ5511
Langcliffe N York 88 SD8264
Langdale End N York 91 SE9391
Langdon Cnwll 5 SX3089
Langdon Beck Dur 95 NY8531
Langdown Hants 13 SU4206
Langdyke Fife 126 NO3304
Langenhoe Essex 41 TM0018
Langford Beds 39 TL1841
Langford Devon 9 ST0203
Langford Essex 40 TL8309
Langford Notts 75 SK8258
Langford Oxon 36 SP2402
Langford Somset 21 ST4560
Langford Budville Somset 20 ST1122
Langford End Beds 52 TL1753
Langham Dorset 22 ST7725
Langham Essex 41 TM0333
Langham Norfk 66 TG0141
Langham Rutlnd 63 SK8411
Langham Suffk 54 TL9769
Langham Moor Essex 41 TM0131
Langham Wick Essex 41 TM0231
Langho Lancs 81 SD7034
Langholm D & G 101 NY3684
Langland Swans 32 SS6087
Langley Berks 26 TQ0178
Langley Ches 79 SJ9471
Langley Derbys 62 SK4445
Langley Gloucs 47 SP0028
Langley Gt Man 79 SD8506
Langley Hants 13 SU4401
Langley Herts 39 TL2122
Langley Kent 28 TQ8052
Langley Nthumb 102 NY8261
Langley Oxon 36 SP2915
Langley Somset 20 ST0828
Langley W Susx 14 SU8029
Langley Warwks 48 SP1962
Langley Burrell Wilts 35 ST9375
Langley Castle Nthumb 102 NY8362
Langley Common Derbys 73 SK2937
Langley Green Derbys 73 SK2738
Langley Green Essex 40 TL8722
Langley Green Warwks 48 SP1962
Langley Lower Green Essex 39 TL4334
Langley Marsh Somset 20 ST0729
Langley Mill Derbys 62 SK4446
Langley Moor Dur 96 NZ2540
Langley Park Dur 96 NZ2145
Langley Street Norfk 67 TG3601
Langley Upper Green Essex 39 TL4434
Langleybury Herts 26 TL0700
Langney E Susx 16 TQ6302
Langold Notts 75 SK5886
Langore Cnwll 5 SX2986
Langport Somset 21 ST4226
Langrick Lincs 77 TF2648
Langridge Somset 35 ST7469
Langridge Ford Devon 19 SS5722
Langrigg Cumb 92 NY1645

Lowe Hill Mansergh

Lowe Hill Staffs 73 SJ9955
Lower Aisholt Somset 20 ST2035
Lower Ansty Dorset 11 ST7603
Lower Apperley Gloucs 47 SO8527
Lower Arncott Oxon 37 SP6018
Lower Ashton Devon 8 SX8484
Lower Assendon Oxon 37 SU7484
Lower Ballam Lancs 80 SD3631
Lower Barewood H & W 46 SO3956
Lower Bartle Lancs 80 SD4933
Lower Beeding W Susx 15 TQ2127
Lower Benefield Nhants 51 SP9988
Lower Bentley H & W 47 SO9865
Lower Beobridge Shrops 60 SO7891
Lower Birchwood Derbys 75 SK4354
Lower Boddington Nhants 49 SP4852
Lower Boscaswell Cnwll 2 SW3734
Lower Bourne Surrey 25 SU8444
Lower Brailes Warwks 48 SP3139
Lower Breakish Highld 129 NG6723
Lower Bredbury Gt Man 79 SJ9191
Lower Broadheath H & W 47 SO8157
Lower Buckenhill H & W 46 SO6033
Lower Bullingham H & W 46 SO5138
Lower Burgate Hants 12 SU1515
Lower Burrowton Devon 9 SY0097
Lower Burton H & W 46 SO4256
Lower Caldecote Beds 52 TL1746
Lower Cam Gloucs 35 SO7400
Lower Canada Somset 21 ST3558
Lower Catesby Nhants 49 SP5159
Lower Chapel Powys 45 SO0235
Lower Chicksgrove Wilts 22 ST9729
Lower Chute Wilts 23 SU3153
Lower Clapton Gt Lon 27 TQ3485
Lower Clent H & W 60 SO9279
Lower Clopton Warwks 48 SP1745
Lower Creedy Devon 8 SS8402
Lower Crossings Derbys 74 SK0480
Lower Cumberworth W York 82 SE2209
Lower Cwmtwrch Powys 32 SN7610
Lower Darwen Lancs 81 SD6825
Lower Dean Beds 51 TL0569
Lower Denby W York 82 SE2307
Lower Diabaig Highld 137 NG7960
Lower Dicker E Susx 16 TQ5511
Lower Dinchope Shrops 59 SO4584
Lower Down Shrops 59 SO3484
Lower Dunsforth N York 89 SE4464
Lower Egleton H & W 47 SO6245
Lower Elkstone Staffs 74 SK0658
Lower Ellastone Staffs 73 SK1142
Lower End Bucks 37 SP6809
Lower End Bucks 38 SP9238
Lower End Nhants 51 SP8861
Lower Everleigh Wilts 23 SU1854
Lower Exbury Hants 13 SZ4299
Lower Eythorne Kent 29 TR2849
Lower Failand Somset 34 ST5173
Lower Farringdon Hants 24 SU7035
Lower Feltham Gt Lon 26 TQ0971
Lower Fittleworth W Susx 14 TQ0118
Lower Foxdale IOM 153 SC2779
Lower Frankton Shrops 59 SJ3732
Lower Freystrop Pembks 30 SM9512
Lower Froyle Hants 24 SU7544
Lower Gabwell Devon 7 SX9169
Lower Gledfield Highld 146 NH5890
Lower Godney Somset 21 ST4742
Lower Gornal W Mids 60 SO9191
Lower Gravenhurst Beds 38 TL1035
Lower Green Gt Man 79 SJ7098
Lower Green Herts 39 TL1832
Lower Green Herts 39 TL4233
Lower Green Kent 16 TQ5640
Lower Green Kent 16 TQ6341
Lower Green Nhants 51 SP8159
Lower Green Norfk 66 TF9837
Lower Green Staffs 60 SJ9007
Lower Green Suffk 53 TL7465
Lower Hacheston Suffk 55 TM3156
Lower Halliford Surrey 26 TQ0866
Lower Halstock Leigh Dorset 10 ST5207
Lower Halstow Kent 28 TQ8567
Lower Hamworthy Dorset 11 SY9990
Lower Hardres Kent 29 TR1553
Lower Harpton H & W 46 SO2760
Lower Hartshay Derbys 74 SK3851
Lower Hartwell Bucks 38 SP7912
Lower Hatton Staffs 72 SJ8236
Lower Hawthwaite Cumb 86 SD2189
Lower Hergest H & W 46 SO2755
Lower Heyford Oxon 49 SP4824
Lower Heysham Lancs 87 SD4160
Lower Higham Kent 28 TQ7172
Lower Holbrook Suffk 54 TM1834
Lower Hordley Shrops 59 SJ3929
Lower Horncroft W Susx 14 TQ0017
Lower Howsell H & W 47 SO7848
Lower Irlam Gt Man 79 SJ7193
Lower Kilburn Derbys 62 SK3744
Lower Kilcott Gloucs 35 ST7889
Lower Killeyan Ag & B 104 NR2742
Lower Kingcombe Dorset 10 SY5599
Lower Kingswood Surrey 26 TQ2453
Lower Kinnerton Ches 71 SJ3462
Lower Langford Somset 21 ST4560
Lower Largo Fife 126 NO4102
Lower Leigh Staffs 73 SK0135
Lower Lemington Gloucs 48 SP2134
Lower Llanfadog Powys 45 SN9567
Lower Lovacott Devon 19 SS5227
Lower Loxhore Devon 19 SS6137
Lower Lydbrook Gloucs 34 SO5916
Lower Lye H & W 46 SO4066
Lower Machen Newpt 34 ST2288
Lower Maes-coed H & W 46 SO3430
Lower Mannington Dorset 12 SU0604
Lower Marston Somset 22 ST7644
Lower Meend Gloucs 34 SO5504
Lower Middleton Cheney Nhants 49 SP5041
Lower Milton Somset 21 ST5347
Lower Moor W Mids 47 SO9747
Lower Morton Gloucs 35 ST6491
Lower Nazeing Essex 39 TL3906
Lower Norton Warwks 48 SP2363
Lower Nyland Dorset 22 ST7521
Lower Penarth V Glam 20 ST1869
Lower Penn Staffs 60 SO8796
Lower Pennington Hants 12 SZ3193
Lower Penwortham Lancs 80 SD5327
Lower Peover Ches 79 SJ7474
Lower Place Gt Man 81 SD9011
Lower Pollicott Bucks 37 SP7013
Lower Pond Street Essex 39 TL4537
Lower Quinton Warwks 48 SP1847
Lower Rainham Kent 28 TQ8167
Lower Raydon Suffk 54 TM0338
Lower Roadwater Somset 20 ST0339
Lower Salter Lancs 87 SD6063
Lower Seagry Wilts 35 ST9580
Lower Sheering Essex 39 TL4914
Lower Shelton Beds 38 SP9942
Lower Shiplake Oxon 37 SU7679
Lower Shuckburgh Warwks 49 SP4862
Lower Slaughter Gloucs 36 SP1622
Lower Soothill W York 82 SE2523
Lower Soudley Gloucs 35 SO6609
Lower Standen Kent 29 TR2340
Lower Stanton St Quintin Wilts 35 ST9180
Lower Stoke Kent 28 TQ8375
Lower Stone Gloucs 35 ST6794
Lower Stonnall Staffs 61 SK0803
Lower Stow Bedon Norfk 66 TL9694
Lower Street Dorset 11 SY8399
Lower Street E Susx 16 TQ7012
Lower Street Norfk 67 TG2635
Lower Street Suffk 53 TL7852
Lower Street Suffk 54 TM1052
Lower Stretton Ches 79 SJ6281
Lower Stroud Dorset 10 SY4598
Lower Sundon Beds 38 TL0526
Lower Swanwick Hants 13 SU4909
Lower Swell Gloucs 48 SP1725
Lower Tadmarton Oxon 48 SP4036
Lower Tale Devon 9 ST0601
Lower Tean Staffs 73 SK0138
Lower Thurlton Norfk 67 TM4299
Lower Town Cnwll 2 SW6528
Lower Town Devon 7 SX7172
Lower Town H & W 47 SO6342
Lower Town Pembks 30 SM9637
Lower Trebullett Cnwll 5 SX3277
Lower Tregantle Cnwll 5 SX3953
Lower Treluswell Cnwll 3 SW7735
Lower Tysoe Warwks 48 SP3445
Lower Ufford Suffk 55 TM2952
Lower Upcott Devon 9 SX8880
Lower Upham Hants 13 SU5219
Lower Upnor Kent 28 TQ7571
Lower Vexford Somset 20 ST1135
Lower Walton Ches 78 SJ6086
Lower Waterston Dorset 11 SY7395
Lower Weare Somset 21 ST4053
Lower Welson H & W 46 SO2950
Lower Westmancote H & W 47 SO9337
Lower Whatcombe Dorset 11 ST8401
Lower Whatley Somset 22 ST7447
Lower Whitley Ches 71 SJ6179
Lower Wick Gloucs 35 ST7096
Lower Wick H & W 47 SO8352
Lower Wield Hants 24 SU6340
Lower Wigginton Herts 38 SP9409
Lower Willingdon E Susx 16 TQ5803
Lower Winchendon Bucks 37 SP7312
Lower Woodend Bucks 37 SU8187
Lower Woodford Wilts 23 SU1235
Lower Wraxhall Dorset 10 ST5700
Lower Wyche H & W 47 SO7743
Lower Wyke W York 82 SE1525
Lowerhouse Lancs 81 SD8032
Lowesby Leics 63 SK7207
Lowestoft Suffk 67 TM5493
Loweswater Cumb 92 NY1421
Lowfield Heath W Susx 15 TQ2739
Lowgill Cumb 87 SD6297
Lowgill Lancs 87 SD6564
Lowick Cumb 86 SD2885
Lowick Nhants 51 SP9881
Lowick Nthumb 111 NU0139
Lowick Bridge Cumb 86 SD2986
Lowick Green Cumb 86 SD2985
Lowlands Dur 96 NZ1325
Lowlands Torfn 34 ST2996
Lowsonford Warwks 48 SP1868
Lowther Cumb 94 NY5323
Lowther Castle Cumb 94 NY5223
Lowthorpe E R Yk 91 TA0860
Lowton Devon 8 SS6604
Lowton Gt Man 78 SJ6197
Lowton Somset 20 ST1918
Lowton Common Gt Man 79 SJ6397
Lowton St Mary's Gt Man 79 SJ6397
Loxbeare Devon 9 SS9116
Loxhill Surrey 25 TQ0038
Loxhore Devon 19 SS6138
Loxhore Cott Devon 19 SS6138
Loxley Warwks 48 SP2553
Loxley Green Staffs 73 SK0630
Loxter H & W 47 SO7140
Loxton Somset 21 ST3755
Loxwood W Susx 14 TQ0331
Lubenham Leics 50 SP7087
Lucas Green Surrey 25 SU9460
Lucasgate Lincs 77 TF4147
Luccombe Somset 20 SS9243
Luccombe Village IOW 13 SZ5879
Lucker Nthumb 111 NU1530
Luckett Cnwll 5 SX3873
Lucking Street Essex 54 TL8134
Luckington Wilts 35 ST8383
Lucknam Wilts 35 ST8272
Luckwell Bridge Somset 20 SS9038
Lucott Somset 19 SS8645
Lucton H & W 46 SO4364
Lucy Cross N York 89 NZ2112
Ludborough Lincs 77 TF2995
Ludbrook Devon 7 SX6654
Ludchurch Pembks 31 SN1411
Luddenden W York 82 SE0426
Luddenden Foot W York 82 SE0325
Luddenham Court Kent 28 TQ9963
Luddesdown Kent 28 TQ6666
Luddington Lincs 84 SE8316
Luddington Warwks 48 SP1652
Luddington in the Brook Nhants 51 TL1083
Ludford Lincs 76 TF1989
Ludford Shrops 46 SO5174
Ludgershall Bucks 37 SP6517
Ludgershall Wilts 23 SU2650
Ludgvan Cnwll 2 SW5033
Ludham Norfk 67 TG3818
Ludlow Shrops 46 SO5175
Ludney Somset 10 ST3812
Ludwell Wilts 22 ST9122
Ludworth Dur 96 NZ3641
Luffenhall Herts 39 TL2928
Luffincott Devon 5 SX3394
Luffness E Loth 118 NT4780
Lugar E Ayrs 107 NS5921
Lugg Green H & W 46 SO4462
Luggate Burn E Loth 118 NT5974
Luggiebank N Lans 116 NS7672
Lugsdale Ches 78 SJ5285
Lugton E Ayrs 115 NS4152
Lugwardine H & W 46 SO5540
Luib Highld 137 NG5627
Lulham H & W 46 SO4141
Lullington Derbys 61 SK2412
Lullington E Susx 16 TQ5202
Lullington Somset 22 ST7851
Lulsgate Bottom Somset 21 ST5165
Lulsley H & W 47 SO7455
Lulworth Camp Dorset 11 SY8381
Lumb Lancs 81 SD8324
Lumb W York 82 SE0221
Lumbutts W York 82 SD9523
Lumby N York 83 SE4830
Lumloch E Duns 116 NS6370
Lumphanan Abers 134 NJ5804
Lumphinnans Fife 117 NT1792
Lumsden Abers 142 NJ4722
Lunan Angus 127 NO6851
Lunanhead Angus 127 NO4752
Luncarty P & K 125 NO0929
Lund E R Yk 84 SE9647
Lund N York 83 SE6532
Lundford Magna Lincs 76 TF1989
Lundie Angus 126 NO2836
Lundie Stirlg 124 NN7304
Lundin Links Fife 126 NO4002
Lundy Green Norfk 67 TM2392
Lunna Shet 155 HU4869
Lunsford Kent 28 TQ6959
Lunsford's Cross E Susx 17 TQ7210
Lunt Mersyd 78 SD3402
Luntley H & W 46 SO3955
Luppitt Devon 9 ST1606
Lupridge Devon 7 SX7153
Lupset W York 82 SE3119
Lupton Cumb 87 SD5581
Lurgashall W Susx 14 SU9326
Lurley Devon 9 SS9215
Lusby Lincs 77 TF3467
Luscombe Devon 7 SX7957
Luson Devon 6 SX6050
Luss Ag & B 115 NS3692
Lusta Highld 136 NG2656
Lustleigh Devon 8 SX7881
Luston H & W 46 SO4863
Luthermuir Abers 135 NO6568
Luthrie Fife 126 NO3319
Lutley W Mids 60 SO9382
Luton Beds 38 TL0921
Luton Devon 9 ST0802
Luton Devon 9 SX9076
Luton Kent 28 TQ7766
Lutterworth Leics 50 SP5484
Lutton Devon 6 SX5959
Lutton Devon 7 SX6961
Lutton Dorset 11 SY8980
Lutton Lincs 65 TF4325
Lutton Nhants 52 TL1187
Luxborough Somset 20 SS9738
Luxulyan Cnwll 4 SX0558
Luzley Gt Man 79 SD9600
Lybster Highld 151 ND2435
Lydbury North Shrops 59 SO3486
Lydcott Devon 19 SS6936
Lydd Kent 17 TR0420
Lydden Kent 29 TR2645
Lydden Kent 29 TR3567
Lyddington Rutlnd 51 SP8797
Lyde Green Hants 24 SU7057
Lydeard St Lawrence Somset 20 ST1332
Lydford Devon 5 SX5185
Lydford on Fosse Somset 21 ST5630
Lydgate Gt Man 82 SD9516
Lydgate W York 81 SD9225
Lydham Shrops 59 SO3391
Lydiard Green Wilts 36 SU0885
Lydiard Millicent Wilts 36 SU0986
Lydiard Tregoze Wilts 36 SU1085
Lydiate Mersyd 78 SD3604
Lydiate Ash H & W 60 SO9775
Lydlinch Dorset 11 ST7413
Lydney Gloucs 35 SO6303
Lydstep Pembks 31 SS0898
Lye W Mids 60 SO9284
Lye Cross Somset 21 ST4962
Lye Green Bucks 38 SP9703
Lye Green E Susx 16 TQ5134
Lye Green Warwks 48 SP1965
Lye Head H & W 60 SO7573
Lye's Green Wilts 22 ST8146
Lyford Oxon 36 SU3994
Lymbridge Green Kent 29 TR1244
Lyme Border 109 NT2041
Lyme Regis Dorset 10 SY3492
Lyminge Kent 29 TR1641
Lymington Hants 12 SZ3295
Lyminster W Susx 14 TQ0204
Lymm Ches 79 SJ6887
Lympne Kent 17 TR1135
Lympsham Somset 21 ST3354
Lympstone Devon 9 SX9984
Lynbridge Devon 19 SS7248
Lynch Somset 20 SS9047
Lynch Green Norfk 66 TG1505
Lynchat Highld 132 NH7801
Lyndhurst Hants 12 SU3008
Lyndon Rutlnd 63 SK9004
Lyndon Green W Mids 61 SP1485
Lyne Surrey 26 TQ0166
Lyne Down H & W 47 SO6431
Lyne of Skene Abers 135 NJ7610
Lyneal Shrops 59 SJ4433
Lyneham Devon 8 SX8579
Lyneham Oxon 36 SP2720
Lyneham Wilts 35 SU0278
Lyneholmford Cumb 101 NY5172
Lynemouth Nthumb 103 NZ2991
Lyness Ork 155 ND3094
Lyng Norfk 66 TG0617
Lyng Somset 21 ST3329
Lynhales H & W 46 SO3255
Lynmouth Devon 19 SS7249
Lynn Shrops 72 SJ7815
Lynn Staffs 61 SK0704
Lynn of Shenval Moray 141 NJ2129
Lynsted Kent 28 TQ9460
Lynstone Cnwll 18 SS2005
Lynton Devon 19 SS7249
Lyon's Gate Dorset 11 ST6505
Lyonshall H & W 46 SO3355
Lytchett Matravers Dorset 11 SY9495
Lytchett Minster Dorset 11 SY9693
Lyth Highld 151 ND2762
Lytham Lancs 80 SD3627
Lytham St Anne's Lancs 80 SD3427
Lythbank Shrops 59 SJ4607
Lythe N York 90 NZ8413
Lythmore Highld 150 ND0566

M

Mabe Burnthouse Cnwll 3 SW7634
Mabie D & G 100 NX9570
Mablethorpe Lincs 77 TF5085
Macclesfield Ches 79 SJ9173
Macclesfield Forest Ches 79 SJ9772
Macduff Abers 142 NJ7064
Macharioch Ag & B 105 NR7309
Machen Caerph 33 ST2189
Machire Ag & B 112 NR2164
Machrie N Ayrs 105 NR8934
Machrihanish Ag & B 104 NR6320
Machrins Ag & B 112 NR3693
Machynlleth Powys 57 SH7400
Machynys Carmth 32 SS5198
Mackworth Derbys 62 SK3137
Macmerry E Loth 118 NT4372
Maddaford Devon 8 SX5494
Madderty P & K 125 NN9522
Maddington Wilts 23 SU0744
Maddiston Falk 116 NS9476
Madehurst W Susx 14 SU9810
Madeley Shrops 60 SJ6904
Madeley Staffs 72 SJ7744
Madeley Heath Staffs 72 SJ7845
Madford Devon 9 ST1411
Madingley Cambs 52 TL3960
Madley H & W 46 SO4238
Madresfield H & W 47 SO8047
Madron Cnwll 2 SW4531
Maen-y-groes Cardgn 42 SN3858
Maenaddwyn Angles 68 SH4684
Maenan A & C 69 SH7965
Maenclochog Pembks 31 SN0827
Maendy V Glam 33 ST0076
Maenporth Cnwll 3 SW7829
Maentwrog Gwynd 57 SH6640
Maer Cnwll 18 SS2008
Maer Staffs 72 SJ7938
Maerdy Carmth 44 SN6527
Maerdy Rhondd 33 SS9798
Maes-glas Newpt 34 ST2985
Maesbrook Shrops 59 SJ3021
Maesbury Shrops 59 SJ3026
Maesbury Marsh Shrops 59 SJ3125
Maesgwynne Carmth 31 SN2024
Maeshafn Denbgs 70 SJ2061
Maesllyn Cardgn 42 SN3644
Maesmynis Powys 45 SO0146
Maesmynis Powys 45 SO0349
Maesteg Brdgnd 33 SS8590
Maesybont Carmth 32 SN5616
Maesycwmmer Caerph 33 ST1594
Magdalen Laver Essex 39 TL5108
Maggieknockater Moray 141 NJ3145
Maggots End Essex 39 TL4827
Magham Down E Susx 16 TQ6011
Maghull Mersyd 78 SD3703
Magor Mons 34 ST4286
Maiden Bradley Wilts 22 ST8038
Maiden Head Somset 21 ST5666
Maiden Law Dur 96 NZ1749
Maiden Newton Dorset 10 SY5997
Maiden Wells Pembks 30 SR9799
Maidencombe Devon 7 SX9268
Maidenhayne Devon 10 SY2795
Maidenhead Berks 26 SU8980
Maidens S Ayrs 106 NS2107
Maidens Green Berks 25 SU8972
Maidenwell Lincs 77 TF3179
Maidford Nhants 49 SP6052
Maids Moreton Bucks 49 SP7035
Maidstone Kent 28 TQ7555
Maidwell Nhants 50 SP7476
Mainclee Newpt 34 ST3288
Mains of Bainakettle Abers 134 NO6274
Mains of Balhall Angus 134 NO5163
Mains of Dalvey Highld 141 NJ1132
Mains of Haulkerton Abers 135 NO7172
Mainsforth Dur 96 NZ3131
Mainsriddle D & G 92 NX9456
Mainstone Shrops 58 SO2787
Maisemore Gloucs 35 SO8121
Major's Green H & W 61 SP1077
Makeney Derbys 62 SK3544
Malborough Devon 7 SX7139
Malcoff Derbys 74 SK0782
Malden Surrey 26 TQ2166
Malden Rushett Gt Lon 26 TQ1761
Maldon Essex 40 TL8506
Malham N York 88 SD9063
Mallaig Highld 129 NM6796
Mallaigvaig Highld 129 NM6897
Malleny Mills C Edin 117 NT1665
Mallows Green Essex 39 TL4726
Malltraeth Angles 68 SH4068
Mallwyd Gwynd 57 SH8612
Malmesbury Wilts 35 ST9387
Malmsmead Somset 19 SS7947
Malpas Ches 71 SJ4847
Malpas Cnwll 3 SW8442
Malpas Newpt 34 ST3090
Maltby Lincs 77 TF3183
Maltby N York 89 NZ4613
Maltby S York 75 SK5392
Maltby le Marsh Lincs 77 TF4681
Malting Green Essex 41 TL9720
Maltman's Hill Kent 28 TQ9043
Malton N York 90 SE7871
Malvern Link H & W 47 SO7947
Malvern Wells H & W 47 SO7742
Malzie D & G 99 NX3754
Mamble H & W 60 SO6871
Mamhilad Mons 34 SO3003
Manaccan Cnwll 3 SW7624
Manafon Powys 58 SJ1102
Manais W Isls 154 NG1089
Manaton Devon 8 SX7581
Manby Lincs 77 TF3986
Mancetter Warwks 61 SP3296
Manchester Gt Man 79 SJ8497
Mancot Flints 71 SJ3167
Mandally Highld 131 NH2900
Manea Cambs 53 TL4789
Maney W Mids 61 SP1195
Manfield N York 89 NZ2113
Mangerton Dorset 10 SY4995
Mangotsfield Gloucs 35 ST6676
Mangrove Green Herts 38 TL1224
Manhay Cnwll 2 SW6930
Manish W Isls 154 NG1089
Mankinholes W York 82 SD9523
Manley Ches 71 SJ5071
Manmoel Caerph 33 SO1803
Mannel Ag & B 120 NL9840
Manning's Heath W Susx 15 TQ2028
Manningford Bohune Wilts 23 SU1357
Manningford Bruce Wilts 23 SU1358
Manningham W York 82 SE1435
Mannington Dorset 12 SU0605
Manningtree Essex 41 TM1031
Mannofield Aber C 135 NJ9104
Manor Park Gt Lon 27 TQ4285
Manorbier Pembks 30 SS0697
Manorbier Newton Pembks 30 SN0400
Manordeilo Carmth 44 SN6726
Manorhill Border 110 NT6632
Manorowen Pembks 30 SM9336
Mansell Gamage H & W 46 SO3944
Mansell Lacy H & W 46 SO4245
Mansergh Cumb 87 SD6082

Mansfield

Middle Rocombe

Mansfield *E Ayrs*	**107**	NS6214
Mansfield *Notts*	**75**	SK5361
Mansfield Woodhouse *Notts*	**75**	SK5363
Mansriggs *Cumb*	**86**	SD2980
Manston *Dorset*	**11**	ST8115
Manston *Kent*	**29**	TR3466
Manston *W York*	**83**	SE3634
Manswood *Dorset*	**11**	ST9708
Manthorpe *Lincs*	**63**	SK9137
Manthorpe *Lincs*	**64**	TF0715
Manton *Lincs*	**84**	SE9302
Manton *Notts*	**75**	SK6078
Manton *Rutlnd*	**63**	SK8704
Manton *Wilts*	**23**	SU1768
Manuden *Essex*	**39**	TL4926
Manwood Green *Essex*	**39**	TL5412
Maperton *Somset*	**22**	ST6726
Maple Cross *Herts*	**26**	TQ0393
Maplebeck *Notts*	**75**	SK7060
Mapledurham *Oxon*	**37**	SU6776
Mapledurwell *Hants*	**24**	SU6851
Maplehurst *W Susx*	**15**	TQ1824
Maplescombe *Kent*	**27**	TQ5664
Mapleton *Derbys*	**73**	SK1647
Mapleton *Kent*	**16**	TQ4649
Mapperley *Derbys*	**62**	SK4342
Mapperley Park *Notts*	**62**	SK5842
Mapperton *Dorset*	**10**	SY5099
Mappleborough Green *Warwks*	**48**	SP0866
Mappleton *E R Yk*	**85**	TA2243
Mapplewell *S York*	**83**	SE3210
Mappowder *Dorset*	**11**	ST7306
Marazanvose *Cnwll*	**3**	SW7950
Marazion *Cnwll*	**2**	SW5130
Marbury *Ches*	**71**	SJ5645
March *Cambs*	**65**	TL4196
March *S Lans*	**108**	NS9914
Marcham *Oxon*	**37**	SU4596
Marchamley *Shrops*	**59**	SJ5929
Marchamley Wood *Shrops*	**59**	SJ5831
Marchington *Staffs*	**73**	SK1330
Marchington Woodlands *Staffs*	**73**	SK1128
Marchros *Gwynd*	**56**	SH3125
Marchwiel *Wrexhm*	**71**	SJ3547
Marchwood *Hants*	**12**	SU3810
Marcross *V Glam*	**20**	SS9269
Marden *H & W*	**46**	SO5146
Marden *Kent*	**28**	TQ7444
Marden *Wilts*	**23**	SU0857
Marden Ash *Essex*	**27**	TL5502
Marden Beech *Kent*	**28**	TQ7442
Marden Thorn *Kent*	**28**	TQ7642
Mardens Hill *E Susx*	**16**	TQ5032
Mardlebury *Herts*	**39**	TL2618
Mardy *Mons*	**34**	SO3015
Marefield *Leics*	**63**	SK7407
Mareham le Fen *Lincs*	**77**	TF2761
Mareham on the Hill *Lincs*	**77**	TF2867
Marehay *Derbys*	**62**	SK3947
Marehill *W Susx*	**14**	TQ0618
Maresfield *E Susx*	**16**	TQ4624
Marfleet *E R Yk*	**85**	TA1429
Marford *Wrexhm*	**71**	SJ3556
Margam *Neath*	**32**	SS7887
Margaret Marsh *Dorset*	**22**	ST8218
Margaretting *Essex*	**40**	TL6701
Margaretting Tye *Essex*	**40**	TL6800
Margate *Kent*	**29**	TR3571
Margnaheglish *N Ayrs*	**105**	NS0332
Margrie *D & G*	**99**	NX5950
Margrove Park *N York*	**97**	NZ6515
Marham *Norfk*	**65**	TF7009
Marhamchurch *Cnwll*	**18**	SS2203
Marholm *Cambs*	**64**	TF1401
Marian-glas *Angles*	**68**	SH5084
Mariansleigh *Devon*	**19**	SS7422
Marine Town *Kent*	**28**	TQ9274
Marionburgh *Abers*	**135**	NJ7006
Marishader *Highld*	**136**	NG4963
Maristow *Devon*	**6**	SX4764
Marjoriebanks *D & G*	**100**	NY0883
Mark *D & G*	**98**	NX1157
Mark *Somset*	**21**	ST3847
Mark Causeway *Somset*	**21**	ST3547
Mark Cross *E Susx*	**16**	TQ5010
Mark Cross *E Susx*	**16**	TQ5831
Mark's Corner *IOW*	**13**	SZ4692
Markbeech *Kent*	**16**	TQ4742
Markby *Lincs*	**77**	TF4878
Markeaton *Derbys*	**62**	SK3237
Market Bosworth *Leics*	**62**	SK4002
Market Deeping *Lincs*	**64**	TF1310
Market Drayton *Shrops*	**72**	SJ6734
Market Harborough *Leics*	**50**	SP7387
Market Lavington *Wilts*	**22**	SU0154
Market Overton *Rutlnd*	**63**	SK8816
Market Rasen *Lincs*	**76**	TF1089
Market Stainton *Lincs*	**76**	TF2279
Market Street *Norfk*	**67**	TG2921
Market Weighton *E R Yk*	**84**	SE8741
Market Weston *Suffk*	**54**	TL9877
Markfield *Leics*	**62**	SK4809
Markham *Caerph*	**33**	SO1601
Markham Moor *Notts*	**75**	SK7173
Markinch *Fife*	**126**	NO2901
Markington *N York*	**89**	SE2865
Marks Tey *Essex*	**40**	TL9023
Marksbury *Somset*	**22**	ST6662
Markshall *Essex*	**40**	TL8425
Markwell *Cnwll*	**5**	SX3758
Markyate *Herts*	**38**	TL0616
Marl Bank *H & W*	**47**	SO7840
Marlborough *Wilts*	**23**	SU1868
Marlbrook *H & W*	**46**	SO5154
Marlbrook *H & W*	**60**	SO9774
Marlcliff *Warwks*	**48**	SP0950
Marldon *Devon*	**7**	SX8663
Marle Green *E Susx*	**16**	TQ5816
Marlesford *Suffk*	**55**	TM3258
Marley *Kent*	**29**	TR1850
Marley *Kent*	**29**	TR3353
Marley Green *Ches*	**71**	SJ5845
Marley Hill *T & W*	**96**	NZ2058
Marlingford *Norfk*	**66**	TG1309
Marloes *Pembks*	**30**	SM7908
Marlow *Bucks*	**26**	SU8486
Marlow *H & W*	**46**	SO4076
Marlpit Hill *Kent*	**16**	TQ4347
Marlpits *E Susx*	**16**	TQ4528
Marlpits *E Susx*	**16**	TQ7013
Marlpool *Derbys*	**62**	SK4345
Marnhull *Dorset*	**22**	ST7818
Marple *Gt Man*	**79**	SJ9588
Marple Bridge *Gt Man*	**79**	SJ9688
Marr *S York*	**83**	SE5105
Marrick *N York*	**88**	SE0798
Marros *Carmth*	**31**	SN2008
Marsden *T & W*	**103**	NZ3964
Marsden *W York*	**82**	SE0411
Marsden Height *Lancs*	**81**	SD8636
Marsett *N York*	**88**	SD9085
Marsh *Bucks*	**38**	SP8109
Marsh *Devon*	**10**	ST2510
Marsh *W York*	**82**	SE0235
Marsh Baldon *Oxon*	**37**	SU5699
Marsh Chapel *Lincs*	**77**	TF3599
Marsh Gibbon *Bucks*	**37**	SP6422
Marsh Green *Devon*	**9**	SY0493
Marsh Green *Kent*	**16**	TQ4344
Marsh Green *Shrops*	**59**	SJ6014
Marsh Green *Staffs*	**72**	SJ8858
Marsh Lane *Derbys*	**74**	SK4079
Marsh Lane *Gloucs*	**34**	SO5807
Marsh Street *Somset*	**20**	SS9944
Marsh The *Powys*	**59**	SO3197
Marshall's Heath *Herts*	**39**	TL1614
Marshalswick *Herts*	**39**	TL1608
Marsham *Norfk*	**67**	TG1923
Marshborough *Kent*	**29**	TR3057
Marshbrook *Shrops*	**59**	SO4489
Marshfield *Gloucs*	**35**	ST7873
Marshfield *Newpt*	**34**	ST2582
Marshgate *Cnwll*	**4**	SX1592
Marshland Green *Gt Man*	**79**	SJ6899
Marshland St James *Norfk*	**65**	TF5209
Marshside *Mersyd*	**80**	SD3619
Marshwood *Dorset*	**10**	SY3899
Marske *N York*	**89**	NZ1000
Marske-by-the-Sea *N York*	**97**	NZ6322
Marston *Ches*	**79**	SJ6775
Marston *H & W*	**46**	SO3557
Marston *Lincs*	**63**	SK8943
Marston *Oxon*	**37**	SP5208
Marston *Staffs*	**60**	SJ8313
Marston *Staffs*	**72**	SJ9227
Marston *Warwks*	**61**	SP2094
Marston *Wilts*	**22**	ST9656
Marston Green *W Mids*	**61**	SP1785
Marston Jabbet *Warwks*	**61**	SP3788
Marston Magna *Somset*	**21**	ST5922
Marston Meysey *Wilts*	**36**	SU1297
Marston Montgomery *Derbys*	**73**	SK1337
Marston Moretaine *Beds*	**38**	SP9941
Marston on Dove *Derbys*	**73**	SK2329
Marston St Lawrence *Nhants*	**49**	SP5341
Marston Stannet *H & W*	**46**	SO5655
Marston Trussell *Nhants*	**50**	SP6985
Marstow *H & W*	**34**	SO5518
Marsworth *Bucks*	**38**	SP9114
Marten *Wilts*	**23**	SU2860
Marthall *Ches*	**79**	SJ7975
Martham *Norfk*	**67**	TG4518
Martin *Hants*	**12**	SU0619
Martin *Kent*	**29**	TR3447
Martin *Lincs*	**76**	TF1259
Martin *Lincs*	**77**	TF2466
Martin Dales *Lincs*	**76**	TF1762
Martin Drove End *Hants*	**12**	SU0520
Martin Hussingtree *H & W*	**47**	SO8860
Martindale *Cumb*	**93**	NY4319
Martinhoe *Devon*	**19**	SS6648
Martinscroft *Ches*	**79**	SJ6589
Martinstown *Dorset*	**11**	SY6489
Martlesham *Suffk*	**55**	TM2547
Martletwy *Pembks*	**30**	SN0310
Martley *H & W*	**47**	SO7560
Martock *Somset*	**21**	ST4619
Marton *Ches*	**71**	SJ6267
Marton *Ches*	**79**	SJ8568
Marton *E R Yk*	**85**	TA1739
Marton *E R Yk*	**91**	TA2069
Marton *Lincs*	**76**	SK8381
Marton *N York*	**97**	NZ5115
Marton *N York*	**89**	SE4162
Marton *N York*	**90**	SE7383
Marton *Shrops*	**58**	SJ2802
Marton *Warwks*	**48**	SP4068
Marton-le-Moor *N York*	**89**	SE3770
Martyr Worthy *Hants*	**24**	SU5132
Martyr's Green *Surrey*	**26**	TQ0857
Marwick *Ork*	**155**	HY2324
Marwood *Devon*	**19**	SS5437
Mary Tavy *Devon*	**5**	SX5079
Marybank *Highld*	**139**	NH4853
Maryburgh *Highld*	**139**	NH5456
Maryculter *Abers*	**135**	NO8599
Marygold *Border*	**119**	NT8159
Maryhill *Abers*	**143**	NJ8245
Maryhill *C Glas*	**115**	NS5669
Marykirk *Abers*	**135**	NO6865
Maryland *Mons*	**34**	SO5105
Marylebone *Gt Lon*	**27**	TQ2782
Marylebone *Gt Man*	**78**	SD5807
Marypark *Moray*	**141**	NJ1938
Maryport *Cumb*	**92**	NY0336
Maryport *D & G*	**98**	NX1434
Marystow *Devon*	**5**	SX4382
Maryton *Angus*	**127**	NO6856
Marywell *Abers*	**134**	NO5895
Marywell *Abers*	**135**	NO9399
Marywell *Angus*	**127**	NO6544
Masham *N York*	**89**	SE2280
Mashbury *Essex*	**40**	TL6511
Mason *T & W*	**103**	NZ2073
Masongill *N York*	**87**	SD6675
Mastin Moor *Derbys*	**75**	SK4575
Matching *Essex*	**39**	TL5212
Matching Green *Essex*	**39**	TL5311
Matching Tye *Essex*	**39**	TL5111
Matfen *Nthumb*	**103**	NZ0371
Matfield *Kent*	**28**	TQ6541
Mathern *Mons*	**34**	ST5290
Mathon *H & W*	**47**	SO7346
Mathry *Pembks*	**30**	SM8832
Matlask *Norfk*	**66**	TG1534
Matlock *Derbys*	**74**	SK3059
Matlock Bank *Derbys*	**74**	SK3060
Matlock Bath *Derbys*	**74**	SK2958
Matlock Dale *Derbys*	**74**	SK2959
Matson *Gloucs*	**35**	SO8515
Matterdale End *Cumb*	**93**	NY3923
Mattersey *Notts*	**75**	SK6889
Mattersey Thorpe *Notts*	**75**	SK6889
Mattingley *Hants*	**24**	SU7357
Mattishall *Norfk*	**66**	TG0511
Mattishall Burgh *Norfk*	**66**	TG0512
Mauchline *E Ayrs*	**107**	NS4927
Maud *Abers*	**143**	NJ9148
Maufant *Jersey*	**152**	JS0000
Maugersbury *Gloucs*	**48**	SP2025
Maughold *IOM*	**153**	SC4991
Mauld *Highld*	**139**	NH4038
Maulden *Beds*	**38**	TL0538
Maulds Meaburn *Cumb*	**94**	NY6216
Maunby *N York*	**89**	SE3586
Maund Bryan *H & W*	**46**	SO5650
Maundown *Somset*	**20**	ST0628
Mautby *Norfk*	**67**	TG4812
Mavesyn Ridware *Staffs*	**73**	SK0816
Mavis Enderby *Lincs*	**77**	TF3666
Maw Green *Ches*	**72**	SJ7057
Maw Green *W Mids*	**60**	SP0196
Mawbray *Cumb*	**92**	NY0846
Mawdesley *Lancs*	**80**	SD4914
Mawdlam *Brdgnd*	**32**	SS8081
Mawgan *Cnwll*	**2**	SW7025
Mawgan Cross *Cnwll*	**2**	SW7024
Mawgan Porth *Cnwll*	**4**	SW8567
Mawla *Cnwll*	**2**	SW7045
Mawnan *Cnwll*	**3**	SW7827
Mawnan Smith *Cnwll*	**3**	SW7728
Mawthorpe *Lincs*	**77**	TF4672
Maxey *Cambs*	**64**	TF1208
Maxstoke *Warwks*	**61**	SP2386
Maxted Street *Kent*	**29**	TR1244
Maxton *Border*	**110**	NT6130
Maxton *Kent*	**29**	TR3041
Maxwell Town *D & G*	**100**	NX9676
Maxworthy *Cnwll*	**5**	SX2593
May Bank *Staffs*	**72**	SJ8547
May's Green *Oxon*	**37**	SU7480
May's Green *Surrey*	**26**	TQ0957
Mayals *Swans*	**32**	SS6089
Maybole *S Ayrs*	**106**	NS2909
Maybury *Surrey*	**26**	TQ0159
Mayes Green *Surrey*	**14**	TQ1239
Mayfield *E Susx*	**16**	TQ5826
Mayfield *Mdloth*	**118**	NT3565
Mayfield *Staffs*	**73**	SK1545
Mayford *Surrey*	**25**	SU9956
Mayland *Essex*	**40**	TL9201
Maynard's Green *E Susx*	**16**	TQ5818
Maypole *Kent*	**29**	TR2064
Maypole *Mons*	**34**	SO4716
Maypole *W Mids*	**61**	SP0778
Maypole Green *Norfk*	**67**	TM4195
Maypole Green *Suffk*	**54**	TL9159
Maypole Green *Suffk*	**55**	TM2767
Mead *Devon*	**18**	SS2217
Meadgate *Somset*	**22**	ST6758
Meadle *Bucks*	**38**	SP8005
Meadowfield *Dur*	**96**	NZ2439
Meadowhall *S York*	**74**	SK3991
Meadowtown *Shrops*	**59**	SJ3001
Meadwell *Devon*	**5**	SX4081
Meal Bank *Cumb*	**87**	SD5495
Mealrigg *Cumb*	**92**	NY1345
Mealsgate *Cumb*	**93**	NY2042
Meamskirk *E Rens*	**115**	NS5455
Meanwood *W York*	**82**	SE2837
Mearbeck *N York*	**88**	SD8160
Meare *Somset*	**21**	ST4541
Meare Green *Somset*	**21**	ST3326
Meare Green *Somset*	**20**	ST2922
Mears Ashby *Nhants*	**51**	SP8366
Measham *Leics*	**62**	SK3311
Meathop *Cumb*	**87**	SD4380
Meaux *E R Yk*	**85**	TA0839
Meavy *Devon*	**6**	SX5467
Medbourne *Leics*	**51**	SP8093
Meddon *Devon*	**18**	SS2717
Meden Vale *Notts*	**75**	SK5870
Medlam *Lincs*	**77**	TF3156
Medlar *Lancs*	**80**	SD4135
Medmenham *Berks*	**37**	SU8084
Medomsley *Dur*	**95**	NZ1154
Medstead *Hants*	**24**	SU6537
Meer Common *H & W*	**46**	SO3652
Meerbrook *Staffs*	**72**	SJ9860
Meesden *Herts*	**39**	TL4332
Meeson *Shrops*	**72**	SJ6421
Meeth *Devon*	**19**	SS5408
Meeting Green *Suffk*	**53**	TL7455
Meeting House Hill *Norfk*	**67**	TG3028
Meidrim *Carmth*	**31**	SN2920
Meifod *Powys*	**58**	SJ1513
Meigle *P & K*	**126**	NO2844
Meikle Carco *D & G*	**107**	NS7813
Meikle Earnock *S Lans*	**116**	NS7053
Meikle Kilmory *Ag & B*	**114**	NS0560
Meikle Obney *P & K*	**125**	NO0337
Meikle Wartle *Abers*	**142**	NJ7230
Meikleour *P & K*	**126**	NO1539
Meinciau *Carmth*	**32**	SN4610
Meir *Staffs*	**72**	SJ9342
Meir Heath *Staffs*	**72**	SJ9240
Melbourn *Cambs*	**39**	TL3844
Melbourne *Derbys*	**62**	SK3825
Melbourne *E R Yk*	**84**	SE7543
Melbury *Devon*	**18**	SS3719
Melbury Abbas *Dorset*	**22**	ST8820
Melbury Bubb *Dorset*	**10**	ST5906
Melbury Osmond *Dorset*	**10**	ST5707
Melbury Sampford *Dorset*	**10**	ST5705
Melchbourne *Beds*	**51**	TL0265
Melcombe Bingham *Dorset*	**11**	ST7602
Meldon *Devon*	**8**	SX5692
Meldon *Nthumb*	**103**	NZ1183
Meldon Park *Nthumb*	**103**	NZ1085
Meldreth *Cambs*	**52**	TL3746
Meldrum *Stirlg*	**116**	NS7299
Meledor *Cnwll*	**3**	SW9254
Melfort *Ag & B*	**122**	NM8313
Melgund Castle *Angus*	**127**	NO5455
Meliden *Denbgs*	**70**	SJ0680
Melin Court *Neath*	**33**	SN8201
Melin-byrhedyn *Powys*	**57**	SN8198
Melin-y-coed *A & C*	**69**	SH8160
Melin-y-ddol *Powys*	**58**	SJ0807
Melin-y-wig *Denbgs*	**70**	SJ0448
Melinau *Pembks*	**31**	SN1613
Melkinthorpe *Cumb*	**94**	NY5525
Melkridge *Nthumb*	**102**	NY7364
Melksham *Wilts*	**22**	ST9063
Mell Green *Berks*	**37**	SU4577
Mellangoose *Cnwll*	**2**	SW6826
Mellguards *Cumb*	**93**	NY4445
Melling *Lancs*	**87**	SD5970
Melling *Mersyd*	**78**	SD3800
Melling Mount *Mersyd*	**78**	SD4001
Mellis *Suffk*	**54**	TM0974
Mellon Charles *Highld*	**144**	NG8491
Mellon Udrigle *Highld*	**144**	NG8996
Mellor *Gt Man*	**79**	SJ9888
Mellor *Lancs*	**81**	SD6530
Mellor Brook *Lancs*	**81**	SD6431
Mells *Somset*	**22**	ST7248
Mells *Suffk*	**55**	TM4076
Melmerby *Cumb*	**94**	NY6137
Melmerby *N York*	**88**	SE0785
Melmerby *N York*	**89**	SE3376
Melness *Highld*	**149**	NC5861
Melon Green *Suffk*	**54**	TL8456
Melplash *Dorset*	**10**	SY4898
Melrose *Border*	**109**	NT5434
Melsetter *Ork*	**155**	ND2689
Melsonby *N York*	**89**	NZ1908
Meltham *W York*	**82**	SE1010
Meltham Mills *W York*	**82**	SE1110
Melton *E R Yk*	**84**	SE9726
Melton *Suffk*	**55**	TM2850
Melton Constable *Norfk*	**66**	TG0432
Melton Mowbray *Leics*	**63**	SK7518
Melton Ross *Lincs*	**84**	TA0610
Meltonby *E R Yk*	**84**	SE7952
Melvaig *Highld*	**144**	NG7486
Melverley *Shrops*	**59**	SJ3316
Melverley Green *Shrops*	**59**	SJ3317
Melvich *Highld*	**150**	NC8764
Membury *Devon*	**10**	ST2803
Memsie *Abers*	**143**	NJ9762
Memus *Angus*	**134**	NO4259
Menabilly *Cnwll*	**3**	SX0951
Menagissey *Cnwll*	**2**	SW7146
Menai Bridge *Angles*	**69**	SH5571
Mendham *Suffk*	**55**	TM2782
Mendlesham *Suffk*	**54**	TM1065
Mendlesham Green *Suffk*	**54**	TM0963
Menheniot *Cnwll*	**5**	SX2863
Menithwood *H & W*	**47**	SO7069
Mennock *D & G*	**108**	NS8107
Menston *W York*	**82**	SE1643
Menstrie *Clacks*	**116**	NS8597
Menthorpe *N York*	**84**	SE7034
Mentmore *Bucks*	**38**	SP9019
Meoble *Highld*	**129**	NM7987
Meole Brace *Shrops*	**59**	SJ4810
Meonstoke *Hants*	**13**	SU6119
Meopham *Kent*	**27**	TQ6466
Meopham Green *Kent*	**27**	TQ6465
Meopham Station *Kent*	**27**	TQ6467
Mepal *Cambs*	**53**	TL4481
Meppershall *Beds*	**38**	TL1336
Mere *Ches*	**79**	SJ7281
Mere *Wilts*	**22**	ST8132
Mere Brow *Lancs*	**80**	SD4218
Mere Green *H & W*	**47**	SO9562
Mere Green *W Mids*	**61**	SP1198
Mere Heath *Ches*	**79**	SJ6670
Mereclough *Lancs*	**81**	SD8730
Meresborough *Kent*	**28**	TQ8264
Mereworth *Kent*	**28**	TQ6553
Meriden *W Mids*	**61**	SP2482
Merkadale *Highld*	**136**	NG3931
Merley *Dorset*	**12**	SZ0297
Merlin's Bridge *Pembks*	**30**	SM9414
Merrifield *Devon*	**7**	SX8147
Merrington *Shrops*	**59**	SJ4720
Merrion *Pembks*	**30**	SR9397
Merriott *Somset*	**10**	ST4412
Merrivale *Devon*	**6**	SX5475
Merrow *Surrey*	**26**	TQ0250
Merry Field Hill *Dorset*	**12**	SU0201
Merry Hill *Herts*	**26**	TQ1394
Merry Hill *W Mids*	**60**	SO9286
Merry Lees *Leics*	**62**	SK4705
Merryhill *W Mids*	**60**	SO8897
Merrymeet *Cnwll*	**5**	SX2766
Mersham *Kent*	**28**	TR0540
Merstham *Surrey*	**27**	TQ2853
Merston *W Susx*	**14**	SU8902
Merstone *IOW*	**13**	SZ5285
Merther *Cnwll*	**3**	SW8644
Merthyr *Carmth*	**31**	SN3520
Merthyr Cynog *Powys*	**45**	SN9837
Merthyr Dyfan *V Glam*	**20**	ST1168
Merthyr Mawr *Brdgnd*	**33**	SS8877
Merthyr Tydfil *Myr Td*	**33**	SO0406
Merthyr Vale *Myr Td*	**33**	ST0799
Merton *Devon*	**19**	SS5212
Merton *Gt Lon*	**27**	TQ2570
Merton *Norfk*	**66**	TL9098
Merton *Oxon*	**37**	SP5717
Meshaw *Devon*	**19**	SS7619
Messing *Essex*	**40**	TL8918
Messingham *Lincs*	**84**	SE8904
Metfield *Suffk*	**55**	TM2980
Metherell *Cnwll*	**5**	SX4069
Metherin *Cnwll*	**4**	SX1174
Metheringham *Lincs*	**76**	TF0661
Methil *Fife*	**118**	NT3799
Methilhill *Fife*	**126**	NO3500
Methleigh *Cnwll*	**2**	SW6226
Methley *W York*	**83**	SE3926
Methley Junction *W York*	**83**	SE3925
Methlick *Abers*	**143**	NJ8537
Methven *P & K*	**125**	NO0225
Methwold *Norfk*	**65**	TL7394
Methwold Hythe *Norfk*	**65**	TL7194
Mettingham *Suffk*	**55**	TM3689
Metton *Norfk*	**67**	TG2037
Mevagissey *Cnwll*	**3**	SX0144
Mexborough *S York*	**75**	SE4700
Mey *Highld*	**151**	ND2872
Meyllteyrn *Gwynd*	**56**	SH2332
Meysey Hampton *Gloucs*	**36**	SP1100
Miabhig *W Isls*	**154**	NB0834
Miavaig *W Isls*	**154**	NB0834
Michaelchurch *H & W*	**46**	SO5225
Michaelchurch Escley *H & W*	**46**	SO3134
Michaelchurch-on-Arrow *Powys*	**46**	SO2450
Michaelston-le-Pit *V Glam*	**33**	ST1572
Michaelstone-y-Fedw *Newpt*	**34**	ST2484
Michaelstow *Cnwll*	**4**	SX0778
Michelcombe *Devon*	**7**	SX6969
Micheldever *Hants*	**24**	SU5139
Micheldever Station *Hants*	**24**	SU5143
Michelmersh *Hants*	**23**	SU3426
Mickfield *Suffk*	**54**	TM1361
Mickle Trafford *Ches*	**71**	SJ4469
Micklebring *S York*	**75**	SK5194
Mickleby *N York*	**90**	NZ8012
Micklefield *W York*	**83**	SE4432
Micklefield Green *Herts*	**26**	TQ0498
Mickleham *Surrey*	**26**	TQ1653
Mickleover *Derbys*	**73**	SK3033
Micklethwaite *Cumb*	**93**	NY2850
Micklethwaite *W York*	**82**	SE1041
Mickleton *Dur*	**95**	NY9623
Mickleton *Gloucs*	**48**	SP1643
Mickletown *W York*	**83**	SE4027
Mickley *Derbys*	**74**	SK3279
Mickley *N York*	**89**	SE2576
Mickley Green *Suffk*	**54**	TL8457
Mickley Square *Nthumb*	**103**	NZ0762
Mid Ardlaw *Abers*	**143**	NJ9463
Mid Beltie *Abers*	**134**	NJ6200
Mid Bockhampton *Hants*	**12**	SZ1796
Mid Calder *W Loth*	**117**	NT0767
Mid Clyth *Highld*	**151**	ND2937
Mid Lavant *W Susx*	**14**	SU8508
Mid Mains *Highld*	**139**	NH4239
Mid Thorpe *Lincs*	**77**	TF2672
Mid Yell *Shet*	**155**	HU5190
Midbea *Ork*	**155**	HY4444
Middle Assendon *Oxon*	**37**	SU7385
Middle Aston *Oxon*	**49**	SP4726
Middle Barton *Oxon*	**49**	SP4325
Middle Chinnock *Somset*	**10**	ST4713
Middle Claydon *Bucks*	**49**	SP7225
Middle Duntisbourne *Gloucs*	**35**	SO9806
Middle Handley *Derbys*	**74**	SK4077
Middle Harling *Norfk*	**54**	TL9885
Middle Kames *Ag & B*	**114**	NR9189
Middle Littleton *H & W*	**48**	SP0847
Middle Madeley *Staffs*	**72**	SJ7745
Middle Maes-coed *H & W*	**46**	SO3333
Middle Mayfield *Staffs*	**73**	SK1444
Middle Mill *Pembks*	**30**	SM8026
Middle Quarter *Kent*	**28**	TQ8938
Middle Rasen *Lincs*	**76**	TF0889
Middle Rocombe *Devon*	**7**	SX9069

Morton New Leeds

Morton *IOW* 13 SZ6085
Morton *Lincs* 75 SK8091
Morton *Lincs* 64 TF0923
Morton *Norfk* 66 TG1216
Morton *Notts* 75 SK7251
Morton *Shrops* 59 SJ2924
Morton Hall *Lincs* 76 SK8863
Morton Tinmouth *Dur* 96 NZ1821
Morton-on-Swale *N York* 89 SE3291
Morvah *Cnwll* 2 SW4035
Morval *Cnwll* 5 SX2556
Morvich *Highld* 138 NG9621
Morville *Shrops* 60 SO6794
Morville Heath *Shrops* 60 SO6893
Morwenstow *Cnwll* 18 SS2015
Mosborough *S York* 74 SK4281
Moscow *E Ayrs* 107 NS4840
Mose *Shrops* 60 SO7590
Mosedale *Cumb* 93 NY3532
Moseley *H & W* 47 SO8159
Moseley *W Mids* 60 SO9498
Moseley *W Mids* 61 SP0783
Moses Gate *Gt Man* 79 SD7306
Moss *Ag & B* 120 NL9544
Moss *S York* 83 SE5914
Moss *Wrexhm* 71 SJ3053
Moss Bank *Mersyd* 78 SJ5197
Moss Edge *Lancs* 80 SD4243
Moss End *Ches* 79 SJ6778
Moss Side *Cumb* 93 NY1952
Moss Side *Lancs* 80 SD3730
Moss Side *Mersyd* 78 SD3802
Moss-side *Highld* 140 NH8555
Mossat *Abers* 142 NJ4719
Mossbank *Shet* 155 HU4575
Mossbay *Cumb* 92 NX9927
Mossblown *S Ayrs* 106 NS4024
Mossbrow *Gt Man* 79 SJ7089
Mossburnford *Border* 110 NT6616
Mossdale *D & G* 99 NX6670
Mossdale *E Ayrs* 107 NS4904
Mossend *N Lans* 116 NS7460
Mosser Mains *Cumb* 92 NY1125
Mossgiel *E Ayrs* 107 NS4828
Mossknowe *D & G* 101 NY2769
Mossley *Ches* 72 SJ8861
Mossley *Gt Man* 82 SD9701
Mosspaul Hotel *Border* 109 NY3999
Mosstodloch *Moray* 141 NJ3259
Mossy Lea *Lancs* 80 SD5312
Mossyard *D & G* 99 NX5451
Mosterton *Dorset* 10 ST4505
Moston *Gt Man* 79 SD8701
Moston *Shrops* 59 SJ5626
Moston Green *Ches* 72 SJ7261
Mostyn *Flints* 70 SJ1580
Motcombe *Dorset* 22 ST8525
Mothecombe *Devon* 6 SX6047
Motherby *Cumb* 93 NY4228
Motherwell *N Lans* 116 NS7457
Motspur Park *Gt Lon* 26 TQ2267
Mottingham *Gt Lon* 27 TQ4272
Mottisfont *Hants* 23 SU3226
Mottistone *IOW* 13 SZ4083
Mottram in Longdendale *Gt Man* 79 SJ9995
Mottram St Andrew *Ches* 79 SJ8778
Mouilpied *Guern* 152 GN0000
Mouldsworth *Ches* 71 SJ5071
Moulin *P & K* 132 NN9459
Moulsecoomb *E Susx* 15 TQ3307
Moulsford *Oxon* 37 SU5883
Moulsoe *Bucks* 38 SP9141
Moultavie *Highld* 146 NH6371
Moulton *Ches* 79 SJ6569
Moulton *Lincs* 64 TF3023
Moulton *N York* 89 NZ2303
Moulton *Nhants* 50 SP7866
Moulton *Suffk* 53 TL6964
Moulton *V Glam* 33 ST0770
Moulton Chapel *Lincs* 64 TF2918
Moulton Seas End *Lincs* 64 TF3227
Moulton St Mary *Norfk* 67 TG3907
Mount *Cnwll* 3 SW7856
Mount *Cnwll* 4 SX1468
Mount *W York* 82 SE0917
Mount Ambrose *Cnwll* 2 SW7043
Mount Bures *Essex* 40 TL9032
Mount Hawke *Cnwll* 2 SW7147
Mount Hermon *Cnwll* 2 SW6915
Mount Lothian *Mdloth* 117 NT2757
Mount Pleasant *Ches* 72 SJ8456
Mount Pleasant *Derbys* 74 SK3448
Mount Pleasant *Dur* 96 NZ2634
Mount Pleasant *E Susx* 16 TQ4216
Mount Pleasant *H & W* 47 SP0064
Mount Pleasant *Norfk* 66 TL9994
Mount Pleasant *Suffk* 53 TL7347
Mount Sorrel *Wilts* 23 SU0324
Mount Tabor *W York* 82 SE0527
Mountain *W York* 82 SE0930
Mountain Ash *Rhondd* 33 ST0499
Mountain Cross *Border* 117 NT1547
Mountain Street *Kent* 29 TR0652
Mountfield *E Susx* 17 TQ7320
Mountgerald House *Highld* 139 NH5661
Mountjoy *Cnwll* 4 SW8760
Mountnessing *Essex* 40 TQ6297
Mounton *Mons* 34 ST5193
Mountsorrel *Leics* 62 SK5814
Mountstuart *Ag & B* 114 NS1159
Mousehill *Surrey* 25 SU9441
Mousehole *Cnwll* 2 SW4626
Mouswald *D & G* 100 NY0672
Mow Cop *Ches* 72 SJ8557
Mowhaugh *Border* 110 NT8120
Mowmacre Hill *Leics* 62 SK5807
Mowsley *Leics* 50 SP6489
Mowtie *Abers* 135 NO8388
Moy *Highld* 140 NH7634
Moy *Highld* 131 NN4282
Moye *Highld* 138 NG8818
Moyles Court *Hants* 12 SU1608
Moylgrove *Pembks* 42 SN1144
Muasdale *Ag & B* 105 NR6840
Much Birch *H & W* 46 SO5030
Much Cowarne *H & W* 46 SO6147
Much Dewchurch *H & W* 46 SO4831
Much Hadham *Herts* 39 TL4219
Much Hoole *Lancs* 80 SD4723
Much Hoole Town *Lancs* 80 SD4722
Much Marcle *H & W* 47 SO6532
Much Wenlock *Shrops* 59 SO6299
Muchalls *Abers* 135 NO9092
Muchelney *Somset* 21 ST4224
Muchelney Ham *Somset* 21 ST4423
Muchlarnick *Cnwll* 5 SX2156
Mucking *Essex* 40 TQ6881
Muckingford *Essex* 40 TQ6779
Muckleford *Dorset* 10 SY6393
Mucklestone *Staffs* 72 SJ7237
Muckley *Shrops* 59 SO6495
Muckton *Lincs* 77 TF3781
Mucomir *Highld* 131 NN1884
Mud Row *Kent* 28 TR0072
Muddiford *Devon* 19 SS5638
Muddles Green *E Susx* 16 TQ5413
Mudeford *Dorset* 12 SZ1892
Mudford *Somset* 21 ST5719
Mudford Sock *Somset* 21 ST5519
Mudgley *Somset* 21 ST4545
Mugdock *Stirlg* 115 NS5577
Mugeary *Highld* 136 NG4439
Mugginton *Derbys* 73 SK2842
Muggintonlane End *Derbys* 73 SK2844
Muggleswick *Dur* 95 NZ0449
Muir of Fowlis *Abers* 134 NJ5612
Muir of Miltonduff *Moray* 141 NJ1859
Muir of Ord *Highld* 139 NH5250
Muir of Thorn *P & K* 125 NO0637
Muirden *Abers* 142 NJ7054
Muirdrum *Angus* 127 NO5637
Muiresk *Abers* 142 NJ6948
Muirhead *Angus* 126 NO3434
Muirhead *Fife* 126 NO2805
Muirhead *N Lans* 116 NS6869
Muirhouses *Falk* 117 NT0180
Muirkirk *E Ayrs* 107 NS6927
Muirmill *Stirlg* 116 NS7283
Muirshearlich *Highld* 131 NN1380
Muirtack *Abers* 143 NJ9937
Muirton *P & K* 125 NN9211
Muirton Mains *Highld* 139 NH4553
Muirton of Ardblair *P & K* 126 NO1643
Muker *N York* 88 SD9097
Mulbarton *Norfk* 67 TG1901
Mulben *Moray* 141 NJ3550
Mulfra *Cnwll* 2 SW4534
Mulindry *Ag & B* 112 NR3659
Mullacott Cross *Devon* 19 SS5144
Mullion *Cnwll* 2 SW6719
Mullion Cove *Cnwll* 2 SW6617
Mumby *Lincs* 77 TF5174
Muncher's Green *Herts* 39 TL3126
Munderfield Row *H & W* 47 SO6451
Munderfield Stocks *H & W* 47 SO6550
Mundesley *Norfk* 67 TG3136
Mundford *Norfk* 66 TL8093
Mundham *Norfk* 67 TM3397
Mundon Hill *Essex* 40 TL8602
Mungrisdale *Cumb* 93 NY3630
Munlochy *Highld* 140 NH6453
Munnoch *N Ayrs* 114 NS2548
Munsley *H & W* 47 SO6640
Munslow *Shrops* 59 SO5287
Murchington *Devon* 8 SX6888
Murcot *H & W* 48 SP0640
Murcott *Oxon* 37 SP5815
Murcott *Wilts* 35 ST9591
Murkle *Highld* 151 ND1668
Murlaggan *Highld* 130 NN0192
Murrell Green *Hants* 24 SU7455
Murroes *Angus* 127 NO4635
Murrow *Cambs* 64 TF3707
Mursley *Bucks* 38 SP8128
Murston *Kent* 28 TQ9264
Murthill *Angus* 134 NO4657
Murthly *P & K* 126 NO1038
Murton *Cumb* 94 NY7221
Murton *Dur* 96 NZ3847
Murton *N York* 83 SE6452
Murton *Nthumb* 111 NT9748
Murton *T & W* 103 NZ3270
Musbury *Devon* 10 SY2794
Muscoates *N York* 90 SE6879
Musselburgh *E Loth* 118 NT3472
Muston *Leics* 63 SK8237
Muston *N York* 91 TA0979
Mustow Green *H & W* 60 SO8774
Muswell Hill *Gt Lon* 27 TQ2889
Mutehill *D & G* 99 NX6848
Mutford *Suffk* 55 TM4888
Muthill *P & K* 125 NN8717
Mutterton *Devon* 9 ST0205
Muxton *Shrops* 60 SJ7114
Mybster *Highld* 151 ND1652
Myddfai *Carmth* 44 SN7730
Myddle *Shrops* 59 SJ4623
Mydroilyn *Cardgn* 42 SN4555
Mylor *Cnwll* 3 SW8135
Mylor Bridge *Cnwll* 3 SW8036
Mynachlog ddu *Pembks* 31 SN1430
Myndd-llan *Flints* 70 SJ1572
Myndtown *Shrops* 59 SO3989
Mynydd Buch *Cardgn* 43 SN7276
Mynydd Isa *Flints* 70 SJ2563
Mynydd Llandygai *Gwynd* 69 SH6065
Mynydd-bach *Mons* 34 ST4894
Mynydd-bach *Swans* 32 SS6597
Mynyddgarreg *Carmth* 31 SN4208
Mynytho *Gwynd* 56 SH3031
Myrebird *Abers* 135 NO7398
Myredykes *Border* 102 NY5998
Mytchett *Surrey* 25 SU8855
Mytholm *W York* 82 SD9827
Mytholmroyd *W York* 82 SE0126
Mythop *Lancs* 80 SD3634
Myton-on-Swale *N York* 89 SE4366

N

Na Buirgh *W Isls* 154 NG0394
Naast *Highld* 144 NG8283
Nab's Head *Lancs* 81 SD6229
Naburn *N York* 83 SE5945
Naccolt *Kent* 28 TR0544
Nackington *Kent* 29 TR1554
Nacton *Suffk* 55 TM2240
Nafferton *E R Yk* 91 TA0559
Nag's Head *Gloucs* 35 ST8898
Nailbridge *Gloucs* 35 SO6415
Nailsbourne *Somset* 20 ST2128
Nailsea *Somset* 34 ST4770
Nailstone *Leics* 62 SK4106
Nailsworth *Gloucs* 35 ST8499
Nairn *Highld* 140 NH8856
Nalderswood *Surrey* 15 TQ2445
Nancegollan *Cnwll* 2 SW6332
Nancledra *Cnwll* 2 SW4936
Nanhoron *Gwynd* 56 SH2731
Nannerch *Flints* 70 SJ1669
Nanpantan *Leics* 62 SK5017
Nanpean *Cnwll* 3 SW9556
Nanquidno *Cnwll* 2 SW3629
Nanstallon *Cnwll* 4 SX0367
Nant Gwynant *Gwynd* 69 SH6350
Nant Peris *Gwynd* 69 SH6058
Nant-ddu *Powys* 33 SO0014
Nant-glas *Powys* 45 SN9965
Nant-y-Bwch *Blae G* 33 SO1210
Nant-y-caws *Carmth* 32 SN4518
Nant-y-derry *Mons* 34 SO3306
Nant-y-gollen *Shrops* 58 SJ2428
Nant-y-moel *Brdgnd* 33 SS9392
Nant-y-pandy *A & C* 69 SH6973
Nanternis *Cardgn* 42 SN3756
Nantgaredig *Carmth* 32 SN4921
Nantgarw *Rhondd* 33 ST1285
Nantglyn *Denbgs* 70 SJ0061
Nantgwyn *Powys* 45 SN9776
Nantlle *Gwynd* 68 SH5153
Nantmawr *Shrops* 58 SJ2524
Nantmel *Powys* 45 SO0366
Nantmor *Gwynd* 57 SH6046
Nantwich *Ches* 72 SJ6552
Nantyffyllon *Brdgnd* 33 SS8492
Naphill *Bucks* 26 SU8496
Napleton *H & W* 47 SO8648
Nappa *N York* 81 SD8553
Napton on the Hill *Warwks* 49 SP4661
Narberth *Pembks* 31 SN1015
Narborough *Leics* 50 SP5497
Narborough *Norfk* 65 TF7412
Narkurs *Cnwll* 5 SX3255
Nasareth *Gwynd* 68 SH4749
Naseby *Nhants* 50 SP6978
Nash *Bucks* 38 SP7833
Nash *Gt Lon* 27 TQ4063
Nash *H & W* 46 SO3062
Nash *Newpt* 34 ST3483
Nash *Shrops* 46 SO6071
Nash End *H & W* 60 SO7781
Nash Lee *Bucks* 38 SP8408
Nash Street *Kent* 27 TQ6469
Nash's Green *Hants* 24 SU6745
Nassington *Nhants* 51 TL0696
Nastend *Gloucs* 35 SO7906
Nasty *Herts* 39 TL3524
Nateby *Cumb* 88 NY7706
Nateby *Lancs* 80 SD4644
Natland *Cumb* 87 SD5289
Naughton *Suffk* 54 TM0249
Naunton *Gloucs* 48 SP1123
Naunton *H & W* 47 SO8739
Naunton Beauchamp *H & W* 47 SO9652
Navenby *Lincs* 76 SK9858
Navestock *Essex* 27 TQ5397
Navestock Side *Essex* 27 TQ5697
Navidale House Hotel *Highld* 147 ND0316
Navity *Highld* 140 NH7864
Nawton *N York* 90 SE6584
Nayland *Suffk* 54 TL9734
Nazeing *Essex* 39 TL4106
Nazeing Gate *Essex* 39 TL4105
Neacroft *Hants* 12 SZ1896
Neal's Green *Warwks* 61 SP3384
Neap *Shet* 155 HU5058
Near Cotton *Staffs* 73 SK0646
Near Sawry *Cumb* 87 SD3795
Neasden *Gt Lon* 26 TQ2185
Neasham *Dur* 89 NZ3210
Neath *Neath* 32 SS7597
Neatham *Hants* 24 SU7440
Neatishead *Norfk* 67 TG3420
Nebo *A & C* 69 SH8355
Nebo *Angles* 68 SH4690
Nebo *Cardgn* 43 SN5465
Nebo *Gwynd* 68 SH4850
Necton *Norfk* 66 TF8709
Nedd *Highld* 148 NC1331
Nedderton *Nthumb* 103 NZ2382
Nedging *Suffk* 54 TL9948
Nedging Tye *Suffk* 54 TM0149
Needham *Norfk* 55 TM2281
Needham Market *Suffk* 54 TM0855
Needham Street *Suffk* 53 TL7265
Needingworth *Cambs* 52 TL3472
Neen Savage *Shrops* 60 SO6777
Neen Sollars *Shrops* 60 SO6672
Neenton *Shrops* 59 SO6387
Nefyn *Gwynd* 56 SH3040
Neilston *E Rens* 115 NS4857
Nelson *Caerph* 33 ST1195
Nelson *Lancs* 81 SD8638
Nemphlar *S Lans* 116 NS8544
Nempnett Thrubwell *Somset* 21 ST5260
Nenthall *Cumb* 94 NY7545
Nenthead *Cumb* 94 NY7743
Nenthorn *Border* 110 NT6837
Neopardy *Devon* 8 SX7999
Nep Town *W Susx* 15 TQ2115
Nercwys *Flints* 70 SJ2360
Nereabolls *Ag & B* 112 NR2255
Nerston *S Lans* 116 NS6456
Nesbit *Nthumb* 111 NT9833
Nesfield *N York* 82 SE0949
Ness *Ches* 71 SJ3076
Nesscliffe *Shrops* 59 SJ3819
Neston *Ches* 71 SJ2977
Neston *Wilts* 22 ST8668
Netchwood *Shrops* 59 SO6291
Nether Alderley *Ches* 79 SJ8476
Nether Blainslie *Border* 109 NT5443
Nether Broughton *Notts* 63 SK6925
Nether Cerne *Dorset* 11 SY6798
Nether Compton *Dorset* 10 ST5917
Nether Crimond *Abers* 143 NJ8222
Nether Dallachy *Moray* 141 NJ3563
Nether Exe *Devon* 9 SS9300
Nether Fingland *S Lans* 108 NS9310
Nether Handley *Derbys* 74 SK4176
Nether Handwick *Angus* 126 NO3641
Nether Haugh *S York* 74 SK4196
Nether Headon *Notts* 75 SK7477
Nether Heage *Derbys* 74 SK3650
Nether Heyford *Nhants* 49 SP6658
Nether Howcleugh *S Lans* 108 NT0212
Nether Kellet *Lancs* 87 SD5068
Nether Kinmundy *Abers* 143 NK0543
Nether Langwith *Notts* 75 SK5370
Nether Moor *Derbys* 74 SK3866
Nether Padley *Derbys* 74 SK2478
Nether Poppleton *N York* 83 SE5654
Nether Row *Cumb* 93 NY3237
Nether Silton *N York* 89 SE4592
Nether Skyborry *Shrops* 46 SO2873
Nether Stowey *Somset* 20 ST1939
Nether Street *Essex* 40 TL5812
Nether Wallop *Hants* 23 SU3036
Nether Wasdale *Cumb* 86 NY1204
Nether Wellwood *E Ayrs* 107 NS6526
Nether Welton *Cumb* 93 NY3545
Nether Westcote *Gloucs* 36 SP2220
Nether Whitacre *Warwks* 61 SP2392
Nether Whitecleuch *S Lans* 108 NS8319
Netheravon *Wilts* 23 SU1448
Netherbrae *Abers* 143 NJ7959
Netherburn *S Lans* 116 NS7947
Netherbury *Dorset* 10 SY4799
Netherby *Cumb* 101 NY3971
Netherby *N York* 83 SE3346
Nethercleuch *D & G* 100 NY1186
Nethercote *Warwks* 49 SP5164
Nethercott *Devon* 18 SS4839
Nethercott *Devon* 5 SX3596
Netherend *Gloucs* 34 SO5900
Netherfield *E Susx* 16 TQ7019
Netherfield *Leics* 62 SK5816
Netherfield *Notts* 62 SK6140
Netherfield Road *E Susx* 17 TQ7417
Nethergate *Lincs* 75 SK7599
Nethergate *Norfk* 66 TG0529
Netherhampton *Wilts* 23 SU1029
Netherhay *Dorset* 10 ST4105
Netherland Green *Staffs* 73 SK1030
Netherlaw *D & G* 99 NX7444
Netherley *Abers* 135 NO8593
Nethermill *D & G* 100 NY0487
Nethermuir *Abers* 143 NJ9044
Netheroyd Hill *W York* 82 SE1419
Netherplace *E Rens* 115 NS5255
Netherseal *Derbys* 61 SK2812
Netherstreet *Wilts* 22 ST9864
Netherthong *W York* 82 SE1309
Netherthorpe *Derbys* 75 SK4474
Netherton *Angus* 134 NO5457
Netherton *Devon* 7 SX8971
Netherton *H & W* 46 SO5226
Netherton *H & W* 47 SO9941
Netherton *Hants* 23 SU3757
Netherton *N Lans* 116 NS7854
Netherton *Nthumb* 111 NT9807
Netherton *Oxon* 36 SU4199
Netherton *P & K* 126 NO1452
Netherton *Shrops* 60 SO7382
Netherton *Stirlg* 115 NS5579
Netherton *W Mids* 60 SO9488
Netherton *W York* 82 SE1213
Netherton *W York* 82 SE2816
Nethertown *Cumb* 86 NX9907
Nethertown *Highld* 151 ND3578
Nethertown *Lancs* 81 SD7236
Nethertown *Staffs* 73 SK1017
Netherwitton *Nthumb* 103 NZ0990
Nethy Bridge *Highld* 141 NJ0020
Netley *Hants* 13 SU4508
Netley Marsh *Hants* 12 SU3313
Nettacott *Devon* 9 SX8999
Nettlebed *Oxon* 37 SU6986
Nettlebridge *Somset* 21 ST6448
Nettlecombe *Dorset* 10 SY5195
Nettlecombe *IOW* 13 SZ5278
Nettleden *Herts* 38 TL0110
Nettleham *Lincs* 76 TF0075
Nettlestead *Kent* 28 TQ6852
Nettlestead Green *Kent* 28 TQ6850
Nettlestone *IOW* 13 SZ6290
Nettlesworth *Dur* 96 NZ2547
Nettleton *Lincs* 76 TA1100
Nettleton *Wilts* 35 ST8278
Nettleton Shrub *Wilts* 35 ST8277
Netton *Devon* 6 SX5546
Netton *Wilts* 23 SU1336
Neuadd *Carmth* 32 SN7021
Neuadd Fawr *Carmth* 44 SN7441
Neuadd-ddu *Powys* 45 SN9175
Nevendon *Essex* 40 TQ7591
Nevern *Pembks* 31 SN0840
Nevill Holt *Leics* 51 SP8193
New Abbey *D & G* 100 NX9666
New Aberdour *Abers* 143 NJ8863
New Addington *Gt Lon* 27 TQ3763
New Alresford *Hants* 24 SU5832
New Alyth *P & K* 126 NO2447
New Arram *E R Yk* 84 TA0344
New Ash Green *Kent* 27 TQ6065
New Balderton *Notts* 75 SK8152
New Barn *Kent* 27 TQ6169
New Barnet *Gt Lon* 27 TQ2695
New Barton *Nhants* 51 SP8564
New Bewick *Nthumb* 111 NU0620
New Bilton *Warwks* 50 SP4875
New Bolingbroke *Lincs* 77 TF3057
New Boultham *Lincs* 76 SK9670
New Bradwell *Bucks* 38 SP8341
New Brampton *Derbys* 74 SK3771
New Brancepeth *Dur* 96 NZ2241
New Bridge *N York* 90 SE8085
New Brighton *Flints* 70 SJ2565
New Brighton *Mersyd* 78 SJ3093
New Brinsley *Notts* 75 SK4550
New Brotton *N York* 97 NZ6920
New Broughton *Wrexhm* 71 SJ3151
New Buckenham *Norfk* 54 TM0890
New Bury *Gt Man* 79 SD7304
New Byth *Abers* 143 NJ8254
New Costessey *Norfk* 66 TG1810
New Cowper *Cumb* 92 NY1245
New Crofton *W York* 83 SE3817
New Cross *Cardgn* 43 SN6376
New Cross *Gt Lon* 27 TQ3676
New Cross *Somset* 21 ST4119
New Cumnock *E Ayrs* 107 NS6213
New Cut *E Susx* 17 TQ8115
New Deer *Abers* 143 NJ8847
New Delaval *Nthumb* 103 NZ2979
New Delph *Gt Man* 82 SD9907
New Denham *Bucks* 26 TQ0484
New Duston *Nhants* 49 SP7162
New Earswick *N York* 83 SE6155
New Eastwood *Notts* 62 SK4646
New Edlington *S York* 75 SK5398
New Elgin *Moray* 141 NJ2261
New Ellerby *E R Yk* 85 TA1639
New Eltham *Gt Lon* 27 TQ4472
New End *H & W* 48 SP0560
New England *Cambs* 64 TF1801
New Farnley *W York* 82 SE2531
New Ferry *Mersyd* 78 SJ3385
New Fletton *Cambs* 64 TL1997
New Fryston *W York* 83 SE4526
New Galloway *D & G* 99 NX6377
New Gilston *Fife* 127 NO4208
New Grimsby *IOS* 2 SV8815
New Hartley *Nthumb* 103 NZ3076
New Haw *Surrey* 26 TQ0563
New Hedges *Pembks* 31 SN1202
New Herrington *T & W* 96 NZ3352
New Holkham *Norfk* 66 TF8839
New Holland *Lincs* 85 TA0823
New Houghton *Derbys* 75 SK4965
New Houghton *Norfk* 66 TF7927
New Houses *Gt Man* 78 SD5502
New Houses *N York* 88 SD8073
New Hutton *Cumb* 87 SD5691
New Hythe *Kent* 28 TQ7159
New Inn *Carmth* 44 SN4736
New Inn *Torfn* 34 ST3099
New Invention *Shrops* 46 SO2976
New Kelso *Highld* 138 NG9442
New Lakenham *Norfk* 67 TG2307
New Lanark *S Lans* 108 NS8842
New Lane *Lancs* 80 SD4212
New Lane End *Ches* 79 SJ6394
New Langholm *D & G* 101 NY3684
New Leake *Lincs* 77 TF4057
New Leeds *Abers* 143 NJ9954

New Longton
North Fambridge

New Longton Lancs 80 SD5025
New Luce D & G 98 NX1764
New Malden Gt Lon 26 TQ2168
New Marske N York 97 NZ6121
New Marston Oxon 37 SP5407
New Marton Shrops 59 SJ3334
New Mill Abers 135 NO7883
New Mill Cnwll 2 SW4534
New Mill Herts 38 SP9212
New Mill W York 82 SE1609
New Mills Cnwll 3 SW8952
New Mills Derbys 79 SK0085
New Mills Powys 58 SJ0901
New Milton Hants 12 SZ2495
New Mistley Essex 41 TM1131
New Moat Pembks 30 SN0625
New Ollerton Notts 75 SK6667
New Oscott W Mids 61 SP0994
New Oxted Surrey 27 TQ3952
New Pitsligo Abers 143 NJ8855
New Polzeath Cnwll 4 SW9379
New Prestwick S Ayrs 106 NS3424
New Quay Cardgn 42 SN3959
New Quay Essex 41 TM0223
New Rackheath Norfk 67 TG2812
New Radnor Powys 45 SO2161
New Rent Cumb 93 NY4536
New Ridley Nthumb 95 NZ0559
New Road Side N York 82 SD9743
New Romney Kent 17 TR0624
New Rossington S York 75 SK6198
New Row Cardgn 43 SN7273
New Row Lancs 81 SD6438
New Scone P & K 126 NO1326
New Sharlston W York 83 SE3819
New Shoreston Nthumb 111 NU1932
New Silksworth T & W 96 NZ3853
New Skelton N York 97 NZ6618
New Somerby Lincs 63 SK9235
New Spilsby Lincs 77 TF4165
New Springs Gt Man 78 SD5906
New Stevenston N Lans 116 NS7659
New Street H & W 46 SO3356
New Swannington Leics 62 SK4215
New Thundersley Essex 40 TQ7789
New Town Beds 52 TL1945
New Town Dorset 22 ST8318
New Town Dorset 11 ST9515
New Town Dorset 11 ST9907
New Town Dorset 22 ST9918
New Town E Loth 118 NT4470
New Town E Susx 16 TQ4720
New Town Nhants 51 SP9677
New Town Somset 10 ST2712
New Town Wilts 36 SU2871
New Tredegar Caerph 33 SO1403
New Trows S Lans 108 NS8038
New Tupton Derbys 74 SK3966
New Village E R Yk 84 SE8530
New Walsoken Cambs 65 TF4609
New Waltham Lincs 85 TA2804
New Whittington Derbys 74 SK3975
New Wimpole Cambs 52 TL3549
New Winton E Loth 118 NT4271
New Yatt Oxon 36 SP3713
New York Lincs 77 TF2455
New York N York 89 SE1963
New York T & W 103 NZ3270
New Zealand Derbys 62 SK3336
Newall W York 82 SE1946
Newark Cambs 64 TF2100
Newark D & G 107 NS7808
Newark Ork 155 HY7142
Newark-on-Trent Notts 75 SK7953
Newarthill N Lans 116 NS7859
Newbarn Kent 29 TR1540
Newbattle Mdloth 118 NT3365
Newbie D & G 101 NY1764
Newbiggin Cumb 93 NY4729
Newbiggin Cumb 94 NY5549
Newbiggin Cumb 94 NY6228
Newbiggin Cumb 86 SD0994
Newbiggin Cumb 86 SD2669
Newbiggin Dur 95 NY9127
Newbiggin Dur 96 NZ1447
Newbiggin N York 88 SD9591
Newbiggin N York 88 SE0086
Newbiggin-by-the-Sea Nthumb 103 NZ3087
Newbiggin-on-Lune Cumb 87 NY7005
Newbigging Angus 126 NO2841
Newbigging Angus 127 NO4237
Newbigging S Lans 117 NT0145
Newbold Derbys 74 SK3672
Newbold Leics 62 SK4019
Newbold on Avon Warwks 50 SP4877
Newbold on Stour Warwks 48 SP2446
Newbold Pacey Warwks 48 SP2957
Newbold Revel Warwks 50 SP4580
Newbold Verdon Leics 62 SK4403
Newborough Angles 68 SH4265
Newborough Cambs 64 TF2005
Newborough Staffs 73 SK1325
Newbottle Nhants 49 SP5236
Newbottle T & W 96 NZ3351
Newbourne Suffk 55 TM2743
Newbridge C Edin 117 NT1272
Newbridge Caerph 33 ST2097
Newbridge Cardgn 44 SN5059
Newbridge Cnwll 2 SW4231
Newbridge Cnwll 3 SW7944
Newbridge D & G 100 NX9479
Newbridge Hants 12 SU2915
Newbridge IOW 13 SZ4187
Newbridge Oxon 36 SP4001
Newbridge Pembks 30 SM9431
Newbridge Wrexhm 70 SJ2841
Newbridge Green H & W 47 SO8439
Newbridge on Wye Powys 45 SO0158
Newbridge-on-Usk Mons 34 ST3894
Newbrough Nthumb 102 NY8767
Newbuildings Devon 8 SS7903
Newburgh Abers 143 NJ9659
Newburgh Abers 143 NJ9925
Newburgh Fife 126 NO2318
Newburgh Lancs 78 SD4810
Newburgh Priory N York 90 SE5476
Newburn T & W 103 NZ1665
Newbury Berks 24 SU4766
Newbury Somset 22 ST6949
Newbury Wilts 22 ST8241
Newby Cumb 94 NY5921
Newby Lancs 81 SD8146
Newby N York 90 NZ5012
Newby N York 88 SD7269
Newby N York 91 TA0190
Newby Bridge Cumb 87 SD3686
Newby Cross Cumb 93 NY3653
Newby East Cumb 93 NY4758
Newby Head Cumb 94 NY5821
Newby West Cumb 93 NY3753
Newby Wiske N York 89 SE3687
Newcastle Mons 34 SO4417
Newcastle Shrops 58 SO2582
Newcastle Emlyn Carmth 31 SN3040
Newcastle upon Tyne T & W 103 NZ2464
Newcastle-under-Lyme Staffs 72 SJ8445
Newcastleton Border 101 NY4887
Newchapel Pembks 31 SN2239
Newchapel Staffs 72 SJ8654
Newchapel Surrey 15 TQ3641
Newchurch Blae G 33 SO1710
Newchurch H & W 46 SO3550
Newchurch IOW 13 SZ5685
Newchurch Kent 17 TR0531
Newchurch Mons 34 ST4597
Newchurch Powys 45 SO2150
Newchurch Staffs 73 SK1423
Newchurch in Pendle Lancs 81 SD8239
Newcraighall C Edin 118 NT3272
Newdigate Surrey 15 TQ1942
Newell Green Berks 25 SU8770
Newenden Kent 17 TQ8327
Newent Gloucs 47 SO7225
Newfield Dur 96 NZ2033
Newfield Dur 96 NZ2452
Newfield Highld 147 NH7877
Newfound Hants 24 SU5851
Newgale Pembks 30 SM8522
Newgate Norfk 66 TG0443
Newgate Street Herts 39 TL3005
Newhall Ches 71 SJ6145
Newhall Derbys 73 SK2820
Newham Nthumb 111 NU1728
Newhaven Derbys 74 SK1660
Newhaven E Susx 16 TQ4401
Newhey Gt Man 82 SD9411
Newholm N York 90 NZ8610
Newhouse N Lans 116 NS7961
Newick E Susx 15 TQ4121
Newingreen Kent 29 TR1236
Newington Kent 28 TQ8564
Newington Kent 29 TR1837
Newington Oxon 37 SU6096
Newington Shrops 59 SO4283
Newington Bagpath Gloucs 35 ST8194
Newland Cumb 86 SD3079
Newland E R Yk 84 TA0631
Newland Gloucs 34 SO5509
Newland H & W 47 SO7948
Newland N York 83 SE6824
Newland E R Yk 84 SE8029
Newland Oxon 36 SP3609
Newland Somset 19 SS8238
Newlandrig Mdloth 118 NT3762
Newlands Border 101 NY5094
Newlands Cumb 93 NY3439
Newlands Nthumb 95 NZ0855
Newlands of Dundurcas Moray 141 NJ2951
Newlyn Cnwll 2 SW4628
Newmachar Abers 143 NJ8919
Newmains N Lans 116 NS8256
Newman's End Essex 39 TL5112
Newman's Green Suffk 54 TL8843
Newmarket Cumb 93 NY3438
Newmarket Suffk 53 TL6463
Newmarket W Isls 154 NB4235
Newmill Border 109 NT4510
Newmill Moray 142 NJ4352
Newmill of Inshewan Angus 134 NO4260
Newmillerdam W York 83 SE3215
Newmills C Edin 117 NT1667
Newmills Fife 117 NT0186
Newmills Mons 34 SO5107
Newmiln P & K 126 NO1230
Newmilns E Ayrs 107 NS5337
Newnes Shrops 59 SJ3834
Newney Green Essex 40 TL6507
Newnham Gloucs 35 SO6911
Newnham H & W 47 SO6469
Newnham Hants 24 SU7053
Newnham Herts 39 TL2437
Newnham Kent 28 TQ9557
Newnham Nhants 49 SP5859
Newnham Paddox Warwks 50 SP4983
Newport Cnwll 5 SX3285
Newport Devon 19 SS5632
Newport Dorset 11 SY8895
Newport Essex 39 TL5234
Newport Gloucs 35 ST7097
Newport Highld 151 ND1324
Newport IOW 13 SZ5089
Newport E R Yk 84 SE8530
Newport Newpt 34 ST3188
Newport Norfk 67 TG5017
Newport Pembks 30 SN0539
Newport Shrops 72 SJ7419
Newport Pagnell Bucks 38 SP8743
Newport-on-Tay Fife 127 NO4228
Newpound Common W Susx 14 TQ0627
Newquay Cnwll 4 SW8161
Newsam Green W York 83 SE3630
Newsbank Ches 72 SJ8366
Newseat Abers 142 NJ7032
Newsham Lancs 80 SD5136
Newsham N York 89 NZ1010
Newsham N York 89 SE3784
Newsham Nthumb 103 NZ3080
Newsholme Lancs 81 SD8451
Newsholme E R Yk 84 SE7129
Newstead Border 109 NT5634
Newstead Notts 75 SK5152
Newstead Nthumb 111 NU1527
Newtack Moray 142 NJ4446
Newthorpe N York 83 SE4632
Newtimber W Susx 15 TQ2613
Newton Ag & B 114 NS0498
Newton Beds 39 TL2344
Newton Border 110 NT6020
Newton Brdgnd 33 SS8377
Newton Cambs 65 TF4314
Newton Cambs 53 TL4349
Newton Cardif 34 ST2378
Newton Ches 71 SJ4167
Newton Ches 71 SJ5059
Newton Ches 71 SJ5375
Newton Ches 71 SJ5278
Newton Cumb 86 SD2271
Newton Derbys 75 SK4459
Newton H & W 46 SO3432
Newton H & W 46 SO3769
Newton H & W 46 SO5153
Newton Highld 139 NH5850
Newton Highld 140 NH7448
Newton Highld 140 NH7866
Newton Lancs 80 SD3436
Newton Lancs 80 SD4430
Newton Lancs 87 SD5974
Newton Lancs 81 SD6950
Newton Lincs 64 TF0436
Newton Moray 141 NJ1663
Newton Moray 141 NJ3362
Newton N York 90 SE8872
Newton Nhants 51 SP8883
Newton Norfk 66 TF8315
Newton Notts 63 SK6841
Newton Nthumb 110 NT9406
Newton Nthumb 103 NZ0364
Newton S Lans 116 NS6760
Newton S Lans 108 NS9331
Newton Shrops 59 SJ4234
Newton Somset 20 ST1038
Newton Staffs 73 SK0325
Newton Suffk 54 TL9240
Newton W Loth 117 NT0977
Newton W Mids 61 SP0393
Newton W York 83 SE4527
Newton Warwks 50 SP5378
Newton Wilts 23 SU2322
Newton Abbot Devon 7 SX8571
Newton Arlosh Cumb 93 NY2055
Newton Aycliffe Dur 96 NZ2724
Newton Bewley Dur 97 NZ4626
Newton Blossomville Bucks 38 SP9251
Newton Bromswold Beds 51 SP9966
Newton Burgoland Leics 62 SK3708
Newton by Toft Lincs 76 TF0487
Newton Ferrers Cnwll 5 SX3466
Newton Ferrers Devon 6 SX5548
Newton Ferry W Isls 154 NF8978
Newton Flotman Norfk 67 TM2198
Newton Green Mons 34 ST5191
Newton Harcourt Leics 50 SP6497
Newton Heath Gt Man 79 SD8700
Newton Hill W York 83 SE3222
Newton Kyme N York 83 SE4644
Newton Longville Bucks 38 SP8431
Newton Mearns E Rens 115 NS5355
Newton Morrell N York 89 NZ2309
Newton Mountain Pembks 30 SM9808
Newton Mulgrave N York 97 NZ7815
Newton of Balcanquhal P & K 126 NO1610
Newton on Ouse N York 90 SE5159
Newton on the Hill Shrops 59 SJ4823
Newton on Trent Lincs 76 SK8373
Newton Poppleford Devon 9 SY0889
Newton Purcell Oxon 49 SP6230
Newton Regis Warwks 61 SK2707
Newton Reigny Cumb 93 NY4731
Newton Row Highld 151 ND3449
Newton Solney Derbys 73 SK2825
Newton St Cyres Devon 9 SX8898
Newton St Faith Norfk 67 TG2217
Newton St Loe Somset 22 ST7064
Newton St Petrock Devon 18 SS4112
Newton Stacey Hants 24 SU4140
Newton Stewart D & G 99 NX4065
Newton Toney Wilts 23 SU2140
Newton Tracey Devon 19 SS5226
Newton under Roseberry N York 90 NZ5713
Newton Underwood Nthumb 103 NZ1486
Newton upon Derwent E R Yk 84 SE7149
Newton Valence Hants 24 SU7232
Newton Wamphray D & G 100 NY1195
Newton-by-the-Sea Nthumb 111 NU2325
Newton-le-Willows Mersyd 78 SJ5995
Newton-le-Willows N York 89 SE2189
Newton-on-the-Moor Nthumb 111 NU1705
Newtongarry Croft Abers 142 NJ5735
Newtongrange Mdloth 118 NT3364
Newtonhill Abers 135 NO9193
Newtonloan Mdloth 118 NT3362
Newtonmill Angus 134 NO6064
Newtonmore Highld 132 NN7098
Newtown Blae G 33 SO1709
Newtown Ches 71 SJ6247
Newtown Ches 72 SJ9060
Newtown Cnwll 2 SW5729
Newtown Cnwll 3 SW7423
Newtown Cnwll 3 SX1052
Newtown Cnwll 5 SX2978
Newtown Cumb 92 NY1048
Newtown Cumb 101 NY5062
Newtown Cumb 94 NY5224
Newtown D & G 107 NS7710
Newtown Derbys 79 SJ9984
Newtown Devon 9 SY0699
Newtown Devon 19 SS7625
Newtown Dorset 10 ST4802
Newtown Dorset 12 SZ0393
Newtown Gloucs 35 SO6702
Newtown Gt Man 78 SD5604
Newtown H & W 46 SO4757
Newtown H & W 46 SO5333
Newtown H & W 46 SO6145
Newtown H & W 47 SO7037
Newtown H & W 47 SO8755
Newtown H & W 60 SO9478
Newtown Hants 12 SU2710
Newtown Hants 24 SU4763
Newtown Hants 13 SU6013
Newtown Highld 131 NH3504
Newtown IOW 13 SZ4290
Newtown Lancs 80 SD5118
Newtown Nthumb 111 NT9631
Newtown Nthumb 103 NU0300
Newtown Nthumb 103 NU0425
Newtown Powys 58 SO1091
Newtown Rhondd 33 ST0598
Newtown Shrops 59 SJ4222
Newtown Shrops 59 SJ4731
Newtown Staffs 60 SJ9904
Newtown Wilts 22 ST9129
Newtown Wilts 23 SU2963
Newtown Linford Leics 62 SK5209
Newtown of Beltrees Rens 115 NS3758
Newtown St Boswells Border 110 NT5732
Newtown Unthank Leics 62 SK4904
Newtyle Angus 126 NO2941
Newyears Green Gt Lon 26 TQ0788
Newyork Ag & B 122 NM9611
Nextend H & W 46 SO3357
Neyland Pembks 30 SM9605
Niarbyl IOM 153 SC2177
Nibley Gloucs 35 SO6606
Nibley Gloucs 35 ST6982
Nibley Green Gloucs 35 ST7396
Nicholashayne Devon 9 ST1016
Nicholaston Swans 32 SS5288
Nickies Hill Cumb 101 NY5367
Nidd N York 89 SE3060
Nigg Aber C 135 NJ9402
Nigg Highld 147 NH8071
Nightcott Somset 19 SS8925
Nimlet Somset 35 ST7470
Nine Elms Wilts 36 SU1085
Nine Wells Pembks 30 SM7924
Ninebanks Nthumb 94 NY7853
Nineveh H & W 47 SO6265
Ninfield E Susx 16 TQ7012
Ningwood IOW 13 SZ3989
Nisbet Border 110 NT6725
Nisbet Hill Border 119 NT7950
Niton IOW 13 SZ5076
Nitshill C Glas 115 NS5260
No Man's Heath Ches 71 SJ5148
No Man's Heath Warwks 61 SK2808
No Man's Land Cnwll 4 SW9470
No Man's Land Cnwll 5 SX2756
Noah's Ark Kent 27 TQ5557
Noak Bridge Essex 40 TQ6990
Noak Hill Essex 27 TQ5494
Noblethorpe W York 82 SE2805
Nobold Shrops 59 SJ4710
Nobottle Nhants 49 SP6763
Nocton Lincs 76 TF0564
Nogdam End Norfk 67 TG3900
Noke Oxon 37 SP5413
Nolton Pembks 30 SM8618
Nolton Haven Pembks 30 SM8618
Nomansland Devon 19 SS8313
Nomansland Wilts 12 SU2517
Noneley Shrops 59 SJ4828
Nonington Kent 29 TR2552
Nook Cumb 101 NY4679
Nook Cumb 87 SD5481
Norbiton Gt Lon 26 TQ1969
Norbreck Lancs 80 SD3140
Norbridge H & W 47 SO7144
Norbury Ches 71 SJ5547
Norbury Derbys 73 SK1241
Norbury Gt Lon 27 TQ3069
Norbury Shrops 59 SO3692
Norbury Staffs 72 SJ7823
Norbury Common Ches 71 SJ5548
Norbury Junction Staffs 72 SJ7923
Norchard H & W 47 SO8568
Norcott Brook Ches 78 SJ6080
Norcross Lancs 80 SD3341
Nordelph Norfk 65 TF5501
Norden Gt Man 81 SD8614
Nordley Shrops 60 SO6996
Norham Nthumb 110 NT9047
Norland Town W York 82 SE0622
Norley Ches 71 SJ5772
Norleywood Hants 12 SZ3597
Norlington E Susx 16 TQ4413
Norman Cross Cambs 52 TL1690
Norman's Bay E Susx 16 TQ6805
Norman's Green Devon 9 ST0503
Normanby Lincs 84 SE8816
Normanby Lincs 76 SK9988
Normanby N York 97 NZ5418
Normanby N York 90 SE7381
Normanby le Wold Lincs 76 TF1295
Normandy Surrey 25 SU9351
Normanton Derbys 62 SK3433
Normanton Leics 63 SK8140
Normanton Lincs 63 SK9446
Normanton Notts 75 SK7054
Normanton Rutlnd 63 SK9305
Normanton W York 83 SE3822
Normanton Wilts 23 SU1340
Normanton le Heath Leics 62 SK3712
Normanton on Soar Notts 62 SK5122
Normanton on the Wolds Notts 62 SK6232
Normanton on Trent Notts 75 SK7868
Normoss Lancs 80 SD3437
Norney Surrey 25 SU9444
Norrington Common Wilts 22 ST8864
Norris Green Cnwll 5 SX4169
Norristhorpe W York 82 SE2123
North Anston S York 75 SK5184
North Aston Oxon 49 SP4828
North Baddesley Hants 13 SU3920
North Ballachulish Highld 130 NN0560
North Barrow Somset 21 ST6129
North Barsham Norfk 66 TF9135
North Benfleet Essex 40 TQ7588
North Bersted W Susx 14 SU9201
North Berwick E Loth 118 NT5485
North Bitchburn Dur 96 NZ1732
North Blyth Nthumb 103 NZ3082
North Boarhunt Hants 13 SU6010
North Bockhampton Hants 12 SZ1797
North Bovey Devon 8 SX7484
North Bradley Wilts 22 ST8555
North Brentor Devon 5 SX4881
North Brewham Somset 22 ST7236
North Bridge Surrey 14 SU9636
North Brook End Cambs 39 TL2944
North Buckland Devon 18 SS4840
North Burlingham Norfk 67 TG3609
North Cadbury Somset 21 ST6327
North Carlton Lincs 76 SK9477
North Carlton Notts 75 SK5984
North Cave E R Yk 84 SE8932
North Cerney Gloucs 35 SP0107
North Charford Hants 12 SU1919
North Charlton Nthumb 111 NU1622
North Cheam Gt Lon 26 TQ2365
North Cheriton Somset 22 ST6925
North Chideock Dorset 10 SY4294
North Cliffe E R Yk 84 SE8736
North Clifton Notts 75 SK8272
North Close Dur 96 NZ2532
North Cockerington Lincs 77 TF3790
North Collingham Notts 76 SK8362
North Common E Susx 15 TQ3921
North Connel Ag & B 122 NM9034
North Cornelly Brdgnd 33 SS8181
North Corner Cnwll 3 SW7818
North Corry Highld 122 NM8353
North Cotes Lincs 77 TA3400
North Country Cnwll 2 SW6943
North Cove Suffk 55 TM4689
North Cowton N York 89 NZ2803
North Crawley Bucks 38 SP9244
North Cray Gt Lon 27 TQ4872
North Creake Norfk 66 TF8538
North Curry Somset 21 ST3125
North Dalton E R Yk 84 SE9351
North Deighton N York 83 SE3951
North Duffield N York 83 SE6837
North Duntulm Highld 136 NG4274
North Elham Kent 29 TR1844
North Elkington Lincs 77 TF2890
North Elmham Norfk 66 TF9820
North Elmsall W York 83 SE4712
North End Cumb 93 NY3259
North End Dorset 22 ST8427
North End E R Yk 85 TA1941
North End E R Yk 85 TA2831
North End Essex 40 TL6618
North End Hants 12 SU1016
North End Hants 24 SU5828
North End Hants 13 SU6502
North End Leics 62 SK5715
North End Lincs 85 TA1022
North End Lincs 85 TA3101
North End Lincs 76 TF0499
North End Lincs 64 TF2341
North End Lincs 77 TF4289
North End Mersyd 78 SD3004
North End Nhants 51 SP9668
North End Norfk 66 TL9992
North End Nthumb 103 NU1301
North End Somset 21 ST4266
North End W Susx 14 SU9703
North End W Susx 14 TQ1109
North Erradale Highld 144 NG7480
North Evington Leics 62 SK6204
North Fambridge Essex 40 TQ8597

Ompton
Pemberton

Ompton Notts 75 SK6865
Once Brewed Nthumb 102 NY7466
Onchan IOM 153 SC3978
One House Suffk 54 TM0159
Onecote Staffs 73 SK0455
Onen Mons 34 SO4314
Ongar Street H & W 46 SO3967
Onibury Shrops 46 SO4579
Onich Highld 130 NN0261
Onllwyn Neath 33 SN8410
Onneley Staffs 72 SJ7542
Onslow Village Surrey 25 SU9849
Onston Ches 71 SJ5873
Openwoodgate Derbys 62 SK3647
Opinan Highld 137 NG7472
Orbliston Moray 141 NJ3057
Orbost Highld 136 NG2543
Orby Lincs 77 TF4967
Orchard Portman Somset 20 ST2421
Orcheston Wilts 23 SU0545
Orcop H & W 46 SO4726
Orcop Hill H & W 46 SO4727
Ord Abers 142 NJ6258
Ordhead Abers 135 NJ6610
Ordie Abers 134 NJ4501
Ordiequish Moray 141 NJ3357
Ordley Nthumb 95 NY9459
Ordsall Notts 75 SK7079
Ore E Susx 17 TQ8311
Oreleton Common H & W 46 SO4768
Oreton Shrops 59 SO6580
Orford Ches 78 SJ6190
Orford Suffk 55 TM4250
Organford Dorset 11 SY9392
Orgreave Staffs 73 SK1415
Orlestone Kent 17 TR0034
Orleton H & W 46 SO4967
Orleton H & W 47 SO7067
Orlingbury Nhants 51 SP8572
Ormathwaite Cumb 93 NY2625
Ormesby N York 97 NZ5317
Ormesby St Margaret Norfk 67 TG4914
Ormesby St Michael Norfk 67 TG4714
Ormiscaig Highld 144 NG8590
Ormiston E Loth 118 NT4169
Ormsaigmore Highld 121 NM4763
Ormsary Ag & B 113 NR7472
Ormskirk Lancs 78 SD4108
Ornsby Hill Dur 96 NZ1648
Oronsay Ag & B 112 NR3588
Orphir Ork 155 HY3404
Orpington Gt Lon 27 TQ4666
Orrell Gt Man 78 SD5303
Orrell Mersyd 78 SJ3496
Orrell Post Gt Man 78 SD5305
Orrisdale IOM 153 SC3292
Orroland D & G 92 NX7746
Orsett Essex 40 TQ6482
Orslow Staffs 72 SJ8015
Orston Notts 63 SK7740
Orthwaite Cumb 93 NY2534
Ortner Lancs 80 SD5354
Orton Cumb 87 NY6208
Orton Nhants 51 SP8079
Orton Staffs 60 SO8795
Orton Longueville Cambs 64 TL1796
Orton Rigg Cumb 93 NY3352
Orton Waterville Cambs 64 TL1595
Orton-on-the-Hill Leics 61 SK3003
Orwell Cambs 52 TL3650
Osbaldeston Lancs 81 SD6431
Osbaldeston Green Lancs 81 SD6432
Osbaldwick N York 83 SE6251
Osbaston Leics 62 SK4204
Osbaston Shrops 59 SJ3222
Osborne IOW 13 SZ5194
Osbournby Lincs 64 TF0638
Oscroft Ches 71 SJ5067
Osgathorpe Leics 62 SK4319
Osgodby Lincs 76 TF0792
Osgodby N York 83 SE6433
Osgodby N York 91 TA0584
Oskaig Highld 137 NG5438
Oskamull Ag & B 121 NM4540
Osmaston Derbys 73 SK1943
Osmington Dorset 11 SY7283
Osmington Mills Dorset 11 SY7381
Osmondthorpe W York 83 SE3333
Osmotherley N York 89 SE4596
Osney Oxon 37 SP4906
Ospringe Kent 28 TR0060
Ossett W York 82 SE2720
Ossington Notts 75 SK7564
Ostend Essex 40 TQ9397
Osterley Gt Lon 26 TQ1577
Osterley Gt Lon 26 TQ1070
Oswaldkirk N York 90 SE6278
Oswaldtwistle Lancs 81 SD7327
Oswestry Shrops 59 SJ2929
Otford Kent 27 TQ5359
Otham Kent 28 TQ7953
Otham Hole Kent 28 TQ8052
Othery Somset 21 ST3831
Otley Suffk 55 TM2055
Otley W York 82 SE2045
Otley Green Suffk 55 TM2156
Otter Ferry Ag & B 114 NR9384
Otterbourne Hants 13 SU4522
Otterburn N York 88 SD8857
Otterburn Nthumb 102 NY8893
Otterham Cnwll 4 SX1690
Otterham Quay Kent 28 TQ8366
Otterhampton Somset 20 ST2443
Ottershaw Surrey 26 TQ0263
Otterswick Shet 155 HU5285
Otterton Devon 9 SY0684
Otterwood Hants 13 SU4102
Ottery Devon 6 SX4475
Ottery St Mary Devon 9 SY1095
Ottinge Kent 29 TR1642
Ottringham E R Yk 85 TA2624
Oughterby Cumb 93 NY2955
Oughtershaw N York 88 SD8780
Oughterside Cumb 92 NY1140
Oughtibridge S York 74 SK3093
Oughtrington Ches 79 SJ6987
Oulston N York 90 SE5474
Oulton Cumb 93 NY2450
Oulton Norfk 66 TG1328
Oulton Staffs 72 SJ7822
Oulton Staffs 72 SJ9035
Oulton Suffk 67 TM5294
Oulton W York 83 SE3628
Oulton Broad Suffk 67 TM5192
Oulton Street Norfk 66 TG1527
Oundle Nhants 51 TL0388
Ounsdale Staffs 60 SO8693
Ousby Cumb 94 NY6134
Ousden Suffk 53 TL7459
Ousefleet E R Yk 84 SE8323
Ouston Dur 96 NZ2554
Ouston Nthumb 103 NZ0770
Out Elmstead Kent 29 TR2050
Out Newton E R Yk 85 TA3821
Out Rawcliffe Lancs 80 SD4041
Outchester Nthumb 111 NU1433
Outgate Cumb 87 SD3599
Outhgill Cumb 88 NY7801
Outhill Warwks 48 SP1066
Outlands Staffs 72 SJ7630
Outlane W York 82 SE0817
Outwell Norfk 65 TF5103
Outwick Hants 12 SU1417
Outwood Surrey 15 TQ3145
Outwood W York 83 SE3323
Outwood Gate Gt Man 79 SD7805
Outwoods Leics 62 SK4018
Outwoods Staffs 72 SJ7817
Outwoods Warwks 61 SP2484
Ouzlewell Green W York 83 SE3326
Ovenden W York 82 SE0827
Over Cambs 52 TL3770
Over Ches 71 SJ6365
Over Gloucs 35 SO8119
Over Gloucs 34 ST5882
Over Burrows Derbys 73 SK2639
Over Compton Dorset 10 ST5816
Over End Cambs 51 TL0893
Over Green Warwks 61 SP1694
Over Haddon Derbys 74 SK2066
Over Kellet Lancs 87 SD5169
Over Kiddington Oxon 36 SP4021
Over Monnow Mons 34 SO5012
Over Norton Oxon 48 SP3128
Over Silton N York 89 SE4493
Over Stowey Somset 20 ST1838
Over Stratton Somset 10 ST4315
Over Tabley Ches 79 SJ7279
Over Wallop Hants 23 SU2838
Over Whitacre Warwks 61 SP2590
Over Woodhouse Derbys 75 SK4671
Over Worton Oxon 49 SP4329
Overbury H & W 47 SO9537
Overcombe Dorset 11 SY6982
Overgreen Derbys 74 SK3273
Overleigh Somset 21 ST4835
Overley Staffs 73 SK1515
Overpool Ches 71 SJ3877
Overscaig Hotel Highld 149 NC4123
Overseal Derbys 73 SK2915
Oversland Kent 28 TR0557
Overstey Green Warwks 48 SP0957
Overstone Nhants 50 SP7966
Overstrand Norfk 67 TG2440
Overstreet Wilts 23 SU0637
Overthorpe Nhants 49 SP4840
Overton Aber C 143 NJ8714
Overton Ches 71 SJ5277
Overton Hants 24 SU5149
Overton Lancs 87 SD4358
Overton N York 83 SE5555
Overton Shrops 46 SO5072
Overton Swans 32 SS4685
Overton W York 82 SE2516
Overton Wrexhm 71 SJ3741
Overton Bridge Wrexhm 71 SJ3542
Overton Green Ches 72 SJ8060
Overtown Lancs 87 SD6275
Overtown N Lans 116 NS8053
Overtown W York 83 SE3516
Overtown Wilts 36 SU1579
Overy Oxon 37 SU5893
Oving Bucks 37 SP7821
Oving W Susx 14 SU9004
Ovingdean E Susx 15 TQ3503
Ovingham Nthumb 103 NZ0863
Ovington Dur 89 NZ1314
Ovington Essex 53 TL7642
Ovington Hants 24 SU5631
Ovington Norfk 66 TF9202
Ovington Nthumb 103 NZ0663
Ower Hants 12 SU3215
Ower Hants 13 SU4702
Owermoigne Dorset 11 SY7685
Owl's Green Suffk 55 TM2869
Owlbury Shrops 59 SO3191
Owlerton S York 74 SK3389
Owlpen Gloucs 35 ST7998
Owlsmoor Berks 25 SU8462
Owlswick Bucks 37 SP7806
Owmby Lincs 85 TA0704
Owmby Lincs 76 TF0087
Owslebury Hants 13 SU5123
Owston Leics 63 SK7707
Owston S York 83 SE5511
Owston Ferry Lincs 75 SE8000
Owstwick E R Yk 85 TA2732
Owthorne E R Yk 85 TA3328
Owthorpe Notts 63 SK6733
Oxborough Norfk 65 TF7401
Oxbridge Dorset 10 SY4797
Oxcombe Lincs 77 TF3177
Oxcroft Derbys 75 SK4873
Oxen End Essex 40 TL6629
Oxen Park Cumb 86 SD3187
Oxenholme Cumb 87 SD5389
Oxenhope W York 82 SE0334
Oxenpill Somset 21 ST4441
Oxenton Gloucs 47 SO9531
Oxenwood Wilts 23 SU3058
Oxford Oxon 37 SP5106
Oxhey Herts 26 TQ1295
Oxhill Dur 96 NZ1852
Oxhill Warwks 48 SP3146
Oxley W Mids 60 SJ9001
Oxley Green Essex 40 TL9014
Oxley's Green E Susx 16 TQ6921
Oxlode Cambs 53 TL4886
Oxnam Border 110 NT6918
Oxnead Norfk 67 TG2224
Oxshott Surrey 26 TQ1460
Oxshott Heath Surrey 26 TQ1361
Oxspring S York 82 SE2601
Oxted Surrey 27 TQ3852
Oxton Border 118 NT4953
Oxton N York 83 SE5042
Oxton Notts 75 SK6351
Oxwich Swans 32 SS4986
Oxwich Green Swans 32 SS4985
Oxwick Norfk 66 TF9125
Oykel Bridge Hotel Highld 145 NC3801
Oyne Abers 142 NJ6725
Oystermouth Swans 32 SS6187
Ozleworth Gloucs 35 ST7993

P

Pabail W Isls 154 NB5231
Packers Hill Dorset 11 ST7110
Packington Leics 62 SK3614
Packmoor Staffs 72 SJ8654
Packmores Warwks 48 SP2866
Padanaram Angus 127 NO4251
Padbury Bucks 49 SP7230
Paddington Ches 79 SJ6389
Paddington Gt Lon 27 TQ2681
Paddlesworth Kent 28 TQ6862
Paddlesworth Kent 29 TR1939
Paddock Wood Kent 28 TQ6744
Paddolgreen Shrops 59 SJ5032
Padeswood Flints 70 SJ2762
Padfield Derbys 74 SK0296
Padgate Ches 79 SJ6389
Padhams Green Essex 40 TQ6497
Padiham Lancs 81 SD7933
Padside N York 89 SE1659
Padstow Cnwll 4 SW9175
Padworth Berks 24 SU6166
Page Bank Dur 96 NZ2335
Pagham W Susx 14 SZ8897
Paglesham Essex 40 TQ9293
Paignton Devon 7 SX8860
Pailton Warwks 50 SP4781
Paine's Cross E Susx 16 TQ6223
Painleyhill Staffs 73 SK0333
Painscastle Powys 45 SO1646
Painshawfield Nthumb 103 NZ0560
Painsthorpe E R Yk 90 SE8158
Painswick Gloucs 35 SO8609
Painter's Forstal Kent 28 TQ9958
Paisley Rens 115 NS4864
Pakefield Suffk 55 TM5390
Pakenham Suffk 54 TL9267
Pale Gwynd 58 SH9836
Pale Green Essex 53 TL6542
Palestine Hants 23 SU2640
Paley Street Berks 26 SU8776
Palfrey W Mids 60 SP0196
Palgrave Suffk 54 TM1178
Pallington Dorset 11 SY7891
Palmers Green Gt Lon 27 TQ3192
Palmersbridge Cnwll 5 SX1977
Palmerston E Ayrs 107 NS5019
Palmerstown V Glam 20 ST1369
Palnackie D & G 92 NX8157
Palnure D & G 99 NX4563
Palterton Derbys 75 SK4768
Pamber End Hants 24 SU6158
Pamber Green Hants 24 SU6159
Pamber Heath Hants 24 SU6162
Pamington Gloucs 47 SO9433
Pamphill Dorset 11 ST9900
Pampisford Cambs 53 TL4948
Panborough Somset 21 ST4745
Panbride Angus 127 NO5635
Pancrasweek Devon 18 SS2905
Pancross V Glam 20 ST0469
Pandy Caerph 33 ST1587
Pandy Gwynd 57 SH6202
Pandy Gwynd 57 SH8729
Pandy Mons 34 SO3322
Pandy Powys 58 SH9004
Pandy Wrexhm 58 SJ1935
Pandy Tudur A & C 69 SH8564
Pandy'r Capel Denbgs 70 SJ0850
Panfield Essex 40 TL7325
Pangbourne Berks 37 SU6376
Pangdean W Susx 15 TQ2911
Panks Bridge H & W 47 SO6248
Pannal N York 82 SE3051
Pannal Ash N York 82 SE2953
Pannanich Wells Hotel Abers 134 NO4097
Pant Shrops 58 SJ2722
Pant Mawr Powys 43 SN8482
Pant-glas Gwynd 68 SH4747
Pant-Gwyn Carmth 44 SN5925
Pant-lasau Swans 32 SN6600
Pant-pastynog Denbgs 70 SJ0461
Pant-y-dwr Powys 45 SN9874
Pant-y-ffridd Powys 58 SJ1502
Pant-y-gog Brdgnd 33 SS9090
Pant-y-mwyn Flints 70 SJ1964
Pantasaph Flints 70 SJ1675
Panteg Pembks 30 SM9234
Pantersbridge Cnwll 4 SX1667
Pantglas Powys 43 SN7797
Panton Lincs 76 TF1778
Pantperthog Gwynd 57 SH7404
Pantyffynnon Carmth 32 SN6210
Pantygasseg Torfn 34 ST2599
Pantymenyn Carmth 31 SN1426
Panxworth Norfk 67 TG3513
Papcastle Cumb 92 NY1031
Papigoe Highld 151 ND3851
Papple E Loth 118 NT5972
Papplewick Notts 75 SK5451
Papworth Everard Cambs 52 TL2862
Papworth St Agnes Cambs 52 TL2664
Par Cnwll 3 SX0753
Paramour Street Kent 29 TR2961
Parbold Lancs 80 SD4911
Parbrook Somset 21 ST5736
Parbrook W Susx 14 TQ0825
Parc Gwynd 57 SH8834
Parc Seymour Newpt 34 ST4091
Parcllyn Cardgn 42 SN2451
Pardshaw Cumb 92 NY0924
Parham Suffk 55 TM3060
Park Abers 135 NO7898
Park D & G 100 NX9091
Park Nthumb 102 NY6861
Park Bottom Cnwll 2 SW6642
Park Bridge Gt Man 79 SD9402
Park Corner Berks 26 SU8582
Park Corner E Susx 16 TQ5336
Park Corner Oxon 37 SU6988
Park End Beds 38 SP9952
Park End Nthumb 102 NY8675
Park End Staffs 72 SJ7851
Park Gate H & W 60 SO9371
Park Gate Hants 13 SU5108
Park Gate W York 82 SE1841
Park Green Essex 39 TL4628
Park Green Suffk 54 TM1364
Park Head Cumb 94 NY5841
Park Head Derbys 74 SK3654
Park Hill Gloucs 34 ST5799
Park Royal Gt Lon 26 TQ1982
Park Street W Susx 14 TQ1131
Parkend Gloucs 34 SO6108
Parkers Green Kent 16 TQ6148
Parkeston Essex 41 TM2332
Parkeston Quay Essex 41 TM2332
Parkfield Bucks 37 SP8002
Parkfield Cnwll 5 SX3167
Parkgate Ches 70 SJ2878
Parkgate Ches 79 SJ7873
Parkgate Cumb 93 NY2146
Parkgate D & G 100 NY0288
Parkgate E Susx 17 TQ7214
Parkgate Essex 40 TL6829
Parkgate Kent 27 TQ5064
Parkgate Kent 17 TQ8534
Parkgate Surrey 15 TQ2043
Parkhall D & Cb 115 NS4871
Parkham Devon 18 SS3921
Parkham Ash Devon 18 SS3620
Parkhill Notts 75 SK6952
Parkhill House Abers 143 NJ8914
Parkhouse Mons 34 SO5003
Parkmill Swans 32 SS5489
Parkside Dur 96 NZ4248
Parkside N Lans 116 NS8058
Parkside Wrexhm 71 SJ3855
Parkstone Dorset 12 SZ0391
Parley Green Dorset 12 SZ1097
Parlington W York 83 SE4235
Parmoor Bucks 37 SU7989
Parndon Essex 39 TL4308
Parr Bridge Gt Man 79 SD7001
Parracombe Devon 19 SS6745
Parrah Green Ches 72 SJ7145
Parrog Pembks 30 SN0539
Parson Drove Cambs 64 TF3708
Parson's Cross S York 74 SK3492
Parson's Heath Essex 41 TM0226
Parson's Hill Derbys 73 SK2926
Parsonby Cumb 92 NY1438
Partick C Glas 115 NS5467
Partington Gt Man 79 SJ7191
Partney Lincs 77 TF4068
Parton Cumb 93 NY2750
Parton Cumb 92 NX9820
Parton D & G 99 NX6970
Partridge Green W Susx 15 TQ1919
Partrishow Powys 34 SO2722
Parwich Derbys 73 SK1854
Paslow Wood Common Essex 27 TL5802
Passenham Nhants 38 SP7839
Passfield Hants 14 SU8234
Passingford Bridge Essex 27 TQ5097
Paston Cambs 64 TF1802
Paston Norfk 67 TG3234
Pasturefields Staffs 73 SJ9924
Patchacott Devon 5 SX4798
Patcham E Susx 15 TQ3008
Patchetts Green Herts 26 TQ1497
Patching W Susx 14 TQ0806
Patchole Devon 19 SS6142
Patchway Gloucs 34 ST6082
Pateley Bridge N York 89 SE1565
Paternoster Heath Essex 40 TL9115
Pateshall H & W 46 SO5262
Path of Condie P & K 125 NO0711
Pathe Somset 21 ST3730
Pathhead E Ayrs 107 NS6114
Pathhead Fife 117 NT2992
Pathhead Mdloth 118 NT3964
Pathlow Warwks 48 SP1758
Patmore Heath Herts 39 TL4425
Patna E Ayrs 106 NS4110
Patney Wilts 23 SU0758
Patrick IOM 153 SC2482
Patrick Brompton N York 89 SE2190
Patricroft Gt Man 79 SJ7597
Patrington E R Yk 85 TA3122
Patrixbourne Kent 29 TR1855
Patterdale Cumb 93 NY3915
Pattingham Staffs 60 SO8299
Pattishall Nhants 49 SP6754
Pattiswick Green Essex 40 TL8124
Patton Shrops 59 SO5895
Paul Cnwll 2 SW4627
Paul's Dene Wilts 23 SU1432
Paulerspury Bucks 49 SP7145
Paull E R Yk 85 TA1626
Paulton Somset 21 ST6556
Paunton H & W 47 SO6650
Pauperhaugh Nthumb 103 NZ1099
Pave Lane Shrops 72 SJ7616
Pavenham Beds 51 SP9955
Pawlett Somset 20 ST2942
Pawston Nthumb 110 NT8532
Paxford Gloucs 48 SP1837
Paxton Border 119 NT9353
Payden Street Kent 28 TQ9254
Payhembury Devon 9 ST0901
Paythorne Lancs 81 SD8251
Paytoe H & W 46 SO4171
Peacehaven E Susx 15 TQ4101
Peak Dale Derbys 74 SK0976
Peak Forest Derbys 74 SK1179
Peak Hill Lincs 64 TF2615
Peakirk Cambs 64 TF1606
Peanmeanach Highld 129 NM7180
Pearson's Green Kent 28 TQ6943
Peartree Green H & W 46 SO5932
Pease Pottage W Susx 15 TQ2633
Peasedown St John Somset 22 ST7057
Peasehill Derbys 74 SK4049
Peaseland Green Norfk 66 TG0516
Peasemore Berks 37 SU4577
Peasenhall Suffk 55 TM3569
Peaslake Surrey 14 TQ0844
Peasley Cross Mersyd 78 SJ5294
Peasmarsh E Susx 17 TQ8822
Peasmarsh Somset 10 ST3312
Peasmarsh Surrey 25 SU9946
Peat Inn Fife 127 NO4509
Peathill Abers 143 NJ9366
Peatling Magna Leics 50 SP5992
Peatling Parva Leics 50 SP5889
Peaton Shrops 59 SO5385
Pebmarsh Essex 40 TL8533
Pebworth H & W 48 SP1347
Pecket Well W York 82 SD9929
Peckforton Ches 71 SJ5356
Peckham Gt Lon 27 TQ3476
Peckleton Leics 62 SK4701
Pedair-ffordd Powys 58 SJ1124
Pedlinge Kent 17 TR1335
Pedmore W Mids 60 SO9182
Pedwell Somset 21 ST4236
Peebles Border 109 NT2540
Peel IOM 153 SC2483
Peel Lancs 80 SD3531
Peel Common Hants 13 SU5703
Peene Kent 29 TR1837
Peening Quarter Kent 17 TQ8828
Pegsdon Beds 38 TL1130
Pegswood Nthumb 103 NZ2287
Pegwell Kent 29 TR3664
Peinchorran Highld 137 NG5233
Peinlich Highld 136 NG4158
Pelcomb Pembks 30 SM9218
Pelcomb Bridge Pembks 30 SM9317
Pelcomb Cross Pembks 30 SM9218
Peldon Essex 41 TL9816
Pell Green E Susx 16 TQ6432
Pelsall W Mids 60 SK0203
Pelsall Wood W Mids 60 SK0204
Pelton Dur 96 NZ2553
Pelton Fell Dur 96 NZ2551
Pelutho Cumb 92 NY1249
Pelynt Cnwll 5 SX2055
Pemberton Carmth 32 SN5300

Pemberton Plumgarths

Pemberton Gt Man	78	SD5503
Pembles Cross Kent	28	TQ8947
Pembrey Carmth	31	SN4301
Pembridge H & W	46	SO3958
Pembroke Pembks	30	SM9801
Pembroke Dock Pembks	30	SM9603
Pembury Kent	16	TQ6240
Pen Rhiwfawr Neath	32	SN7410
Pen-bont Rhydybeddau Cardgn	43	SN6783
Pen-ffordd Pembks	31	SN0722
Pen-groes-oped Mons	34	SO3106
Pen-llyn Angles	68	SH3582
Pen-lon Angles	68	SH4365
Pen-rhiw Pembks	31	SN2440
Pen-twyn Caerph	33	SO2000
Pen-twyn Mons	34	SO5209
Pen-twyn Torfn	34	SO2603
Pen-y-bont Powys	58	SJ2123
Pen-y-Bont-Fawr Powys	58	SJ0824
Pen-y-bryn Neath	33	SS8384
Pen-y-bryn Pembks	31	SN1742
Pen-y-cae Powys	33	SN8413
Pen-y-cae-mawr Mons	34	ST4195
Pen-y-cefn Flints	70	SJ1175
Pen-y-clawdd Mons	34	SO4507
Pen-y-coedcae Rhondd	33	ST0587
Pen-y-cwn Pembks	30	SM8523
Pen-y-darren Myr Td	33	SO0506
Pen-y-fai Brdgnd	33	SS8981
Pen-y-felin Flints	70	SJ1569
Pen-y-garn Cardgn	43	SN6285
Pen-y-genffordd Powys	45	SO1729
Pen-y-graig Gwynd	56	SH2033
Pen-y-Gwryd Hotel Gwynd	69	SH6655
Pen-y-lan V Glam	33	SS9976
Pen-y-pass Gwynd	69	SH6455
Pen-y-stryt Denbgs	70	SJ1952
Pen-yr-Heol Mons	34	SO4311
Pen-yr-Heolgerrig Myr Td	33	SO0306
Penair Cnwll	3	SW8445
Penallt Mons	34	SO5210
Penally Pembks	31	SS1199
Penalt H & W	46	SO5629
Penare Cnwll	3	SW9940
Penarth V Glam	33	ST1871
Penblewin Pembks	31	SN1216
Penbryn Cardgn	42	SN2951
Pencader Carmth	31	SN4436
Pencaenewydd Gwynd	56	SH4040
Pencaitland E Loth	118	NT4468
Pencalenick Cnwll	3	SW8545
Pencarnisiog Angles	68	SH3573
Pencarreg Carmth	44	SN5445
Pencarrow Cnwll	4	SX1082
Pencelli Powys	45	SO0925
Penclawdd Swans	32	SS5495
Pencoed Brdgnd	33	SS9581
Pencombe H & W	46	SO5952
Pencoyd H & W	46	SO5126
Pencraig H & W	34	SO5620
Pencraig Powys	58	SJ0426
Pendeen Cnwll	2	SW3834
Penderyn Rhondd	33	SN9408
Pendine Carmth	31	SN2208
Pendlebury Gt Man	79	SD7802
Pendleton Lancs	81	SD7539
Pendock H & W	47	SO7832
Pendoggett Cnwll	4	SX0279
Pendomer Somset	10	ST5210
Pendoylan V Glam	33	ST0576
Pendre Brdgnd	33	SS9181
Penegoes Powys	57	SH7600
Penelewey Cnwll	3	SW8140
Pengam Caerph	33	ST1597
Pengam Cardif	33	ST2177
Penge Gt Lon	27	TQ3570
Pengelly Cnwll	3	SW8551
Pengelly Cnwll	4	SX0783
Pengorffwysfa Angles	68	SH4692
Pengover Green Cnwll	5	SX2765
Pengrugla Cnwll	3	SW9947
Pengwern Denbgs	70	SJ0276
Penhale Cnwll	2	SW6918
Penhale Cnwll	4	SW9057
Penhale Cnwll	4	SX0860
Penhale Cnwll	5	SX4153
Penhallow Cnwll	3	SW7651
Penhalurick Cnwll	3	SW7038
Penhalvean Cnwll	2	SW7038
Penhill Wilts	36	SU1588
Penhow Newpt	34	ST4290
Penhurst E Susx	16	TQ6916
Peniarth Gwynd	57	SH6105
Penicuik Mdloth	117	NT2359
Peniel Carmth	31	SN4324
Peniel Denbgs	70	SJ0362
Penifiler Highld	136	NG4841
Peninver Ag & B	105	NR7524
Penisar Waun Gwynd	69	SH5563
Penistone S York	82	SE2403
Penjerrick Cnwll	3	SW7730
Penkelly Cnwll	4	SX1854
Penketh Ches	78	SJ5587
Penkill S Ayrs	106	NX2398
Penkridge Staffs	60	SJ9213
Penlean Cnwll	5	SX2098
Penley Wrexhm	71	SJ4040
Penllergaer Swans	32	SS6198
Penllyn V Glam	33	SS9775
Penmachno A & C	69	SH7950
Penmaen Caerph	33	ST1897
Penmaen Swans	32	SS5288
Penmaenan A & C	69	SH7175
Penmaenmawr A & C	69	SH7276
Penmaenpool Gwynd	57	SH6918
Penmark V Glam	20	ST0568
Penmon Angles	69	SH6280
Penmorfa Gwynd	57	SH5540
Penmynydd Angles	68	SH5074
Penn Bucks	26	SU9193
Penn W Mids	60	SO8895
Penn Street Bucks	26	SU9295
Pennal Gwynd	57	SH6900
Pennan Abers	143	NJ8465
Pennant Denbgs	58	SJ0234
Pennant Powys	43	SN8897
Pennant-Melangell Powys	58	SJ0226
Pennard Swans	32	SS5688
Pennerley Shrops	59	SO3599
Pennicott Devon	9	SS8701
Pennington Cumb	86	SD2677
Pennington Hants	12	SZ3195
Pennington Green Gt Man	79	SD6206
Pennorth Powys	45	SO1125
Pennsylvania Gloucs	35	ST7473
Penny Bridge Cumb	86	SD3083
Penny Bridge Pembks	30	SN0001
Penny Green Notts	75	SK5475
Penny Hill Lincs	64	TF3526
Pennycross Ag & B	121	NM5025
Pennygate Norfk	67	TG3423
Pennyghael Ag & B	121	NM5125
Pennyglen S Ayrs	106	NS2710
Pennymoor Devon	19	SS8611
Penparc Cardgn	42	SN2047
Penparcau Cardgn	43	SN5980
Penpedairheol Caerph	33	ST1497
Penpedairheol Mons	34	SO3303
Penperlleni Mons	34	SO3204
Penpethy Cnwll	4	SX0886
Penpillick Cnwll	3	SX0856
Penpol Cnwll	3	SW8139
Penpoll Cnwll	3	SX1454
Penponds Cnwll	2	SW6339
Penpont D & G	100	NX8494
Penpont Powys	45	SN9728
Penquit Devon	7	SX6454
Penrest Cnwll	5	SX3377
Penrherber Carmth	31	SN2938
Penrhiw-pal Cardgn	42	SN3445
Penrhiwceiber Rhondd	33	ST0597
Penrhiwllan Cardgn	31	SN3641
Penrhos Angles	68	SH2781
Penrhos Gwynd	56	SH3433
Penrhos Mons	34	SO4111
Penrhos Powys	32	SN8011
Penrhos garnedd Gwynd	69	SH5670
Penrhyn Bay A & C	69	SH8281
Penrhyn-side A & C	69	SH8181
Penrhyncoch Cardgn	43	SN6384
Penrhyndeudraeth Gwynd	57	SH6139
Penrice Swans	32	SS4987
Penrioch N Ayrs	105	NR8744
Penrith Cumb	94	NY5130
Penrose Cnwll	4	SW8770
Penrose Cnwll	5	SX2589
Penruddock Cumb	93	NY4227
Penryn Cnwll	3	SW7834
Pensarn A & C	70	SH9578
Pensarn Carmth	31	SN4119
Pensax H & W	47	SO7269
Pensby Mersyd	78	SJ2782
Penselwood Somset	22	ST7531
Pensford Somset	21	ST6263
Pensham H & W	47	SO9444
Penshaw T & W	96	NZ3253
Penshurst Kent	16	TQ5243
Penshurst Station Kent	16	TQ5246
Pensilva Cnwll	5	SX2970
Pensnett W Mids	60	SO9189
Pensont Cnwll	4	SX0874
Penstone Devon	8	SS7700
Penstrowed Powys	58	SO0691
Pentewan Cnwll	3	SX0147
Pentir Gwynd	69	SH5766
Pentire Cnwll	4	SW7961
Pentlepoir Pembks	31	SN1105
Pentlow Essex	54	TL8146
Pentlow Street Essex	54	TL8245
Pentney Norfk	65	TF7214
Penton Grafton Hants	23	SU3247
Penton Mewsey Hants	23	SU3247
Pentraeth Angles	68	SH5278
Pentre Denbgs	70	SJ0862
Pentre Flints	71	SJ3267
Pentre Mons	34	SO3106
Pentre Powys	58	SO0685
Pentre Powys	58	SO1589
Pentre Rhondd	33	SS9696
Pentre Shrops	59	SJ3617
Pentre Wrexhm	70	SJ2840
Pentre bach Cardgn	44	SN5547
Pentre Bach Flints	70	SJ2175
Pentre Berw Angles	68	SH4772
Pentre Ffwrndan Flints	70	SJ2572
Pentre Gwynfryn Gwynd	57	SH5927
Pentre Halkyn Flints	70	SJ2072
Pentre Hodrey Shrops	46	SO3277
Pentre Isaf A & C	70	SH9871
Pentre Llanrhaeadr Denbgs	70	SJ0863
Pentre Llifior Powys	58	SO1598
Pentre Meyrick V Glam	33	SS9675
Pentre Saron Denbgs	70	SJ0260
Pentre ty gwyn Carmth	44	SN8135
Pentre'r Felin A & C	69	SH8069
Pentre'r-felin Cardgn	44	SN6148
Pentre'r-felin Powys	45	SN9230
Pentre'rbryn Cardgn	42	SN3954
Pentre-ba^ch Powys	45	SN9132
Pentre-bont A & C	69	SH7351
Pentre-cagel Cardgn	31	SN3340
Pentre-celyn Denbgs	70	SJ1453
Pentre-celyn Powys	57	SH8905
Pentre-chwyth Swans	32	SS6794
Pentre-clawdd Shrops	59	SJ2931
Pentre-cwrt Carmth	31	SN3838
Pentre-dwr Swans	32	SS6995
Pentre-Gwenlais Carmth	32	SN6016
Pentre-llwyn-llwyd Powys	45	SN9654
Pentre-llyn Cardgn	43	SN6175
Pentre-llyn-cymmer A & C	70	SH9752
Pentre-Maw Powys	57	SH8803
Pentre-piod Torfn	34	SO2601
Pentre-poeth Newpt	34	ST2686
Pentre-tafarn-y-fedw A & C	69	SH8162
Pentrebach Myr Td	33	SO0604
Pentrebeirdd Powys	58	SJ1813
Pentredwr Denbgs	70	SJ1946
Pentrefelin Angles	68	SH4392
Pentrefelin Gwynd	57	SH5239
Pentrefoelas A & C	69	SH8751
Pentregalar Pembks	31	SN1831
Pentregat Cardgn	42	SN3551
Pentrich Derbys	74	SK3852
Pentridge Hill Dorset	12	SU0317
Pentyrch Cardif	33	ST1081
Penwithick Cnwll	3	SX0256
Penwood Hants	24	SU4461
Penwyllt Powys	33	SN8515
Penybanc Carmth	44	SN6123
Penybont Powys	45	SO1164
Penycae Wrexhm	70	SJ2745
Penycaerau Gwynd	56	SH1927
Penyffordd Flints	71	SJ3061
Penygarnedd Powys	58	SJ1023
Penygraig Rhondd	33	ST0090
Penygroes Carmth	32	SN5813
Penygroes Gwynd	68	SH4752
Penysarn Angles	68	SH4590
Penywaun Rhondd	33	SN9804
Penywern Neath	32	SN7609
Penzance Cnwll	2	SW4730
Peopleton H & W	47	SO9350
Peover Heath Ches	79	SJ7973
Peper Harow Surrey	25	SU9344
Peplow Shrops	59	SJ6224
Pepper's Green Essex	40	TL6110
Peppershill Oxon	37	SP6709
Pepperstock Beds	38	TL0817
Perceton N Ayrs	106	NS3540
Percie Abers	134	NO5992
Percyhorner Abers	143	NJ9665
Perelle Guern	152	GN0000
Periton Somset	20	SS9545
Perivale Gt Lon	26	TQ1682
Perkins Village Devon	9	SY0291
Perkinsville Dur	96	NZ2553
Perlethorpe Notts	75	SK6470
Perran Wharf Cnwll	3	SW7738
Perranarworthal Cnwll	3	SW7738
Perranporth Cnwll	3	SW7554
Perranuthnoe Cnwll	2	SW5329
Perranwell Cnwll	3	SW7739
Perranwell Cnwll	3	SW7752
Perranzabuloe Cnwll	3	SW7752
Perrott's Brook Gloucs	35	SP0106
Perry W Mids	61	SP0792
Perry Barr W Mids	61	SP0791
Perry Green Essex	40	TL8022
Perry Green Herts	39	TL4317
Perry Green Wilts	35	ST9689
Perry Street Somset	10	ST3305
Pershall Staffs	72	SJ8129
Pershore H & W	47	SO9446
Pertenhall Beds	51	TL0865
Perth P & K	126	NO1123
Perthy Shrops	59	SJ3633
Perton H & W	46	SO5940
Perton Staffs	60	SO8699
Pertwood Wilts	22	ST8936
Pet Street Kent	29	TR0846
Peter Tavy Devon	5	SX5177
Peter's Green Herts	38	TL1419
Peterborough Cambs	64	TL1998
Peterchurch H & W	46	SO3438
Peterculter Aber C	135	NJ8300
Peterhead Abers	143	NK1246
Peterlee Dur	96	NZ4241
Peters Marland Devon	18	SS4713
Petersfield Hants	13	SU7423
Petersham Gt Lon	26	TQ1873
Peterston-Super-Ely V Glam	33	ST0876
Peterstone Wentlooge Newpt	34	ST2679
Peterstow H & W	46	SO5624
Petham Kent	29	TR1251
Petherwin Gate Cnwll	5	SX2889
Petrockstow Devon	19	SS5109
Petsoe End Bucks	38	SP8949
Pett E Susx	17	TQ8714
Pett Bottom Kent	29	TR1552
Pettaugh Suffk	54	TM1659
Petterden Angus	127	NO4240
Pettinain S Lans	108	NS9543
Pettistree Suffk	55	TM3055
Petton Devon	20	ST0124
Petton Shrops	59	SJ4326
Petts Wood Gt Lon	27	TQ4567
Petty France Gloucs	35	ST7885
Pettycur Fife	117	NT2686
Pettymuk Abers	143	NJ9023
Petworth W Susx	14	SU9721
Pevensey E Susx	16	TQ6405
Pevensey Bay E Susx	16	TQ6504
Pewsey Wilts	23	SU1660
Pheasant's Hill Bucks	37	SU7887
Phepson H & W	47	SO9459
Philadelphia T & W	96	NZ3352
Philham Devon	18	SS2522
Philiphaugh Border	109	NT4327
Phillack Cnwll	2	SW5638
Philleigh Cnwll	3	SW8639
Philpot End Essex	40	TL6118
Philpstoun W Loth	117	NT0577
Phocle Green H & W	47	SO6326
Phoenix Green Hants	24	SU7555
Phoines Highld	132	NN7093
Pibsbury Somset	21	ST4426
Pica Cumb	92	NY0222
Piccadilly Warwks	61	SP2398
Piccotts End Herts	38	TL0409
Pickering N York	90	SE7984
Picket Piece Hants	23	SU3947
Picket Post Hants	12	SU1906
Pickford W Mids	61	SP2881
Pickford Green W Mids	61	SP2781
Pickhill N York	89	SE3483
Picklescott Shrops	59	SO4399
Pickmere Ches	79	SJ6977
Pickney Somset	20	ST1929
Pickstock Shrops	72	SJ7223
Pickup Bank Lancs	81	SD7122
Pickwell Devon	18	SS4540
Pickwell Leics	63	SK7811
Pickwick Wilts	35	ST8670
Pickworth Lincs	63	SK9913
Pickworth Lincs	64	TF0433
Pict's Cross H & W	46	SO5526
Pictillum Abers	142	NJ7317
Picton Ches	71	SJ4371
Picton Flints	70	SJ1182
Picton N York	89	NZ4107
Picton Ferry Carmth	31	SN2717
Piddinghoe E Susx	16	TQ4303
Piddington Bucks	37	SU8094
Piddington Nhants	51	SP8054
Piddington Oxon	37	SP6317
Piddlehinton Dorset	11	SY7197
Piddletrenthide Dorset	11	SY7099
Pidley Cambs	52	TL3377
Pie Corner H & W	47	SO6461
Piercebridge Dur	96	NZ2115
Pierowall Ork	155	HY4348
Piff's Elm Gloucs	47	SO9026
Pig Oak Dorset	12	SU0202
Pig Street H & W	46	SO3647
Pigdon Nthumb	103	NZ1588
Pigeon Green Warwks	48	SP2260
Pikehall Derbys	74	SK1959
Pilford Dorset	12	SU0301
Pilgrims Hatch Essex	27	TQ5895
Pilham Lincs	76	SK8693
Pill Somset	34	ST5275
Pillaton Cnwll	5	SX3664
Pillatonmill Cnwll	5	SX3663
Pillerton Hersey Warwks	48	SP2948
Pillerton Priors Warwks	48	SP2947
Pilleth Powys	46	SO2667
Pilley Hants	12	SZ3298
Pilley S York	74	SE3300
Pilley Bailey Hants	12	SZ3398
Pillgwenlly Newpt	34	ST3186
Pillhead Devon	18	SS4726
Pilling Lancs	80	SD4048
Pilling Lane Lancs	80	SD3749
Pilning Gloucs	34	ST5684
Pilot Inn Kent	17	TR0818
Pilsbury Derbys	74	SK1163
Pilsdon Dorset	10	SY4199
Pilsgate Cambs	64	TF0605
Pilsley Derbys	74	SK2371
Pilsley Derbys	74	SK4262
Pilson Green Norfk	67	TG3713
Piltdown E Susx	16	TQ4422
Pilton Devon	19	SS5534
Pilton Nhants	51	TL0284
Pilton Rutlnd	63	SK9102
Pilton Somset	21	ST5941
Pilton Green Swans	32	SS4487
Pimlico Lancs	81	SD7443
Pimlico Nhants	49	SP6140
Pimperne Dorset	11	ST9009
Pin Green Herts	39	TL2525
Pinchbeck Lincs	64	TF2425
Pinchbeck Bars Lincs	64	TF1925
Pinchbeck West Lincs	64	TF2024
Pincheon Green S York	83	SE6517
Pinchinthorpe N York	90	NZ5714
Pincock Lancs	80	SD5417
Pindon End Bucks	38	SP7847
Pinfold Lancs	80	SD3811
Pinford End Suffk	54	TL8459
Pinged Carmth	31	SN4203
Pingewood Berks	24	SU6969
Pinhoe Devon	9	SX9694
Pinkett's Booth W Mids	61	SP2781
Pinkney Wilts	35	ST8686
Pinley W Mids	61	SP3577
Pinley Green Warwks	48	SP2066
Pinmill Suffk	55	TM2037
Pinminnoch S Ayrs	106	NX1993
Pinmore S Ayrs	106	NX2091
Pinn Devon	9	SY1086
Pinner Gt Lon	26	TQ1289
Pinner Green Gt Lon	26	TQ1289
Pinsley Green Ches	71	SJ5846
Pinvin H & W	47	SO9549
Pinwherry S Ayrs	98	NX2086
Pinxton Derbys	75	SK4554
Pipe and Lyde H & W	46	SO5043
Pipe Gate Shrops	72	SJ7340
Pipehill Staffs	61	SK0907
Piperhill Highld	140	NH8650
Pipers Pool Cnwll	5	SX2584
Pipewell Nhants	51	SP8485
Pippacott Devon	19	SS5237
Pippin Street Lancs	81	SD5924
Pipton Powys	45	SO1637
Pirbright Surrey	25	SU9455
Pirbright Camp Surrey	25	SU9356
Pirnie Border	110	NT6528
Pirnmill N Ayrs	105	NR8744
Pirton H & W	47	SO8847
Pirton Herts	38	TL1431
Pishill Oxon	37	SU7389
Pistyll Gwynd	56	SH3241
Pitagowan P & K	132	NN8165
Pitblae Abers	143	NJ9864
Pitcairngreen P & K	125	NO0627
Pitcalnie Highld	147	NH8072
Pitcaple Abers	142	NJ7225
Pitcarity Angus	134	NO3365
Pitch Green Bucks	37	SP7703
Pitch Place Surrey	25	SU8839
Pitch Place Surrey	25	SU9852
Pitchcombe Gloucs	35	SO8508
Pitchcott Bucks	37	SP7720
Pitcher Row Lincs	64	TF2933
Pitchford Shrops	59	SJ5303
Pitchroy Moray	141	NJ1738
Pitcombe Somset	22	ST6732
Pitcot V Glam	33	SS8974
Pitcox E Loth	118	NT6475
Pitfichie Abers	142	NJ6716
Pitglassie Abers	142	NJ6943
Pitgrudy Highld	147	NH7991
Pitkennedy Angus	127	NO5454
Pitlessie Fife	126	NO3309
Pitlochry P & K	132	NN9458
Pitmachie Abers	142	NJ6728
Pitmain Highld	132	NH7400
Pitmedden Abers	143	NJ8827
Pitmuies Angus	127	NO5649
Pitmunie Abers	142	NJ6614
Pitney Somset	21	ST4528
Pitroddie P & K	126	NO2125
Pitscottie Fife	126	NO4112
Pitsea Essex	40	TQ7488
Pitses Gt Man	79	SD9403
Pitsford Nhants	50	SP7567
Pitstone Bucks	38	SP9415
Pitt Devon	9	ST0316
Pitt Hants	24	SU4528
Pitt Court Gloucs	35	ST7496
Pitt's Wood Kent	16	TQ6149
Pittarrow Abers	135	NO7274
Pittenweem Fife	127	NO5502
Pitteuchar Fife	117	NT2899
Pittington Dur	96	NZ3244
Pittodrie House Hotel Abers	142	NJ6924
Pitton Wilts	23	SU2131
Pittulie Abers	143	NJ9567
Pity Me Dur	96	NZ2645
Pityme Cnwll	4	SW9576
Pivington Kent	28	TQ9146
Pixey Green Suffk	55	TM2475
Pixham Surrey	26	TQ1750
Plain Street Cnwll	4	SW9778
Plains N Lans	116	NS7966
Plaish Shrops	59	SO5296
Plaistow Derbys	74	SK3456
Plaistow Gt Lon	27	TQ4082
Plaistow H & W	47	SO6939
Plaistow W Susx	14	TQ0030
Plaitford Hants	12	SU2719
Plank Lane Gt Man	79	SJ6399
Plas Cymyran Angles	68	SH2975
Plastow Green Hants	24	SU5361
Platt Kent	27	TQ6257
Platt Bridge Gt Man	78	SD6002
Platt Lane Shrops	59	SJ5136
Platts Heath Kent	28	TQ8750
Plawsworth Dur	96	NZ2647
Plaxtol Kent	27	TQ6053
Play Hatch Oxon	37	SU7376
Playden E Susx	17	TQ9221
Playford Suffk	55	TM2147
Playing Place Cnwll	3	SW8141
Playley Green Gloucs	47	SO7631
Plealey Shrops	59	SJ4206
Plean Stirlg	116	NS8386
Pleasance Fife	126	NO2312
Pleasington Lancs	81	SD6426
Pleasley Derbys	75	SK5064
Pleasleyhill Notts	75	SK5064
Pleck Dorset	11	ST7010
Pledgdon Green Essex	40	TL5626
Pledwick W York	83	SE3316
Pleinheaume Guern	152	GN0000
Plemont Jersey	152	JS0000
Plemstall Ches	71	SJ4570
Plenmeller Nthumb	102	NY7163
Pleshey Essex	40	TL6614
Plockton Highld	137	NG8033
Ploughfield H & W	46	SO3841
Plowden Shrops	59	SO3887
Ploxgreen Shrops	59	SJ3604
Pluckley Kent	28	TQ9245
Pluckley Station Kent	28	TQ9243
Pluckley Thorne Kent	28	TQ9244
Plucks Gutter Kent	29	TR2663
Plumbland Cumb	92	NY1539
Plumgarths Cumb	87	SD4994

Pyleigh — Ridgewell

Pyleigh *Somset* 20 ST1330
Pylle *Somset* 21 ST6038
Pymore *Cambs* 53 TL4986
Pymore *Dorset* 10 SY4694
Pyrford *Surrey* 26 TQ0358
Pyrton *Oxon* 37 SU6896
Pytchley *Nhants* 51 SP8574
Pyworthy *Devon* 18 SS3102

Q

Quabbs *Shrops* 58 SO2180
Quadring *Lincs* 64 TF2233
Quadring Eaudike *Lincs* 64 TF2433
Quainton *Bucks* 37 SP7420
Quaker's Yard *Myr Td* 33 ST0995
Quaking Houses *Dur* 96 NZ1850
Quarley *Hants* 23 SU2743
Quarndon *Derbys* 62 SK3340
Quarr Hill *IOW* 13 SZ5792
Quarrier's Homes *Inver* 115 NS3666
Quarrington *Lincs* 64 TF0544
Quarrington Hill *Dur* 96 NZ3337
Quarry Bank *Ches* 71 SJ5465
Quarry Bank *W Mids* 60 SO9386
Quarrywood *Moray* 141 NJ1763
Quarter *N Ayrs* 114 NS1961
Quarter *S Lans* 116 NS7251
Quatford *Shrops* 60 SO7391
Quatt *Shrops* 60 SO7588
Quebec *Dur* 96 NZ1743
Quedgeley *Gloucs* 35 SO8014
Queen Adelaide *Cambs* 53 TL5681
Queen Camel *Somset* 21 ST5924
Queen Charlton *Somset* 21 ST6367
Queen Dart *Devon* 19 SS8316
Queen Oak *Dorset* 22 ST7831
Queen Street *Kent* 28 TQ6845
Queen Street *Wilts* 35 SU0287
Queen's Bower *IOW* 13 SZ5684
Queen's Head *Shrops* 59 SJ3327
Queen's Park *Beds* 38 TL0349
Queen's Park *Nhants* 49 SP7562
Queenborough *Kent* 28 TQ9172
Queenhill *H & W* 47 SO8537
Queensbury *W York* 82 SE1030
Queensferry *Flints* 71 SJ3168
Queenslie *C Glas* 116 NS6565
Queenzieburn *N Lans* 116 NS6977
Quendon *Essex* 39 TL5130
Queniborough *Leics* 63 SK6412
Quenington *Gloucs* 36 SP1404
Quernmore *Lancs* 87 SD5160
Quernmore Park Hall *Lancs* 87 SD5162
Queslett *W Mids* 61 SP0695
Quethiock *Cnwll* 5 SX3164
Quick's Green *Berks* 37 SU5876
Quidenham *Norfk* 54 TM0287
Quidhampton *Hants* 24 SU5150
Quidhampton *Wilts* 23 SU1030
Quina Brook *Shrops* 59 SJ5232
Quinberry End *Nhants* 49 SP6250
Quinton *Nhants* 49 SP7754
Quinton *W Mids* 60 SO9984
Quinton Green *Nhants* 50 SP7853
Quintrell Downs *Cnwll* 4 SW8460
Quither *Devon* 5 SX4481
Quixhall *Staffs* 73 SK1041
Quixwood *Border* 119 NT7863
Quoditch *Devon* 5 SX4097
Quorndon *Leics* 62 SK5616
Quothquan *S Lans* 108 NS9939
Quoyburray *Ork* 155 HY5005
Quoyloo *Ork* 155 HY2420

R

Rabbit's Cross *Kent* 28 TQ7847
Rableyheath *Herts* 39 TL2319
Raby *Cumb* 93 NY1951
Raby *Mersyd* 71 SJ3179
Rachan Mill *Border* 108 NT1134
Rachub *Gwynd* 69 SH6267
Rackenford *Devon* 19 SS8518
Rackham *W Susx* 14 TQ0413
Rackheath *Norfk* 67 TG2814
Rackwick *Ork* 155 ND2099
Radbourne *Derbys* 73 SK2836
Radcliffe *Gt Man* 79 SD7806
Radcliffe *Nthumb* 103 NU2602
Radcliffe on Trent *Notts* 63 SK6439
Radclive *Bucks* 49 SP6734
Radcot *Oxon* 36 SU2899
Raddington *Somset* 20 ST0225
Radernie *Fife* 127 NO4609
Radford Semele *Warwks* 48 SP3464
Radlet *Somset* 20 ST2038
Radlett *Herts* 26 TL1600
Radley *Devon* 19 SS7323
Radley *Oxon* 37 SU5398
Radley Green *Essex* 40 TL6205
Radmore Green *Ches* 71 SJ5955
Radnage *Bucks* 37 SU7897
Radstock *Somset* 22 ST6854
Radstone *Nhants* 49 SP5840
Radway *Warwks* 48 SP3648
Radway Green *Ches* 72 SJ7754
Radwell *Beds* 51 TL0057
Radwell *Herts* 39 TL2335
Radwinter *Essex* 53 TL6037
Radwinter End *Essex* 53 TL6139
Radyr *Cardif* 33 ST1280
RAF College (Cranwell) *Lincs* 76 TF0049
Rafford *Moray* 141 NJ0556
Raftra *Cnwll* 2 SW3723
Ragdale *Leics* 63 SK6619
Ragdon *Shrops* 59 SO4591
Raginnis *Cnwll* 2 SW4625
Raglan *Mons* 34 SO4107
Ragnall *Notts* 75 SK8073
Raigbeg *Highld* 140 NH8128
Rainbow Hill *H & W* 47 SO8555
Rainford *Mersyd* 78 SD4700
Rainham *Gt Lon* 27 TQ5282
Rainham *Kent* 28 TQ8165
Rainhill *Mersyd* 78 SJ4991
Rainhill Stoops *Mersyd* 78 SJ5090
Rainow *Ches* 79 SJ9475
Rainsough *Gt Man* 79 SD8002
Rainton *N York* 89 SE3675
Rainworth *Notts* 75 SK5858
Raisbeck *Cumb* 87 NY6407
Raise *Cumb* 94 NY7046
Raisthorpe *N York* 90 SE8561
Rait *P & K* 126 NO2226
Raithby *Lincs* 77 TF3084
Raithby *Lincs* 77 TF3766
Raithwaite *N York* 90 NZ8611
Rake *W Susx* 14 SU8027
Rakewood *Gt Man* 82 SD9414
Ralia *Highld* 132 NN7097
Ram *Carmth* 44 SN5846
Ram Hill *Gloucs* 35 ST6779
Ram Lane *Kent* 28 TQ9646
Ramasaig *Highld* 136 NG1644
Rame *Cnwll* 3 SW7233
Rame *Cnwll* 6 SX4249
Rampisham *Dorset* 10 ST5602
Rampside *Cumb* 86 SD2366
Rampton *Cambs* 53 TL4267
Rampton *Notts* 75 SK8078
Ramridge End *Beds* 38 TL1023
Ramsbottom *Gt Man* 81 SD7916
Ramsbury *Wilts* 36 SU2771
Ramscraigs *Highld* 151 ND1427
Ramsdean *Hants* 13 SU7022
Ramsdell *Hants* 24 SU5857
Ramsden *H & W* 47 SO9246
Ramsden *Oxon* 36 SP3515
Ramsden Bellhouse *Essex* 40 TQ7194
Ramsden Heath *Essex* 40 TQ7095
Ramsey *Cambs* 52 TL2885
Ramsey *Essex* 41 TM2130
Ramsey *IOM* 153 SC4594
Ramsey Forty Foot *Cambs* 52 TL3087
Ramsey Heights *Cambs* 52 TL2484
Ramsey Island *Essex* 40 TL9405
Ramsey Mereside *Cambs* 52 TL2889
Ramsey St Mary's *Cambs* 52 TL2587
Ramsgate *Kent* 29 TR3865
Ramsgill *N York* 89 SE1170
Ramshaw *Dur* 95 NY9547
Ramsholt *Suffk* 55 TM3141
Ramshope *Nthumb* 102 NT7304
Ramshorn *Staffs* 73 SK0845
Ramsley *Devon* 8 SX6593
Ramsnest Common *Surrey* 14 SU9432
Ranby *Lincs* 76 TF2278
Ranby *Notts* 75 SK6580
Rand *Lincs* 76 TF1078
Randwick *Gloucs* 35 SO8306
Ranfurly *Rens* 115 NS3865
Rangemore *Staffs* 73 SK1822
Rangeworthy *Gloucs* 35 ST6986
Rank's Green *Essex* 40 TL7418
Rankinston *E Ayrs* 107 NS4513
Ranksborough *Rutlnd* 63 SK8311
Rann *Lancs* 81 SD7124
Rannoch Station *P & K* 124 NN4257
Ranochan *Highld* 129 NM8282
Ranscombe *Somset* 20 SS9443
Ranskill *Notts* 75 SK6587
Ranton *Staffs* 72 SJ8524
Ranton Green *Staffs* 72 SJ8423
Ranworth *Norfk* 67 TG3514
Raploch *Stirlg* 116 NS7894
Rapness *Ork* 155 HY5141
Rapps *Somset* 10 ST3316
Rascarrel *D & G* 92 NX7948
Rashfield *Ag & B* 114 NS1483
Rashwood *H & W* 47 SO9165
Raskelf *N York* 90 SE4971
Rassau *Blae G* 33 SO1511
Rastrick *W York* 82 SE1421
Ratagan *Highld* 138 NG9119
Ratby *Leics* 62 SK5105
Ratcliffe Culey *Leics* 61 SP3299
Ratcliffe on Soar *Notts* 62 SK4928
Ratcliffe on the Wreake *Leics* 63 SK6314
Ratfyn *Wilts* 23 SU1642
Rathen *Abers* 143 NJ9960
Rathillet *Fife* 126 NO3620
Rathmell *N York* 88 SD8059
Ratho *C Edin* 117 NT1370
Rathven *Moray* 142 NJ4465
Ratlake *Hants* 13 SU4123
Ratley *Warwks* 48 SP3847
Ratling *Kent* 29 TR2453
Ratlinghope *Shrops* 59 SO4096
Rattan Row *Norfk* 65 TF5114
Rattar *Highld* 151 ND2673
Ratten Row *Cumb* 93 NY3240
Ratten Row *Cumb* 93 NY3949
Ratten Row *Lancs* 80 SD4241
Rattery *Devon* 7 SX7461
Rattlesden *Suffk* 54 TL9758
Ratton Village *E Susx* 16 TQ5901
Rattray *P & K* 126 NO1845
Raughton *Cumb* 93 NY3947
Raughton Head *Cumb* 93 NY3745
Raunds *Nhants* 51 SP9972
Raven Meols *Mersyd* 78 SD2905
Ravenfield *S York* 75 SK4895
Ravenglass *Cumb* 86 SD0896
Ravenhills Green *H & W* 47 SO7454
Raveningham *Norfk* 67 TM3996
Ravenscar *N York* 91 NZ9801
Ravenscliffe *Staffs* 72 SJ8452
Ravensdale *IOM* 153 SC3592
Ravensden *Beds* 51 TL0754
Ravenshead *Notts* 75 SK5654
Ravensmoor *Ches* 71 SJ6150
Ravensthorpe *Nhants* 50 SP6670
Ravensthorpe *W York* 82 SE2220
Ravenstone *Bucks* 38 SP8451
Ravenstone *Leics* 62 SK4013
Ravenstonedale *Cumb* 88 NY7203
Ravenstruther *S Lans* 116 NS9245
Ravensworth *N York* 89 NZ1308
Raw *N York* 91 NZ9305
Rawcliffe *N York* 83 SE5854
Rawcliffe *E R Yk* 83 SE6822
Rawcliffe Bridge *E R Yk* 83 SE6921
Rawdon *W York* 82 SE2139
Rawling Street *Kent* 28 TQ9059
Rawmarsh *S York* 75 SK4396
Rawnsley *Staffs* 60 SK0212
Rawreth *Essex* 40 TQ7893
Rawridge *Devon* 9 ST2006
Rawtenstall *Lancs* 81 SD8123
Raydon *Suffk* 54 TM0438
Raylees *Nthumb* 102 NY9291
Rayleigh *Essex* 40 TQ8090
Raymond Hill *Devon* 10 SY3296
Rayne *Essex* 40 TL7222
Raynes Park *Gt Lon* 26 TQ2368
Rea *Gloucs* 35 SO8016
Reach *Cambs* 53 TL5666
Read *Lancs* 81 SD7634
Reading *Berks* 24 SU7173
Reading Street *Kent* 17 TQ9230
Reading Street *Kent* 29 TR3869
Reagill *Cumb* 94 NY6017
Rearquhar *Highld* 146 NH7492
Rearsby *Leics* 63 SK6514
Rease Heath *Shrops* 72 SJ6454
Reay *Highld* 150 NC9664
Reculver *Kent* 29 TR2269
Red Ball *Somset* 9 ST0917
Red Bull *Ches* 72 SJ8254
Red Cross *Cambs* 53 TL4754
Red Cross *Cnwll* 18 SS2605
Red Dial *Cumb* 93 NY2546
Red Hill *Dorset* 12 SZ0995
Red Hill *Warwks* 48 SP1356
Red Lodge *Suffk* 53 TL6970
Red Lumb *Gt Man* 81 SD8415
Red Rock *Gt Man* 78 SD5809
Red Roses *Carmth* 31 SN2011
Red Row *T & W* 103 NZ2599
Red Street *Staffs* 72 SJ8251
Red Wharf Bay *Angles* 68 SH5281
Redberth *Pembks* 31 SN0804
Redbourn *Herts* 38 TL1012
Redbourne *Lincs* 76 SK9799
Redbrook *Gloucs* 34 SO5309
Redbrook *Wrexhm* 71 SJ5041
Redbrook Street *Kent* 28 TQ9336
Redburn *Highld* 140 NH9447
Redburn *Nthumb* 102 NY7764
Redcar *N York* 97 NZ6024
Redcastle *D & G* 100 NX8165
Redcastle *Highld* 139 NH5849
Redding *Falk* 116 NS9278
Reddingmuirhead *Falk* 116 NS9177
Reddish *Gt Man* 79 SJ8993
Redditch *H & W* 48 SP0467
Rede *Suffk* 54 TL8055
Redenhall *Norfk* 55 TM2684
Redenham *Hants* 23 SU3049
Redesmouth *Nthumb* 102 NY8682
Redford *Abers* 135 NO7570
Redford *Angus* 127 NO5644
Redford *W Susx* 14 SU8626
Redfordgreen *Border* 109 NT3616
Redgate *Rhondd* 33 ST0188
Redgorton *P & K* 125 NO0828
Redgrave *Suffk* 54 TM0477
Redhill *Abers* 135 NJ7704
Redhill *Herts* 39 TL3033
Redhill *Somset* 21 ST4962
Redhill *Surrey* 27 TQ2750
Redisham *Suffk* 55 TM4084
Redland *Bristl* 34 ST5775
Redland *Ork* 155 HY3724
Redlingfield *Suffk* 54 TM1870
Redlingfield Green *Suffk* 54 TM1871
Redlynch *Somset* 22 ST7033
Redlynch *Wilts* 12 SU2021
Redmain *Cumb* 92 NY1333
Redmarley *H & W* 47 SO7666
Redmarley D'Abitot *Gloucs* 47 SO7531
Redmarshall *Dur* 96 NZ3821
Redmile *Leics* 63 SK7935
Redmire *N York* 88 SE0491
Redmyre *Abers* 135 NO7575
Rednal *Shrops* 59 SJ3628
Rednal *W Mids* 60 SP0076
Redpath *Border* 110 NT5835
Redpoint *Highld* 137 NG7368
Redruth *Cnwll* 2 SW6942
Redstocks *Wilts* 22 ST9362
Redstone *P & K* 126 NO1834
Redstone Cross *Pembks* 31 SN1015
Redvales *Gt Man* 79 SD8008
Redwick *Gloucs* 34 ST5486
Redwick *Newpt* 34 ST4184
Redworth *Dur* 96 NZ2423
Reed *Herts* 39 TL3636
Reedham *Norfk* 67 TG4201
Reedness *E R Yk* 84 SE7923
Reeds Holme *Lancs* 81 SD8024
Reepham *Lincs* 76 TF0473
Reepham *Norfk* 66 TG1022
Reeth *N York* 88 SE0399
Reeves Green *W Mids* 61 SP2677
Regaby *IOM* 153 SC4397
Reiff *Highld* 144 NB9614
Reigate *Surrey* 27 TQ2550
Reighton *N York* 91 TA1375
Reisque *Abers* 143 NJ8819
Reiss *Highld* 151 ND3354
Rejerrah *Cnwll* 3 SW7956
Releath *Cnwll* 2 SW6532
Relubbus *Cnwll* 2 SW5631
Relugas *Moray* 141 NH9948
Remenham *Berks* 37 SU7684
Remenham Hill *Berks* 37 SU7882
Rempstone *Notts* 62 SK5724
Rendcomb *Gloucs* 35 SP0209
Rendham *Suffk* 55 TM3464
Renfrew *Rens* 115 NS5067
Renhold *Beds* 38 TL0952
Renishaw *Derbys* 75 SK4577
Rennington *Nthumb* 111 NU2118
Renton *D & Cb* 115 NS3877
Renwick *Cumb* 94 NY5943
Repps *Norfk* 67 TG4217
Repton *Derbys* 73 SK3026
Resaurie *Highld* 140 NH7045
Rescassa *Cnwll* 3 SW9842
Rescorla *Cnwll* 3 SW9848
Resipole *Highld* 121 NM7264
Reskadinnick *Cnwll* 2 SW6341
Resolis *Highld* 140 NH6765
Resolven *Neath* 33 SN8302
Rest and be Thankful *Ag & B* 123 NN2307
Reston *Border* 119 NT8862
Restronguet *Cnwll* 3 SW8136
Reswallie *Angus* 127 NO5051
Reterth *Cnwll* 4 SW9463
Retew *Cnwll* 4 SW9257
Retford *Notts* 75 SK7081
Retire *Cnwll* 4 SX0064
Rettendon *Essex* 40 TQ7698
Retyn *Cnwll* 4 SW8858
Revesby *Lincs* 77 TF2961
Rew *Devon* 7 SX7570
Rew *Devon* 7 SX7138
Rew Street *IOW* 13 SZ4794
Rewe *Devon* 9 SX9499
Rexon *Devon* 5 SX4188
Reydon *Suffk* 55 TM4977
Reymerston *Norfk* 66 TG0206
Reynalton *Pembks* 31 SN0908
Reynoldston *Swans* 32 SS4889
Rezare *Cnwll* 5 SX3677
Rhadyr *Mons* 34 SO3602
Rhandirmwyn *Carmth* 44 SN7843
Rhayader *Powys* 45 SN9768
Rheindown *Highld* 139 NH5147
Rhes-y-cae *Flints* 70 SJ1871
Rhewl *Denbgs* 70 SJ1060
Rhewl *Denbgs* 70 SJ1744
Rhewl Mostyn *Flints* 70 SJ1580
Rhewl-fawr *Flints* 70 SJ1381
Rhicarn *Highld* 148 NC0825
Rhiconich *Highld* 148 NC2552
Rhicullen *Highld* 146 NH6971
Rhigos *Rhondd* 33 SN9205
Rhireavach *Highld* 144 NH0295
Rhives *Highld* 147 NC8200
Rhiwbina *Cardif* 33 ST1682
Rhiwbryfdir *Gwynd* 57 SH6946
Rhiwderyn *Newpt* 34 ST2687
Rhiwen *Gwynd* 69 SH5763
Rhiwinder *Rhondd* 33 ST0287
Rhiwlas *Gwynd* 69 SH5765
Rhiwlas *Gwynd* 58 SH9237
Rhiwlas *Powys* 58 SJ1932
Rhiwsaeson *Cardif* 33 ST0682
Rhode *Somset* 20 ST2734
Rhoden Green *Kent* 28 TQ6845
Rhodes *Gt Man* 79 SD8505
Rhodes Minnis *Kent* 29 TR1542
Rhodesia *Notts* 75 SK5679
Rhodiad-y-brenin *Pembks* 30 SM7627
Rhonehouse *D & G* 99 NX7459
Rhoose *V Glam* 20 ST0666
Rhos *Carmth* 31 SN3835
Rhos *Denbgs* 70 SJ1261
Rhos *Neath* 32 SN7302
Rhos *Powys* 45 SO1741
Rhos Haminiog *Cardgn* 43 SN5464
Rhos Lligwy *Angles* 68 SH4886
Rhos y-brithdir *Powys* 58 SJ1323
Rhos-fawr *Gwynd* 56 SH3838
Rhos-on-Sea *A & C* 69 SH8480
Rhos-y-garth *Cardgn* 43 SN6373
Rhos-y-gwaliau *Gwynd* 58 SH9434
Rhos-y-llan *Gwynd* 56 SH2337
Rhos-y-meirch *Powys* 46 SO2769
Rhosbeirio *Angles* 68 SH3991
Rhoscefnhir *Angles* 68 SH5276
Rhoscolyn *Angles* 68 SH2675
Rhoscrowther *Pembks* 30 SM9002
Rhosesmor *Flints* 70 SJ2168
Rhosgadfan *Gwynd* 68 SH5057
Rhosgoch *Angles* 68 SH4089
Rhosgoch *Powys* 45 SO1847
Rhoshill *Pembks* 31 SN1940
Rhoshirwaun *Gwynd* 56 SH2029
Rhoslan *Gwynd* 56 SH4840
Rhoslefain *Gwynd* 57 SH5705
Rhosllanerchrugog *Wrexhm* 71 SJ2946
Rhosmaen *Carmth* 44 SN6423
Rhosmeirch *Angles* 68 SH4677
Rhosneigr *Angles* 68 SH3173
Rhosnesni *Wrexhm* 71 SJ3550
Rhosrobin *Wrexhm* 71 SJ3252
Rhossili *Swans* 31 SS4187
Rhostryfan *Gwynd* 68 SH4957
Rhostyllen *Wrexhm* 71 SJ3148
Rhosybol *Angles* 68 SH4288
Rhosygadfa *Shrops* 59 SJ3234
Rhosymedre *Wrexhm* 70 SJ2842
Rhu *Ag & B* 115 NS2684
Rhuallt *Denbgs* 70 SJ0775
Rhubodach *Ag & B* 114 NS0273
Rhuddall Heath *Ches* 71 SJ5562
Rhuddlan *Denbgs* 70 SJ0278
Rhulen *Powys* 45 SO1349
Rhunahaorine *Ag & B* 105 NR7048
Rhyd *Gwynd* 57 SH6341
Rhyd-Ddu *Gwynd* 69 SH5652
Rhyd-lydan *A & C* 69 SH8950
Rhyd-uchaf *Gwynd* 58 SH9037
Rhyd-y pennau *Cardgn* 43 SN6385
Rhyd-y-clafdy *Gwynd* 56 SH3234
Rhyd-y-foel *A & C* 70 SH9176
Rhyd-y-groes *Gwynd* 69 SH5867
Rhyd-y-meirch *Mons* 34 SO3107
Rhyd-y-sarn *Gwynd* 57 SH6842
Rhyd-yr-onnen *Gwynd* 57 SH6102
Rhydargaeau *Carmth* 31 SN4326
Rhydcymerau *Carmth* 44 SN5738
Rhydd *H & W* 47 SO8345
Rhydding *Neath* 32 SS7499
Rhyddlan *Cardgn* 44 SN4943
Rhydgaled *A & C* 70 SH9964
Rhydlanfair *A & C* 69 SH8252
Rhydlewis *Cardgn* 42 SN3447
Rhydlios *Gwynd* 56 SH1929
Rhydowen *Cardgn* 42 SN4445
Rhydrosser *Cardgn* 43 SN5667
Rhydspence *H & W* 46 SO2447
Rhydtalog *Flints* 70 SJ2354
Rhydycroesau *Shrops* 58 SJ2430
Rhydyfelin *Cardgn* 43 SN5979
Rhydyfelin *Rhondd* 33 ST0988
Rhydyfro *Neath* 32 SN7105
Rhydymain *Gwynd* 57 SH7821
Rhydymwyn *Flints* 70 SJ2066
Rhyl *Denbgs* 70 SJ0081
Rhymney *Caerph* 33 SO1107
Rhynd *P & K* 126 NO1520
Rhynie *Abers* 142 NJ4927
Rhynie *Highld* 147 NH8479
Ribbesford *H & W* 60 SO7874
Ribbleton *Lancs* 81 SD5631
Ribby *Lancs* 80 SD4031
Ribchester *Lancs* 81 SD6535
Riber *Derbys* 74 SK3059
Riby *Lincs* 85 TA1807
Riccall *N York* 83 SE6237
Riccarton *Border* 101 NY5494
Riccarton *E Ayrs* 107 NS4236
Rich's Holford *Somset* 20 ST1434
Richards Castle *H & W* 46 SO4969
Richings Park *Bucks* 26 TQ0278
Richmond *N York* 89 NZ1701
Richmond *S York* 74 SK4085
Richmond Fort *Guern* 152 GN0000
Richmond upon Thames *Gt Lon* 26 TQ1774
Rickerscote *Staffs* 72 SJ9220
Rickford *Somset* 21 ST4859
Rickham *Devon* 7 SX7537
Rickinghall *Suffk* 54 TM0475
Rickling *Essex* 39 TL4931
Rickling Green *Essex* 39 TL5129
Rickmansworth *Herts* 26 TQ0694
Riddell *Border* 109 NT5124
Riddings *Cumb* 101 NY4075
Riddings *Derbys* 74 SK4252
Riddlecombe *Devon* 19 SS6113
Riddlesden *W York* 82 SE0742
Ridge *Dorset* 11 SY9386
Ridge *Herts* 26 TL2100
Ridge *Somset* 21 ST5556
Ridge *Wilts* 22 ST9531
Ridge Green *Surrey* 15 TQ3048
Ridge Lane *Warwks* 61 SP2994
Ridge Row *Kent* 29 TR2042
Ridgebourne *Powys* 45 SO0560
Ridgehill *Somset* 21 ST5462
Ridgeway *Derbys* 74 SK3551
Ridgeway *Derbys* 74 SK4081
Ridgeway *H & W* 48 SP0461
Ridgeway Cross *H & W* 47 SO7147
Ridgewell *Essex* 53 TL7340

Ridgewood
Ryton

Ridgewood E Susx	16	TQ4719
Ridgmont Beds	38	SP9736
Riding Mill Nthumb	103	NZ0161
Ridley Kent	27	TQ6164
Ridley Nthumb	102	NY7963
Ridley Green Ches	71	SJ5554
Ridlington Norfk	67	TG3430
Ridlington Rutlnd	63	SK8402
Ridlington Street Norfk	67	TG3430
Ridsdale Nthumb	102	NY9084
Rievaulx N York	90	SE5785
Rigg D & G	101	NY2966
Riggend N Lans	116	NS7670
Righoul Highld	140	NH8851
Rigmadon Park Cumb	87	SD6184
Rigsby Lincs	77	TF4375
Rigside S Lans	108	NS8735
Riley Green Lancs	81	SD6225
Rileyhill Staffs	61	SK1114
Rilla Mill Cnwll	5	SX2973
Rillaton Cnwll	5	SX2973
Rillington N York	90	SE8574
Rimington Lancs	81	SD8045
Rimpton Somset	21	ST6121
Rimswell E R Yk	85	TA3128
Rinaston Pembks	30	SM9825
Rindleford Shrops	60	SO7395
Ring o'Bells Lancs	78	SD4510
Ring's End Cambs	65	TF3902
Ringford D & G	99	NX6957
Ringinglow Derbys	74	SK2883
Ringland Norfk	66	TG1313
Ringles Cross E Susx	16	TQ4722
Ringlestone Kent	28	TQ8755
Ringley Gt Man	79	SD7605
Ringmer E Susx	16	TQ4412
Ringmore Devon	7	SX6546
Ringmore Devon	7	SX9272
Ringorm Moray	141	NJ2644
Ringsfield Suffk	55	TM4088
Ringsfield Corner Suffk	55	TM4087
Ringshall Bucks	38	SP9814
Ringshall Suffk	54	TM0452
Ringshall Stocks Suffk	54	TM0551
Ringstead Nhants	51	SP9875
Ringstead Norfk	65	TF7040
Ringwood Hants	12	SU1505
Ringwould Kent	29	TR3548
Rinsey Cnwll	2	SW5927
Rinsey Croft Cnwll	2	SW6028
Ripe E Susx	16	TQ5110
Ripley Derbys	74	SK3950
Ripley Hants	12	SZ1698
Ripley N York	89	SE2860
Ripley Surrey	26	TQ0556
Riplingham E R Yk	84	SE9631
Riplington Hants	13	SU6623
Ripon N York	89	SE3171
Rippingale Lincs	64	TF0927
Ripple H & W	47	SO8737
Ripple Kent	29	TR3550
Ripponden W York	82	SE0319
Risabus Ag & B	104	NR3143
Risbury H & W	46	SO5455
Risby Lincs	84	SE9114
Risby Suffk	54	TL8066
Risca Caerph	34	ST2391
Rise E R Yk	85	TA1542
Riseden E Susx	16	TQ6130
Riseden Kent	28	TQ7036
Risegate Lincs	64	TF2129
Riseholme Lincs	76	SK9775
Risehow Cumb	92	NY0234
Riseley Beds	51	TL0462
Riseley Berks	24	SU7263
Rishangles Suffk	54	TM1668
Rishton Lancs	81	SD7230
Rishworth W York	82	SE0318
Rising Bridge Lancs	81	SD7825
Risley Ches	79	SJ6592
Risley Derbys	62	SK4535
Risplith N York	89	SE2468
Rivar Wilts	23	SU3161
Rivenhall End Essex	40	TL8316
River Kent	29	TR2943
River W Susx	14	SU9323
River Bank Cambs	53	TL5368
Riverford Highld	139	NH5454
Riverhead Kent	27	TQ5156
Rivers Corner Dorset	11	ST7712
Rivington Lancs	81	SD6214
Roachill Devon	19	SS8522
Road Ashton Wilts	22	ST8856
Road Green Norfk	67	TM2693
Road Weedon Nhants	49	SP6359
Roade Nhants	49	SP7651
Roadhead Cumb	101	NY5174
Roadmeetings S Lans	116	NS8649
Roadside E Ayrs	107	NS5717
Roadside Highld	151	ND1560
Roadwater Somset	20	ST0338
Roag Highld	136	NG2644
Roan of Craigoch S Ayrs	106	NS2904
Roast Green Essex	39	TL4632
Roath Cardif	33	ST1977
Roberton Border	109	NT4214
Roberton S Lans	108	NS9428
Robertsbridge E Susx	17	TQ7423
Roberttown W York	82	SE1922
Robeston Wathen Pembks	31	SN0815
Robgill Tower D & G	101	NY2471
Robin Hill Staffs	72	SJ9057
Robin Hood Lancs	80	SD5211
Robin Hood W York	83	SE3227
Robin Hood's Bay N York	91	NZ9505
Robinhood End Essex	53	TL7036
Roborough Devon	19	SS5717
Roborough Devon	6	SX5062
Roby Mersyd	78	SJ4390
Roby Mill Lancs	78	SD5107
Rocester Staffs	73	SK1039
Roch Pembks	30	SM8821
Roch Gate Pembks	30	SM8720
Rochdale Gt Man	81	SD8913
Roche Cnwll	4	SW9860
Rochester Kent	28	TQ7468
Rochester Nthumb	102	NY8298
Rochford Essex	40	TQ8790
Rochford H & W	47	SO6268
Rochville Ag & B	114	NS2390
Rock Cnwll	4	SW9375
Rock H & W	60	SO7371
Rock Neath	32	SS7893
Rock Nthumb	111	NU2020
Rock W Susx	14	TQ1213
Rock Ferry Mersyd	78	SJ3386
Rock Hill H & W	47	SO9569
Rockbeare Devon	9	SY0194
Rockbourne Hants	12	SU1118
Rockcliffe Cumb	101	NY3561
Rockcliffe D & G	92	NX8454
Rockcliffe Cross Cumb	101	NY3463
Rockesta Cnwll	2	SW3722
Rockfield Highld	147	NH9282
Rockfield Mons	34	SO4814
Rockford Devon	19	SS7547
Rockford Hants	12	SU1607
Rockgreen Shrops	46	SO5275
Rockhampton Gloucs	35	ST6593
Rockhead Cnwll	4	SX0784
Rockhill Shrops	46	SO2978
Rockingham Nhants	51	SP8691
Rockland All Saints Norfk	66	TL9996
Rockland St Mary Norfk	67	TG3104
Rockland St Peter Norfk	66	TL9897
Rockley Notts	75	SK7174
Rockley Wilts	36	SU1571
Rockliffe Lancs	81	SD8722
Rockwell End Bucks	37	SU7988
Rockwell Green Somset	20	ST1220
Rodborough Gloucs	35	SO8404
Rodbourne Wilts	36	SU1485
Rodbourne Wilts	35	ST9383
Rodd H & W	46	SO3262
Roddam Nthumb	111	NU0220
Rodden Dorset	10	SY6184
Roddymoor Dur	96	NZ1536
Rode Somset	22	ST8053
Rode Heath Ches	72	SJ8056
Rode Heath Ches	72	SJ8767
Rodel W Isls	154	NG0483
Roden Shrops	59	SJ5716
Rodhuish Somset	20	ST0139
Rodington Shrops	59	SJ5814
Rodington Heath Shrops	59	SJ5814
Rodley Gloucs	35	SO7411
Rodley W York	82	SE2236
Rodmarton Gloucs	35	ST9498
Rodmell E Susx	15	TQ4106
Rodmersham Kent	28	TQ9261
Rodmersham Green Kent	28	TQ9161
Rodney Stoke Somset	21	ST4849
Rodsley Derbys	73	SK2040
Rodway Somset	20	ST2540
Roe Cross Gt Man	79	SJ9896
Roe Green Gt Man	79	SD7501
Roe Green Herts	39	TL2107
Roe Green Herts	39	TL3133
Roecliffe N York	89	SE3765
Roehampton Gt Lon	26	TQ2273
Roffey W Susx	15	TQ1932
Rogart Highld	146	NC7202
Rogate W Susx	14	SU8023
Roger Ground Cumb	87	SD3597
Rogerstone Newpt	34	ST2787
Roghadal W Isls	154	NG0483
Rogiet Mons	34	ST4587
Roke Oxon	37	SU6293
Roker T & W	96	NZ4058
Rollesby Norfk	67	TG4416
Rolleston Leics	63	SK7300
Rolleston Notts	75	SK7452
Rolleston Staffs	73	SK2327
Rolston E R Yk	85	TA2144
Rolstone Somset	21	ST3962
Rolvenden Kent	17	TQ8431
Rolvenden Layne Kent	17	TQ8530
Romaldkirk Dur	95	NY9922
Romanby N York	89	SE3693
Romanno Bridge Border	117	NT1647
Romansleigh Devon	19	SS7220
Romden Castle Kent	28	TQ8941
Romesdal Highld	136	NG4053
Romford Dorset	12	SU0709
Romford Gt Lon	27	TQ5188
Romiley Gt Man	79	SJ9490
Romney Street Kent	27	TQ5561
Romsey Hants	12	SU3521
Romsley H & W	60	SO9680
Romsley Shrops	60	SO7883
Ronachan Ag & B	113	NR7454
Rookhope Dur	95	NY9342
Rookley IOW	13	SZ5084
Rookley Green IOW	13	SZ5083
Rooks Bridge Somset	21	ST3652
Rooks Nest Somset	20	ST0933
Rookwith N York	89	SE2086
Roos E R Yk	85	TA2830
Roose Cumb	86	SD2269
Roosebeck Cumb	86	SD2567
Roothams Green Beds	51	TL0957
Ropley Hants	24	SU6431
Ropley Dean Hants	24	SU6232
Ropley Soke Hants	24	SU6533
Ropsley Lincs	63	SK9933
Rora Abers	143	NK0650
Rorrington Shrops	59	SJ3000
Roscarie Moray	141	NJ3850
Roscroggan Cnwll	2	SW6542
Rose Cnwll	3	SW7754
Rose Ash Devon	19	SS7921
Rose Green Essex	40	TL9028
Rose Green Suffk	54	TL9337
Rose Green Suffk	54	TL9744
Rose Green W Susx	14	SZ9099
Rose Hill E Susx	16	TQ4516
Rose Hill Lancs	81	SD8231
Roseacre Lancs	80	SD4336
Rosebank S Lans	116	NS8049
Rosebush Pembks	31	SN0729
Rosecare Cnwll	4	SX1695
Rosecliston Cnwll	4	SW8159
Rosedale Abbey N York	90	SE7296
Roseden Nthumb	111	NU0321
Rosehall Highld	146	NC4702
Rosehearty Abers	143	NJ9267
Rosehill Shrops	59	SJ4715
Roseisle Moray	141	NJ1466
Roselands E Susx	16	TQ6200
Rosemarket Pembks	30	SM9508
Rosemarkie Highld	140	NH7357
Rosemary Lane Devon	9	ST1514
Rosemount P & K	126	NO1843
Rosenannon Cnwll	4	SW9566
Rosenithon Cnwll	3	SW8021
Roser's Cross E Susx	16	TQ5420
Rosevean Cnwll	4	SX0258
Rosevine Cnwll	3	SW8736
Rosewarne Cnwll	2	SW6036
Rosewell Mdloth	117	NT2862
Roseworth Dur	96	NZ4221
Roseworthy Cnwll	2	SW6139
Rosgill Cumb	94	NY5316
Roshven Highld	129	NM7078
Roskhill Highld	136	NG2744
Roskorwell Cnwll	3	SW7923
Roskrow Cnwll	3	SW7635
Rosley Cumb	93	NY3245
Roslin Mdloth	117	NT2763
Rosliston Derbys	73	SK2416
Rosneath Ag & B	114	NS2583
Ross D & G	99	NX6444
Ross Nthumb	111	NU1337
Ross-on-Wye H & W	46	SO5923
Rossett Wrexhm	71	SJ3657
Rossett Green N York	82	SE2952
Rossington S York	75	SK6298
Rosskeen Highld	146	NH6869
Rossland Rens	115	NS4370
Roster Highld	151	ND2639
Rostherne Ches	79	SJ7483
Rosthwaite Cumb	93	NY2514
Roston Derbys	73	SK1340
Rosudgeon Cnwll	2	SW5529
Rosyth Fife	117	NT1082
Rothbury Nthumb	103	NU0501
Rotherby Leics	63	SK6716
Rotherfield E Susx	16	TQ5529
Rotherfield Greys Oxon	37	SU7282
Rotherfield Peppard Oxon	37	SU7182
Rotherham S York	75	SK4392
Rothersthorpe Nhants	49	SP7156
Rotherwick Hants	24	SU7156
Rothes Moray	141	NJ2749
Rothesay Ag & B	114	NS0864
Rothiebrisbane Abers	142	NJ7437
Rothiemay Moray	142	NJ5548
Rothiemurchus Lodge Highld	133	NH9407
Rothienorman Abers	142	NJ7235
Rothley Leics	62	SK5812
Rothley Nthumb	103	NZ0488
Rothmaise Abers	142	NJ6832
Rothwell Lincs	76	TF1499
Rothwell Nhants	51	SP8181
Rothwell W York	83	SE3428
Rothwell Haigh W York	83	SE3328
Rotsea E R Yk	84	TA0651
Rottal Lodge Angus	134	NO3769
Rottingdean E Susx	15	TQ3602
Rottington Cumb	92	NX9613
Roucan D & G	100	NY0277
Roud IOW	13	SZ5180
Rough Close Staffs	72	SJ9239
Rough Common Kent	29	TR1259
Rougham Norfk	66	TF8320
Rougham Green Suffk	54	TL9061
Roughlee Lancs	81	SD8440
Roughley W Mids	61	SP1399
Roughpark Abers	134	NJ3412
Roughton Lincs	77	TF2464
Roughton Norfk	67	TG2136
Roughton Shrops	60	SO7594
Roughway Kent	27	TQ6153
Round Bush Herts	26	TQ1498
Round Green Beds	38	TL1022
Round Street Kent	28	TQ6568
Roundbush Essex	40	TL8501
Roundbush Green Essex	40	TL5814
Roundham Somset	10	ST4209
Roundhay W York	83	SE3337
Rounds Green W Mids	60	SO9889
Roundstreet Common W Susx	14	TQ0528
Roundway Wilts	22	SU0163
Roundyhill Angus	126	NO3750
Rous Lench H & W	47	SP0153
Rousdon Devon	10	SY2991
Rousham Oxon	49	SP4724
Rout's Green Bucks	37	SU7898
Routenbeck Cumb	93	NY1930
Routenburn N Ayrs	114	NS1961
Routh E R Yk	85	TA0942
Row Cnwll	4	SX0976
Row Cumb	94	NY6234
Row Cumb	87	SD4589
Row Ash Hants	13	SU5413
Row Green Essex	40	TL7420
Rowanburn D & G	101	NY4177
Rowardennan Hotel Stirlg	115	NS3698
Rowardennan Lodge Stirlg	115	NS3598
Rowarth Derbys	79	SK0189
Rowberrow Somset	21	ST4558
Rowborough IOW	13	SZ4684
Rowde Wilts	22	ST9762
Rowden Devon	8	SX6499
Rowen A & C	69	SH7671
Rowfield Derbys	73	SK1948
Rowfoot Nthumb	102	NY6860
Rowford Somset	20	ST2327
Rowhedge Essex	41	TM0221
Rowhook W Susx	14	TQ1234
Rowington Warwks	48	SP2069
Rowland Derbys	74	SK2172
Rowland's Castle Hants	13	SU7310
Rowland's Gill T & W	96	NZ1658
Rowledge Surrey	25	SU8243
Rowley Dur	95	NZ0848
Rowley E R Yk	84	SE9732
Rowley Shrops	59	SJ3006
Rowley Green W Mids	61	SP3483
Rowley Hill W York	82	SE1914
Rowley Regis W Mids	60	SO9787
Rowlstone H & W	46	SO3727
Rowly Surrey	14	TQ0440
Rowner Hants	13	SU5801
Rowney Green H & W	61	SP0471
Rownhams Hants	12	SU3817
Rowrah Cumb	92	NY0518
Rows of Trees Ches	79	SJ8379
Rowsham Bucks	38	SP8417
Rowsley Derbys	74	SK2565
Rowstock Oxon	37	SU4789
Rowston Lincs	76	TF0856
Rowthorne Derbys	75	SK4764
Rowton Ches	71	SJ4464
Rowton Shrops	59	SJ3612
Rowton Shrops	59	SJ6119
Rowton Shrops	59	SO4180
Rowtown Surrey	26	TQ0363
Roxburgh Border	110	NT6930
Roxby Lincs	84	SE9116
Roxby N York	97	NZ7616
Roxton Beds	52	TL1554
Roxwell Essex	40	TL6408
Roy Bridge Highld	131	NN2681
Royal Oak Dur	96	NZ2023
Royal Oak Lancs	78	SD4103
Royal's Green Ches	71	SJ6242
Roydhouse W York	82	SE2112
Roydon Essex	39	TL4010
Roydon Norfk	65	TF7023
Roydon Norfk	54	TM1080
Roydon Hamlet Essex	39	TL4107
Royston Herts	39	TL3540
Royston S York	83	SE3611
Royton Gt Man	79	SD9107
Rozel Jersey	152	JS0000
Ruabon Wrexhm	71	SJ3043
Ruaig Ag & B	120	NM0747
Ruan High Lanes Cnwll	3	SW9039
Ruan Lanihorne Cnwll	3	SW8942
Ruan Major Cnwll	2	SW7016
Ruan Minor Cnwll	2	SW7115
Ruardean Gloucs	35	SO6217
Ruardean Hill Gloucs	35	SO6317
Ruardean Woodside Gloucs	35	SO6216
Rubery H & W	60	SO9977
Ruckcroft Cumb	94	NY5344
Ruckhall H & W	46	SO4637
Ruckhall Common H & W	46	SO4539
Ruckinge Kent	17	TR0233
Ruckland Lincs	77	TF3378
Ruckley Shrops	59	SJ5300
Rudby N York	89	NZ4706
Rudchester Nthumb	103	NZ1167
Ruddington Notts	62	SK5732
Ruddle Gloucs	35	SO6811
Ruddlemoor Cnwll	3	SX0054
Rudford Gloucs	35	SO7721
Rudge Somset	22	ST8251
Rudgeway Gloucs	35	ST6386
Rudgwick W Susx	14	TQ0834
Rudhall H & W	47	SO6225
Rudheath Ches	79	SJ6772
Rudley Green Essex	40	TL8303
Rudloe Wilts	35	ST8470
Rudry Caerph	33	ST2086
Rudston E R Yk	91	TA0967
Rudyard Staffs	72	SJ9557
Ruecastle Border	110	NT6120
Rufford Lancs	80	SD4615
Rufforth N York	83	SE5251
Rug Denbgs	70	SJ0543
Rugby Warwks	50	SP5075
Rugeley Staffs	73	SK0418
Ruggaton Devon	19	SS5545
Ruishton Somset	20	ST2625
Ruislip Gt Lon	26	TQ0987
Ruletown Head Border	110	NT6113
Rumbach Moray	141	NJ3852
Rumbling Bridge P & K	117	NT0199
Rumburgh Suffk	55	TM3481
Rumby Hill Dur	96	NZ1634
Rumford Cnwll	4	SW8970
Rumford Falk	116	NS9377
Rumney Cardif	33	ST2178
Rumwell Somset	20	ST1923
Runcorn Ches	78	SJ5182
Runcton W Susx	14	SU8802
Runcton Holme Norfk	65	TF6109
Runfold Surrey	25	SU8647
Runhall Norfk	66	TG0507
Runham Norfk	67	TG4610
Runham Norfk	67	TG5108
Runnington Somset	20	ST1221
Runsell Green Essex	40	TL7905
Runshaw Moor Lancs	80	SD5319
Runswick N York	97	NZ8016
Runtaleave Angus	133	NO2867
Runwell Essex	40	TQ7594
Ruscombe Berks	37	SU7976
Rush Green Ches	79	SJ6987
Rush Green Essex	41	TM1515
Rush Green Gt Lon	27	TQ5187
Rush Green Herts	39	TL2123
Rush Green Herts	39	TL3325
Rushall H & W	47	SO6435
Rushall Norfk	55	TM1982
Rushall W Mids	60	SK0200
Rushall Wilts	23	SU1255
Rushbrooke Suffk	54	TL8961
Rushbury Shrops	59	SO5191
Rushden Herts	39	TL3031
Rushden Nhants	51	SP9566
Rushenden Kent	28	TQ9071
Rusher's Cross E Susx	16	TQ6028
Rushett Common Surrey	14	TQ0242
Rushford Devon	5	SX4576
Rushford Norfk	54	TL9281
Rushlake Green E Susx	16	TQ6218
Rushmere Suffk	55	TM4986
Rushmere St Andrew Suffk	55	TM1946
Rushmoor Surrey	25	SU8740
Rushock H & W	46	SO3058
Rushock H & W	60	SO8871
Rusholme Gt Man	79	SJ8594
Rushton Ches	71	SJ5863
Rushton Nhants	51	SP8482
Rushton Shrops	59	SJ6008
Rushton Spencer Staffs	72	SJ9362
Rushwick H & W	47	SO8254
Rushyford Dur	96	NZ2728
Ruskie Stirlg	116	NN6200
Ruskington Lincs	76	TF0851
Rusland Cumb	87	SD3488
Rusper W Susx	15	TQ2037
Ruspidge Gloucs	35	SO6611
Russ Hill Surrey	15	TQ2240
Russel's Green Suffk	55	TM2572
Russell Green Essex	40	TL7413
Russell's Green E Susx	16	TQ7011
Russell's Water Oxon	37	SU7089
Rusthall Kent	16	TQ5639
Rustington W Susx	14	TQ0402
Ruston N York	91	SE9583
Ruston Parva E R Yk	91	TA0661
Ruswarp N York	90	NZ8809
Ruthall Shrops	59	SO5990
Rutherford Border	110	NT6430
Rutherglen S Lans	116	NS6161
Ruthernbridge Cnwll	4	SX0166
Ruthin Denbgs	70	SJ1258
Ruthrieston Aber C	135	NJ9204
Ruthven Abers	142	NJ5046
Ruthven Angus	126	NO2848
Ruthven Highld	140	NH8132
Ruthven Highld	132	NN7699
Ruthven House Angus	126	NO3047
Ruthvoes Cnwll	4	SW9260
Ruthwaite Cumb	93	NY2336
Ruthwell D & G	100	NY0967
Ruxley Corner Gt Lon	27	TQ4770
Ruxton Green H & W	34	SO5419
Ruyton-XI-Towns Shrops	59	SJ3922
Ryal Nthumb	103	NZ0174
Ryall Dorset	10	SY4095
Ryall H & W	47	SO8640
Ryarsh Kent	28	TQ6660
Rycote Oxon	37	SP6705
Rydal Cumb	87	NY3606
Ryde IOW	13	SZ5992
Rye E Susx	17	TQ9220
Rye Cross H & W	47	SO7735
Rye Foreign E Susx	17	TQ8922
Rye Harbour E Susx	17	TQ9319
Rye Street H & W	47	SO7835
Ryebank Shrops	59	SJ5131
Ryeford H & W	35	SO6322
Ryehill E R Yk	85	TA2225
Ryeish Green Nhants	24	SU7267
Ryhall Rutlnd	64	TF0310
Ryhill W York	83	SE3814
Ryhope T & W	96	NZ4152
Rylah Derbys	75	SK4667
Ryland Lincs	76	TF0179
Rylands Notts	62	SK5335
Rylstone N York	88	SD9658
Ryme Intrinseca Dorset	10	ST5810
Ryther N York	83	SE5539
Ryton N York	90	SE7975
Ryton Shrops	60	SJ7602
Ryton T & W	103	NZ1564
Ryton Warwks	61	SP4086

Ryton Woodside
Scorborough

Ryton Woodside *T & W* 96 NZ1462
Ryton-on-Dunsmore *Warwks* 61 SP3874

S

Sabden *Lancs* 81 SD7837
Sabine's Green *Essex* 27 TQ5496
Sacombe *Herts* 39 TL3319
Sacombe Green *Herts* 39 TL3419
Sacriston *Dur* 96 NZ2447
Sadberge *Dur* 96 NZ3416
Saddell *Ag & B* 105 NR7832
Saddington *Leics* 50 SP6691
Saddle Bow *Norfk* 65 TF6015
Saddlescombe *W Susx* 15 TQ2711
Sadgill *Cumb* 87 NY4805
Saffron Walden *Essex* 39 TL5438
Sageston *Pembks* 30 SN0503
Saham Hills *Norfk* 66 TF9003
Saham Toney *Norfk* 66 TF8901
Saighton *Ches* 71 SJ4462
St Abbs *Border* 119 NT9167
St Agnes *Border* 118 NT6763
St Agnes *Cnwll* 2 SW7150
St Albans *Herts* 38 TL1407
St Allen *Cnwll* 3 SW8250
St Andrew *Guern* 152 GN0000
St Andrew's Major *V Glam* 33 ST1371
St Andrews *Fife* 127 NO5116
St Andrews Well *Dorset* 10 SY4793
St Ann's *D & G* 100 NY0793
St Ann's Chapel *Cnwll* 5 SX4170
St Ann's Chapel *Devon* 7 SX6647
St Anne's *Lancs* 80 SD3228
St Anthony *Cnwll* 3 SW7825
St Anthony's Hill *E Susx* 16 TQ6201
St Arvans *Mons* 34 ST5296
St Asaph *Denbgs* 70 SJ0374
St Athan *V Glam* 20 ST0167
St Aubin *Jersey* 152 JS0000
St Austell *Cnwll* 3 SX0152
St Bees *Cumb* 86 NX9711
St Blazey *Cnwll* 3 SX0654
St Blazey Gate *Cnwll* 3 SX0653
St Boswells *Border* 110 NT5930
St Brelade *Jersey* 152 JS0000
St Brelades Bay *Jersey* 152 JS0000
St Breock *Cnwll* 4 SW9771
St Breward *Cnwll* 4 SX0977
St Briavels *Gloucs* 34 SO5604
St Bride's Major *V Glam* 33 SS8974
St Brides *Pembks* 30 SM8010
St Brides Netherwent *Mons* 34 ST4289
St Brides super-Ely *Cardif* 33 ST0977
St Brides Wentlooge *Newpt* 34 ST2982
St Budeaux *Devon* 6 SX4558
St Buryan *Cnwll* 2 SW4025
St Catherine *Somset* 35 ST7769
St Catherines *Ag & B* 123 NN1207
St Chloe *Gloucs* 35 SO8401
St Clears *Carmth* 31 SN2816
St Cleer *Cnwll* 5 SX2468
St Clement *Cnwll* 3 SW8543
St Clement *Jersey* 152 JS0000
St Clether *Cnwll* 5 SX2084
St Colmac *Ag & B* 114 NS0467
St Columb Major *Cnwll* 4 SW9163
St Columb Minor *Cnwll* 4 SW8362
St Columb Road *Cnwll* 4 SW9159
St Combs *Abers* 143 NK0563
St Cross South Elmham *Suffk* 55 TM2984
St Cyrus *Abers* 135 NO7464
St David's *P & K* 125 NN9420
St Davids *Pembks* 30 SM7525
St Day *Cnwll* 3 SW7242
St Decumans *Somset* 20 ST0642
St Dennis *Cnwll* 4 SW9557
St Devereux *H & W* 46 SO4431
St Dogmaels *Cardgn* 42 SN1645
St Dogwells *Pembks* 30 SM9727
St Dominick *Cnwll* 5 SX4067
St Donats *V Glam* 20 SS9368
St Edith's Marsh *Wilts* 22 ST9764
St Endellion *Cnwll* 4 SW9978
St Enoder *Cnwll* 3 SW8956
St Erme *Cnwll* 3 SW8449
St Erney *Cnwll* 5 SX3759
St Erth *Cnwll* 2 SW5535
St Erth Praze *Cnwll* 2 SW5735
St Ervan *Cnwll* 4 SW8970
St Ewe *Cnwll* 3 SW9746
St Fagans *Cardif* 33 ST1277
St Fergus *Abers* 143 NK0952
St Fillans *P & K* 124 NN6924
St Florence *Pembks* 31 SN0801
St Gennys *Cnwll* 4 SX1497
St George *A & C* 70 SH9775
St George's *V Glam* 33 ST1076
St George's Hill *Surrey* 26 TQ0862
St Georges *Somset* 21 ST3762
St Germans *Cnwll* 5 SX3657
St Giles in the Wood *Devon* 19 SS5319
St Giles-on-the-Heath *Cnwll* 5 SX3690
St Harmon *Powys* 45 SN9872
St Helen Auckland *Dur* 96 NZ1826
St Helena *Norfk* 66 TG1816
St Helens *Cumb* 92 NY0232
St Helens *E Susx* 17 TQ8212
St Helens *IOW* 13 SZ6289
St Helens *Mersyd* 78 SJ5195
St Helier *Gt Lon* 27 TQ2567
St Helier *Jersey* 152 JS0000
St Hilary *Cnwll* 2 SW5431
St Hilary *V Glam* 33 ST0173
St Hill *Devon* 9 ST0908
St Hill *W Susx* 15 TQ3835
St Illtyd *Blae G* 34 SO2202
St Ippollitts *Herts* 39 TL1927
St Ishmaels *Pembks* 30 SM8307
St Issey *Cnwll* 4 SW9271
St Ive *Cnwll* 5 SX3167
St Ives *Cambs* 52 TL3171
St Ives *Cnwll* 2 SW5140
St Ives *Dorset* 12 SU1204
St Jame's End *Nhants* 49 SP7460
St James *Norfk* 67 TG2720
St James South Elmham *Suffk* 55 TM3281
St John *Cnwll* 5 SX4053
St John *Jersey* 152 JS0000
St John's *IOM* 153 SC2781
St John's Chapel *Devon* 19 SS5329
St John's Chapel *Dur* 95 NY8837
St John's Fen End *Norfk* 65 TF5312
St John's Highway *Norfk* 65 TF5214
St John's Kirk *S Lans* 108 NS9836
St John's Town of Dalry *D & G* 99 NX6281
St John's Wood *Gt Lon* 27 TQ2683
St Johns *Dur* 95 NZ0633
St Johns *H & W* 47 SO8454
St Johns *Kent* 27 TQ5356
St Johns *Surrey* 25 SU9857
St Jude's *IOM* 153 SC3996
St Just *Cnwll* 2 SW3731
St Just Lane *Cnwll* 3 SW8535
St Just-in-Roseland *Cnwll* 3 SW8435
St Katherines *Abers* 142 NJ7834
St Keverne *Cnwll* 3 SW7921
St Kew *Cnwll* 4 SX0276
St Kew Highway *Cnwll* 4 SX0375
St Keyne *Cnwll* 5 SX2461
St Laurence *Kent* 29 TR3665
St Lawrence *Cnwll* 4 SX0466
St Lawrence *Essex* 41 TL9604
St Lawrence *IOW* 13 SZ5376
St Lawrence *Jersey* 152 JS0000
St Leonard's Street *Kent* 28 TQ6756
St Leonards *Bucks* 38 SP9007
St Leonards *Dorset* 12 SU1103
St Leonards *E Susx* 17 TQ8009
St Levan *Cnwll* 2 SW3822
St Lythans *V Glam* 33 ST1072
St Mabyn *Cnwll* 4 SX0473
St Madoes *P & K* 126 NO1921
St Margaret South Elmham *Suffk* 55 TM3183
St Margaret's at Cliffe *Kent* 29 TR3544
St Margarets *H & W* 46 SO3533
St Margarets *Herts* 39 TL3811
St Margarets Hope *Ork* 155 ND4493
St Marks *IOM* 153 SC2974
St Martin *Cnwll* 5 SX2555
St Martin *Guern* 152 GN0000
St Martin *Jersey* 152 JS0000
St Martin's *P & K* 126 NO1530
St Martin's Green *Cnwll* 3 SW7323
St Martin's Moor *Shrops* 59 SJ3135
St Martins *Shrops* 59 SJ3236
St Mary *Jersey* 152 JS0000
St Mary Bourne *Hants* 24 SU4250
St Mary Church *V Glam* 33 ST0071
St Mary Cray *Gt Lon* 27 TQ4768
St Mary Hill *V Glam* 33 SS9678
St Mary in the Marsh *Kent* 17 TR0627
St Mary's *Ork* 155 HY4701
St Mary's Bay *Kent* 17 TR0827
St Mary's Grove *Somset* 21 ST4669
St Mary's Hoo *Kent* 28 TQ8076
St Marychurch *Devon* 7 SX9166
St Maughans *Mons* 34 SO4617
St Maughans Green *Mons* 34 SO4717
St Mawes *Cnwll* 3 SW8433
St Mawgan *Cnwll* 4 SW8765
St Mellion *Cnwll* 5 SX3965
St Mellons *Cardif* 34 ST2281
St Merryn *Cnwll* 4 SW8874
St Mewan *Cnwll* 3 SW9951
St Michael Caerhays *Cnwll* 3 SW9642
St Michael Church *Somset* 20 ST3030
St Michael Penkevil *Cnwll* 3 SW8541
St Michael South Elmham *Suffk* 55 TM3483
St Michael's on Wyre *Lancs* 80 SD4641
St Michaels *H & W* 46 SO5865
St Michaels *Kent* 17 TQ8835
St Minver *Cnwll* 4 SW9677
St Monans *Fife* 127 NO5201
St Neot *Cnwll* 4 SX1868
St Neots *Cambs* 52 TL1860
St Newlyn East *Cnwll* 3 SW8256
St Nicholas *Pembks* 30 SM9035
St Nicholas *V Glam* 33 ST0974
St Nicholas at Wade *Kent* 29 TR2666
St Ninians *Stirlg* 116 NS7991
St Olaves *Norfk* 67 TM4599
St Osyth *Essex* 41 TM1215
St Ouen *Jersey* 152 JS0000
St Owens Cross *H & W* 46 SO5324
St Paul's Walden *Herts* 39 TL1922
St Pauls Cray *Gt Lon* 27 TQ4768
St Peter *Jersey* 152 JS0000
St Peter Port *Guern* 152 GN0000
St Peter's *Guern* 152 GN0000
St Peter's *Kent* 29 TR3868
St Peter's Hill *Cambs* 52 TL2372
St Petrox *Pembks* 30 SR9797
St Pinnock *Cnwll* 5 SX2063
St Quivox *S Ayrs* 106 NS3723
St Ruan *Cnwll* 2 SW7115
St Sampson *Guern* 152 GN0000
St Saviour *Guern* 152 GN0000
St Saviour *Jersey* 152 JS0000
St Stephen *Cnwll* 3 SW9453
St Stephen's Coombe *Cnwll* 3 SW9451
St Stephens *Cnwll* 5 SX3285
St Stephens *Cnwll* 5 SX4158
St Teath *Cnwll* 4 SX0680
St Tudy *Cnwll* 4 SX0676
St Twynnells *Pembks* 30 SR9597
St Veep *Cnwll* 3 SX1455
St Vigeans *Angus* 127 NO6443
St Wenn *Cnwll* 4 SW9664
St Weonards *H & W* 46 SO4924
Saintbury *Gloucs* 48 SP1139
Salachail *Ag & B* 123 NN0551
Salcombe *Devon* 7 SX7439
Salcombe Regis *Devon* 9 SY1588
Salcott *Essex* 40 TL9413
Sale *Gt Man* 79 SJ7991
Sale Green *H & W* 47 SO9358
Saleby *Lincs* 77 TF4578
Salehurst *E Susx* 17 TQ7524
Salem *Cardgn* 43 SN6684
Salem *Carmth* 44 SN6226
Salem *Gwynd* 69 SH5456
Salen *Ag & B* 121 NM5743
Salen *Highld* 121 NM6864
Salesbury *Lancs* 81 SD6832
Salford *Beds* 38 SP9339
Salford *Gt Man* 79 SJ8197
Salford *Oxon* 48 SP2828
Salford Priors *Warwks* 48 SP0751
Salfords *Surrey* 15 TQ2846
Salhouse *Norfk* 67 TG3114
Saline *Fife* 117 NT0292
Salisbury *Wilts* 23 SU1429
Salkeld Dykes *Cumb* 94 NY5437
Salle *Norfk* 66 TG1024
Salmonby *Lincs* 77 TF3273
Salperton *Gloucs* 36 SP0720
Salph End *Beds* 38 TL0852
Salsburgh *N Lans* 116 NS8262
Salt *Staffs* 72 SJ9527
Salt Cotes *Cumb* 93 NY1853
Salta *Cumb* 92 NY0845
Saltaire *W York* 82 SE1438
Saltash *Cnwll* 6 SX4258
Saltburn *Highld* 146 NH7270
Saltburn-by-the-Sea *N York* 97 NZ6621
Saltby *Leics* 63 SK8526
Saltcoats *Cumb* 86 SD0797
Saltcoats *N Ayrs* 106 NS2441
Saltcotes *Lancs* 80 SD3728
Saltdean *E Susx* 15 TQ3802
Salterbeck *Cumb* 92 NX9926
Salterforth *Lancs* 81 SD8845
Salterswall *Ches* 71 SJ6266
Salterton *Wilts* 23 SU1236
Saltfleet *Lincs* 77 TF4593
Saltfleetby All Saints *Lincs* 77 TF4590
Saltfleetby St Clements *Lincs* 77 TF4691
Saltfleetby St Peter *Lincs* 77 TF4489
Saltford *Somset* 22 ST6867
Salthouse *Norfk* 66 TG0743
Saltley *W Mids* 61 SP1088
Saltmarsh *Newpt* 34 ST3482
Saltmarshe *E R Yk* 84 SE7824
Saltney *Flints* 71 SJ3865
Salton *N York* 90 SE7179
Saltrens *Devon* 18 SS4522
Saltwick *Nthumb* 103 NZ1780
Saltwood *Kent* 29 TR1535
Salvington *W Susx* 14 TQ1205
Salwarpe *H & W* 47 SO8762
Salwayash *Dorset* 10 SY4596
Sambourne *Warwks* 48 SP0662
Sambrook *Shrops* 72 SJ7124
Samlesbury *Lancs* 81 SD5930
Samlesbury Bottoms *Lancs* 81 SD6228
Sampford Arundel *Somset* 20 ST1118
Sampford Brett *Somset* 20 ST0741
Sampford Courtenay *Devon* 8 SS6301
Sampford Moor *Somset* 20 ST1118
Sampford Peverell *Devon* 9 ST0314
Sampford Spiney *Devon* 6 SX5372
Samson's Corner *Essex* 41 TM0818
Samsonlane *Ork* 155 HY6526
Samuelston *E Loth* 118 NT4870
Sanaigmore *Ag & B* 112 NR2370
Sancreed *Cnwll* 2 SW4129
Sancton *E R Yk* 84 SE8939
Sand *Somset* 21 ST4346
Sand Cross *E Susx* 16 TQ5820
Sand Hills *W York* 83 SE3739
Sand Hole *E R Yk* 84 SE8137
Sand Hutton *N York* 90 SE6958
Sand Side *Cumb* 86 SD2282
Sandaig *Highld* 129 NG7102
Sandal Magna *W York* 83 SE3417
Sandale *Cumb* 93 NY2440
Sandavore *Highld* 128 NM4785
Sandbach *Ches* 72 SJ7560
Sandbank *Ag & B* 114 NS1680
Sandbanks *Dorset* 12 SZ0487
Sandend *Abers* 142 NJ5566
Sanderstead *Gt Lon* 27 TQ3461
Sandford *Cumb* 94 NY7316
Sandford *Devon* 8 SS8202
Sandford *Dorset* 11 SY9289
Sandford *Hants* 12 SU1601
Sandford *IOW* 13 SZ5381
Sandford *S Lans* 107 NS7143
Sandford *Shrops* 59 SJ3423
Sandford *Shrops* 59 SJ5833
Sandford *Somset* 21 ST4259
Sandford Orcas *Dorset* 21 ST6220
Sandford St Martin *Oxon* 49 SP4226
Sandford-on-Thames *Oxon* 37 SP5301
Sandgate *Kent* 29 TR2035
Sandhaven *Abers* 143 NJ9667
Sandhead *D & G* 98 NX0949
Sandhill *S York* 75 SK4496
Sandhills *Dorset* 10 ST5800
Sandhills *Dorset* 11 ST6810
Sandhills *Oxon* 37 SP5507
Sandhills *Surrey* 14 SU9337
Sandhills *W Mids* 61 SK0604
Sandhoe *Nthumb* 102 NY9666
Sandhole *Ag & B* 114 NS0098
Sandholme *Lincs* 64 TF3337
Sandholme *E R Yk* 84 SE8230
Sandhurst *Berks* 25 SU8361
Sandhurst *Gloucs* 47 SO8223
Sandhurst *Kent* 17 TQ8028
Sandhurst Cross *Kent* 17 TQ7827
Sandhutton *N York* 89 SE3881
Sandiacre *Derbys* 62 SK4736
Sandilands *Lincs* 77 TF5280
Sandiway *Ches* 71 SJ6070
Sandleheath *Hants* 12 SU1215
Sandleigh *Oxon* 37 SP4701
Sandley *Dorset* 22 ST7724
Sandling *Kent* 28 TQ7557
Sandlow Green *Ches* 72 SJ7865
Sandness *Shet* 155 HU1957
Sandon *Essex* 40 TL7404
Sandon *Herts* 39 TL3234
Sandon *Staffs* 72 SJ9429
Sandon Bank *Staffs* 72 SJ9428
Sandown *IOW* 13 SZ5984
Sandplace *Cnwll* 5 SX2557
Sandridge *Herts* 39 TL1710
Sandridge *Wilts* 22 ST9465
Sandringham *Norfk* 65 TF6928
Sands *Bucks* 26 SU8493
Sandsend *N York* 90 NZ8612
Sandside *Cumb* 87 SD4780
Sandtoft *Lincs* 84 SE7408
Sandway *Kent* 28 TQ8950
Sandwich *Kent* 29 TR3358
Sandwick *Cumb* 93 NY4219
Sandwick *Shet* 155 HU4323
Sandwick *W Isls* 154 NB4432
Sandwith *Cumb* 92 NX9614
Sandwith Newtown *Cumb* 92 NX9614
Sandy *Beds* 52 TL1649
Sandy Bank *Lincs* 77 TF2655
Sandy Cross *H & W* 47 SO6757
Sandy Haven *Pembks* 30 SM8507
Sandy Lane *W York* 82 SE1135
Sandy Lane *Wilts* 22 ST9668
Sandy Lane *Wrexhm* 71 SJ4040
Sandy Park *Devon* 8 SX7189
Sandycroft *Flints* 71 SJ3366
Sandyford *D & G* 101 NY2093
Sandygate *Devon* 7 SX8674
Sandygate *IOM* 153 SC3797
Sandyhills *D & G* 92 NX8855
Sandylands *Lancs* 87 SD4263
Sandylane *Staffs* 72 SJ7035
Sandylane *Swans* 32 SS5589
Sandyway *H & W* 46 SO4925
Sangobeg *Highld* 149 NC4266
Sangomore *Highld* 149 NC4067
Sankey Bridges *Ches* 78 SJ5887
Sankyn's Green *H & W* 47 SO7965
Sanna Bay *Highld* 128 NM4469
Sanndabhaig *W Isls* 154 NB4432
Sannox *N Ayrs* 105 NS0145
Sanquhar *D & G* 107 NS7809
Santon *Cumb* 86 NY1001
Santon *IOM* 153 SC3273
Santon Bridge *Cumb* 86 NY1101
Santon Downham *Suffk* 54 TL8187
Sapcote *Leics* 50 SP4893
Sapey Common *H & W* 47 SO7064
Sapiston *Suffk* 54 TL9175
Sapley *Cambs* 52 TL2474
Sapperton *Derbys* 73 SK1834
Sapperton *Gloucs* 35 SO9403
Sapperton *Lincs* 64 TF0133
Saracen's Head *Lincs* 64 TF3427
Sarclet *Highld* 151 ND3443
Sarisbury *Hants* 13 SU5008
Sarn *Brdgnd* 33 SS9083
Sarn *Gwynd* 56 SH2432
Sarn *Powys* 58 SN9597
Sarn *Powys* 58 SO2090
Sarn-bach *Gwynd* 56 SH3026
Sarn-wen *Powys* 58 SJ2718
Sarnau *Cardgn* 42 SN3150
Sarnau *Carmth* 31 SN3318
Sarnau *Gwynd* 70 SH9639
Sarnau *Powys* 58 SJ2315
Sarnau *Powys* 45 SO0232
Sarnesfield *H & W* 46 SO3750
Saron *Carmth* 31 SN3737
Saron *Carmth* 32 SN6012
Saron *Gwynd* 69 SH5365
Saron *Gwynd* 68 SH4658
Sarratt *Herts* 26 TQ0499
Sarre *Kent* 29 TR2565
Sarsden *Oxon* 36 SP2822
Sarson *Hants* 23 SU3044
Satley *Dur* 95 NZ1143
Satmar *Kent* 29 TR2539
Satron *N York* 88 SD9397
Satterleigh *Devon* 19 SS6622
Satterthwaite *Cumb* 86 SD3392
Satwell *Oxon* 37 SU7083
Sauchen *Abers* 135 NJ7011
Saucher *P & K* 126 NO1933
Sauchieburn *Abers* 135 NO6669
Saul *Gloucs* 35 SO7409
Saundby *Notts* 75 SK7888
Saundersfoot *Pembks* 31 SN1304
Saunderton *Bucks* 37 SP7901
Saunton *Devon* 18 SS4637
Sausthorpe *Lincs* 77 TF3868
Saveock Water *Cnwll* 3 SW7645
Saverley Green *Staffs* 72 SJ9638
Savile Town *W York* 82 SE2420
Sawbridge *Warwks* 50 SP5065
Sawbridgeworth *Herts* 39 TL4814
Sawdon *N York* 91 SE9485
Sawley *Derbys* 62 SK4631
Sawley *Lancs* 81 SD7746
Sawley *N York* 89 SE2467
Sawston *Cambs* 53 TL4849
Sawtry *Cambs* 52 TL1683
Saxby *Leics* 63 SK8219
Saxby *Lincs* 76 TF0086
Saxby All Saints *Lincs* 84 SE9816
Saxelbye *Leics* 63 SK6921
Saxham Street *Suffk* 54 TM0861
Saxilby *Lincs* 76 SK8975
Saxlingham *Norfk* 66 TG0239
Saxlingham Green *Norfk* 67 TM2396
Saxlingham Nethergate *Norfk* 67 TM2297
Saxlingham Thorpe *Norfk* 67 TM2197
Saxmundham *Suffk* 55 TM3863
Saxon Street *Cambs* 53 TL6759
Saxondale *Notts* 63 SK6839
Saxtead *Suffk* 55 TM2665
Saxtead Green *Suffk* 55 TM2564
Saxtead Little Green *Suffk* 55 TM2466
Saxthorpe *Norfk* 66 TG1130
Saxton *N York* 83 SE4736
Sayers Common *W Susx* 15 TQ2618
Scackleton *N York* 90 SE6472
Scaftworth *Notts* 75 SK6691
Scagglethorpe *N York* 90 SE8372
Scalasaig *Ag & B* 112 NR3993
Scalby *E R Yk* 84 SE8429
Scalby *N York* 91 TA0090
Scald End *Beds* 51 TL0457
Scaldwell *Nhants* 50 SP7672
Scale Houses *Cumb* 94 NY5845
Scaleby *Cumb* 101 NY4463
Scalebyhill *Cumb* 101 NY4463
Scales *Cumb* 93 NY3426
Scales *Cumb* 86 SD2772
Scales *Lancs* 80 SD4531
Scalesceugh *Cumb* 93 NY4449
Scalford *Leics* 63 SK7624
Scaling *N York* 90 NZ7413
Scaling Dam *N York* 90 NZ7412
Scalloway *Shet* 155 HU4039
Scamblesby *Lincs* 77 TF2778
Scammonden *W York* 82 SE0515
Scamodale *Highld* 129 NM8373
Scampston *N York* 90 SE8575
Scampton *Lincs* 76 SK9579
Scaniport *Highld* 140 NH6239
Scapegoat Hill *W York* 82 SE0916
Scarborough *N York* 91 TA0488
Scarcewater *Cnwll* 3 SW9154
Scarcliffe *Derbys* 75 SK4968
Scarcroft *W York* 83 SE3541
Scarcroft Hill *W York* 83 SE3741
Scarfskerry *Highld* 151 ND2674
Scargill *Dur* 88 NZ0510
Scarinish *Ag & B* 120 NM0444
Scarisbrick *Lancs* 80 SD3713
Scarness *Cumb* 93 NY2230
Scarning *Norfk* 66 TF9512
Scarrington *Notts* 63 SK7341
Scarth Hill *Lancs* 78 SD4206
Scarthingwell *N York* 83 SE4937
Scartho *Lincs* 85 TA2606
Scawby *Lincs* 84 SE9605
Scawsby *S York* 83 SE5404
Scawthorpe *S York* 83 SE5506
Scawton *N York* 90 SE5483
Scayne's Hill *W Susx* 15 TQ3623
Scethrog *Powys* 45 SO1025
Scholar Green *Staffs* 56 SJ8356
Scholar Green *Staffs* 72 SJ8357
Scholes *Gt Man* 78 SD5905
Scholes *S York* 74 SK3895
Scholes *W York* 82 SE1507
Scholes *W York* 82 SE1625
Scholes *W York* 83 SE3736
Scholey Hill *W York* 83 SE3825
School Aycliffe *Dur* 96 NZ2523
School Green *Ches* 72 SJ6464
School Green *W York* 82 SE1132
School House *Dorset* 10 ST3602
Schoolgreen *Berks* 24 SU7367
Scissett *W York* 82 SE2410
Scleddau *Pembks* 30 SM9434
Sco Ruston *Norfk* 67 TG2821
Scofton *Notts* 75 SK6280
Scole *Norfk* 54 TM1579
Sconser *Highld* 137 NG5132
Scoonie *Fife* 126 NO3801
Scopwick *Lincs* 76 TF0757
Scoraig *Highld* 144 NH0096
Scorborough *E R Yk* 84 TA0145

Sutcombemill
Thearne

Sutcombemill *Devon* 18 SS3411
Suton *Norfk* 66 TM0999
Sutterby *Lincs* 77 TF3872
Sutterton *Lincs* 64 TF2835
Sutton *Beds* 52 TL2247
Sutton *Cambs* 51 TL0998
Sutton *Cambs* 53 TL4479
Sutton *Devon* 8 SS7202
Sutton *Devon* 7 SX7042
Sutton *E Susx* 16 TV4999
Sutton *Gt Lon* 27 TQ2564
Sutton *Kent* 29 TR3349
Sutton *Mersyd* 78 SJ5393
Sutton *N York* 83 SE4925
Sutton *Norfk* 67 TG3823
Sutton *Notts* 75 SK6784
Sutton *Notts* 63 SK7637
Sutton *Oxon* 36 SP4106
Sutton *Pembks* 30 SM9115
Sutton *S York* 83 SE5512
Sutton *Shrops* 59 SJ3527
Sutton *Shrops* 59 SJ5010
Sutton *Shrops* 72 SJ6631
Sutton *Shrops* 60 SO7386
Sutton *Staffs* 72 SJ7622
Sutton *Suffk* 55 TM3046
Sutton *W Susx* 14 SU9715
Sutton at Hone *Kent* 27 TQ5569
Sutton Bassett *Nhants* 50 SP7790
Sutton Benger *Wilts* 35 ST9478
Sutton Bingham *Somset* 10 ST5410
Sutton Bonington *Notts* 62 SK5024
Sutton Bridge *Lincs* 65 TF4721
Sutton Cheney *Leics* 50 SK4100
Sutton Coldfield *W Mids* 61 SP1295
Sutton Courtenay *Oxon* 37 SU5094
Sutton Crosses *Lincs* 65 TF4321
Sutton Fields *Notts* 62 SK4926
Sutton Grange *N York* 89 SE2873
Sutton Green *Oxon* 36 SP4107
Sutton Green *Surrey* 25 TQ0054
Sutton Green *Wrexhm* 71 SJ4048
Sutton Howgrave *N York* 89 SE3179
Sutton in Ashfield *Notts* 75 SK4958
Sutton in the Elms *Leics* 50 SP5193
Sutton Lane Ends *Ches* 79 SJ9270
Sutton Maddock *Shrops* 60 SJ7201
Sutton Mallet *Somset* 21 ST3736
Sutton Mandeville *Wilts* 22 ST9828
Sutton Manor *Mersyd* 78 SJ5190
Sutton Marsh *H & W* 46 SO5544
Sutton Montis *Somset* 21 ST6224
Sutton on Sea *Lincs* 77 TF5281
Sutton on the Hill *Derbys* 73 SK2333
Sutton on Trent *Notts* 75 SK7965
Sutton Poyntz *Dorset* 11 SY7083
Sutton Scansdale *Derbys* 75 SK4468
Sutton Scotney *Hants* 24 SU4639
Sutton St Edmund *Lincs* 64 TF3613
Sutton St James *Lincs* 65 TF3918
Sutton St Nicholas *H & W* 46 SO5245
Sutton Street *Kent* 28 TQ8055
Sutton upon Derwent *E R Yk* 84 SE7047
Sutton Valence *Kent* 28 TQ8149
Sutton Veny *Wilts* 22 ST9041
Sutton Waldron *Dorset* 11 ST8615
Sutton Weaver *Ches* 71 SJ5479
Sutton Wick *Oxon* 37 SU4894
Sutton Wick *Somset* 21 ST5759
Sutton-in-Craven *N York* 82 SE0043
Sutton-on-Hull *E R Yk* 85 TA1232
Sutton-on-the-Forest *N York* 90 SE5864
Sutton-under-Brailes *Warwks* 48 SP3037
Sutton-under-Whitestonecliffe *N York* 90 SE4882
Swaby *Lincs* 77 TF3877
Swadlincote *Derbys* 73 SK2919
Swaffham *Norfk* 66 TF8108
Swaffham Bulbeck *Cambs* 53 TL5562
Swaffham Prior *Cambs* 53 TL5764
Swafield *Norfk* 67 TG2832
Swainby *N York* 89 NZ4701
Swainshill *H & W* 46 SO4641
Swainsthorpe *Norfk* 67 TG2101
Swainswick *Somset* 22 ST7668
Swalcliffe *Oxon* 48 SP3737
Swalecliffe *Kent* 29 TR1367
Swallow *Lincs* 85 TA1703
Swallow Beck *Lincs* 76 SK9467
Swallow Nest *S York* 75 SK4585
Swallowcliffe *Wilts* 22 ST9627
Swallowfield *Berks* 24 SU7264
Swallows Cross *Essex* 40 TQ6198
Swampton *Hants* 24 SU4150
Swan Green *Ches* 79 SJ7373
Swan Street *Essex* 40 TL8927
Swan Village *W Mids* 60 SO9892
Swanage *Dorset* 12 SZ0378
Swanbourne *Bucks* 38 SP8026
Swanbridge *V Glam* 20 ST1667
Swancote *Shrops* 60 SO7494
Swanland *E R Yk* 84 SE9928
Swanley *Kent* 27 TQ5168
Swanley Village *Kent* 27 TQ5369
Swanmore *Hants* 13 SU5716
Swannington *Leics* 62 SK4116
Swannington *Norfk* 66 TG1319
Swanpool Garden Suberb *Lincs* 76 SK9569
Swanscombe *Kent* 27 TQ6074
Swansea *Swans* 32 SS6592
Swanton Abbot *Norfk* 67 TG2625
Swanton Morley *Norfk* 66 TG0117
Swanton Novers *Norfk* 66 TG0231
Swanton Street *Kent* 28 TQ8759
Swanwick *Derbys* 74 SK4053
Swanwick *Hants* 13 SU5109
Swarby *Lincs* 64 TF0440
Swardeston *Norfk* 67 TG2002
Swarkestone *Derbys* 62 SK3728
Swarland *Nthumb* 103 NU1602
Swarland Estate *Nthumb* 103 NU1603
Swarraton *Hants* 24 SU5636
Swartha *W York* 82 SE0546
Swarthmoor *Cumb* 86 SD2777
Swaton *Lincs* 64 TF1337
Swavesey *Cambs* 52 TL3668
Sway *Hants* 12 SZ2798
Swayfield *Lincs* 63 SK9922
Swaythling *Hants* 13 SU4416
Sweet Green *H & W* 47 SO6462
Sweetham *Devon* 9 SX8899
Sweethaws *E Susx* 16 TQ5028
Sweetlands Corner *Kent* 28 TQ7845
Sweets *Cnwll* 4 SX1595
Sweetshouse *Cnwll* 4 SX0861
Swefling *Suffk* 55 TM3463
Swepstone *Leics* 62 SK3610
Swerford *Oxon* 48 SP3731
Swettenham *Ches* 72 SJ8067
Swffryd *Blae G* 33 ST2198
Swift's Green *Kent* 28 TQ8744
Swiftsden *E Susx* 17 TQ7328
Swilland *Suffk* 54 TM1852
Swillbrook *Lancs* 80 SD4834
Swillington *W York* 83 SE3830
Swimbridge *Devon* 19 SS6230
Swimbridge Newland *Devon* 19 SS6030
Swinbrook *Oxon* 36 SP2812
Swincliffe *N York* 89 SE2458
Swincliffe *W York* 82 SE2027
Swincombe *Devon* 19 SS6941
Swinden *N York* 81 SD8554
Swinderby *Lincs* 76 SK8663
Swindon *Gloucs* 47 SO9325
Swindon *Nthumb* 102 NY9799
Swindon *Staffs* 60 SO8690
Swindon *Wilts* 36 SU1484
Swine *E R Yk* 85 TA1335
Swinefleet *E R Yk* 84 SE7621
Swineford *Gloucs* 35 ST6969
Swineshead *Beds* 51 TL0565
Swineshead *Lincs* 64 TF2340
Swineshead Bridge *Lincs* 64 TF2242
Swiney *Highld* 151 ND2335
Swinford *Leics* 50 SP5679
Swinford *Oxon* 37 SP4408
Swingfield Minnis *Kent* 29 TR2142
Swingfield Street *Kent* 29 TR2343
Swingleton Green *Suffk* 54 TL9647
Swinhill *S Lans* 116 NS7748
Swinhoe *Nthumb* 111 NU2128
Swinhope *Lincs* 76 TF2196
Swinithwaite *N York* 88 SE0489
Swinmore Common *H & W* 47 SO6741
Swinscoe *Staffs* 73 SK1247
Swinside *Cumb* 93 NY2421
Swinstead *Lincs* 64 TF0122
Swinthorpe *Lincs* 76 TF0680
Swinton *Border* 110 NT8347
Swinton *Gt Man* 79 SD7701
Swinton *N York* 89 SE2179
Swinton *N York* 90 SE7573
Swinton *S York* 75 SK4599
Swithland *Leics* 62 SK5512
Swordale *Highld* 139 NH5765
Swordland *Highld* 129 NM7891
Swordly *Highld* 150 NC7463
Sworton Heath *Ches* 79 SJ6884
Swydd-ffynnon *Cardgn* 43 SN6966
Swynnerton *Staffs* 72 SJ8535
Swyre *Dorset* 10 SY5288
Sycharth *Powys* 58 SJ2025
Sychnant *Powys* 45 SN9777
Sychtyn *Powys* 58 SH9907
Sydallt *Flints* 71 SJ3055
Syde *Gloucs* 35 SO9511
Sydenham *Gt Lon* 27 TQ3671
Sydenham *Oxon* 37 SP7301
Sydenham Damerel *Devon* 5 SX4176
Sydenhurst *Surrey* 14 SU9534
Syderstone *Norfk* 66 TF8332
Sydling St Nicholas *Dorset* 10 SY6399
Sydmonton *Hants* 24 SU4857
Sydnal Lane *Shrops* 60 SJ8005
Syerston *Notts* 63 SK7447
Syke *Gt Man* 81 SD8915
Sykehouse *S York* 83 SE6316
Syleham *Suffk* 55 TM2078
Sylen *Carmth* 32 SN5106
Symbister *Shet* 155 HU5462
Symington *S Ayrs* 106 NS3831
Symington *S Lans* 108 NS9935
Symonds Yat *H & W* 34 SO5515
Symondsbury *Dorset* 10 SY4493
Sympson Green *W York* 82 SE1838
Synderford *Dorset* 10 ST3803
Synod Inn *Cardgn* 42 SN4054
Syre *Highld* 149 NC6943
Syreford *Gloucs* 35 SP0220
Syresham *Nhants* 49 SP6241
Syston *Leics* 62 SK6211
Syston *Lincs* 63 SK9240
Sytchampton *H & W* 47 SO8466
Sywell *Nhants* 51 SP8267

T

Tabley Hill *Ches* 79 SJ7379
Tackley *Oxon* 37 SP4719
Tacolneston *Norfk* 66 TM1495
Tadcaster *N York* 83 SE4843
Taddington *Derbys* 74 SK1471
Taddington *Gloucs* 48 SP0831
Taddiport *Devon* 18 SS4818
Tadley *Hants* 24 SU6061
Tadlow *Cambs* 52 TL2847
Tadmarton *Oxon* 48 SP3937
Tadwick *Somset* 35 ST7470
Tadworth *Surrey* 26 TQ2257
Tafarn-y-bwlch *Pembks* 31 SN0834
Tafarn-y-Gelyn *Denbgs* 70 SJ1961
Tafarnaubach *Blae G* 33 SO1210
Taff's Well *Cardif* 33 ST1283
Tafolwern *Powys* 57 SH8902
Tai'r Bull *Powys* 45 SN9925
Taibach *Neath* 32 SS7788
Tain *Highld* 151 ND2266
Tain *Highld* 147 NH7781
Tairbeart *W Isls* 154 NB1500
Takeley *Essex* 40 TL5621
Takeley Street *Essex* 39 TL5421
Tal-y-Bont *A & C* 69 SH7668
Tal-y-bont *Gwynd* 57 SH5921
Tal-y-bont *Gwynd* 69 SH6070
Tal-y-cafn *A & C* 69 SH7871
Tal-y-coed *Mons* 34 SO4115
Tal-y-garn *Rhondd* 33 ST0379
Tal-y-llyn *Gwynd* 57 SH7109
Tal-y-Waun *Torfn* 34 SO2604
Talachddu *Powys* 45 SO0833
Talacre *Flints* 70 SJ1183
Talaton *Devon* 9 SY0699
Talbenny *Pembks* 30 SM8411
Talbot Green *Rhondd* 33 ST0382
Talbot Village *Dorset* 12 SZ0793
Taleford *Devon* 9 SY0997
Talerddig *Powys* 58 SH9300
Talgarreg *Cardgn* 42 SN4251
Talgarth *Powys* 45 SO1533
Taliesin *Cardgn* 43 SN6591
Talisker *Highld* 136 NG3230
Talke *Staffs* 72 SJ8253
Talke Pits *Staffs* 72 SJ8353
Talkin *Cumb* 94 NY5557
Talla Linnfoots *Border* 108 NT1320
Talladale *Highld* 144 NG9170
Tallaminnock *S Ayrs* 106 NX4098
Tallarn Green *Wrexhm* 71 SJ4444
Tallentire *Cumb* 92 NY1035
Talley *Carmth* 44 SN6332
Tallington *Lincs* 64 TF0908
Tallwrn *Wrexhm* 71 SJ2947
Talmine *Highld* 149 NC5863
Talog *Carmth* 31 SN3325
Talsarn *Cardgn* 44 SN5456
Talsarnau *Gwynd* 57 SH6135
Talskiddy *Cnwll* 4 SW9165
Talwrn *Angles* 68 SH4877
Talwrn *Wrexhm* 71 SJ3847
Talybont *Cardgn* 43 SN6589
Talybont-on-Usk *Powys* 33 SO1122
Talysarn *Gwynd* 68 SH4952
Talywern *Powys* 57 SH8200
Tamer Lane End *Gt Man* 79 SD6401
Tamerton Foliot *Devon* 6 SX4761
Tamworth *Staffs* 61 SK2003
Tamworth Green *Lincs* 64 TF3842
Tan Hill *N York* 88 NY8906
Tan Office Green *Suffk* 53 TL7858
Tan-y-Bwlch *Gwynd* 57 SH6540
Tan-y-fron *A & C* 70 SH9564
Tan-y-fron *Wrexhm* 71 SJ2952
Tan-y-groes *Cardgn* 42 SN2849
Tancred *N York* 89 SE4558
Tancredston *Pembks* 30 SM8826
Tandlemuir *Rens* 115 NS3361
Tandridge *Surrey* 27 TQ3750
Tanfield *Dur* 96 NZ1855
Tanfield Lea *Dur* 96 NZ1854
Tangiers *Pembks* 30 SM9518
Tangley *Hants* 23 SU3252
Tangmere *W Susx* 14 SU9006
Tankerness *Ork* 155 HY5109
Tankersley *S York* 74 SK3499
Tankerton *Kent* 29 TR1166
Tannach *Highld* 151 ND3247
Tannachie *Abers* 135 NO7884
Tannadice *Angus* 134 NO4758
Tanner Green *H & W* 61 SP0874
Tannington *Suffk* 55 TM2467
Tannochside *N Lans* 116 NS7061
Tansley *Derbys* 74 SK3259
Tansor *Nhants* 51 TL0590
Tantobie *Dur* 96 NZ1754
Tanton *N York* 90 NZ5210
Tanwood *H & W* 60 SO9074
Tanworth in Arden *Warwks* 61 SP1170
Tanygrisiau *Gwynd* 57 SH6945
Taobh Tuath *W Isls* 154 NF9989
Taplow *Bucks* 26 SU9182
Tarbert *Ag & B* 113 NR6551
Tarbert *Ag & B* 113 NR8668
Tarbert *W Isls* 154 NB1500
Tarbet *Ag & B* 123 NN3104
Tarbet *Highld* 148 NC1649
Tarbet *Highld* 129 NM7992
Tarbock Green *Mersyd* 78 SJ4687
Tarbolton *S Ayrs* 107 NS4327
Tarbrax *S Lans* 117 NT0255
Tardebigge *H & W* 47 SO9969
Tardy Gate *Lancs* 80 SD5425
Tarfside *Angus* 134 NO4879
Tarland *Abers* 134 NJ4804
Tarleton *Lancs* 80 SD4520
Tarlscough *Lancs* 80 SD4314
Tarlton *Gloucs* 35 ST9599
Tarnock *Somset* 21 ST3752
Tarns *Cumb* 92 NY1248
Tarnside *Cumb* 87 SD4390
Tarporley *Ches* 71 SJ5562
Tarr *Somset* 19 SS8632
Tarr *Somset* 20 ST1030
Tarrant Crawford *Dorset* 11 ST9203
Tarrant Gunville *Dorset* 11 ST9213
Tarrant Hinton *Dorset* 11 ST9311
Tarrant Keynston *Dorset* 11 ST9204
Tarrant Launceston *Dorset* 11 ST9409
Tarrant Monkton *Dorset* 11 ST9408
Tarrant Rawston *Dorset* 11 ST9306
Tarrant Rushton *Dorset* 11 ST9305
Tarring Neville *E Susx* 16 TQ4403
Tarrington *H & W* 46 SO6140
Tarskavaig *Highld* 129 NG5810
Tarves *Abers* 143 NJ8631
Tarvie *P & K* 133 NO0164
Tarvin *Ches* 71 SJ4966
Tarvin Sands *Ches* 71 SJ4967
Tasburgh *Norfk* 67 TM1996
Tasley *Shrops* 60 SO6894
Taston *Oxon* 36 SP3521
Tatenhill *Staffs* 73 SK2021
Tathall End *Bucks* 38 SP8246
Tatham *Lancs* 87 SD6069
Tathwell *Lincs* 77 TF3182
Tatsfield *Surrey* 27 TQ4156
Tattenhall *Ches* 71 SJ4858
Tatterford *Norfk* 66 TF8628
Tattersett *Norfk* 66 TF8429
Tattershall *Lincs* 76 TF2157
Tattershall Bridge *Lincs* 76 TF1956
Tattershall Thorpe *Lincs* 76 TF2159
Tattingstone *Suffk* 54 TM1337
Tattingstone White Horse *Suffk* 54 TM1338
Tatworth *Somset* 10 ST3205
Tauchers *Moray* 141 NJ3749
Taunton *Somset* 20 ST2224
Taverham *Norfk* 66 TG1613
Taverners Green *Essex* 40 TL5618
Tavernspite *Pembks* 31 SN1812
Tavistock *Devon* 6 SX4874
Taw green *Devon* 8 SX6597
Tawstock *Devon* 19 SS5529
Taxal *Derbys* 79 SK0079
Taychreggan Hotel *Ag & B* 123 NN0421
Tayinloan *Ag & B* 105 NR6946
Taynton *Gloucs* 35 SO7222
Taynton *Oxon* 36 SP2313
Taynuilt *Ag & B* 122 NN0031
Tayport *Fife* 127 NO4628
Tayvallich *Ag & B* 113 NR7487
Tealby *Lincs* 76 TF1590
Team Valley *T & W* 103 NZ2459
Teangue *Highld* 129 NG6609
Teanord *Highld* 140 NH5964
Tebay *Cumb* 87 NY6104
Tebworth *Beds* 38 SP9926
Tedburn St Mary *Devon* 8 SX8194
Teddington *Gloucs* 47 SO9633
Teddington *Gt Lon* 26 TQ1670
Tedstone Delamere *H & W* 47 SO6958
Tedstone Wafer *H & W* 47 SO6759
Teesport *N York* 97 NZ5423
Teesside Park *N York* 97 NZ4618
Teeton *Nhants* 50 SP6970
Teffont Evias *Wilts* 22 ST9931
Teffont Magna *Wilts* 22 ST9932
Tegryn *Pembks* 31 SN2233
Teigh *Rutlnd* 63 SK8615
Teigncombe *Devon* 8 SX6787
Teigngrace *Devon* 7 SX8574
Teignmouth *Devon* 7 SX9473
Teindside *Border* 109 NT4408
Telford *Shrops* 60 SJ6908
Tellisford *Somset* 22 ST8055
Telscombe *E Susx* 15 TQ4003
Telscombe Cliffs *E Susx* 15 TQ4001
Tempar *P & K* 124 NN6857
Templand *D & G* 100 NY0886
Temple *C Glas* 115 NS5469
Temple *Cnwll* 4 SX1473
Temple *Mdloth* 117 NT3158
Temple Balsall *W Mids* 61 SP2076
Temple Bar *Cardgn* 44 SN5354
Temple Cloud *Somset* 21 ST6257
Temple End *Suffk* 53 TL6650
Temple Ewell *Kent* 29 TR2844
Temple Grafton *Warwks* 48 SP1255
Temple Guiting *Gloucs* 48 SP0928
Temple Hirst *N York* 83 SE6024
Temple Normanton *Derbys* 74 SK4167
Temple Pier *Highld* 139 NH5330
Temple Sowerby *Cumb* 94 NY6127
Templecombe *Somset* 22 ST7022
Templeton *Devon* 19 SS8813
Templeton *Pembks* 31 SN1111
Templetown *Dur* 95 NZ1050
Tempsford *Beds* 52 TL1653
Ten Mile Bank *Norfk* 65 TL5996
Tenbury Wells *H & W* 46 SO5968
Tenby *Pembks* 31 SN1300
Tendring *Essex* 41 TM1424
Tendring Green *Essex* 41 TM1325
Tendring Heath *Essex* 41 TM1326
Tenpenny Heath *Essex* 41 TM0820
Tenterden *Kent* 17 TQ8833
Terling *Essex* 40 TL7715
Tern *Shrops* 59 SJ6216
Ternhill *Shrops* 59 SJ6332
Terregles *D & G* 100 NX9377
Terrington *N York* 90 SE6770
Terrington St Clement *Norfk* 65 TF5520
Terrington St John *Norfk* 65 TF5314
Terry's Green *Warwks* 61 SP1073
Teston *Kent* 28 TQ7053
Testwood *Hants* 12 SU3514
Tetbury *Gloucs* 35 ST8993
Tetbury Upton *Gloucs* 35 ST8895
Tetchill *Shrops* 59 SJ3932
Tetcott *Devon* 5 SX3396
Tetford *Lincs* 77 TF3374
Tetney *Lincs* 77 TA3100
Tetney Lock *Lincs* 85 TA3402
Tetsworth *Oxon* 37 SP6801
Tettenhall *W Mids* 60 SJ8800
Tettenhall Wood *W Mids* 60 SO8899
Tetworth *Cambs* 52 TL2253
Teversal *Notts* 75 SK4861
Teversham *Cambs* 53 TL4958
Teviothead *Border* 109 NT4005
Tewel *Abers* 135 NO8085
Tewin *Herts* 39 TL2714
Tewkesbury *Gloucs* 47 SO8932
Teynham *Kent* 28 TQ9662
Thackley *W York* 82 SE1738
Thackthwaite *Cumb* 92 NY1423
Thackthwaite *Cumb* 93 NY4225
Thakeham *W Susx* 14 TQ1017
Thame *Oxon* 37 SP7005
Thames Ditton *Surrey* 26 TQ1567
Thamesmead *Gt Lon* 27 TQ4780
Thanington *Kent* 29 TR1356
Thankerton *S Lans* 108 NS9738
Tharston *Norfk* 66 TM1894
Thatcham *Berks* 24 SU5167
Thatto Heath *Mersyd* 78 SJ5093
Thaxted *Essex* 40 TL6131
The Bank *Ches* 72 SJ8457
The Bank *Shrops* 59 SO6199
The Beeches *Gloucs* 36 SP0302
The Biggins *Cambs* 53 TL4788
The Blythe *Staffs* 73 SK0428
The Bourne *H & W* 47 SO9856
The Braes *Highld* 137 NG5234
The Bratch *Staffs* 60 SO8693
The Broad *H & W* 46 SO4961
The Brunt *E Loth* 118 NT6873
The Bungalow *IOM* 153 SC3986
The Bush *Kent* 28 TQ6649
The Butts *Gloucs* 35 SO8916
The Chequer *Wrexhm* 71 SJ4840
The City *Beds* 52 TL1159
The City *Bucks* 37 SU7896
The Common *Oxon* 48 SP2927
The Common *Wilts* 35 SU0285
The Corner *Kent* 28 TQ7041
The Corner *Shrops* 59 SO4387
The Cronk *IOM* 153 SC3395
The Den *N Ayrs* 115 NS3251
The Flatt *Cumb* 101 NY5678
The Forge *H & W* 46 SO3459
The Forstal *E Susx* 16 TQ5435
The Forstal *Kent* 28 TQ8946
The Forstal *Kent* 28 TR0438
The Fouralls *Shrops* 72 SJ6831
The Green *Cumb* 86 SD1884
The Green *Essex* 40 TL7719
The Grove *H & W* 47 SO8741
The Haven *W Susx* 14 TQ0830
The Haw *Gloucs* 47 SO8427
The Hill *Cumb* 86 SD1783
The Hirsel *Border* 110 NT8240
The Holt *Berks* 37 SU8078
The Leacon *Kent* 17 TQ9833
The Lee *Bucks* 38 SP9004
The Lhen *IOM* 153 NX3801
The Lochs *Moray* 141 NJ3062
The Middles *Dur* 96 NZ2051
The Moor *Kent* 17 TQ7529
The Mumbles *Swans* 32 SS6187
The Mythe *Gloucs* 47 SO8934
The Narth *Mons* 34 SO5206
The Neuk *Abers* 135 NO7397
The Quarry *Gloucs* 35 ST7499
The Quarter *Kent* 28 TQ8844
The Reddings *Gloucs* 35 SO9121
The Rookery *Staffs* 72 SJ8555
The Ross *P & K* 124 NN7621
The Sands *Surrey* 25 SU8846
The Shoe *Wilts* 35 ST8074
The Smithies *Shrops* 60 SO6897
The Spike *Cambs* 53 TL4848
The Spring *Warwks* 61 SP2873
The Square *Torfn* 34 ST2796
The Stair *Kent* 16 TQ6047
The Stocks *Kent* 17 TQ9127
The Straits *Hants* 25 SU7839
The Strand *Wilts* 22 ST9259
The Thrift *Herts* 39 TL3139
The Towans *Cnwll* 2 SW5538
The Vauld *H & W* 46 SO5349
The Wyke *Shrops* 60 SJ7206
Theakston *N York* 89 SE3085
Thealby *Lincs* 84 SE8917
Theale *Berks* 24 SU6471
Theale *Somset* 21 ST4646
Thearne *E R Yk* 85 TA0736

Torbryan Tunstall

Torbryan *Devon* 7 SX8266
Torcastle *Highld* 131 NN1378
Torcross *Devon* 7 SX8241
Tore *Highld* 140 NH6052
Torfrey *Cnwll* 3 SX1154
Torinturk *Ag & B* 113 NR8164
Torksey *Lincs* 76 SK8378
Tormarton *Gloucs* 35 ST7678
Tormitchell *S Ayrs* 106 NX2394
Tormore *N Ayrs* 105 NR8932
Tornagrain *Highld* 140 NH7650
Tornaveen *Abers* 134 NJ6106
Torness *Highld* 139 NH5826
Tornewton *Devon* 7 SX8167
Toronto *Dur* 96 NZ1930
Torosay Castle *Ag & B* 122 NM7335
Torpenhow *Cumb* 93 NY2039
Torphichen *W Loth* 117 NS9672
Torphins *Abers* 134 NJ6202
Torpoint *Cnwll* 6 SX4355
Torquay *Devon* 7 SX9164
Torquhan *Border* 118 NT4448
Torr *Devon* 6 SX5851
Torran *Highld* 137 NG5949
Torrance *E Duns* 116 NS6173
Torranyard *N Ayrs* 115 NS3544
Torre *Somset* 20 ST0439
Torridon *Highld* 138 NG9055
Torridon House *Highld* 138 NG8657
Torrin *Highld* 129 NG5721
Torrisdale *Highld* 149 NC6761
Torrisdale Square *Ag & B* 105 NR7936
Torrish *Highld* 147 NC9718
Torrisholme *Lancs* 87 SD4563
Torrobull *Highld* 146 NC5904
Torry *Aber C* 135 NJ9405
Torryburn *Fife* 117 NT0286
Tortan *H & W* 60 SO8472
Torteval *Guern* 152 GN0000
Torthorwald *D & G* 100 NY0378
Tortington *W Susx* 14 TQ0004
Tortworth *Gloucs* 35 ST7093
Torvaig *Highld* 136 NG4944
Torver *Cumb* 86 SD2894
Torwood *Falk* 116 NS8385
Torwoodlee *Border* 109 NT4738
Torworth *Notts* 75 SK6586
Toscaig *Highld* 137 NG7138
Toseland *Cambs* 52 TL2462
Tosside *N York* 81 SD7656
Tostock *Suffk* 54 TL9563
Totaig *Highld* 136 NG2050
Tote *Highld* 136 NG4149
Tote *Highld* 137 NG5160
Tote Hill *W Susx* 14 SU8624
Tothill *Lincs* 77 TF4181
Totland *IOW* 12 SZ3287
Totley *S York* 74 SK3079
Totley Brook *S York* 74 SK3180
Totnes *Devon* 7 SX8060
Toton *Notts* 62 SK5034
Totronald *Ag & B* 120 NM1656
Totscore *Highld* 136 NG3866
Tottenham *Gt Lon* 27 TQ3390
Tottenhill *Norfk* 65 TF6411
Totteridge *Gt Lon* 26 TQ2494
Totternhoe *Beds* 38 SP9821
Tottington *Gt Man* 81 SD7712
Tottleworth *Lancs* 81 SD7331
Totton *Hants* 12 SU3613
Touchen End *Berks* 26 SU8776
Toulston *N York* 83 SE4543
Toulton *Somset* 20 ST1931
Toulvaddie *Highld* 147 NH8880
Tovil *Kent* 28 TQ7554
Tow Law *Dur* 95 NZ1138
Towan *Cnwll* 4 SW8774
Towan *Cnwll* 3 SX0148
Toward *Ag & B* 114 NS1368
Toward Quay *Ag & B* 114 NS1167
Towcester *Nhants* 49 SP6948
Towednack *Cnwll* 2 SW4838
Towersey *Oxon* 37 SP7305
Towie *Abers* 134 NJ4312
Town End *Cambs* 65 TL4195
Town End *Cumb* 87 NY3406
Town End *Cumb* 87 NY6325
Town End *Cumb* 87 SD3687
Town End *Cumb* 87 SD4483
Town Green *Lancs* 78 SD4005
Town Green *Norfk* 67 TG3612
Town Head *Cumb* 87 NY4103
Town Head *N York* 88 SD8258
Town Head *N York* 82 SE1748
Town Kelloe *Dur* 96 NZ3536
Town Lane *Gt Man* 79 SJ6999
Town Littleworth *E Susx* 15 TQ4117
Town Moor *T & W* 103 NZ2465
Town of Lowdon *Mersyd* 78 SJ6196
Town Row *E Susx* 16 TQ5630
Town Street *Suffk* 53 TL7785
Town Yetholm *Border* 110 NT8128
Townend *D & Cb* 115 NS3976
Towngate *Cumb* 94 NY5246
Towngate *Lincs* 64 TF1310
Townhead *Cumb* 92 NY0735
Townhead *Cumb* 94 NY6334
Townhead *D & G* 100 NY0088
Townhead *S York* 82 SE1602
Townhead of Greenlaw *D & G* 99 NX7464
Townhill *Fife* 117 NT1089
Townlake *Devon* 5 SX4074
Towns End *Hants* 24 SU5659
Townsend *Somset* 10 ST3614
Townshend *Cnwll* 2 SW5932
Townwell *Gloucs* 35 ST7090
Towthorpe *E R Yk* 91 SE8962
Towthorpe *N York* 90 SE6258
Towton *N York* 83 SE4839
Towyn *A & C* 70 SH9779
Toxteth *Mersyd* 78 SJ3588
Toy's Hill *Kent* 27 TQ4651
Toynton All Saints *Lincs* 77 TF3963
Toynton Fen Side *Lincs* 77 TF3961
Toynton St Peter *Lincs* 77 TF4063
Trabboch *E Ayrs* 107 NS4421
Trabbochburn *E Ayrs* 107 NS4621
Traboe *Cnwll* 3 SW7421
Tracebridge *Somset* 20 ST0621
Tradespark *Highld* 140 NH8656
Traethsaith *Cardgn* 42 SN2851
Trafford Park *Gt Man* 79 SJ7896
Trallong *Powys* 45 SN9629
Tranent *E Loth* 118 NT4072
Tranmere *Mersyd* 78 SJ3187
Trannack *Cnwll* 2 SW5633
Trantelbeg *Highld* 150 NC8952
Trantlemore *Highld* 150 NC8953
Tranwell *Nthumb* 103 NZ1883
Trap *Carmth* 32 SN6518
Trap's Green *Warwks* 48 SP1069
Trapshill *Berks* 23 SU3763
Traquair *Border* 109 NT3334
Trash Green *Berks* 24 SU6569
Traveller's Rest *Devon* 19 SS6127
Trawden *Lancs* 81 SD9138
Trawscoed *Cardgn* 43 SN6672
Trawsfynydd *Gwynd* 57 SH7035
Tre Aubrey *V Glam* 33 ST0372
Tre'R-Ddol *Cardgn* 43 SN6692
Tre-gagle *Mons* 34 SO5207
Tre-Gibbon *Rhondd* 33 SN9905
Tre-groes *Cardgn* 42 SN4044
Tre-Mostyn *Flints* 70 SJ1479
Tre-Vaughan *Carmth* 31 SN3921
Tre-wyn *Mons* 34 SO3222
Trealaw *Rhondd* 33 ST0092
Treales *Lancs* 80 SD4332
Treamble *Cnwll* 3 SW7856
Trearddur Bay *Angles* 68 SH2579
Treaslane *Highld* 136 NG3953
Treator *Cnwll* 4 SW9075
Trebanog *Rhondd* 33 ST0190
Trebanos *Neath* 32 SN7103
Trebartha *Cnwll* 5 SX2677
Trebarvah *Cnwll* 2 SW7130
Trebarwith *Cnwll* 4 SX0586
Trebeath *Cnwll* 5 SX2587
Trebehor *Cnwll* 2 SW3724
Trebelzue *Cnwll* 4 SW8464
Trebetherick *Cnwll* 4 SW9378
Treborough *Somset* 20 ST0136
Trebudannon *Cnwll* 4 SW8961
Trebullett *Cnwll* 5 SX3278
Treburgett *Cnwll* 4 SX0579
Treburick *Cnwll* 4 SW8971
Treburley *Cnwll* 5 SX3577
Treburrick *Cnwll* 4 SW8670
Trebyan *Cnwll* 4 SX0763
Trecastle *Powys* 45 SN8829
Trecogo *Cnwll* 5 SX3080
Trecott *Devon* 8 SS6300
Trecwn *Pembks* 30 SM9632
Trecynon *Rhondd* 33 SN9903
Tredaule *Cnwll* 5 SX2381
Tredavoe *Cnwll* 2 SW4528
Tredegar *Blae G* 33 SO1408
Tredethy *Cnwll* 4 SX0672
Tredington *Gloucs* 47 SO9029
Tredington *Warwks* 48 SP2543
Tredinnick *Cnwll* 4 SW9270
Tredinnick *Cnwll* 4 SX0459
Tredinnick *Cnwll* 4 SX1666
Tredinnick *Cnwll* 5 SX2357
Tredinnick *Cnwll* 5 SX2957
Tredomen *Powys* 45 SO1231
Tredrissi *Pembks* 31 SN0742
Tredrizzick *Cnwll* 4 SW9577
Tredunhock *Mons* 34 ST3794
Tredustan *Powys* 45 SO1332
Treen *Cnwll* 2 SW4337
Treen *Cnwll* 2 SW3923
Treesmill *Cnwll* 3 SX0855
Treeton *S York* 75 SK4387
Trefacca *Powys* 45 SO1431
Trefasser *Pembks* 30 SM8938
Trefdraeth *Angles* 68 SH4170
Trefeglwys *Powys* 58 SN9690
Trefenter *Cardgn* 43 SN6068
Treffgarne *Pembks* 30 SM9523
Treffgarne Owen *Pembks* 30 SM8625
Trefforest *Rhondd* 33 ST0888
Treffynnon *Pembks* 30 SM8528
Trefil *Blae G* 33 SO1212
Trefilan *Cardgn* 44 SN5456
Treflach Wood *Shrops* 58 SJ2625
Trefnannau *Powys* 58 SJ2316
Trefnant *Denbgs* 70 SJ0570
Trefonen *Shrops* 58 SJ2526
Trefor *Angles* 68 SH3780
Treforda *Cnwll* 4 SX0988
Trefrew *Cnwll* 4 SX1084
Trefriw *A & C* 69 SH7863
Tregadillett *Cnwll* 5 SX2983
Tregaian *Angles* 68 SH4580
Tregare *Mons* 34 SO4110
Tregarne *Cnwll* 3 SW7823
Tregaron *Cardgn* 44 SN6759
Tregarth *Gwynd* 69 SH6067
Tregaswith *Cnwll* 4 SW8962
Tregatta *Cnwll* 4 SX0587
Tregawne *Cnwll* 4 SX0066
Tregear *Cnwll* 3 SW8650
Tregeare *Cnwll* 5 SX2486
Tregeiriog *Wrexhm* 58 SJ1733
Tregele *Angles* 68 SH3592
Tregellist *Cnwll* 4 SX0177
Tregenna *Cnwll* 3 SW8743
Tregenna *Cnwll* 4 SX0973
Tregeseal *Cnwll* 2 SW3731
Tregew *Cnwll* 3 SW8034
Tregidden *Cnwll* 3 SW7523
Tregiddle *Cnwll* 2 SW6723
Tregidgeo *Cnwll* 3 SW9647
Tregiskey *Cnwll* 3 SX0146
Treglemais *Pembks* 30 SM8229
Tregole *Cnwll* 5 SX1998
Tregolls *Cnwll* 3 SW7335
Tregonce *Cnwll* 4 SW9373
Tregonetha *Cnwll* 4 SW9563
Tregony *Cnwll* 3 SW9244
Tregoodwell *Cnwll* 4 SX1183
Tregoose *Cnwll* 2 SW6823
Tregoss *Cnwll* 4 SW9660
Tregowris *Cnwll* 3 SW7722
Tregoyd *Powys* 45 SO1937
Tregrehan Mills *Cnwll* 3 SX0453
Tregullon *Cnwll* 4 SX0664
Tregunna *Cnwll* 4 SW9673
Tregunnon *Cnwll* 5 SX2283
Tregurrian *Cnwll* 4 SW8565
Tregustick *Cnwll* 4 SW9866
Tregynon *Powys* 58 SO0998
Trehafod *Rhondd* 33 ST0490
Trehan *Cnwll* 5 SX4058
Treharris *Myr Td* 33 ST0996
Treharrock *Cnwll* 4 SX0178
Trehemborne *Cnwll* 4 SW8773
Treherbert *Carmth* 44 SN5847
Treherbert *Rhondd* 33 SS9498
Treheveras *Cnwll* 3 SW8046
Trehunist *Cnwll* 5 SX3263
Trekelland *Cnwll* 5 SX3480
Trekenner *Cnwll* 5 SX3478
Treknow *Cnwll* 4 SX0586
Trelan *Cnwll* 3 SW7418
Trelash *Cnwll* 4 SX1890
Trelassick *Cnwll* 3 SW8752
Trelawne *Cnwll* 5 SX2154
Trelawnyd *Flints* 70 SJ0979
Treleague *Cnwll* 3 SW7821
Treleaver *Cnwll* 3 SW7716
Trelech *Carmth* 31 SN2830
Trelech a'r Betws *Carmth* 31 SN3026
Treleddyd-fawr *Pembks* 30 SM7528
Trelew *Cnwll* 3 SW8135
Trelewis *Myr Td* 33 ST1096
Treligga *Cnwll* 4 SX0484
Trelights *Cnwll* 4 SW9979
Trelill *Cnwll* 4 SX0478
Trelinnoe *Cnwll* 5 SX3181
Trelion *Cnwll* 3 SW9252
Trelissick *Cnwll* 3 SW8339
Trelleck *Mons* 34 SO5005
Trelleck Grange *Mons* 34 SO4901
Trelogan *Flints* 70 SJ1180
Trelonk *Cnwll* 3 SW8941
Trelow *Cnwll* 4 SW9269
Trelowarren *Cnwll* 2 SW7124
Trelowia *Cnwll* 5 SX2956
Treluggan *Cnwll* 3 SW8838
Trelystan *Powys* 58 SJ2503
Tremadog *Gwynd* 57 SH5640
Tremail *Cnwll* 4 SX1686
Tremaine *Cnwll* 5 SX2389
Tremar *Cnwll* 5 SX2568
Trematon *Cnwll* 5 SX3959
Trembraze *Cnwll* 5 SX2565
Tremeirchion *Denbgs* 70 SJ0873
Tremethick Cross *Cnwll* 2 SW4430
Tremollett *Cnwll* 5 SX2975
Tremore *Cnwll* 4 SX0164
Trenance *Cnwll* 3 SW8022
Trenance *Cnwll* 4 SW8568
Trenance *Cnwll* 4 SW9270
Trenarren *Cnwll* 3 SX0348
Trenault *Cnwll* 5 SX2683
Trench *Shrops* 60 SJ6912
Trench Green *Oxon* 37 SU6877
Trencreek *Cnwll* 4 SW8260
Trencreek *Cnwll* 4 SX1896
Trendeal *Cnwll* 3 SW8952
Trendrine *Cnwll* 2 SW4739
Treneague *Cnwll* 4 SW9871
Trenear *Cnwll* 2 SW6731
Treneglos *Cnwll* 5 SX2088
Trenerth *Cnwll* 2 SW6035
Trenewan *Cnwll* 4 SX1753
Trenewth *Cnwll* 4 SX0778
Trengothal *Cnwll* 2 SW3724
Trengune *Cnwll* 4 SX1893
Treninnick *Cnwll* 4 SW8160
Trenowah *Cnwll* 4 SW7959
Trenoweth *Cnwll* 3 SW7533
Trent *Dorset* 10 ST5918
Trent Port *Lincs* 76 SK8381
Trent Vale *Staffs* 72 SJ8643
Trentham *Staffs* 72 SJ8740
Trentishoe *Devon* 19 SS6448
Trentlock *Derbys* 62 SK4831
Treoes *V Glam* 33 SS9478
Treorchy *Rhondd* 33 SS9597
Trequite *Cnwll* 4 SX0377
Trerhyngyll *V Glam* 33 ST0077
Trerulefoot *Cnwll* 5 SX3358
Tresahor *Cnwll* 3 SW7431
Tresawle *Cnwll* 3 SW8846
Trescott *Staffs* 60 SO8597
Trescowe *Cnwll* 2 SW5731
Tresean *Cnwll* 4 SW7858
Tresham *Gloucs* 35 ST7991
Tresillian *Cnwll* 3 SW8646
Tresinney *Cnwll* 4 SX1081
Treskinnick Cross *Cnwll* 5 SX2098
Treslea *Cnwll* 4 SX1368
Tresmeer *Cnwll* 5 SX2387
Tresparrett *Cnwll* 4 SX1491
Tressait *P & K* 132 NN8160
Tresta *Shet* 155 HU3650
Tresta *Shet* 155 HU6090
Treswell *Notts* 75 SK7879
Treswithian *Cnwll* 2 SW6241
Trethawle *Cnwll* 5 SX2662
Trethevey *Cnwll* 4 SX0789
Trethewey *Cnwll* 2 SW3823
Trethomas *Caerph* 33 ST1888
Trethosa *Cnwll* 3 SW9454
Trethurgy *Cnwll* 3 SX0355
Tretio *Pembks* 30 SM7829
Tretire *H & W* 46 SO5123
Tretower *Powys* 33 SO1821
Treuddyn *Flints* 70 SJ2557
Trevadlock *Cnwll* 5 SX2679
Trevague *Cnwll* 5 SX2379
Trevalga *Cnwll* 4 SX0890
Trevalyn *Wrexhm* 71 SJ3856
Trevanger *Cnwll* 4 SW9677
Trevanson *Cnwll* 4 SW9773
Trevarrack *Cnwll* 2 SW4731
Trevarren *Cnwll* 4 SW9160
Trevarrian *Cnwll* 4 SW8566
Trevarrick *Cnwll* 3 SW9843
Trevarth *Cnwll* 3 SW7240
Trevaughan *Carmth* 31 SN2015
Treveal *Cnwll* 2 SW4740
Treveal *Cnwll* 4 SW7858
Treveale *Cnwll* 3 SW8751
Treveighan *Cnwll* 4 SX0779
Trevellas Downs *Cnwll* 3 SW7452
Trevelmond *Cnwll* 5 SX2063
Trevempor *Cnwll* 4 SW8159
Treveneague *Cnwll* 2 SW5432
Treveor *Cnwll* 3 SW9841
Treverbyn *Cnwll* 3 SW8849
Treverbyn *Cnwll* 4 SX0157
Treverva *Cnwll* 3 SW7531
Trevescan *Cnwll* 2 SW3524
Trevethin *Torfn* 34 SO2801
Trevia *Cnwll* 4 SX0983
Trevigro *Cnwll* 5 SX3369
Trevilla *Cnwll* 3 SW8239
Trevilledor *Cnwll* 4 SW8867
Trevilson *Cnwll* 3 SW8455
Trevine *Pembks* 30 SM8432
Treviscoe *Cnwll* 3 SW9455
Treviskey *Cnwll* 3 SW9340
Trevissick *Cnwll* 3 SX0248
Trevithal *Cnwll* 2 SW4626
Trevithick *Cnwll* 4 SW8862
Trevithick *Cnwll* 3 SW9645
Trevivian *Cnwll* 4 SX1785
Trevoll *Cnwll* 4 SW8358
Trevone *Cnwll* 4 SW8975
Trevor *Denbgs* 70 SJ2742
Trevor *Gwynd* 56 SH3746
Trevorgans *Cnwll* 2 SW4025
Trevorrick *Cnwll* 4 SW8672
Trevorrick *Cnwll* 4 SW9273
Trevose *Cnwll* 4 SW8675
Trew *Cnwll* 2 SW6129
Trewalder *Cnwll* 4 SX0782
Trewalkin *Powys* 45 SO1531
Trewarlett *Cnwll* 5 SX3380
Trewarmett *Cnwll* 4 SX0686
Trewarthenick *Cnwll* 3 SW9044
Trewassa *Cnwll* 4 SX1486
Trewaves *Cnwll* 2 SW5926
Treween *Cnwll* 5 SX2182
Trewellard *Cnwll* 2 SW3733
Trewen *Cnwll* 5 SX2583
Trewen *Cnwll* 4 SX0577
Trewennack *Cnwll* 2 SW6728
Trewent *Pembks* 30 SS0197
Trewern *Powys* 58 SJ2811
Trewetha *Cnwll* 4 SX0080
Trewethern *Cnwll* 4 SX0076
Trewidland *Cnwll* 5 SX2559
Trewillis *Cnwll* 3 SW7717
Trewince *Cnwll* 3 SW8633
Trewint *Cnwll* 4 SX1072
Trewint *Cnwll* 5 SX2180
Trewint *Cnwll* 5 SX2963
Trewirgie *Cnwll* 3 SW8845
Trewithian *Cnwll* 3 SW8737
Trewoodloe *Cnwll* 5 SX3271
Trewoofe *Cnwll* 2 SW4425
Trewoon *Cnwll* 2 SW6819
Trewoon *Cnwll* 3 SW9952
Treworgan *Cnwll* 3 SW8349
Treworlas *Cnwll* 3 SW8938
Treworld *Cnwll* 4 SX1190
Treworthal *Cnwll* 3 SW8839
Treyarnon *Cnwll* 4 SW8673
Treyford *W Susx* 14 SU8218
Triangle *W York* 82 SE0422
Trickett's Cross *Dorset* 12 SU0800
Triermain *Cumb* 102 NY5966
Triffleton *Pembks* 30 SM9724
Trillacott *Cnwll* 5 SX2689
Trimdon *Dur* 96 NZ3634
Trimdon Colliery *Dur* 96 NZ3735
Trimdon Grange *Dur* 96 NZ3635
Trimingham *Norfk* 67 TG2838
Trimley *Suffk* 55 TM2737
Trimley Heath *Suffk* 55 TM2738
Trimley Lower Street *Suffk* 55 TM2636
Trimpley *H & W* 60 SO7978
Trims Green *Herts* 39 TL4717
Trimsaran *Carmth* 32 SN4504
Trimstone *Devon* 19 SS5043
Trinafour *P & K* 132 NN7264
Trinant *Caerph* 33 ST2099
Tring *Herts* 38 SP9211
Tring Wharf *Herts* 38 SP9212
Tringford *Herts* 38 SP9113
Trinity *Angus* 134 NO6061
Trinity *Jersey* 152 JS0000
Trinity Gask *P & K* 125 NN9718
Triscombe *Somset* 20 SS9237
Triscombe *Somset* 20 ST1535
Trislaig *Highld* 130 NN0874
Trispen *Cnwll* 3 SW8450
Tritlington *Nthumb* 103 NZ2092
Troan *Cnwll* 4 SW8957
Trochry *P & K* 125 NN9740
Troedrhiwfuwch *Caerph* 33 SO1204
Troedyraur *Cardgn* 42 SN3245
Troedyrhiw *Myr Td* 33 SO0702
Trofarth *A & C* 69 SH8571
Trois Bois *Jersey* 152 JS0000
Troon *Cnwll* 2 SW6638
Troon *S Ayrs* 106 NS3230
Troston *Suffk* 54 TL8972
Troswell *Cnwll* 5 SX2592
Trotshill *H & W* 47 SO8855
Trottiscliffe *Kent* 27 TQ6460
Trotton *W Susx* 14 SU8322
Trough Gate *Lancs* 81 SD8821
Troughend *Nthumb* 102 NY8692
Troutbeck *Cumb* 93 NY3927
Troutbeck *Cumb* 87 NY4002
Troutbeck Bridge *Cumb* 87 NY4000
Troway *Derbys* 74 SK3879
Trowbridge *Wilts* 22 ST8558
Trowell *Notts* 62 SK4839
Trowle Common *Wilts* 22 ST8458
Trowse Newton *Norfk* 67 TG2406
Troy *W York* 82 SE2439
Trudoxhill *Somset* 22 ST7443
Trull *Somset* 20 ST2122
Trumfleet *S York* 83 SE6011
Trumpan *Highld* 136 NG2261
Trumpet *H & W* 47 SO6539
Trumpington *Cambs* 53 TL4454
Trumpsgreen *Surrey* 25 SU9967
Trunch *Norfk* 67 TG2834
Trunnah *Lancs* 80 SD3442
Truro *Cnwll* 3 SW8244
Truscott *Cnwll* 5 SX2985
Trusham *Devon* 8 SX8582
Trusley *Derbys* 73 SK2535
Trusthorpe *Lincs* 77 TF5183
Trysull *Staffs* 60 SO8594
Tubney *Oxon* 36 SU4399
Tuckenhay *Devon* 7 SX8156
Tuckhill *Shrops* 60 SO7888
Tuckingmill *Cnwll* 2 SW6540
Tuckingmill *Wilts* 22 ST9329
Tuckton *Dorset* 12 SZ1492
Tucoyse *Cnwll* 3 SW9645
Tuddenham *Suffk* 53 TL7371
Tuddenham *Suffk* 55 TM1948
Tudeley *Kent* 16 TQ6245
Tudhoe *Dur* 96 NZ2535
Tudorville *H & W* 46 SO5922
Tudweiloig *Gwynd* 56 SH2436
Tuesley *Surrey* 25 SU9642
Tuffley *Gloucs* 35 SO8314
Tufton *Hants* 24 SU4546
Tufton *Pembks* 30 SN0428
Tugby *Leics* 63 SK7601
Tugford *Shrops* 59 SO5587
Tughall *Nthumb* 111 NU2126
Tullibody *Clacks* 116 NS8595
Tullich *Ag & B* 123 NN0815
Tullich *Highld* 140 NH6328
Tullich *Highld* 147 NH8576
Tulliemet *P & K* 125 NO0052
Tulloch *Abers* 143 NJ8031
Tulloch *Stirlg* 124 NN5120
Tulloch Station *Highld* 131 NN3580
Tullochgorm *Ag & B* 114 NR9695
Tullybeagles Lodge *P & K* 125 NO0136
Tullynessle *Abers* 142 NJ5519
Tulse Hill *Gt Lon* 27 TQ3172
Tumble *Carmth* 32 SN5411
Tumbler's Green *Essex* 40 TL8025
Tumby *Lincs* 76 TF2359
Tumby Woodside *Lincs* 77 TF2757
Tummel Bridge *P & K* 132 NN7659
Tunbridge Wells *Kent* 16 TQ5839
Tundergarth *D & G* 101 NY1780
Tungate *Norfk* 67 TG2629
Tunstall *E R Yk* 85 TA3031
Tunstall *Kent* 28 TQ8961
Tunstall *Lancs* 87 SD6073
Tunstall *N York* 89 SE2196
Tunstall *Norfk* 67 TG4107
Tunstall *Staffs* 72 SJ7727
Tunstall *Staffs* 72 SJ8651
Tunstall *Suffk* 55 TM3655
Tunstall *T & W* 96 NZ3953

Vennington

Wellesbourne Mountford

Vennington *Shrops* 59 SJ3309
Venny Tedburn *Devon* 8 SX8297
Venterdon *Cnwll* 5 SX3675
Ventnor *IOW* 13 SZ5677
Venton *Devon* 6 SX5956
Vernham Dean *Hants* 23 SU3356
Vernham Street *Hants* 23 SU3457
Vernolds Common *Shrops* 59 SO4780
Verwood *Dorset* 12 SU0809
Veryan *Cnwll* 3 SW9139
Veryan Green *Cnwll* 3 SW9140
Vickerstown *Cumb* 86 SD1868
Victoria *Blae G* 33 SO1707
Victoria *Cnwll* 4 SW9861
Victoria *S York* 82 SE1705
Vidlin *Shet* 155 HU4765
Viewfield *Moray* 141 NJ2864
Viewpark *N Lans* 116 NS7061
Vigo *Kent* 27 TQ6361
Ville la Bas *Jersey* 152 JS0000
Villiaze *Guern* 152 GN0000
Vinehall Street *E Susx* 17 TQ7520
Vines Cross *E Susx* 16 TQ5917
Virginia Water *Surrey* 25 TQ0067
Virginstow *Devon* 5 SX3792
Virley *Essex* 40 TL9414
Vobster *Somset* 22 ST7048
Voe *Shet* 155 HU4062
Vowchurch *H & W* 46 SO3636
Vulcan Village *Ches* 78 SJ5894

W

Wackerfield *Dur* 96 NZ1522
Wacton *Norfk* 66 TM1791
Wadborough *H & W* 47 SO9047
Waddesdon *Bucks* 37 SP7416
Waddeton *Devon* 7 SX8756
Waddicar *Mersyd* 78 SJ3999
Waddingham *Lincs* 76 SK9896
Waddington *Lancs* 81 SD7343
Waddington *Lincs* 76 SK9764
Waddon *Devon* 9 SX8879
Waddon *Dorset* 10 SY6285
Wadebridge *Cnwll* 4 SW9972
Wadeford *Somset* 10 ST3110
Wadenhoe *Nhants* 51 TL0183
Wadesmill *Herts* 39 TL3617
Wadhurst *E Susx* 16 TQ6431
Wadshelf *Derbys* 74 SK3170
Wadswick *Wilts* 22 ST8467
Wadworth *S York* 75 SK5696
Waen *Denbgs* 70 SH9962
Waen *Denbgs* 70 SJ1065
Waen *Powys* 58 SJ2319
Waen Fach *Powys* 58 SJ2017
Waen-pentir *Gwynd* 69 SH5766
Waen-wen *Gwynd* 69 SH5768
Wagbeach *Shrops* 59 SJ3602
Wainfelin *Torfn* 34 SO2701
Wainfleet All Saints *Lincs* 77 TF4959
Wainfleet Bank *Lincs* 77 TF4759
Wainford *Norfk* 55 TM3490
Wainhouse Corner *Cnwll* 4 SX1895
Wains Hill *Somset* 34 ST3970
Wainscott *Kent* 28 TQ7470
Wainstalls *W York* 82 SE0428
Waitby *Cumb* 88 NY7508
Waithe *Lincs* 77 TA2800
Wake Green *W Mids* 61 SP0982
Wakefield *W York* 83 SE3320
Wakerley *Nhants* 51 SP9599
Wakes Colne *Essex* 40 TL8928
Wal-wen *Flints* 70 SJ2076
Walberswick *Suffk* 55 TM4974
Walberton *W Susx* 14 SU9705
Walbottle *T & W* 103 NZ1666
Walbutt *D & G* 99 NX7468
Walby *Cumb* 101 NY4460
Walcombe *Somset* 21 ST5546
Walcot *Lincs* 84 SE8720
Walcot *Lincs* 64 TF0635
Walcot *Lincs* 76 TF1356
Walcot *Shrops* 59 SJ5912
Walcot *Shrops* 59 SO3485
Walcot *Warwks* 48 SP1358
Walcot *Wilts* 36 SU1684
Walcot Green *Norfk* 54 TM1280
Walcote *Leics* 50 SP5683
Walcott *Norfk* 67 TG3532
Walden *N York* 88 SE0082
Walden Head *N York* 88 SD9880
Walden Stubbs *N York* 83 SE5516
Walderslade *Kent* 28 TQ7663
Walderton *W Susx* 14 SU7910
Walditch *Dorset* 10 SY4892
Waldley *Derbys* 73 SK1236
Waldridge *Dur* 96 NZ2549
Waldringfield *Suffk* 55 TM2845
Waldron *E Susx* 16 TQ5419
Wales *S York* 75 SK4882
Wales *Somset* 21 ST5824
Walesby *Lincs* 76 TF1392
Walesby *Notts* 75 SK6870
Walford *H & W* 46 SO3872
Walford *H & W* 34 SO5820
Walford *Shrops* 59 SJ4320
Walford *Staffs* 72 SJ8133
Walford Heath *Shrops* 59 SJ4419
Walgherton *Ches* 72 SJ6948
Walgrave *Nhants* 51 SP8071
Walhampton *Hants* 12 SZ3396
Walk Mill *Lancs* 81 SD8729
Walkden *Gt Man* 79 SD7302
Walker *T & W* 103 NZ2864
Walker Fold *Lancs* 81 SD6741
Walker's Green *H & W* 46 SO5247
Walker's Heath *W Mids* 61 SP0578
Walkerburn *Border* 109 NT3637
Walkeringham *Notts* 75 SK7792
Walkerith *Lincs* 75 SK7892
Walkern *Herts* 39 TL2826
Walkerton *Fife* 126 NO2301
Walkhampton *Devon* 6 SX5369
Walkington *E R Yk* 84 SE9936
Walkley *S York* 74 SK3388
Walkwood *H & W* 48 SP0364
Wall *Cnwll* 2 SW6036
Wall *Nthumb* 102 NY9168
Wall *Staffs* 61 SK1006
Wall End *Cumb* 86 SD2383
Wall End *H & W* 46 SO4457
Wall Heath *W Mids* 60 SO8889
Wall Houses *Nthumb* 103 NZ0368
Wall under Haywood *Shrops* 59 SO5092
Wallacetown *S Ayrs* 106 NS2703
Wallacetown *S Ayrs* 106 NS3422
Wallands Park *E Susx* 15 TQ4010
Wallasey *Mersyd* 78 SJ2992
Wallend *Kent* 28 TQ8775
Waller's Green *H & W* 47 SO6739
Wallhead *Cumb* 101 NY4660
Wallingford *Oxon* 37 SU6089
Wallington *Gt Lon* 27 TQ2864
Wallington *Hants* 13 SU5806
Wallington *Herts* 39 TL2933
Wallington Heath *W Mids* 60 SJ9903
Wallis *Pembks* 30 SN0125
Wallisdown *Dorset* 12 SZ0694
Walliswood *W Susx* 14 TQ1138
Walls *Shet* 155 HU2449
Wallsend *T & W* 103 NZ2966
Wallthwaite *Cumb* 93 NY3526
Wallyford *E Loth* 118 NT3671
Walmer *Kent* 29 TR3750
Walmer Bridge *Lancs* 80 SD4724
Walmersley *Gt Man* 81 SD8013
Walmestone *Kent* 29 TR2559
Walmley *W Mids* 61 SP1393
Walmley Ash *W Mids* 61 SP1492
Walmsgate *Lincs* 77 TF3677
Walpole *Somset* 20 ST3042
Walpole *Suffk* 55 TM3674
Walpole Cross Keys *Norfk* 65 TF5119
Walpole Highway *Norfk* 65 TF5114
Walpole St Andrew *Norfk* 65 TF5017
Walpole St Peter *Norfk* 65 TF5016
Walrow *Somset* 21 ST3447
Walsall *W Mids* 60 SP0198
Walsall Wood *W Mids* 61 SK0403
Walsden *W York* 81 SD9321
Walsgrave on Sowe *W Mids* 61 SP3881
Walshall Green *Herts* 39 TL4430
Walsham le Willows *Suffk* 54 TM0071
Walshaw *Gt Man* 81 SD7711
Walshaw *W York* 82 SD9731
Walshford *N York* 83 SE4153
Walsoken *Norfk* 65 TF4710
Walston *S Lans* 117 NT0545
Walsworth *Herts* 39 TL1930
Walter Ash *Bucks* 37 SU8398
Walters Green *Kent* 16 TQ5140
Walterston *V Glam* 33 ST0671
Walterstone *H & W* 46 SO3425
Waltham *Kent* 29 TR1048
Waltham *Lincs* 85 TA2603
Waltham Abbey *Essex* 27 TL3800
Waltham Chase *Hants* 13 SU5614
Waltham Cross *Herts* 27 TL3600
Waltham on the Wolds *Leics* 63 SK8024
Waltham St Lawrence *Berks* 37 SU8276
Waltham's Cross *Essex* 40 TL6930
Walthamstow *Gt Lon* 27 TQ3689
Walton *Bucks* 38 SP8936
Walton *Cambs* 64 TF1702
Walton *Cumb* 101 NY5264
Walton *Derbys* 74 SK3568
Walton *Leics* 50 SP5987
Walton *Powys* 46 SO2559
Walton *Shrops* 59 SJ5818
Walton *Shrops* 46 SO4679
Walton *Somset* 21 ST4636
Walton *Staffs* 72 SJ8528
Walton *Staffs* 72 SJ8932
Walton *Suffk* 55 TM2935
Walton *W Susx* 14 SU8104
Walton *W York* 83 SE3516
Walton *W York* 83 SE4447
Walton *Warwks* 48 SP2853
Walton Cardiff *Gloucs* 47 SO9032
Walton East *Pembks* 30 SN0223
Walton Elm *Dorset* 11 ST7717
Walton Grounds *Nhants* 49 SP5135
Walton Lower Street *Suffk* 55 TM2834
Walton on the Hill *Surrey* 26 TQ2255
Walton on the Naze *Essex* 41 TM2522
Walton on the Wolds *Leics* 62 SK5919
Walton Park *Somset* 34 ST4172
Walton West *Pembks* 30 SM8612
Walton-in-Gordano *Somset* 34 ST4273
Walton-le-Dale *Lancs* 81 SD5628
Walton-on-Thames *Surrey* 26 TQ1066
Walton-on-the-Hill *Staffs* 72 SJ9520
Walton-on-Trent *Derbys* 73 SK2118
Walwen *Flints* 70 SJ1179
Walwen *Flints* 70 SJ1771
Walwick *Nthumb* 102 NY9070
Walworth *Dur* 96 NZ2318
Walworth *Gt Lon* 27 TQ3277
Walworth Gate *Dur* 96 NZ2320
Walwyn's Castle *Pembks* 30 SM8711
Wambrook *Somset* 10 ST2907
Wampool *Cumb* 93 NY2454
Wanborough *Surrey* 25 SU9348
Wanborough *Wilts* 36 SU2082
Wandel *S Lans* 108 NS9427
Wandon End *Herts* 38 TL1322
Wandsworth *Gt Lon* 27 TQ2574
Wangford *Suffk* 55 TM4679
Wanlip *Leics* 62 SK5910
Wanlockhead *D & G* 108 NS8712
Wannock *E Susx* 16 TQ5703
Wansford *Cambs* 64 TL0799
Wansford *E R Yk* 84 TA0656
Wanshurst Green *Kent* 28 TQ7645
Wanstead *Gt Lon* 27 TQ4088
Wanstrow *Somset* 22 ST7141
Wanswell *Gloucs* 35 SO6801
Wantage *Oxon* 36 SU3988
Wants Green *H & W* 47 SO7557
Wapley *Gloucs* 35 ST7179
Wappenbury *Warwks* 48 SP3769
Wappenham *Nhants* 49 SP6245
Warbleton *E Susx* 16 TQ6018
Warborough *Oxon* 37 SU5993
Warboys *Cambs* 52 TL3080
Warbreck *Lancs* 80 SD3238
Warbstow *Cnwll* 5 SX2090
Warburton *Gt Man* 79 SJ7089
Warcop *Cumb* 94 NY7415
Ward End *W Mids* 61 SP1188
Ward Green *Suffk* 54 TM0464
Warden *Kent* 28 TR0271
Warden *Nthumb* 102 NY9166
Warden Law *T & W* 96 NZ3649
Warden Street *Beds* 38 TL1244
Wardhedges *Beds* 38 TL0635
Wardington *Oxon* 49 SP4846
Wardle *Ches* 71 SJ6156
Wardle *Gt Man* 81 SD9116
Wardley *Gt Man* 79 SD7602
Wardley *Rutlnd* 51 SK8300
Wardley *T & W* 96 NZ3061
Wardlow *Derbys* 74 SK1874
Wardsend *Ches* 79 SJ9382
Wardy Hill *Cambs* 53 TL4782
Ware *Herts* 39 TL3514
Ware Street *Kent* 28 TQ7956
Wareham *Dorset* 11 SY9287
Warehorne *Kent* 17 TQ9832
Waren Mill *Nthumb* 111 NU1434
Warenford *Nthumb* 111 NU1328
Warenton *Nthumb* 111 NU1030
Wareside *Herts* 39 TL3915
Waresley *Cambs* 52 TL2554
Waresley *H & W* 60 SO8470
Warfield *Berks* 25 SU8872
Warfleet *Devon* 7 SX8750
Wargate *Lincs* 64 TF2330
Wargrave *Berks* 37 SU7978
Warham *H & W* 46 SO4838
Warham All Saints *Norfk* 66 TF9541
Warham St Mary *Norfk* 66 TF9441
Wark *Nthumb* 110 NT8238
Wark *Nthumb* 102 NY8577
Warkleigh *Devon* 19 SS6422
Warkton *Nhants* 51 SP8979
Warkworth *Nhants* 49 SP4840
Warkworth *Nthumb* 111 NU2406
Warlaby *N York* 89 SE3491
Warland *W York* 82 SD9420
Warleggan *Cnwll* 4 SX1569
Warleigh *Somset* 22 ST7964
Warley Town *W York* 82 SE0524
Warlingham *Surrey* 27 TQ3658
Warmanbie *D & G* 101 NY1969
Warmbrook *Derbys* 73 SK2853
Warmfield *W York* 83 SE3720
Warmingham *Ches* 72 SJ7061
Warmington *Nhants* 51 TL0790
Warmington *Warwks* 49 SP4147
Warminster *Wilts* 22 ST8745
Warmley *Gloucs* 35 ST6673
Warmsworth *S York* 75 SE5400
Warmwell *Dorset* 11 SY7585
Warndon *H & W* 47 SO8856
Warnford *Hants* 13 SU6223
Warnham *W Susx* 15 TQ1533
Warnham Court *W Susx* 15 TQ1533
Warningcamp *W Susx* 14 TQ0307
Warninglid *W Susx* 15 TQ2426
Warren *Ches* 79 SJ8870
Warren *Pembks* 30 SR9397
Warren Row *Berks* 37 SU8180
Warren Street *Kent* 28 TQ9252
Warren's Green *Herts* 39 TL2628
Warrenby *N York* 97 NZ5825
Warrenhill *S Lans* 108 NS9438
Warrington *Bucks* 51 SP8953
Warrington *Ches* 78 SJ6088
Warriston *C Edin* 117 NT2575
Warsash *Hants* 13 SU4906
Warslow *Staffs* 74 SK0858
Warsop *Notts* 75 SK5667
Warsop Vale *Notts* 75 SK5467
Warter *E R Yk* 84 SE8750
Warter Priory *E R Yk* 84 SE8449
Warthermaske *N York* 89 SE2078
Warthill *N York* 83 SE6755
Wartling *E Susx* 16 TQ6509
Wartnaby *Leics* 63 SK7123
Warton *Lancs* 80 SD4128
Warton *Lancs* 87 SD4972
Warton *Nthumb* 103 NU0002
Warton *Warwks* 61 SK2803
Warwick *Cumb* 93 NY4656
Warwick *Warwks* 48 SP2865
Warwick Bridge *Cumb* 93 NY4756
Warwicksland *Cumb* 101 NY4577
Wasbister *Ork* 155 HY3932
Wasdale Head *Cumb* 86 NY1808
Wash *Derbys* 74 SK0682
Wash *Devon* 7 SX7665
Washaway *Cnwll* 4 SX0369
Washbourne *Devon* 7 SX7954
Washbrook *Somset* 21 ST4250
Washbrook *Suffk* 54 TM1142
Washfield *Devon* 9 SS9315
Washfold *N York* 88 NZ0502
Washford *Somset* 20 ST0541
Washford Pyne *Devon* 19 SS8111
Washingborough *Lincs* 76 TF0170
Washington *T & W* 96 NZ3155
Washington *W Susx* 14 TQ1112
Washwood Heath *W Mids* 61 SP1088
Wasing *Berks* 24 SU5764
Waskerley *Dur* 95 NZ0445
Wasperton *Warwks* 48 SP2658
Wasps Nest *Lincs* 76 TF0764
Wass *N York* 90 SE5579
Watchet *Somset* 20 ST0743
Watchfield *Oxon* 36 SU2490
Watchfield *Somset* 21 ST3446
Watchgate *Cumb* 87 SD5398
Watchill *Cumb* 93 NY1842
Watcombe *Devon* 7 SX9267
Watendlath *Cumb* 93 NY2716
Water *Devon* 8 SX7580
Water *Lancs* 81 SD8425
Water Eaton *Oxon* 37 SP5112
Water Eaton *Staffs* 60 SJ9011
Water End *Beds* 38 TL0637
Water End *Beds* 38 TL1047
Water End *Beds* 38 TL1051
Water End *Essex* 53 TL5840
Water End *Herts* 38 TL0310
Water End *Herts* 39 TL2304
Water End *E R Yk* 84 SE7938
Water Fryston *W York* 83 SE4726
Water Newton *Cambs* 51 TL1097
Water Orton *Warwks* 61 SP1790
Water Stratford *Bucks* 49 SP6534
Water Street *Neath* 32 SS8083
Water Yeat *Cumb* 86 SD2889
Water's Nook *Gt Man* 79 SD6605
Waterbeach *Cambs* 53 TL4965
Waterbeach *W Susx* 14 SU8908
Waterbeck *D & G* 101 NY2477
Watercombe *Dorset* 11 SY7585
Waterden *Norfk* 66 TF8836
Waterend *Cumb* 92 NY1122
Waterfall *Staffs* 73 SK0851
Waterfoot *Lancs* 81 SD8321
Waterfoot *S Lans* 115 NS5655
Waterford *Herts* 39 TL3114
Watergate *Cnwll* 4 SX1181
Waterhead *Cumb* 87 NY3703
Waterhead *E Ayrs* 107 NS5411
Waterheads *Border* 117 NT2451
Waterhouses *Dur* 96 NZ1841
Waterhouses *Staffs* 73 SK0850
Wateringbury *Kent* 28 TQ6853
Waterlane *Gloucs* 35 SO9204
Waterloo *Cnwll* 4 SX1072
Waterloo *Derbys* 74 SK4163
Waterloo *Dorset* 11 SZ0193
Waterloo *H & W* 46 SO3447
Waterloo *Highld* 129 NG6623
Waterloo *Mersyd* 78 SJ3298
Waterloo *N Lans* 116 NS8154
Waterloo *Norfk* 67 TG2219
Waterloo *P & K* 125 NO0537
Waterloo *Pembks* 30 SM9803
Waterloo Cross *Devon* 9 ST0514
Waterloo Port *Gwynd* 68 SH4964
Waterlooville *Hants* 13 SU6809
Watermillock *Cumb* 93 NY4422
Waterperry *Oxon* 37 SP6206
Waterrow *Somset* 20 ST0525
Waters Upton *Shrops* 59 SJ6319
Watersfield *W Susx* 14 TQ0115
Waterside *Bucks* 26 SP9600
Waterside *Cumb* 93 NY2245
Waterside *E Ayrs* 107 NS4308
Waterside *E Ayrs* 107 NS4843
Waterside *E Duns* 116 NS6773
Waterside *Lancs* 81 SD7123
Waterside *S York* 83 SE6714
Waterstock *Oxon* 37 SP6305
Waterston *Pembks* 30 SM9305
Watford *Herts* 26 TQ1196
Watford *Nhants* 50 SP6069
Wath *N York* 89 SE1467
Wath *N York* 89 SE3277
Wath upon Dearne *S York* 75 SE4300
Watlington *Norfk* 65 TF6111
Watlington *Oxon* 37 SU6894
Watnall *Notts* 62 SK5046
Watten *Highld* 151 ND2454
Wattisfield *Suffk* 54 TM0074
Wattisham *Suffk* 54 TM0151
Watton *Dorset* 10 SY4591
Watton *E R Yk* 84 TA0150
Watton *Norfk* 66 TF9100
Watton Green *Norfk* 66 TF9201
Watton-at-Stone *Herts* 39 TL3019
Wattons Green *Essex* 27 TQ5295
Wattston *N Lans* 116 NS7770
Wattstown *Rhondd* 33 ST0193
Wattsville *Caerph* 33 ST2091
Wauldby *E R Yk* 84 SE9629
Waulkmill *Abers* 135 NO6492
Waunarlwydd *Swans* 32 SS6095
Waunfawr *Cardgn* 43 SN6081
Waunfawr *Gwynd* 68 SH5259
Waungron *Swans* 32 SN5901
Waunlwyd *Blae G* 33 SO1806
Wavendon *Bucks* 38 SP9137
Waverbridge *Cumb* 93 NY2249
Waverton *Ches* 71 SJ4663
Waverton *Cumb* 93 NY2247
Wawne *E R Yk* 85 TA0936
Waxham *Norfk* 67 TG4426
Waxholme *E R Yk* 85 TA3229
Way *Kent* 29 TR3265
Way Village *Devon* 19 SS8810
Way Wick *Somset* 21 ST3862
Waye *Devon* 7 SX7771
Wayford *Somset* 10 ST4006
Waytown *Dorset* 10 SY4797
Weacombe *Somset* 20 ST1140
Weald *Cambs* 52 TL2259
Weald *Oxon* 36 SP3002
Wealdstone *Gt Lon* 26 TQ1589
Wear Head *Dur* 95 NY8539
Weardley *W York* 82 SE2944
Weare *Somset* 21 ST4152
Weare Giffard *Devon* 18 SS4721
Wearne *Somset* 21 ST4228
Weasdale *Cumb* 87 NY6903
Weasenham All Saints *Norfk* 66 TF8421
Weasenham St Peter *Norfk* 66 TF8522
Weaste *Gt Man* 79 SJ8098
Weatheroak Hill *H & W* 61 SP0674
Weaverham *Ches* 71 SJ6174
Weaverslake *Staffs* 73 SK1319
Weaverthorpe *N York* 91 SE9670
Webb's Heath *Gloucs* 35 ST6873
Webbington *Somset* 21 ST3855
Webheath *H & W* 48 SP0266
Webton *H & W* 46 SO4136
Wedderlairs *Abers* 143 NJ8532
Wedding Hall Fold *N York* 82 SD9445
Weddington *Kent* 29 TR2959
Weddington *Warwks* 61 SP3693
Wedhampton *Wilts* 23 SU0557
Wedmore *Somset* 21 ST4347
Wednesbury *W Mids* 60 SO9895
Wednesfield *W Mids* 60 SJ9400
Weecar *Notts* 75 SK8266
Weedon *Bucks* 38 SP8118
Weedon Lois *Nhants* 49 SP6046
Weeford *Staffs* 61 SK1403
Week *Devon* 19 SS5727
Week *Devon* 19 SS7316
Week *Devon* 7 SX7862
Week *Somset* 20 SS9133
Week St Mary *Cnwll* 5 SX2397
Weeke *Devon* 8 SS7606
Weeke *Hants* 24 SU4630
Weekley *Nhants* 51 SP8881
Weel *E R Yk* 84 TA0639
Weeley *Essex* 41 TM1422
Weeley Heath *Essex* 41 TM1520
Weem *P & K* 125 NN8449
Weeping Cross *Staffs* 72 SJ9421
Weethley *Warwks* 48 SP0555
Weeting *Norfk* 53 TL7788
Weeton *E R Yk* 85 TA3520
Weeton *Lancs* 80 SD3834
Weeton *N York* 82 SE2847
Weetwood *W York* 82 SE2737
Weir *Lancs* 81 SD8625
Weir Quay *Devon* 6 SX4365
Weirbrook *Shrops* 59 SJ3424
Welbeck Abbey *Notts* 75 SK5574
Welborne *Norfk* 66 TG0610
Welbourn *Lincs* 76 SK9654
Welburn *N York* 90 SE7267
Welbury *N York* 89 NZ3902
Welby *Lincs* 63 SK9738
Welches Dam *Cambs* 53 TL4686
Welcombe *Devon* 18 SS2318
Weldon Bridge *Nthumb* 103 NZ1398
Welford *Berks* 24 SU4073
Welford *Nhants* 50 SP6480
Welford-on-Avon *Warwks* 48 SP1452
Welham *Leics* 50 SP7692
Welham *Notts* 75 SK7281
Welham Green *Herts* 39 TL2305
Well *Hants* 25 SU7646
Well *Lincs* 77 TF4473
Well *N York* 89 SE2681
Well End *Bucks* 26 SU8888
Well End *Herts* 26 TQ2098
Well Fold *W York* 82 SE2024
Well Head *Herts* 39 TL1727
Well Hill *Kent* 27 TQ4963
Well Town *Devon* 9 SS9009
Welland *H & W* 47 SO7940
Welland Stone *H & W* 47 SO8138
Wellbank *Angus* 127 NO4737
Wellbury *Herts* 38 TL1329
Wellesbourne *Warwks* 48 SP2855
Wellesbourne Mountford *Warwks* 48 SP2755

Wellhouse

Westwood

Wellhouse *Berks*	24	SU5272
Welling *Gt Lon*	27	TQ4675
Wellingborough *Nhants*	51	SP8967
Wellingham *Norfk*	66	TF8722
Wellingore *Lincs*	76	SK9856
Wellington *Cumb*	86	NY0704
Wellington *H & W*	46	SO4948
Wellington *Shrops*	59	SJ6511
Wellington *Somset*	20	ST1320
Wellington Heath *H & W*	47	SO7140
Wellington Marsh *H & W*	46	SO4946
Wellow *IOW*	12	SZ3888
Wellow *Notts*	75	SK6766
Wellow *Somset*	22	ST7458
Wellpond Green *Herts*	39	TL4122
Wells *Somset*	21	ST5445
Wells Green *Ches*	72	SJ6853
Wells Head *W York*	82	SE0833
Wells-Next-The-Sea *Norfk*	66	TF9143
Wellsborough *Leics*	62	SK3602
Wellstye Green *Essex*	40	TL6318
Welltree *P & K*	125	NN9622
Wellwood *Fife*	117	NT0988
Welney *Norfk*	65	TL5293
Welsh Bicknor *H & W*	34	SO5917
Welsh End *Shrops*	59	SJ5135
Welsh Frankton *Shrops*	59	SJ3533
Welsh Hook *Pembks*	30	SM9327
Welsh Newton *H & W*	34	SO5017
Welsh St Donats *V Glam*	33	ST0276
Welshampton *Shrops*	59	SJ4335
Welshpool *Powys*	58	SJ2207
Welton *Cumb*	93	NY3544
Welton *E R Yk*	84	SE9627
Welton *Lincs*	76	TF0179
Welton *Nhants*	50	SP5865
Welton le Marsh *Lincs*	77	TF4768
Welton le Wold *Lincs*	77	TF2787
Welwick *E R Yk*	85	TA3421
Welwyn *Herts*	39	TL2316
Welwyn Garden City *Herts*	39	TL2312
Wem *Shrops*	59	SJ5128
Wembdon *Somset*	20	ST2837
Wembley *Gt Lon*	26	TQ1885
Wembury *Devon*	6	SX5248
Wembworthy *Devon*	19	SS6609
Wemyss Bay *Inver*	114	NS1969
Wenallt *Cardgn*	43	SN6771
Wendens Ambo *Essex*	39	TL5136
Wendlebury *Oxon*	37	SP5619
Wendling *Norfk*	66	TF9312
Wendover *Bucks*	38	SP8607
Wendron *Cnwll*	2	SW6731
Wendy *Cambs*	52	TL3247
Wenfordbridge *Cnwll*	4	SX0875
Wenhaston *Suffk*	55	TM4275
Wennington *Cambs*	52	TL2379
Wennington *Gt Lon*	27	TQ5381
Wennington *Lancs*	87	SD6170
Wensley *Derbys*	74	SK2661
Wensley *N York*	89	SE0989
Wentbridge *W York*	83	SE4817
Wentnor *Shrops*	59	SO3892
Wentworth *Cambs*	53	TL4878
Wentworth *S York*	74	SK3898
Wentworth Castle *S York*	83	SE3202
Wenvoe *V Glam*	33	ST1272
Weobley *H & W*	46	SO4051
Weobley Marsh *H & W*	46	SO4151
Wepham *W Susx*	14	TQ0408
Wereham *Norfk*	65	TF6801
Wergs *Staffs*	60	SJ8700
Wern *Gwynd*	57	SH5439
Wern *Powys*	58	SH9612
Wern *Powys*	58	SJ2513
Wern *Powys*	33	SO1217
Wern *Shrops*	58	SJ2734
Wern-y-gaer *Flints*	70	SJ2068
Werneth Low *Gt Man*	79	SJ9592
Wernffrwd *Swans*	32	SS5194
Werrington *Cambs*	64	TF1603
Werrington *Cnwll*	5	SX3287
Werrington *Staffs*	72	SJ9447
Wervin *Ches*	71	SJ4271
Wesham *Lancs*	80	SD4133
Wessington *Derbys*	74	SK3757
West Aberthaw *V Glam*	20	ST0266
West Acre *Norfk*	65	TF7815
West Allerdean *Nthumb*	111	NT9646
West Alvington *Devon*	7	SX7243
West Amesbury *Wilts*	23	SU1341
West Anstey *Devon*	19	SS8527
West Appleton *N York*	89	SE2294
West Ashby *Lincs*	77	TF2672
West Ashling *W Susx*	14	SU8107
West Ashton *Wilts*	22	ST8755
West Auckland *Dur*	96	NZ1826
West Ayton *N York*	91	SE9884
West Bagborough *Somset*	20	ST1733
West Balsdon *Cnwll*	5	SX2798
West Bank *Blae G*	33	SO2105
West Bank *Ches*	78	SJ5183
West Barkwith *Lincs*	76	TF1580
West Barnby *N York*	90	NZ8212
West Barns *E Loth*	118	NT6578
West Barsham *Norfk*	66	TF9033
West Bay *Dorset*	10	SY4690
West Beckham *Norfk*	66	TG1439
West Bedfont *Surrey*	26	TQ0674
West Bergholt *Essex*	40	TL9527
West Bexington *Dorset*	10	SY5386
West Bilney *Norfk*	65	TF7115
West Blatchington *E Susx*	15	TQ2707
West Boldon *T & W*	96	NZ3561
West Bourton *Dorset*	22	ST7629
West Bowling *W York*	82	SE1630
West Brabourne *Kent*	29	TR0842
West Bradenham *Norfk*	66	TF9108
West Bradford *Lancs*	81	SD7444
West Bradley *Somset*	21	ST5536
West Bretton *W York*	82	SE2813
West Bridgford *Notts*	62	SK5836
West Briscoe *Dur*	95	NY9619
West Bromwich *W Mids*	60	SP0091
West Buccleigh Hotel *Border*	109	NT3214
West Buckland *Devon*	19	SS6531
West Buckland *Somset*	20	ST1720
West Burton *N York*	88	SE0186
West Burton *W Susx*	14	SU9914
West Butsfield *Dur*	95	NZ1044
West Butterwick *Lincs*	84	SE8305
West Byfleet *Surrey*	26	TQ0461
West Cairngaan *D & G*	98	NX1231
West Caister *Norfk*	67	TG5011
West Calder *W Loth*	117	NT0163
West Camel *Somset*	21	ST5724
West Chaldon *Dorset*	11	SY7782
West Challow *Oxon*	36	SU3688
West Charleton *Devon*	7	SX7542
West Chelborough *Dorset*	10	ST5405
West Chevington *Nthumb*	103	NZ2297
West Chiltington *W Susx*	14	TQ0818
West Chinnock *Somset*	10	ST4613
West Chisenbury *Wilts*	23	SU1352
West Clandon *Surrey*	26	TQ0452
West Cliffe *Kent*	29	TR3444
West Coker *Somset*	10	ST5113
West Combe *Devon*	7	SX7662
West Compton *Dorset*	10	SY5694
West Compton *Somset*	21	ST5942
West Cottingwith *N York*	83	SE6942
West Cowick *E R Yk*	83	SE6421
West Cross *Swans*	32	SS6189
West Curry *Cnwll*	5	SX2893
West Curthwaite *Cumb*	93	NY3249
West Dean *W Susx*	14	SU8612
West Dean *Wilts*	23	SU2526
West Deeping *Lincs*	64	TF1008
West Derby *Mersyd*	78	SJ3993
West Dereham *Norfk*	65	TF6500
West Down *Devon*	19	SS5142
West Drayton *Gt Lon*	26	TQ0579
West Drayton *Notts*	75	SK7074
West Dunnet *Highld*	151	ND2171
West Ella *E R Yk*	84	TA0029
West End *Beds*	51	SP9853
West End *Berks*	37	SU8275
West End *Berks*	25	SU8671
West End *Caerph*	33	ST2195
West End *Cambs*	52	TL3168
West End *Cumb*	93	NY3258
West End *E R Yk*	84	SE9130
West End *E R Yk*	85	TA1830
West End *E R Yk*	85	TA2627
West End *Gloucs*	35	ST7188
West End *Hants*	13	SU4614
West End *Hants*	24	SU6335
West End *Herts*	39	TL2608
West End *Herts*	39	TL3306
West End *Lancs*	81	SD7328
West End *Lincs*	77	TF3598
West End *N York*	89	SE1457
West End *N York*	83	SE5140
West End *Norfk*	66	TF9009
West End *Norfk*	67	TG5011
West End *Oxon*	37	SU5886
West End *Somset*	21	ST4569
West End *Somset*	22	ST6734
West End *Surrey*	25	SU9461
West End *Surrey*	26	TQ1263
West End *W Susx*	15	TQ2016
West End *W York*	82	SE2238
West End *Wilts*	22	ST9124
West End *Wilts*	35	ST9777
West End *Wilts*	22	ST9824
West End Green *Hants*	24	SU6661
West Ewell *Surrey*	26	TQ2063
West Farleigh *Kent*	28	TQ7152
West Farndon *Nhants*	49	SP5251
West Felton *Shrops*	59	SJ3425
West Firle *E Susx*	16	TQ4707
West Firsby *Lincs*	76	SK9784
West Flotmanby *N York*	91	TA0779
West Garforth *W York*	83	SE3932
West Ginge *Oxon*	37	SU4486
West Grafton *Wilts*	23	SU2460
West Green *Hants*	24	SU7456
West Grimstead *Wilts*	23	SU2026
West Grinstead *W Susx*	15	TQ1720
West Haddlesey *N York*	83	SE5626
West Haddon *Nhants*	50	SP6371
West Hagbourne *Oxon*	37	SU5187
West Hagley *H & W*	60	SO9080
West Hallam *Derbys*	62	SK4341
West Hallam Common *Derbys*	62	SK4241
West Halton *Lincs*	84	SE9020
West Ham *Gt Lon*	27	TQ3983
West Handley *Derbys*	74	SK3977
West Hanney *Oxon*	36	SU4092
West Hanningfield *Essex*	40	TQ7399
West Harnham *Wilts*	23	SU1329
West Harptree *Somset*	21	ST5556
West Harting *W Susx*	14	SU7820
West Hatch *Somset*	20	ST2821
West Hatch *Wilts*	22	ST9227
West Haven *Angus*	127	NO5735
West Head *Norfk*	65	TF5705
West Heath *Hants*	24	SU5858
West Heath *W Mids*	60	SP0277
West Helmsdale *Highld*	147	ND0115
West Hendred *Oxon*	37	SU4488
West Heslerton *N York*	91	SE9176
West Hewish *Somset*	21	ST3963
West Hill *Devon*	9	SY0794
West Hoathly *W Susx*	15	TQ3632
West Holme *Dorset*	11	SY8885
West Horndon *Essex*	40	TQ6288
West Horrington *Somset*	21	ST5747
West Horsley *Surrey*	26	TQ0752
West Horton *Nthumb*	111	NU0230
West Hougham *Kent*	29	TR2640
West Howe *Dorset*	12	SZ0595
West Howetown *Somset*	20	SS9134
West Huntingtower *P & K*	125	NO0724
West Huntspill *Somset*	20	ST3044
West Hyde *Beds*	38	TL1117
West Hyde *Herts*	26	TQ0391
West Hythe *Kent*	17	TR1234
West Ilkerton *Devon*	19	SS7046
West Ilsley *Berks*	37	SU4782
West Itchenor *W Susx*	14	SU7901
West Keal *Lincs*	77	TF3663
West Kennett *Wilts*	23	SU1168
West Kilbride *N Ayrs*	114	NS2048
West Kingsdown *Kent*	27	TQ5763
West Kington *Wilts*	35	ST8077
West Kirby *Mersyd*	78	SJ2186
West Knapton *N York*	90	SE8775
West Knighton *Dorset*	11	SY7387
West Knoyle *Wilts*	22	ST8632
West Lambrook *Somset*	10	ST4118
West Langdon *Kent*	29	TR3247
West Laroch *Highld*	130	NN0758
West Lavington *W Susx*	14	SU8920
West Lavington *Wilts*	22	SU0052
West Layton *N York*	89	NZ1410
West Leake *Notts*	62	SK5226
West Learmouth *Nthumb*	110	NT8437
West Lees *N York*	89	NZ4702
West Leigh *Devon*	8	SS6805
West Leigh *Devon*	7	SX7557
West Leigh *Somset*	20	ST1230
West Lexham *Norfk*	66	TF8417
West Lilling *N York*	90	SE6465
West Linton *Border*	117	NT1551
West Littleton *Gloucs*	35	ST7675
West Lockinge *Oxon*	36	SU4187
West Lulworth *Dorset*	11	SY8280
West Lutton *N York*	91	SE9369
West Lydford *Somset*	21	ST5631
West Lyn *Devon*	19	SS7248
West Lyng *Somset*	21	ST3128
West Lynn *Norfk*	65	TF6120
West Malling *Kent*	28	TQ6757
West Malvern *H & W*	47	SO7646
West Marden *W Susx*	14	SU7713
West Markham *Notts*	75	SK7272
West Marsh *Lincs*	85	TA2509
West Marton *N York*	81	SD8950
West Melbury *Dorset*	22	ST8720
West Melton *S York*	83	SE4201
West Meon *Hants*	13	SU6423
West Meon Hut *Hants*	13	SU6526
West Meon Woodlands *Hants*	13	SU6426
West Mersea *Essex*	41	TM0112
West Milton *Dorset*	10	SY5096
West Minster *Kent*	28	TQ9073
West Molesey *Surrey*	26	TQ1368
West Monkton *Somset*	20	ST2628
West Moors *Dorset*	12	SU0802
West Morden *Dorset*	11	SY9095
West Morriston *Border*	110	NT6040
West Morton *W York*	82	SE0942
West Mudford *Somset*	21	ST5620
West Ness *N York*	90	SE6879
West Newbiggin *Dur*	96	NZ3518
West Newton *E R Yk*	85	TA2037
West Newton *Norfk*	65	TF6928
West Newton *Somset*	20	ST2829
West Norwood *Gt Lon*	27	TQ3171
West Ogwell *Devon*	7	SX8270
West Orchard *Dorset*	11	ST8216
West Overton *Wilts*	23	SU1267
West Panson *Devon*	5	SX3491
West Parley *Dorset*	12	SZ0896
West Peckham *Kent*	27	TQ6452
West Pelton *Dur*	96	NZ2353
West Pennard *Somset*	21	ST5438
West Pentire *Cnwll*	4	SW7760
West Perry *Cambs*	52	TL1466
West Porlock *Somset*	19	SS8747
West Prawle *Devon*	7	SX7637
West Preston *W Susx*	14	TQ0602
West Pulham *Dorset*	11	ST7008
West Putford *Devon*	18	SS3616
West Quantoxhead *Somset*	20	ST1141
West Raddon *Devon*	9	SS8902
West Rainton *Dur*	96	NZ3246
West Rasen *Lincs*	76	TF0689
West Ravendale *Lincs*	76	TF2299
West Raynham *Norfk*	66	TF8725
West Retford *Notts*	75	SK6981
West Rounton *N York*	89	NZ4103
West Row *Suffk*	53	TL6775
West Rudham *Norfk*	66	TF8127
West Runton *Norfk*	66	TG1842
West Saltoun *E Loth*	118	NT4667
West Sandford *Devon*	8	SS8102
West Sandwick *Shet*	155	HU4588
West Scrafton *N York*	88	SE0783
West Sleekburn *Nthumb*	103	NZ2884
West Somerton *Norfk*	67	TG4620
West Stafford *Dorset*	11	SY7289
West Stockwith *Notts*	75	SK7895
West Stoke *W Susx*	14	SU8208
West Stonesdale *N York*	88	NY8801
West Stoughton *Somset*	21	ST4148
West Stour *Dorset*	22	ST7822
West Stourmouth *Kent*	29	TR2562
West Stow *Suffk*	54	TL8171
West Stowell *Wilts*	23	SU1361
West Stratton *Hants*	24	SU5240
West Street *Kent*	28	TQ7376
West Street *Kent*	28	TQ9054
West Street *Kent*	29	TR3254
West Street *Suffk*	54	TL9871
West Tanfield *N York*	89	SE2678
West Taphouse *Cnwll*	4	SX1463
West Tarbert *Ag & B*	113	NR8467
West Tarring *W Susx*	14	TQ1103
West Thorney *W Susx*	14	SU7602
West Thorpe *Notts*	62	SK6225
West Thurrock *Essex*	27	TQ5877
West Tilbury *Essex*	40	TQ6678
West Tisted *Hants*	24	SU6529
West Torrington *Lincs*	76	TF1381
West Town *H & W*	46	SO4361
West Town *Hants*	13	SZ7199
West Town *Somset*	21	ST4868
West Town *Somset*	21	ST5160
West Town *Somset*	21	ST5335
West Town *Somset*	22	ST7042
West Tytherley *Hants*	23	SU2729
West Tytherton *Wilts*	35	ST9474
West Walton *Norfk*	65	TF4613
West Walton Highway *Norfk*	65	TF4913
West Weetwood *Nthumb*	111	NU0028
West Wellow *Hants*	12	SU2819
West Wembury *Devon*	6	SX5249
West Wemyss *Fife*	118	NT3294
West Wick *Somset*	21	ST3761
West Wickham *Cambs*	53	TL6149
West Wickham *Gt Lon*	27	TQ3766
West Williamston *Pembks*	30	SN0305
West Winch *Norfk*	65	TF6316
West Winterslow *Wilts*	23	SU2331
West Wittering *W Susx*	14	SZ7898
West Witton *N York*	88	SE0588
West Woodburn *Nthumb*	102	NY8987
West Woodhay *Berks*	23	SU3963
West Woodlands *Somset*	22	ST7743
West Woodside *Cumb*	93	NY3049
West Worldham *Hants*	24	SU7436
West Worthing *W Susx*	15	TQ1302
West Wratting *Essex*	53	TL6052
West Wycombe *Bucks*	37	SU8294
West Wylam *Nthumb*	103	NZ1063
West Yatton *Wilts*	35	ST8575
West Yoke *Kent*	27	TQ6065
West Youlstone *Cnwll*	18	SS2615
Westbere *Kent*	29	TR1961
Westborough *Lincs*	63	SK8544
Westbourne *W Susx*	13	SU7507
Westbrook *Berks*	24	SU4272
Westbrook *Kent*	29	TR3470
Westbrook *Wilts*	22	ST9565
Westbury *Bucks*	49	SP6235
Westbury *Shrops*	59	SJ3509
Westbury *Wilts*	22	ST8751
Westbury Leigh *Wilts*	22	ST8649
Westbury on Severn *Gloucs*	35	SO7114
Westbury-on-Trym *Bristl*	34	ST5777
Westbury-sub-Mendip *Somset*	21	ST5049
Westby *Lancs*	80	SD3831
Westcliff-on-Sea *Essex*	40	TQ8685
Westcombe *Somset*	22	ST6739
Westcote *Gloucs*	36	SP2120
Westcott *Bucks*	37	SP7116
Westcott *Devon*	9	ST0204
Westcott *Somset*	19	SS8720
Westcott *Surrey*	15	TQ1448
Westcott Barton *Oxon*	49	SP4325
Westcourt *Wilts*	23	SU2261
Westdean *E Susx*	16	TV5299
Westdown Camp *Wilts*	23	SU0447
Westdowns *Cnwll*	4	SX0582
Wested *Kent*	27	TQ5166
Westend *Gloucs*	35	SO7807
Westend Town *Nthumb*	102	NY7865
Westenhanger *Kent*	29	TR1237
Wester Drumashie *Highld*	140	NH6032
Wester Essenside *Border*	109	NT4320
Wester Ochiltree *W Loth*	117	NT0374
Wester Pitkierie *Fife*	127	NO5505
Westerdale *Highld*	151	ND1251
Westerdale *N York*	90	NZ6605
Westerfield *Suffk*	54	TM1747
Westergate *W Susx*	14	SU9305
Westerham *Kent*	27	TQ4454
Westerhope *T & W*	103	NZ1966
Westerland *Devon*	7	SX8662
Westerleigh *Gloucs*	35	ST6979
Westerton *Angus*	127	NO6754
Westerton *W Susx*	14	SU8807
Westfield *Cumb*	92	NX9926
Westfield *E Susx*	17	TQ8115
Westfield *N Lans*	116	NS7273
Westfield *Norfk*	66	TF9909
Westfield *Somset*	22	ST6753
Westfield *W Loth*	116	NS9472
Westfield Sole *Kent*	28	TQ7761
Westfields *Dorset*	11	ST7206
Westfields *H & W*	46	SO4941
Westfields of Rattray *P & K*	126	NO1746
Westford *Somset*	20	ST1220
Westgate *Dur*	95	NY9038
Westgate *Lincs*	84	SE7707
Westgate *Norfk*	66	TF9740
Westgate Hill *W York*	82	SE2029
Westgate on Sea *Kent*	29	TR3270
Westgate Street *Norfk*	67	TG1921
Westhall *Suffk*	55	TM4280
Westham *Dorset*	11	SY6679
Westham *E Susx*	16	TQ6404
Westham *Somset*	21	ST4046
Westhampnett *W Susx*	14	SU8806
Westhay *Somset*	21	ST4342
Westhead *Lancs*	78	SD4407
Westhide *H & W*	46	SO5843
Westhill *Abers*	135	NJ8307
Westholme *Somset*	21	ST5741
Westhope *H & W*	46	SO4651
Westhope *Shrops*	59	SO4786
Westhorp *Nhants*	49	SP5152
Westhorpe *Lincs*	64	TF2231
Westhorpe *Suffk*	54	TM0468
Westhoughton *Gt Man*	79	SD6506
Westhouse *N York*	87	SD6773
Westhouses *Derbys*	74	SK4157
Westhumble *Surrey*	26	TQ1651
Westlake *Devon*	6	SX6253
Westland Green *Herts*	39	TL4222
Westleigh *Devon*	18	SS4728
Westleigh *Devon*	9	ST0617
Westleton *Suffk*	55	TM4369
Westley *Shrops*	59	SJ3607
Westley *Suffk*	54	TL8264
Westley Waterless *Cambs*	53	TL6156
Westlington *Bucks*	37	SP7610
Westlinton *Cumb*	101	NY3964
Westmarsh *Kent*	29	TR2761
Westmeston *E Susx*	15	TQ3313
Westmill *Herts*	39	TL3627
Westminster *Gt Lon*	27	TQ2979
Westmuir *Angus*	126	NO3652
Westnewton *Cumb*	92	NY1344
Westoe *T & W*	103	NZ3765
Weston *Berks*	36	SU3973
Weston *Ches*	78	SJ5080
Weston *Ches*	72	SJ7352
Weston *Devon*	9	ST1400
Weston *Devon*	9	SY1688
Weston *Dorset*	11	SY6871
Weston *H & W*	46	SO3656
Weston *Hants*	13	SU7221
Weston *Herts*	39	TL2530
Weston *Lincs*	64	TF2924
Weston *N York*	82	SE1747
Weston *Nhants*	49	SP5846
Weston *Notts*	75	SK7767
Weston *Shrops*	59	SO6093
Weston *Shrops*	59	SJ2927
Weston *Shrops*	59	SJ5629
Weston *Shrops*	46	SO3273
Weston *Somset*	22	ST7366
Weston *Staffs*	72	SJ9726
Weston Beggard *H & W*	46	SO5841
Weston by Welland *Nhants*	50	SP7791
Weston Colley *Hants*	24	SU5039
Weston Colville *Cambs*	53	TL6153
Weston Corbett *Hants*	24	SU6846
Weston Coyney *Staffs*	72	SJ9343
Weston Favell *Nhants*	50	SP7962
Weston Green *Cambs*	53	TL6252
Weston Heath *Shrops*	60	SJ7713
Weston Hills *Lincs*	64	TF2720
Weston in Arden *Warwks*	61	SP3886
Weston Jones *Staffs*	72	SJ7624
Weston Longville *Norfk*	66	TG1115
Weston Lullingfields *Shrops*	59	SJ4224
Weston Patrick *Hants*	24	SU6946
Weston Rhyn *Shrops*	58	SJ2835
Weston Subedge *Gloucs*	48	SP1241
Weston Turville *Bucks*	38	SP8510
Weston under Penyard *H & W*	35	SO6322
Weston under Wetherley *Warwks*	48	SP3669
Weston Underwood *Bucks*	38	SP8650
Weston Underwood *Derbys*	73	SK2942
Weston-in-Gordano *Somset*	34	ST4474
Weston-on-the-Green *Oxon*	37	SP5318
Weston-Super-Mare *Somset*	21	ST3260
Weston-under-Lizard *Staffs*	60	SJ8010
Weston-upon-Trent *Derbys*	62	SK4027
Westonbirt *Gloucs*	35	ST8589
Westoning *Beds*	38	TL0332
Westoning Woodend *Beds*	38	TL0232
Westonzoyland *Somset*	21	ST3534
Westow *N York*	90	SE7565
Westpeek *Devon*	5	SX3493
Westport *Somset*	21	ST3820
Westquarter *Falk*	116	NS9178
Westra *V Glam*	33	ST1470
Westridge Green *Berks*	37	SU5679
Westrigg *W Loth*	116	NS9067
Westrop *Wilts*	36	SU2093
Westruther *Border*	110	NT6349
Westry *Cambs*	65	TL4098
Westthorpe *Derbys*	75	SK4579
Westward *Cumb*	93	NY2744
Westward Ho! *Devon*	18	SS4329
Westwell *Kent*	28	TQ9947
Westwell *Oxon*	36	SP2209
Westwell Leacon *Kent*	28	TQ9647
Westwick *Cambs*	53	TL4265
Westwick *Dur*	95	NZ0715
Westwick *Norfk*	67	TG2726
Westwood *Devon*	9	SY0199
Westwood *Kent*	27	TQ6070
Westwood *Kent*	29	TR3667
Westwood *Notts*	75	SK4551
Westwood *Wilts*	22	ST8059

Westwood Heath

Windygates

Westwood Heath *W Mids* 61 SP2776
Westwoodside *Lincs* 75 SE7400
Wetham Green *Kent* 28 TQ8468
Wetheral *Cumb* 93 NY4654
Wetherby *W York* 83 SE4048
Wetherden *Suffk* 54 TM0062
Wetheringsett *Suffk* 54 TM1266
Wethersfield *Essex* 40 TL7131
Wetherup Street *Suffk* 54 TM1464
Wetley Rocks *Staffs* 72 SJ9649
Wettenhall *Ches* 71 SJ6261
Wetton *Staffs* 73 SK1055
Wetwang *E R Yk* 91 SE9359
Wetwood *Staffs* 72 SJ7733
Wexcombe *Wilts* 23 SU2758
Wexham *Bucks* 26 SU9882
Wexham Street *Bucks* 26 SU9883
Weybourne *Norfk* 66 TG1142
Weybread *Suffk* 55 TM2480
Weybread Street *Suffk* 55 TM2479
Weybridge *Surrey* 26 TQ0764
Weycroft *Devon* 10 SY3099
Weydale *Highld* 151 ND1564
Weyhill *Hants* 23 SU3146
Weymouth *Dorset* 11 SY6779
Whaddon *Bucks* 38 SP8034
Whaddon *Cambs* 52 TL3546
Whaddon *Gloucs* 35 SO8313
Whaddon *Wilts* 22 ST8861
Whaddon *Wilts* 23 SU1926
Whale *Cumb* 94 NY5221
Whaley *Derbys* 75 SK5171
Whaley Bridge *Derbys* 79 SK0180
Whaley Thorns *Derbys* 75 SK5271
Whaligoe *Highld* 151 ND3140
Whalley *Lancs* 81 SD7336
Whalley Banks *Lancs* 81 SD7335
Whalton *Nthumb* 96 NZ1318
Whamley *Nthumb* 102 NY8766
Whaplode *Lincs* 64 TF3224
Whaplode Drove *Lincs* 64 TF3213
Wharf *Warwks* 49 SP4352
Wharfe *N York* 88 SD7869
Wharles *Lancs* 80 SD4435
Wharley End *Beds* 38 SP9442
Wharncliffe Side *S York* 74 SK2994
Wharram-le-Street *N York* 90 SE8665
Wharton *Ches* 72 SJ6666
Wharton *H & W* 46 SO5055
Whashton Green *N York* 89 NZ1405
Whasset *Cumb* 87 SD5080
Whaston *N York* 89 NZ1506
Whatcote *Warwks* 48 SP2944
Whateley *Warwks* 61 SP2299
Whatfield *Suffk* 54 TM0246
Whatley *Somset* 10 ST3607
Whatley *Somset* 22 ST7347
Whatley's End *Gloucs* 35 ST6581
Whatlington *E Susx* 17 TQ7618
Whatsole Street *Kent* 29 TR1144
Whatstandwell *Derbys* 74 SK3354
Whatton *Notts* 63 SK7439
Whauphill *D & G* 99 NX4049
Whaw *N York* 88 NY9804
Wheal Rose *Cnwll* 2 SW7144
Wheatacre *Norfk* 67 TM4694
Wheatfield *Oxon* 37 SU6899
Wheathampstead *Herts* 39 TL1714
Wheathill *Shrops* 59 SO6282
Wheathill *Somset* 21 ST5830
Wheatley *Hants* 25 SU7840
Wheatley *Oxon* 37 SP5905
Wheatley *W York* 82 SE0726
Wheatley Hill *Dur* 96 NZ3738
Wheatley Hills *S York* 83 SE5904
Wheatley Lane *Lancs* 81 SD8337
Wheaton Aston *Staffs* 60 SJ8512
Wheatsheaf *Wrexhm* 71 SJ3253
Wheddon Cross *Somset* 20 SS9238
Wheel Inn *Cnwll* 2 SW6921
Wheelbarrow Town *Kent* 29 TR1445
Wheeler's Green *Oxon* 24 SU7672
Wheeler's Street *Kent* 28 TQ8444
Wheelerend Common *Bucks* 37 SU8093
Wheelerstreet *Surrey* 25 SU9440
Wheelock *Ches* 72 SJ7559
Wheelock Heath *Ches* 72 SJ7557
Wheelton *Lancs* 81 SD6021
Wheldale *W York* 83 SE4526
Weldrake *N York* 83 SE6844
Whelford *Gloucs* 36 SU1699
Whelpley Hill *Bucks* 38 SP9904
Whelpo *Cumb* 93 NY3139
Whelston *Flints* 70 SJ2076
Whempstead *Herts* 39 TL3221
Whenby *N York* 90 SE6369
Whepstead *Suffk* 54 TL8358
Wherstead *Suffk* 54 TM1540
Wherwell *Hants* 23 SU3841
Wheston *Derbys* 74 SK1376
Whetsted *Kent* 28 TQ6646
Whetstone *Gt Lon* 27 TQ2693
Whetstone *Leics* 50 SP5597
Wheyrigg *Cumb* 93 NY1948
Whicham *Cumb* 86 SD1382
Whichford *Warwks* 48 SP3134
Whickham *T & W* 96 NZ2061
Whiddon *Devon* 18 SX4799
Whiddon Down *Devon* 8 SX6992
Whight's Corner *Suffk* 54 TM1242
Whigstreet *Angus* 127 NO4844
Whilton *Nhants* 49 SP6364
Whimble *Devon* 18 SS3503
Whimple *Devon* 9 SY0497
Whimpwell Green *Norfk* 67 TG3829
Whin Lane End *Lancs* 80 SD3941
Whinburgh *Norfk* 66 TG0009
Whinnie Liggate *D & G* 99 NX7252
Whinnow *Cumb* 93 NY3051
Whinny Hill *Dur* 96 NZ3818
Whinnyfold *Abers* 143 NK0733
Whippingham *IOW* 13 SZ5193
Whipsnade *Beds* 38 TL0117
Whipton *Devon* 9 SX9493
Whisby *Lincs* 76 SK9067
Whissendine *Rutlnd* 63 SK8214
Whissonsett *Norfk* 66 TF9123
Whistlefield *Ag & B* 114 NS2393
Whistlefield Inn *Ag & B* 114 NS1492
Whistley Green *Berks* 25 SU7974
Whiston *Mersyd* 78 SJ4791
Whiston *Nhants* 51 SP8460
Whiston *S York* 75 SK4489
Whiston *Staffs* 60 SJ8914
Whiston *Staffs* 73 SK0347
Whiston Cross *Shrops* 60 SJ7903
Whiston Eaves *Staffs* 73 SK0446
Whiston Lane End *Mersyd* 78 SJ4690
Whitacre Fields *Warwks* 61 SP2592
Whitbeck *Cumb* 86 SD1184
Whitbourne *H & W* 47 SO7257
Whitburn *T & W* 96 NZ4062
Whitburn *W Loth* 116 NS9464
Whitby *Ches* 71 SJ3975
Whitby *N York* 91 NZ8910
Whitbyheath *Ches* 71 SJ3974
Whitchester *Border* 119 NT7159
Whitchurch *Bucks* 38 SP8020
Whitchurch *Cardif* 33 ST1579
Whitchurch *Devon* 6 SX4972
Whitchurch *H & W* 34 SO5517
Whitchurch *Hants* 24 SU4648
Whitchurch *Oxon* 37 SU6377
Whitchurch *Pembks* 30 SM8025
Whitchurch *Shrops* 71 SJ5341
Whitchurch *Somset* 21 ST6167
Whitchurch Canonicorum *Dorset* 10 SY3995
Whitchurch Hill *Oxon* 37 SU6378
Whitcombe *Dorset* 11 SY7188
Whitcot *Shrops* 59 SO3791
Whitcott Keysett *Shrops* 58 SO2782
White Ball *Somset* 20 ST1019
White Chapel *H & W* 48 SP0740
White Chapel *Lancs* 81 SD5541
White Colne *Essex* 40 TL8729
White Coppice *Lancs* 81 SD6118
White Cross *Cnwll* 2 SW6821
White End *H & W* 47 SO7834
White Kirkley *Dur* 95 NZ0235
White Lackington *Dorset* 11 SY7198
White Ladies Aston *H & W* 47 SO9252
White Mill *Carmth* 32 SN4621
White Notley *Essex* 40 TL7818
White Ox Mead *Somset* 22 ST7258
White Pit *Lincs* 77 TF3777
White Roding *Essex* 40 TL5613
White Stake *Lancs* 80 SD5125
White Stone *H & W* 46 SO5642
White Waltham *Berks* 26 SU8577
White-le-Head *Dur* 96 NZ1654
Whiteacre *Kent* 29 TR1148
Whiteacre Heath *Warwks* 61 SP2292
Whiteash Green *Essex* 40 TL7930
Whitebirk *Lancs* 81 SD7028
Whitebridge *Highld* 139 NH4815
Whitebrook *Mons* 34 SO5306
Whitecairns *Abers* 143 NJ9218
Whitechapel *Gt Lon* 27 TQ3381
Whitechurch *Pembks* 31 SN1536
Whitecliffe *Gloucs* 34 SO5609
Whitecraig *E Loth* 118 NT3470
Whitecroft *Gloucs* 35 SO6206
Whitecrook *D & G* 98 NX1656
Whitecross *Cnwll* 2 SW5234
Whitecross *Cnwll* 4 SW9672
Whitecross *Falk* 117 NS9676
Whiteface *Highld* 146 NH7088
Whitefarland *N Ayrs* 105 NR8642
Whitefaulds *S Ayrs* 106 NS2909
Whitefield *Devon* 19 SS7035
Whitefield *Gt Man* 79 SD8006
Whitefield *Somset* 20 ST0729
Whitefield Lane End *Mersyd* 78 SJ4589
Whiteford *Abers* 142 NJ7126
Whitegate *Ches* 71 SJ6269
Whitehall *Hants* 24 SU7452
Whitehall *Ork* 155 HY6528
Whitehall *W Susx* 15 TQ1321
Whitehaven *Cumb* 92 NX9718
Whitehill *Hants* 14 SU7934
Whitehill *Kent* 28 TR0059
Whitehills *Abers* 142 NJ6565
Whitehouse *Abers* 142 NJ6114
Whitehouse *Ag & B* 113 NR8161
Whitehouse Common *W Mids* 61 SP1397
Whitekirk *E Loth* 118 NT5981
Whitelackington *Somset* 10 ST3815
Whiteley *Hants* 13 SU5209
Whiteley Bank *IOW* 13 SZ5581
Whiteley Green *Ches* 79 SJ9278
Whiteley Village *Surrey* 26 TQ0962
Whitemans Green *W Susx* 15 TQ3025
Whitemire *Moray* 140 NH9854
Whitemoor *Cnwll* 4 SW9757
Whitemoor *Derbys* 62 SK3647
Whitemoor *Notts* 62 SK5441
Whitemoor *Staffs* 72 SJ8861
Whitenap *Hants* 12 SU3620
Whiteness *Shet* 155 HU3844
Whiteoak Green *Oxon* 36 SP3414
Whiteparish *Wilts* 23 SU2423
Whiterashes *Abers* 143 NJ8523
Whiterow *Highld* 151 ND3648
Whiterow *Moray* 141 NJ0257
Whiteshill *Gloucs* 35 SO8406
Whitesmith *E Susx* 16 TQ5213
Whitestaunton *Somset* 10 ST2810
Whitestone *Devon* 9 SX8694
Whitestone Cross *Devon* 9 SX8993
Whitestreet Green *Suffk* 54 TL9739
Whitewall Corner *N York* 90 SE7969
Whiteway *Gloucs* 35 SO9110
Whiteway *Somset* 22 ST7264
Whitewell *Lancs* 81 SD6646
Whiteworks *Devon* 6 SX6171
Whitfield *Gloucs* 35 ST6791
Whitfield *Kent* 29 TR3045
Whitfield *Nhants* 49 SP6039
Whitfield *Nthumb* 94 NY7857
Whitfield Hall *Nthumb* 94 NY7756
Whitford *Devon* 10 SY2595
Whitford *Flints* 70 SJ1478
Whitgift *E R Yk* 84 SE8122
Whitgreave *Staffs* 72 SJ9028
Whithorn *D & G* 99 NX4440
Whiting Bay *N Ayrs* 105 NS0425
Whitington *Norfk* 65 TL7199
Whitkirk *W York* 83 SE3633
Whitland *Carmth* 31 SN1916
Whitlaw *Border* 109 NT5012
Whitletts *S Ayrs* 106 NS3623
Whitley *Berks* 24 SU7270
Whitley *N York* 83 SE5620
Whitley *S York* 74 SK3494
Whitley *Wilts* 22 ST8866
Whitley Bay *T & W* 103 NZ3571
Whitley Chapel *Nthumb* 95 NY9257
Whitley Heath *Staffs* 72 SJ8126
Whitley Lower *W York* 82 SE2217
Whitley Row *Kent* 27 TQ4952
Whitlock's End *W Mids* 61 SP1076
Whitlow *S York* 74 SK3182
Whitminster *Gloucs* 35 SO7708
Whitmore *Dorset* 12 SU0609
Whitmore *Staffs* 72 SJ8140
Whitnage *Devon* 9 ST0215
Whitnash *Warwks* 48 SP3263
Whitney-on-Wye *H & W* 46 SO2747
Whitrigg *Cumb* 93 NY2038
Whitrigg *Cumb* 93 NY2257
Whitrigglees *Cumb* 93 NY2457
Whitsbury *Hants* 12 SU1219
Whitsford *Devon* 19 SS6633
Whitsome *Border* 119 NT8650
Whitson *Newpt* 34 ST3883
Whitstable *Kent* 29 TR1066
Whitstone *Cnwll* 5 SX2698
Whittingehame *E Loth* 118 NT6073
Whittingham *Nthumb* 111 NU0611
Whittingslow *Shrops* 59 SO4388
Whittington *Derbys* 74 SK3875
Whittington *Gloucs* 35 SP0120
Whittington *H & W* 47 SO8753
Whittington *Lancs* 87 SD6075
Whittington *Shrops* 59 SJ3231
Whittington *Staffs* 61 SK1508
Whittington *Staffs* 60 SO8682
Whittington *Warwks* 61 SP2999
Whittington Moor *Derbys* 74 SK3773
Whittle-le-Woods *Lancs* 81 SD5821
Whittlebury *Nhants* 49 SP6943
Whittlesey *Cambs* 64 TL2697
Whittlesford *Cambs* 53 TL4748
Whittlestone Head *Lancs* 81 SD7119
Whitton *Dur* 96 NZ3822
Whitton *Lincs* 84 SE9024
Whitton *Nthumb* 103 NU0501
Whitton *Powys* 46 SO2767
Whitton *Shrops* 46 SO5772
Whitton *Suffk* 54 TM1447
Whittonditch *Wilts* 36 SU2872
Whittonstall *Nthumb* 95 NZ0757
Whitway *Hants* 24 SU4559
Whitwell *Derbys* 75 SK5276
Whitwell *Herts* 39 TL1820
Whitwell *IOW* 13 SZ5277
Whitwell *N York* 89 SE2899
Whitwell *Rutlnd* 63 SK9208
Whitwell Street *Norfk* 66 TG1022
Whitwell-on-the-Hill *N York* 90 SE7265
Whitwick *Leics* 62 SK4315
Whitwood *W York* 83 SE4024
Whitworth *Lancs* 81 SD8818
Whixall *Shrops* 59 SJ5134
Whixley *N York* 89 SE4458
Whorlton *Dur* 95 NZ1014
Whorlton *N York* 90 NZ4802
Whyle *H & W* 46 SO5561
Whyteleafe *Surrey* 27 TQ3358
Wibdon *Gloucs* 34 ST5797
Wibsey *W York* 82 SE1430
Wibtoft *Warwks* 50 SP4887
Wichenford *H & W* 47 SO7860
Wichling *Kent* 28 TQ9256
Wick *Devon* 9 ST1704
Wick *Dorset* 12 SZ1591
Wick *Gloucs* 35 ST7072
Wick *H & W* 47 SO9645
Wick *Highld* 151 ND3650
Wick *Somset* 20 ST2144
Wick *Somset* 21 ST4026
Wick *V Glam* 33 SS9271
Wick *W Susx* 14 TQ0203
Wick *Wilts* 12 SU1621
Wick End *Beds* 38 SP9850
Wick St Lawrence *Somset* 21 ST3665
Wicken *Cambs* 53 TL5770
Wicken *Nhants* 49 SP7439
Wicken Bonhunt *Essex* 39 TL4933
Wickenby *Lincs* 76 TF0982
Wicker Street Green *Suffk* 54 TL9742
Wickersley *S York* 75 SK4791
Wickford *Essex* 40 TQ7493
Wickham *Berks* 36 SU3971
Wickham *Hants* 13 SU5711
Wickham Bishops *Essex* 40 TL8412
Wickham Green *Berks* 24 SU4072
Wickham Green *Suffk* 54 TM0969
Wickham Heath *Berks* 24 SU4169
Wickham Market *Suffk* 55 TM3055
Wickham Skeith *Suffk* 54 TM0969
Wickham St Paul *Essex* 54 TL8336
Wickham Street *Suffk* 53 TL7654
Wickham Street *Suffk* 54 TM0869
Wickhambreaux *Kent* 29 TR2158
Wickhambrook *Suffk* 53 TL7554
Wickhamford *H & W* 48 SP0641
Wickhampton *Norfk* 67 TG4205
Wicklewood *Norfk* 66 TG0702
Wickmere *Norfk* 66 TG1733
Wickstreet *E Susx* 16 TQ5308
Wickwar *Gloucs* 35 ST7288
Widdington *Essex* 39 TL5331
Widdop *Lancs* 81 SD9233
Widdrington *Nthumb* 103 NZ2595
Widdrington Station *T & W* 103 NZ2494
Wide Open *T & W* 103 NZ2472
Widecombe in the Moor *Devon* 8 SX7176
Widegates *Cnwll* 5 SX2858
Widemouth Bay *Cnwll* 18 SS2002
Widford *Essex* 40 TL6904
Widford *Herts* 39 TL4216
Widford *Oxon* 36 SP2712
Widham *Wilts* 36 SU0988
Widmer End *Bucks* 26 SU8896
Widmerpool *Notts* 63 SK6327
Widmore *Gt Lon* 27 TQ4268
Widnes *Ches* 78 SJ5184
Widworthy *Devon* 9 SY2199
Wigan *Gt Man* 78 SD5805
Wigborough *Somset* 10 ST4415
Wiggaton *Devon* 9 SY1093
Wiggenhall St Germans *Norfk* 65 TF5914
Wiggenhall St Mary Magdalen *Norfk* 65 TF5911
Wiggenhall St Mary the Virgin *Norfk* 65 TF5813
Wiggens Green *Essex* 53 TL6642
Wiggenstall *Staffs* 74 SK0960
Wiggington *Shrops* 59 SJ3335
Wigginton *Herts* 38 SP9310
Wigginton *N York* 90 SE6058
Wigginton *Oxon* 48 SP3833
Wigginton *Staffs* 61 SK2006
Wigglesworth *N York* 81 SD8156
Wiggold *Gloucs* 36 SP0404
Wiggonby *Cumb* 93 NY2952
Wiggonholt *W Susx* 14 TQ0616
Wighill *N York* 83 SE4746
Wighton *Norfk* 66 TF9439
Wigley *Derbys* 74 SK3171
Wigley *Hants* 12 SU3217
Wigmore *H & W* 46 SO4169
Wigmore *Kent* 28 TQ7964
Wigsley *Notts* 76 SK8570
Wigsthorpe *Nhants* 51 TL0482
Wigston *Leics* 50 SP6198
Wigston Fields *Leics* 50 SK6000
Wigston Parva *Leics* 50 SP4689
Wigthorpe *Notts* 75 SK5983
Wigtoft *Lincs* 64 TF2636
Wigton *Cumb* 93 NY2548
Wigtown *D & G* 99 NX4355
Wigtwizzle *S York* 74 SK2495
Wike *W York* 83 SE3342
Wilbarston *Nhants* 51 SP8188
Wilberfoss *E R Yk* 84 SE7350
Wilburton *Cambs* 53 TL4775
Wilby *Nhants* 51 SP8666
Wilby *Norfk* 54 TM0389
Wilby *Suffk* 55 TM2472
Wilcot *Wilts* 23 SU1360
Wilcrick *Newpt* 34 ST4088
Wilday Green *Derbys* 74 SK3274
Wildboarclough *Ches* 79 SJ9868
Wilden *Beds* 51 TL0955
Wilden *H & W* 60 SO8272
Wildhern *Hants* 23 SU3550
Wildhill *Herts* 39 TL2606
Wildmanbridge *S Lans* 116 NS8253
Wildmoor *H & W* 60 SO9575
Wildsworth *Lincs* 75 SK8097
Wilford *Notts* 62 SK5637
Wilkesley *Ches* 71 SJ6241
Wilkhaven *Highld* 147 NH9486
Wilkieston *W Loth* 117 NT1268
Wilkin's Green *Herts* 39 TL1907
Wilksby *Lincs* 77 TF2862
Willand *Devon* 9 ST0310
Willards Hill *E Susx* 17 TQ7124
Willaston *Ches* 71 SJ3377
Willaston *Ches* 72 SJ6852
Willcott *Shrops* 59 SJ3718
Willen *Bucks* 38 SP8741
Willenhall *W Mids* 60 SO9798
Willenhall *W Mids* 61 SP3676
Willerby *E R Yk* 84 TA0230
Willerby *N York* 91 TA0079
Willersey *Gloucs* 48 SP1039
Willersley *H & W* 46 SO3147
Willesborough *Kent* 28 TR0441
Willesborough Lees *Kent* 28 TR0342
Willesden *Gt Lon* 26 TQ2284
Willesleigh *Devon* 19 SS6033
Willesley *Wilts* 35 ST8588
Willett *Somset* 20 ST1033
Willey *Shrops* 60 SO6799
Willey *Warwks* 50 SP4984
Willey Green *Surrey* 25 SU9351
Williamscot *Oxon* 49 SP4845
Williamstown *Rhondd* 33 ST0090
Willian *Herts* 39 TL2230
Willicote *Warwks* 48 SP1849
Willingale *Essex* 40 TL5907
Willingdon *E Susx* 16 TQ5902
Willingham *Cambs* 52 TL4070
Willingham *Lincs* 76 SK8784
Willingham Green *Cambs* 53 TL6254
Willington *Beds* 52 TL1150
Willington *Ches* 71 SJ5266
Willington *Derbys* 73 SK2928
Willington *Dur* 96 NZ1935
Willington *Kent* 28 TQ7853
Willington *Warwks* 48 SP2639
Willington Quay *T & W* 103 NZ3267
Willitoft *E R Yk* 84 SE7434
Williton *Somset* 20 ST0840
Willoughby *Lincs* 64 TF0537
Willoughby *Lincs* 77 TF4771
Willoughby *Warwks* 50 SP5167
Willoughby Hills *Lincs* 64 TF3545
Willoughby Waterleys *Leics* 50 SP5792
Willoughby-on-the-Wolds *Notts* 63 SK6325
Willoughton *Lincs* 76 SK9293
Willow Green *Ches* 71 SJ6076
Willows Green *Essex* 40 TL7219
Willsbridge *Gloucs* 35 ST6670
Willsworthy *Devon* 8 SX5381
Willtown *Somset* 21 ST3924
Wilmcote *Warwks* 48 SP1658
Wilmington *Devon* 9 SY2199
Wilmington *E Susx* 16 TQ5404
Wilmington *Kent* 27 TQ5372
Wilmington *Somset* 22 ST6962
Wilmslow *Ches* 79 SJ8481
Wilnecote *Staffs* 61 SK2200
Wilpshire *Lancs* 81 SD6832
Wilsden *W York* 82 SE0936
Wilsford *Lincs* 63 TF0042
Wilsford *Wilts* 23 SU1057
Wilsford *Wilts* 23 SU1339
Wilsham *Devon* 19 SS7548
Wilshaw *W York* 82 SE1109
Wilsill *N York* 89 SE1864
Wilsley Green *Kent* 28 TQ7736
Wilsley Pound *Kent* 28 TQ7837
Wilson *H & W* 46 SO5523
Wilson *Leics* 62 SK4024
Wilsontown *S Lans* 116 NS9455
Wilstead *Beds* 38 TL0643
Wilsthorpe *Lincs* 64 TF0913
Wilstone *Herts* 38 SP9014
Wilstone Green *Herts* 38 SP9013
Wilton *Cumb* 86 NY0311
Wilton *H & W* 46 SO5824
Wilton *N York* 97 NZ5819
Wilton *N York* 90 SE8582
Wilton *Wilts* 23 SU0931
Wilton *Wilts* 23 SU2661
Wilton Dean *Border* 109 NT4914
Wimbish *Essex* 53 TL5936
Wimbish Green *Essex* 53 TL6035
Wimblebury *Staffs* 60 SK0111
Wimbledon *Gt Lon* 26 TQ2370
Wimblington *Cambs* 65 TL4192
Wimborne Minster *Dorset* 11 SZ0199
Wimborne St Giles *Dorset* 12 SU0311
Wimbotsham *Norfk* 65 TF6205
Wimpstone *Warwks* 48 SP2148
Wincanton *Somset* 22 ST7128
Winceby *Lincs* 77 TF3268
Wincham *Ches* 79 SJ6775
Winchburgh *W Loth* 117 NT0975
Winchcombe *Gloucs* 48 SP0228
Winchelsea *E Susx* 17 TQ9017
Winchelsea Beach *E Susx* 17 TQ9116
Winchester *Hants* 24 SU4829
Winchet Hill *Kent* 28 TQ7340
Winchfield *Hants* 24 SU7654
Winchmore Hill *Bucks* 26 SU9395
Winchmore Hill *Gt Lon* 27 TQ3194
Wincle *Ches* 72 SJ9566
Wincobank *S York* 74 SK3891
Winder *Cumb* 92 NY0417
Windermere *Cumb* 87 SD4098
Winderton *Warwks* 48 SP3240
Windhill *Highld* 139 NH5348
Windlehurst *Gt Man* 79 SJ9586
Windlesham *Surrey* 25 SU9364
Windmill *Cnwll* 4 SW8974
Windmill *Derbys* 74 SK1677
Windmill Hill *E Susx* 16 TQ6412
Windmill Hill *Somset* 10 ST3116
Windrush *Gloucs* 36 SP1913
Windsole *Abers* 142 NJ5560
Windsor *Berks* 26 SU9576
Windsor Green *Suffk* 54 TL8954
Windsoredge *Gloucs* 35 SO8400
Windy Arbour *Warwks* 61 SP2971
Windy Hill *Wrexhm* 71 SJ3054
Windygates *Fife* 118 NO3400